Professional SQL Server™ 2005
Integration Services

Professional SQL Server™ 2005 Integration Services

Brian Knight, Allan Mitchell, Darren Green, Douglas Hinson,
Kathi Kellenberger, Andy Leonard, Erik Veerman,
Jason Gerard, Haidong Ji, Mike Murphy

Wiley Publishing, Inc.

Professional SQL Server™ 2005 Integration Services

Published by
Wiley Publishing, Inc.
10475 Crosspoint Boulevard
Indianapolis, IN 46256
www.wiley.com

Copyright © 2006 by Wiley Publishing, Inc., Indianapolis, Indiana

Published simultaneously in Canada

ISBN-13: 978-0-7645-8435-0
ISBN-10: 0-7645-8435-9

Manufactured in the United States of America

10 9 8 7 6 5 4 3 2

1B/QZ/QR/QW/IN

Library of Congress Cataloging-in-Publication Data:

Professional SQL Server 2005 integration services / Brian Knight ... [et al.].
  p. cm.
 Includes index.
 ISBN-13: 978-0-7645-8435-0 (paper/website)
 ISBN-10: 0-7645-8435-9 (paper/website)
 1. SQL server. 2. Database management. I. Knight, Brian, 1976-
 QA76.9.D3P767 2005
 005.75'85 — dc22

                    2005026347

About the Authors

Brian Knight, SQL Server MVP, MCSE, MCDBA, is the cofounder of SQLServerCentral.com and was recently on the Board of Directors for the Professional Association for SQL Server (PASS). He runs the local SQL Server users group in Jacksonville, Florida (JSSUG). Brian is a contributing columnist for *SQL Server Standard* and also maintains a weekly column for the database Web site SQLServerCentral.com. He is the author of *Admin911: SQL Server* (Osborne/McGraw-Hill Publishing) and coauthor of *Professional SQL Server DTS* and *Professional SQL Server 2005 SSIS* (Wiley Publishing). Brian has spoken at such conferences as PASS, SQL Connections, and TechEd. His blog can be found at www.whiteknighttechnology.com.

Allan Mitchell is joint owner of a UK-based consultancy, Konesans, specializing in ETL implementation and design. He is currently working on a project for one of the UK's leading investment banks doing country credit risk profiling as well as designing custom SSIS components for clients.

Darren Green is the joint owner of Konesans, a UK-based consultancy specializing in SQL Server, and of course DTS and SSIS solutions. Having managed a variety of database systems from version 6.5 onwards, he has extensive experience in many aspects of SQL Server. He also manages the resource sites SQLDTS.com and SQLIS.com, as well as being a Microsoft MVP.

Douglas Hinson, MCP splits his time between database and software development as a Senior Architect for Hinson & Associates Consulting in Jacksonville, Florida. Douglas specializes in conceptualizing and building insurance back-end solutions for payroll deduction, billing, payment, and claims processing operations in a multitude of development environments. He also has experience developing logistics and postal service applications.

Kathi Kellenberger is a database administrator at Bryan Cave LLP, an international law firm headquartered in St. Louis, Missouri. She fell in love with computers the first time she used a Radio Shack TRS-80, many years ago while in college. Too late to change majors, she spent 16 years in a health care field before switching careers. She lives in Edwardsville, Illinois, with her husband, Dennis, college-age son, Andy, and many pets. Her grown-up daughter, Denise, lives nearby. When she's not working or writing articles for SQLServerCentral.com, you'll find her spending time with her wonderful sisters, hiking, cycling, or singing at the local karaoke bar.

Andy Leonard is a SQL Server DBA, MCSD, and engineer who lives in Jacksonville, Florida. Andy manages a SQL Server DBA Team. He has a passion for developing enterprise solutions of all types and a fondness for business intelligence solutions in industrial enterprises. Learn more at www.andyleonard.net and reach Andy at andy@andyleonard.net.

Erik Veerman is a mentor with Solid Quality Learning and is based out of Atlanta, Georgia. Erik has been developing Microsoft-based Business Intelligence and ETL-focused solutions since the first release of DTS and OLAP Server in SQL Server 7.0, working with a wide range of customers and industries. His industry recognition includes Microsoft's Worldwide BI Solution of the Year and *SQL Server Magazine*'s Innovator Cup winner. Erik led the ETL architecture and design for the first production implementation of Integration Services and participated in developing ETL standards and best practices for Integration Services through Microsoft's SQL Server 2005 reference initiative, Project REAL.

Jason Gerard is President of Object Future Consulting, Inc., a software development and mentoring company located in Jacksonville, Florida (www.objectfuture.com). Jason is an expert with .NET and J2EE technologies and has developed enterprise applications for the health care, financial, and insurance industries. When not developing enterprise solutions, Jason spends as much time as possible with his wife Sandy, son Jakob, and Tracker, his extremely lazy beagle.

Haidong Ji (季海东), MCSD and MCDBA, is a Senior Database Administrator in Chicago, Illinois. He manages enterprise SQL Server systems, along with some Oracle and MySQL systems on Unix and Linux. He has worked extensively with DTS 2000. He was a developer prior to his current role, focusing on Visual Basic, COM and COM+, and SQL Server. He is a regular columnist for SQLServerCentral.com, a popular and well-known portal for SQL Server.

Mike Murphy is a .NET developer, MCSD, and in a former life an automated control systems engineer currently living in Jacksonville, Florida. Mike enjoys keeping pace with the latest advances in computer technology, meeting with colleagues at Jacksonville Developer User Group meetings (www.jaxdug.com) and, when time allows, flying R/C Helicopters. To contact Mike, e-mail him at mike@murphysgeekdom.com or visit www.murphysgeekdom.com.

Credits

Excecutive Editor
Bob Elliott

Development Editor
Brian MacDonald

Technical Editors
Slobodan M. Bojanic
James K. Howey
Ted Lee
Runying Mao
Ashwani Nanda
Ashvini Sharma

Production Editor
William A. Barton

Copy Editor
Publication Services

Editorial Manager
Mary Beth Wakefield

Production Manager
Tim Tate

Vice President and Executive Group Publisher
Richard Swadley

Vice President and Publisher
Joseph B. Wikert

Project Coordinator
Ryan Steffen

Graphics and Production Specialists
Denny Hager
Joyce Haughey
Jennifer Heleine
Barbara Moore
Alicia B. South

Quality Control Technicians
John Greenough
Brian H. Walls

Media Development Specialists
Angela Denny
Kit Malone
Travis Silvers

Proofreading and Indexing
TECHBOOKS Production Services

To my eternally patient wife, Jennifer

Acknowledgments

First and foremost, thanks to my wife for taking on the two small children for the months while I was writing this book. As always, nothing would be possible without my wife, Jennifer. I'm sorry that all I can dedicate to her is a technical book. Thanks to my two boys Colton and Liam for being so patient with their Dad. Thanks to all the folks at Microsoft (especially Ash) for their technical help while we were writing this. This book was turned good to great with the help of our excellent Development Editor Brian MacDonald. Once again, I must thank the Pepsi Cola Company for supplying me with enough caffeine to make it through long nights and early mornings. —*Brian Knight*

I would like to thank my wife, with whom all things are possible, and our son Ewan, who is the cutest baby ever, but I would say that, wouldn't I? I would also like to thank the SSIS team at Microsoft, in particular Donald Farmer, Ashvini Sharma, and Kirk Haselden, because let's face it, without them this book would not need to be written. —*Allan Mitchell*

I'd like to thank my wife Teri for being so patient and not spending too much time out shopping while I was holed up writing this. Thanks also go to the team in Redmond for answering all my questions and being so generous with their time. —*Darren Green*

First, I'd like to thank God for his continuous blessings. To my beautiful wife Misty, thank you for being so supportive and understanding during this project and always. You are a wonderful wife and mother whom I can always count on. To my son Kyle and daughter Mariah, you guys are my inspirations. I love you both. To my parents, thanks for instilling in me the values of persistence and hard work. Thanks, Jenny, for being my sister and my friend, and thanks to all my family for your love and support. Thanks to Brian MacDonald, Ashvini Sharma, and Allen Mitchell for doing the hard work of reading these long chapters and offering your advice and perspectives. A big thanks to the Team and Brian Knight for asking me to come along on this project in the first place and giving me this opportunity, which I have thoroughly enjoyed. —*Douglas Hinson*

I would like to thank my extended family, friends, and coworkers for their encouragement and sharing of my excitement about this project. Thanks to Doug Wilmsmeyer who advised me over 10 years ago to learn VB and SQL Server. Thanks to my brother, Bill Morgan, Jr., who taught me programming logic and gave me my first break programming ASP back in 1996. But most of all, thank you to Dennis, my husband, my partner, and love of my life. Because of all you do for me, I am able to live my dreams. —*Kathi Kellenberger*

I would first like to thank my wonderful wife. Christy signed on to this project when I did, and did as much to contribute to my part of this book. Christy, thank you for your unwavering support. Thanks to our son, Stevie, for giving up some playtime so Dad could write, and to Emma for just being cute. Thanks also to Manda and Penny for their support and prayers. Thanks to the team at work for their flexibility and inspiration, especially Mike Potts, Jason Gerard, Doug Hinson, Mike Murphy, and Ron Pizur. Finally, I would like to thank Brian Knight for his example, friendship, leadership, and the opportunity to write some of this book. —*Andy Leonard*

Acknowledgments

Thanks are in order to the Microsoft Integration Services development team for a few reasons. First, thank you for your vision and execution of a great product, one that has already made a big splash in the industry. Also, thanks to Donald Farmer and Ashvini Sharma (on the Microsoft development team) for your partnership since my first introduction to Integration Services in the summer of 2003; this includes putting up with my oftentimes nagging and ignorant questions, and talking through design scenarios and working with clients to make success stories. Much of those discussions and real-world lessons learned have been captured in the chapter I've contributed. A thanks needs to go to Mark Chaffin, a great contributor in the industry, for pulling me into this effort and for the many white-board design sessions we had putting this product into action. —*Erik Veerman*

Thanks go to my wife, Sandy, for putting up with my many late-night writing sessions. You were awesome during this whole experience. I would like to thank my son, Jakob, for making me laugh when I needed it. Many thanks to Doug Hinson for looking over my work and to Chad Crisostomo for critiquing my grammar. Thanks to Mike Potts for your support. Finally, thanks to Brian Knight for presenting me with this opportunity and to Andy Leonard for convincing me to do it. —*Jason Gerard*

I'd like to thank a lot of people who've helped me over the years. Thanks to my parents for their hard work and perseverance and for giving us an education in very difficult circumstances. Thanks to my brothers and their families for their help and care. Thanks to Brian Knight for introducing me to technical writing; I am very grateful for that. Thanks to Brian MacDonald, our editor, for his patience and excellent editing guidance. Finally, thanks to Maria and Benjamin, who are absolutely and positively the best thing that ever happened to my life. Maria, thank you for all you have done and for putting up with me. Benjamin, thank you for bringing so much joy and fulfillment into our lives. We are incredibly proud of you. —*Haidong Ji*

I would like to thank my parents, Barb and Jim, and my brother Tom for all their support throughout my life. Thanks to Sheri and Nichole for always believing in me. I would also like to thank Brian Knight for offering me this opportunity to expand my horizons into the world of writing, and Andy Leonard for keeping me motivated. And finally, thanks so much to all my friends and colleagues at work.
—*Mike Murphy*

Contents

Acknowledgments   xi

Foreword   xxiii

Introduction   xxv

Who This Book Is For   xxv

How This Book Is Structured   xxv

What You Need to Use This Book   xxvi

Conventions   xxvii

Source Code   xxvii

Errata   xxvii

p2p.wrox.com   xxviii

Chapter 1: Welcome to SQL Server Integration Services   1

What's New in SQL Server 2005 SSIS   1

    Import and Export Wizard   2

    The Business Intelligence Development Studio   3

Architecture   3

    Packages   5

    Tasks   5

    Data Source Elements   6

    Data Source Views   8

Precedence Constraints   9

    Constraint Value   9

    Conditional Expressions   9

Containers   10

Variables   10

Data Flow Elements   11

    Sources   11

    Destinations   12

    Transformations   13

Error Handling and Logging   14

Editions of SQL Server 2005   16

Summary   17

Contents

Chapter 2: The SSIS Tools   19

Import and Export Wizard   **19**
  Using the Import and Export Wizard   19
Package Installation Wizard   **25**
Business Intelligence Development Studio   **25**
Creating Your First Package   **27**
The Solution Explorer Window   **28**
  The Toolbox   29
  The Properties Windows   30
  Navigation Pane   31
  Other Windows   32
The SSIS Package Designer   **32**
  Controller Flow   33
  Connection Managers   36
  Variables   37
  Data Flow   38
  Event Handlers   39
  Package Explorer   40
  Executing a Package   41
Summary   **41**

Chapter 3: SSIS Tasks   43

Shared Properties   **43**
Execute SQL Task   **44**
Bulk Insert Task   **46**
Using the Bulk Insert and Execute SQL Tasks   **48**
Data Flow Task   **51**
Execute Process Task   **51**
File System Task   **52**
FTP Task   **54**
Using the File System and FTP Task   **55**
Execute Package Task   **59**
Script and ActiveX Tasks   **60**
Send Mail Task   **62**
Message Queue Task   **63**
Web Service Task   **63**
WMI Data Reader and Event Watcher Task   **65**
XML Task   **68**
SQL Server Analysis Services Execute DDL and Processing Tasks   **70**
Data Mining Query Task   **71**

Contents

The Expression Page   **72**

Summary   **72**

Chapter 4: Containers and Data Flow   73

Containers   **73**

Task Host Containers   73

Sequence Containers   73

For Loop Container   74

Foreach Loop Container   78

Sources   **80**

OLE DB Source   80

Excel Source   83

Flat File Source   84

Raw File Source   84

XML Source   84

Data Reader Source   84

Destinations   **84**

Data Mining Model Training   86

DataReader Destination   86

Dimension and Partition Processing   87

Excel Destination   87

Flat File Destination   88

OLE DB Destination   88

Raw File Destination   89

Recordset Destination   89

SQL Server and Mobile Destinations   90

Transformations   **90**

Aggregate   91

Audit   93

Character Map   94

Conditional Split   94

Copy Column   97

Data Conversion   97

Data Mining Query   98

Derived Column   99

Export Column   100

Fuzzy Grouping and Lookup   101

Import Column   101

Lookup   101

Merge   102

Merge Join   103

Contents

Multicast 104

OLE DB Command 105

Percentage and Row Sampling 105

Pivot and Unpivot 106

Row Count 107

Script Component 107

Slowly Changing Dimension 107

Sort 107

Term Extraction and Lookup 108

Union All 109

Data Flow Example **110**

Data Viewers **116**

Summary **117**

Chapter 5: Creating an End-to-End Package **119**

Basic Transformation Tutorial **119**

Creating Connections 120

Creating the Tasks 122

Creating the Data Flow 123

Completing the Package 124

Saving the Package 125

Executing the Package 125

Typical Mainframe ETL with Data Scrubbing **125**

Creating the Data Flow 129

Handling Dirty Data 129

Finalizing 133

Handling More Bad Data 134

Looping and the Dynamic Task **138**

Looping 139

Making the Package Dynamic 140

Summary **142**

Chapter 6: Advanced Tasks and Transforms **143**

Execute SQL Task **144**

Variables 145

Expressions 146

Using SQL Output Parameters to Change Runtime Settings 148

Import Column **150**

Import Column Example 151

Import Column Example Using File Iteration 155

Using Temp Tables in SSIS Package Development   **157**
Export Column   **159**
Row Count   **160**
OLE DB Command   **162**
Term Extraction   **165**
Term Lookup   **171**
Fuzzy Lookup   **173**
Fuzzy Grouping   **178**
Pivot Transform   **182**
Unpivot   **186**
Slowly Changing Dimension   **189**
Database Object-Level Tasks   **201**
Transfer Database Task   201
Transfer Logins Task   202
Transfer Master Stored Procedures Task   203
Transfer SQL Server Objects Task   204
Summary   **205**

Chapter 7: Scripting in SSIS   207

Scripting Overview   **207**
Expressions   **208**
Dynamic Properties   208
Expressions in Tasks   211
Script Tasks   **213**
The Dts Object   218
Accessing Variables   219
Events   220
Logging   222
Script Task Debugging   222
Using .NET Assemblies   **225**
Structured Exception Handling   **227**
Script Component   **228**
Using the Script Component   229
Debugging the Script Component   235
Summary   **237**

Chapter 8: Accessing Heterogeneous Data   239

Excel   **240**
Exporting to Excel   240
Importing from Excel   244

Contents

Access   **250**

    Understanding Access Security   250

    Configuring an Access Connection Manager   251

    Importing from Access   253

    Using a Parameter   255

Oracle   **259**

    Client Setup   259

    Importing Oracle Data   259

Web Services   **262**

    The Hyperlink Extractor Service   262

    The Currency Conversion Service   265

XML Data   **272**

Summary   **278**

Chapter 9: Reliability and Scalability   **279**

Restarting Packages   **279**

    Simple Control Flow   280

    Containers within Containers and Checkpoints   285

    Variations on a Theme   288

    Inside the Checkpoint File   290

Package Transactions   **292**

    Single Package, Single Transaction   293

    Single Package, Multiple Transactions   296

    Two Packages, One Transaction   298

    Single Package Using a Native Transaction in SQL Server 299

Error Outputs   **301**

Scaling Out   **304**

    Scale Out Memory Pressures   304

    Scale Out by Staging Data   305

Summary   **310**

Chapter 10: Understanding the Integration Services Engine **311**

The Integration Services Engine: An Analogy   **311**

Understanding the SSIS Data Flow and Control Flow   **312**

    Comparing and Contrasting the Data Flow and Control Flow 312

    SSIS Package Execution Times from Package Start to Package Finish 314

Enterprise Workflows with the Control Flow   **315**

Enterprise Data Processing with the Data Flow **317**
Memory Buffer Architecture 317
Types of Transformations 318
Advanced Data Flow Execution Concepts 329
Summary **339**

Chapter 11: Applying the Integration Services Engine **341**

That Was Then: DTS **341**
DTS Solution Architecture 342
Common DTS Processing Practices 343
DTS Limitations 345
This Is Now: Integration Services **346**
Integration Services Design Practices 347
Optimizing Package Processing 360
Pipeline Performance Monitoring **366**
Summary **369**

Chapter 12: DTS 2000 Migration and Metadata Management **371**

Migrating DTS 2000 Packages to SSIS **371**
Using the Package Migration Wizard **373**
Running DTS 2000 Packages under SSIS **380**
Package Metadata and Storage Management **384**
Managing SSIS Packages within SQL Server Management Studio 386
Managing DTS 2000 Packages within SQL Server Management Studio 388
Summary **389**

Chapter 13: Error and Event Handling **391**

Precedence Constraints **391**
Precedence Constraints and Expressions 393
Multiple Constraints 397
Event Handling **398**
Events 398
Inventory Example 399
Event Bubbling 406
Breakpoints **408**
Checkpoints **411**
Logging **412**
Summary **416**

Contents

Chapter 14: Programming and Extending SSIS   **417**

  The Sample Components   **417**
    Component 1: Source Adapter   418
    Component 2: Transformation   418
    Component 3: Destination Adapter   419
  The Pipeline Component Methods   **419**
    Design-Time   419
    Runtime   423
    Connection Time   425
  Building the Components   **425**
    Preparation   426
    Building the Source Adapter   432
    Building the Transform   443
    Building the Destination Adapter   454
  Debugging Components   **461**
    Design-Time   462
    Runtime   463
  Summary   **466**

Chapter 15: Adding a User Interface to Your Component   **467**

  Three Key Steps   **467**
  Building the User Interface   **468**
    Adding the Project   468
    Implementing IDtsComponentUI   471
    Setting the UITypeName   475
    Building the Form   476
  Further Development   **481**
    Runtime Connections   482
    Component Properties   484
    Handling Errors and Warnings   486
    Column Properties   488
  Summary   **490**

Chapter 16: External Management and WMI Task Implementation   **491**

  External Management with Managed Code   **491**
  Application Object Maintenance Operations   **492**
    Package Maintenance Operations   493
    Server Folder Maintenance   494
    Package Role Maintenance   495

Contents

Package Monitoring   495

A Package Management Example   496

Package Log Providers   **505**

Specifying Events to Log   506

Programming Log Providers   507

Package Configurations   **509**

Creating a Configuration   510

Programming the Configuration Object   511

Configuration Object   512

Windows Management Instrumentation Tasks   **512**

WMI Reader Task Explained   513

WMI Event Watcher Task   514

WMI Data Reader Example   515

WMI Event Watcher Task Example   521

Summary   **522**

Chapter 17: Using SSIS with External Applications   523

RSS In, Reporting Services Report Out   **524**

InfoPath Document   **532**

ASP.NET Application   **540**

Summary   **545**

Chapter 18: SSIS Software Development Life Cycle   547

Introduction to Software Development Life Cycles   **548**

Software Development Life Cycles: A Brief History   548

Types of Software Development Life Cycles   549

Versioning and Source Code Control   **550**

Microsoft Visual SourceSafe   550

Team Foundation Server, Team System, and SSIS   565

MSF Agile and SSIS   570

The Project Portal   573

Putting It to Work   573

Code Deployment and Promotion from Development to Test to Production   **587**

The Deployment Wizard   588

Import a Package   589

Summary   **591**

Contents

Chapter 19: Case Study: A Programmatic Example   593

Background   **593**
Business Problem   **594**
Solution Summary   **594**
Solution Architecture   **595**
Data Architecture   **599**
    File Storage Location Setup   599
    Bank ACH Payments   599
    Lockbox Files   600
    PayPal or Direct Credits to Corporate Account   601
    Case Study Database Model   601
    Database Setup   602
Case Study Load Package   **610**
    Naming Conventions and Tips   611
    Package Setup and File System Tasks   612
    Lockbox Control Flow Processing   616
    Lockbox Validation   622
    Lockbox Processing   631
    ACH Control Flow Processing   635
    ACH Validation   639
    ACH Processing   643
    E-mail Payment Processing   645
    E-mail Data Flow Processing   648
    Testing   651
Case Study Process Package   **651**
    Package Setup   652
    High-Confidence Data Flow   654
    Medium-Confidence Data Flow   659
    Interpreting the Results   663
Running in SQL Agent   **664**
Summary   **665**

Index   **667**

Foreword

It was back in 2001 when I first started to manage the then data transformation services team. At that time, I'd just moved over from working on the Analysis Services team. I did not have much of a background in DTS but was a great fan of the product and was willing to learn and eager to get started. The question was, What is the best way to get up to speed with the product in a short amount of time?

As I asked around, almost all my new teammates recommended "the red book," which of course was Brian Knight and Mark Chaffin's *Professional DTS* book. And right they were; this book is comprehensive, detailed, and easy to follow with clear examples. I think that it has been invaluable to anyone who wanted to get started with DTS.

Since then a few years have passed, and DTS has evolved into SQL Server Integration Services (SSIS). The philosophical foundations and the customer-centric focus of both these products are the same; their origins undeniably are the same. But SSIS is a totally different product that plays in a very different space than DTS. Indeed DTS is a very popular functionality of SQL Server. It is used by almost everyone who has a need to move data or tables in any from. In fact, according to some surveys, more than 70 percent of all SQL Server users use DTS. Given the popularity of DTS, one might ask why we chose to pretty much rewrite this product and build SSIS.

The answer lies in what most defines the SSIS/DTS team: listening to our customers. We had been hearing again and again from customers that while they loved DTS, they still felt the need to buy a complementary ETL product, especially in the higher-end/enterprise space. We heard a repeating theme around performance, scalability, complexity, and extensibility. Customers just wanted more from DTS. Among those providing us this feedback were the authors of this book, and I personally have had a lot of feedback from Mark Chaffin on the evolution of DTS into SSIS. Along with the need to greatly expand the functionality, performance, and scalability of the product, there was the implicit need to adapt to the emerging .NET and managed code architectures that were beginning to sweep our industry. All this together led to the only logical conclusion, and this was to build a new product from the ground up, not just to tweak DTS or even to build on the legacy architecture. After we shipped SQL 2000, this effort to take DTS to the next level slowly began.

Luckily for us, we had some great vision and direction on what this new product should be. Euan Garden, who had been the program manager for DTS, Gert Drapers, who was then architect/manager for DTS, Jag Bhalla, whose company we had acquired, and Bill Baker, the general manager for all of SQL Server's Business Intelligence efforts, provided that initial direction and set the course for what was to become SSIS. The DTS team was still part of the Management Tools team, and it was only in 2001 that it became a separate team. It was still a very small team, but one with a clear and very important mission: complete the SQL BI "stack" by developing an industry-leading ETL/data integration platform.

So here I was in the summer of 2001, taking over the team with a huge mission and just one thing to do: deliver on this mission! The initial team was quite small but extremely talented. They included Mark Blaszczak, the most prolific developer I have ever met; Jag Bhalla, a business-savvy data warehouse industry veteran; James Howey, a deeply technical PM with an intuitive grasp of the data pipeline;

Kirk Haselden, a natural leader and highly structured developer; and Ted Lee, a veteran developer of two previous versions of SQL Server (just about the only one who really understood the legacy DTS code base!). We built the team up both via external hiring and internal "poaching" and soon had most of our positions filled. Notable additions to the team included Donald Farmer, the incredibly talented and customer-facing GPM who now is in many ways most identified with SSIS; Ashvini Sharma, the UI dev lead with a never-say-die attitude and incredible customer empathy; and Jeff Bernhard, the dev manager whose pet projects caused much angst but significantly enhanced the functionality of the product. Before we knew it, Beta 1 was upon us. After Beta 1 we were well on our way to deliver what is now SSIS. Somewhere along the way, it became clear that the product we were building was no longer DTS; it was a lot more in every way possible. After much internal debate, we decided to rename the product. But what to call it? There were all sorts of names suggested (e.g., METL) and we went through all kinds of touchy-feely interviews about the emotional responses evoked by candidate names. In the end, we settled on a simple yet comprehensive name that had been suggested very early on in the whole naming process: Integration Services (with the SQL Server prefix to clarify that this was about SQL Server data).

That DTS was part of the larger SQL BI group helped immensely, and the design of SSIS reflects this pedigree on many levels. My earliest involvement with DTS was during the initial planning for Yukon (SQL 2005) when I was part of a small sub-team involved in mocking up the user experience for the evolution of the DTS designer. The incredible potential of enabling deep integration with the OLAP and Data Mining technologies fascinated me right from the beginning (and this fascination of going "beyond ETL" still continues — check out www.beyondetl.com). Some of this integration is covered in Chapter 6 of this book along with Chapter 4, which provides a very good introduction to the new Data Flow task and its components. Another related key part of SSIS is its extensibility, both in terms of scripting as well as building custom components (tasks and transforms). Chapter 14 of this book, written by Darren and Allen (who also run SQLIS.com and who are our MVPs), is a great introduction to this.

I should add that while I have written this foreword in the first person and tried to provide some insight into the development of SSIS, my role on the team is a supporting one at best, and the product is the result of an absolutely incredible team: hardworking, dedicated, customer-focused, and unassuming. In fact, many of them (Runying Mao, James Howey, Ashvini Sharma, Bob Bojanic, Ted Lee, and Grant Dickinson) helped review this book for technical accuracy. In the middle of a very hectic time (trying to wrap up five years' worth of development takes a lot), they found time to review this book!

I am assuming that by the time you read this book, we will have signed off on the final bits for SQL 2005. It's been a long but rewarding journey, delivering what I think is a great product with some great features. SSIS is a key addition to SQL Server 2005, and this book will help you to become proficient with it. SSIS is easy to get started with, but it is a very deep and rich product with subtle complexities. This book will make it possible for you to unlock the vast value that is provided by SSIS. I sincerely hope you enjoy both this book and working with SQL Server 2005 Integration Services.

Kamal Hathi
Product Unit Manager
SQL Server Integration Services

Introduction

SQL Server Integration Services (SSIS) is now in its third and largest evolution since its invention. It has gone from a side-note feature of SQL Server to a major player in the Extract Transform Load (ETL) market. With that evolution comes an evolving user base to the product. What once was a DBA feature has now grown to be used by SQL Server developers and casual users that may not even know they're using the product.

The best thing about SSIS is its price tag: free with your SQL Server purchase. Many ETL vendors charge hundreds of thousands of dollars for what you will see in this book. SSIS is also a great platform for you to expand and integrate into, which many ETL vendors do not offer. Once you get past the initial learning curve, you'll be amazed with the power of the tool, and it can take weeks off your time to market.

Who This Book Is For

Having used SSIS for years through its evolution, the idea of writing this book was quite compelling. If you've used DTS in the past, I'm afraid you'll have to throw out your old knowledge and start nearly anew. Very little from the original DTS was kept in this release. Microsoft has spent the five years between releases making the SSIS environment a completely new enterprise-strength ETL tool. So, if you considered yourself pretty well-versed in DTS, you're now back to square one.

This book is intended for developers, DBAs, and casual users who hope to use SSIS for transforming data, creating a workflow, or maintaining their SQL Server. This book is a *professional* book, meaning that the authors assume that you know the basics of how to query a SQL Server and have some rudimentary programming skills. Not much programming skills will be needed or assumed, but it will help with your advancement. No skills in the prior release of SSIS (called DTS then) are required, but we do reference it throughout the book when we call attention to feature enhancements.

How This Book Is Structured

The first four chapters of this book are structured more as instructional, laying the groundwork for the later chapters. From Chapter 5 on, we show you how to perform a task as we explain the feature. SSIS is a very feature-rich product, and it took a lot to cover the product:

Chapter 1 introduces the concepts that we're going to discuss throughout the remainder of this book. We talk about the SSIS architecture and give a brief overview of what you can do with SSIS.

Chapter 2 shows you how to quickly learn how to import and export data by using the Import and Export Wizard and then takes you on a tour of the Business Intelligence Development Studio (BIDS).

Chapter 3 goes into each of the tasks that are available to you in SSIS.

Chapter 4 covers how to use containers to do looping in SSIS and describes how to configure each of the basic transforms.

Now that you know how to configure most of the tasks and transforms, Chapter 5 puts it all together with a large example that lets you try out your SSIS experience.

Chapter 6 is where we cover each of the more advanced tasks and transforms that were too complex to talk about in much depth in the previous three chapters.

Chapter 7 shows you some of the ways you can use the Script task in SSIS. This chapter also speaks to expressions.

Sometimes you connect to systems other than SQL Server. Chapter 8 shows you how to connect to systems other than SQL Server like Excel, XML, and Web Services.

Chapter 9 demonstrates how to scale SSIS and make it more reliable. You can use the features in this chapter to show you how to make the package restartable if a problem occurs.

Chapter 10 teaches the Data Flow buffer architecture and how to monitor the Data Flow execution.

Chapter 11 shows how to performance tune the Data Flow and some of the best practices.

Chapter 12 shows how to migrate DTS 2000 packages to SSIS and if necessary how to run DTS 2000 packages under SSIS. It also discusses metadata management.

Chapter 13 discusses how to handle problems with SSIS with error and event handling.

Chapter 14 shows the SSIS object model and how to use it to extend SSIS. The chapter goes through creating your own components, and then Chapter 15 adds a user interface to the discussion.

Chapter 16 walks through creating an application that interfaces with the SSIS to manage the environment. It also discusses the WMI set of tasks.

Chapter 17 teaches you how to expose the SSIS Data Flow to other programs like InfoPath, Reporting Services, and your own .NET application.

Chapter 18 introduces a software development life cycle methodology to you. It speaks to how SSIS can integrate with Visual Studio Team Systems.

Chapter 19 is a programmatic case study that creates three SSIS packages for a banking application.

What You Need to Use This Book

To follow this book, you will only need to have SQL Server 2005 and the Integration Services component installed. You'll need a machine that can support the minimum hardware requirements to run SQL Server 2005. You'll also want to have the AdventureWorks and AdventureWorksDW databases installed. (For Chapters 14 and 15, you will also need Visual Studio 2005 and C# to run the samples.)

Conventions

To help you get the most from the text and keep track of what's happening, we've used a number of conventions throughout the book.

❏   We *highlight* new terms and important words when we introduce them.

❏   We show keyboard strokes like this: Ctrl+A.

❏   We show file names, URLs, and code within the text like so: `persistence.properties`.

❏   We present code in two different ways:

```
In code examples we highlight new and important code with a gray background.
```

```
The gray highlighting is not used for code that's less important in the present
context or that has been shown before.
```

Source Code

As you work through the examples in this book, you may choose either to type in all the code manually or to use the source code files that accompany the book. All of the source code used in this book is available for download at `http://www.wrox.com`. Once at the site, simply locate the book's title (either by using the Search box or by using one of the title lists) and click the Download Code link on the book's detail page to obtain all the source code for the book.

Because many books have similar titles, you may find it easiest to search by ISBN; this book's ISBN is 0-7645-8435-9 (changing to 978-0-7645-8435-0, as the new industry-wide 13-digit ISBN numbering system will be phased in by January 2007).

Once you download the code, just decompress it with your favorite compression tool. Alternately, you can go to the main Wrox code download page at `www.wrox.com/dynamic/books/download.aspx` to see the code available for this book and all other Wrox books.

Errata

We make every effort to ensure that there are no errors in the text or in the code. However, no one is perfect, and mistakes do occur. If you find an error in one of our books, like a spelling mistake or faulty piece of code, we would be very grateful for your feedback. By sending in errata, you may save another reader hours of frustration, and at the same time you will be helping us provide even higher-quality information.

To find the errata page for this book, go to `http://www.wrox.com` and locate the title using the Search box or one of the title lists. Then, on the book details page, click the Book Errata link. On this page you can view all errata that has been submitted for this book and posted by Wrox editors. A complete book list including links to each book's errata is also available at `www.wrox.com/misc-pages/booklist.shtml`.

If you don't spot "your" error on the Book Errata page, go to www.wrox.com/contact/techsupport .shtml and complete the form there to send us the error you have found. We'll check the information and, if appropriate, post a message to the book's errata page and fix the problem in subsequent editions of the book.

p2p.wrox.com

For author and peer discussion, join the P2P forums at p2p.wrox.com. The forums are a Web-based system for you to post messages relating to Wrox books and related technologies and to interact with other readers and technology users. The forums offer a subscription feature to e-mail you topics of interest of your choosing when new posts are made to the forums. Wrox authors, editors, other industry experts, and your fellow readers are present on these forums.

At http://p2p.wrox.com you will find a number of different forums that will help you not only as you read this book but also as you develop your own applications. To join the forums, just follow these steps:

1. Go to p2p.wrox.com and click the Register link.

2. Read the terms of use and click Agree.

3. Complete the required information to join as well as any optional information you wish to provide and click Submit.

4. You will receive an e-mail with information describing how to verify your account and complete the joining process.

You can read messages in the forums without joining P2P, but in order to post your own messages, you must join.

Once you join, you can post new messages and respond to messages other users post. You can read messages at any time on the Web. If you would like to have new messages from a particular forum e-mailed to you, click the Subscribe to this Forum icon by the forum name in the forum listing.

For more information about how to use the Wrox P2P, be sure to read the P2P FAQs for answers to questions about how the forum software works as well as many common questions specific to P2P and Wrox books. To read the FAQs, click the FAQ link on any P2P page.

Welcome to SQL Server Integration Services

SQL Server Integration Services (SSIS) is one of the most powerful features in SQL Server 2005. It is technically classified as a business intelligence feature and is a robust way to load data and perform tasks in a workflow. Even though it's mainly used for data loads, you can use it to do other tasks in a workflow like executing a program or a script, or it can be extended. This chapter describes much of the architecture of SSIS and covers the basics of tasks.

What's New in SQL Server 2005 SSIS

In SQL Server 7.0, Microsoft had a small team of developers work on a much understated feature of SQL Server called Data Transformation Services (DTS). DTS was the backbone of the Import/Export Wizard, and the DTS's primary purpose was to transform data from almost any OLE DB–compliant data source to another destination. It also had the ability to execute programs and run scripts, making workflow a minor feature.

By the time that SQL Server 2000 was released, DTS had a strong following of DBAs and developers. Microsoft included in the release new features like the Dynamic Properties task to help you dynamically alter the package at runtime. It also had extended logging and broke a transformation into many phases, called the multiphase data pump. Usability studies still showed that at this point developers had to create elaborate scripts to extend DTS to do what they wanted. For example, if you wanted DTS to conditionally load data based on the existence of a file, you would have to use the ActiveX Script task and VBScript to dynamically do this. The problem here was that most DBAs didn't have this type of scripting experience.

After five years, Microsoft released the much touted SQL Server 2005, where DTS is no longer an understated feature, but one of the main business intelligence (BI) foundations. It's been given so much importance now that it has its own service. DTS has also been renamed to SQL Server Integration Services (SSIS). So much has been added to SSIS that the rename of the product was most appropriate. Microsoft made a huge investment in usability and making it so that there is no longer a need for scripting.

Most of this book will assume that you know nothing about the past releases of SQL Server DTS and will start with a fresh look at SQL Server 2005 SSIS. After all, when you dive into the new features, you'll realize how little knowing anything about the old release actually helps you when learning this one. The learning curve can be considered steep at first, but once you figure out the basics, you'll be creating what would have been complex packages in SQL Server 2000 in minutes.

You can start differentiating the new SSIS by looking at the toolbox that you now have at your fingertips as an SSIS developer. The names of the tools and how you use them have changed dramatically, but the tools all existed in a different form in SQL Server 2000. This section introduces you briefly to each of the tools, but you will explore them more deeply beginning in the next chapter.

Import and Export Wizard

If you need to move data quickly from almost any OLE DB–compliant data source to a destination, you can use the SSIS Import and Export Wizard (shown in Figure 1-1). The wizard is a quick way to move the data and perform very light transformations of data. It has not changed substantially from SQL Server 2000. Like SQL Server 2000, it still gives you the option of checking all the tables you'd like to transfer. You also get the option now of encapsulating the entire transfer of data into a single transaction.

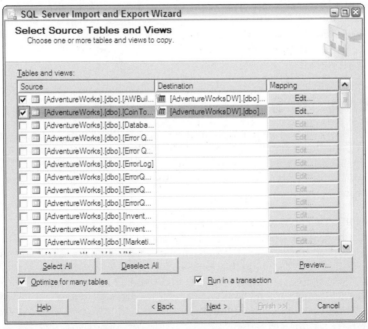

Figure 1-1

The Business Intelligence Development Studio

The Business Intelligence Development Studio (BIDS) is the central tool that you'll spend most of your time in as a SQL Server 2005 SSIS developer. Like the rest of SQL Server 2005, the tool's foundation is the Visual Studio 2005 interface (shown in Figure 1-2), which is the equivalent of the DTS Designer in SQL Server 2000. The nicest thing about the tool is that it's not bound to any particular SQL Server. In other words, you won't have to connect to a SQL Server to design a SSIS package. You can design the package disconnected from your SQL Server environment and then deploy it to your target SQL Server you'd like it to run on. This interface will be discussed in much more detail in Chapter 3.

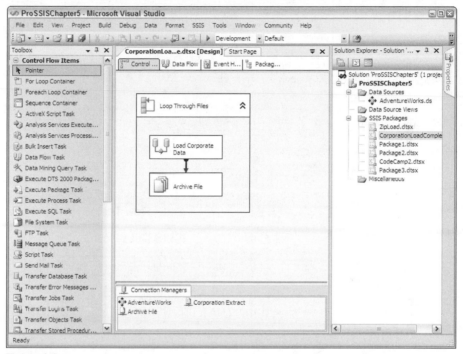

Figure 1-2

Architecture

SQL Server 2005 has truly evolved SSIS into a major player in the extraction, transformation, and loading (ETL) market. It was a complete code rewrite from SQL Server 2000 DTS. What's especially nice about SSIS is its price tag, which is free with the purchase of SQL Server. Other ETL tools can cost hundreds of thousands of dollars based on how you scale the software. The SSIS architecture has also expanded dramatically, as you can see in Figure 1-3. The SSIS architecture consists of four main components:

- ❑ The SSIS Service
- ❑ The SSIS runtime engine and the runtime executables
- ❑ The SSIS data flow engine and the data flow components
- ❑ The SSIS clients

3

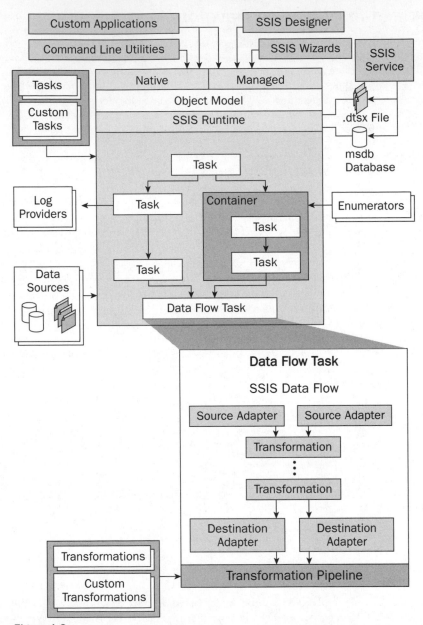

Figure 1-3

The SSIS Service handles the operational aspects of SSIS. It is a Windows service that is installed when you install the SSIS component of SQL Server 2005, and it tracks the execution of packages (a collection of work items) and helps with the storage of the packages. Don't worry; you'll learn more about what packages are momentarily. The SSIS Service is turned off by default and is set to disabled. It only turns on when a package is executed for the first time. You don't need the SSIS service to run SSIS packages, but if the service is stopped, all the SSIS packages that are currently running will in turn stop.

The SSIS runtime engine and its complementary programs actually run your SSIS packages. The engine saves the layout of your packages and manages the logging, debugging, configuration, connections, and transactions. Additionally, it manages handling your events when one is raised in your package. The runtime executables provide the following functionality to a package that you'll explore in more detail later in this chapter:

❑ **Containers:** Provide structure and scope to your package

❑ **Tasks:** Provide the functionality to your package

❑ **Event Handlers:** Respond to raised events in your package

❑ **Precedence Constraints:** Provide ordinal relationship between various items in your package

In Chapter 3, you'll spend a lot of time in each of these architecture sections, but the vital ones are introduced here.

Packages

A core component of SSIS and DTS is the notion of a *package*. A package best parallels an executable program in Windows. Essentially, a package is a collection of tasks that execute in an orderly fashion. Precedence constraints help manage which order the tasks will execute in. A package can be saved onto a SQL Server, which in actuality is saved in the msdb database. It can also be saved as a .DTSX file, which is an XML-structured file much like .RDL files are to Reporting Services. Of course, there is much more to packages than that, but you'll explore the other elements of packages, like event handlers, later in this chapter.

Tasks

A *task* can best be described as an individual unit of work. They provide functionality to your package, in much the same way that a method does in a programming language. The following are some of the tasks available to you:

❑ **ActiveX Script Task:** Executes an ActiveX script in your SSIS package. This task is mostly for legacy DTS packages.

❑ **Analysis Services Execute DDL Task:** Executes a DDL task in Analysis Services. For example, this can create, drop, or alter a cube.

❑ **Analysis Services Processing Task:** This task processes a SQL Server Analysis Services cube, dimension, or mining model.

❑ **Bulk Insert Task:** Loads data into a table by using the BULK INSERT SQL command.

❑ **Data Flow Task:** This very specialized task loads and transforms data into an OLE DB destination.

❑ **Data Mining Query Task:** Allows you to run predictive queries against your Analysis Services data-mining models.

❑ **Execute DTS 2000 Package Task:** Exposes legacy SQL Server 2000 DTS packages to your SSIS 2005 package.

- ❑ **Execute Package Task:** Allows you to execute a package from within a package, making your SSIS packages modular.

- ❑ **Execute Process Task:** Executes a program external to your package, such as one to split your extract file into many files before processing the individual files.

- ❑ **Execute SQL Task:** Executes a SQL statement or stored procedure.

- ❑ **File System Task:** This task can handle directory operations such as creating, renaming, or deleting a directory. It can also manage file operations such as moving, copying, or deleting files.

- ❑ **FTP Task:** Sends or receives files from an FTP site.

- ❑ **Message Queue Task:** Send or receives messages from a Microsoft Message Queue (MSMQ).

- ❑ **Script Task:** Slightly more advanced than the ActiveX Script task. This task allows you to perform more intense scripting in the Visual Studio programming environment.

- ❑ **Send Mail Task:** Send a mail message through SMTP.

- ❑ **Web Service Task:** Executes a method on a Web service.

- ❑ **WMI Data Reader Task:** This task can run WQL queries against the Windows Management Instrumentation. This allows you to read the event log, get a list of applications that are installed, or determine hardware that is installed, to name a few examples.

- ❑ **WMI Event Watcher Task:** This task empowers SSIS to wait for and respond to certain WMI events that occur in the operating system.

- ❑ **XML Task:** Parses or processes an XML file. It can merge, split, or reformat an XML file.

There is also an array of tasks that can be used to maintain your SQL Server environment. These tasks perform functions such as transferring your SQL Server databases, backing up your database, or shrinking the database. Each of the tasks available to you is described in Chapter 3 in much more detail, and those tasks will be used in many examples throughout the book. Tasks are extensible, and you can create your own tasks in a language like C# to perform tasks in your environment, such as reading data from your proprietary mainframe.

Data Source Elements

The main purpose of SSIS remains lifting data, transforming it, and writing it to a destination. Data sources are the connections that can be used for the source or destination to transform that data. A data source can be nearly any OLE-DB-compliant data source such as SQL Server, Oracle, DB2, or even nontraditional data sources such as Analysis Services and Outlook. The data sources can be localized to a single SSIS package or shared across multiple packages in BIDS.

A connection is defined in the Connection Manager. The Connection Manager dialog box may vary vastly based on the type of connection you're trying to configure. Figure 1-4 shows you what a typical connection to SQL Server would look like.

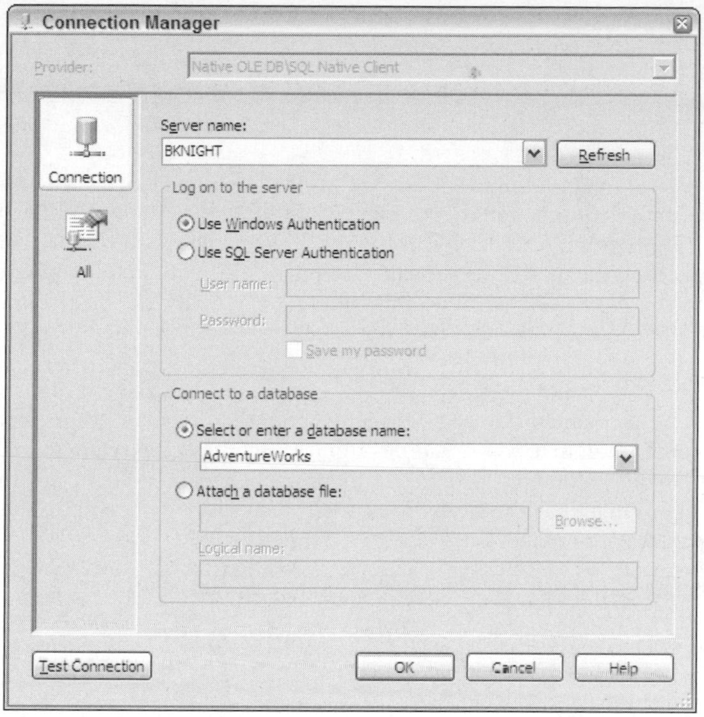

Figure 1-4

You can configure the connection completely offline, and the SSIS package will not use it until you begin to instantiate it in the package. The nice thing about this is that you can develop in an airport and then connect as needed.

Data Source Views

Data source views (DSVs) are a new concept to SQL Server 2005. This feature allows you to create a logical view of your business data. They are a collection of tables, views, stored procedures, and queries that can be shared across your project and leveraged in Analysis Services and Report Builder.

This is especially useful in large complex data models that are prevalent in ERP systems like Siebel or SAP. These systems have column names like ER328F2 to make the data model flexible to support nearly any environment. This complex model naming convention creates positions of people in companies who specialize in just reading the model for reports. The business user, though, would never know what a column like this means, so a DSV may map this column to an entity like LastPaymentDate. It also maps the relationships between the tables that may not necessarily exist in the physical model.

DSVs also allow you to segment a large data model into more bite-sized chunks. For example, your Siebel system may be segmented into a DSV called Accounting, Human Resource, and Inventory. One example called Human Resource can be seen in Figure 1-5. As you can see in this figure, a friendly name has been assigned to one column called Birth Date (previously named BirthDate without the space) in the Employee entity. While this is a simplistic example, it's especially useful for the ER328F2 column previously mentioned.

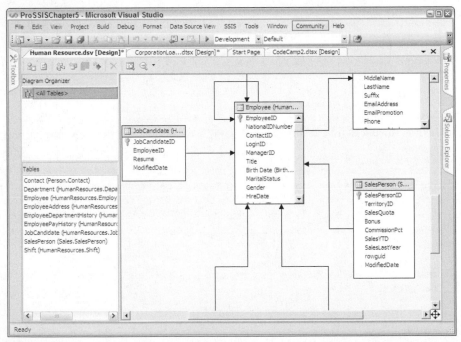

Figure 1-5

DSVs are deployed as a connection manager. There are a few key things to remember with data source views. Like data sources, DSVs allow you to define the connection logic once and reuse it across your SSIS packages. Unlike connections, though, DSVs are disconnected from the source connection and are not refreshed as the source structure changes. For example, if you change the Employee table in a connection to Resources, the DSV will not pick up the change. Where this type of caching is a huge benefit is in development. DSVs allow you to utilize cached metadata in development, even if you're in an airport, disconnected. It also speeds up package development. Since your DSV is most likely a subset of the actual data source, your SSIS connection dialog boxes will load much faster.

Precedence Constraints

Precedence constraints direct the tasks to execute in a given order. They direct the workflow of your SSIS package based on given conditions. Precedence constraints have been enhanced dramatically in SQL Server 2005 Integration Services conditional branching of your workflow based on conditions.

Constraint Value

Constraint values are the type of precedence constraint that you may be familiar with in SQL Server 2000. There are three types of constraint values:

❑ **Success:** A task that's chained to another task with this constraint will execute only if the prior task completes successfully.

❑ **Completion:** A task that's chained to another task with this constraint will execute if the prior task completes. Whether the prior task succeeds or fails is inconsequential.

❑ **Failure:** A task that's chained to another task with this constraint will execute only if the prior task fails to complete. This type of constraint is usually used to notify an operator of a failed event or write bad records to an exception queue.

Conditional Expressions

The nicest improvement to precedence constraints in SSIS 2005 is the ability to dynamically follow workflow paths based on certain conditions being met. These conditions use the new conditional expressions to drive the workflow. An *expression* allows you to evaluate whether certain conditions have been met before the task is executed and the path followed. The *constraint* evaluates only the success or failure of the previous task to determine whether the next step will be executed. The SSIS developer can set the conditions by using evaluation operators. Once you create a precedence constraint, you can set the EvalOp property to any one of the following options:

❑ **Constraint:** This is the default setting and specifies that only the constraint will be followed in the workflow.

❑ **Expression:** This option gives you the ability to write an expression (much like VB.NET) that allows you to control the workflow based on conditions that you specify.

❑ **ExpressionAndConstraint:** Specifies that both the expression and the constraint must be met before proceeding.

❑ **ExpressionOrConstraint:** Specifies that either the expression or the constraint can be met before proceeding.

An example workflow can be seen in Figure 1-6. This package first copies files using the File System task, and if that is successful and meets certain criteria in the expression, it will transform the files using the Data Flow task. If the first step fails, then a message will be sent to the user by using the Send Mail task. You can also see the small *fx* icon above the Data Flow task. This is graphically showing the developer that this task will not execute unless an expression has also been met and the previous step has successfully completed. The expression can check anything, such as looking at a checksum, before running the Data Flow task.

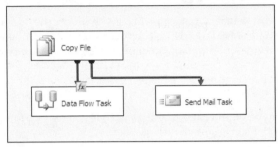

Figure 1-6

Containers

Containers are a new concept in SSIS that didn't previously exist in SQL Server. They are a core unit in the SSIS architecture that help you logically group tasks together into units of work or create complex conditions. By using containers, SSIS variables and event handlers (these will be discussed in a moment) can be defined to have the scope of the container instead of the package. There are four types of containers that can be employed in SSIS:

❑ **Task host container:** The core type of container that every task implicitly belongs to by default. The SSIS architecture extends variables and event handlers to the task through the task host container.

❑ **Sequence container:** Allows you to group tasks into logical subject areas. In BIDS, you can then collapse or expand this container for usability.

❑ **For loop container:** Loops through a series of tasks for a given amount of time or until a condition is met.

❑ **For each loop container:** Loops through a series of files or records in a data set and then executes the tasks in the container for each record in the collection.

As you read through this book, you'll gain lots of experience with the various types of containers.

Variables

Variables are one of the most powerful components of the SSIS architecture. In SQL Server 7.0 and 2000 DTS, these were called global variables, but they've been drastically improved on in SSIS. Variables allow you to dynamically configure a package at runtime. Without variables, each time you wanted to deploy a package from development to production, you'd have to open the package and change all the hard-coded connection settings to point to the new environment. Now with variables, you can just change the variables at deployment time, and anything that uses those variables will in turn be changed. Variables have the scope of an individual container, package, or system.

Data Flow Elements

Once you create a Data Flow task, it spawns a new data flow. Just as the Controller Flow handles the main workflow of the package, the data flow handles the transformation of data. Almost anything that manipulates data falls into the data flow category. As data moves through each step of the data flow, the data changes based on what the transform does. For example in Figure 1-7, a new column is derived using the Derived Column transform, and that new column is then available to subsequent transformations or to the destination.

In this section, each of the sources, destinations, and transformations will be briefly covered. These areas are covered in much more detail in Chapters 3 and 4.

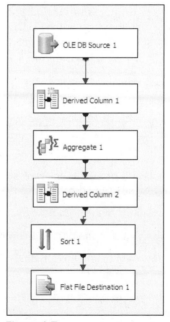

Figure 1-7

Sources

A *source* is where you specify the location of your source data to pull from in the data pump. Sources will generally point to the Connection Manager in SSIS. By pointing to the Connection Manager, you can reuse connections throughout your package, because you need only change the connection in one place. There are six sources altogether that can be used out of the box with SSIS:

❑ **OLE DB Source:** Connects to nearly any OLE DB data source, such as SQL Server, Access, Oracle, or DB2, to name just a few.

❑ **Excel Source:** Source that specializes in receiving data from Excel spreadsheets. This source also makes it easy to run SQL queries against your Excel spreadsheet to narrow the scope of the data that you wish to pass through the flow.

❑ **Flat File Source:** Connects to a delimited or fixed-width file.

❑ **Raw File Source:** A specialized file format that was produced by a Raw File Destination (discussed momentarily). The Raw File Source usually represents data that is in transit and is especially quick to read.

❑ **XML Source:** Can retrieve data from an XML document.

❑ **Data Reader Source:** The DataReader source is an ADO.NET connection much like the one you see in the .NET Framework when you use the DataReader interface in your application code to connect to a database.

Destinations

Inside the data flow, destinations accept the data from the data sources and from the transformations. The flexible architecture can send the data to nearly any OLE DB–compliant data source or to a flat file. Like sources, destinations are managed through the Connection Manager. The following destinations are available to you in SSIS:

❑ **Data Mining Model Training:** This destination trains an Analysis Services mining model by passing in data from the data flow to the destination.

❑ **DataReader Destination:** Allows you to expose data to other external processes, such as Reporting Services or your own .NET application. It uses the ADO.NET DataReader interface to do this.

❑ **Dimension Processing:** Loads and processes an Analysis Services dimension. It can perform a full, update, or incremental refresh of the dimension.

❑ **Excel Destination:** Outputs data from the data flow to an Excel spreadsheet.

❑ **Flat File Destination:** Enables you to write data to a comma-delimited or fixed-width file.

❑ **OLE DB Destination:** Outputs data to an OLE DB data connection like SQL Server, Oracle, or Access.

❑ **Partition Processing:** Enables you to perform incremental, full, or update processing of an Analysis Services partition.

❑ **Raw File Destination:** This destination outputs data that can later be used in the Raw File Source. It is a very specialized format that is very quick to output to.

❑ **Recordset Destination:** Writes the records to an ADO record set.

❑ **SQL Server Destination:** The destination that you use to write data to SQL Server most efficiently.

❑ **SQL Server Mobile Destination:** Inserts data into a SQL Server running on a Pocket PC.

Transformations

Transformations are key components to the data flow that change the data to a desired format. For example, you may want your data to be sorted and aggregated. Two transformations can accomplish this task for you. The nicest thing about transformations in SSIS is that it's all done in-memory and it no longer requires elaborate scripting as in SQL Server 2000 DTS. The transformation is covered in Chapters 4 and 6. Here's a complete list of transforms:

- ❑ **Aggregate:** Aggregates data from transform or source.

- ❑ **Audit:** The transformation that exposes auditing information to the package, such as when the package was run and by whom.

- ❑ **Character Map:** This transformation makes string data changes for you, such as changing data from lowercase to uppercase.

- ❑ **Conditional Split:** Splits the data based on certain conditions being met. For example, this transformation could be instructed to send data down a different path if the State column is equal to Florida.

- ❑ **Copy Column:** Adds a copy of a column to the transformation output. You can later transform the copy, keeping the original for auditing purposes.

- ❑ **Data Conversion:** Converts a column's data type to another data type.

- ❑ **Data Mining Query:** Performs a data-mining query against Analysis Services.

- ❑ **Derived Column:** Creates a new derived column calculated from an expression.

- ❑ **Export Column:** This transformation allows you to export a column from the data flow to a file. For example, you can use this transformation to write a column that contains an image to a file.

- ❑ **Fuzzy Grouping:** Performs data cleansing by finding rows that are likely duplicates.

- ❑ **Fuzzy Lookup:** Matches and standardizes data based on fuzzy logic. For example, this can transform the name Jon to John.

- ❑ **Import Column:** Reads data from a file and adds it into a data flow.

- ❑ **Lookup:** Performs a lookup on data to be used later in a transformation. For example, you can use this transformation to look up a city based on the zip code.

- ❑ **Merge:** Merges two sorted data sets into a single data set in a data flow.

- ❑ **Merge Join:** Merges two data sets into a single data set using a join function.

- ❑ **Multicast:** Sends a copy of the data to an additional path in the workflow.

- ❑ **OLE DB Command:** Executes an OLE DB command for each row in the data flow.

- ❑ **Percentage Sampling:** Captures a sampling of the data from the data flow by using a percentage of the total rows in the data flow.

- ❑ **Pivot:** Pivots the data on a column into a more non-relational form. *Pivoting* a table means that you can slice the data in multiple ways, much like in OLAP and Excel.

❑ **Row Count:** Stores the row count from the data flow into a variable.

❑ **Row Sampling:** Captures a sampling of the data from the data flow by using a row count of the total rows in the data flow.

❑ **Script Component:** Uses a script to transform the data. For example, you can use this to apply specialized business logic to your data flow.

❑ **Slowly Changing Dimension:** Coordinates the conditional insert or update of data in a slowly changing dimension. You'll learn the definition of this term and study the process in Chapter 6.

❑ **Sort:** Sorts the data in the data flow by a given column.

❑ **Term Extraction:** Looks up a noun or adjective in text data.

❑ **Term Lookup:** Looks up terms extracted from text and references the value from a reference table.

❑ **Union All:** Merges multiple data sets into a single data set.

❑ **Unpivot:** Unpivots the data from a non-normalized format to a relational format.

Error Handling and Logging

In SSIS, the package events are exposed in the user interface, with each event having the possibility of its own event handler design surface. This *design surface* is the pane in Visual Studio where you can specify a series of tasks to be performed if a given event happens. There are a multitude of event handlers to help you develop packages that can self-fix problems. For example, the OnError error handler triggers an event whenever an error occurs anywhere in scope. The scope can be the entire package or an individual container. Event handlers are represented as a workflow, much like any other workflow in SSIS. An ideal use for event handlers would be to notify an operator if any component fails inside the package. You'll learn much more about event handlers in Chapter 13.

Handling errors in your data is easy now in SSIS 2005. In the data flow, you can specify in a transformation or connection what you wish to happen if an error exists in your data. You can select that the entire transformation fails and exits upon an error, or the bad rows can be redirected to a failed data flow branch. You can also choose to ignore any errors. An example of an error handler can be seen in Figure 1-8, where if an error occurs during the Derived Column transformation, it will be outputted to the data flow. You can then use that outputted information to write to an output log.

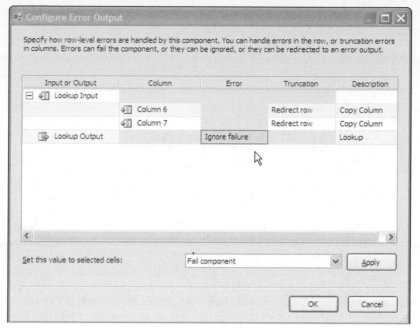

Figure 1-8

Once configured, you can specify that the bad records be written to another connection, as shown in Figure 1-9. The On Failure precedence constraint can be seen as a red line that connects the Derived Column 1 task to the SQL Server Destination. The green arrows are the On Success precedence constraints. You can see the On Success constraint between the OLE DB Source and the Derived Column transform.

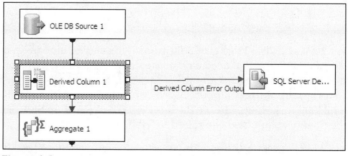

Figure 1-9

Logging has also been improved in SSIS 2005. It is now at a much finer detail than in SQL Server 2000 DTS. There are more than a dozen events that can be logged for each task or package. You can enable partial logging for one task and enable much more detailed logging for billing tasks. Some of the events that can be monitored are OnError, OnPostValidate, OnProgress, and OnWarning, to name just a few. The logs can be written to nearly any connection: SQL Profiler, text files, SQL Server, the Windows Event log, or an XML file.

Editions of SQL Server 2005

The available features in SSIS and SQL Server vary widely based on what edition of SQL Server you're using. As you can imagine, the more high-end the edition of SQL Server, the more features are available. In order from high-end to low-end, the following SQL Server editions are available:

❑ **SQL Server 2005 Enterprise Edition:** The edition of SQL Server for large enterprises that need higher availability and more advanced features in SQL Server and business intelligence. For example, there is no limit on processors or RAM in this edition. You're bound only by the number of processors and amount of RAM that the OS can handle. This edition is available for an estimated retail price (ERP) of $24,999 (U.S.) per processor or $13,499 (U.S.) per server (25 CALs). Microsoft will also continue to support Developer Edition, which lets developers develop SQL Server solutions at a much reduced price. That edition has all the features of Enterprise Edition but is licensed for development purposes only.

❑ **SQL Server 2005 Standard Edition:** This edition of SQL Server has a lot more value in SQL Server 2005. For example, you can now create a highly available system in Standard Edition by using clustering, database mirroring, and integrated 64-bit support. These features were available only in Enterprise Edition in SQL Server 2000 and caused many businesses to purchase Enterprise Edition when Standard Edition was probably sufficient for them. Like Enterprise Edition in SQL Server 2005, it also offers unlimited RAM! Thus, you can scale it as high as your physical hardware and OS will allow. There is a cap of four processors, though. Standard Edition is available for an ERP of $5,999 (U.S.) per processor or $2,799 (U.S.) per server (10 CALs).

❑ **SQL Server 2000 and 2005 Workgroup Editions:** This new edition is designed for small and medium-sized businesses that need a database server with limited business intelligence and Reporting Services. Available for an ERP of $3,899 (U.S.) per processor or $739 (U.S.) per server (5 CALs), Workgroup Edition supports up to two processors with unlimited database size. In SQL Server 2000 Workgroup Edition, the limit is 2 GB of RAM. In SQL Server 2005 Workgroup Edition, the memory limit has been raised to 3 GB.

❑ **SQL Server 2005 Express Edition:** This edition is the equivalent of Desktop Edition (MSDE) in SQL Server 2000 but with several enhancements. For example, MSDE never offered any type of management tool, and this is included in 2005. Also included are the Import and Export Wizard and a series of other enhancements. This remains a free addition of SQL Server for small applications. It has a database size limit of 4 GB. Most important, the query governor has been removed from this edition, allowing for more people to query the instance at the same time.

As for SSIS, you'll have to use at least Standard Edition to receive the bulk of the SSIS features. In the Express and Workgroup Editions, only the Import and Export Wizard is available to you. You'll have to upgrade to Enterprise or Developer Edition to see some features in SSIS. The following advanced transformations are available only with Enterprise Edition:

❑   Analysis Services Partition Processing Destination

❑   Analysis Services Dimension Processing Destination

❑   Data Mining Training Destination

❑   Data Mining Query Component

❑   Fuzzy Grouping

❑   Fuzzy Lookup

❑   Term Extraction

❑   Term Lookup

Half of the above transformations are used in servicing Analysis Services. To continue that theme, one task is available only in Enterprise Edition — the Data Mining Query task.

Summary

In this chapter, you were introduced to the SQL Server Integration Services (SSIS) architecture and some of the different elements you'll be dealing with in SSIS. Tasks are individual units of work that are chained together with precedence constraints. Packages are executable programs in SSIS that are a collection of tasks. Lastly, transformations are the data flow items that change the data to the form you request, such as sorting the data.

In Chapter 2, you'll study some of the wizards you have at your disposal to expedite tasks in SSIS, and in Chapter 3, you'll dive deeper into the various SSIS tasks.

2

The SSIS Tools

As with any Microsoft product, SQL Server ships with a myriad of wizards to make your life easier and reduce your time to market. In this chapter you'll learn about some of the wizards that are available to you. These wizards make transporting data and deploying your packages much easier and can save you hours of work in the long run. The focus will be on the Import and Export Wizard. This wizard allows you to create a package for importing or exporting data quickly. As a matter of fact, you may run this in your day-to-day work without even knowing that SSIS is the back-end for the wizard. The latter part of this chapter will explore other tools that are available to you, such as the Business Intelligence Development Studio.

Import and Export Wizard

The Import and Export Wizard is the easiest method to move data from sources like Oracle, DB2, SQL Server, and text files to nearly any destination. This wizard, which uses SSIS on the back-end, isn't much different from its SQL Server 2000 counterpart. The wizard is a fantastic way to create a shell of a SSIS package that you can later add to. Oftentimes as a SSIS developer, you'll want to relegate the grunt work and heavy lifting to the wizard and then do the more complex coding yourself.

Using the Import and Export Wizard

To get to the Import and Export Wizard, right-click on the database you want to import data from or export data to in SQL Server Management Studio and select Tasks ➪ Import Data (or Export Data based on what task you're performing). You can also open the wizard by right-clicking SSIS Packages in BIDS and selecting SSIS Import and Export Wizard. The last way to open the wizard is by typing **dtswizard.exe** at the command line or Run prompt. No matter whether you need to import or export the data, the first few screens will look very similar.

Once the wizard comes up, you'll see the typical Microsoft wizard welcome screen. Click Next to begin specifying the source connection. In this screen you'll specify where your data is coming from in the Source drop-down box. Once you select the source, the rest of the options on the dialog box may vary based on the type of connection. The default source is SQL Native Client, and it looks like Figure 2-1. You have OLE DB sources like SQL Server, Oracle, and Access available out of the box. You can also use text files, Excel files, and XML files. After selecting the source, you'll have to fill in the provider-specific information. For SQL Server, you must enter the server name, as well as the user name and password you'd like to use. If you're going to connect with your Windows account, simply select Use Windows Authentication. Lastly, choose a database that you'd like to connect to. For most of the examples in this book, you'll use the AdventureWorks database.

Additional sources such as Sybase and DB2 can also become available if you install the vendor's OLE DB providers. Installing Host Integration Services by Microsoft also includes common providers like DB2.

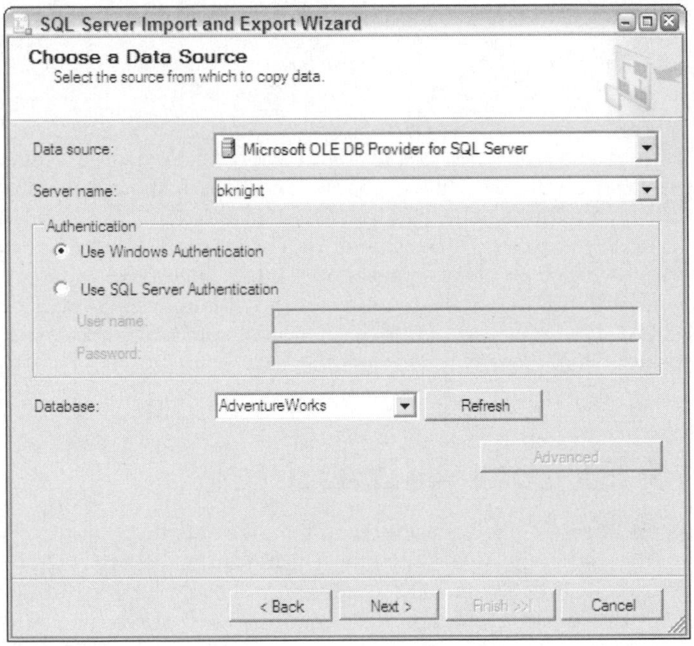

Figure 2-1

After you click Next, you'll be taken to the next screen in the wizard, where you specify the destination for your data. The properties for this screen are exactly identical to those for the previous screen. Click Next again to be taken to the Specify Table Copy or Query screen (see Figure 2-2). On the next screen, if you select "Copy data from one or more tables or views," you'll simply check the tables you want. If you select "Write a query to specify the data to transfer," then you'll be able to write an ad hoc query (after clicking Next) of where to select the data from or what stored procedure to use to retrieve your data.

For the purpose of this example, select "Copy data from one or more tables or views" and click Next. This takes you to the screen where you can check the tables or views that you'd like to transfer to the destination (see Figure 2-3). For this tutorial, check all the tables that belong to the HumanResources schema in the AdventureWorks database.

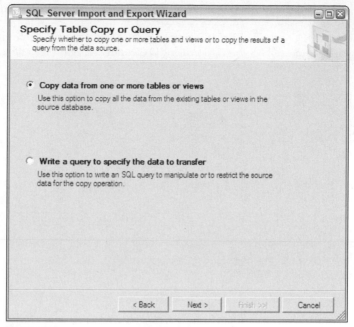

Figure 2-2

You can optionally check the "Optimize for Many Tables" and "Run in a Transaction" checkboxes to encapsulate the entire data move in a single transaction that would roll back if a problem occurs.

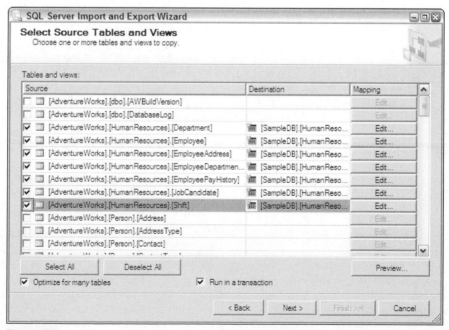

Figure 2-3

If you wish, you can click the Edit buttons to go to the Column Mappings dialog box (see Figure 2-4) for each table. Here you can change the mapping between each source and destination column. For example, if you want the DepartmentID column to go to the DepartmentID2 column on the destination, simply select the Destination cell for the DepartmentID column and point it to the new column, or choose SSIS to ignore the column altogether.

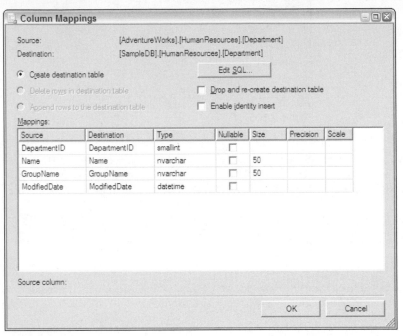

Figure 2-4

Notice that since you're moving the data to a new database that doesn't have the Department table already there, the Create Destination Table option is one of the few options enabled by default. This will create the Department table on the destination before populating it with data from the source. If the table did already exist, you could select that all the rows in the destination table will be deleted before populating it. The default setting if you already have the table there is to append the data from the source to the destination. You can also specify that you want the table to be dropped and re-created. The Edit SQL option allows you to specify the schema for the destination table that will be created.

Finally, you can enable the Identity Insert option if the table you're going to move data into has an identity column. If the table did have an identity column in it, then the wizard will automatically enable this option. If you don't have the option enabled and you try to move data into an identity column, the wizard will fail to execute.

Click OK to apply the settings from the Column Mappings dialog box and Next to proceed to the Save and Execute Package screen. Here you can specify whether you want the package to execute only once or whether you'd like to save the package off for later use. As you saw earlier, you don't necessarily have to execute the package here. You can uncheck Execute Immediately and just save the package for later modification. In this example, set the wizard to Execute Immediately, save the package as a File System file, and click Next. You'll learn more about where to save your SSIS packages in Chapter 3.

You will then be asked how you wish to protect the sensitive data in your package. Again, you'll learn more about this in Chapter 3, so for the time being, specify that you'd like to protect your sensitive data with a password and give the dialog box a password (as shown in Figure 2-5).

Figure 2-5

You will then be taken to the Save SSIS Package screen, where you can type the name of the package and the location to which you'd like to save the package. Optionally, you can add a description to the package. This helps you later operationally when you need to identify the purpose of the package (see Figure 2-6).

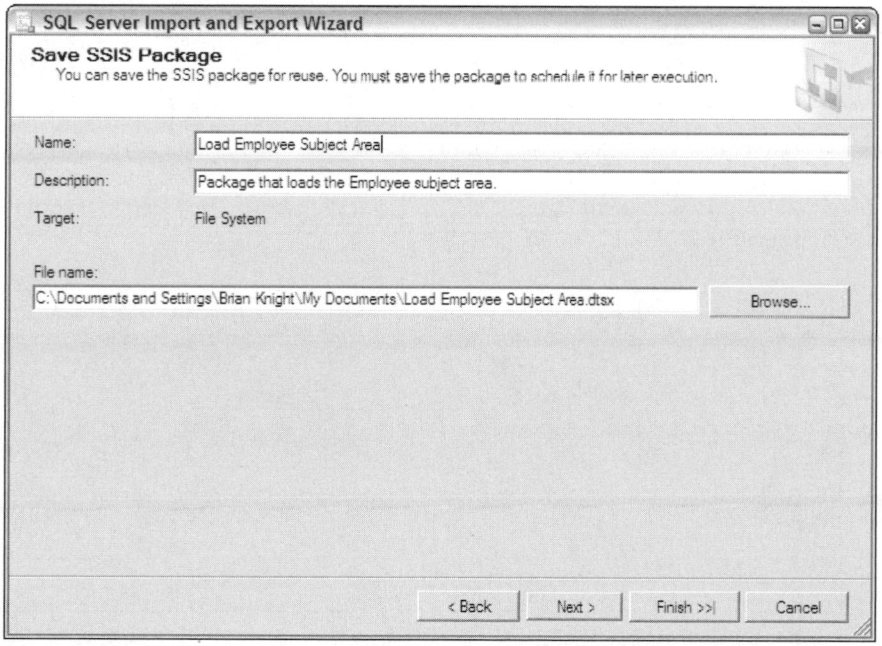

Figure 2-6

Click Next and confirm what tasks you wish the wizard to perform. The package will then execute when you click Finish, and you'll see the page in Figure 2-7. Any errors will be displayed in the Message column. You can also see how many rows were copied over in this column. You can also double-click on an entry that failed to see why it failed.

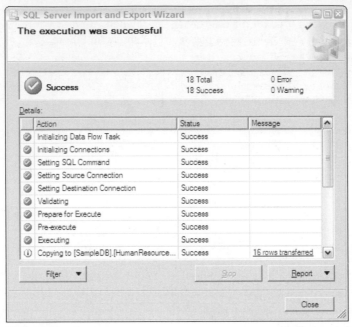

Figure 2-7

After the wizard executes, the package can be found in the location that you have specified, but the default is in the My Documents directory. You can open the package that executed in BIDS. You can see the Data Flow tab for the package in Figure 2-8. There is also a control flow step that contains the preparation steps, such as creating the tables.

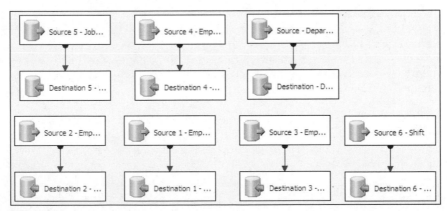

Figure 2-8

You'll also see in the package that there are only two connections: one for the destination and another for the source. Even though it's a shared connection, each transformation runs in parallel, which is a marked improvement from SQL Server 2000, where this would be a serial operation when using a single connection.

Package Installation Wizard

Another wizard that you may see and use regularly is the Package Installation Wizard, which walks you through installing your SSIS project onto a new server. You may receive a .SSISDeploymentManifest file from a vendor or from a developer to run. If you double-click on the file ProSSISChapter5 .SSISDeploymentManifest, for example, it would launch the Package Installation Wizard to install the SSIS project called ProSSISChapter5 into a new environment.

After the wizard's introduction screen, you must choose whether you'd like the wizard to install the packages onto the SQL Server (msdb database) or install them as files on the server. If you select files, you will be prompted for the location you'd like them placed. If you select SQL Server, you'll be prompted for the SQL Server onto which you'd like to install the package.

This wizard will be covered in greater detail in Chapter 18 when deployments are discussed. Until then, you can create a manifest file yourself by right-clicking on a project and selecting Yes for the CreateDeploymentUtility option in the Deployment Utility page.

Business Intelligence Development Studio

The Business Intelligence Development Studio (BIDS) is where most of your time is spent as a SSIS developer. It is where you create, deploy, and manage your SSIS projects.

BIDS uses a light version of Visual Studio 2005. If you have the full version of Visual Studio 2005 and SQL Server 2005 installed, you can create business intelligence projects there as well in the full interface. Either way, the user experience is the same. In SQL Server 2005, the SSIS development environment is detached from SQL Server, so you can develop your SSIS solution offline and then deploy it to wherever you'd like in a single click. Previously, in SQL Server 2000, you had to connect to a SQL Server instance in Enterprise Manager and then open the DTS Designer to create a package.

BIDS can be seen in the root of the SQL Server program group. Once you start BIDS, you'll be taken to the Start Page. An example of a Start Page is shown in Figure 2-9. You can see that a few windows are already open by default: Solution Explorer, Toolbox, Output, and Class View. You can open more windows (you'll learn about these various windows in a moment) by clicking their corresponding icon in the upper-right corner or under the View menu.

The Start Page contains key information about your BIDS environment, such as the last few projects that you had open under the Recent Projects box. In the Getting Started box, you can click Import and Export settings to import your Visual Studio settings from another computer or standardize your development organization's settings. You can also see the latest MSDN news under the MSDN: Visual Studio 2005 box.

The nicest thing about SSIS development in the Visual Studio environment is that it gives you full access to the Visual Studio feature set, such as debugging, automatic integration with Source Safe, and integrated help. It is a familiar environment for developers and makes deployments easy.

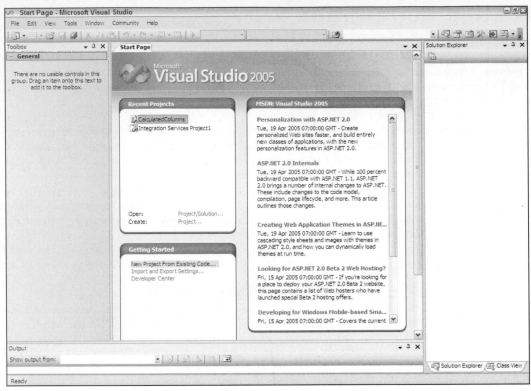

Figure 2-9

To start a new SSIS project, you will first need to open BIDS and select File ➪ New ➪ Project. You'll notice a series of new templates (shown in Figure 2-10) in your template list now that you've installed SQL Server 2005. Select Integration Services Project, and name your project and solution whatever you'd like.

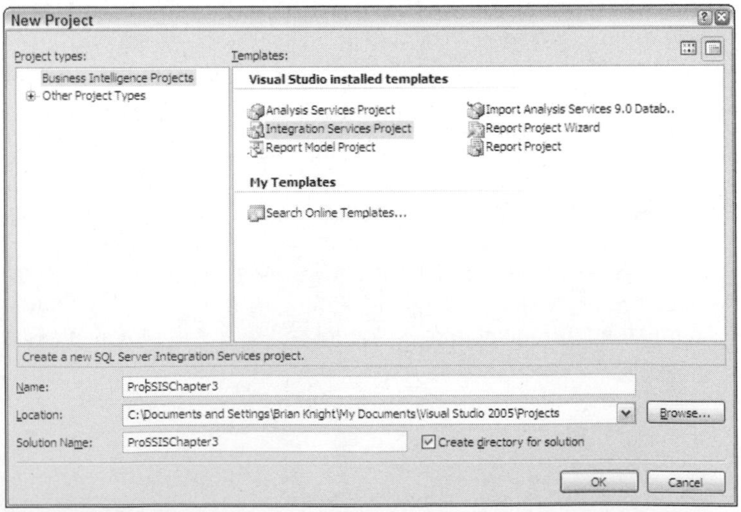

Figure 2-10

Creating Your First Package

Before you jump into the fundamentals of the toolset, you should exercise some of the BIDS features by creating a very basic package. If you don't understand some of this, don't worry yet. It will make much more sense later in this chapter and in Chapter 3. This quick example will show you how to configure a task and how to chain tasks together with precedence constraints.

Start by opening BIDS by selecting Start ⇨ Programs ⇨ Microsoft SQL Server 2005 ⇨ SQL Server Business Intelligence Development Studio. Once BIDS is open, select New ⇨ Project from the File menu. Under the Business Intelligence Project Type on the left, select Integration Services Project. Call the project "Basic Package" for the Name option, and then click OK.

In the Solution Explorer to the right of BIDS, you'll see that an empty package called Package1.dtsx was created. On the left of BIDS is your Toolbox, which contains all of the work items that you can accomplish in whatever tab you're in. In the Toolbox, drag the Execute Process task over to the empty design pane in the middle. Double-click on the task to configure it. This opens the editor for the given task, transformation, or data connection you wish to configure. Name the task Notepad, and you can optionally enter a description in the General page. Select the Process page in the left pane, and for the Executable option, select Notepad .exe. Click OK to exit the editor.

Drag another Execute Process task over and double-click on it to open the editor again. Name this task Calc. In the Process page, type **calc.exe** for the Executable option. Click OK to exit the editor. Click the first Notepad task and you'll see a green arrow pointing downward from the task. This is a precedence constraint, which was mentioned in Chapter 1. Left-click on the arrow and drag it onto the Calc task. These tasks are now connected, and the Calc task will not execute until the first task succeeds.

Click the Save icon to save the package. Select Debug ⇨ Start Debugging or hit F5. This will execute the package. You should first see Notepad open, and once you close Notepad, the Windows calculator will open (as shown in Figure 2-11). Once you close the calculator, the package will complete. The two tasks should also show as green in color, which means they successfully executed. You can click the Stop button or select Stop Debugging under the Debug menu to complete the package's execution.

Congratulations, you have created your first package. Granted, this package will never be used in a production environment, but it does show you the basic concepts in SSIS. It's important to note that you will not develop packages that have interactive windows like this. If you were to execute this in production, it would wait for a user's interaction to close the window before the package would complete. The concepts you were introduced to here will be described in greater detail in each upcoming chapter, and now you'll learn about the features that are available to you in BIDS.

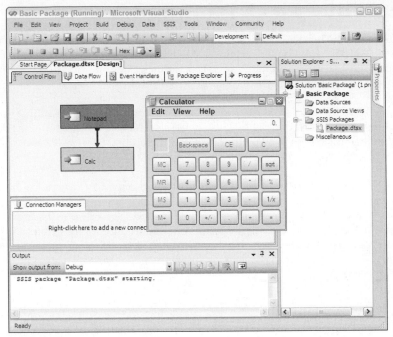

Figure 2-11

The Solution Explorer Window

The Solution Explorer Window is where you can find all of your created SSIS packages, connections, and Data Source Views. A *solution* is a container that holds a series of projects. Each project holds a myriad of objects for whatever type of project you're working in. For SSIS, it will hold your packages and shared connections. Once you create a solution, you can store many projects inside of it. For example, you may have a solution that has your VB.NET application and all the SSIS packages that support that package. In this example, you would probably have two projects: one for VB and another for SSIS.

After creating a new project, your Solution Explorer Window will contain a series of empty folders. Figure 2-12 shows you a partially filled Solution Explorer. In this screenshot, there's a solution and a project called CalculatedColumns. Inside that project, there are two SSIS packages.

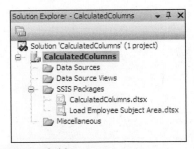

Figure 2-12

To create a new project inside an existing open solution, right-click the solution name in the Solution Explorer Window and select New Project. To create a new item to your project in the folder, right-click on the folder that holds the type of item that you wish to add and select New Data Source, New Data Source View, or New SSIS Package.

If you look into the directory that contains your solution and project files, you'll see all the files that are represented in the Solution Explorer Window. Some of the base files you may see will have the following extensions:

❑   .dtsx — A SSIS package, which uses its legacy extension from the early beta cycles of SQL Server 2005 when SSIS was still called DTS

❑   .ds — A shared data source file

❑   .dsv — A data source view

❑   .sln — A solution file that contains one or more projects

❑   .dtproj — A SSIS project file

The Toolbox

The Toolbox contains all the items that you can use in the design pane at any given point in time. For example, the Control Flow tab has the items shown in Figure 2-13. This list may grow based on what custom tasks are installed. The list will be completely different when you're in a different tab, such as the Data Flow tab. All the tasks you see in Figure 2-13 will be covered in Chapter 3.

Figure 2-13

The Toolbox is organized into tabs such as Maintenance Tasks and Control Flow Items. These tabs can be collapsed and expanded for usability. As you use the Toolbox, you may want to customize your view by removing tasks or tabs from the default view. You can remove or customize the list of items in your Toolbox by right-clicking on an item and selecting Choose Items. This takes you to the Choose Toolbox Items dialog box shown in Figure 2-14. To customize the list that you see when you're in the Control Flow, select the SSIS Control Flow Items tab, and check the tasks you'd like to see.

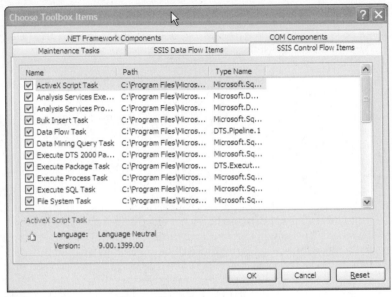

Figure 2-14

If you right-click on a particular task, you'll get a menu that will let you customize your view by adding or removing tabs and adding, renaming, or removing items. You can also change the order in which the items or tabs appear just by clicking and dragging from the source to the destination or by right-clicking and selecting Sort Alphabetically.

The Properties Windows

The Properties Window (shown in Figure 2-15) is where you can customize almost any item that you have selected. For example, if you select a task in the design pane, you'll receive a list of properties to configure, such as the task's name and what query it's going to use. The view will vary widely based on what item you have selected. Figure 2-15 shows a Send Mail task.

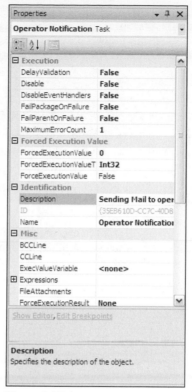

Figure 2-15

Navigation Pane

One of the nice usability features that have been added in BIDS is the ability to navigate quickly through the package by using the navigation pane (as shown in Figure 2-16) in the bottom-right corner of the package. The pane is visible only when your package is more than one screen in size, and it allows you to quickly navigate through the package. To access the pane, left-click and hold on the cross-arrow in the bottom-right corner of the screen. You can then scroll up and down a large package with ease.

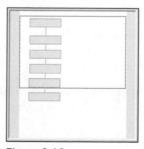

Figure 2-16

Other Windows

At design time, the BIDS has several other windows that you can choose to dock, undock, show, hide, or auto-hide based on your needs or what stage you are at in development. These supplementary windows include the following:

❑ **Error List window:** Shows errors and warnings that have been detected in the package. Double-clicking on an entry in this window will open the editor of the object causing the error.

❑ **Output window:** Shows the results from when you build or execute a package in the BIDS environment. For example, the Output window will show any errors that occur during building or deploying or during runtime.

❑ **Task List window:** Shows tasks that a developer can create for descriptive purpose or as a follow-up for later development.

As you begin to test your packages, you will want to execute them inside of the BIDS. This will shift the mode into runtime, and no editing will be allowed until the package has completed execution. During runtime, the following windows will also appear:

❑ **Call Stack window:** Shows the names of functions or tasks on the stack.

❑ **Breakpoints window:** Shows all of the breakpoints set in the current project.

❑ **Command window:** Used to execute commands or aliases directly in the BIDS.

❑ **Immediate window:** Used to debug and evaluate expressions, execute statements, and print variable values.

❑ **Autos window:** Displays variables used in the current statement and the previous statement.

❑ **Locals window:** Shows all of the local variables in the current scope.

❑ **Watch windows:** Allow you to add specific variables to the window that can be viewed as package execution takes place. You can also directly modify read/write variables in this window. You'll learn more about these in Chapter 13.

The SSIS Package Designer

The SSIS Package Designer contains the design panes that you'll use to create a SSIS package. The tool contains all the items you need to move data or create a workflow with minimal or no code. The Package Designer contains four tabs: Control Flow, Data Flow, Event Handlers, and Package Explorer. One additional tab, Progress, also appears when you execute packages. In this chapter, you'll mainly explore the Controller Flow tab. Unlike SQL Server 2000 DTS, where control and data flow were intermingled, control flow and data flow editors are completely separated by these tabs. This usability feature gives you greater control when creating and editing packages. The task that binds the control flow and data flow together is the Data Flow task, which you'll study in depth over the next two chapters.

Controller Flow

The controller flow is most similar to SQL Server 2000 DTS, since it contains most of the tasks you're used to in SQL Server 2000. It contains the workflow parts of the package, which include the tasks and precedence constraints. SSIS has introduced the new concept of containers, which was briefly discussed in Chapter 1. In the Control Flow tab, you can click and drag a task from the Toolbox into the Controller Flow designer pane. Once you have a task created, you can double-click the task to configure it. Until the task is configured, you may see a yellow warning on the task.

After you configure the task, you can link it to other tasks by using precedence constraints. Once you click on the task, you'll notice a green arrow pointing down from the task, as shown in Figure 2-17.

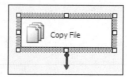

Figure 2-17

To create an On Success precedence constraint, click on the arrow and drag it to the task you wish to link to the first task. In Figure 2-18, you can see the On Success precedence constraint between a File System task and a Data Flow task. (Notice the warning icon on the Data Flow task, because it hasn't been configured yet.) You can also see an On Failure constraint, which is represented as a red arrow between the File System task and the Send Mail task. This type of controller flow may send a message to an operator in the event that the file operation fails.

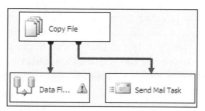

Figure 2-18

When you click on a transformation in the Data Flow tab, you'll also see a red arrow pointing down, enabling you to quickly direct your bad data to a separate output. In the Controller Flow, though, you'll need to use a different approach. If you'd like the next task to execute only if the first task has failed, create a precedence constraint as was shown earlier for the On Success constraint. After the constraint is created, double-click on the constraint arrow and you'll be taken to the Precedence Constraint Editor (shown in Figure 2-19).

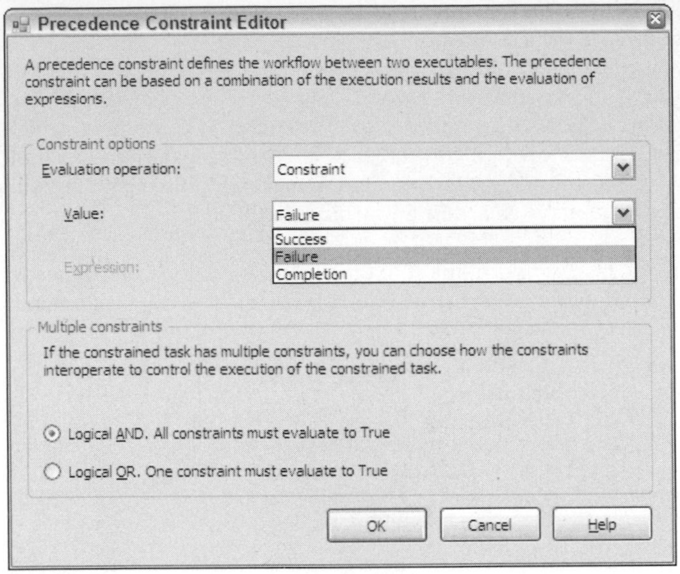

Figure 2-19

In this editor, you can set what type of constraint you'll be using in the Value drop-down field: Success, Failure, or Completion. In SSIS 2005, you have the option of adding a logical AND or OR when a task has multiple constraints. In DTS 2000, a task with multiple constraints would execute only if all constraints evaluated to True. This, of course, was a problem when a task had two or more error constraints that preceded it because both tasks had to fail before the subsequent task would execute. In the Precedence Constraint Editor in SSIS 2005, you can configure the task to only execute if the group of predecessor tasks has completed (AND) or if any one of the predecessor tasks has completed (OR). If a constraint is a logical AND, the precedence constraint line is solid. If it is set to OR, the line is dotted. This is useful if you want to be notified if any one of the tasks fails by using the logical OR constraint.

In the Evaluation Operation drop-down box, you can edit how the task will be evaluated.

❏ **Constraint:** Evaluates the success, failure, or completion of the predecessor task or tasks

❏ **Expression:** Evaluates the success of a customized condition that is programmed using an expression

❏ **Expression and Constraint:** Evaluates both the expression and the constraint before moving to the next task

❏ **Expression or Constraint:** Determines if either the expression or the constraint has been successfully met before moving to the next task

If you select Expression or one of its variants as your option, you'll be able to type an expression in the Expression box. An expression is usually used to evaluate a variable before proceeding to the next task. For example, if you want to ensure that Variable1 is equal to Variable2, you would use the following syntax in the Expression box:

```
@Variable1 == @Variable2
```

You can also single-click on the constraint and use the Properties Window to the right to set these properties if you prefer not to use the editor.

Task Grouping

A very nice usability feature in SSIS is the ability to group tasks logically in containers. For example, if you have a group of tasks that create and purge the staging environment, you can group them together so that your package is not cluttered visually. For example, in Figure 2-20 there are two tasks to create and purge staging. To group them, select both tasks by clicking one task and holding the CTRL key down while you select the second task. Then, right-click on the tasks and select Group.

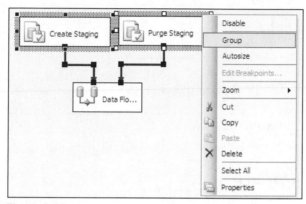

Figure 2-20

Once you have the two tasks grouped, you'll see a box container around the tasks. This container will be called Group by default. To rename the group, simply double-click on the container and type the new name over the old one. You can also collapse the group so that your package isn't cluttered. To do this, just click the arrows that are pointing downward in the group. Once collapsed, your grouping will look like Figure 2-21. You can also ungroup the tasks by right-clicking on the group and selecting Ungroup.

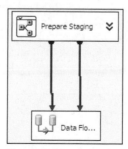

Figure 2-21

Annotation

Annotation is a key part of any package that a good developer never wants to leave out. An *annotation* is a comment that you place in your package to help others and yourself understand what is happening in the package. To add an annotation, right-click where you'd like to place the comment and select Add

Annotation. It is a good idea to always add an annotation to your package that shows the title and version your package is on. Most SSIS developers like to also put a version history annotation note in the package so that they can see what's changed in the package between releases and who performed the change. You can see both of these examples in Figure 2-22. Note that the group from Figure 2-21 has been expanded.

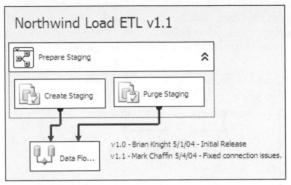

Figure 2-22

Connection Managers

You may have already noticed that there is a Connection Managers tab at the bottom of your Package Designer pane. This tab contains a list of data connections that both control flow and data flow tasks can use. Whether the connection is an FTP address or a connection to an Analysis Services server, you'll see a reference to it here. These connections can be referenced as either source or targets in any of the operations and can connect to relational or Analysis Services databases, flat files, or other data sources.

When you create a new package, there are no connections defined. You can create connections by right-clicking in the Connections area and choosing the appropriate data connection type. Once the connection is created, you can rename it to fit your naming conventions or to better describe what is contained in the connection. Even if you have a shared connection defined for your project, it won't be usable in the package until you add it to the Connection Managers tab. Nearly any task or transformation that uses data will require a Connection Manager. There are a few exceptions, such as the Raw File destination and source that you'll learn about in the next chapter, that allow you to define your connection inline. Figure 2-23 shows two connections: one to a relational database (AdventureWorks) and another to a flat file (Sample Data).

Figure 2-23

Variables

Variables are a powerful piece of the SSIS architecture; they allow you to dynamically control the package at runtime, much like you do in any .NET language. In SQL Server 2000 terms, variables are closest to global variables, but they've been improved on greatly, as you'll see in Chapters 5 and 6. There are two types of variables: system and user. *System variables* are ones that are built into SSIS, whereas *user variables* are created by the SSIS developer. Variables can also have varying scope, with the default scope being the entire package. They can also be set to be in scope of a container, task, or event handler inside the package. The addition of scope to variables is the main differentiating factor between SSIS variables and DTS global variables.

One of the optional design-time windows can display a list of variables. To access the Variables Window, right-click in the design pane and select Variables. The Variables Window (shown in Figure 2-24) will appear where the Toolbox was, and you can toggle between the two windows by selecting the corresponding tab below the window. By default, you will see only the user variables; to see the system variables as well, select the Show System Variables icon in the top of the window. To add a new variable, click the Add Variable icon in the Variables Window and type the name.

Figure 2-24

You'll find yourself using system variables throughout your package habitually for auditing or error handling. Some of the system variables that are in the scope of a package that you may find interesting for auditing purposes are listed in the following table.

Variable Name	Data Type	Description
CreationDate	DateTime	The date when the package was created.
InteractiveMode	Boolean	Indicates how the package was executed. If the package was executed from BIDS, this would be set to true. If it was executed as a job, it would be set to false.
MachineName	String	The computer where the package is running.
PackageID	String	The unique identifier (GUID) for the package.
PackageName	String	The name of the package.
StartTime	DateTime	The time when the package started.
UserName	String	The user that started the package.
VersionBuild	Int32	The version of the package.

Variables will be discussed in greater detail in each chapter. For a full list of system variables, please refer to Books Online under "System Variables."

Data Flow

When you create a Data Flow task in the Controller flow, a subsequent data flow is created in the Data Flow tab. You can expand the data flow by double-clicking on the task or by going to the Data Flow tab and selecting the appropriate Data Flow task from the top drop-down box (shown in Figure 2-25). The data flow key components are sources, destinations, transformations, and paths. The green and red arrows that were the precedence constraints in the Control Flow tab are now called *paths*.

When you first start defining the data flow, you will create a source to a data source and then a destination to go to. The transformations (also known as transforms throughout this book) modify the data before it is written to the destination. As the data flows through the path from transform to transform, the data changes based on what transform you have selected. The red arrow that connects the transforms named Fix Bad Records and Add Audit Info in Figure 2-25 writes the bad records to a destination such as an error queue or moves data down a different path if an error occurs. This entire process is covered in much more detail in Chapter 4.

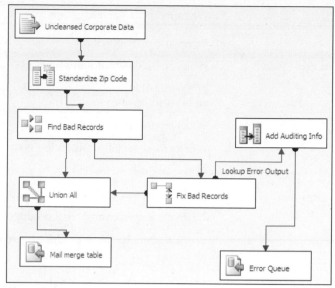

Figure 2-25

Event Handlers

The Event Handlers tab allows you to create workflows to handle errors or changes in events. If you wanted to handle errors in SQL Server 2000, you had to create an On Failure precedence constraint that led to an error-handling task off of each task you wanted to monitor. Now in SQL Server 2005 SSIS, you can do this globally across your entire package. For example, if you want to trap any errors and have them e-mailed to you, you could create an OnError event handler and configure it to send a message out to an operator, as shown in Figure 2-26.

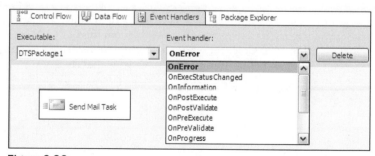

Figure 2-26

You can configure the event handler scope under the Executable drop-down box. An executable can be a package, Foreach Loop, For Loop, Sequence, or task host container. In the Event Handler box, you can specify the event you wish to monitor for. The events you can select are in the following table.

Event	When Event Is Raised
OnError	When an error occurs
OnExecStatusChanged	When an executable's status changes
OnInformation	When informational event is raised during the validation and execution of an executable
OnPostExecute	When an executable completes
OnPostValidate	When an executable's validation is complete
OnPreExecute	Before an executable runs
OnPreValidate	Before an executable's validation begins
OnProgress	When measurable progress has happened on an executable
OnQueryCancel	When a query has been instructed to cancel
OnTaskFailed	When a task fails
OnVariableValueChanged	When a variable is changed at runtime
OnWarning	When a warning occurs in your package

Event handlers are critically important to developing a package that is "self-healing" and can correct its own problems. You'll learn more about event handlers in Chapter 13.

Package Explorer

The final tab in the SSIS Package Designer is the Package Explorer tab. This tab consolidates all the design panes into a single view. It's similar to the disconnected edit dialog box in SQL Server 2000 DTS. The Package Explorer tab (shown in Figure 2-27) lists all the tasks, connections, containers, event handlers, variables, and transforms in your package, and you can double-click on any item here to configure it easily. You can also modify the properties for the item in the right Properties Window after selecting the item you wish to modify.

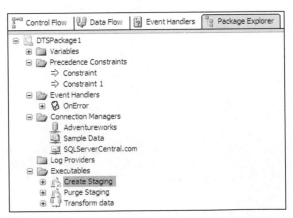

Figure 2-27

Executing a Package

When you want to execute a package, you can click on the Play icon on the toolbar, press F5, or choose Start from the Debug menu. This puts the design environment into execution mode, opens several new windows, enables several new menu and toolbar items, and begins to execute the package. When the package finishes running, BIDS doesn't immediately go back to design mode but rather stays in execution mode to allow you to inspect any runtime variables or to view any execution output. This also means that you can't make any changes to the objects within the package, but you can modify variables and objects' read/write properties. You may already be familiar with this concept from executing .NET projects.

To get back to design mode, you must click on the Stop icon on the debugging toolbar, press Shift+F5, or choose Debug ⇨ Stop Debugging.

Summary

This chapter's goal was to get you acclimated with the main SSIS wizards. The Import and Export Wizard is a quick way to create a package that does a simple import or export of data. The wizard can produce a package that can be run multiple times. The Package Installation Wizard is a method to deploy your SSIS project after its development is complete.

You were then taken on a tour of the Business Intelligence Development Studio (BIDS), which is where you'll be spending most of your time as you develop packages. You looked at the key parts of the interface and learned how to create your first simple package.

Now that you've gotten your feet wet, it's time to see the real power of SSIS, which lies in the multitude of tasks you can use in your packages. You'll learn about some of the more common ones in Chapter 3 and about the advanced transforms in Chapter 4.

3

SSIS Tasks

Tasks are the foundation of the controller flow in SSIS. Even the data flow is tied to the controller flow by a task. A task can be anything from moving a file to moving data. More advanced tasks enable you to execute SQL commands, send mail, run ActiveX scripts, and access Web services. You already used the Execute Process task in the simple example in Chapter 2, and you'll be using various tasks throughout the rest of the book as you work through the examples. This chapter will introduce you to the more common tasks you'll be using and give you some examples of how to use them.

All tasks have some common features. To add a task to the controller flow pane, click and drag it from the Toolbox onto the pane. You can then double-click on the task to configure it. You may see a red or yellow warning on the task until you configure it with the required fields. You'll find out more about these fields in the next section. Some of the advanced tasks in SSIS will be covered lightly in this chapter and covered in more detail in Chapter 6.

Shared Properties

No matter what task you use in your package, there is a standard set of properties for each task in the SSIS environment that you will have available to you. Many of the same properties have been carried over from SQL Server 2000 DTS, but most are new and complete the vision of an enter-prise-ready ETL tool. Here is a list of the properties that you will use:

❑ **Disable:** If set to true, then the task is disabled and will not execute.

❑ **DelayValidation:** If set to true, SSIS will not validate any of the properties set in the task until runtime. This is useful if you are operating in a disconnected mode and you want to enter a value for production that cannot be validated until the package is deployed. The default value for this property is false.

❑ **Description:** The description of what the instance of the task does. The default name for this is <task name>, or if you have multiple tasks of the same type, it would read <task name 1> (where the number 1 increments). This property does not have to be unique and should accurately describe what the task does for people who may be monitoring the package in your operations group.

❑ **ExecValueVariable:** Contains the name of the custom variable that will store the output of the task's execution. The default value of this property is <none>, which means that the execution output is not stored.

❑ **FailPackageonFailure:** If set to true, the entire package will fail if the individual task fails. By default, this property is set to false.

❑ **FailParentonFailure:** If set to true, the task's parent will fail if the individual task reports an error. The task's parent can be a package or container. You'll read more about containers later.

❑ **ID:** Automatically generated unique ID that is associated to an instance of a task. The ID is in GUID format and looks like this: {BK4FH3I-RDN3-I8RF-KU3F-JF83AFJRLS}

❑ **IsolationLevel:** Specifies the isolation level of the transaction, if transactions are enabled in the TransactionMode property. The values are Chaos, ReadCommitted, ReadUncommitted, RepeatableRead, Serializable, Unspecified, and Snapshot. The default value of this property is Serializable. These options correspond with standard SQL Server transactions.

❑ **LoggingMode:** Specifies the type of logging that will be performed for this task. The values are UseParentSetting, Enabled, and Disabled. The default value of this property is UseParentSetting, which tells the task to use the logging mechanism for the package or container.

❑ **Name:** The name associated with the task. The default name for this is <task name>, or if you have multiple tasks of the same type, it would read <task name 1> (where the number 1 increments). As a SSIS designer, you should probably change this name to make it more readable to an operator at runtime, but it must be unique inside your package.

❑ **TransactionOption:** Specifies the transaction attribute for the task. The values are NotSupported, Supported, and Required. The default value of this property is Supported, which enables the option for you to use transactions in your task.

Each task also has an Expression page in its editor that helps make the task dynamic. You'll look at this after you look at each of the tasks.

Execute SQL Task

The Execute SQL task will execute one or a series of SQL statements or stored procedures. The task has been greatly improved in SSIS and now allows you to execute scripts that are in a file. Most of the configuration this time is in the General page (shown in Figure 3-1). The Timeout option specifies the number of seconds before the task will time-out. A value of 0 means it can run for an infinite amount of time.

The ResultSet option sets what format you'd like the results of the query to be outputted in. By default, the results of the query will be ignored by setting the option to none. This is great when you want the SQL statement to prepare a staging table. You can also output the results to a single row, full result set, or XML format. Once you set this option to something other than none, you'll be able to map where you want the results to go in the Result Set page. This page maps the result set to a user parameter and lets you create a new one. The variable you output the results to can be in the scope of a single container or the entire package.

You can then later use those results somewhere else in your package. An example of this may be to check a value in a table that was set by another package. If the value is set to 1, that package has completed and you can proceed to the next task. Otherwise, you may loop back to the beginning of the package and try again.

The ConnectionType option, as its name implies, specifies what type of connection you'd like to run your SQL query against. Valid options include OLE DB, ODBC, ADO, ADO.NET, EXCEL, and SQLMOBILE. For SQL Server connections, select OLE DB and specify the Connection Manager below in the Connection option. Your query can be stored as a variable or input file or it can be directly inputted. You can specify the location of your SQL query under the SQLSourceType option. Then type or select the query or source of the query in the next option down. That next option may be called SQLStatement if you selected direct input in the SQLSourceType option. The option may also be called SourceVariable or FileConnection.

If you have selected the ADO connection type, then the IsQueryStoredProcedure option, which specifies whether the query is a stored procedure, will also be available. If you're not using the ADO connection type, then there's no reason to set this option. If your OLE DB source supports prepared queries, then you can select the BypassPrepare option to have this step bypassed (if set to true). Preparing a query will cache the query and its execution plan to help speed it up the next time it runs. You also have the option to parse the query or build a query by clicking these options at the bottom. By selecting Build Query, you have the familiar Query Builder tool in Visual Studio to develop your query in.

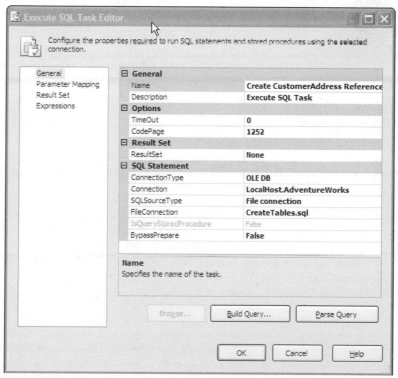

Figure 3-1

Bulk Insert Task

The Bulk Insert task allows you to insert data from a text file (also called a flat file) into a SQL Server in the same manner as a BULK INSERT statement or the bcp.exe command-line tool. This task is in the controller flow only, and it does not generate a data flow. A disadvantage to the task is that it does not allow any transformations to occur to the data in flight. In exchange for this, you have the fastest way to load a lot of data into a SQL Server since it's done in a bulk fashion.

When you create a Bulk Insert task and go to configure it, the Bulk Insert Task Editor will open (shown in Figure 3-2). As in most tasks, the General page allows you to name and describe the task. Make sure you name it something that describes its unit of work, like "Prepare Staging." This will help you later when you deploy the package and troubleshoot problems.

The most important page, which is shown in Figure 3-2, is the Connection page. This page lets you specify the source and destination for the data. Select the destination from the Connection drop-down box in the Destination Connection group. Next, specify a destination table from the next drop-down box below the destination connection. While you're specifying connections, also specify the source connection's file name in the File drop-down box. Both the source and destination connections use the Connection Manager. If you haven't already created the shared connections, you'll need to create a new one from the source or destination connection drop-down box by selecting <New Connection...>.

After you specify the connections, you can set what type of file you're importing and how it's delimited. You can select Use File or Specify from the format drop-down box. If you select Use File, you'll have to select a Bulk Insert format file, which tells the task how the file is formatted (text and row delimiters). Generally, you're going to want to specify a file format by selecting Specify from the Format drop-down box. The Specify option gives you the control to specify what the delimiters are. For the most part, the default delimiter options are perfect for specifying a file format. One that you may have to change on a regular basis is the column delimiter, which tells the task what character separates each column. The default here is tab-delimited, but another common one you'll see is comma-delimited.

> *The format file must be on the SQL Server, since the operation occurs there when a bulk insert task is used. You may also wish to use a UNC path (\\MachineName\ShareName\FileName.csv) if the source or format file is not going to be on the executing server.*

In the Options page of the Bulk Insert Task Editor, you'll be able to use some lesser-known options. Here you can specify the code page for the source file. You will rarely want to change the code page from RAW, which is the default. The DataFileType option can specify what type of file the source file is. Options here include char, native, widechar, and widenative. Generally, files you receive will be the default char option, but in some cases you may see a file with native format. You'll see this if the file was created from an instance of SQL Server by using the bcp.exe program with the –n (native) switch.

In the Options page, you can also specify the first and last row to copy if you'd like only a sampling of the rows or if you want to skip a header row. The BatchSize option shows how many records will be written to SQL Server before committing the batch. If you have a BatchSize of 0 (the default), this means that all the records will be written to SQL Server in a single batch. If you have more than 100,000 records, then you may want to adjust this setting to 50,000 or adjust based on your need. The adjustment may vary based on the width of your file.

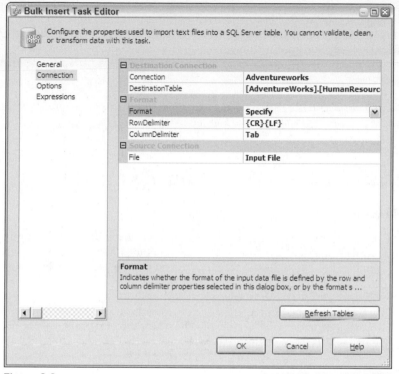

Figure 3-2

The options drop-down box contains five options that you can turn off and on.

❑ **Check Constraints:** The option that checks table and column constraints before committing the record. This option is the only one turned on by default.

❑ **Keep Nulls:** By selecting this option, the Bulk Insert task will replace any empty columns in the source file with NULLs in SQL Server.

❑ **Enable Identity Insert:** Enable this option if your destination table has an identity column that you're inserting into. Otherwise, you will receive an error.

❑ **Table Lock:** This option creates a SQL Server lock on the target table from insert and updates other than the records you're inserting. This option will speed up your process but may cause a production outage since others will be blocked from modifying the table. If you check this option, SSIS will not have to compete for locks to insert massive amounts of data into the target table. Set this option only if you're certain that no other process will be competing with your task for table access.

❑ **Fire Triggers:** By default, the Bulk Insert task will ignore triggers for maximum speed. By checking this option, the task will no longer ignore triggers and will fire the insert triggers for the table you're inserting into.

There are a few other options you can set in the Options page. The SortedData option specifies what column you wish to sort by while inserting the data. This option defaults to nothing, which means false. You'll almost never have a need to set this option, but if you do, type the column name that you wish to sort by. The MaxErrors option specifies how many errors are acceptable before the task is stopped with an error. Each row that does not insert is considered an error; by default, if a single row has a problem, the entire task fails.

> The Bulk Insert task does not log error-causing rows. If you want your bad records to be written to an error file or table, it's better to use the Data Flow task.

Using the Bulk Insert and Execute SQL Tasks

Take a time-out briefly to exercise a few of the tasks that were just discussed. First, go ahead and create a new SSIS project called Chapter3 as you saw in the last chapter. Rename the package called Package.dtsx that's created with the project to BulkLoadZip.dtsx. If you're prompted to rename the package as well, select Yes.

Before you tackle the bulk of the tutorial, go to the page for this book at www.wrox.com and download the example extract ZipCode.txt file. Place the file into a new directory called C:\SSISDemos. Then, create the following table in the AdventureWorks database in SQL Management Studio or in the tool of your choice. You will be inserting into this table momentarily.

```
CREATE TABLE Chapter3 (
    ZipCode CHAR(5),
    State CHAR(2),
    ZipName VARCHAR(16)
)
```

Back in BIDS, drag the Bulk Insert task onto the Control Flow design pane. Notice that the task has a red icon on it telling you that the task hasn't been configured yet. Double-click on the task to open the editor. In the General page, type the name "Load Zip Codes" for the Name option. For the Description option, type "Loads zip codes from a flat file."

Click the Connection page. From the Connection drop-down box, select <New connection...>. This will open the Configure OLE DB Connection Manager dialog box. You're going to now create a connection to the AdventureWorks database that can be reused throughout this chapter. Click New to add a new Connection Manager. For the Server Name option, select the server that contains your AdventureWorks database. For the database, select the AdventureWorks database. Your final configuration should look like Figure 3-3, but your login information will vary based on your server's security configuration. Click OK to go back to the previous screen, and click OK again to go back to the Bulk Insert Task Editor.

You'll now see that the Connection Manager you just created has been transposed into the Connection drop-down box. For the DestinationTable option, select the [AdventureWorks].[dbo].[Chapter3] table. The other options will remain to be the default options. The RowDelimiter option will be {CR}{LF} (a carriage return) and the ColumnDelimiter option will be Tab. For the File option, you will again select <New connection...> to create a new Connection Manager. This will open the File Connection Manager Editor. For the Usage Type, select Existing File. Then point to C:\SSISDemos\ZipCode.txt for the File option. Your final screen should look something like Figure 3-4.

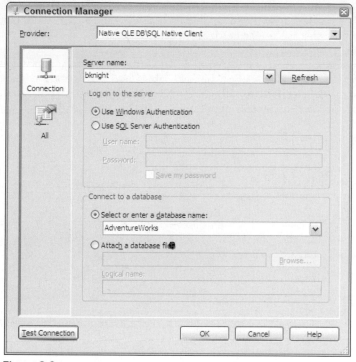

Figure 3-3

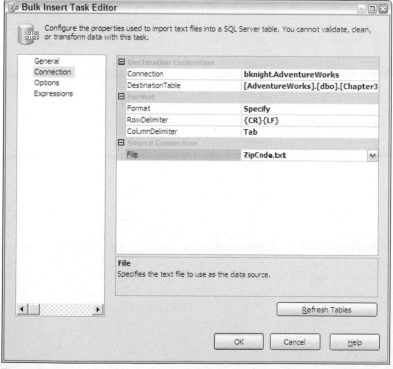

Figure 3-4

Next, go to the Options page and change the FirstRow option to 2. If you open the ZipCode.txt file, you'll notice that there is a header row with the column names before the data. By changing the FirstRow option to 2, you have told the task to skip the header row. Click OK to exit the editor.

With the first task configured, drag the Execute SQL task onto the design pane. Double-click on the task to open the editor. Name the task "Purge Chapter3 Table," and you can add whatever description you'd like this time. For the Connection drop-down box, select the AdventureWorks Connection Manager that you created earlier. For the SQLStatement option, type the following SQL code:

```
DELETE FROM Chapter3
```

Your final configuration of the General page should look like Figure 3-5. Click OK to exit the editor.

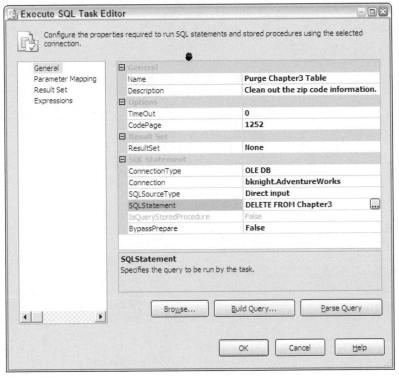

Figure 3-5

Click the task named "Purge Chapter3 Table" and drag the green arrow onto the task named "Load Zip Codes." This creates an On Success precedence constraint between the two tasks. The Bulk Insert task will not be executed unless the first task successfully executes. At this point, the package is complete. Save the package and execute it. When the package executes, the table will be purged using the Execute SQL task and then the table will be repopulated using the Bulk Insert task. A successful execution will look like what's shown in Figure 3-6.

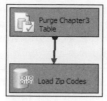

Figure 3-6

To stop the package's execution, click the Stop button. In Chapter 5, you'll see a similar example but you'll use the Data Flow task. The disadvantage in using the Bulk Insert task is its lack of error handling and its all-or-nothing nature. If a single row fails to insert, then your task may fail (based on your setting for the maximum number of allowed errors).

Data Flow Task

If you are familiar with SQL Server 2000 DTS, you won't recognize the Data Flow task in SSIS, as it is a very specialized task in SSIS and is treated differently than the other tasks. This is generally how you're going to insert data into your target system. It's such a large task that most of the next chapter is dedicated to it. The largest improvement is that you don't have to create staging tables to perform common tasks such as aggregating data. Instead, all of this can be done in-memory.

Execute Process Task

The Execute Process task will execute a Windows or console application inside of the controller flow. It's been much improved on since SQL Server 2000, and now it is more robust in its error handling. For example, you can now write any errors from the execution to a variable that can be read later. Also, any output from the command file can be written to a variable.

The Process page in the Execute Process Task Editor (shown in Figure 3-7) contains most of the important configuration items for this task. The RequireFullFileName property tells the task whether it needs the full path to execute the command. If the file is not found at the full path, the task will fail. This is useful only when you're worried about a second copy of the file existing in a folder somewhere that is referenced by the Windows PATH. For example, if the file exists in the System32 directory, you wouldn't have to type the full path to the file.

The Executable option is the path and file name to the executable you'd like to run. This does not contain any types of switches or parameters you'd like to pass. The Arguments option contains those types of items. For example, Figure 3-7 shows that the task will execute expand.exe and pass in the cabinet from which you want to extract and where you'd like it to be extracted. The WorkingDirectory option contains the path from which the executable or command file will work.

The StandardInputVariable parameter is the variable you'd like to pass into the process as an argument. It is a way to make that one option dynamic. You can also capture the result of the execution with the StandardOutputVariable and any errors that occurred from the execution in the StandardErrorVariable. You can later use this to determine if you should go to the next task by using expression validation in the precedence constraint. For example, if the result of the execution of the expand.exe program was a sharing violation, you can loop back to the beginning and try again.

There are some other minor options in this page of the editor. One of those is the FailTaskIfReturnCodeIsNotSuccessValue option, which indicates that the task will fail if the exit code passed from the program is different from the SuccessValue option. The default value that indicates success is 0. The Timeout option determines the number of seconds that must elapse before the program is considered a runaway process and has stalled. A value of 0, which is the default, means the process can run for an infinite amount of time. This option is used in conjunction with the TerminateProcessAfterTimeOut option, which, if set to true, will terminate the process after the timeout has been surpassed. The last option is WindowStyle, which can set the executable to be run minimized, maximized, hidden, or normal. If this is set to any option other than hidden, the user will be able to see windows potentially pop up and may interact with them if the user catches them in time.

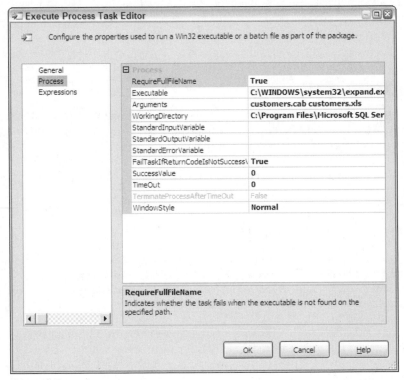

Figure 3-7

File System Task

Consider a typical ETL process from a mainframe system. Typically when you want to automate a data load of a system nightly, the process would look like this:

❑ You receive a file from a mainframe or source system via FTP.

❑ Your package would see the file in the directory and react by moving it to another working directory.

❑ The data would then be extracted out of the file and the file would be archived to another directory.

Previously in SQL Server 2000, each of the preceding steps would have taken lots of scripting by using the ActiveX Script task. You would have had to write one task in VBScript to poll the directory to see if the file had arrived. Another script would see the file and move it to another directory. The last script would archive the file. Typically this would take dozens, if not hundreds, of lines of code once you write all the error checking, and it would be a nightmare to update.

In SQL Server 2005, this process is much simpler with the addition of the File System task. This task allows you to perform file operations such as copying, moving, renaming, and deleting a file. It also can perform directory functions such as creating, deleting, copying, moving, or renaming a directory. It can also set operating system attributes and delete all the contents in a directory.

Most of the properties in this task are set in the General page of the File System Task Editor, which is shown in Figure 3-8. The contents of this page may vary widely based on what you set in the Operation option. This option specifies what you'd like the task to accomplish. Your options are all the previously mentioned items that can perform file, directory, and SET operations. Once you set the option, the page dynamically molds itself to that operation. For example, if you select Delete Files, there's no need for the DestinationPath options.

The IsDestinationPathVariable option allows you to specify whether the destination path will be set to a SSIS variable. If this is set to true, the dynamic property DestinationVariable sets the destination path to a variable. If it's set to false, then the DestinationConnection option will be available for you to select the Connection Manager that contains your file or directory. These same properties exist for the source connection in the bottom of the page. The OverwriteDestination option is set to false by default and specifies whether the task will overwrite the destination file or directory if it already exists. You'll be using this task a lot in Chapter 5's tutorials.

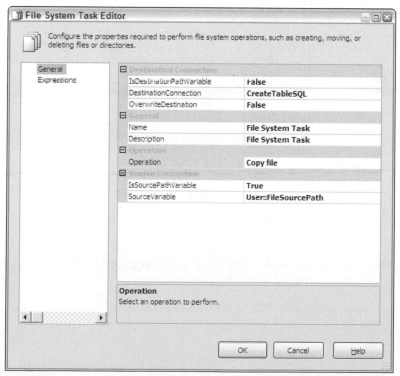

Figure 3-8

FTP Task

The FTP task allows you to receive or send files over the File Transfer Protocol (FTP). In SQL Server 2000, you could only receive files through FTP. In SSIS, this has been drastically improved. You can now receive, send, and delete local or remote files. You can also create and delete remote and local directories.

The General page in the FTP Task Editor is where you specify which FTP Connection Manager contains your FTP site information. If you haven't specified one yet, select New Connection under the FTPConnection option. This will open the FTP Connection Manager option. It's quite a bit different from the OLE DB Connection Managers you've been using up to this point, as you can see in Figure 3-9. The Server Name option contains the FTP address for where you'd like to connect. The default port for most FTP sites is 21. The other important option to note here is the Use Passive Mode option. You may have to select this option if the server you're connecting to is only configured to communicate passively. This was a constant issue in SQL Server 2000 since it didn't have this option.

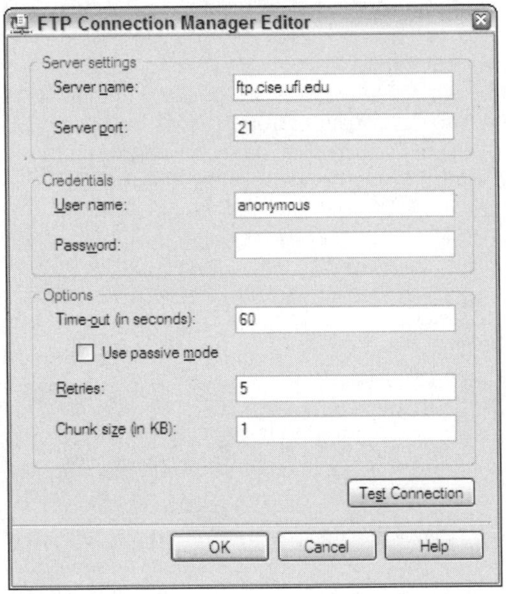

Figure 3-9

Once you have the FTP connection configured, there are some notable options in the File Transfer page (as shown in Figure 3-10). The options here are almost identical to the options in the File System task. The IsRemotePathVariable and IsLocalPathVariable options allow the paths to be set to a variable. The RemotePath option sets what directory or files on the remote FTP system you want to perform the action on. The LocalPath option is the Connection Manager that contains a directory on the SSIS side that is going to receive or send the files via FTP. The OverwriteFileAtDestination option sets whether the file at the destination will be overwritten if a conflict exists. Like many FTP clients, you can set the files to be transported using ASCII format by setting the IsTransferAscii option to true. The most important option, of course, is the Operation option, which selects what type of action you'd like to perform.

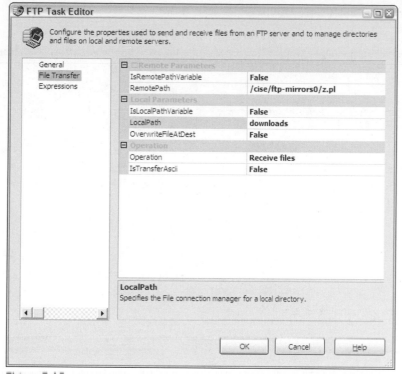

Figure 3-10

Using the File System and FTP Task

You should pause again and try out a few of the tasks. In this example, you're going to try to FTP a file from a university and then copy the file to an archive folder. Create a new directory if it doesn't exist yet called C:\SSISDemos\Archive. Then, create a new package in your Chapter3 SSIS project. Change the name of the package to FileCopy.dtsx.

Drag over the FTP task from the Toolbox to the design pane. Double-click on FTP task to open the editor, as shown in Figure 3-11. Name the task "FTP a File" and type any description. For the FTPConnection drop-down box, select <New connection...>. This will open the FTP Connection Editor. For the Server Name option, type **ftp.microsoft.com** and click Test Connection. Click OK to go back to the FTP Task Editor.

Next, go to the File Transfer page and type **/bussys/readme.txt** for the remote path. You can also click the ellipsis button to point to the file. For the Local Path option, select <New connection...> to open the File Connection Manager Editor. Select Existing Folder for the Usage Type and type **C:\SSISDemos** for the Folder.

The Operation drop-down box should be set to Receive Files. For the OverwriteFileAtDest option, select True. Click OK to exit the editor (shown in Figure 3-12).

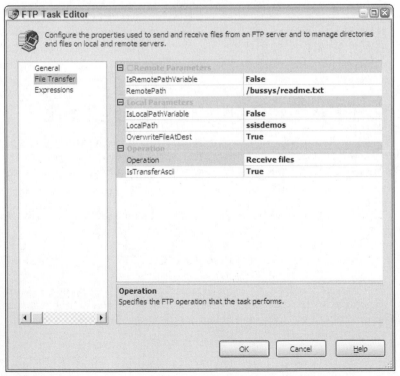

Figure 3-11

Figure 3-12

Now that the file will be downloaded, go ahead and archive it. In a real-world scenario, chances are you'd download the file, load it into a SQL Server, and then archive it, but you'll see that complete example in Chapter 5's tutorial. To copy the file into an archive directory, you'll use the File System task. Drag it onto the design pane and double-click on it to open the editor.

For the DestinationConnection option in the General page, select <New connection...>. Once the File Connection Manager Editor opens, select the usage type of Existing Folder and type **C:\SSISDemos\ Archive** for the folder name. Click OK to go back to the General page. Change the OverwriteDestination option to True.

For the Name option, type **Archive File** and type whatever description you'd like. The Operation option should be set to Copy File. Select True for the IsSourcePathVariable option and select <New variable...> for the SourceVariable drop-down box. This will open the Add Variable dialog box. The name of your variable will be SourceFile, and the value will be set to C:\SSISDemos\Readme.txt as shown in Figure 3-13.

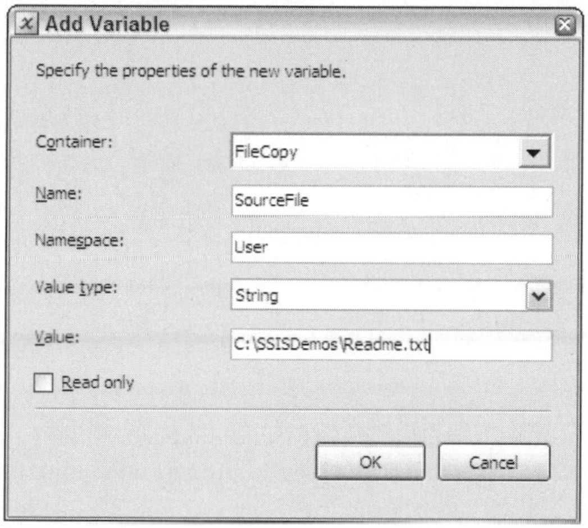

Figure 3-13

Click OK to go back to the General page. The SourceFile variable will be transposed into the SourceVariable drop-down box. The path to your destination file will be pulled dynamically from this variable. The reason you may wish to do this is to point to a file that does not exist yet. Your configuration of the task is now complete (shown in Figure 3-14). Click OK to go back to the design pane.

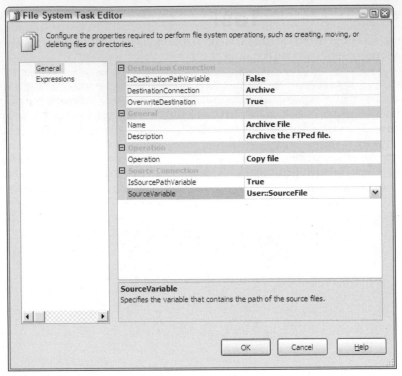

Figure 3-14

Back in the Control Flow tab, connect the FTP file task to the File System task with a precedence constraint. This way, the file will be FTPed first and then copied to the archive folder. Execute the package, and the final results should look something like Figure 3-15. Click Stop after the package has successfully executed and save the package. You should be able to see a Readme.txt file in the C:\SSISDemos\ directory and in the C:\SSISDemos\Archive directory now.

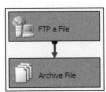

Figure 3-15

Execute Package Task

The Execute Package task executes another child package from a parent package. While this task did exist in SQL Server 2000 DTS, several improvements have simplified the task. In the Package page of the task editor (shown in Figure 3-16), you can see the new ExecuteOutofProcess property, which if set to true will execute the package in its own process and memory space. The default behavior of this property is to be set to true, which will require more memory but will improve performance. Another key difference between this version and the SQL Server 2000 version of the task is that this task no longer pushes parameters to the child package. Instead, the child package will reach into the parent package and pull the configuration values.

Again, the bulk of the configuration is done in the Package page in the Execute Package Task Editor. You first point to where the package is going to be. Your options here are File System and SQL Server. A File System task is a .dtsx file, and a SQL Server package is stored in the msdb database of a SQL Server instance. If you select File System, you must first create a new Connection Manager connection to the package by selecting New Connection from the Connection drop-down box. If you select SQL Server, you'll simply point it to the OLE DB Connection Manager to the SQL Server that holds your package.

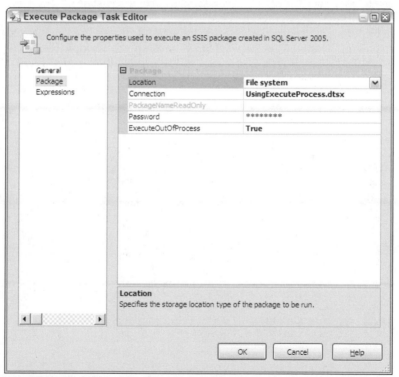

Figure 3-16

Script and ActiveX Tasks

The Script task allows you to access the Microsoft Visual Studio for Applications (VSA) environment to write and execute scripts by using the VB.NET language. The ActiveX Script task allows you to continue using your legacy ActiveX scripts from SQL Server 2000. There are some key advantages to using the Script task over the ActiveX Script task. The Script task gives you these extra functional advantages:

❑ An integrated Visual Studio design environment with Intellisense.

❑ You can easily pass parameters into the script.

❑ You can easily add breakpoints into your code.

❑ You can pre-compile your script into binary format for a speed advantage.

The Script task is configured through the Script page in the Script Task Editor (shown in Figure 3-17). Even though there's a ScriptLanguage option that lets you select what .NET language you'd like to use, only VB.NET is available in this release of SQL Server. If the PreCompileScriptIntoBinaryCode option is set to true, the code will compile and speed up your runtime of the task significantly. The side effect of this, though, is that your package will be larger than its uncompiled state.

The EntryPoint option sets the entry point class that the task will call. The ReadOnlyVariables and ReadWriteVariables options allow you to pass SSIS variables into the script. The former is for read-only parameters, and variables can be written to the latter. With each option, you can separate each SSIS variable by commas. Once you're ready to write the script, click Design Script.

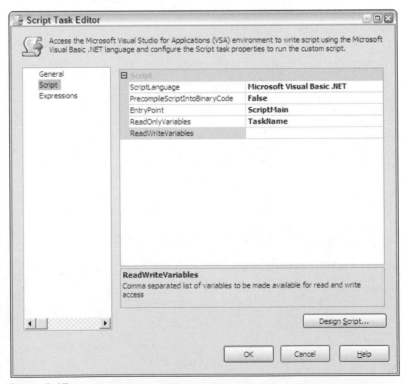

Figure 3-17

When you click Design Script, the Visual Studio environment opens, which lets you use advanced debugging tactics, breakpoints, and Intellisense. The following example shows you how to call the TaskName system variable that was passed into the script. The script firsts sees if the variable exists and then pops up a message box with the task name.

```
Imports System
Imports System.Data
Imports System.Math
Imports Microsoft.SqlServer.Dts.Runtime

Public Class ScriptMain
    Public Sub Main()
        Dim variables As Variables
        If Dts.Variables.Contains("TaskName") = True Then
            Dts.VariableDispenser.LockOneForRead("TaskName", variables)
            Dim TaskName As Object = variables("TaskName").Value

        End If

        MsgBox("You are in the task: " & CStr(variables("TaskName").Value))
        Dts.TaskResult = Dts.Results.Success
    End Sub

End Class
```

The results of the task execution would look like Figure 3-18.

Figure 3-18

With regard to scripting, take a look at the ActiveX Script task. This is in SSIS largely for backward compatibility with SQL Server 2000 DTS. You'll find that it's not a very advanced task, but it does have some advantages. Like the Script task, the task is configured through the Script page. As in its SQL Server 2000 predecessor, it supports more languages than just VBScript with the Language option. It will support whatever language is installed on the SSIS machine, such as JScript in addition to VBScript. The EntryMethod option specifies the class that you'd like the script to execute. Click the ellipsis button next to the Script option to type in your script. You can also click Browse to locate the script file.

Browsing to a script will overwrite any script that you already have in the Script option.

Send Mail Task

The Send Mail task can send out an e-mail message via SMTP. In SQL Server 2000, you had to send messages out through MAPI, which meant you had to install Outlook on the server that the package was running on. Now, that's no longer a requirement. The Mail page (shown in Figure 3-19) in the Send Mail Task Editor is where the configuration of this task takes place. The SMTPConnection option is where you select the SMTP Connection Manager or where you create a new one to an SMTP server.

Most of the configuration options are pretty self-explanatory in this task. One that is of special interest is the MessageSourceType option, which specifies whether the message source will be read from a file or a variable or whether it will be directly inputted into the MessageSource option.

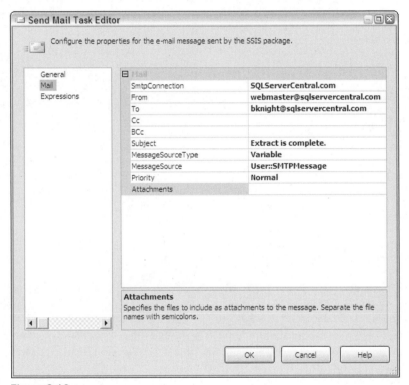

Figure 3-19

Message Queue Task

The Message Queue task allows you to send or receive messages from Microsoft Message Queuing (MSMQ). A message can be a string, file, or variable. The main benefit to using this task is the ability to make packages communicate with each other at runtime. You can use this to scale out your packages, having multiple packages executing in parallel with each loading a subset of the data and then checking in with the parent package after they're at certain checkpoints. You can also use this task to distribute files across your network. For example, a package running at your home office can send an inventory file to each of the message queues at the satellite offices, and then those SSIS packages could load the files into their SQL Servers.

In the General page, you specify the MSMQ Connection Manager under the MSMQConnection option. Then, you specify whether you'd like to send or receive a message under the Message option. In this page, you can also select whether you'd like to use the Windows 2000 version of MSMQ, which is by default set to false.

The bulk of the configuration is under the Send or Receive page (the one you see varies based on the Message option you selected in the General page). If you're on the Receive page, you can configure the task to remove the message from the queue after it has read it. You can also set the time-out properties here, such as whether the task will produce an error if it experiences a time-out.

No matter whether you're sending or receiving messages, you'll be able to select what type of message you wish to send under the MessageType option. You can either send or receive a string message, a variable, or a data file. Additionally, if you're receiving a message, you can immediately convert the message you receive into a variable by selecting String Message to Variable and then specifying a variable in the Variable option.

Web Service Task

The Web Service task is a new task in SSIS to connect to a Web service and execute a method. Once you execute the method, you can write the results from the Web service to a file or to a variable. This would be useful for trading information with third-party applications. For example, you can execute a Web service method to retrieve a list of updated products at Amazon. Then, you can write those products to a file and input them into your database to make them live.

To use the task, you'll need to open the Web Service Task Editor and specify a HTTP Connection Manager in the General tab. The HTTP Connection Manager looks quite a bit different from the OLE DB Connection Managers you're used to. In the Server URL option, point to the .ASMX file of the Web service. If you're just experimenting with the task and want a Web service to try, go to www.xmethods .net/ for a myriad of free Web services. Most won't require a key or authentication of any type. If the Web service does require credentials, then you'll need to modify the HTTP Connection Manager. The one being used in Figure 3-20 will extract the hyperlinks from a given Web page and would be handy for creating a package that can spider a Web site.

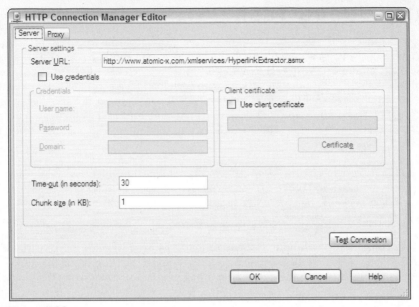

Figure 3-20

Once your HTTP Connection Manager is configured, go back to the General page to select the Web Service Description Language (WSDL) for the service. This file describes to the task how to use the service. If you do point to an external Web site, you must copy the WSDL file locally. On this page, you can also select whether the WSDL file can be overwritten.

The Web service you connect to may or may not require input parameters. Input parameters are passed to the method in the Input page of the task. In this page, you select the service you wish to call from a drop-down box in the Service option and then the method you'd like to execute from the Method drop-down box. The WebMethodDocumentation option will then automatically fill in to describe the method. The inputs will then appear at the bottom in the Service box. Type in the parameters you'd like to send to the service and go to the Output tab to configure where you'd like the results to be sent. You can have them sent to a file connection or to a variable. In the example in Figure 3-21, the Web service is sent a URL to spider, and the results are outputted to a variable, which is configured in the Output page. If you output to a file, you would use the File Connection Manager.

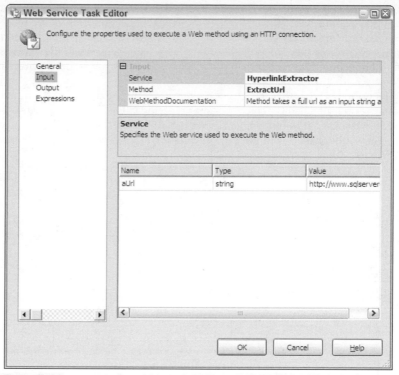

Figure 3-21

WMI Data Reader and Event Watcher Task

Windows Management Instrumentation (WMI) is one of the best-kept secrets in Windows. WMI allows you to manage Windows servers and workstations through a scripting interface. The WMI Data Reader task allows you to interface with this environment by writing WQL queries (the query language for WMI) against the server or workstation (to look at the Application Event Log, for example). The output of this query can be written to a file or variable for later consumption. The following are some applications for which you could use the WMI Data Reader task:

❑   Read the event log looking for a given error.

❑   Query the list of applications that are running.

❑   Query to see how much RAM is available at package execution for debugging.

❑   Determine the amount of free space on a hard drive.

You can configure this task in the WMI Data Reader Task Editor in the WMI Options tab (Figure 3-22). First, select the WMI Connection Manager under the WMIConnection drop-down box. The WQLQuerySourceType option selects whether your query will be directly inputted, retrieved from a variable, or retrieved from a file. The WQLQuerySource is where you select the query that you wish to run against the connection. This may be a variable name, a text file name, or the query itself.

The OutputType option is where you specify whether you want the output of the query to retrieve just the values from the query or also the column names with the values. The OverwriteDestination option sets whether you wish the destination to be overwritten each time it is run or whether you want it to just append to the connection. Lastly, configure the destination as you have in every other task.

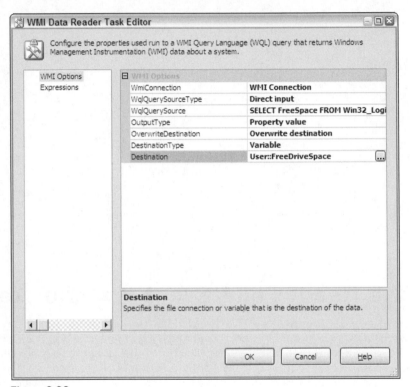

Figure 3-22

WQL queries look much like any SQL query. For example, the following query selects the free space, name, and a few other metrics about the C: drive:

```
SELECT FreeSpace, DeviceId, Size, SystemName, Description FROM Win32_LogicalDisk
WHERE DeviceID = 'C:'
```

The output of this type of query would look like this in a table:

```
Description, Local Fixed Disk
DeviceID, C:
FreeSpace, 32110985216
```

```
Size, 60003381248
SystemName, BKNIGHT
```

This example of a WQL query selects information written to the Application Event Log after a certain date and about the SQL Server and SSIS services:

```
SELECT * FROM Win32_NTLogEvent WHERE LogFile = 'Application' AND
(SourceName='SQLISService' OR SourceName='SQLISPackage') AND TimeGenerated >
'20050117'
```

The results would look like this:

```
0
BKNIGHT
12289
1073819649
3
System.String[]
Application
3738
SQLISPackage
20050430174924.000000-240
20050430174924.000000-240
information
BKNIGHT\Brian Knight
0
```

The WMI Event Watcher Task empowers SSIS to wait for and respond to certain WMI events that occur in the operating system. The task operates in much the same way as the WMI Data Reader task operates. The following are some of the useful things you can do with this task:

❑   Watch a directory for a certain file to be written

❑   Wait for a given service to start

❑   Wait for the memory of a server to reach a certain level before executing the rest of the package or before transferring files to the server

❑   Watch for the CPU to be free

The last CPU example would look like the following query, which detects whether the CPU is less than 50% utilized:

```
SELECT * from __InstanceModificationEvent WITHIN 2 WHERE TargetInstance ISA
'Win32_Processor' and TargetInstance.LoadPercentage < 50
```

You configure this task in much the same way as the WMI Data Reader task. Open the task editor (shown in Figure 3-23) and go to the WMI Options page. The AfterEvent option shows whether the task will succeed, fail, or keep querying if the condition is met. You can also configure what will happen if a time-out occurs under the ActionAtTimeout and AfterTimeout settings. The NumberOfEvents option configures the number of events to watch for. Lastly, the Timeout option determines how long the task will wait for the event to be met.

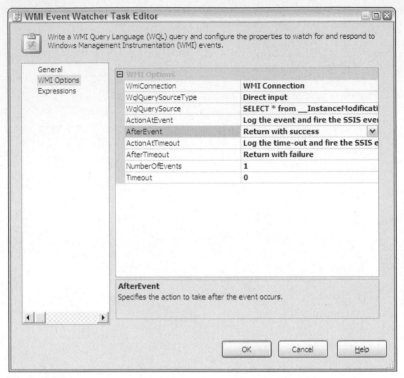

Figure 3-23

XML Task

The XML task is a new comprehensive task that can perform many different functions with your XML files. It allows SSIS to dynamically modify, merge, or create XML files at runtime. The functions this task can perform include the following:

- ❑ Take a series of XML files and merge them into a single file
- ❑ Prepare an XML file for a report by applying an XSLT style sheet to it
- ❑ Select out pieces of an XML file using XPATH
- ❑ Compare two XML files and write the differences to an XML Diffgram
- ❑ Validate the XML files against a Document Type Definition (DTD)

You configure the task through the XML Task Editor in the General tab. This very large dialog box changes based on what OperationType you select. The OperationType option has several different types of settings:

- ❑ **Validate:** Validates the XML document against the Document Type Definition (DTD) document or the XML Schema Definition (XSD) schema

- ❑ **XSLT:** Performs an XSL transformation against your XML document

- ❑ **XPATH:** Performs an XPATH query against the XML document

- ❑ **Merge:** Merges two XML documents into a single file

- ❑ **Diff:** Compares two XML documents

- ❑ **Patch:** Creates a new document from the previously mentioned Diff operation

If you're using the XPATH OperationType, you can set the XPathStringSource option to determine what options you'd like to query in the XML file. Figure 3-24 shows an example of how to use the XPATH operation to pull certain countries out of the orders.xml file and output the results to a variable called XPathResult.

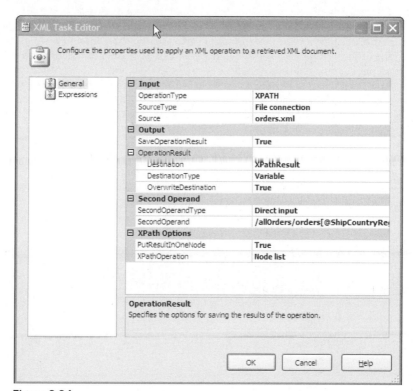

Figure 3-24

SQL Server Analysis Services Execute DDL and Processing Tasks

The SQL Server Analysis Services Execute DDL task is the Analysis Services equivalent of the Execute SQL task, but it is not quite as robust. The task simply executes a DDL statement against an Analysis Services system. The results of the DDL statement cannot be outputted to a variable as we showed in the Execute SQL task. Typically you would use something like DDL statements to create a cube, a dimension, or any other OLAP object.

To configure the task, go to the DDL page and select the Connection Manager that you wish to execute the DDL statement against in the Connection option. Then select whether the DDL statement will be directly inputted, pulled from a file, or pulled from a variable in the SourceType option. The last option is dynamic and will vary based on what you selected for the source of the DDL statement in the previous option. Essentially that option selects the variable or file where the DDL statement is stored or allows you to directly input the statement.

The SQL Server Analysis Services Processing task takes care of the processing of Analysis Services objects. The configuration of the task is done in the Analysis Services Processing Task Editor in the Analysis Services page. First, select the Analysis Services Connection Manager that you wish to process. Next, click the Add button and select the Analysis Services objects you'd like to process. After clicking OK, you'll be taken back to the Analysis Services page (Figure 3-25), where you can change the type of processing you will be performing. To do this, right-click on each object and select the process option you'd like. The option varies based on the type of object.

If you click Impact Analysis, analysis is performed on the selected objects, showing you the objects that will be affected by the processing. The Change Settings button lets you configure the batch settings for the task. For example, here you can change whether you want the objects to be processed in sequential order or in parallel. You also can specify how you want errors handled.

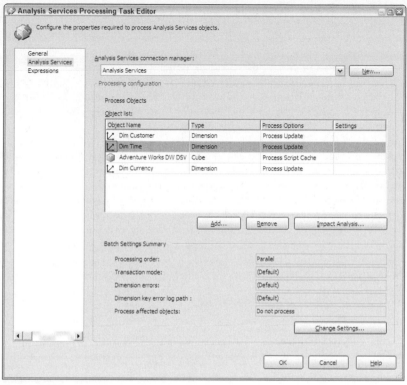

Figure 3-25

Data Mining Query Task

The Data Mining Query task is an evolution of its SQL Server 2000 predecessor. The Data Mining Query task allows you to run predictive queries against your Analysis Services data-mining models and output the results to a data source. This will be covered extensively in Chapter 6, as this is a detailed task.

The Expression Page

Common to all the tasks you've seen to date is an Expressions page in each of the editors. The Expression page is where you can make a task dynamic at runtime. In SQL Server 2000, you would use the Dynamic Properties task to do this, but that task no longer exists in 2005. In the Expression page, you can set properties of the task to be equal to an expression. The expression can be a constant value that you key in or a SSIS variable. This is extremely useful to a SSIS developer. For example, you could read a series of variables from a configuration file (these will be discussed later) and then dynamically set properties such as the Execute Process task working directories property.

To use the Expression page, click the ellipsis (...) button next to the Expressions option. This will take you to the Property Expressions Editor where you can delete properties that are already mapped or you can create new ones. To create a new one, select the property you wish to set from the Property column and then type the expression into the Expression column. Optionally, you can also select the ellipsis button in the Expression column to open the Expression Builder (shown in Figure 3-26). Here you can easily create expressions by dragging and dropping them from the various windows. You can also click Evaluate to see what the expression's value would be if it were to run as you have typed it.

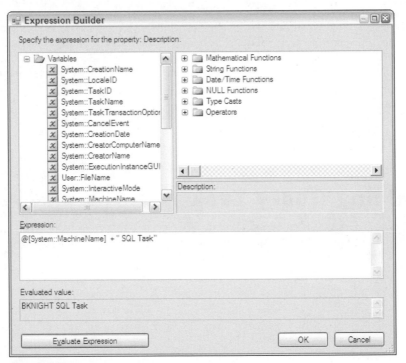

Figure 3-26

Summary

In this chapter, you looked at each task and learned how to configure it. You saw a number of examples of how to use the tasks. In the next chapter, you'll continue to look at the control flow by exploring containers, which enable you to loop through tasks. You'll also dive much deeper into data flow and learn about each transformation option you have there.

4

Containers and Data Flow

In the last chapter you were introduced to the Package Designer. In this chapter, you'll continue along those lines with an exploration of the Control Flow tab and spend most of your time in the Data Flow task. The Data Flow task is where the bulk of your data heavy lifting will occur. This chapter walks you through how each transformation in the Data Flow task can help you move and clean your data.

Containers

Containers are objects that help SSIS provide structure to one or more tasks. They can help you loop through a set of tasks until a criterion has been met or can help you group a set of tasks logically. Containers can also be nested, containing other containers. Containers are set in the Control Flow tab in the Package Designer. There are four types of containers in the Control Flow tab: Task Host, Sequence, For Loop, and Foreach containers.

Task Host Containers

The task host container is the default container that single tasks fall into. You'll notice that this type of container is not in the Toolbox in Visual Studio. In fact, even if you don't specify a container for a task, it will be placed in a task host container. The SSIS architecture extends variables and event handlers to the task through the task host container.

Sequence Containers

Sequence containers handle the flow of a subset of a package and can help you divide a package into smaller, more-manageable pieces. Some nice applications that you can use sequence containers for include the following:

❑ Grouping tasks so that you can disable a part of the package that's no longer needed

❑ Narrowing the scope of the variable to a container

❑ Managing the properties of multiple tasks in one step by setting the properties of the container

❑ Using one method to ensure that multiple tasks have to execute successfully before the next task executes

Sequence containers show up like any other task in your Control Flow tab. Once you drag and drop any container from your Toolbox onto the design pane, you just have to drag the tasks you'd like to use into the container. Figure 4-1 gives you an example of two containers. The left container is a Sequence container where two tasks must execute successfully before the Foreach Loop container will be executed.

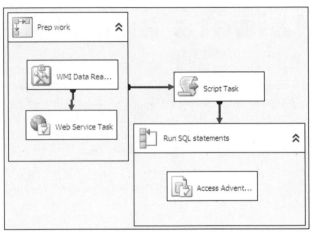

Figure 4-1

For Loop Container

The For Loop container is a method to create looping in your package similar to how you would in nearly any programming language, using the `for` looping. In this looping style, SSIS optionally initializes an expression and continues to evaluate it until the expression evaluates to false.

In the example in Figure 4-2, you can see that the Message Queue task is continuously looped through until a condition is evaluated as false. Once the loop is broken, the Script task is executed. This is useful when you'd like to try retrieving a message from a Microsoft Message Queue five times. By default, the Message Queue task will execute indefinitely until it retrieves the queue. With this method, you could set the time-out of the Message Queue task to 30 seconds and let it retry four times until it either retrieves the message or fails. In a more advanced example, you could build logic into the precedence constraints to state that if the variable was retrieved from the queue, you want to execute the Script task, and if not, to send a message.

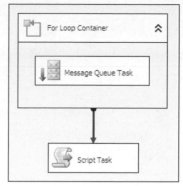

Figure 4-2

To set the properties of a For Loop container, double-click on the container box and the For Loop Editor will open, as shown in Figure 4-3. The InitExpression option, which is optional in the For Loop page, initializes the loop. The initial expression can also be set elsewhere when the expression is declared. The EvalExpression is the expression that will be evaluated each loop. Once this expression returns false, the loop will be stopped. The last parameter, the AssignExpression option, optionally can change the expression each time the loop repeats.

You can now try out some of the containers that have just been demonstrated. In this example, you'll see how to use a For Loop container to iterate through a script five times. While this example is pretty rudimentary, you can plug whatever task you want in place of the Script task.

1. Create a new SSIS project called Chapter4, and change the name of the default package to ForLoop.dtsx.

2. Open the ForLoop.dtsx package, create a new variable, and call it Counter. You may have to open the Variable window if it isn't already open. To do this, right-click in the design pane and select Variables. Once the window is open, click the Add Variable button. Accept all the defaults for the variable (int32).

3. Drag the For Loop container to the control flow and double-click on it to open the editor. Set the InitExpression option to @Counter = 0. This will initialize the loop by setting the Counter variable to 0. Next, in the EvalExpression option, type **@Counter < 5 and @Counter = @Counter + 1** for the AssignExpression. This means that the loop will iterate as long as the Counter variable is less than 5, and each time it loops, 1 will be added to the variable. The last step to configure the For Loop page is to type for the name option "Iterate through a Script" (shown in Figure 4-3) and click OK.

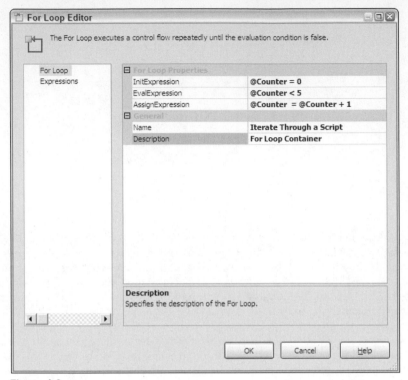

Figure 4-3

4. Next, drag a Script task into the For Loop container and double-click on the task to edit it. In the General tab, name the task "Pop Up the Iteration."

5. In the Script tab, set the ReadOnlyVariables (Figure 4-4) to Counter and click Design Script. By typing **Counter** for that option, you're going to pass in the Counter parameter to be used by the Script task.

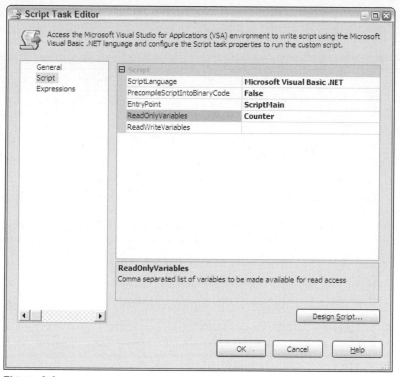

Figure 4-4

6. When you click Design Script, the Visual Studio 2005 design environment will open. Replace the Main() subroutine with the following code. This code will read the variable and pop up a message box that tells you what the value of the Counter variable is.

```
Public Sub Main()
    Dim variables As Variables
    If Dts.Variables.Contains("Counter") = True Then
        Dts.VariableDispenser.LockOneForRead("Counter", variables)
    End If

    MsgBox("You are in iteration: " & CStr(variables("Counter").Value))
    Dts.TaskResult = Dts.Results.Success

End Sub
```

7. Exit the Visual Studio design environment and click OK to exit the Script task. When you execute the package, you should see results similar to Figure 4-5. You should see five pop-up boxes starting at iteration 0 and proceeding through iteration 4. You'll see the Script task go green and then back to yellow as it transitions between each iteration of the loop. After the loop is complete, the For Loop container and the Script task will both be green.

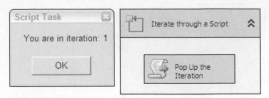

Figure 4-5

Foreach Loop Container

The Foreach Loop is a powerful looping mechanism that allows you to loop through a collection of objects. As you loop through the collection, the container will assign the value from the collection to a task or connection inside the container as shown below. You can also map the value to a variable. The type of objects that you will loop through can vary based on the enumerator you set in the editor in the Collection page. The editor varies widely based on what you set for this option. You can set this to one of the following options:

- ❑ **For Each File Enumerator:** Performs an action for each file in a directory with a given file extension

- ❑ **For Each Item Enumerator:** Loops through a list of items that are set manually in the container

- ❑ **For Each ADO Enumerator:** Loops through a list of tables or rows in a table from an ADO record set

- ❑ **For Each ADO.NET Schema Rowset Enumerator:** Loops through an ADO.NET schema

- ❑ **For Each From Variable Enumerator:** Loops through a SSIS variable

- ❑ **For Each Nodelist Enumerator:** Loops through a node list in an XML document

- ❑ **For Each SMO Enumerator:** Enumerates a list of SQL Management Objects (SMO)

You will use an example similar to your For Loop for the Foreach Loop. In this example, you'll iterate through a collection of files in a directory and pop up a message for each file in the directory. Again, in reality you'd have the script perform some type of more meaningful action, but you can plug in that action easily later. In Chapter 5, you will dive into a detailed example using this container.

1. Add a new package to your Chapter4 project, and rename it ForeachLoop.dtsx.

2. Drag a Foreach Loop container into the control flow and double-click it to open the editor. In the General page, name the container "Iterate through Files" and type whatever description you'd like.

3. In the Collection page, keep the default Enumerator "Foreach File Enumerator." For the Folder option, select a folder that has only a few files. Your files will not be harmed or moved in any way, but a message will pop up for each file. For the Files option, keep the default *.* value as shown in Figure 4-6.

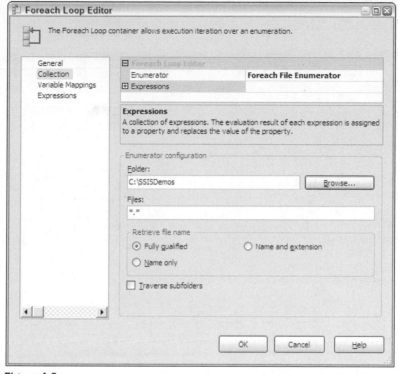

Figure 4-6

4. Go to the Variable Mapping page. In the Variable column drop-down box, select <New variable...>, which will open the Add Variable dialog box.

Name the variable FileName, and do not assign any value to it. Click OK to go back to the Variable Mapping page. You'll now see that the variable name has been transposed into the Variable column and that a 0 is in the Index column. The Foreach File Enumerator has only one column in its index, so this is fine. Click OK to exit the editor.

5. Drag a Script task onto the design pane and double-click it to open the editor. Name the task "Read Files" and type any description.

6. Go to the Script page and type the value of FileName for the ReadOnlyVariable option. Then, click Design Script to open the Visual Studio environment. Replace the Main() subroutine with the following code:

```
Public Sub Main()
    Dim variables As Variables
    If Dts.Variables.Contains("FileName") = True Then
        Dts.VariableDispenser.LockOneForRead("FileName", variables)
    End If

    MsgBox("Found the file: " & CStr(variables("FileName").Value))
```

```
         Dts.TaskResult = Dts.Results.Success

  End Sub
```

7. Exit the script designer and click OK to exit back into the control flow. Execute the package and
    you should see results similar to Figure 4-7 (depending on what directory you pointed to).

Figure 4-7

Sources

A *source* is where you specify the location of your source data. Most sources will point to the Connection
Manager in SSIS. By pointing to the Connection Manager, you can reuse connections throughout your
package, because you need only change the connection in one place. There are six sources altogether that
can be used out of the box with SSIS. To reach the Data Flow tab, create a new Data Flow task in the
Control tab. You can then drag the source from the Toolbox.

OLE DB Source

The OLE DB source is the most common type of source, and it can point to any OLE DB–compliant data
source. To configure the OLE DB source, double-click the source once you've added it to the design pane.
In the Configuration Manager page of the OLE DB Source Editor (Figure 4-8), select the Configuration
Manager of your OLE DB source from the OLE DB Connection Manager drop-down box.

The Data Access Mode option sets how you wish to retrieve the data. Your options here are Table/View
or SQL Command, or you can pull either from variables. Once you select the Data Access Mode, you
will need the table or view, or you can type a query.

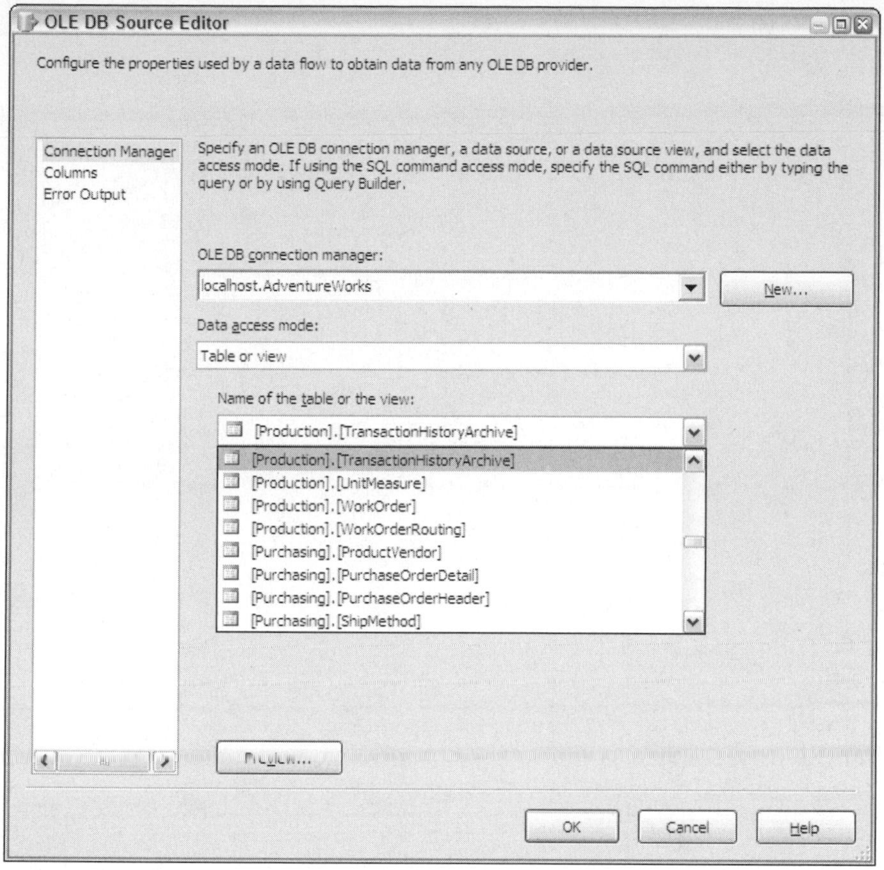

Figure 4-8

Like the other sources, you can go to the Columns page to set columns that you wish to output, as shown in Figure 4-9. Simply check the columns you wish to output, and you can then assign the name you wish to send down the data flow in the Output column. Select only the columns that you will want to use, as the smaller the data set, the better performance you will receive.

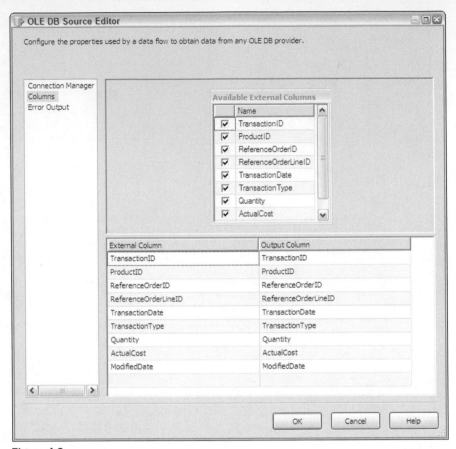

Figure 4-9

Optionally, you can go to the Error Output page (Figure 4-10) and specify how you wish to handle rows that have errors. For example, you may wish to output any rows that have a data type conversion issue to a different path in the data flow. On each column, you can specify that if an error occurs, you wish the row to be ignored, be redirected, or fail. The Truncation column specifies what to do if a data truncation occurs. You have the same options available to you for Truncation as you do for the Error option.

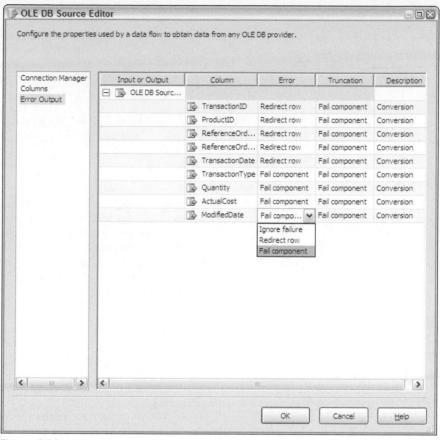

Figure 4-10

Excel Source

The Excel source is a source that points to an Excel spreadsheet, just as it sounds. Once you point to an Excel Connection Manager, you can select the sheet from the Name of the Excel Sheet drop-down box or you can run a query by changing the Data Access Mode.

Flat File Source

The Flat File source provides a data source for connections that are not relational. Flat File sources are typically comma- or tab-delimited files, or they could be fixed-width. A fixed-width file is typically received from the mainframe, and it has fixed start and stop points for each column. This method makes for a fast load but takes longer at design-time for the developer to map each column. You specify a Flat File source the same way you specify an OLE DB source. Once you add it to your data flow pane, you point it to a Connection Manager connection that is a flat file or a multi-flat file. After that, you go to the Columns tab to specify what columns you want to be presented to the data flow. All the specifications for the flat file, such as delimiter type, were previously set in the Flat File Connection Manager.

Raw File Source

The Raw File source is a specialized type of flat file that is optimized for quick usage from SSIS. A Raw File source is created by a Raw File destination (this will be discussed later in this chapter). You can't add columns to the Raw File source, but you can remove unused columns from the source in much the same way you do in the other sources. Because the Raw File source requires little translation, it can load data much faster than the Flat File source, but the price of this is that you have little flexibility. Typically, you see raw files used to capture data at checkpoints to be used later in case of a package failure.

XML Source

The XML source is a powerful SSIS source that can use a local or remote (via HTTP or UNC) XML file as the source. This data source is a bit different from the OLE DB source in its configuration. First, you point to the XML file locally on your machine or at a UNC path. You can also point to a remote HTTP address for an XML file. This is useful for interaction with a vendor. This source is very useful when used in conjunction with the Web Service task or the XML task. Once you point the data item to an XML file, you must generate an XSD file (XML Schema Definition) by clicking the Generate XSD button or point to an existing XSD file. The schema definition can also be an in-line XML file, so you don't necessarily have to have an XSD file. The rest of the source resembles the other sources, where you can filter the columns you don't want to see down the chain.

Data Reader Source

The Data Reader source allows you to make a .NET provider a source and allows you to make it available for consumption inside the package. The source uses an ADO.NET Connection Manager to connect to the provider. Consuming and contributing to external systems by using this source and destination will be discussed in much more detail in Chapter 17.

Destinations

Inside the data flow, *destinations* accept the data from the data sources and from the transformations. The architecture can send the data to nearly any OLE DB–compliant data source, a flat file, or Analysis Services. Like sources, destinations are managed through the Connection Manager. The configuration difference between sources and destinations is that in destinations, you have a Mappings page (shown in Figure 4-11), where you specify how the inputed data from the data flow maps to the destination.

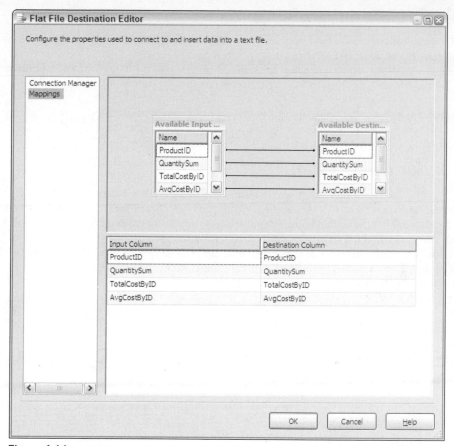

Figure 4-11

You won't be able to configure the destination until it is connected to the data flow. To do this, select the source or a transformation and drag the green arrow to the destination. If you want to output the bad data to a destination, you would drag the red arrow to that destination. If you try to configure the destination before attaching it to the transformation or source, you would see the error in Figure 4-12.

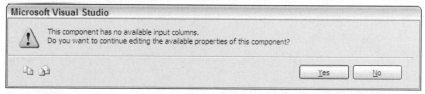

Figure 4-12

Data Mining Model Training

The Data Mining Model Training destination can train an Analysis Services data mining model by passing it data from the data flow. You can train multiple mining models from a single destination and data flow. To use this destination, you would select an Analysis Services Connection Manager and the mining model.

> *The data you pass into the Data Mining Model Training destination must be presorted. To do this, you would use the Sort transformation, which will be discussed in the next section.*

DataReader Destination

The DataReader destination is a way of extending SSIS data flows to external packages or programs that can use the DataReader interface, such as Reporting Services. When you configure this destination, you should make sure that the name of your destination is something that's easy to recognize later in your program, because you will be calling that name later. You can see in Figure 4-13 that the destination's name is RowSampling Output. After you've configured the name and basic properties, check the columns you'd like outputted to the destination in the Input Columns tab.

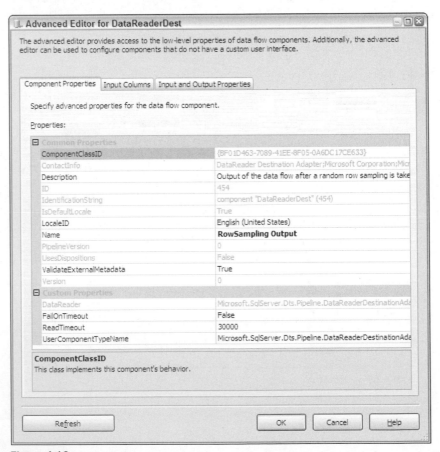

Figure 4-13

If you'd like to use this destination now in Reporting Services, you'd have to ensure that it has this type of connection (SSIS) available to it. In Reporting Services, ensure that the SSIS extension is in the <DATA> section of the RSReportDesigner.config file. In the Report Designer, you'll now see a new connection type called SSIS. Select this data source, and then type the fully qualified name of the package like this:

```
-f C:\Packages\RSSPartnerFeed.dtsx
```

In the Query box for the connection, specify the DataReader destination that you'd like to retrieve data from. Every time the report needs data, the DTS package will be executed, and you will see DataReader destination data wherever it is exposed in the data flow. As you can imagine, you won't be able to use this feature unless you have a data flow in your package. It is also important to performance-tune your package before implementing this enterprise-wide, as your program will be awaiting a response from a SSIS package before it can proceed.

Using SSIS as a data source would be especially useful when you'd like to display non–SQL Server data in Reporting Services or in your application after it was transformed. For example, if you'd like to display an RSS feed (a news feed standard) in a clean tabular format in Reporting Services, this type of function would be especially useful. If you were to design this, users could then subscribe to the RSS feed in Reporting Services and have their data also pushed to them using subscriptions. This will be discussed in much more detail in Chapter 17.

Dimension and Partition Processing

The Dimension Processing destination loads and processes an Analysis Services dimension. You have the option to perform full, incremental, or update processing. To configure the destination, select the Analysis Services Connection Manager that contains the dimension that you'd like to process on the Connection Manager page in the Dimension Processing Destination Editor. You will then see a list of dimensions and fact tables in the box, as shown in Figure 4-14. Select the dimension you'd like to load and process and go to the Mappings page, where you'll map the data from the data flow to the selected dimension. Lastly, you can configure how you'd like to handle errors such as unknown keys in the Advanced page. Generally, the default options are fine for this page unless you have special needs for error handling.

The Partition Processing destination has identical options, but it processes an Analysis Services partition instead of a dimension.

Excel Destination

The Excel destination is identical to the Excel source, except that the destination accepts data instead of sending data. First, select the Excel Connection Manager from the Connection Manager page and then specify which worksheet you wish to load data to.

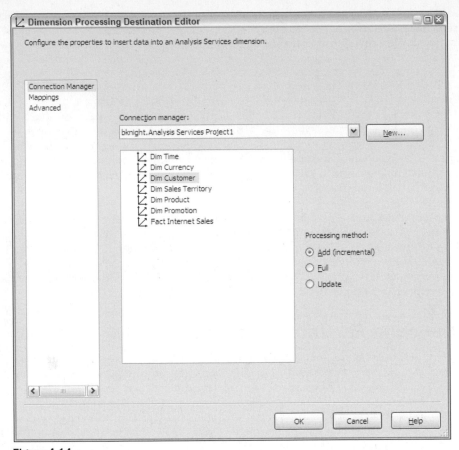

Figure 4-14

Flat File Destination

The commonly used Flat File destination sends data to a flat file and can be fixed-width or delimited. The destination uses a Flat File Connection Manager. You can also add a custom header to the file by typing it into the Header option in the Connection Manager page. Lastly, you can specify on this page that the destination file will be overwritten each time the data flow is run.

OLE DB Destination

The most commonly used destination for you will probably be the OLE DB destination (Figure 4-15). It can write data from the data flow to OLE DB–compliant data sources such as Oracle, Access, and SQL Server. It configures like any other destination and source, using OLE DB Connection Managers. A dynamic option it does have is the Data Access Mode. If you select Table or View — Fast Load, or its variable equivalent, then you will have a number of options below, such as Table Lock. This Fast Load option is available only for SQL Server database instances. A few options of note here are the Rows Per Batch option, which specifies how many rows are allowed before a batch is committed. The other option is the Maximum Insert Commit Size, which specifies how large the batch size will be when inserting using the Fast Load option. The Table Lock option will place a lock on the destination table to speed up the load. As you can imagine, this will cause grief for your users if they're trying to read from the table at the same time. The other important option is Keep Identity. This option allows you to insert into a column that has the identity property set on it.

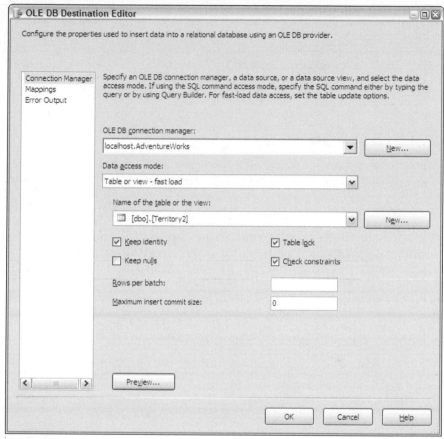

Figure 4-15

Raw File Destination

The Raw File destination is an especially speedy data destination that does not use a Connection Manager to configure. Instead, you point to the file on the server in the editor. The destination is written to typically as an intermediate point for partially transformed data. Once written to, other packages could read the data in by using the Raw File source. The file is written in native format and so is very fast.

Recordset Destination

The Recordset destination populates an ADO record set that can be used outside the transformation. For example, you can populate the ADO record set, and then a Script task could read that record set by reading a variable later in the control flow. This type of destination does not support an error output like some of the other destinations.

SQL Server and Mobile Destinations

The SQL Server destination is the destination that is optimized for SQL Server. It gains its speed advantages by using the bulk insert features that are built into SQL Server. What's nice about this destination is that you can perform transformations earlier in the data flow and actually load data quickly in bulk into SQL Server after it has been transformed. Through the Advanced tab in the destination, you can configure the same features that are available in the bulk insert feature, such as executing triggers or locking the table. Note that this destination can be used only if the package is running on the same machine as SQL Server, because it uses an interface that's in-memory. Lastly, the SQL Server Mobile destination is a destination that can direct data to a Pocket PC device.

Transformations

Transformations (the term *transform* will be used throughout this book) are key components to the data flow that transform the data to a desired format as you move from step to step. For example, you may wish a sampling of your data to be sorted and aggregated. Three transforms can accomplish this task for you. The nicest thing about transforms in SSIS is that it is all done in-memory and it no longer requires elaborate scripting as in SQL Server 2000 DTS. As you add a transform, the data is altered and passed down the path in the data flow. Also, since this is done in-memory, you no longer have to create staging tables to perform most functions. When dealing with very large data sets, though, you may still choose to create staging tables.

You set up the transform by dragging it onto the data flow tab design area. Then, click the source or transform you'd like to connect it to, and drag the green arrow to the target transform or destination. If you drag the red arrow, then rows that fail to transform will be directed to that target. After you have the transform connected, you can double-click it to configure the transform.

In this chapter you will look at each of the transforms at a basic level. In the next chapter, you'll take some of the common tasks and transformation on a test drive and use them in a few real-world scenarios. There are a few transformations that are more advanced, which will be described briefly here but will be covered in much more detail in Chapter 6. Those transformations include the following:

- ❑ Slowly Changing Dimension
- ❑ Pivot and Unpivot
- ❑ Row Count
- ❑ Import and Export Column
- ❑ Term Extraction and Lookup
- ❑ Fuzzy Grouping and Matching
- ❑ Data Mining
- ❑ OLE DB Command

A few of these transformations are not advanced in functionality or complexity; they just don't have a custom UI implemented in SSIS. If a custom UI hasn't been implemented for a transform, it uses the Advanced Editor.

Aggregate

The aggregate transform allows you to aggregate data from the data flow to apply certain T-SQL functions like GROUP BY, Average, Minimum, Maximum, and Count. For example, in Figure 4-13, you can see that the data is grouped together on the ProductID column and then the other two columns are summed. This produces three new columns that can be consumed down the path, or future actions can be performed on them.

The Aggregate transform is configured in the Aggregate Transformation Editor (see Figure 4-16). To configure it, first check the column that you wish to perform the action on. After you check the column, the input column will be filled below in the grid. Optionally, type an alias in the Output Alias column that you wish to give the column when it's outputted to the next transform or destination. For example, if the column now holds the total money per customer, you may change the name of the column that's outputted from InvoiceAmt to TotalCustomerSaleAmt. This will make it easier for you to recognize what the column is along the path of the data. The most important option is the Operation drop-down box. For this option, you can select the following:

❑ **Group By:** Breaks the data set into groups by the column you specify

❑ **Average:** Averages the selected column's numeric data

❑ **Count:** Counts the records in a group

❑ **Count Distinct:** Counts the distinct non-NULL values in a group

❑ **Minimum:** Returns the minimum numeric value in the group

❑ **Maximum:** Returns the maximum numeric value in the group

❑ **Sum:** Returns sum of the selected column's numeric data in the group

You can click the Advanced tab to see the options that allow you to configure multiple outputs from the transform. After you click Advanced, you can type a new Aggregation Name to create a new output. You will then be able to check the columns you'd like to aggregate again as if it were a new transform.

Figure 4-16

In the Advanced tab, the Key Scale option sets an approximate number of keys. The option is set to Unspecified by default and optimizes the transform's cache to the appropriate level. For example, setting it to Low will optimize the transform to write 500,000 keys. Setting it to Medium will optimize it for 5,000,000 keys, and High will optimize the transform for 25,000,000 keys. You can also set the exact number of keys by using the Number of Keys option.

The Count Distinct Scale option will optionally set the amount of distinct values that can be written by the transform. The default value is unspecified, but if you set it to Low, the transform will be optimized to write 500,000 distinct values. Setting the option to Medium will set it to 5,000,000 values, and High will optimize the transform to 25,000,000.

The Auto Extend Factor specifies to what factor your memory can be extended by the transform. The default option is 25%, and you can specify other settings to keep your RAM from getting away from you. The last option is the Warn On Division by Zero checkbox. This option helps you handle division-by-zero errors such as averaging a value of zero. If this option is not checked, the transform will fail instead of giving a warning.

Audit

The Audit transform allows you to add auditing data to your data flow. In the age of HIPPA and Sarbanes-Oxley (SOX) audits, you often must be able to track who inserted the data into a table and when. This transform helps you with that function. For example, if you'd like to track what task inserted data into the table, you can add those columns to the data flow path with this transform.

The task is easy to configure. All other columns are passed through to the path as an output, and any auditing item you add will also be added to the path. Simply select the type of data you'd like to audit in the Audit Type column (shown in Figure 4-17), and then name the column that will be outputted to the flow. The following are some of the options you'll have available to you:

- **Execution Instance GUID:** The GUID that identifies the execution instance of the package
- **PackageID:** The unique ID for the package
- **PackageName:** The name of the package
- **VersionID:** The version GUID of the package
- **ExecutionStartTime:** The time the package began
- **MachineName:** The machine that the package ran on
- **UserName:** The user that started the package
- **TaskName:** The Data Flow task name that holds the audit task
- **TaskID:** The unique identifier for the data flow task that holds the audit task

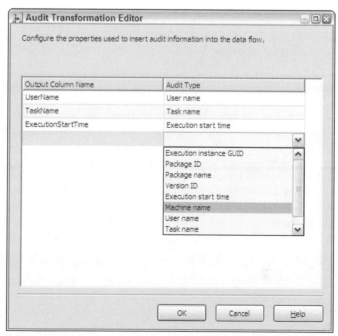

Figure 4-17

Character Map

The Character Map transform (shown in Figure 4-18) performs common character translations in the flow. This simple transform can be configured in a single tab. To do so, check the columns you wish to transform. Then, select whether you want this modified column to be added as a new column or whether you want to update the original column. You can give the column a new name under the Output Alias column. Lastly, select the operation you wish to perform on the inputted column. The available operation types are as follows:

- ❑ **Byte Reversal:** Reverses the order of the bytes. For example, for the data 0x1234 0x9876, the result is 0x4321 0x6789. This uses the same behavior as LCMapString with the LCMAP_BYTEREV option.

- ❑ **Full Width:** Converts the half-width character type to full width.

- ❑ **Half Width:** Converts the full-width character type to half width.

- ❑ **Hiragana:** Converts the Katakana style of Japanese characters to Hiragana.

- ❑ **Katakana:** Converts the Hiragana style of Japanese characters to Katakana.

- ❑ **Linguistic Casing:** Applies the regional linguistic rules for casing.

- ❑ **Lowercase:** Changes all letters in the input to lowercase.

- ❑ **Traditional Chinese:** Converts the simplified Chinese characters to traditional Chinese.

- ❑ **Simplified Chinese:** Converts the traditional Chinese characters to simplified Chinese.

- ❑ **Uppercase:** Changes all letters in the input to uppercase.

In the screenshot in Figure 4-15, you can see that two columns are being transformed. Both columns will be transformed to uppercase. For the TaskName input, a new column is added and the original is kept. The UserName column is replaced in-line.

Conditional Split

The Conditional Split transform is a fantastic way to add complex logic into your data flow. The transform allows you to send the path to various outputs or paths based on conditions. For example, you could configure the transform to send all products with sales that have a quantity greater than 500 to one path and products that have fewer sales down another path. This exact situation is shown in Figure 4-19. You can drag and drop the column or code snippets from the tree above. After you complete the condition, you will need to name it something logical rather than the default name of Case 1. You'll use this case name later. You also can configure the Default Output Column Name, which will output any data that does not fit any case.

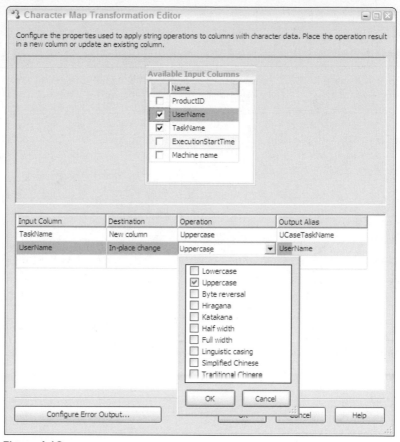

Figure 4-18

You can also conditionally read string data by using expressions like the following example, which reads the first letter of the City column:

```
SUBSTRING(City,1,1) == "F"
```

Once you connect the transform to the next transform in the path or destination, you'll see a pop-up dialog box that lets you select which case you wish to flow down this path, as shown in Figure 4-20. In this figure, you can see two cases. The GoodSales can go down one path, and the Default down another. After you complete the configuration of the first case, you can create a path for each case in the conditional split.

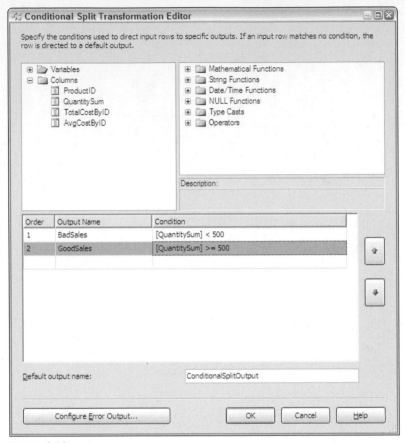

Figure 4-19

Figure 4-20

If you have two cases, and a default case to catch any other conditions, your path may look like Figure 4-21.

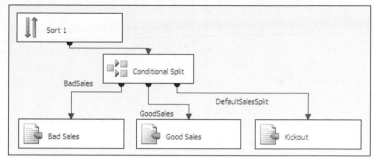

Figure 4-21

A much more detailed example will be given in Chapter 5.

Copy Column

The Copy Column transform is a very simple transformation that copies the output of a column to a clone of itself. This is useful if you wish to create a copy of a column before you perform some elaborate transformations. You could then keep the original value as your control subject and the copy as the modified column. To configure this transform, go to the Copy Column Transformation Editor and check the column you'd like to clone. Then assign a name to the new column.

Many transforms will allow you to transform the data from a column to a new column inherently.

Data Conversion

The Data Conversion transform performs a similar function to the CONVERT or CAST functions in T-SQL. The transform is configured in the Data Conversion Transformation Editor (Figure 4-22), where you would check each column that you wished to convert and then assign what you wish to convert it to under the Data Type column. The Output Alias is the column name you want to assign to the column after it is transformed. If you don't assign it a new name, it will show as Data Conversion: ColumnName later in the data flow.

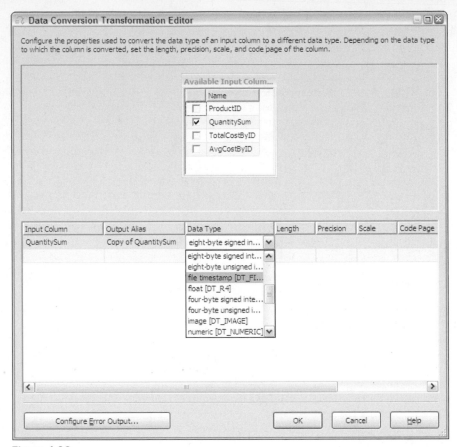

Figure 4-22

Data Mining Query

The Data Mining Query transformation typically is used to fill in gaps in your data or predict a new column for your data flow. This transformation runs a data-mining query and adds the output to the data flow. It also can optionally add columns, such as the probability of a certain condition being true. A few great scenarios for this transformation would be the following:

❑ You could take columns such as number of children, household income, and marital income to predict a new column that states whether the person owns a house or not.

❑ You could predict what customers would want to buy based on their shopping cart items.

❑ You could fill in the blank holes in your data where customers didn't enter all the fields in a questionnaire.

The possibilities are endless with this. This topic will be covered extensively throughout the book, and you'll learn how to configure it in Chapter 6.

Derived Column

The Derived Column transform creates a new column that is derived from the output of another column. You may wish to use this transformation, for example, to multiply the quantity of orders by the cost of the order to derive the total cost of the order, as shown in Figure 4-23. You can also use it to find out the current date or to fill in the blanks in the data by using the ISNULL function. This is one of the top five transforms that you'll find yourself using to alleviate the need for T-SQL scripting in the package.

To configure this transform, drag the column or variable into the Expression column as shown in Figure 4-23. Then add any functions to it. A list of functions can be found in the top-right corner of the Derive Column Transformation Editor. You must then specify, in the Derived Column drop-down box, if you want the output to replace an existing column in the data flow or to create a new column. If you create a new column, specify the name in the Derived Column Name column.

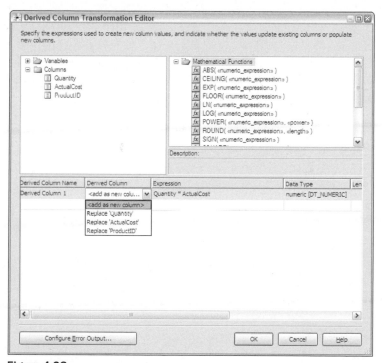

Figure 4-23

Export Column

The Export Column transformation is a transformation that exports an image or a file from the data flow. Unlike the other transformations, the Export Column transform doesn't need a destination to create the file. To configure it, go to the Export Column Transformation Editor, which is shown in Figure 4-24. Select the column that contains the file from the Extract Column drop-down box. Select the column that contains the path and file name to send the files to in the File Path Column drop-down box.

The other options specify where the file will be overwritten or dropped. The Allow Append checkbox specifies whether the output will be appended to the existing file, if one exists. If you check Force Truncate, the existing file will be overwritten if it exists. The Write BOM option specifies whether a byte-order mark is written to the file if it is a DT_NTEXT data type.

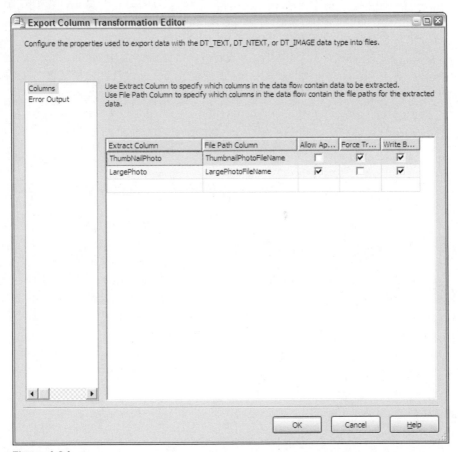

Figure 4-24

If you do not check the Append or Truncate options and the file exists, the package will fail if the error is not handled. The following error is a subset of the complete error you'd receive:

```
Error: 0xC02090A6 at Data Flow Task, Export Column [61]: Opening the file
"wheel_small.gif" for writing failed. The file exists and cannot be overwritten. If
the AllowAppend property is FALSE and the ForceTruncate property is set to FALSE,
the existence of the file will cause this failure.
```

Fuzzy Grouping and Lookup

The Fuzzy Grouping transformation is a very handy transform in your Toolbox that helps you find patterns in your data that could represent duplicated data. For example, it can match a row like "Main St." with "Main Street" to point out a duplicate and condense it down to one record. The Fuzzy Lookup transformation looks at your data input and attempts to clean dirty data. It's very similar to a T-SQL join, but it operates in a fuzzy fashion. This type of transformation typically follows a Lookup transform. The Lookup transformation would attempt to find an exact match, and then you would attempt to look up the records that can't be found with the Fuzzy Lookup transform. Both of these transforms are rather large and will be discussed in much greater detail in Chapter 6.

Import Column

The Import Column transformation is the opposite of the Export Column transform. It can take image or text files stored in a directory and import them as columns into the data flow. You'll learn more about this transformation in Chapter 6.

Lookup

The Lookup transformation performs the same function as the Lookup tab in the Data Pump Task in SQL Server 2000. For example, if you had a column called ZipCode in the data flow and wanted to derive the two columns called State and City, you could use this transformation to perform this type of lookup if you had a mapping table somewhere to reference. As in SQL Server 2000, this should be used sparingly and is no substitute to a good join in a SQL query, as it will cause some latency as each row is looked up.

To configure the Lookup transform, open the editor (Figure 4-25) and first select the Connection Manager that contains the lookup table. You can then select the table or type the query that will represent the lookup information. Instead of typing the query, you can also click Build Query to build a query in an easy interface.

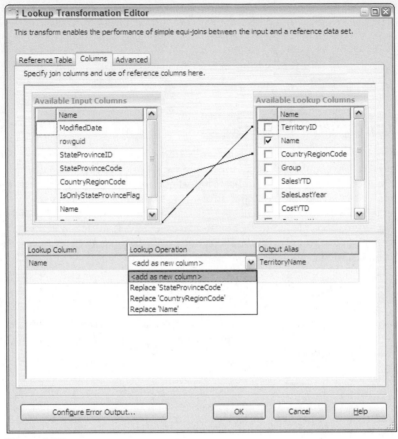

Figure 4-25

Merge

The Merge transformation can merge data from two paths into a single output. The transform is useful when you wish to break out your data flow into a path that handles certain errors and then merge it back into the main data flow downstream after the errors have been handled. It's also useful if you wish to merge data from two data sources.

The transform is similar to the Union All transformation, which you'll learn about in a moment, but the Merge transform has some restrictions that may cause you to lean toward using Union All:

❑ The data must be sorted before the Merge transform. You can do this by using the Sort transform prior to the merge or by specifying an ORDER BY clause in the source connection.

❑ The metadata must be the same between both paths. For example, the CustomerID column can't be a numeric column in one path and a character column in another path.

❑ If you have more than two paths, you should choose the Union All transformation.

To configure the transform, ensure that the data is sorted exactly the same on both paths and drag the path onto the transform. You'll be asked if the path you'd like to merge is Merge Input 1 or 2. If this is the first path you're connecting to the transform, select Merge Input 1. Next, connect the second path into the transform. The transformation will automatically configure itself, as you can see in Figure 4-26. Essentially, it will map each of the columns to the column from the other path, and you have the choice to ignore a certain column's data.

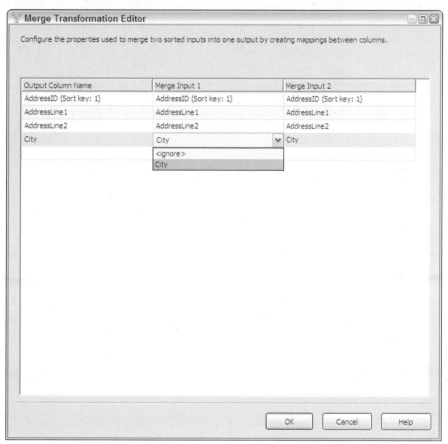

Figure 4-26

Merge Join

One of the overriding themes of SSIS is that you shouldn't have to write any code to create your transformation. One case to prove this is the Merge Join transformation. This transformation will merge the output of two inputs and perform an INNER or OUTER join on the data. An example of where this would be useful is if you have an HR system in one data stream that has an EmployeeID in it and you have a payroll system in another data stream with the payments data. You could merge the two data inputs together and output the employee's name from the HR system and paycheck data from the payroll system into a single path. You can see a variation of this in Figure 4-27, where the employee's name is merged from one system and hire date from another system.

If both inputs are in the same database, it would be faster to perform a join at the OLE DB Source level instead of using a transformation. This transformation is useful when you have two different data sources you wish to merge or when you don't want to write your own join code.

To configure the Merge Join transformation, connect your two inputs into the Merge Join transform and then select what represents the right and left join as you connect each input. Open the Merge Join Transformation Editor and verify the linkage between the two tables. You can see an example of this in Figure 4-28, where the ContactID is the linkage. You can right-click on the arrow to delete a linkage or drag a column from the left input onto the right input to create a new linkage if one is missing. Lastly, check each of the columns you want to be passed as output to the path and select the type of join you wish to make (LEFT, INNER, or FULL).

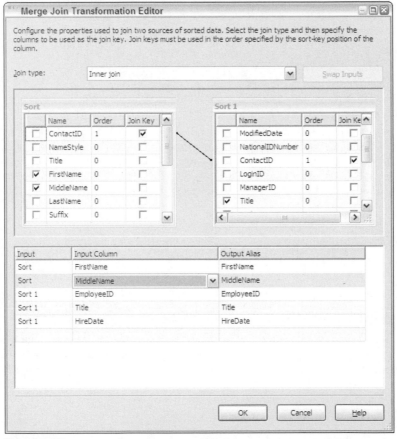

Figure 4-27

Multicast

The Multicast transformation, as the name implies, can send a single data input to multiple output paths easily. You may want to use this transformation to send a path to multiple destinations sliced in different ways, as shown in Figure 4-28. To configure the transform, simply connect the transform to your input, and then drag the output path from the Multicast transform onto your next destination or transform. After you connect the Multicast transform to your first destination or transform, you can keep connecting it to other transforms or destinations. There is nothing to configure in the Multicast Transformation Editor other than the names of the outputs.

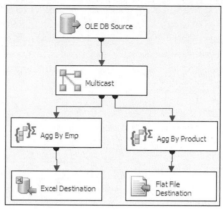

Figure 4-28

The Multicast transformation is similar to the Split transformation in that both transformations send data to multiple outputs. The Multicast will send all the rows from the path, whereas the Split will conditionally send part of the data to the path.

OLE DB Command

The OLE DB Command transformation executes an OLE DB command against each row in your data flow. It's quite useful for cleaning up child tables before you perform your insert. This transform uses the Advanced Editor and is covered in Chapter 6.

Percentage and Row Sampling

The Percentage and Row Sampling transformations give you the ability to take the data from the source and randomly select a subset of data. The transformation produces two outputs that you can select. One output is the data that was randomly selected, and the other is the data that was not selected. You can use this to send a subset of data to a development or test server. The most useful application of this transform is to train a data-mining model. You can use one output path to train your data-mining model and the sampling to validate your data-mining model.

To configure the transformation, select the percentage or number of rows you wish to be sampled (as shown in Figure 4-29). As you can imagine, the Percentage Sampling transformation allows you to select the percentage of rows, and the Row Sampling transformation allows you to specify how many rows you wish to be outputted randomly. Next, you can optionally name each of the outputs from the transformation. The last option is to specify the seed that will randomize the data. If you select a seed and run the transformation multiple times, the same data will be outputted to the destination. If you uncheck this option, which is the default, the seed will be automatically incremented by one each at runtime and you will see random data each time.

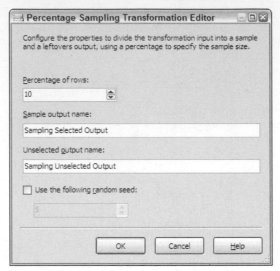

Figure 4-29

Pivot and Unpivot

The Pivot transformation denormalizes a normalized data set to make it more viewable for reporting. This output is similar to how OLAP displays data or how the matrix report looks in Reporting Services. You will now look at a quick example of how a pivot table would use data. Say, for example, you have a list of employees and the number of items they sold by date. This view, as shown in the following table, may not be as useful as a pivoted view:

Employee	Date	Items Sold
Mary	9/1/2005	180
Mary	9/2/2005	2
Mary	9/3/2005	140
John	9/1/2005	88
John	9/3/2005	60
John	9/4/2005	12

Once you pivot the data by the date as shown in the following table, you can quickly see the number of orders that each employee had per date. The dates where the employee had no orders just show a NULL.

	9/1/2005	9/2/2005	9/3/2005	9/4/2005
Mary	180	2	140	
John	88		60	12

The Pivot transformation performs this function for you. The Unpivot transformation performs exactly the opposite. You'll learn much more about how to configure these two transformations in Chapter 6.

Row Count

The Row Count transformation simply counts the rows that flow through the transform and outputs the number to a variable. The variable is in the scope of the Data Flow task. Typically, you would see this used to feed an e-mail that is sent to a user about the number of records that were loaded. The configuration of this transform will be discussed in Chapter 6.

Script Component

The Script Component transform allows you to write custom scripts as transforms, sources, or destinations. Some of the things you can do with this transform include the following:

❑ Create a custom transform that would use a .NET assembly to validate credit card numbers or mailing addresses.

❑ Validate data and skip records that don't seem reasonable. For example, you can use it in a human resource recruitment system to pull out candidates that don't match the salary requirement at a job code level.

❑ Write a custom component to integrate with a third-party vendor.

Scripts used as sources can support multiple outputs, and you have the option of precompiling the scripts for runtime efficiency. You'll learn much more about the Scripting Component transform in Chapter 7.

Slowly Changing Dimension

The Slowly Changing Dimension transform coordinates the updating and inserting of a dimension in a data warehouse. This transformation is coordinated through the Slowly Changing Dimension Wizard. The wizard will produce all the transforms necessary to update or add to your dimension. This was once a very arduous process for a DTS developer and now can be done in minutes. This transform will be explained in much more detail in Chapter 6.

Sort

The Sort transformation allows you to sort data based on any column in the path. This will probably be one of the top five transformations you use on a regular basis because some other transforms require sorted data. To configure the transform, open the Sort Transformation Editor once it's connected to the path and check the column that you wish to sort by. Then, uncheck any column you don't want passed through to the path from the Pass Through column. By default, every column will be passed through the pipeline. You can see this in Figure 4-30, where the user is sorting by ProductID and passing all other columns in the path as output.

In the bottom grid, you can specify the alias that you wish to output and whether you're going to sort in ascending or descending order. The Sort Order column shows which column will be sorted on first, second, third, and so on. You can optionally check the Remove Rows with Duplicate Sort Values option to remove any rows that have duplicate values.

Figure 4-30

Term Extraction and Lookup

The Term Extraction transformation pulls out keywords from a data set. For example, you can use the Term Extraction transform to look at a series of articles and pull out keywords from each article. Another great use for it would be to analyze e-mail messages from a company support mailbox to find common issues and terms. The transform works only with English words and linguistics.

Common pronouns and articles are not extracted from the input. For example, "bicycle" would be extracted but not the words "the bicycle." Two new output columns are extracted from the input: term and score. The term output column is the term that was extracted from the input, and the score is how often it shows in the input. All other input columns are dropped. If you want to keep your original data, you may have to use the Multicast transformation and send one path to the Term Extraction and the other wherever you wish to output the data. You can also specify data that you wish to exclude from the transformation's inspection.

The Term Lookup transformation pulls out rows that meet keywords that you predefine. For example, if you have a support e-mail system that logs messages into a database, you could have this transformation comb through the e-mail messages and automatically pull out any message that talks about problems with your product. It uses a Connection Manager to point to a table that contains the terms that you wish to use as your reference.

You'll learn much more about this in Chapter 6.

Union All

The Union All transform works much the opposite way as the Merge transform. It takes the outputs from multiple sources or transforms and combines them into a single result set. For example, in Figure 4-31, the user combines the data from two XML sources on the Internet into a single output using the Union All transform and then sends the single result set into the Term Extraction transform.

To configure the transform, connect the first source or transformation to the Union All transform and then continue to connect the other sources or transforms to it until you are complete. You can optionally open the Union All Editor to make sure the columns map correctly, but SSIS will take care of that for you automatically. The transform fixes minor metadata issues. For example, if you have one input that is a 20-character string and another that is 50 characters, the output of this from the Union All transform will be the longer 50-character column.

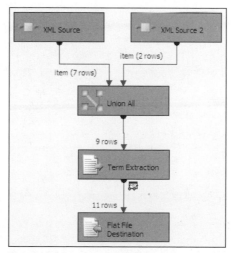

Figure 4-31

Data Flow Example

Now you can practice what you've learned in this chapter and pull together some of the transforms and connections to create a small ETL process. This process will pull transactional data from the AdventureWorks database and then massage the data by aggregating, sorting, and calculating new columns. This extract may be used by another vendor or an internal organization.

1. Create a new package and rename it AdventureWorksExtract.dtsx. Start by dragging a Data Flow task onto the control flow. Double-click on the task to go to the Data Flow tab.

2. In the Data Flow tab, drag an OLE DB Source onto the design pane. Right-click on the source and rename it TransactionHistory. Double-click on it to open the editor. The connection to the AdventureWorks database may already be in the Data Connections list on the left. If it is, select it, and click OK. If it's not there yet, click New to add a new connection to the AdventureWorks database on any server.

3. When you click OK, you'll be taken back to the OLE DB Source Editor. Ensure that the Data Access Mode option is set to "Table or View." Select the [Production].[TransactionHistoryArchive] table from the Name of the Table drop-down box as shown in Figure 4-32.

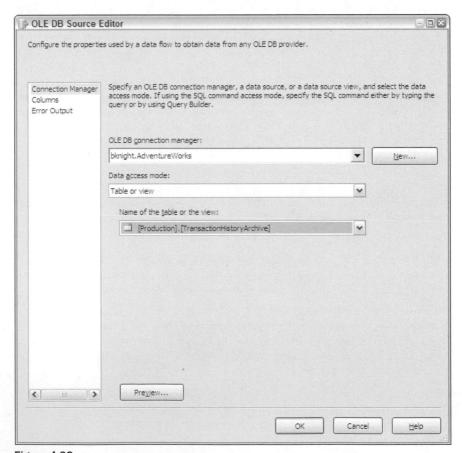

Figure 4-32

4. Go to the Columns page (shown in Figure 4-33) and uncheck every column except for ProductID, Quantity, and ActualCost. Click OK to exit the editor.

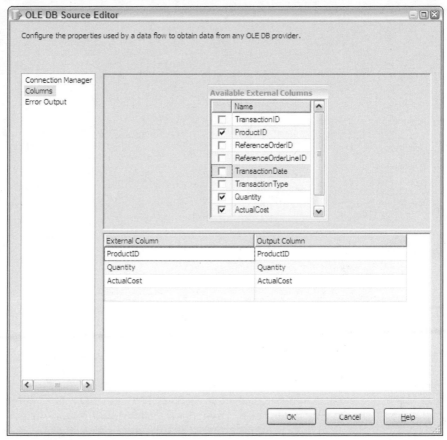

Figure 4-33

5. Drag a Derived Column transform onto the data flow, right-click on it, and select Rename. Rename the transform "Calculate Total Cost." Click the TransactionHistory OLE DB source and drag the green arrow (the data path) onto the Derived Column transform.

6. Double-click on the Derived Column transform to open the editor (shown in Figure 4-34). For the Expression column, type the following code or drag and drop the column names from the upper-left box: **[Quantity]* [ActualCost]**. The Derived Column should have the <add as a new column> option selected, and type **TotalCost** for the Derived Column Name option. Click OK to exit the editor.

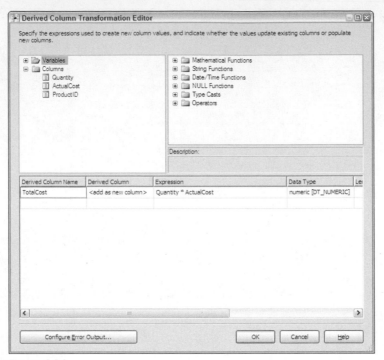

Figure 4-34

7. Drag an Aggregate transform onto the data flow and rename it "Aggregate Data." Drag the green arrow from the Derived Column transform onto this transform. Double-click the Aggregate transform to open the editor (shown in Figure 4-35). Select the ProductID column and note that it is transposed into the bottom section. The ProductID column should have Group By for the Operation column. Next, check the Quantity and TotalCost columns and set the operation of both of these columns to Sum. Click OK to exit the editor.

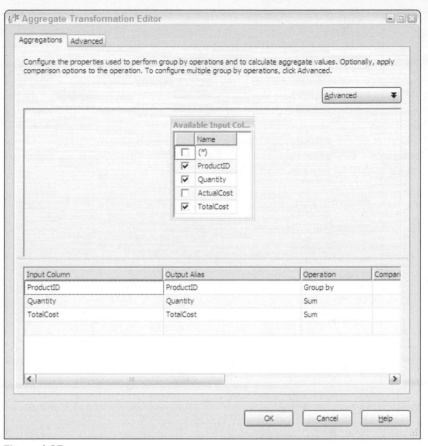

Figure 4-35

8. Drag a Sort transform onto the data flow and rename it "Sort by ProductID." Connect the Aggregate transform to this transform by the green arrow as in the last step. Double-click on the Sort transform to configure it in the editor. You can sort by the most popular products by checking the Quantity column and selecting Descending for the Sort Type drop-down box. Click OK to exit the editor.

9. You've now done enough massaging of the data and are ready to export the data to a flat file that can be consumed by another vendor. Drag a Flat File Destination onto the data flow. Connect it to the Sort transform by using the green arrow as you saw in the last few steps. Rename the Flat File Destination "Vendor Extract."

10. Double-click on the destination to open the Flat File Destination Editor. You're going to output the data to a new Connection Manager, so click New. When prompted for the Flat File Format, select Delimited. Name the Connection Manager "Vendor Extract" also and type whatever description you'd like. If you have the directory, point the File Name option to C:\SSISDemos\ VendorExtract.csv (make sure this directory is created before proceeding). Check the Column Names in the First Data Row option. Your final screen should look like Figure 4-36. Click OK to go back to the Flat File Destination Editor.

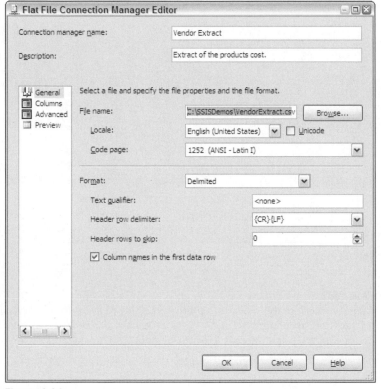

Figure 4-36

11. Go to the mappings page and make sure that each column in the Inputs table is mapped to the Destination table, as shown in Figure 4-37. Click OK to exit the editor and go back to the data flow.

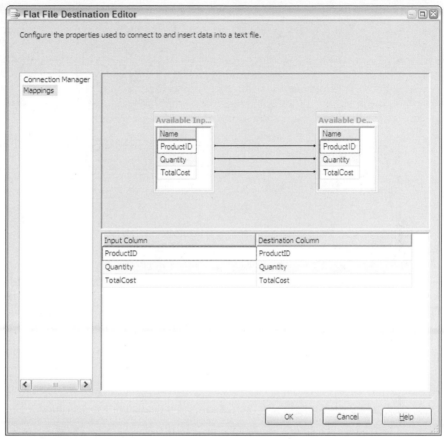

Figure 4-37

12. Now, your first larger ETL package is complete! This package is very typical of what you'll be doing day-to-day inside of SSIS, and you will see this expanded on greatly in Chapter 5. Execute the package and you should see the rows flow through the data flow as shown in Figure 4-38. Note that as the data flows from transform to transform you can see how many records were passed through the transform.

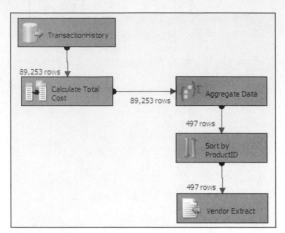

Figure 4-38

Data Viewers

Data viewers are a very important feature in SSIS for debugging your data pump pipeline. They allow you to view data at points in time at runtime. If you place a data viewer before and after the Aggregate transform, you can see at runtime the data flowing into the transform and what it looks like after the transform happens. Once you deploy your package and run it on the server as a job or with the service, the data viewers do not show. Anytime the package is executed outside the designer, the data viewers won't show. There are four types of data viewers:

❏   **Grid:** Shows a snapshot of the data in grid format at that point in time

❏   **Histogram:** Shows the distribution of numeric data in a histogram graph

❏   **Scatter Plot:** Shows the distribution of numeric data using an x- and y-axis

❏   **Column Chart:** Displays the occurrence count of discrete values in a selected column

To place a data viewer in your pipeline, right-click on one of the paths (red or green arrows leaving a transform or source) and select Data Viewers. The Configure Data Viewer dialog box will appear, as shown in Figure 4-39. Select what type of data viewer you wish to use and optionally give it a name. You can go to the other tab that's named after what type of data viewer you're using to select what columns will be used in the data viewer.

Once you run the package, you'll see the data viewers open and populate with data when the package runs the transform that it's attached to, as shown in Figure 4-40. The package will not proceed until you click the > button. You can also copy the data for further investigation by clicking Copy Data.

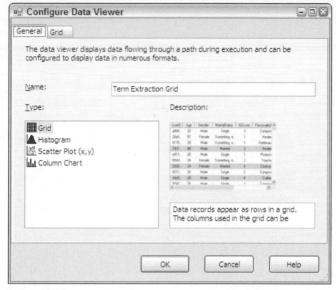

Figure 4-39

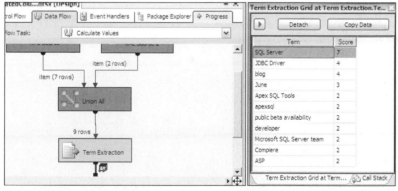

Figure 4-40

Summary

In this chapter, you learned about containers and transformations. Containers allow you as an SSIS developer to group tasks or loop through a series of tasks. Transformations allow you to change the data from a source or another transform and pass the results as output to a destination or another transformation in the path. In the next chapter, you will use what you have learned over the past two chapters to create a few packages that will perform typical ETL tasks for you.

Creating an End-to-End Package

Now that you've learned about all the basic tasks and transforms in SSIS, you can jump into some practical applications for SSIS. You'll first start with a normal transformation of data from a series of flat files into SQL Server. Next you'll add some complexity to a transformation by archiving the files automatically. The last example will show you how to make a package that handles basic errors and makes the package more dynamic. As you run through the tutorials, remember to save your package and project often to avoid any loss of work.

Basic Transformation Tutorial

As you can imagine, the primary reason that people use SSIS is to read the data from a source and write it to a destination after it's massaged. This tutorial will walk you through a common scenario where you want to copy data from a flat file source to a SQL Server table without massaging the data. Don't worry; things will get much more complex later in your next package.

Start the tutorial by going online to the Wiley Web site and downloading the sample extract that contains zip code information about cities in Florida. The zip code extract was retrieved from public record data from the 1990 census and has been filtered down to just Florida cities to save on your download time. You'll use this in the next tutorial as well, so it's very important not to skip this tutorial. You can download the sample extract file called ZipCode.txt from this book's Web page at www.wrox.com. Place the file into a directory called C:\SSISDemos.

Open Business Information Development Studio (BIDS) and select File ⇨ New ⇨ Project. Then select Integration Services Project as your project type. Type **ProSSISChapter5** as the project name, and accept the rest of the defaults (as shown in Figure 5-1).

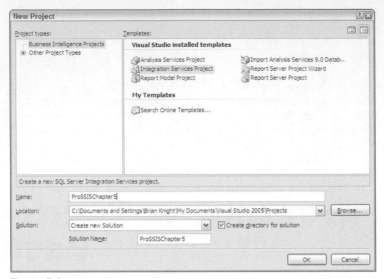

Figure 5-1

The project will be created, and you'll see a default Package.dtsx package file in the Solution Explorer. Right-click on the Package.dtsx file in the Solution Explorer and select Rename. Rename the file ZipLoad.dtsx. When you're asked if you'd like to rename the package as well, click Yes. If the package isn't opened yet, double-click on it to open it in the Package Designer.

Creating Connections

Now that you have the package ready to begin, you need to create a shared connection that can be used across multiple packages. In the Solution Explorer, right-click on Data Sources and select New Data Source. This opens the Data Source Wizard. Select the "Create a data source based on an existing or new connection" radio box and click New, which opens the window to create a new Connection Manager.

There are many ways you could have created the connection. For example, you could have created it as you're creating each source and destination. Once you're more experienced with the tool, you'll find what works best for you.

Your first Connection Manager will be to SQL Server, so select Native OLE DB\SQL Native Client. For the Server Name option, type the name of your SQL Server and enter the authentication mode that is necessary for you to read and write to the database. Lastly, select the AdventureWorks database and click OK. If you don't have the AdventureWorks database, you can pick any other database on the server. You can optionally test the connection. You will then have a data source in the Data Source box that should be selected. Click Next and name the data source AdventureWorks.

You'll use other connections as well, but for those, you'll create connections that will be local to the package only and not shared. With the ZipLoad package open, right-click in the Connection Managers box below and select New Connection from Data Source. You should see the AdventureWorks data source you created earlier. Select that data source and click OK. Once the Connection Manager is created, right-click on it and rename it AdventureWorks if it's not already named that. This is, of course, optional and just keeps us all on the same page.

Next, create a Flat File connection and point it to the ZipCode.txt file in your C:\SSISDemos directory. Right-click in the Connection Manager area of Package Designer, and select New Flat File Connection. Name the connection ZipCode Extract and type any description you like. Point the File Name option to C:\SSISDemos\ZipCode.txt or browse to the correct location by clicking Browse.

You need to set the Format drop-down box to Delimited with <none> set for the Text Qualifier option. The Text Qualifier option allows you to specify that character data is wrapped in quotes or some type of qualifier. This helps you when you have a file that is delimited by commas and you also have commas inside some of the text data that you do not wish to separate by. Setting a Text Qualifier will ignore those commas inside the text data. Lastly, select "Tab {t}" from the Header Row Qualifier drop-down box and check the "Column names in first data row" option. This states that your first row contains the column names for the file. Your final configuration for this page should look like Figure 5-2.

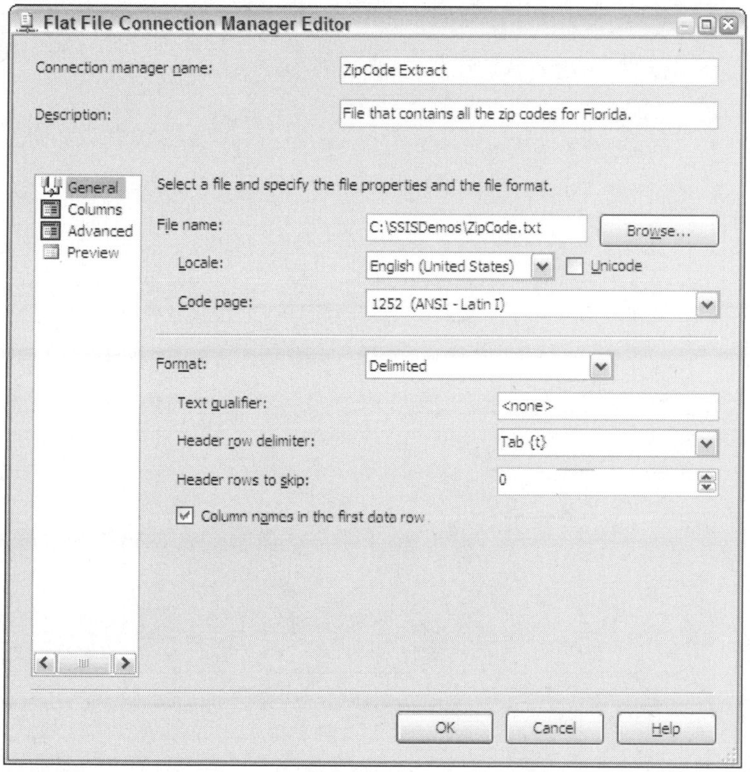

Figure 5-2

You can go to the Columns page to view a preview of the first 101 rows and set the row and column delimiters. The defaults are generally fine for this screen. The Row Delimiter option should be set to {CR}{LF}, which means that a carriage return separates each row. The Column Delimiter option should have carried over from the first page and will again be set to "Tab {t}". In some extracts that you may receive, the header record may be different from the data records and the configurations won't be exactly the same as in the example.

The Advanced page is where you can specify the data types for each of the three columns. The default for this type of data is a 50-character string, which is excessive in this case. Click Suggest Types to comb through the data and find the best data type fit for the data. This will open the Suggest Column Types dialog box, where you should accept the default options and click OK.

You can now see that the data types in the Advanced page have changed for each column. One column in particular was incorrectly changed. When combing through the first 100 records, the Suggest Column Types dialog box selected a "two-byte signed integer [DT_I2]" for the zip code column. While this would work for the data extract you have, it won't work once you get to some states that have zip codes that begin with a zero. Change this column to a string by selecting string [DT_STR] from the DataType drop-down box, and change the length of the column to 5 by changing the OutputColumnWidth option (shown in Figure 5-3). The last configuration change is to change the TextQualified option to False and click OK.

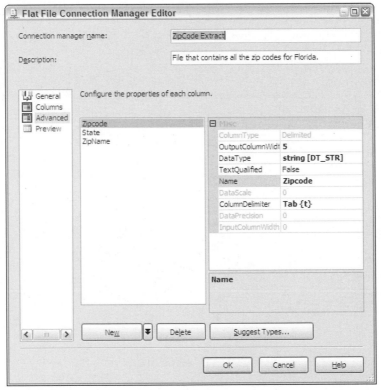

Figure 5-3

Creating the Tasks

With the first few connections created, you can go ahead and create your first task. In this tutorial, you'll have only a single task, which will be the Data Flow task. In the Toolbox, drag the Data Flow task over to the design pane in the Control Flow tab. Next, right-click on the task and select Rename to rename the task "Load ZipCode Info."

Creating the Data Flow

Now comes the more detailed portion of almost all of your packages. Double-click on the task to drill into the data flow. This will automatically take you to the Data Flow tab. You'll see that "Load ZipCode Info" was transposed to the Data Flow Task drop-down box. If you had more than this one Data Flow task, then more would appear as options in the drop-down box.

Drag and drop a Flat File Source onto the data flow design pane, and then rename it "Florida ZipCode File." All the rename instructions in these tutorials are optional, but they will keep you on the same page and make your operational people happier because they'll understand what's failing. Open the "Florida ZipCode File" source and point it to the Connection Manager called ZipCode Extract. Go to the Columns page and take notice of the columns that you'll be outputting to the path. You've now configured the source, and you can click OK.

Next, drag and drop a SQL Server Destination onto the design pane and rename it AdventureWorks. Connect the path (green arrow) from the "Florida ZipCode File" source to the AdventureWorks destination. Double-click on the destination and select AdventureWorks from the Connection Manager drop-down box. For the Use a Table or View option, click the New button next to the drop-down box. This is how you can create a table inside BIDS without having to go back to SQL Server Management Studio. The default DDL for creating the table will use the destination's name (AdventureWorks), and the data types may not be exactly what you'd like, as shown below:

```
CREATE TABLE [AdventureWorks] (
    [Zipcode] VARCHAR(5),
    [State] VARCHAR(2),
    [ZipName] VARCHAR(16)
)
```

Suppose this won't do for your picky DBA, who is concerned about performance. In this case, you should rename the table ZipCode (taking out the brackets) and change each column's data type to a more suitable size and type:

```
CREATE TABLE ZipCode (
    Zipcode CHAR(5),
    State CHAR(2),
    ZipName VARCHAR(16)
)
```

Once you have completed changing the DDL, click OK and the table name will be transposed into the table drop-down box. Finally, go to the Mapping page to ensure that the inputs are mapped to the outputs correctly. SSIS attempts to map the columns based on name, and in this case, since you just created the table with the same column names, it should be a direct match, as shown in Figure 5-4.

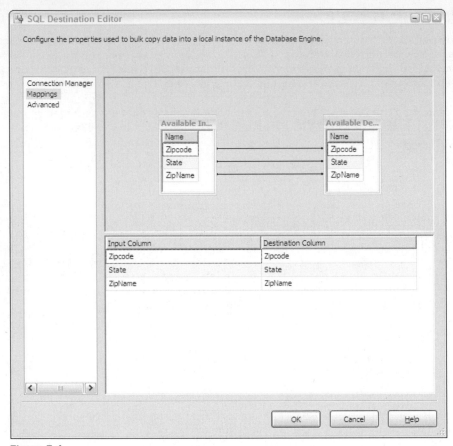

Figure 5-4

Once you've confirmed that the mappings look like Figure 5-4, click OK.

Completing the Package

With the basic framework of the package now constructed, you need to add one more task into the control flow to ensure that you can run this package multiple times. To do this, click on the Control Flow tab and drag an Execute SQL task over to the design pane. Rename the task "Purge ZipCode Table." Double-click on the task and select AdventureWorks from the Connection drop-down box. Finally, type the following query for the SQLStatement option (you can also click the ellipsis button and enter the query):

```
DELETE FROM ZipCode
```

Click OK to complete the task configuration. Connect the task as a parent to the "Load ZipCode Info" task. To do this, click the "Purge ZipCode Table" task and drag the green arrow onto the "Load ZipCode Info" task.

Saving the Package

Your first package is now complete. Go ahead and save the package by clicking the Save icon in the top menu or by selecting File ⇨ Save Selected Items. It's important to note here that by clicking Save, you're saving the .DTSX file to the project, but you have not saved it to the server yet. To do that, you'll have to deploy the solution or package. The tutorial will cover that in the last section of this chapter.

Executing the Package

With the package complete, you can attempt to execute it. Do this by selecting the green arrow in the upper menu. You can also right-click on the ZipCode.dtsx package file in the Solution Explorer and select Execute Package. The package will take a few moments to compile and validate, and then it will execute.

You can see the progress under the Progress tab or in the Output window. In the Controller Flow tab, you'll see the two tasks go from yellow to green (hopefully). If both turn green, then the package execution was successful. In the event your package failed, you can look in the Output window to see why. The Output window should be open by default, but in case it's not, you can open it by clicking View ⇨ Other Windows ⇨ Output.

You can go to the Data Flow tab to see how many records were copied over. You can see the Controller tab in the left image in Figure 5-5 and the Data Flow tab in the right image. Notice the number of records displays in the path as SSIS moves from transform to transform.

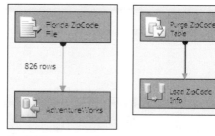

Figure 5-5

By default, when you execute a package, you'll be placed in debug mode. Changes you make in this mode will not be made available until you run the package again. To break out of this mode, click the square stop icon or click Stop Debugging under the Debug menu.

Typical Mainframe ETL with Data Scrubbing

With the basic ETL out of the way, you will now jump into a more complex SSIS package that attempts to scrub data. You can start this scenario by downloading some public data from the Florida Department of Corporations at ftp://dossftp.dos.state.fl.us/public/doc/cor/. Manually download the file 010305c.dat from the FTP site and place the file into a directory called C:\SSISDemos.

In this scenario, you run a credit card company that's interested in marketing to newly formed domestic corporations in Florida. You want to prepare a data extract each day for the marketing department to perform a mail merge and perform a bulk mailing. Yes, your company is an old-fashioned, snail-mail spammer.

Luckily the Department of State for Florida has an interesting extract you can use to empower your marketing department. As with most extracts that come from a legacy system, this extract unfortunately is in a fixed-width format. This means that the file is not delimited by any symbol, and you'll have to manually configure each column's width. In these types of events, your mainframe group or the third party would send you a record layout for the file extract. In this case, you can see the record layout here: http://www.sunbiz.org/corpweb/inquiry/corfile.html. The record layout for this extract would look like this:

```
01   ANNUAL_MICRO_DATA_REC.
       03   ANNUAL_COR_NUMBER                  PIC X(12).
       03   ANNUAL_COR_NAME                    PIC X(48).
       03   ANNUAL_COR_STATUS                  PIC X(01).
       03   ANNUAL_COR_FILING_TYPE             PIC X(15).
       03   ANNUAL_COR_2ND_MAIL_ADD_1          PIC X(42).
       03   ANNUAL_COR_2ND_MAIL_ADD_2          PIC X(42).
       03   ANNUAL_COR_2ND_MAIL_CITY           PIC X(28).
       03   ANNUAL_COR_2ND_MAIL_STATE          PIC X(02).
       03   ANNUAL_COR_2ND_MAIL_ZIP            PIC X(10).
       03   ANNUAL_COR_2ND_MAIL_COUNTRY        PIC X(02).
       03   ANNUAL_COR_FILE_DATE               PIC X(08).
       03   ANNUAL_COR_FEI_NUMBER              PIC X(14).
       03   ANNUAL_MORE_THAN_SIX_OFF_FLAG      PIC X(01).
       03   ANNUAL_LAST_TRX_DATE               PIC X(08).
       03   ANNUAL_STATE_COUNTRY               PIC X(02).
       03   ANNUAL_REPORT_YEAR_1               PIC X(04).
       03   ANNUAL_HOUSE_FLAG_1                PIC X(01).
       03   ANNUAL_REPORT_DATE_1               PIC X(08).
       03   ANNUAL_REPORT_YEAR_2               PIC X(04).
       03   ANNUAL_HOUSE_FLAG_2                PIC X(01).
       03   ANNUAL_REPORT_DATE_2               PIC X(08).
       03   ANNUAL_REPORT_YEAR_3               PIC X(04).
       03   ANNUAL_HOUSE_FLAG_3                PIC X(01).
       03   ANNUAL_REPORT_DATE_3               PIC X(08).
       03   ANNUAL_RA_NAME                     PIC X(42).
       03   ANNUAL_RA_NAME_TYPE                PIC X(01).
       03   ANNUAL_RA_ADD_1                    PIC X(42).
       03   ANNUAL_RA_CITY                     PIC X(28).
       03   ANNUAL_RA_STATE                    PIC X(02).
       03   ANNUAL_RA_ZIP5                     PIC X(05).
       03   ANNUAL_RA_ZIP4                     PIC X(04).
       03   ANNUAL_PRINCIPALS                  OCCURS 6 TIMES.
            05   ANNUAL_PRINC_TITLE               PIC X(04).
            05   ANNUAL_PRINC_NAME_TYPE           PIC X(01).
            05   ANNUAL_PRINC_NAME                PIC X(42).
            05   ANNUAL_PRINC_ADD_1               PIC X(42).
            05   ANNUAL_PRINC_CITY                PIC X(28).
            05   ANNUAL_PRINC_STATE               PIC X(02).
            05   ANNUAL_PRINC_ZIP5                PIC X(05).
            05   ANNUAL_PRINC_ZIP4                PIC X(04).
       03   FILLER                             PIC X(04).
```

Each row represents another column, and you can see the length of each column after the word PIC. This type of format is very typical from legacy systems and even from newer ones. You won't be using all the columns in this example, so you won't have to define them all. The business goals of this package are as follows:

❏ Create a package that finds the files in the C:\SSISDemos directory and loads the file into your relational database.

❏ Archive the file after you load it to prevent it from being loaded twice.

❏ The package must self-heal. If a column is missing data, the data should be added automatically.

❏ If the package encounters an error in its attempt to self-heal, output the row to an error queue.

Start a new package in your existing ProSSISChapter5 BIDS project from the first tutorial. Right-click in the Solution Explorer and select Add ➪ New Item. From the New Item dialog box, choose "New SSIS Package." This will create Package1.dtsx, or some numeric variation on that name. Rename the file CorporationLoad.dtsx, and the package should also be renamed. Double-click on the package to open it.

Just like the last package you created, right-click in the Connection Managers area and select a new Connection Manager from the Data Source that points to the AdventureWorks data connection. You now have two packages using the same Shared Connection. Next, create a new Flat File Connection Manager just as you did in the last tutorial. When the configuration screen opens, call the connection "Corporation Extract" in the General page. Type any description you'd like. For this Connection Manager, you're going to configure the file slightly differently. This time, the file will not be delimited by any character or tab. Instead, select Fixed Width from the Format drop-down box. You will also not have any type of column headers this time, so there's no need to check the same "Column names in the first data row" option.

A fixed-width file means that each column is not delimited by any character or tab. Instead, you have to manually specify where each column begins and ends. Most mainframe files you receive will be sent to you in this format. As you'll see in a moment, it's not nearly as easy to configure. You can take the record layout that was discussed earlier and deduce how you should set the starting points of each column. To do this, go to the Columns page in the Flat File Connection Manager Editor (shown in Figure 5-6). Then, start by entering a Row Width of 1172 characters for this file (this number would be given to you by the originator of the file typically).

Next, specify where each column ends by adding a vertical bar at each column end point. Add that bar by left-clicking on the spot where the column ends. The ruler above the data shows you what character you're on before adding a new vertical bar, and the data preview in the Source Data Columns area may help guide you. For this example, you can use the following table as a hint to remind you where you need to place lines. To remove the vertical bar, you can double-click on it, or to move it, just click and drag it to the proper spot.

Position Stops at	Field Description
12	Corporate number
60	Corporation name
61	Corporate status
65	Filing Type

Table continued on following page

127

Position Stops at	Field Description
118	Mailing address line 1
160	Mailing address line 2
188	City
190	State
200	Zip code
202	Country
210	Filing date
224	FEI number
1172	Records you'll throw out

Notice that for this example, you're throwing out most of the data. It is grouped in one column that you'll remove in the path.

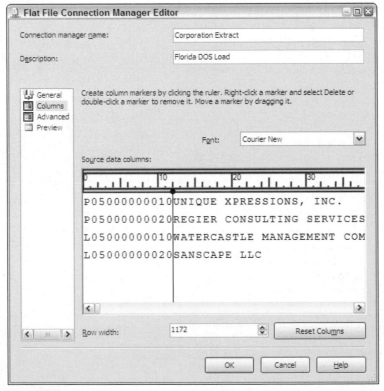

Figure 5-6

After you finish adding all the columns, go to the Advanced tab. Click Suggest Types as you did in the last example. In the Suggest Column Types dialog box, click OK to accept the defaults. Again, this dialog box will accomplish most of the data type discovery for you, but it will make some mistakes that you will have to repair. The first mistake is Column 8 (ZipCode column). You may need to change this DataType option to String [DT_STR] and the OutputColumnWidth to 10 characters. Finally, you'll want to change Column 10 to String [DT_STR]. After you've properly set these two columns, click OK to save the Connection Manager.

Creating the Data Flow

With the mundane work of creating the connections now out of the way, you can go ahead and create the fun transformation. As you did in the last package, you must first create a Data Flow task by dragging it from the Toolbox. Name this task "Load Corporate Data." Double-click on the task to go to the Data Flow tab.

Drag and drop onto the design pane a Flat File source and rename it "Uncleansed Corporate Data." Double-click the source and select Corporate Extract as your Connection Manager that you'll be using. Next, go to the Columns tab and uncheck Column 11 and Column 12 since the marketing department won't need that data. You'll add the destination and transformation in a moment after the scenario is expanded a bit.

Handling Dirty Data

Before you go deeper into this scenario, you should take a time-out to look more closely at this data. As you were creating the connection, a very observant person (I did not notice this until it was too late) may have noticed that some of the important data that you'll need is missing. For example, the city and state are missing from some of the records.

To fix this for the marketing department, you'll use some of the transforms that were discussed in the last chapter to send the good records down one path and the bad records down a different path. You will then attempt to cleanse the bad records and then send those back through the main path. There may be some records you can't cleanse (such as corporations with foreign postal codes) that you'll just have to write to an error log and deal with at a later date.

First, standardize the postal code to a five-digit format. Currently, some have five digits and some have the full 10-digit zip code with a dash (five digits, a dash, and four more digits). Some are nine-digit zip codes without the dash. To standardize the zip code, you use the Derived Column transform. Drag the transform over from the Toolbox and rename it "Standardize Zip Code."

Connect the source to the transformation and double-click on the transform to configure it. Expand the Columns tree in the upper-left corner, find [Column 8], and drag it onto the grid below. This will pre-fill some of the information for you in the derived columns grid area. You now need to create an expression that will take the various zip codes formats in the [Column 8] output column and output only the first five characters. One way of doing this is with the SUBSTRING function. If you choose to solve the business problem with that method, the code would look like this:

```
SUBSTRING([Column 8],1,5)
```

This code should be typed into the Expression column in the grid. Next, select that the derived column will replace the existing Column 8 output by selecting that option from the Derived Column drop-down box. You can see what the options should look like in Figure 5-7. Once you've completed the transformation, click OK.

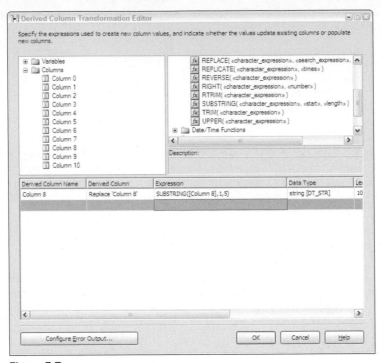

Figure 5-7

The Conditional Split Transformation

Now that you've standardized the data slightly, drag and drop the Conditional Split transformation onto the design pane and connect the green arrow from the source to the Conditional Split. Rename the transform "Find Bad Records." The Conditional Split transformation will enable you to push certain bad records into a data-cleansing process.

To cleanse the data that has no city or state, you'll write a condition that says that any row that is missing a city or state will be moved to a cleansing path in the data flow. Double-click on the Conditional Split transform after you have connected it from the Derived Column transform to edit the transformation. Create a condition called "Missing State or City" by typing its name in the Output Name column. You will now need to write an expression that looks for empty records. One method of doing this is to use the LTRIM function. The two vertical bars (|) in the following code are the same as an OR login in your code. The following code will check for a blank Column 6 or Column 7:

```
LTRIM([Column 6]) == "" || LTRIM([Column 7]) == ""
```

The last thing you'll need to do is give a name to the default output if the coded condition is not met. Call that output "Good Data," as shown in Figure 5-8. The default output is the name of the output that will contain the data that did not meet your conditions.

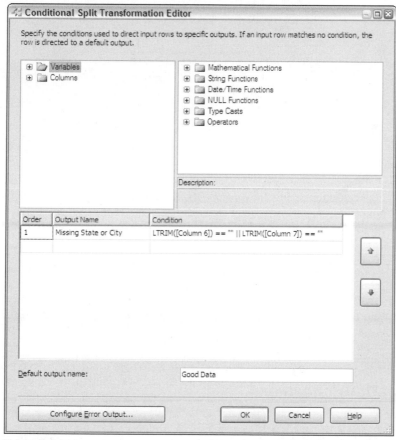

Figure 5-8

If you have multiple cases, always place conditions that you feel will capture most of the records at the top of the list.

The Lookup Transformation

Next, drag and drop the Lookup transformation onto the design pane. When you connect to it from the Conditional Split transformation, you'll see the Input Output Selection dialog box (shown in Figure 5-9). Select "Missing State or Zip" and click OK. This will send any bad records to the lookup transformation from the Conditional Split. Rename the Lookup transformation "Fix Bad Records."

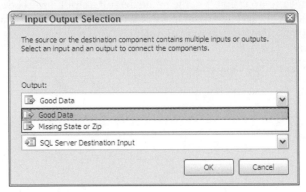

Figure 5-9

The Lookup transformation allows you to map a city and state to the rows that are missing that information by looking the record up against the ZipCode table you loaded earlier. Open up the transformation editor for the Lookup transform, and in the Reference Table page, select AdventureWorks as the Connection Manager that contains your lookup table. Select ZipCode from the Use Table or View drop-down box.

Next, go to the Columns page and drag Column 8 from the left Available Input Columns to the right ZipCode column in the Available Lookup Columns table. This will create an arrow between the two tables as shown in Figure 5-10. Then, check the State and City columns that you wish to output. This will transfer their information to the bottom grid. Select that you wish for these columns to replace the existing Column 6 and Column 7. The ZipName column will replace Column 6 and the State column will replace Column 7 as shown in the grid in Figure 5-10. Click OK to exit the transform editor. There are many more options here, but you should stick with the basics for the time being.

The Union All Transformation

Now that your dirty data is cleansed, go ahead and send the sanitized data back into the main data path by using a Union All transformation. Drag and drop the Union All transform onto the design pane and connect the "Fix Bad Records" Lookup transform and the "Find Bad Records" Conditional Split transform onto the Union All transform. There is nothing more to configure with the Union All transformation.

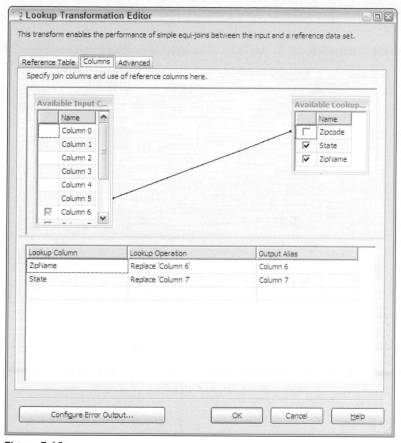

Figure 5-10

Finalizing

The last step in the data flow is to send the data to an OLE DB destination. Drag the OLE DB destination to the design pane and rename it "Mail Merge Table." Connect the Union All transform to the destination. Double-click on the destination and select AdventureWorks from the Connection Manager drop-down box. For the Use a Table or View option, select the New button next to the drop-down box. The default DDL for creating the table will use the destination's name (AdventureWorks), and the data types may not be exactly what you'd like, as shown here:

```
CREATE TABLE [Mail Merge Table] (
    [Column 0] VARCHAR(12),
    [Column 1] VARCHAR(48),
    [Column 2] VARCHAR(1),
    [Column 3] VARCHAR(4),
    [Column 4] VARCHAR(53),
    [Column 5] VARCHAR(42),
    [Column 6] VARCHAR(28),
    [Column 7] VARCHAR(2),
    [Column 8] VARCHAR(10),
    [Column 9] VARCHAR(2),
    [Column 10] VARCHAR(10)
)
```

Go ahead and change the schema to something a bit more useful. Change the table name and each column to a more logical name like this:

```
CREATE TABLE MarketingCorporation(
    CorporateNumber varchar(12),
    CorporationName varchar(48),
    FilingStatus char(1),
    FilingType char(4),
    AddressLine1 varchar(53),
    AddressLine2 varchar(42),
    City varchar(28),
    State char(2),
    ZipCode varchar(10),
    Country char(2),
    FilingDate varchar(10) NULL
)
```

You may have to map the columns this time because the column names are different. Go to the mappings page and map each column to its new name.

Handling More Bad Data

The unpolished package is essentially complete, but it has one fatal flaw that you're about to discover. Go ahead and execute the package. Depending on the year you're performing this demo, it may fail (it was written in 2005, and each year in the file is overwritten with a new year). Don't panic if your package fails. In 2005, the 010305c.dat file contained some superfluous data from individuals outside the country. You can see this by adding a grid data viewer between the "Find Bad Records" and "Fix Bad Records" transforms.

If you do this, you can see, for example, that in the 010305c.dat file, four records were sent to be cleansed by the Lookup transformation. Of those, only two had the potential to be cleansed. The other two records were for companies outside the country and could not be located in the Lookup transform that contained only Florida zip codes. You may remember that the business requirement was to only send marketing a list of domestic addresses for their mail merge product. They didn't care about the international addresses because you didn't have a business presence in those countries. The grid data viewer pointed out the problem in the last two records, though, and it looks something like Figure 5-11.

Column 6	Column 7	Column 8	Column 9
JACKSONVILLE, FLORIDA		32207	
BOYNTON BEACH		33436	US
CARACAS, 1062, VENEZUE...			
BELIZE CITY			BZ

Figure 5-11

The error you'd see in the output window when you executed the package would look something like this:

```
Error: 0xC020901E at Load Corporate Data, Fix Bad Records [87]: Row yielded no
match
during lookup.

Error: 0xC0209029 at Load Corporate Data, Fix Bad Records [87]: The "component "Fix
Bad
Records" (87)" failed because error code 0xC020901E occurred, and the error row
disposition on "output "Lookup Output" (89)" specifies failure on error. An error
occurred on the specified object of the specified component.

Error: 0xC0047022 at Load Corporate Data, DTS.Pipeline: The ProcessInput method on
component "Fix Bad Records" (87) failed with error code 0xC0209029. The identified
component returned an error from the ProcessInput method. The error is specific to
the
component, but the error is fatal and will cause the Data Flow task to stop
running.

Error: 0xC0047021 at Load Corporate Data, DTS.Pipeline: Thread "WorkThread0" has
exited
with error code 0xC0209029.

Error: 0xC0047039 at Load Corporate Data, DTS.Pipeline: Thread "WorkThread1"
received a
shutdown signal and is terminating. The user requested a shutdown, or an error in
another
thread is causing the pipeline to shutdown.

Error: 0xC0047021 at Load Corporate Data, DTS.Pipeline: Thread "WorkThread1" has
exited
with error code 0xC0047039.
```

You need to not fail the package on these types of problems, so send the bad records to an error queue that can be reviewed and cleaned out manually. To do this properly, you'll audit each record that fails and create an ErrorQueue table on the SQL Server. Drag over the Audit transformation from your Toolbox. Rename the Audit transformation "Add Auditing Info" and connect the failure path (the red arrow coming out of the "Fix Bad Records" transform after you click it) to the Audit transform.

You'll immediately see the Configure Error Output dialog box (shown in Figure 5-12). This screen allows you to tell SSIS how to react if certain errors occur in the transformation. The rows under the Truncation column distinguish what would happen if a row is too large to be added to the transform. The Error column tells SSIS how to react in the event of a transformation error. You can see to the right in the Description column what type of error it's expecting to handle for that particular transformation. For example, for the Lookup transformation the expected error this will trap is a lookup failure, meaning the

Lookup transformation was unable to find a match for the inputted record. For this example, select each of the error types to redirect the row as shown in Figure 5-10. The default is to fail the component, which would fail the entire package, or you can choose to just ignore the error completely by selecting Ignore from the same drop-down box.

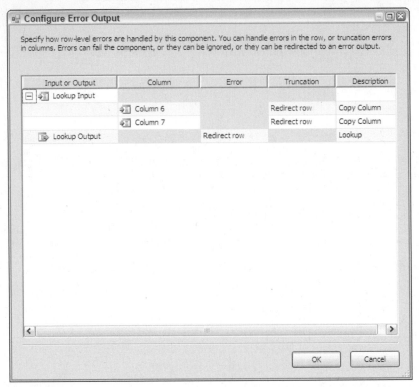

Figure 5-12

Once you've configured the Error Output handling as shown in Figure 5-12, click OK.

When you redirect bad rows, as you did here, two additional columns are added to the data flow: the Error Code and Error Description columns. This can tell someone who's expected to clean the queue what column caused the problem and the description of the error.

With the errors now being handled, double-click the Audit transform to configure that transformation. Go ahead and add two additional columns to the output. Select Task Name and Package Name from the drop-down boxes in the Audit Type column. This will transpose a default Output Column Name. Take out the spaces in each output column name, as shown in Figure 5-13, to make it easier to query later. You'll want to output this auditing information because you may have multiple packages and tasks loading data into the corporation table, and you'll want to track which package actually originated the error.

Figure 5-13

The last thing you need to do to polish up the package is to send the bad rows to the SQL Server ErrorQueue table. Drag another OLE DB destination over to the design pane and connect the Audit transformation to it. Rename the destination "Error Queue." Double-click on the destination and select AdventureWorks as the Connection Manager, and click New to add the ErrorQueue table. Name the table "ErrorQueue" and follow a similar schema to the one below:

```
CREATE TABLE ErrorQueue(
    CorporateNumber varchar(12),
    CorporationName varchar(48),
    FilingStatus char(1),
    FilingType char(4),
    AddressLine1 varchar(53),
    AddressLine2 varchar(42),
    City varchar(28),
    State char(2),
    ZipCode varchar(10),
    Country char(2),
    FilingDate varchar(10) NULL,
    ErrorCode INT,
    ErrorColumn INT,
    TaskName NVARCHAR(19),
    PackageName NVARCHAR(30)
)
```

In error queue tables like the one just illustrated, be very generous when defining the schema. In other words, you don't want to create another transformation error trying to write into the error queue table. Instead, you may want to define everything as a varchar column and give more space than is actually needed.

You may have to map the columns this time due to the column names being different. Go to the mappings page and map each column to its new name.

You are now ready to re-execute the package. This time, in my data file, four records needed to be fixed, and two of those were sent to the error queue. The final package would look something like the one shown in Figure 5-14 when executed. Again, your data may vary widely based on what corporation file you downloaded from the Department of State.

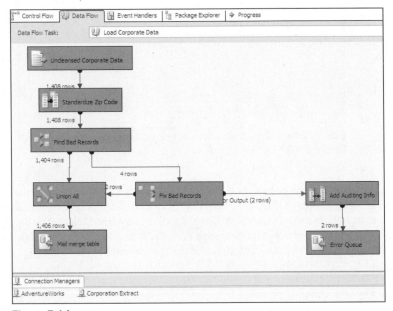

Figure 5-14

Looping and the Dynamic Task

You've come a long way in this chapter to creating a self-healing package, but it's not terribly reusable yet. Your next task in the business requirements is to configure the package so that it reads a directory for any .DAT file and performs the previous tasks to that collection of files. To simulate this example, go ahead and download a few files again from ftp://dossftp.dos.state.fl.us/public/doc/cor/. They can be whatever .DAT file you'd like, but make sure you download at least two more.

Looping

Your first task is to loop through any set of .DAT files in the C:\SSISDemos directory and load them into your database. To meet this business requirement, you'll need to use the Foreach Loop container. Go to the Control Flow tab in the same package that you've been working in, and drag the container onto the design pane. Then, drag the "Load Corporate Data" Data Flow task onto the container. Rename the container "Loop Through Files."

Double-click on the container to configure it. Go to the Collection page and select Foreach File Enumerator from the Enumerator drop-down box. Next, specify that the folder will be C:\SSISDemos and that the files will have the *.DAT extension, as shown in Figure 5-15.

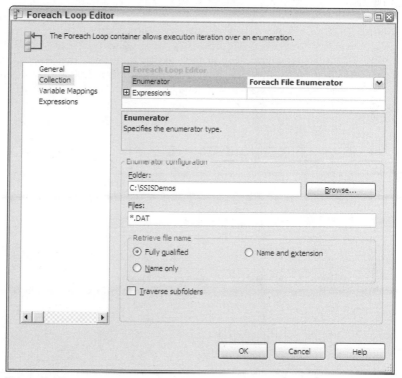

Figure 5-15

You need to now map the variables to the results of the Foreach File Enumeration. Go to the Variable Mappings page inside the Foreach Loop Editor and select <New Variable...> from the Variable column drop-down box. This will open the Add Variable dialog box. For the container, you'll remain at the package level. You could assign the scope of the variable to the container, but you should keep things simple for this example. Name the variable "ExtractFileName" in the Name option and click OK, leaving the rest of the options at their default settings.

You will then see the User::ExtractFileName variable in the Variable column and the number 0 in the Index option. Since the Foreach File Enumerator option has only one column, you'll only see an index of 0 for this column. If you used a different enumerator option, you would have the ability to enter a number for each column that was returned from the enumerator. Click OK to leave the Foreach Loop editor.

Making the Package Dynamic

Now with the loop created, you need to set the file name in the Corporation Extract Connection Manager to be equal to the file name that the enumerator retrieves dynamically. To meet this business requirement, right-click on the Corporation Extract Connection Manager and select Properties (note that you're clicking on Properties, not on Edit as you've done in the past). In the Properties pane for this Connection Manager, click the ellipsis button next to the Expressions option.

By clicking the ellipsis button, you open the Property Expressions Editor. Select ConnectionString from the Property drop-down box, as shown in Figure 5-16. You can either type in **@[User::ExtractFileName]** in the Expression column or click the ellipsis button and then drag and drop the variable into the expression window. By typing **@[User::ExtractFileName]**, you are setting the file name in the Connection Manager to be equal to the ExtractFileName variable that you set in the Foreach Loop earlier. Click OK to exit the Property Expression Editor. You'll now see in the Property window that there is a single expression by clicking the plus sign.

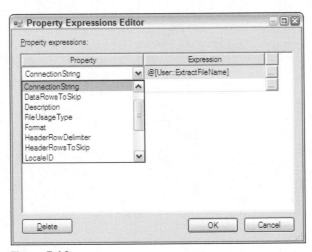

Figure 5-16

As it stands right now, each time the loop finds a .DAT file in the C:\SSISDemos directory, it will set the ExtractFileName variable to that path and file name. Then, the Connection Manager will use that variable as its file name and run the Data Flow task one time for each file it finds. You now have a reusable package that can be run against any file in the format you designated earlier.

The only missing technical solution to complete is the archiving of the files after you load them. Before you begin solving that problem, manually create an archive directory under C:\SSISDemos called C:\SSISDemos\Archive. Right-click in the Connection Manager window and select Create New File Connection. Select Existing Folder for the Usage Type, and point the file to the C:\SSISDemos\Archive directory. Click OK and rename the newly created Connection Manager "Archive File."

Next, drag a File System task into the "Loop Through Files" container and connect it to the "Load Corporate Data" Data Flow task with an On Success constraint (the green arrow should be attached to the File System task). Rename that task "Archive File."

Double-click on the "Archive File" File System task to open the editor (shown in Figure 5-17). Set the Operation drop-down box to Move File. Next, specify that the Destination Connection not be a variable and that it be set to the Archive File Connection Manager that you just created. The SourceConnection drop-down box should be set to the "Corporation Extract" Connection Manager that you created a long time ago. Essentially, what you're configuring is that the file that was pulled earlier from the loop will be moved to whatever directory and file name is in the Archive File Connection Manager.

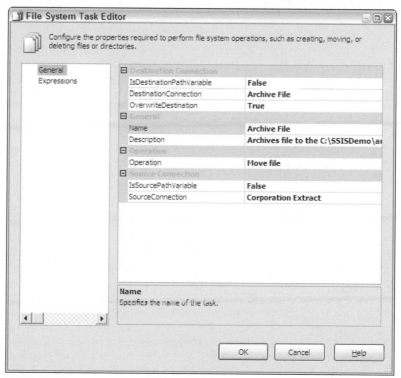

Figure 5-17

Your complete package should now be ready to execute. Go ahead and save the package first before you execute it. If you successfully implemented the solution, your control flow should look something like Figure 5-18 when executed. When you execute the package, you'll see the control flow items flash green once for each .DAT file in the directory.

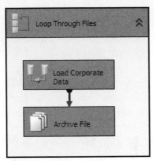

Figure 5-18

Summary

This chapter focused on driving home the basic SSIS transforms, tasks, and containers. You performed a basic ETL procedure and then expanded the ETL to self-heal when bad data arrived from your data supplier. You then set the package to loop through a directory, find each .DAT file, and load it into the database. The finale was archiving the file automatically after it was loaded. With this type of package now complete, you could throw any .DAT file that matched the format you configured and it will load with reasonable certainty. In the upcoming chapter, you'll dive into some more advanced tasks and transforms that use the Advanced Editor.

6

Advanced Tasks and Transforms

In Chapter 4 you learned about a few tasks and briefly looked over some of the common transformations that you will need in your everyday package development toolkit. If you have some experience with the old SQL Server 2000 DTS, you should be getting a little more comfortable now with the idea that the old dark-arrow data-pump task is gone. The paradigm of hiding transformation-level ActiveX script and embedding connectivity in the transformation task is no more. No longer will you be likely to forget to change the transformation destination when you point packages to other databases on the same server — even though you changed the destination connection. Connections are now created and stored globally. Transformation activity, now managed more easily, has exploded with options that can be viewed in their own design surface in the Data Flow tab.

In a lot of ways you are going to have to restrain yourself in your approach to SSIS package development. It is not necessary to start every new package by opening up an ActiveX script task and using brute force to get things done. In fact, if at first you find yourself in the guts of a script task, just stop. There are so many new tasks and transforms that handle things like removing ragged edges from flat files, splitting incoming content, and looping through tasks in a package that chances are you'll most likely find something that can get the job done. You may still run into things that push past the limit of canned SSIS capabilities. If this happens, open up a .NET script task and access the full power of the .NET framework.

This chapter is about the nuts and bolts of getting thing done. You are going to put these new tools to work on some real-world problems. Do you need to retrieve settings from stored procedure output parameters? Conditionally branch into logic based on a row count? Generate some meaningful statistics from free-form text data? How about using fuzzy logic to standardize data for lookup tables while you load it? You'll look at these and other advanced implementations of some of the tasks, and then later you'll explore some of the more complex transformations. It is assumed that you are familiar enough with the BIDS environment to build packages, so this chapter will not explain how to do this in detail.

Execute SQL Task

The Execute SQL task is probably not one of the more advanced SSIS tasks, but it is one of the most used task in SQL Server 2000 DTS. You'll use it as a jumping-off point to cover variables, expressions, and some advanced techniques of runtime property management.

The Execute SQL task is a task often used to truncate staging data table prior to import. Another common use is to call stored procedures to take on the task of performing complicated business logic that couldn't be modeled in the DTS package environment. The SSIS version can provide these same services, but now with a better configuration editor and methods to map stored procedure parameters and to read back result and output values.

Create an SSIS package and drag an Execute SQL task on the Control Flow design surface. The control will show a red icon on the task, and an error message appears in the error list to inform you that there is no connection associated with this task. You'll have to open up the Execute SQL task editor and set that up to satisfy that error condition. Double-click the task, and your editor should look similar to Figure 6-1.

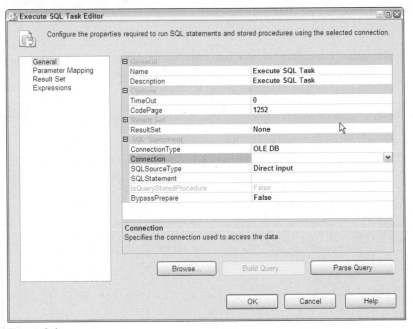

Figure 6-1

The task has four sections in the Execute SQL task editor:

❑ **General:** Contains the properties to allow the setting of the task name, description, connection-related settings, setting to indicate how to execute the SQL statement, and the SQL statement to execute.

❑ **Parameter Mapping:** Contains a collection of parameters that can be matched to package- or container-level variables. Parameters allow the ability to provide variable input to a stored procedure or a prepared SQL statement at runtime.

- ❑ **Result Set:** Contains the collection of mapped variables to values returned in the row set formed as a result of executing the SQL statement in the SQLSourceProperty.

- ❑ **Expressions:** Contains the collection of expressions that can be used to configure properties of this task.

The General tab contains the core properties of the task. They include the following:

- ❑ **ConnectionType and Connection:** These properties are connection-related settings such as the type and name of the connection. (Providing the type of connection allows the component to validate the type of connection against the selected connection.)

- ❑ **SQLStatement:** This property holds the SQL statement for the task to execute. This statement can be a simple SELECT statement, the content of a large SQL script separated with GO statements, or a call to a stored procedure.

- ❑ **SQLSourceType:** This property is a new addition from the old DTS SQL task. It provides the option of populating the SQLStatement property at development or loading at runtime using either a variable or a file that contains a SQL script.

- ❑ **ResultSet property:** This property can be set to expect as a result of executing the SQL statement either no result set, a singleton result set, a full result set (multiple rows), or an XML string. Setting the property to NONE will deactivate the Result Set tab from accepting result set mappings.

There are plenty of examples in Books Online and elsewhere about setting up and configuring input parameters with in-line SQL and stored procedures as well as demonstrations using the task to load and execute SQL scripts using the File Connection property SQLSourceType. The example will demonstrate how to configure this task to retrieve Output parameters from stored procedures.

However, before you jump right into the example, you need to understand how SSIS design-time engines deal with variables, and you need to understand the power of something new to DTS: expressions.

Variables

In DTS 2000, all variables were basically global. In SSIS, variables have scope, starting with package scope (that works almost like a global) and ending with scope at a task or transformation task level. Variables can be created with separate namespaces (not shown in Figure 6-2). The default namespace is User. Variables are also case-sensitive. Why does all this matter? Because you can create some logic bugs if you aren't paying attention. Figure 6-2 shows an example of two variables named sSQL coexisting in a package.

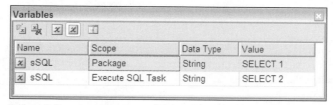

Name	Scope	Data Type	Value
sSQL	Package	String	SELECT 1
sSQL	Execute SQL Task	String	SELECT 2

Figure 6-2

The variable in the Execute SQL task will override the package-level variable, and the package-level variable value will take over after the task completes. It seems like common sense when you think about it, but even then it is easy to create scoped variables accidentally. You'll need to pay careful attention to the scope column when you create a variable. The scope is automatically provided based on the object you currently have selected in BIDS when you create the variable. Adding a variable while in a container, on a task, on a transform, or even in the Data Flow design surface creates local object-level scope variables. If you are on the package design surface, then a variable is created by default at the scope level of the package.

Why talk about variable scope in a chapter on advanced task and transformations? Because the old method of using the ActiveX task to set connection or other package properties is really not necessary anymore. Even though this method provided a great way to change properties at runtime, the whole way of doing things in SSIS has changed. First, there is a whole set of configuration tools that allow packages to be configured using XML files, environmental variables, and even registry settings. These techniques are much more manageable for multiple-environment deployments when the package settings are static and are known prior to runtime. However, if you retrieve settings from your input streams or need to alter a property using information provided during runtime, configurations are not going to help you. Three examples of using nonstatic configurations are calling packages with parameters, changing an output file name to a sequential naming scheme, or setting a connection property during execution. To do any of these three, you'll have to use a technique that is going to involve variables.

Variables can store values retrieved in one task and then can be passed to other tasks. Variables can be used to set properties of most Integrated Service (IS) components by using a new idea to SSIS called Property Expressions. Variables allow the setting and configuration of component tasks that use these values to exchange bits of information: flags, counts, or strings settings that control settings of the package itself. With this level of flexibility, you are going to be using a lot more variables than ever before.

Expressions

Most IS tasks, transforms, and containers have a collection of potential property expressions — this even includes the package itself. The expressions collection is designed to expose container properties to be set by a logical expression. An Execute SQL Task property that is exposed by an expression is the SQLStatementSource property, which is the SQL statement to be executed. Another property, ConnectionString, exposes the OLE DB connection string for an OLE DB connection object. To review the available properties exposed for any container, click on the container and view the property named "expressions" in the property window. A click on the ellipsis will bring up the property expressions editor. (Make sure the property window has refreshed and your intended container is displayed in the window.)

Figure 6-3 shows the property expressions editor for an Execute SQL Task property with a partial set of properties exposed in the drop-down view.

There are two columns in the property expressions editor: one for selecting the property and another for defining an expression that can be evaluated. The result of the evaluated expression will be substituted into the value of the property at runtime.

Creating an expression starts with clicking on the ellipsis in the expression column. Figure 6-4 is an example of the Expression Builder. This tool guides you through building a logic statement using items such as literals, system and user variables, columns, operators, and built-in functions. The operators and functions in the expression language will be familiar to C#, C, and TSQL programmers, as they are similar to all three — but not exactly. Visual Basic brothers and sisters will need to remember things like ==

mean "equals" and && means "AND." TSQL brothers and sisters will need to wrap literals in double quotes instead of single. The expression language is not case-sensitive, so the C# and C programmers can do a little extra work keeping track of uppercase and lowercase variables that won't matter. Spend a little time with the expression builder and you'll quickly work out the differences as compared to your preferred languages.

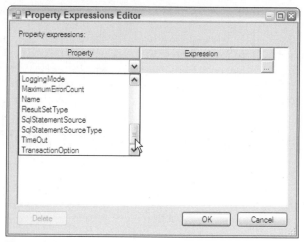

Figure 6-3

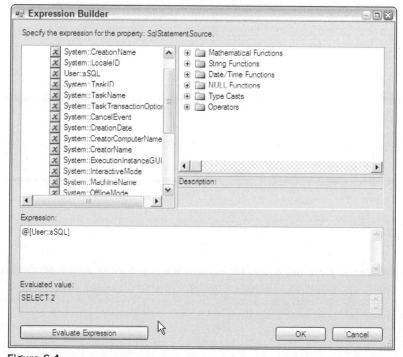

Figure 6-4

Now continue with an Execute SQL task using the two differently scoped variables discussed in the section on variables. Figure 6-4 shows the Expression Builder opened up for the SQLStatementSource property, and the variables node has been expanded to show all the available variables for this current expression.

You must click on the variable User::sSQL and drag it onto the expression window to create the expression. The value of that expression will be substituted into the property SQLStatementSource at runtime and will become the statement that is executed in the task. To find out the evaluated result of this variable, click the Evaluate Expression button on the lower left. Notice that the evaluated value displayed is "SELECT 2." In the variables section of this chapter, you looked at two variables with the same name "sSQL" but with different scope. The variable scoped to the Execute SQL task with the value of "SELECT 2" takes precedence inside this task. Although this was a quick introduction to variables and expressions, you will be using them heavily during this chapter and in more advanced ways. See Chapter 7 for more information and detail on using expressions.

Using SQL Output Parameters to Change Runtime Settings

Now you will return to the stored procedure output parameter example. In this example, you will set up a simple export of the [HumanResources].[Shift] table from the AdventureWorks database but change the destination file at runtime. You will use the Execute SQL task to retrieve the new export location from an output parameter.

Your client requires you to integrate SSIS packages with a proprietary database that contains all package and software settings. This database sits on each environment: development, quality control, and production. Settings are moved into the different environments during turnover with your packages. When the package loads, all settings should be pulled from the database at runtime using a set of standardized stored procedures.

Since you have to retrieve your settings at runtime and you have to interact with a set of stored procedures to retrieve the settings, the configuration options in SSIS are not available. (Remember, these options can only set up the package before the package is processed in runtime.) You do have expressions that can help you out, so see if you can come up with a solution.

1. If you don't have an SSIS package open with an Execute SQL task, set up one now.

2. Add a package-level variable by right-clicking on the Control Flow design surface and selecting Variables. Name the variable "MyFile." Set the data type to string and set the value to
    `c:\Execute SQL Sample.txt`.

    Don't put quotation marks around the contents of string variable values. Think of the value in the variables collection as being the result of the variable assignment.

3. To simulate the proprietary stored procedure that you are required to use, you need to create it. For simplicity, you'll put your sample retrieval proc in the same database. Run the following script in the AdventureWorks database on the server. This script will create the procedure that will allow you to retrieve your connection.

```
USE adventureworks
go
CREATE PROC dbo.usp_GetConfigParamValue (
        @ApplicationName   Varchar(30),          -- the name of the application.
```

```
@ParameterName      Varchar(50),        -- the name of the parameter
@ParameterTypeName Varchar(30),         -- the name of the parameter type
@ParameterValueVar Varchar(255) OUTPUT -- output buffer for value
)

AS

      Set NOCOUNT ON

      --Dummy proc to simulate the real usp_GetConfigParamValue
      --Always outputs 'c:\ Execute SQL Sample Changed.txt'
      SET @PARAMETERVALUEVAR='c:\Execute SQL Sample Changed.txt'

      Set NOCOUNT OFF
```

4. Set the ConnectionType property of the Execute SQL Task to ADO.NET using the .NET SQL Client provider. Then select <New Connection> from the Connection property. Create an ADO.NET connection object using the server name "." for the local machine. Use the drop-down to select your SQL Server instance and leave the default as NT Authentication. Select the database "AdventureWorks." Save this connection.

An OLE DB connection for this example will not work properly. Each provider will handle stored procedure parameters differently.

5. Set the Execute SQL SQLStatement property to the following:

```
EXEC usp_GetConfigParamValue 'MYAPP', 'MYPARM', 'STRING', @MYVALUE OUTPUT
```

6. In the Parameter Mapping tab, add a mapping to the variable named MyFile to the parameter in the SQLStatement @MyValue by setting the variable name to User::MyFile, the direction to Output, the data type to String, and the parameter to MyValue. Click OK to save settings.

7. To finish out the package, drop a Data Flow task onto the Control Flow surface. Connect the output of the Execute SQL task to the Data Flow task.

8. In the Data Flow design surface, add a DataReader Source and a Flat File Destination.

Make sure you don't add a Flat File Source. The source and destination transforms are at first easy to get confused.

9. Configure the DataReader Source to use the AdventureWorks connection and set SQLCommand property to the following:

```
Select * from [HumanResources].[Shift]
```

10. Connect the DataReader transformation to the Flat File Destination.

11. Configure the Flat File Destination by creating a new connection to a delimited file in the Destination File editor. Set the file name to "c:\myfile.txt." Click the Mappings tab to populate the default mapping and accept the rest of the defaults.

12. What you want to do is show that you can change the Flat File Destination at runtime. Right now this package is set up to pull all records from the [HumanResources].[Shift] table and dump to C:\Execute SQL Sample.txt in a delimited format. The Execute SQL task retrieves a string "C:\Execute SQL Sample Changed.txt" from the stored procedure. You want this file name to change at runtime. To do this, you're going to need an expression that changes the ConnectionString property on the Flat File Connection.

13. Locate and click on the Flat File Connection Manager—not the Flat File Destination. In the property window, locate the Expressions property and click the ellipsis to add an expression to a property. The property you want evaluated at runtime is ConnectionString. Use the Expression Builder to select the variable @[User::MyFile] or type this in. This expression will be evaluated at runtime and will change the ConnectionString property to the value stored in the variable MyFile.

Run the package and check your local drive. You should see the file "Execute SQL Sample Changed.txt" in the root of the c:\ drive. A quick look at the package execution steps shows that the output is changed and directed to the new location. Remember, you originally set the file to "Execute SQL Sample.txt."

This technique is used to output a flat file to one location in the development environment and then to another location in the production environment using a proprietary set of database utilities that store and retrieve application settings. An advantage to this method is that once the settings have been moved into the different environments, packages can be altered while testing and moved into production without having to keep track of all the embedded settings. More importantly, the example highlights the power of SSIS expressions and variables and demonstrates the use of output parameters using the ADO.NET provider. There are several things to notice that you may have passed over quickly:

❑ If your data provider doesn't recognize OUTPUT parameter by name or position, a work-around is to have the stored procedure return a result set and map the results to variables. If you can't modify the stored procedure, you can use the old-school method of executing and retrieving the value of the output variable in the SQLStatement and mapping the variables. The following would be the SQLStatement property setting for the preceding example:

```
DECLARE @MYVALUE AS VARCHAR(255)
EXEC usp_GetConfigParamValue 'MYAPP', 'MYPARM', 'STRING', @MYVALUE OUTPUT
SELECT @MYVALUE AS MyValue
```

❑ The IsQueryStoredProcedure property was left FALSE. It seems as though this should be true since you are using a stored procedure. But setting this property to true will create an error message that the stored procedure could not be found. This occurs with or without the addition of the EXEC statement.

Import Column

The Import Column transform was named the File Inserter transform in the beta releases of SQL Server 2005, and it is a partner to the Export Column transform, which was renamed from File Extractor. After discovering what they do, you may find that the former names are more intuitive. These transforms do the work of translating physical files from system file storage paths into database blob-type fields and vice versa. The trick to understanding the Import Column transform is that its input source requires at least one column that is the fully qualified path to the file you are going to store in the database, and you need a destination column name for the output of the resulting blob and file path string. This transform also has to be configured using the Advanced Editor—something you've only briefly looked at in earlier chapters.

The Advanced Editor is not intuitive, nor wizard-like in appearance, hence the name "Advanced," which you will incidentally be once you figure it out. In the editor, you won't have the ability to merge two incoming column sources into the full file path, so if your source data for the file paths have the file name separate from the file path, you should use the Merge transforms to concatenate the columns before connecting that stream to the Import Column transform.

Import Column Example

Now you'll do an example where you'll import some images into your AdventureWorks database. Create a new SSIS project named "Import Column Example." Transforms live in the Data Flow tab, so add a Data Flow task to the Control Flow, and then add an Import Column transform to the Data Flow surface. To make this easy, you're going to need to complete the following short tasks:

1. Create a directory called c:\import\images\.

2. Find a small JPEG file and copy it three times into c:\import\images. Change the file names to 1.jpg, 2.jpg, and 3.jpg.

3. Create a text file with the following content and save in c:\import\images\ as filelist.txt.

```
C:\import\images\1.JPG
C:\import\images\2.JPG
C:\import\images\3.JPG
```

4. Run the following SQL script in AdventureWorks to create a storage location for the image files.

```
use AdventureWorks
Go
CREATE TABLE dbo.tblmyImages
(
    [StoredFilePath] [varchar](50) NOT NULL,
    [Document] image
)
```

5. You are going to use the filelist.txt file as your input stream for the files that you need to load into your database, so add a Flat File Source to your Data Flow surface and configure it to read one column from your filelist.txt flat file. Name the column "ImageFilePath."

Take advantage of the opportunity to open up the Advanced Editor on the Flat File transform by clicking on the Show Advanced Editor link in the property window or by right-clicking on the transform and selecting Advanced Editor. Look at the difference between this editor and the normal Flat File Editor. The Advanced Editor is stripped down to the core of the transform object—no custom wizards, just an interface sitting directly over the object properties themselves. It is possible to mess these properties up beyond recognition, but even in the worst case you can just drop and re-create the transform task. Look particularly at the Input and Output Properties of the Advanced Editor. Expand the nodes out until the editor looks like Figure 6-5.

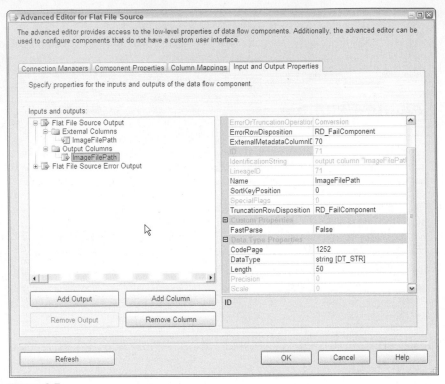

Figure 6-5

You didn't have to use the Advanced Editor to set up the import of the filelist.txt file. However, looking at the way the Advanced Editor displays the information will be really helpful when you configure the Import Column transform. Notice that you have an External Columns (Input) and Output Columns collection with one node in each collection named "ImageFilePath." This reflects that your connection describes a field called "ImageFilePath" and that this transform will simply output data with the same field name. The Column Mappings tab shows a visual representation of this mapping. If you changed the Name property value to myImageFilePath, you'll see the column mappings morph to reflect the new name. Notice also that the ID property for the one output column is 71 and its ExternalMetaDataColumnID is set to 70. Clicking on the one External Column reveals that its ID property is 70. From this, you can determine that if you had to create this transform using the Advanced Editor, you would have had to add both columns and link the external source (input) to the output source. Secondly you'd notice that you can add or remove outputs, but you are limited in this editor by the transformation as to what you can do to the output. You can't, for example, apply an expression against the output to transform the data as it flows through this transform. That makes sense because this transform has a specific task. It moves data from a flat file into a stream.

Connect the Flat File Source to the Import Column transform task. Open the Advanced Editor for the Import Column transform and click on the Input Columns tab. The input stream for this task is the output stream for the Flat File. Select the one available column, move to the Input and Output Properties tab, and expand these nodes. This time you don't have much help. An example of this editor can be seen in Figure 6-6. The input columns collection has a column named ImageFilePath, but there are no output columns. On the Flat File task, you could ignore some of the inputs. In the Import Column transform, all inputs have to be re-output. In fact, if you don't map an output, you'll get the following error:

```
Validation error. Data Flow Task: Import Column [1]: The "input column
"ImageFilePath" (164)" references output column ID 0, and that column is not found
on the output.
```

Add an output column by clicking on the output columns folder icon and click on the Add Column button. Name the column "myImage." Notice that the DataType property is [DT_IMAGE] by default. That is because producing image outputs is what this transform does. You can also pass DT_TEXT, DT_NTEXT, or DT_IMAGE types as outputs from this task. Your last task is to connect the input to the output. Take note of the output column property ID for myImage. This ID will need to be updated in the FileDataColumnID property of the input column ImageFilePath. If you fail to link the output column, you'll get this error:

```
Validation error. Data Flow Task: Import Column [1]: The "output column "myImage"
(207)" is not referenced by any input column. Each output column must be referenced
by exactly one input column.
```

The Advanced Editor for each of the different transforms follows a similar layout but may have other properties available. Another property of interest in this task is Expect BOM, which you would set to True if you expect a byte-order mark at the beginning of the file path. A completed editor would resemble Figure 6-6.

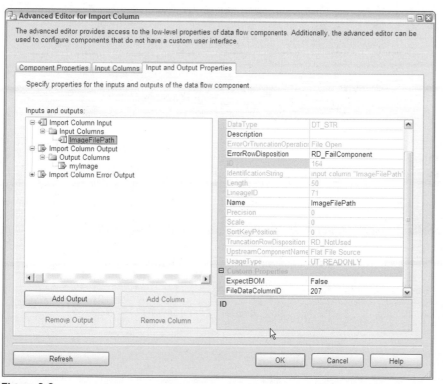

Figure 6-6

Complete this example by adding an OLE Destination to the Data Flow design surface. Connect the data from the Import Column to the OLE Destination. Configure the OLE destination to the AdventureWorks database and to the tblmyImages structure that was created for database storage. Click on the Mappings setting. Notice that you have two available input columns from the Import Column task. One is the full path and the other will be the file as DT_IMAGE type. Connect the input and destination columns to complete the transform. Your final Data Flow design surface should look like Figure 6-7. Go ahead and run it.

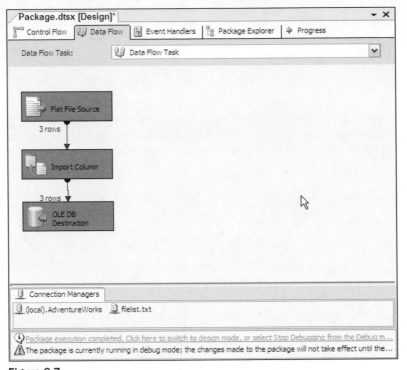

Figure 6-7

Take a look at the destination table to see the results:

```
FullFileName              Document
---------------------     -----------------------------------
C:\import\images\1.JPG    0xFFD8FFE120EE45786966000049492A00...
C:\import\images\2.JPG    0xFFD8FFE125FE45786966000049492A00...
C:\import\images\3.JPG    0xFFD8FFE1269B45786966000049492A00...
(3 row(s) affected)
```

Import Column Example Using File Iteration

In the real world, you'd never get a list of image files to import in a nice, neat text file for your input stream. What you are going to get is a file path where someone has FTP'd, copied, or dumped files into a folder that need to be loaded into a database. You're going to have to generate your own stream. You can use a Foreach task that can iterate and build a list of files. The problem is finding a stream that you can fill with this list of files. To start, take a look at the sources that you can use. There is a neat connection that can handle multiple files, but that doesn't convert into a transformation source. You could jump into a script and generate your nice, neat text file, but there's a better way. Use your earlier Input Column example and your database server and create a file list that will replace the flat file source. Your strategy will be to read the files that are in the c:\import\images\ directory and save each file into a temporary staged table on the server. Then you'll use an OLE DB Source to query these results and stream them into the ImportColumn task, which will store your file contents.

1. Using the previous Import Column example, first create a temporary table by running the following SQL code in the Adventure Works database.

```
USE AdventureWorks
GO
CREATE TABLE stgfilelist
(
    [FullFileName] [varchar](50) NOT NULL,
)
```

2. Add a Foreach container to the Control Flow surface. Set the Foreach container enumerator to Foreach File Enumerator, the Folder property to "c:\import\images\," the Files property to "*.jpg," and the Retrieve File Name setting to Fully qualified.

3. Click on Variable Mappings in the Foreach Loop editor. Create a string variable at the package scope level named myFilePath. Leave the value blank. Save the variable by closing the variable editor. Set the Variable Index in the task to 0. This will allow the Foreach Loop to save the value of each file name it finds in the directory into the variable myFilePath. Save the Foreach Loop.

4. Now add an Execute SQL task to the Control Flow surface inside the Foreach container. Configure the Connection in the SQLtask to the Adventure Works database.

5. Click on the Expressions option in the Execute SQL task editor. Find the property SQLStatementSource. Set up an expression that will build an INSERT statement to store the name of the current file path retrieved by the Foreach loop that will be stored in the variable myFilePath. The expression should look like this, including quotes:

```
"INSERT INTO stgFileList SELECT '" +  @[User::myFilePath] + "'"
```

6. Click on the Foreach Loop container and connect to the Data Flow task using the green successful-completion arrow. The Data Flow so far should look like Figure 6-8.

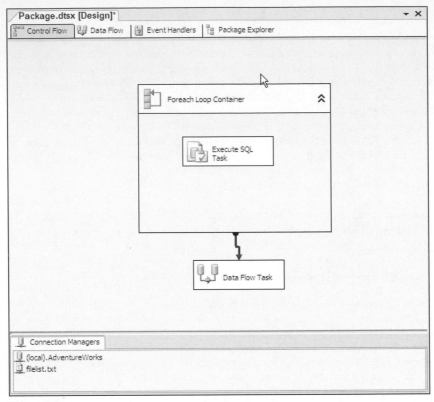

Figure 6-8

7. In the Data Flow surface, remove the Flat File Source. Add a new OLE DB Source. Set its connection to Adventure Works. Set the data access mode to Table or View. Select stgFileList as the table or view. Click on columns to refresh the transform mappings and save.

8. You'll notice that the Import Column task now has an issue with the fact that you've changed around the import source for the task. Either hold the mouse over the transform or look in the error output window. You'll see an error similar to the following:

```
Validation error. Data Flow Task: DTS.Pipeline: input column "FullFileName" (336)
has lineage ID 319 that was not previously used in the Data Flow task
```

9. Reconfigure the import source of the Import Column task by attempting to reopen the Advanced Editor. You'll see the Restore Invalid References Editor instead. See Figure 6-9 for an example of this editor. In the list, you'll see any invalid references with a drop-down to allow you to remap the reference if you'd like. You can also select any invalid mappings, or select all mappings if that is more efficient, and delete them, attempt to remap by column name, or simply ignore them and continue. In this example, you replaced the source column FullFileName from a flat file to a column FullFileName from an OLE DB Source. SSIS recognizes each of these as separate columns since each has its own ID column. Since the column names are similar, the default in the available columns drop-down is set to your new column. Leave the defaults, select Apply, and close the editor.

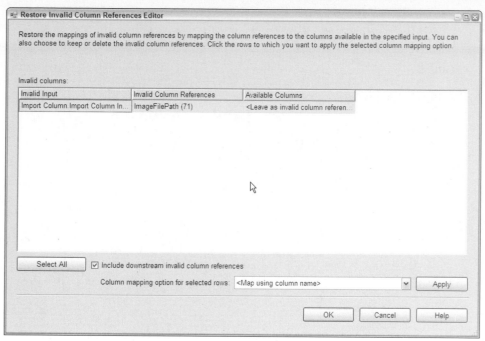

Figure 6-9

Finally, open the OLE DB destination and ensure that the mappings for the destination still exist. Map the resulting FullFileName column from the Import Column transform task to the OLE same column name. Execute the package and you'll see that the files are enumerated into your temporary storage location and that they have been turned into a stream of fully qualified file paths as input into an Import Columns task; the result is that you store both the path and the digitized document into the database in a data field.

Using Temp Tables in SSIS Package Development

In the Import Column example, you created a physical table in your production database to stage a list of files. In a production environment, you may not want to create and destroy objects in the production database and might prefer to use temp tables instead. Seems easy, right? It is, but there is a trick and a little surprise in the default behavior of one of the components. Figure 6-10 shows a quick example of a package with two Execute SQL tasks. The Create Temp Table task executes a SQL command to create a temporary table named #tmpMyData. The Drop Temp Table task executes a SQL command to drop table #tmpMyData.

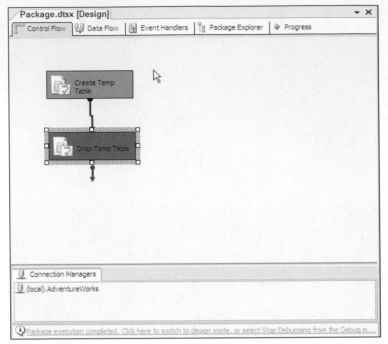

Figure 6-10

Notice that the drop portion of the package failed. If you review the package progress tab, the error message reports that the table doesn't exist. Obviously both of these Execute SQL tasks do not share the same connection—even though they share the same graphical connection. You'll notice in the regular property window of the OLE DB connection (as shown in Figure 6-11) that there is a property RetainSameConnection that is set to "FALSE" as a default.

Figure 6-11

Each task using a connection will build its own connection using the properties provided by the Connection Manager for that property. A temp table can only live in one connection and it is automatically destroyed when that connection is closed. However, if you change this property to "TRUE," both Execute SQL tasks will share the same connection and both will be able to use the temp table. This trick can also be useful if you are going to be performing a task requiring a connection within a loop. Otherwise, imagine how many openings and closings are going to occur during that loop.

Export Column

The Export Column transformation task is used to extract blob-type data from fields in a database and create files in their original formats to be stored in a file system or viewed by a format viewer, such as Microsoft Word or Microsoft Paint. The trick to understanding the Export Column transformation is that it requires an input stream field that contains digitized document data and another field that can be used for a fully qualified path. The Export Column transformation will convert the digitized data into a physical file on the file system for each row in the input stream using the fully qualified path. In Chapter 4 you studied this transformation in detail, so in this chapter you'll just look at a quick example.

In this example, you'll use existing data in the AdventureWorks database to output some stored documents from the database back to file storage. The AdventureWorks database has a table named [production] .[document] that contains a file path and a field containing an embedded Microsoft Word document. Pull these documents out of the database and save them into a directory on the file system.

1. Create a directory with an easy name like "c:\exports\" that you can use when exporting these documents.

2. Create a new SSIS package named Export Column Example. Add a Data Flow task to the Control Flow design surface.

3. On the Data Flow design surface, add an OLE DB Data Source configured to the AdventureWorks database table [production].[document].

4. If you preview the data in this table, you'll notice that the FileName field in the table is a super-long file path. Modify that path so that it points to your directory "c:\exports\."

5. Add a Derived Column transformation task to the Data Flow design surface. Connect the output of the OLE DB Data to the task.

6. Create a Derived Column Name named "NewFilePath." Use the Derived Column setting of <add as new column>. To derive a new file name, just use the primary key for the file name and add your path to it. To do this, set the expression to the following:

```
"c:\\exports\\" + (DT_WSTR,50)DocumentID + ".doc"
```

The "\\" is required in the expressions editor instead of "\" because of its use as an escape sequence.

7. Add an Export Column transformation task to the Data Flow design surface. Connect the output of the Derived Column task to the Export Column task. The Export Columns task will consume the input stream and separate all the fields into two usable categories: fields that can possibly be in digitized data formats, and fields that can possibly be used as file names. Figure 6-12 is a graphic that has been created to show the contents of both categories for this example.

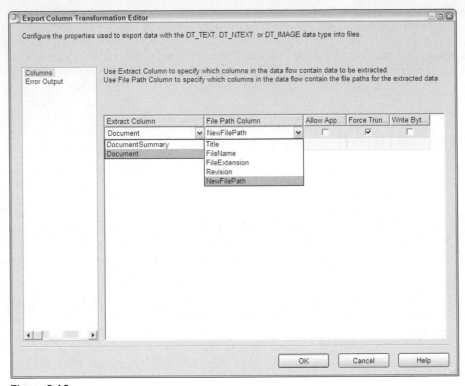

Figure 6-12

Notice that fields like the primary key [DocumentID] do not appear in either collection. This field doesn't contain embedded data, and it cannot be resolved to a file name.

8. Set the Extract Column equal to the [Document] field, since this contains the embedded MS Word object. Set the File Path Column equal to the field name [NewFilePath]. This field is the one that you derived in Derived Column task.

9. Check the Force Truncate option to rewrite the files if they exist. (This will allow you to run the package again without an error if the files already exist.)

10. Run the package and check the contents of the "c:\exports\" directory. You should see a list of MS Word files in sequence from 1 to 9. Open one and you'll be able to read the document in MS Word.

Row Count

The Row Count transformation task provides the ability to count rows in a stream that is directed to its input source. This transformation must place that count into a variable. This transformation is useful for tasks that require knowing "How many?" It is especially valuable since you don't physically have to commit stream data to a physical table to retrieve the count. If you need to know how many rows are split during the Conditional Split transformation, direct the output of each side of the split to a separate Row Count transformation. Each Row Count transformation is designed for an input stream and will output a row count into a Long or compatible data type. You can then use this variable to log information into storage, to build e-mail messages, or to conditionally run steps in your packages.

This transformation uses the Advanced Editor. As you recall, you used this editor in the Import Columns section of this chapter. Configuring this transformation is much easier. All you really need to provide in terms of configuration is the name of the variable to store the count of the input stream.

You will now simulate a situation where you have a conditional step in a package that should run only if an input stream row count is evaluated to have a row count greater than zero. You could use this type of logic to implement conditional execution of any task, but for simplicity, you'll conditionally execute a SQL Statement.

1. Create an SSIS package named Row Count Example. Add a Data Flow task to the Control Flow design surface.

2. Add a Variable named MyRowCount. Ensure that the variable is package scoped and of type Int32.

3. Add an OLE DB Data Source to the Data Flow design surface. Configure the source to point to your AdventureWorks database and the table [ErrorLog].

4. Add a Row Count transformation task to the Data Flow design surface. Open the Advanced Editor. Provide the variable name MyRowCount as the VariableName property. Your editor should resemble Figure 6-13.

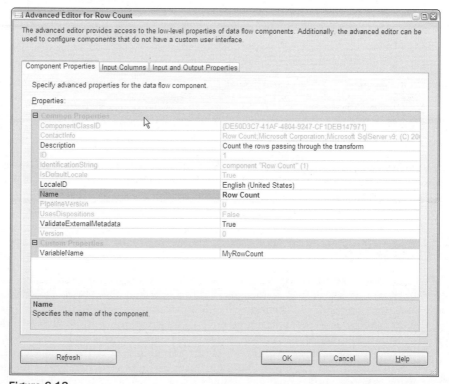

Figure 6-13

5. Return to the Control Flow tab and add an Execute SQL task. Configure the connection to the same OLE DB connection and set the SQLStatement to SELECT 1. This task is not really going to perform any action. It will be used to show the conditional ability to perform steps based on the value returned by the Row Count transformation.

6. Connect the Data Flow task to the Execute SQL task.

7. Right-click the arrow connecting the Data Flow and Execute SQL tasks. Select the Edit menu. In the Precedence Constraint Editor, change the Evaluation Operation to Expression. Set the Expression to @MyRowCount>0. Your editor should look like Figure 6-14.

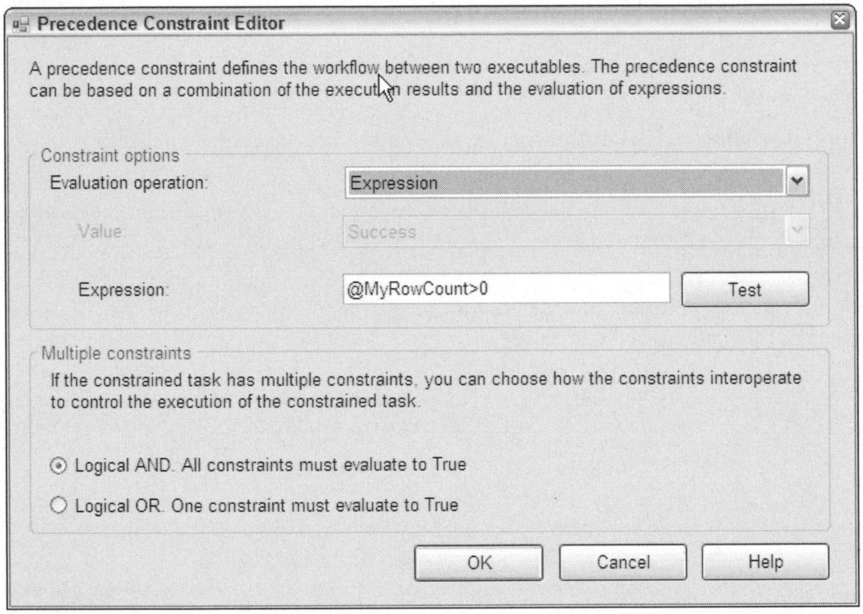

Figure 6-14

When you run the package, you'll see that the Execute SQL task is not executed. If you are curious, insert a row into the [ErrorLog] table and rerun the package. You'll see that the Execute SQL task will turn green, indicating that it was executed.

OLE DB Command

The OLE DB Command transformation is a component designed to execute a SQL statement for each row in an input stream. This task is analogous to an ADO Command object being created, prepared, and executed for each row of a result set. The input stream provides the data for parameters that can be set into the SQL statement that is either an in-line statement or a stored procedure call. Now I don't know about you, but just hearing the "for each row" phrase in the context of SQL makes me think of another phrase — "performance degradation." This involves firing an update, insert, or delete statement, prepared or unprepared some unknown number of times. This doesn't mean there aren't any good reasons to use this transformation — you'll actually be doing a few in this chapter. Just understand the impact and think about your use of this transformation. Pay specific attention to the volume of input rows that will be fed into it. Weigh the performance and scalability aspects during your design phases against a solution that would cache the stream into a temporary table and use set-based logic instead.

To use the OLE DB Command transform task, you basically need to determine how to set up the connection where the SQL statement will be run, provide the SQL statement to be executed, and configure the mapping of any parameters in the input stream to the SQL statement. Take a look at the settings for the OLE DB Command transformation by opening its editor. The OLE DB Command transform is another component that uses the Advanced Editor. There are four tabs in the editor:

❑ **Connection Manager:** Allows the selection of an OLE DB Connection. This connection is where the SQL Statement will be executed. This also doesn't have to be the same connection that is used to provide the input stream.

❑ **Component Properties:** Here you can set the SQL Command statement to be executed in the SQLCommand property and set the amount of time to allow for a timeout in the CommandTimeout property in seconds. The property works the same way as the ADO Command object. The value for the CommandTimeout of 0 indicates no time-out. You can also name the task and provide a description in this tab.

❑ **Column Mappings:** This tab will display columns available in the input stream and the destination columns, which will be the parameters available in the SQL command. You can map the columns by clicking on a column in the input columns and dragging it onto the matching destination parameter. It is a one-to-one mapping, so if you need to use a value for two parameters, you'll need use a Derived Column transform to duplicate the column in the input stream prior to configuring the columns in this transform.

❑ **Input and Output Properties:** Most of the time you'll be able to map your parameters in the Column Mappings tab. However, if the OLE DB provider doesn't provide support for deriving parameter information (parameter refreshing), you'll have to come here to manually set up your output columns using specific parameter names and DBParamInfoFlags.

The easiest way to learn this task is by example. Suppose you have a requirement to process a small daily volume of validated, electronically sent deposit entries and to run them through logic to create deposit entries in your accounting database. You also have to build payment transactions that will need to be reviewed by accounting personnel using the accounting software, which applies the money to each customer's account. Fortunately, you don't need to know how to create deposit transactions or payment transactions. You've been given two stored procedures that will do the work of building the transactions, so you'll use them in the example.

1. Create an SSIS package named "OLE DB Command." Add a Data Flow component to the Control Flow.

2. Create a text file containing the following entries and save it to "c:\ole db eft data.txt."

```
CustomerID,DepositAmt,DepositDate,Invoice
XY-111-222,$100.00,07/13/2005,222-063105
XX-Z11-232,$1000.00,07/13/2005,232-063105
XX-Y88-233,$555.00,07/13/2005,233-053105
```

3. Run the following SQL Scripts to create the simulated stored procedures in your AdventureWorks database.

```
USE ADVENTUREWORKS
GO
CREATE PROC usp_DepositTrans_Add (
        @CUSTOMERID varchar(10),
```

```
        @DEPOSITAMT money,
        @DEPOSITDATE smalldatetime,
        @INVOICE  varchar(15))

AS

    ---THIS IS A DUMMY PROCEDURE FOR DEMO PURPOSES
GO
CREATE PROC usp_PaymentTrans_Add (
        @CUSTOMERID varchar(10),
        @DEPOSITAMT money,
        @DEPOSITDATE smalldatetime,
        @INVOICE  varchar(15))

AS

    --THIS IS A DUMMY PROCEDURE FOR DEMO PURPOSES
```

4. Add a Flat File Source to your Data flow to consume the text file "c:\ole db eft file.txt."

5. Add an OLE DB Command transform task to the Data Flow design surface. Connect the output of the Flat File Source to the OLE DB command transform.

6. Configure the OLE DB Command transform task to a connection to AdventureWorks. Update the SQLCommand property for the transform to add a deposit for each input row by setting the property to usp_DepositTrans_Add ?, ?, ?, ?. Each of the "?" marks stand in place of a parameter. Click refresh to pull the parameters from the proc. The completed tab should look like Figure 6-15.

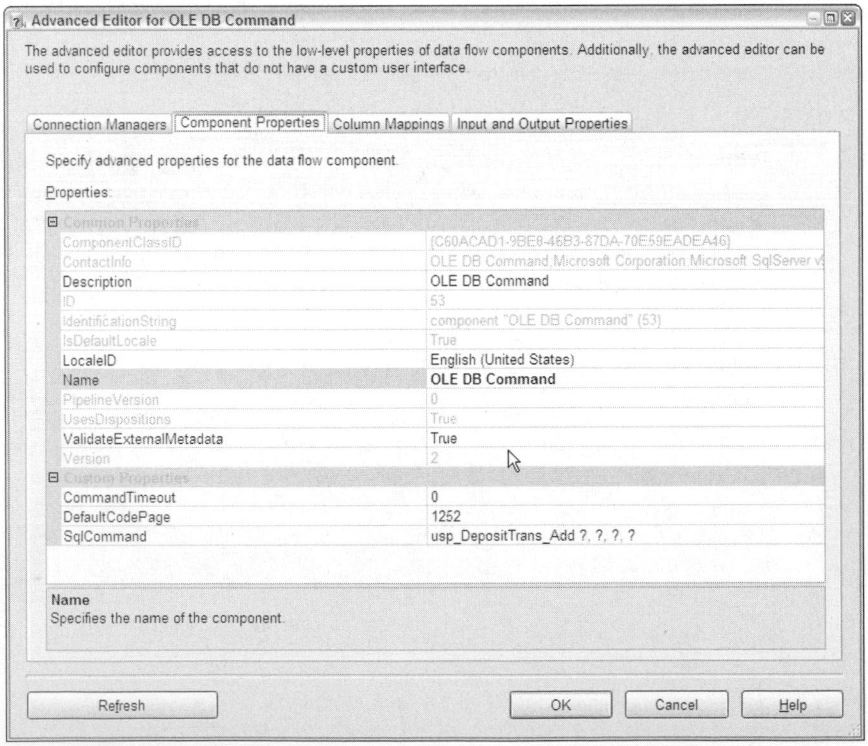

Figure 6-15

7. In the Column Mappings tab, map each column in the input columns collection to a column in the destination columns collection. This should look like Figure 6-16.

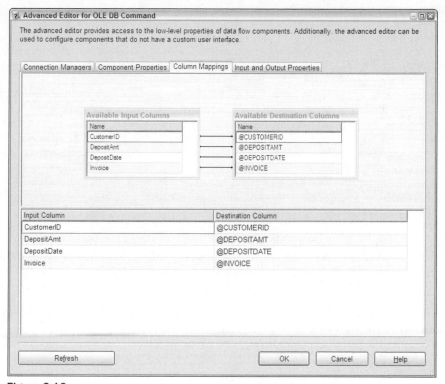

Figure 6-16

8. Add another OLE DB Command transform task to the Data Flow design surface. Connect the output of the first OLE DB Command transform to the second and then go through the same configuration as for the deposit command, but this time set the SQLCommand property to `usp_PaymentTrans_Add ?, ?, ?, ?`.

When you run this package, you'll see that three rows were processed by each OLE DB Command transform. If the procedures were functional, they would have created three deposit and three payment transactions. In this example, you found a good reason to use this task — reusability. It may be more efficient to process these transactions in a SQL batch, but then you'd have to stage the data and code the batch transaction. In this example, you were able to reuse existing logic that was designed for manual or one-at-a-time data entry and bundle that into an automated SSIS package fairly quickly.

Term Extraction

If you have done some word and phrase analysis on Web sites for better search engine placement, you will be familiar with the job that this transformation task performs. The Term Extraction transformation is a tool to mine free-flowing text for word and phrase frequency. You can feed any text-based input stream into the transformation and it will output two columns: a text phrase and a statistical value for the phrase relative to the total input stream. The statistical values or scores that can be calculated can be as simple as a count of the frequency of the words and phrases, or they can be a little more complicated as the result of a formula named TFIDF score. The TFIDF acronym stands for Term Frequency and Inverse Document Frequency, and it is a formula designed to balance the frequency of the distinct words and phrases relative to the total text sampled. If you're interested, here's the formula:

```
TDIDF (of a term or phrase) = (frequency of term) * log((# rows in sample)/(# rows
with term or phrase))
```

The results generated by the Term Extraction transformation are based on internal algorithms and statistical models that are encapsulated in the component. You can't alter or gain any insight into this logic by examining the code. However, some of the core rules for how the logic breaks apart the text to determine word and phrase boundaries are documented in Books Online. What you can do is tweak some external settings and make adjustments to the extraction behavior by examining the resulting output. Since text extraction is domain-specific, the transform also provides the ability to store terms and phrases that you have predetermined are noisy or insignificant in your final results. You can then automatically remove these items from future extractions. Within just a few testing iterations, you can have the transform producing meaningful results.

Before you write this transformation off as a cool utility that you'll never use, consider this: How useful would it be to query into something like a customer service memo field stored in your data warehouse and generate some statistics about the comments that are being made? This is the type of use for which the Term Extraction transform is perfectly suited. The trick to understanding how to use the component is to remember that it has one input. That input must be either a NULL-terminated ANSI (DT_WSTR) or Unicode (DT_NTEXT) string. If your input stream is not one of these two types, you can use the Data Conversion transform to convert it. Since this transformation can best be learned by playing around with all the settings, put this transform to work on exactly what was proposed before — mining some customer service memo fields.

You have a set of comment fields from a customer service database for an appliance manufacture. In this field, the customer service representative will record a note that summarizes the contact with the customer. For simplicity sake, you'll create these comment fields in a text file and analyze them in the Term Extraction transformation.

1. Create the customer service text file using the following text (cut and paste into Notepad). Save as "c:\custsvc.txt."

```
Ice maker in freezer stopped working model XX-YY3
Door to refrigerator is coming off model XX-1
Ice maker is making a funny noise XX-YY3
Handle on fridge falling off model XX-Z1
Freezer is not getting cold enough XX-1
Ice maker grinding sound fridge XX-YY3
Customer asking how to get the ice maker to work model XX-YY3
Customer complaining about dent in side panel model XX-Z1
Dent in model XX-Z1
Customer wants to exchange model XX-Z1 because of dent in door
Handle is wiggling model XX-Z1
```

2. Create a SSIS project named Term Extraction. Add a Data Flow task to the Control Flow design surface.

3. Create a Flat File connection to "c:\custsvc.txt." Change the output column named in the Advanced tab to "CustSvcNote." Change OutputColumnWidth to 100 to account for the length of the field.

4. Add a Flat File Source to the Data Flow design surface. Configure the source to use the Flat File connection.

5. Since the Flat File Source output is string (DT_STR), you'll need to convert the string to either the DT_WSTR or DT_NTEXT data type. Add a Data Conversion Transform to the Data Flow design surface and connect the output of the Flat File Source. Set the Input Column to CustSvcNote, the Output Alias to ConvCustSvcNote, and the Data Type to Unicode string [DT_WSTR]. Click OK to save.

6. Add a Term Extraction task to the Data Flow design surface. Connect the output of the Data Conversion transform to its input. Open the Term Extraction Editor. Figure 6-17 shows the available input columns from the input stream and the two default-named output columns. You can change the named output columns if you wish. Only one input column can be chosen. Click the column ConvCustSvcNote, since this is the column that is converted to a Unicode string. If you click the unconverted column, you'll see a validation error like the following:

```
The input column can only have DT_WSTR or DT_NTEXT as its data type.
```

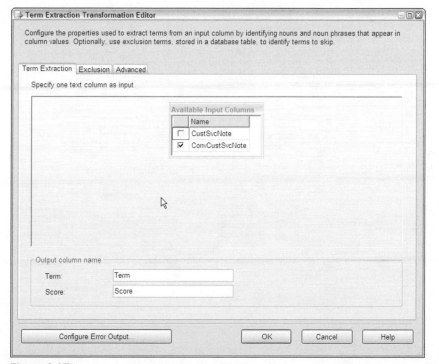

Figure 6-17

7. Close the Term Extraction Editor. Ignore the cautionary warnings about rows sent to error outputs. You didn't configure an error location for bad rows to be saved, but it's not necessary for this example.

8. Add an OLE DB Destination to the Data Flow. Connect the output of the Term Extraction task to the OLE DB Destination. Configure the OLE DB Destination to use your AdventureWorks connection.

9. Click on the New button to configure the Name of Table or View property. A window will come up with a CREATE TABLE DDL statement. Notice that the data types are a Unicode text field and a double. Alter the statement to read:

```
CREATE TABLE [TermResults] (
    [Term] NVARCHAR(128),
    [Score] DOUBLE PRECISION
)
```

10. When you click OK, the new table TermResults will be created in the AdventureWorks database. Click the Mappings tab to confirm the mapping between the Term Extract outputs of Term and Score to the table [TermResults].

11. Add a Data Viewer by right-clicking the Data Flow between the Term Extract transform and the OLE DB destination. Set the type to grid and accept defaults.

12. Run the package.

The package will stop on the Data Viewer to allow you to view the results of the Term Extract transform. You should see a list of terms and an associated score for each word. Since you just accepted all of the Term Extraction settings, the default score is a simple count of frequency. Stop the package, open the Term Extraction Transformation Editor, and view the Advanced tab. See Figure 6-18 for an example of the properties on this tab.

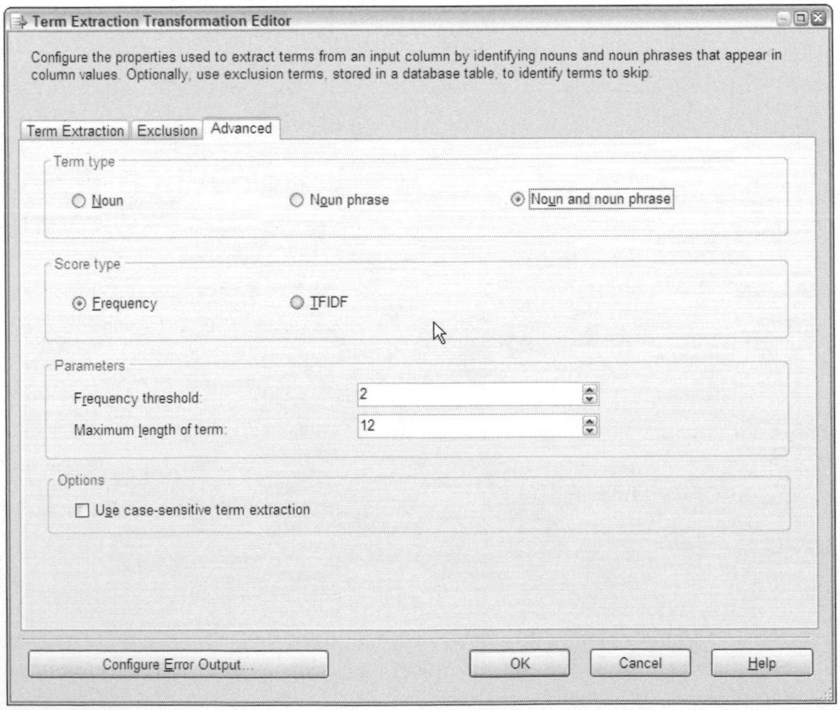

Figure 6-18

The Advanced tab allows for some configuration of the task and can be divided into four categories:

❑ **Term Type:** Settings that control how the input stream should be broken into bits called *tokens*. The Noun Term Type will focus the transform on nouns only, Noun Phrases will extract noun phrases, and Noun and Noun Phrases will extract both.

❑ **Score Type:** Choose between analyzing words by frequency or by a weighted frequency.

❑ **Parameters:** Frequency threshold is the minimum number of times a word or phrase must appear in tokens. Maximum length of term is the maximum number of words that should be combined together for evaluation.

❑ **Options:** Check this option to consider case-sensitivity or leave unchecked to disregard.

This is where the work really starts. How you set the transform up really affects the results you'll see. Figure 6-19 shows an example of the results using each of the different Term Type settings combined with the different score types.

Term	Noun		Noun Phrase		Both	
	Score (f)	Score (tdidf)	Score (f)	Score (tdidf)	Score (f)	Score (tdidf)
dent	3	3.897848			3	3.897848
customer	3	3.897848			3	3.897848
freezer	2	3.409496			2	3.409496
door	2	3.409496			2	3.409496
XX-YY3	4	* 4.046403				
ice	4	* 4.046403				
maker	4	* 4.046403				
XX-Z1	5	3.942286				
XX-1	2	3.409496				
model	*8	2.547629				
ice maker			*4	*4.046403	*4	*4.046403
model XX-Z1			3	3.897848	3	3.897848
model XX-YY3			2	3.409496	2	3.409496

* - Indicates highest-scoring item

Figure 6-19

One of the unusual things to notice is that the term "model XX-Z1" shows a frequency score of 3 when the Term Type option is set to "Both," even though you can physically count five instances of this phrase in the customer service data. However, the term "XX-Z1" is counted with the correct frequency when you break the source text into nouns only. This demonstrates that the statistical models are sensitive to where and how noun phrases are used. As a consequence, the tagging of noun phrases may not be completely accurate.

At the moment, using a combination of these statistics, you can report that customer service is logging a high percentage of calls concerning the terms "model," "model XX-Z1," "model XX-YY3," "ice maker," "dent," and "customer." An assumption can be made that there may be some issues with models XX-Z1 and XX-YY3 that your client needs to look into.

In evaluating this data, you may determine that some words over time are just not of interest to the analysis. In this example, the words "model" and "customer" really serve no purpose but to dampen the scores for other words. To remove these words from your analysis, take advantage of the exclusion features in the Term Extraction transform by adding these words to a table with a single Unicode NULL-terminated string column. Figure 6-20 shows a properly configured exclusion table in the Exclusion tab of the Term Extraction Editor. Rerun the package and review the new results.

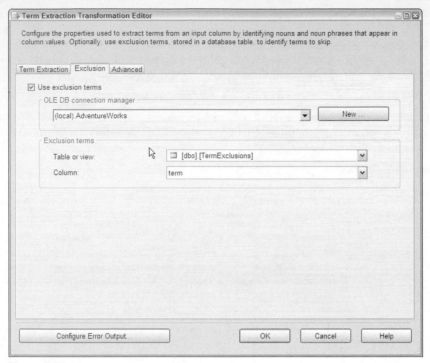

Figure 6-20

Notice that the results of your noun-term extraction have suffered a setback. No longer do the phrases "model XX-Z1" or "model XX-YY3" even appear in the results. Huh? Well, you did tell the transform to exclude the term "model." You meant the word. You didn't intend for the phase including the word to also be removed. You'll need to remove the word "model" from your exclusion table because it is too restrictive. A different way to look at the Term Extraction transform is that it is a utility that will build a word list. To really make sense of that word list, you need to add some human intervention and the next transform — Term Lookup.

Term Lookup

The Term Lookup transform uses the same algorithms and statistical models as the Term Extraction transform to break up an incoming stream into noun or noun phrase tokens, but it is designed to compare those tokens to a stored word list and output a matching list of terms and phrases with simple frequency counts. Now a strategy for working with both term-based transforms should become clear. Periodically use the Term Extraction transform to mine the text data and to generate lists of statistical phrases. Store these phrases in a word list, along with phrases that you think the term extraction process should identify. Remove the phrases that you don't want identified. Use the Term Lookup Transform to reprocess the text input to generate your final statistics. This way, you are generating statistics on known phrases of importance.

You can use results from the Term Extraction example by removing the word "model" from the [TermExclusions] table for future Term Extractions. You would then want to review all of the terms stored in the [TermResults] table, sort them out, remove the duplicates, and add back terms that make sense to your subject matter experts reading the text. Since you want to generate some statistics about which model numbers are generating customer service calls, but you don't want to restrict your extractions to only the occurrences of the model number in conjunction with the word "model," remove phrases combining the word "model" and the model number. The final [TermResults] table should look something like the following:

```
  term
  -----------
dent
door
freezer
ice
ice maker
maker
XX-1
XX-YY3
XX-Z1
```

Take a copy of the package you built in the Extraction example, but exchange the Term Extraction transform for a Term Lookup transform and change the OLE Destination to output to a table [TermReport].

Open the Term Lookup Editor. It should look similar to Figure 6-21. There are three basic tabs used to set up this task:

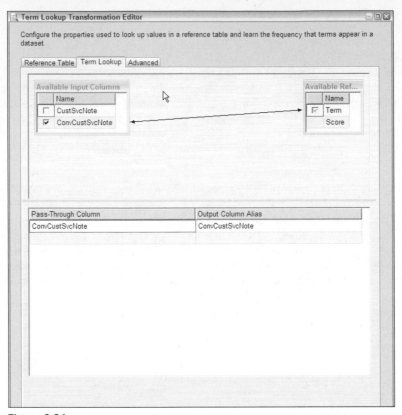

Figure 6-21

❑ **Reference Table:** This is where you will configure the connection to the reference table. The Term Lookup task should be used to validate each tokenized term that it finds in the input stream.

❑ **Term Lookup:** After selecting the lookup table, you will map the field from the input stream to the reference table for matching.

❑ **Advanced:** This tab has one setting to check if the matching is case-sensitive.

The results of running this package will be a list of phrases that you are expecting from your stored word list. A sample of the first six rows is displayed below. Notice that this result set doesn't summarize the findings. You are just given a blow-by-blow report on the number of terms in the word list that were found for each row of the customer service notes. In this text sample, it is just a coincidence that each term appears only once in each note.

```
Term           Frequency  ConvCustSvcNote
-------------  ---------  -------------------------------------------------
freezer            1      ice maker in freezer stopped working model XX-YY3
ice maker          1      ice maker in freezer stopped working model XX-YY3
XX-YY3             1      ice maker in freezer stopped working model XX-YY3
door               1      door to refrigerator is coming off model XX-1
```

```
XX-1              1         door to refrigerator is coming off model XX-1
ice maker         1         ice maker is making a funny noise XX-YY3
(Only first six rows of resultset are displayed)
```

To complete the report, add an Aggregate transform between the Term Lookup transform and the OLE DB Destination transform. Set up the Aggregate transform to ignore the ConvCustSvcNote column, group by the Term column, and summarize the Frequency Column. Connect the Aggregate Transform to the OLE DB Destination and remap the columns in the OLE DB transform.

Although this is a very rudimentary example, you will start to see the possibilities of using SSIS for very raw and unstructured data sources like this customer service comment data. In a short period of time, you have pulled some meaningful results from the data. Already you can provide the intelligence that model XX-Z1 is generating 45% of your sample calls and that 36% of your customer calls are related to the ice maker. Figure 6-22 shows some sample data that you can generate with what you know so far. Pretty cool results from what is considered unstructured data.

Analysis of Customer Service Data Calls Received 07/15/05		
Total Number of Calls		11
Appliance Models		% Calls
XX-Z1	5	45%
XX-YY3	4	36%
XX-1	2	18%
Totals	11	100%
Key Issues:		
ice maker	4	36%
dent	3	27%
door	2	18%
freezer	2	18%
Totals	11	100%

Figure 6-22

Fuzzy Lookup

If you've done some work in the world of extract, transfer, and load processes (ETL), you've run into the proverbial crossroads of handling bad data. The test data is staged, but all attempts to retrieve a foreign key from a dimension table result in no matches for a number of rows. This is the crossroads of bad data. At this point, there are a finite set of options. You could create a set of Astro-Physics-based lookup functions using SQL Sound-Ex, full-text searching, or distance-based word calculation formulas. This strategy is time-consuming to create and test, complicated to implement, and dependent on language lexicon, and it isn't always consistent or reusable (not to mention that everyone from now on will be scared to alter the code for fear of breaking it). You could just give up and divert the row for manual processing by subject matter experts (that's a way to make some new friends). You could just add the new data to the lookup tables and retrieve the new keys. If you just add the data, the foreign key retrieval issue gets solved, but you could be adding an entry into the dimension table that will skew data-mining results downstream. This is what I like to call a *lazy-add*. This is a descriptive, not a technical, term. A lazy-add would import a misspelled job title like "prasedent" into the dimension table when there is already an entry of "president." It was added, but it was lazy.

The Fuzzy Lookup and Fuzzy Grouping transformations add one more road to take at the crossroads of bad data. These transformations allow the addition of a step to the process that is easy to use, consistent, scalable, and reusable, and they will reduce your unmatched rows significantly — maybe even altogether. If you've already allowed bad data in your dimension tables, or you are just starting a new ETL process, you'll want to put the Fuzzy Grouping transformation to work on your data to find data redundancy. This transformation can examine the contents of a suspect field in a staged or committed table and provide possible groupings of similar words based on provided tolerances. This matching information can then be used to clean up that table. Fuzzy Grouping will be discussed later in this chapter.

If you are correcting data during an ETL process, use the Fuzzy Lookup transformation — my suggestion is to do so *only* after attempting to perform a regular lookup on the field. This best practice is recommended because Fuzzy Lookups don't come cheap. Fuzzy Lookups build specialized indexes of the input stream and the reference data for comparison purposes. You can store them for efficiency, but these indexes can use up some disk space or can take up some memory if you choose to rebuild them on each run. Storing matches made by the Fuzzy Lookups over time in a translation or pre-dimension table is a great design. Regular Lookup transforms can first be run against this translation table and then divert only those items in the Data Flow that can't be matched to a Fuzzy Lookup. This technique uses Lookup transforms and translation tables to find matches using INNER JOINS. Fuzzy Lookups whittle the remaining unknowns down if similar matches can be found with a high level of confidence. Finally, if your last resort is to have the item diverted to a subject matter expert, you can save that decision into the translation table so that the ETL process can match it next time in the first iteration.

Using the Fuzzy Lookup transformation requires an input stream of at least one field that is a string. Unlike the Term Lookup transformation, which requires a NULL-terminated Unicode string, this transform just needs a text input and most any text data type will do. Internally the transform has to be configured to connect to a reference table that will be used for comparison. The output to this transform will be a set of columns containing the following:

❑ **Input and Pass-Through Field Names and Values:** This column contains the name and value of the text input provided to the Fuzzy Lookup transform task or passed through during the lookup.

❑ **Reference Field Name and Value:** This column contains the name and value(s) of the matched results from the reference table.

❑ **Similarity:** This column contains a number between 0 and 1 representing similarity. Similarity is a threshold that you set when configuring the Fuzzy Lookup task. The closer this number is to 1, the closer the two text fields must match.

❑ **Confidence:** This column contains a number between 0 and 1 representing confidence of the match relative to the set of matched results. Confidence is different from similarity, because it is not calculated by examining just one word against another but rather by comparing the chosen word match against all the other possible matches. Confidence gets better the more accurately your reference data represents your subject domain, and it can change based on the sample of the data coming into the ETL process.

The Fuzzy Lookup Transformation Editor has three configuration tabs.

❑ **Reference Table:** This tab sets up the OLE DB Connection to the source of the reference data. The Fuzzy Lookup takes this reference data and builds a token-based index out of it before it can begin to compare items. In this tab are the options to save that index or to use an existing index from a previous process. There is also an option to maintain the index, which will detect changes from run to run and keep the index current. Note that if you are processing large amounts of potential data, this index can grow large.

❏ **Columns:** This tab allows mapping of the one text field in the input stream to the field in the reference table for comparison. Drag and drop a field from the Available Input Column onto the matching field in the Available Lookup Column. You can also click on the two fields to be compared and right-click to create a relationship. Another neat feature is the ability to add the foreign key of the lookup table to the output stream. To do this, just click on that field in the Available Input Columns. A complete Columns tab should look something like Figure 6-23.

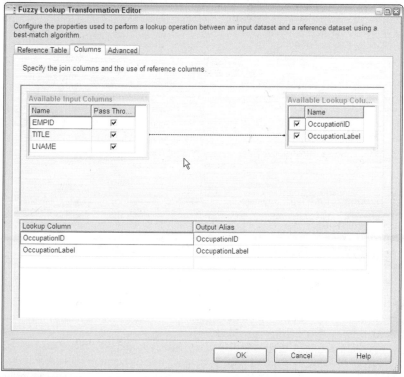

Figure 6-23

❏ **Advanced:** This tab contains the settings that control the fuzzy logic algorithms. You can set the maximum number of matches to output per incoming row. The default is set to 1. Incrementing this setting higher than this may generate more results that you'll have to sift through, but it may be required if there are too many closely matching strings in your domain data. A slider controls the Similarity threshold. A recommendation is to start this setting in the middle at .50 when experimenting and move up or down as you review the results. The token delimiters can also be set if, for example, you don't want the comparison process to break incoming strings up by "." or spaces. The default for this setting is all common delimiters. See Figure 6-24 for an example of an Advanced tab.

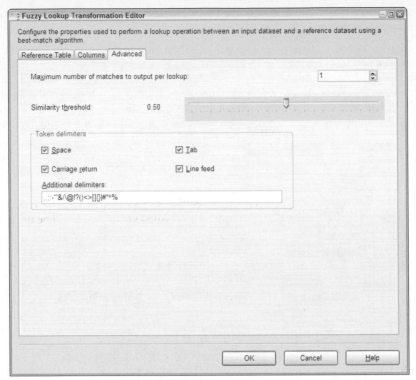

Figure 6-24

Although this transform neatly packages some highly complex logic in an easy-to-use component, the results won't be perfect. You'll need to spend some time experimenting with the configurable setting and monitoring the results. You will now look at an example and put this transform to work.

You are going to create a quick demonstration of the Fuzzy Lookup transform's capabilities by setting up a small table of occupation titles that will represent your dimension table. You will then import a set of person records that will require a lookup on the occupation to your dimension table. Not all will match, of course. The Fuzzy Lookup transformation will be employed to find matches, and you will experiment with the settings to learn about its capabilities.

1. First copy the following data into a text file named "c:\import\empdata.txt." This data will represent employee data that you are going to import. Notice that some of the occupation titles are cut off in the text file because of the positioning within the layout. Also notice that this file has an uneven right margin. Both of these issues are typical ETL situations that are especially painful.

```
EMPIDTITLE              LNAME
00001EXECUTIVE VICE PRESIDENWASHINGTON
00002EXEC VICE PRES      PIZUR
00003EXECUTIVE VP        BROWN
00005EXEC VP             MILLER
00006EXECUTIVE VICE PRASIDENSWAMI
00007FIELDS OPERATION MGR  SKY
```

```
00008FLDS OPS MGR          JEAN
00009FIELDS OPS MGR         GANDI
00010FIELDS OPERATIONS MANAGHINSON
00011BUSINESS OFFICE MANAGERBROWN
00012BUS OFFICE MANAGER      GREEN
00013BUS OFF MANAGER         GATES
00014BUS OFF MGR             HALE
00015BUS OFFICE MNGR         SMITH
00016BUS OFFICE MGR          AI
00017X-RAY TECHNOLOGIST      CHIN
00018XRAY TECHNOLOGIST       ABULA
00019XRAY TECH               HOGAN
00020X-RAY TECH              ROBERSON
```

2. Run the following SQL code in AdventureWorks or in a database of your choice. This code will create your dimension table and add the accepted entries that will be used for reference purposes.

```
CREATE TABLE [Occupation](
  [OccupationID] [smallint] IDENTITY(1,1) NOT NULL,
  [OccupationLabel] [varchar] (50) NOT NULL
 CONSTRAINT [PK_Occupation_OccupationID] PRIMARY KEY CLUSTERED
(
  [OccupationID] ASC
) ON [PRIMARY]
) ON [PRIMARY]

GO


INSERT INTO [Occupation] Select 'EXEC VICE PRES'
INSERT INTO [Occupation] Select 'FIELDS OPS MGR'
INSERT INTO [Occupation] Select 'BUS OFFICE MGR'
INSERT INTO [Occupation] Select 'X-RAY TECH'
```

3. Create a new SSIS project named Fuzzy Lookup Example. Drop a Data Flow task on the Control Flow design surface and click on the Data Flow tab.

4. Add a Flat File Connection to the Connection Manager. Name it "Employee Data," and then set the file name to "c:\import\empdata.txt." Set the Format property to Ragged Right. (By the way, for those of you who use flat files, the addition of the ability to process a ragged-right file is a welcome addition.) Set the option to pull the column names from the first data row. Click on the Columns tab and set the columns to break at positions 5 and 28. Click on the Advanced tab and set the OuputColumnWidth property for the TITLE field to 50. Save the connection.

5. Add a Flat File Source to the Data Flow surface and configure it to use the Employee Data connection. Add an OLE DB Destination and configure it to point to the AdventureWorks database or to the database of your choice.

6. Add a Fuzzy Lookup transform task to the Data Flow design surface. Connect the output of the Flat File source to the Fuzzy Lookup and the output of the Fuzzy Lookup to the OLE DB Destination.

7. Open the Fuzzy Lookup Transformation Editor. Set the OLE DB Connection Manager in the Reference tab to use the AdventureWorks database connection and the Occupation table. Set up the Columns tab connecting the input to the reference table columns as in Figure 6-23, and set up the Advanced tab with a Similarity threshold of 50 (.50).

177

8. Open the editor for the OLE DB Destination. Set the OLE DB connection to the AdventureWorks database. Click New to create a new table to store the results. Change the table name in the DDL statement to [FuzzyResults]. Click on the Mappings tab, accept the defaults, and save.

9. Add a Data View of type grid to the Data Flow between the Fuzzy Lookup and the OLE DB Destination.

Run the package, and your results at the Data View should resemble those in Figure 6-25. Notice that the logic has matched 100% of the items at a 50% similarity threshold — and you have the foreign key OccupationID added to your input for free! Had you used a strict INNER JOIN or Lookup Transform, you would have made only four matches, a dismal 21% hit ratio. These items can be seen in the Fuzzy Lookup output where the values are 1 for similarity and confidence.

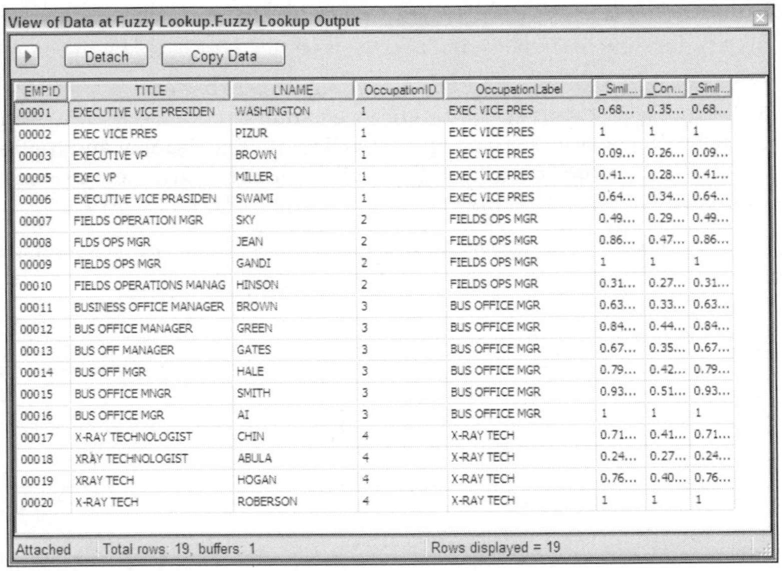

EMPID	TITLE	LNAME	OccupationID	OccupationLabel	_Simil...	_Con...	_Simil...
00001	EXECUTIVE VICE PRESIDEN	WASHINGTON	1	EXEC VICE PRES	0.68...	0.35...	0.68...
00002	EXEC VICE PRES	PIZUR	1	EXEC VICE PRES	1	1	1
00003	EXECUTIVE VP	BROWN	1	EXEC VICE PRES	0.09...	0.26...	0.09...
00005	EXEC VP	MILLER	1	EXEC VICE PRES	0.41...	0.28...	0.41...
00006	EXECUTIVE VICE PRASIDEN	SWAMI	1	EXEC VICE PRES	0.64...	0.34...	0.64...
00007	FIELDS OPERATION MGR	SKY	2	FIELDS OPS MGR	0.49...	0.29...	0.49...
00008	FLDS OPS MGR	JEAN	2	FIELDS OPS MGR	0.86...	0.47...	0.86...
00009	FIELDS OPS MGR	GANDI	2	FIELDS OPS MGR	1	1	1
00010	FIELDS OPERATIONS MANAG	HINSON	2	FIELDS OPS MGR	0.31...	0.27...	0.31...
00011	BUSINESS OFFICE MANAGER	BROWN	3	BUS OFFICE MGR	0.63...	0.33...	0.63...
00012	BUS OFFICE MANAGER	GREEN	3	BUS OFFICE MGR	0.84...	0.44...	0.84...
00013	BUS OFF MANAGER	GATES	3	BUS OFFICE MGR	0.67...	0.35...	0.67...
00014	BUS OFF MGR	HALE	3	BUS OFFICE MGR	0.79...	0.42...	0.79...
00015	BUS OFFICE MNGR	SMITH	3	BUS OFFICE MGR	0.93...	0.51...	0.93...
00016	BUS OFFICE MGR	AI	3	BUS OFFICE MGR	1	1	1
00017	X-RAY TECHNOLOGIST	CHIN	4	X-RAY TECH	0.71...	0.41...	0.71...
00018	XRAY TECHNOLOGIST	ABULA	4	X-RAY TECH	0.24...	0.27...	0.24...
00019	XRAY TECH	HOGAN	4	X-RAY TECH	0.76...	0.40...	0.76...
00020	X-RAY TECH	ROBERSON	4	X-RAY TECH	1	1	1

View of Data at Fuzzy Lookup.Fuzzy Lookup Output

Detach   Copy Data

Attached   Total rows: 19, buffers: 1   Rows displayed = 19

Figure 6-25

Fuzzy Grouping

In the previous section, you learned about situations where bad data creep into your dimension tables. The blame was placed on the "lazy-add" ETL processes that add data to dimension tables to avoid rejecting rows when there are no natural key matches. Processes like these are responsible for state abbreviations like "XX" and entries that look to the human eye like duplicates but are stored as two separate entries. The occupation titles "X-Ray Tech" and "XRay Tech" are good examples of duplicates that humans can see but computers have a harder time with.

The Fuzzy Grouping transformation can look through a list of similar text and group the results using the same logic as the Fuzzy Lookup. You can use these groupings in a transformation table to clean up source and destination data or to crunch fact tables into more meaningful results without altering the underlying data. The Fuzzy Group transformation also expects an input stream of text. It also requires a connection to an OLE DB data source because it creates in that source a set of structures to use during the analysis of the input stream.

The Fuzzy Lookup Editor has three configuration tabs:

- **Connection Manager:** This tab sets the OLE DB connection that the transform will use to write the storage tables that it needs.

- **Columns:** This tab displays the Available Input Columns and allows the selection of any or all input columns for fuzzy grouping analysis. See Figure 6-26 for a completed Columns tab.

  Each column selected will be analyzed and grouped into logical matches resulting in a new column representing that group match for each data row. Each column can also be selected for Pass-Through — meaning the data is not analyzed but is available in the output stream. You can choose the names of any of the output columns: Group Output Alias, Output Alias, Clean Match, and Similarity Alias score column.

  The minimum similarity evaluation is available at the column level if you select more than one column.

  The numerals option (which is not visible in Figure 6-26 but can be found by scrolling to the right) allows configuration of the significance of numbers in the input stream when grouping text logically. The options are to consider leading, trailing, leading and trailing, or neither leading nor trailing numbers significant. This option would need to be considered when comparing address or similar types of information.

  Comparison flags are the same options to ignore or pay attention to case, kana type, nonspacing characters, character width, symbols, and punctuation.

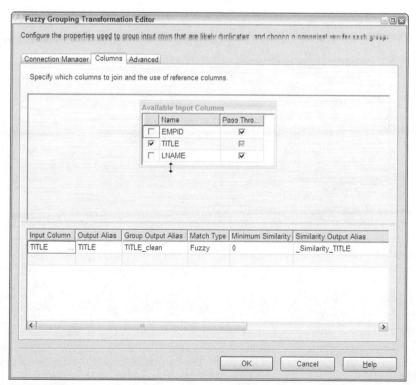

Figure 6-26

❑ **Advanced:** This tab contains the settings controlling the fuzzy logic algorithms that assign groupings to text in the input stream. You can set the names of the three additional fields that will be added automatically to the output of this transform. These fields are named "_key_out," "_key_in," and "_score" by default. A slider controls the Similarity threshold. A recommendation for this transform is to start this setting at 0.5 while experimenting and then move it up or down as you review the results. The token delimiters can also be set if, for example, you don't want the comparison process to break incoming strings up by "." or spaces. The default for this setting is all common delimiters. See Figure 6-27 for a completed Advanced tab.

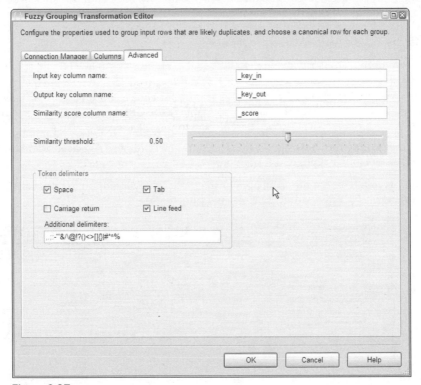

Figure 6-27

Suppose you are tasked with creating a brand-new occupations table using the employee occupations text file you imported in the Fuzzy Lookup example. Using only this data, create a new employee occupations table with occupation titles that can serve as natural keys and that best represent this sample. Use the Fuzzy Grouping transform to develop the groupings for the dimension table.

1. Create a new SSIS project named Fuzzy Grouping Example. Drop a Data Flow task on the Control Flow design surface and click on the Data Flow tab.

2. Add a Flat File Connection to the Connection Manager. Name it "Employee Data." Set the file name to "c:\import\empdata.txt." (Use the empdata.txt file from the Fuzzy Lookup example.) Set the Format property to Ragged Right. Set the option to pull the column names from the first data row. Click on the Columns tab and set the columns to break at positions 5 and 28. Click on the Advanced tab and set the OuputColumnWidth property for the TITLE field to 50. Save the connection.

3. Add a Flat File Source to the Data Flow surface and configure to use the Employee Data connection. Add an OLE DB Destination.

4. Add a Fuzzy Grouping transform task to the Data Flow design surface. Connect the output of the Flat File source to the Fuzzy Lookup and the output of the Fuzzy Lookup to the OLE DB Destination.

5. Open the Fuzzy Grouping Editor and set the OLE DB Connection Manager to the AdventureWorks connection.

6. In the Columns tab, select the Title column in the Available Input Columns. Accept the other defaults. Figure 6-26 is an example of a completed Columns tab for this example.

7. In the Advanced tab, set the Similarity threshold to .50. This will be your starting point for similarity comparisons.

8. Add an OLE DB Destination to the Data Flow design surface. Configure the destination to use the AdventureWorks database or database of your choice. For the Name of Table or View, click the New button. Change the name of the table in the CREATE table statement to [FuzzyGrouping]. Click on the Mapping tab to complete the task and save it.

9. Add a Data Viewer in the pipe between the Fuzzy Grouping transform and the OLE DB Destination. Set the type to grid so that you can review the data at this point. Run the package. The output shown at multiple similarity thresholds would look similar to Figure 6-28.

| | SIMILARITY THRESHOLD SETTINGS | | |
| | 75% | 50% | 25% |
RAW INPUT TITLE	FUZZY GROUPED TITLE	FUZZY GROUPED TITLE	FUZZY GROUPED TITLE
EXECUTIVE VICE PRESIDEN	EXECUTIVE VICE PRESIDEN	EXECUTIVE VICE PRESIDEN	EXECUTIVE VICE PRESIDEN
EXEC VICE PRES	EXEC VICE PRES	EXEC VICE PRES	EXECUTIVE VICE PRESIDEN
EXECUTIVE VP	EXEC VP	EXECUTIVE VP	EXEC VP
EXEC VP	EXEC VP	EXEC VP	EXEC VP
EXECUTIVE VICE PRASIDEN	EXECUTIVE VICE PRESIDEN	EXECUTIVE VICE PRASIDEN	EXECUTIVE VICE PRESIDEN
FIELDS OPERATION MGR	FIELDS OPERATION MGR	FIELDS OPERATION MGR	FLDS OPS MGR
FLDS OPS MGR	FLDS OPS MGR	FLDS OPS MGR	FLDS OPS MGR
FIELDS OPS MGR	FLDS OPS MGR	FIELDS OPS MGR	FLDS OPS MGR
FIELDS OPERATIONS MANAG	FIELDS OPERATIONS MANAG	FIELDS OPERATIONS MANAG	BUS OFFICE MANAGER
BUSINESS OFFICE MANAGER	BUSINESS OFFICE MANAGER	BUSINESS OFFICE MANAGER	BUS OFFICE MANAGER
BUS OFFICE MANAGER	BUS OFF MANAGER	BUS OFFICE MANAGER	BUS OFFICE MANAGER
BUS OFF MANAGER	BUS OFF MANAGER	BUS OFF MANAGER	BUS OFFICE MANAGER
BUS OFF MGR	BUS OFF MANAGER	BUS OFF MGR	BUS OFFICE MANAGER
BUS OFFICE MNGR	BUS OFFICE MNGR	BUS OFFICE MNGR	BUS OFFICE MANAGER
BUS OFFICE MGR	BUS OFFICE MNGR	BUS OFFICE MGR	BUS OFFICE MANAGER
X-RAY TECHNOLOGIST	X-RAY TECHNOLOGIST	X-RAY TECHNOLOGIST	X-RAY TECH
XRAY TECHNOLOGIST	XRAY TECHNOLOGIST	XRAY TECHNOLOGIST	XRAY TECHNOLOGIST
XRAY TECH	XRAY TECH	XRAY TECH	X-RAY TECH
X-RAY TECH	X-RAY TECH	X-RAY TECH	X-RAY TECH
19	13	19	6

Figure 6-28

Now you can look at these results and see more logical groupings and a few issues even at the lowest level of similarity. The title of "X-Ray Tech" is similar to the title "Xray Technologist." The title "Executive Vice Presiden" isn't really a complete title, and really should be grouped with "Exec VP." But this is pretty good for about five minutes of work.

To build a dimension table from this output, look at the two fields in the Data View named "_key_in" and "_key_out." If these two values match, then the grouped value is the "best" representative candidate for the natural key in a dimension table. Separate the rows in the stream using a Conditional Split transform where these two values match, and use an OLE Command transform to insert the values in the dimension table. Remember that the more data, the better the grouping.

The output of the Fuzzy Grouping transform is also a good basis for a translation table in your ETL processes. By saving both the original value and the Fuzzy Grouping value — with a little subject matter expert editing — you can use a Lookup transform and this table to provide much-improved foreign key lookup results. You'll be able to improve on this idea with the Slowly Changing Dimension transform later in the chapter.

Pivot Transform

Do you ever get the feeling that pivot tables are the modern day Rosetta Stone for translating data to your business owners? You store it relationally, but they ask for it in a format that you have to write a complex case statement to generate. Well, not anymore. Now you can use a SSIS transformation to generate the results. A *pivot table* is a result of cross-tabulated columns generated by summarizing data from a row format. Prior to SQL Server 2005, a pivot table could be generated only by using a SELECT...CASE statement to build summary columns based on one field in the row.

Typically a Pivot is generated using the following input columns:

❑ **Pivot Column:** A Pivot column is the element of input data to "pivot." The word "pivot" is another way of saying "to create a column for each unique instance of." However, this data must be under control. Think about creating columns in a table. You wouldn't create 1000 uniquely named columns in a table. So for best results when choosing a data element to pivot, pick an element that can be run through a GROUP BY statement that will generate 15 or fewer columns. If you are dealing with dates, use something like a DATENAME function to convert to the month or day of the year.

❑ **Row Columns:** Row columns are elements of input data that act as row (not column) identifiers. Just like any GROUP BY statement, some of the data are needed to define the group (row), whereas other data are just along for the ride.

❑ **Value Columns:** These columns are aggregations for data that provide the results in the matrix between the row columns and the pivot columns.

The Pivot Transform task can accept an input stream, use your definitions of the columns above, and generate a pivot table output. It helps if you are familiar with your input needs and format your data prior to this transform. Aggregate the data using GROUP BY statements. Pay special attention to sorting by row columns — this can significantly alter your results.

The Pivot Transform task uses the Advanced Editor to set up pivot rules. To set your expectations properly, you are going to have to define each of your literal pivot columns. A common misconception, and source of confusion, is approaching the Pivot transform with the idea that you can simply set the pivot column to pivot by the month of the purchase date column and the transformation should automatically build 12 pivot columns with the month of the year for you. It will not. It is your task to create an output column for each month of the year. If you are using colors as your pivot column, you'll need to add an output column for every possible color. What happens if columns are set up for Blue, Green, and Yellow and the color Red appears in the input source? The Pivot transform task will fail. So plan ahead and know the possible pivots that can result from your choice of a pivot column or provide for an error output for data that doesn't match your expected pivot values.

Use some of the AdventureWorks product and transactional history to generate a quick pivot table to show product quantities sold by month. This is a typical upper-management request and you can cover all the options with this example. Adventure Works Management wants a listing of each product with the total quantity of transactions by month for the year 2003.

First identify the Pivot Column. The month of the year looks like the data that is driving the creation of the pivot columns. The row data columns will be the product name and the product number. The value field will be the total number of transactions for the product in a matrix by month. Now you are ready to set up the Pivot transformation.

1. Create a new SSIS project named "Pivot Example." Add a Data Flow task to the Control Flow design surface.

2. Add an OLE DB Source transform to the Data Flow design surface. Configure the connection to the AdventureWorks database. Set the Data Access Mode to SQL Command. Add the following SQL statement into the SQL Command text box:

```
SELECT p.[Name] as ProductName, p.ProductNumber,
       datename(mm, t.TransactionDate) as TransMonth,
       sum(t.quantity) as TotQuantity
FROM production.product p
INNER JOIN production.transactionhistory t
ON t.productid = p.productid
WHERE t.transactiondate between '01/01/03' and '12/31/03'
GROUP BY p.[name], p.productnumber, datename(mm,t.transactiondate)
ORDER BY productname, datename(mm, t.transactiondate)
```

3. Add the Pivot transform and connect the output of the OLE DB Source to the input of the transform. Open the Advanced Editor and navigate to the Input Columns tab. In many of the transforms, you have the option of passing through some values from the input to the output. In the Pivot transform, you have to select all the columns that will be included in the output of the Pivot. All nonselected input columns will be ignored. Select all the input columns for this example.

4. Move to the Input and Output Properties tab. There is a collection of input, output, and error outputs. Remember that the input columns are the raw data coming in. The output columns will be the pivot data coming out. Figure 6-29 shows the input columns expanded and a view of the properties for the ProductName column. There are two important properties in that property editor:

   ❑ The LineageID property can't be changed, but you will need to know it in order to map output columns to an input column.

   ❑ The PivotUsage has to be set using the following codes:

   0: The column is just passed through as a row attribute.

   1: The column is the row column identifier (BOL calls this the Set Key).

   2: The pivot column.

   3: The value column.

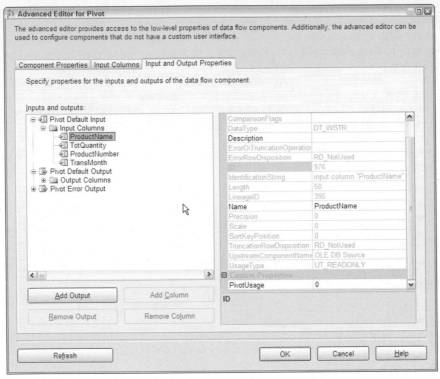

Figure 6-29

5. Set the PivotUsage properties for each of the Input Columns to match these codes:

❑ ProductName: 0 — A row attribute

❑ ProductNumber: 1 — A row identifier

❑ TransMonth: 2 — The pivot column

❑ TotQuantity: 3 — The value column

6. Expand the Output Column Nodes. Click the Add Column button to add a column to the output column collection. Set the name of the new output column to ProductName. Set the SourceColumn value to the LineageID of the same-named input column. Do the same thing for the ProductNumber Column. Figure 6-30 shows an example of the properties that appear for the output column. There are some new properties here:

❑ **Comparison Flags:** Allows ignoring of case, kana type, nonspacing characters, character width, and symbols when sorting the field. The defaults use each of these setting when sorting.

❑ **SortKeyPosition:** Provides for custom sorting by position. Each field has a number that indicates the order by which it is sorted. A zero (0) indicates that it is nonsorted. A one (1) indicates that it is sorted.

❑ **PivotKeyValue:** This property is important only for the output columns that you define for the Pivot Column. In this column, you'll place the exact text or an expression that will resolve to the groupings that you want to appear as your pivot columns. When pivoting on colors, this value would be Blue, Green, or Red.

❏ **SourceColumn:** This property requires the LineageID (not the ID) of the source column. This is a "poor man's" way of connecting the input columns to the output columns.

The output columns will be generated in exactly the same order that they appear on the output columns collection. You can't move them once they are added either, so pay attention to this as you add output columns.

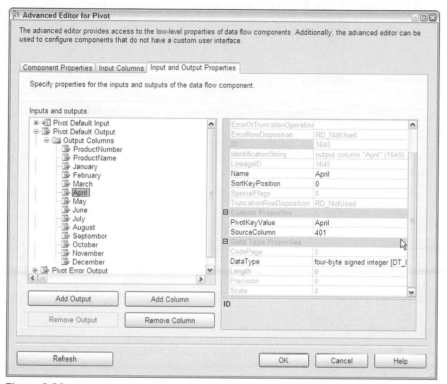

Figure 6-30

7. Add an output column named "January." Now for the big secret to making the whole thing work: Set the source column value to the LineageID of the TotQuantity column—*not* the TransMonth column. Remember that you are building a two-dimensional grid. The TransMonth field dictates one of the dimensions. The value in the column should be the total quantity at that dimension. Set the PivotKeyValue to "January" (without quotes). The pivot key is the literal value that will be examined in the data to determine when to put a value in a column. It is important that the incoming data sorts on this column to get consistent results. Repeat this process of creating an output column for each month of the year.

Do not use the LineageID values that you see in any of these figures. LineageIDs are specific to your own examples.

8. To finish the example, add an OLE DB Destination. Configure to the AdventureWorks connection. Connect the Pivot Default Output to the input of the OLE DB Destination. Click on the New Button to alter the CREATE TABLE statement to build a table named PivotTable.

9. Add a Data Viewer in the pipe between the PIVOT and OLE DB destination and run the package. You'll see the data in a pivot table in the Data Viewer as in Figure 6-31.

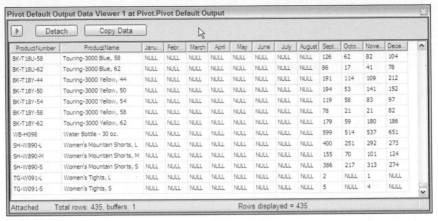

Figure 6-31

Unpivot

The Unpivot transform performs the reverse of the Pivot transform. Use this transform to reengineer pivoted data quickly into a relational state. All the same ideas about pivots apply, but you'll be applying them in reverse. Use a view in the AdventureWorks works database named [Sales].[vSalespersonsalesbyfiscalyears] to demonstrate returning a pivot table back into its named columns. See Figure 6-32 for a sample set of the rows in this pivot table.

	SalesPersonID	FullName	Title	SalesTerritory	2002	2003	2004
1	275	Michael G Blythe	Sales Representative	Northeast	1951086.8256	4743906.8935	4557045.0459
2	276	Linda C Mitchell	Sales Representative	Southwest	2800029.1538	4647225.4431	5200475.2311
3	277	Jillian Carson	Sales Representative	Central	3308895.8507	4991867.7074	3857163.6331
4	278	Garrett R Vargas	Sales Representative	Canada	1135639.2632	1480136.0065	1764938.9857
5	279	Tsvi Michael Reiter	Sales Representative	Southeast	3242697.0127	2661156.2418	2811012.715
6	280	Pamela O Ansman-Wolfe	Sales Representative	Northwest	1473076.9138	900368.5797	1656492.8626
7	281	Shu K Ito	Sales Representative	Southwest	2040118.6229	2870320.8578	3018725.4858

Figure 6-32

Your task, as with the Pivot transform, is to break the columns down into their pivot functions. Which column appears to define the row? The column labeled "SalesPersonID" is the best candidate for your row (or set) column since it meets the criteria of uniquely defining the row. The columns labeled "2002," "2003," and "2004" appear to be items in a series and meet the requirement of unique instances of columns. Columns [2002], [2003], and [2004] are the best candidates to be combined into your Unpivot column. Intuitively, if you are combining three different named columns, you'll need only one column and one column name. Name your Unpivot column "SalesYear." Determining the value column is not a function of choosing an available column heading. The value column is defined by the data in the matrix—the result of the row and pivot column combinations. Since your data is sales data, you can assume that this is total sales information (although it is peculiar that this data is stored at the ten-thousands place).

Call your value column "YearlySales." The remaining columns — "FullName," "Title," and "SalesTerritory" — play no significant role in the pivot process. These columns are just attributes to the row column identifier "SalesPersonID." Now you are ready to configure the Unpivot transform to extract these columns from the pivot table.

1. Create a new SSIS project named "Unpivot Example." Add a Data Flow task to the Control Flow design surface.

2. Add an OLE DB transform to the Data Flow design surface. Configure the transform to connect to the AdventureWorks database and to table [Sales].[vSalespersonsalesbyfiscalyears].

3. Add an Unpivot transform to the Data Flow design surface. Connect the output of the OLE DB Source to the transform. Click on the task to invoke the Unpivot Transform Editor. An example of this editor is shown in Figure 6-33. The key to understanding how to configure the transform is to understand that regardless of the number of input columns, *only* the columns that represent the pivot are to be selected in the Available Input Columns collection. All columns can be selected for pass-through, but only the pivot columns should appear in the grid. The grid contains three columns:

   ❏ **Input Column:** Each candidate Unpivot column should be selected as an input column.

   ❏ **Destination Column:** The name you have chosen to use when combining all your unpivot columns.

   ❏ **Pivot Key Value:** This is the unique value that generated the pivot and will now be placed into your new destination column. Usually the default will be the same as the original pivot column. You can also put expressions in this property.

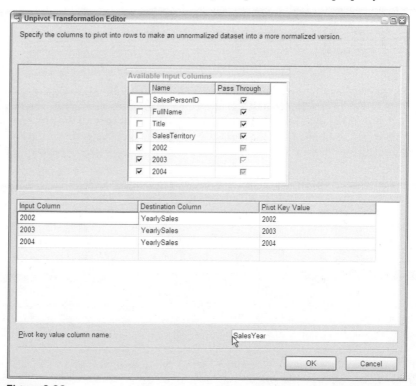

Figure 6-33

4. Configure the Pivot Key Value Column Name property. This is simply the pivot column name that represents your value column. Earlier you named this column "YearlySales." The Unpivot transform will use this name as your field name and move the data from this column in the pivot table into this field. The transform doesn't need the data type provided, since that can be inferred from the source data. All the other fields should be set to pass-through for this transformation. This will make these fields available as transformation output.

5. Add an OLE DB Destination to the Data Flow design surface. Connect the transform to the AdventureWorks database. Click on the New button to create a new Name of table or view. Change the `CREATE TABLE` statement table name to "UnPivotData." Save. Click on the Mappings tab and save the transform.

6. Add a data view of type grid to the pipe between the Unpivot and the OLE DB Destination. Run the package. The results should be similar to those in Figure 6-34. Notice that the SalesYear column is filled with the unpivoted column values of "2002," "2003," and "2004."

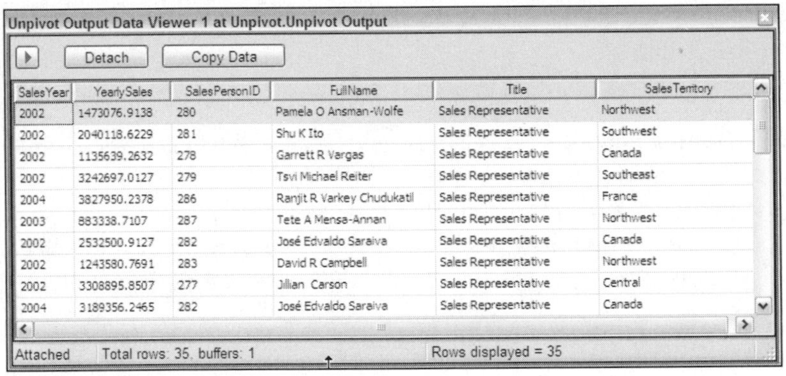

SalesYear	YearlySales	SalesPersonID	FullName	Title	SalesTerritory
2002	1473076.9138	280	Pamela O Ansman-Wolfe	Sales Representative	Northwest
2002	2040118.6229	281	Shu K Ito	Sales Representative	Southwest
2002	1135639.2632	278	Garrett R Vargas	Sales Representative	Canada
2002	3242697.0127	279	Tsvi Michael Reiter	Sales Representative	Southeast
2004	3827950.2378	286	Ranjit R Varkey Chudukatil	Sales Representative	France
2003	883338.7107	287	Tete A Mensa-Annan	Sales Representative	Northwest
2002	2532500.9127	282	José Edvaldo Saraiva	Sales Representative	Canada
2002	1243580.7691	283	David R Campbell	Sales Representative	Northwest
2002	3308895.8507	277	Jillian Carson	Sales Representative	Central
2004	3189356.2465	282	José Edvaldo Saraiva	Sales Representative	Canada

Figure 6-34

Take a side trip and review the Advanced Editor. The Advanced Editor (see Figure 6-35) is essentially the same as the Pivot transform—but configured in reverse. The input columns are the pivot table columns and the output columns are the relational columns. Notice that for each of the pivot columns [2002], [2003], and [2004] the DestinationColumn is set to 317. This is the LineageID for the [YearlySales] column and your value field.

If you view the properties for the SalesYear output column, you'll see that this column is defined as the PivotKey. The word "Pivot Key" is appropriate since the result of packaging the unpivot columns [2002], [2003], and [2004] is to create a column that can be used as a Pivot to unpack back into the separate column names.

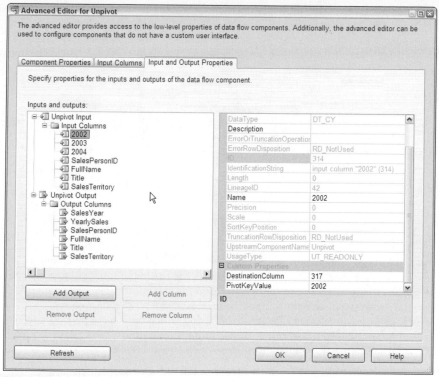

Figure 6-35

Slowly Changing Dimension

The Slowly Changing Dimension (SCD) transform provides a great head start in helping to solve a common, classic changing-dimension problem that occurs in the outer edge of your data model — the dimension or lookup tables. The changing-dimension issue in online transaction and analytical processing database designs is too big to cover in this chapter, but a little background may be necessary to help you understand the value of service the SCD transformation provides.

A dimension table contains a set of discrete values with a description and often other measurable attributes such as price, weight, or sales territory. The classic problem is what to do in your dimension data when an attribute in a row changes, particularly when you are loading data automatically through an ETL process. Take for example something as simple as a product defined in AdventureWorks (see Figure 6-36).

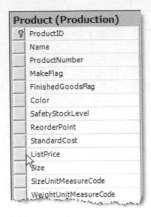

Figure 6-36

Typically in an On-Line Transaction Processing system (OLTP) you'd store one row for the product. If the price of the product changes from $10.00 to $15.00, the field StandardCost gets updated to $15.00. This accomplishes the mission of providing the answer to the question "How much does it cost now?" but you lose the historical perspective about the increases in the price of product. To solve this problem, you have really three basic options. The key to choosing which option comes down to what ultimately matters to your subject domain and can even result in the alteration of your data model. Each option is known by a common name: Type I, II, and III slowly changing dimensions.

- ❑ **Type I: Overwrite History** — Implements the dimensional attribute change by potentially updating the current value with the new value. However, as discussed above, you'd lose your historical perspective on this attribute.

- ❑ **Type II: Maintain History** — Implements the new change by adding a completely new row to the dimension table. This preserves the historical perspective but has side effects including complicating the lookup process and adding size to the dimension table.

- ❑ **Type III: Preserve Last History** — Implements the new change by adding additional attributes to the dimension table to store the last value in the same row. This saves some history but only the last historical change. This is not typically used, but it can be a great solution to store something like a marital name change in a customer or employee dimension table. This way, both names are available in the same row.

The Slowly Changing Dimension doesn't provide an automated method of handling Type III changes, but it can identify these candidates and divert to a specific output stream to be handled by other tasks.

The Slowly Changing Dimension transform provides a wizard-like UI that will walk you through a series of questions to guide the decisions about how to handle changes in the dimension table. An Advanced Editor provides more configurability but takes a little getting used to before you can become proficient with it. The wizard will start automatically after clicking the SCD object or the Show Editor link. Once configured, the SCD will generate several transformation tasks to accomplish the task of updating and inserting the target dimension table. Figure 6-37 is an example of the types of tasks that will be generated by this transform. You can see that it is not like the other transform tasks, which are completely contained when you drop them onto the Data Flow design surface.

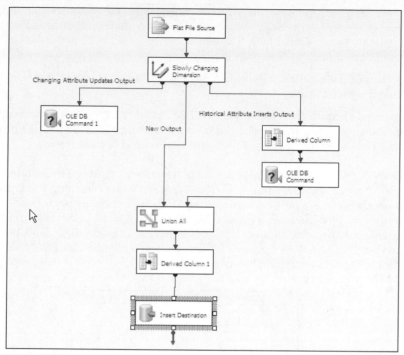

Figure 6-37

The SCD creates all these tasks because it is automating a task that is quite busy. In a nutshell, the SCD essentially consumes both an incoming data source and an OLE DB–connected dimension table, examines both sources using the results of your settings, generates at least two of six possible output streams, and then creates an OLE DB Command object for relevant stream to perform the database update. If it doesn't create exactly the scenario you need, you are at least in the neighborhood. The possible types of output steams or pipes are as follows:

❑ **Changing Attributes Updates Output:** Essentially these are Type I changes. All attributes that were selected in the SCD as changeable will be examined in the incoming data source and compared to the dimension table. If the incoming data source and dimension table match by the business (natural) keys but the attribute values are different, then the input row is diverted to this output stream.

❑ **Historical Attributes Inserts Output:** Essentially these are Type II changes. All attributes defined in the SCD as historical will be examined in the incoming data source and compared to the dimension table. If the incoming data source and dimension table match by the business (natural) keys but the attribute values are different, then the input row is diverted to this output stream.

❑ **Fixed Attributes Output:** All attributes defined in the SCD as fixed will be examined in the incoming data source and compared to the dimension table. If the incoming data source and dimension table match by the business (natural) keys but the attribute values are different, then the input row is diverted to this output stream. This stream can be used to deal with Type III changes, but you have to code your own OLE DB Command. (See the earlier section on OLE DB Command transforms.)

❏ **Inferred Member Updates:** This output is created when the option to enable inferred member support is selected in the SCD. You want to use this option if you want to load the dimension table using a fact or similar table. The output can be used to add to the dimension table rows that will be updated in a later process.

❏ **New Output:** This is the same output stream as the historical output and is used to add rows into the destination table.

❏ **Unchanged Output:** This output is not created by default. If the SCD detects no change in the input source and dimension tables based on the rules provided, then no action is taken. You can create a Data Flow for this output if you have an interest in these rows.

Before you go any further, you should make a point of reference by picking a real-world example and then follow through setting up an SCD transform for each type. You'll use something you know something about — your paychecks — in a rather unconventional SCD example. Every payroll cycle something gets subtracted from your checks before you get it: federal taxes, FICA taxes, health insurance premiums, 401K contributions, voluntary benefits, and even mass-transit tickets. To model these deductions, you might have a table in your OLTP database similar to Figure 6-38. You'd call this table PayrollDeductItem and it would be referenced by a Payroll Event Fact table.

Column Name	Data Type	Allow Nulls
PayrollDeductItemID	int	☐
EmployeePlanIDNbr	nchar(10)	☑
DeductionAmount	money	☑
EmployeeID	int	☑
PayDeductType	nchar(10)	☑

Figure 6-38

A year has gone by and now everyone is signing up for new benefits. Your task is to import the new benefits and update these payroll deduction records in the PayrollDeductItem table. When you examine the import file with the new employee benefits, you'll notice that some benefits have changed in the amount of deduction, some have been added, and if the deduction has been dropped, the amount is now zero. You can schedule an update of your data to run prior to the start of the first payroll for the new benefits period. But if you just update the benefits in place, you'll lose the ability to see trends in employee benefit elections. With this scenario in place, use the SCD transform to import the new records and experiment with the different options available. To prepare for the scenarios, run through the next few setup steps:

1. One thing you'll have to do is add some fields to allow for historical tracking. Even though you use only certain combinations depending on the type of slowly changing dimension logic, go ahead and create all the different fields now. As you work through the options, the purpose of each will become clear. Create the PayrollDeductItem table and add the current employee deductions using the following script:

```
Use AdventureWorks
GO
CREATE TABLE [dbo].[PayrollDeductItem](
    [PayrollDeductItemID] [int] IDENTITY(1,1) NOT NULL,
    [EmployeePlanIDNbr] [varchar](50) NULL,
    [DeductionAmount] [money] NULL,
    [EmployeeID] [int] NULL,
```

```
        [PayDeductType] [char](10) NULL,
        [HistTextStatus] [char](10) NULL
            CONSTRAINT [DF_PDI_HistTxtStatus] DEFAULT ('CURRENT'),
        [HistBitStatus] [bit] NULL
            CONSTRAINT [DF_PDI_HistBitStatus] DEFAULT ('TRUE'),
        [HistStartDate] [smalldatetime] NULL,
        [HistEndDate] [smalldatetime] NULL,
 CONSTRAINT [PK_POLICY] PRIMARY KEY CLUSTERED
(
   [PayrollDeductItemID] ASC
) ON [PRIMARY]
) ON [PRIMARY]
GO
 INSERT INTO PAYROLLDEDUCTITEM(EmployeePlanIDNbr, DEDUCTIONAMOUNT, EMPLOYEEID,
        PAYDEDUCTTYPE, HISTSTARTDATE)
SELECT '000000001', 200.00, 1, '401K', '01/01/2004'
UNION
SELECT 'ZZ0-10001', 10.00, 1, 'LIFE', '01/01/2004'
UNION
SELECT '000000002', 220.00, 2, '401K', '01/01/2004'
UNION
SELECT 'DC001-111', 10.00, 2, 'BUSPASS', '01/01/2004'
UNION
SELECT '000000003', 300.00, 3, '401K', '01/01/2004'
UNION
SELECT 'ZZ0-10003', 10.00, 3, 'LIFE', '01/01/2004'
GO
```

2. Create a text file to represent the new benefits that have been enrolled. Some are the same, some are new, and some have changed.

```
EMPLOYEEID,EMPLOYEEPLANIDNBR,DEDUCTIONAMOUNT,PAYDEDUCTTYPE,ENROLLDATE,COMMENT
1,000000001,225,401K,'01/01/05',INCREASED 401K DEDUCTION
1,ZZ0-10001,15,LIFE,'01/01/05',INCREASED LIFE DEDUCTION
2,000000002,220,401K,'01/01/05',NO CHANGE
2,DC001-111,0,BUSPASS,'01/01/05',TERMINATED BUSPASS DEDUCTION
3,000000003,250,401K,'01/01/05',DECREASED DEDUCTION
3,ZZ0-10003,10,LIFE,'01/01/05',NO CHANGE
4,000000004,175,401K, '01/01/05',NEW 401K DEDUCTION
```

3. Create a package with a Data Flow task and configure a Flat File connection to the text file as a delimited file. Select the option to use the column names in the first data row. Change the sizes of the EmployeePlanNbr and PayDeductType columns in the Advanced tab to Size=10. Set the data type of EmployeeID to a 32-bit Integer [DT_I4]. Set the data type of DeductionAmount to currency [DT_CY].

4. Import the file with a Flat File Source in the Data Flow tab that uses the Flat File connector.

5. Add a Slowly Changing Dimension transform to the Data Flow design surface and connect the output of the flat file to the SCD.

For reference, the completed PayrollDeductItem table should look like Figure 6-39. One thing you might be wondering is why there are extra columns: HistTextStatus, HistBitStatus, HistStartDate, and HistEndDate. You don't need all these columns to use the SCD transform. You'll use different columns throughout this section, and the differences will be explained as you go along.

	PayrollDeductItemID	EmployeePlanIDNbr	DeductionAmount	EmployeeID	PayDeductType	HistTextStatus	HistBitStatus	HistStartDate	HistEndDate
1	1	000000001	200.00	1	401K	CURRENT	1	2004-01-01 00:00:00	NULL
2	2	000000002	220.00	2	401K	CURRENT	1	2004-01-01 00:00:00	NULL
3	3	000000003	300.00	3	401K	CURRENT	1	2004-01-01 00:00:00	NULL
4	4	DC001-111	10.00	2	BUSPASS	CURRENT	1	2004-01-01 00:00:00	NULL
5	5	ZZ0-10001	10.00	1	LIFE	CURRENT	1	2004-01-01 00:00:00	NULL
6	6	ZZ0-10003	10.00	3	LIFE	CURRENT	1	2004-01-01 00:00:00	NULL

Figure 6-39

The SCD Wizard will guide you through four steps to configure the SCD transform. The steps can be categorized into the following:

1. **Dimension Table and Business Key Wizard Selection step:** This step requires the location of the dimension table, the mapping of the input fields from your source data to the dimension table for comparison, and a decision about what to use for a business key for this data. What fields do you need to map? Map any field that contains data to overwrite dimension field data or that makes up a natural or business key to the dimension field data. If the mapping is considered a part of the natural or business key for the dimension table, then each field should be denoted as a Business Key in the Key Type column.

2. **Slowly Changing Dimension Wizard Selection step:** This step focuses only on those fields mapped in the first step that aren't business keys. This step needs a decision for each of these fields to determine how to update the dimension table. Each field (or attribute) should fit into one of these categories (or should not be selected) when a row is matched using the business key:

   ❑ **Fixed Attribute:** The value in the dimension table should be fixed. If the value in the incoming source doesn't match, this should create an error.

   ❑ **Changing Attribute:** The value in the dimension table can always be overwritten by new values from the source. If only changing attributes are selected, the slowly changing dimension would be classified as a Type I change.

   ❑ **Historical Attribute:** The value in the incoming source doesn't match the dimension table, but the change in value is significant and should be stored. If a historical attribute is selected, this implies a Type II slowly changing dimension.

3. **Fixed and Changing Attribute Options:** If you have selected any attribute that is fixed, there is the option to fail or ignore on a change in that attribute. Another choice selects whether overwrites of data are allowed only on active rows or whether overwrites on both active and outdated rows are allowed.

4. **Historical Attribute Wizard Selection step:** This step appears only if a historical attribute is selected. If there is a historical attribute, you are dealing with a Type II solution to a slowly changing dimension. There are two ways to store the historical change. Each way results in a new row being created and each way is represented in the wizard with separate option buttons:

   ❑ **Use a single column to show current and expired records.** This option allows selection of a column in the dimension table that can be used to turn on or off or mark in some way to denote that one record is old and another more current. In the SCD transform, there are only two choices: True/False and Current/Expired.

   ❑ **Use start and end dates to identify current and expired records.** This option requires the selection of one start date and one end date column. An option also requires a date variable to be chosen that will mark the end date of the old historical record and the start date of the new record.

5. **Inferred Member selections Wizard Selection step:** This step is used if you are loading your dimension tables from your fact table and you don't have all the attribute data from the dimension table or plan to load it later. Turning on inferred member support will allow you to fill the dimension table with what you have and mark these separately from any data you may have already loaded. An example of an inferred member would be a new benefit like a grocery store discount card that you don't yet have loaded in your database, but you are now receiving data about your employees who have chosen this benefit.

6. **Finish Wizard Selection step:** This step will go over all the decisions that you have selected prior to building the transforms. This step is the "Are you sure?" dialog box.

In the payroll deduction example, you have to make a decision about how to identify a row in your dimension table using the columns in the data as a natural or business key. Your knowledge of the subject domain tells you that the [EmployeeIDNbr] rarely changes but also that each plan selected by the employee has a unique number that doesn't change, even if the benefit amount changes. The combination of [EmployeeIDNbr] and [EmployeePlanIDNbr] would probably be your strongest business key. The primary key [PayrollDeductItemID] is not used for comparison purposes because it has no relevance outside the database. When comparing to rows in an unconnected database source, [PayrollDeductItemID] doesn't help you decide whether a row should be inserted or updated.

Your other decision is what to do if you find a match from your new enrollment data source in your dimension table. When you process the first row of the input file, what do you do with the [EmployeePlanIDNbr] of "0000000001," [EmployeeID] of "1," and [PayDeductType] of "401" when the amount of $225.00 is different for the existing benefit? Do you update the current row using the business key of [EmployeeID]=1 and [EmployeePlanIDNbr] = "0000000001" to $225.00? Figure 6-40 will give you a good idea what results you might expect based on the choices available.

Business Key	Changing Attributes	Historical Attributes	Historical Change Type	SCD Type	Results
EmployeePlanIDNbr EmployeeID	DeductionAmount PayDeductType	N/A	N/A	Type I	Overwrites Current Row
	PayDeductType	DeductionAmount	Single Column Current/Expired	Type II	Old Row Marked Expired New Row Marked Current
			Single Column True/False	Type II	Old Row Marked False New Row Marked True
			Date Columns Start/End	Type II	Old Row End Date Marked w/Variable New Row Start Date Marked w/Variable

Figure 6-40

Take this information in Figure 6-40 and proceed with the SCD transform. When you first open the editor, you automatically get the wizard and a start page. Click Next to navigate to the Dimension Table and Business Key Wizard Selection step. First you must select an OLE DB data source and the table that represents the dimension table. The dimension table will be the PayrollDeductItem table. All incoming source columns that either will be used as business keys or will update the dimension columns should be selected and mapped to the matching dimension columns. The Key Type for each input column defaults to "Not a key column." The columns [EmployeePlanIDNbr] and [EmployeeID] that you chose earlier as business keys should both have Key Type property values of "Business Key." Notice that the wizard requires the selection of at least one business key to move to the next step. The wizard should look like Figure 6-41. Click Next to continue.

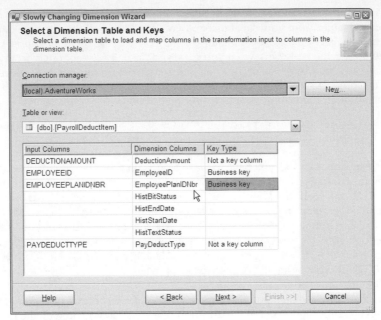

Figure 6-41

The next step will display all remaining fields that are not part of the business key. These are the only fields that are candidates for updating in the dimension table. For each field, select whether the field will be a changing or a historical attribute. If a field is selected as a Changing Attribute, column data in the dimension table will be replaced when a match is made by business key. Fields selected as a Historical Attribute column will be evaluated for changes. If a change is detected in any of these columns, a new row will be created and marked based on the type of Historical Change chosen. Experiment by setting up both columns — [DeductionAmount] and [PayDeductType] — as changing attributes and click Next. You should see the Fixed and Changing Attribute Options step as in Figure 6-42. If the attribute value for field [PayDeductType] is changed to Fixed, the Fixed attributes section would be enabled. Go back and set up the [DeductionAmount] field as a historical attribute and the [PayDeductType] as a changing attribute.

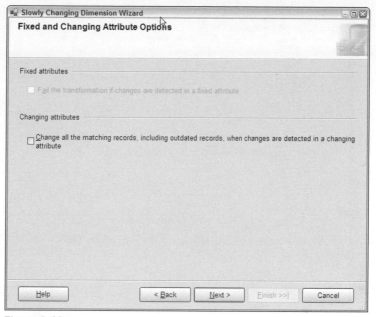

Figure 6-42

Since you've chosen one historical attribute, the Historical Attribute Wizard Selection step will be next. You have the option of choosing one of two methods to store the information historically if the DeductionAmount field changes. Now the extra fields on the PayrollDeductItem table start to make sense. All these fields are not necessary, but they are provided for you to experiment with the different storage options. The HistStartDate and HistEndDate fields would be used for the date-based historical storage option. Use HistBitStatus or HistTextStatus when using the single-column method. This method will update the old record to False or Expired. The new record will have the value of True or Current. Figure 6-43 is an example of the step with the options to use start and end dates enabled. The option to set the date value is expanded to show the available options. You can also use the value of your own variable. Set this step to System::StartTime and continue.

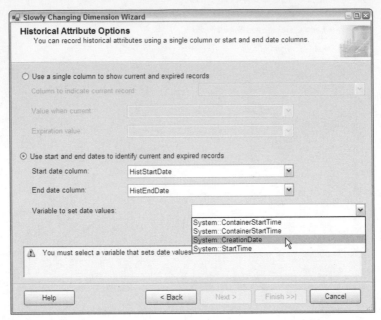

Figure 6-43

The next step is the Inferred Member selections Wizard Selection step. In this example, you should not have any deductions coming from employees that are not in the payroll system, so you don't really need any inferred member support. This option would be useful if you were loading the dimension data from this enrollment input and just needed a placeholder in the dimension data. The inferred member selection step looks like Figure 6-44. If inferred member support is enabled, you must choose to either set the values of all the attributes designated as historical or changing attributes to NULL or use a Boolean column to indicate that the data was loaded as an inferred member.

The completion of the Inferred Member support step brings up a confirmation and final step. Earlier you had gone over all the different outputs that were available in the SCD transform. This step will give you a preview of what outputs will be used based on the settings of the SCD transform. It is against these outputs that you can intercept the stream from the SCD transform and provide your own custom logic prior to, or in place of, the automatically generated OLE Command tasks. However, note that once you add customization, you should not use the wizard again. The wizard will automatically regenerate the components, wiping out any customization that you have added. The completion of the example should look similar to Figure 6-45.

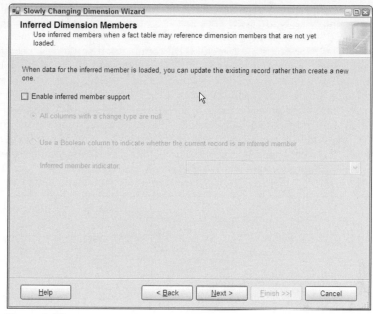

Figure 6-44

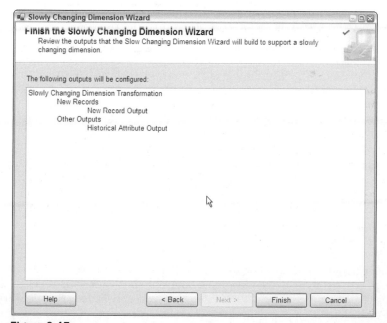

Figure 6-45

After completing the SCD Wizard, your Data Flow design page should have exploded with transform objects to look something like Figure 6-46. There are three pipes coming from the SCD transform. Starting from the left, the pipe updates all matching business key rows in the dimension table with the field contents of the Flat File Source using an OLE DB command. If you have a need to create a Type III SCD, this pipe is the one you want to intercept and use to code your own update. In the middle, the New Output pipe will contain all incoming rows that are identified as new rows. These rows will be combined in the Union All transform with the rows being created as a result of the historical attribute rules and be inserted into the dimension table. In the far-right pipe, the old rows where the historically named attributes show differences will be updated with the markings that identify that the row has expired. Since you selected to use the date ranges, the Derived Column transform generates the expiration date, and the OLE DB command updates each matching row. The second Derived Column task creates the start date and updates each incoming row with that date.

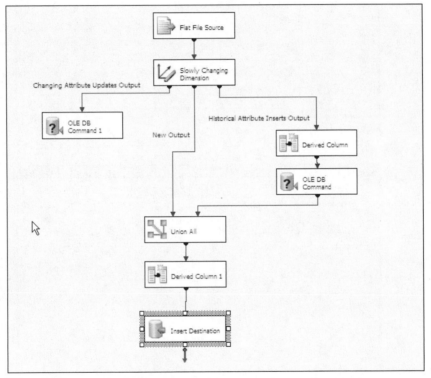

Figure 6-46

To complete the example for production use, I'd recommend examining the OLE DB commands to determine how much you are going to trust incoming data to update your dimensions. If you are updating a data warehouse with data from your OLTP system, you probably have very little work to do. If you are using the SCD transform to import data as was done in this example, the OLE DB commands need to be more discriminatory. For example, fields that have data shouldn't be replaced with missing attributes from the input source. But even with these disclaimers, it should be clear that the SCD Wizard has given you a great start and has generated most of the heavy lifting.

Database Object-Level Tasks

The last section of this chapter is reserved for a set of tasks that are going to be convenient for copying or moving schema and data-level information. These tasks are similar to the Transfer SQL Objects tasks from DTS and should be compatible if you transfer any packages using these tasks from DTS to SSIS. These tasks can do the following:

❑ Move or copy entire databases. This can be accomplished by detaching the database and moving the files (faster) or by moving the schema and content (slower).

❑ Transfer error messages from one server to another.

❑ Move or copy selected or entire SQL Agent jobs.

❑ Move or copy server-level or database-level logins.

❑ Move or copy objects such as tables, views, stored procedures, functions, defaults, user-defined data types, partition functions, partition schemas, schemas (or roles), sql assemblies, user-defined aggregates, user-defined types, and xml schemas. These objects can be copied over by selecting all, by individually selecting each desired object types, or even by selecting individual objects themselves.

❑ Move or copy master stored procedures between two servers.

Transfer Database Task

The Transfer Database task has, as you would expect, a source and destination connection and a database property. The other properties address how the transfer should take place. Figure 6-47 is an example of the Transfer Database task filled out to copy the AdventureWorks database on the same server as a test instance.

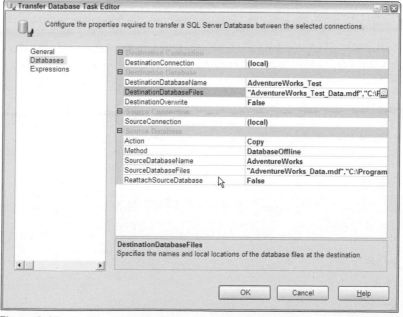

Figure 6-47

Notice that the destination and source are set to the same server. For this copy to work, the DestinationDatabaseFiles property has to be set to new mdf and ldf file names. The property is set by default to the SourceDatabaseFiles property. To set the new destination database file names, click on the ellipsis and then change the Destination File or Destination Folder properties.

The Action property controls whether the task should copy or move the Source Database. The Method property controls whether the database should be copied while the source database is kept online, using SQL Server Management Objects (SMO), or by detaching the database, moving the files, and then reattaching the database. The DestinationOverwrite property controls whether the creation of the destination database should be allowed to overwrite. This includes deleting the database in the destination if it is found. This is useful in the case where you want to copy a database from production into a quality-control or production test environment and the new database should replace any existing similar database. The last property is the ReattachSourceDatabase, which allows control over what action should be taken upon failure of the copy. Use this property if you have a package running on a schedule that takes a production database offline to copy it and you need to guarantee that the database goes back online even if the copy fails.

What's really great about the Transfer Database task is that the logins, roles, object permissions, and even the data come along too. This task may in some instances be too big of a hammer. You may find it more advantageous to just transfer specific sets of objects from one database to another. The next four tasks will give you these abilities.

Transfer Logins Task

The Transfer Logins task focuses only on the security aspects of your databases. Have you ever backed up and restored a database or used the SQL 2000 DTS to transfer logins only to find that the SIDs associated with the logins don't match? Now you can transfer the logins from one database and have them corrected at the destination.

Of course, you'll have your obligatory source and destination connection properties in this editor. You also have the choice to move logins from all databases or selected databases, or you can select individual logins to transfer. Make this choice in the LoginsToTransfer property. The default is SelectedLogIns. The partner properties to LoginsToTransfer are the LogInsList and DatabasesList. One will be activated based on your choice of logins to transfer. Figure 6-48 shows an example Transfer LogIns Task Editor with the selection to copy selected logins.

Two last properties to cover relate to what you want the transfer logins process to do if it encounters an existing login in the destination. If you want the login to be replaced, set the IfObjectExists property to Overwrite. Other options are to fail the task or to skip that login. The long-awaited option to resolve unmatched user security IDs is found in the property CopySids and can be true or false.

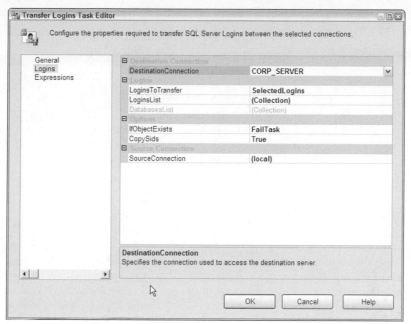

Figure 6-48

Transfer Master Stored Procedures Task

This task is used to transfer master stored procedures. If you need to transfer your own stored procedure, use the Transfer SQL Server Objects task instead. To use this task, set the source and destination connections, and then set the property TransferAllStoredProcedures to true or false. If you set this property to false, you'll be able to select individual master stored procedures to transfer. The remaining property, IfObjectExists, allows you to select what action should take place if a transferring object exists in the destination. Again the choices are to Overwrite, FailTask, or Skip. Figure 6-49 is an example of a completed Transfer Master Stored Procedures Task Editor.

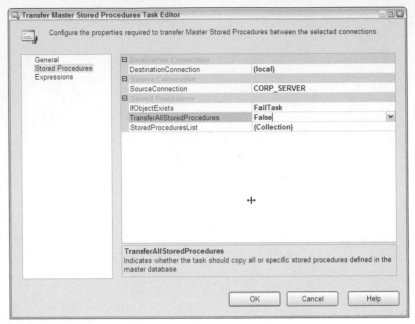

Figure 6-49

Transfer SQL Server Objects Task

The Transfer SQL Server Objects Task is the most flexible of the Transfer tasks. Within this task lies the ability to transfer all types of database objects. To use this task, set the properties to connect to a source and destination database; if the properties aren't visible, expand the Connection category. As you can see in Figure 6-50, there are many options available in this task. Some may be hidden until categories are expanded.

This task exists for those instances when selective object copying is needed. The selectivity is why this is not called the Transfer Database task. You specifically have to set the property CopyData to true to get the bulk transfers of data. The Property CopyAllObjects means that only the tables, views, stored procedures, defaults, rules, and UDFs will be transferred. If you want the table indexes, triggers, primary keys, foreign keys, full-text indexes, or extended properties, you'll have to select these individually. By expanding the ObjectsToCopy category, you'll expose properties that allow individual selections for tables, views, and other programmable objects. The security options give you some of the same abilities as the Transfer Database task. You can transfer Database users, roles, logins, and object-level permissions by selecting true for these properties.

The power lies in the complexity, since this task can be customized and used in packages to move only specific items, for example, during the promotion of objects from one environment to another, or to be less discriminate and copy all tables, views, and other database objects, with or without the data.

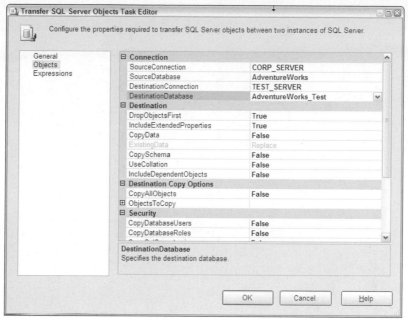

Figure 6-50

Summary

This chapter attempted to stick with the everyday nuts-and-bolts uses of some of the tasks and transforms so that you'll at least be aware of how your old DTS has changed and get a feel for what is now available. Overall there was only enough space for a few simple examples, but you looked at some background concepts of variable scope and the use of expressions in runtime property management.

When you put down this book and begin applying these tasks and transforms to real problems, you may find that your packages are becoming quite involved. Not only do the components need to work together, but you also need to provide error handling, to log activity, and to address the issues of moving packages from environment to environment. Refer to the case study in Chapter 19 to see a more complete picture of all these pieces coming together to transform, load, and then process three completely different formats of payment data. This case study is unique in its use of the SSIS environment as both an ETL and a programming solution to a business problem. The case study also makes use of both the Script task and the Script Component transform to retrieve and set variables that control both the logic flow and the transformation flow in the package. Both the Script task and the Script Component transform are indispensable when you need to do something for which a ready-made task or transform does not yet exist. Read on to Chapter 7 to discover the power and capabilities of the new scripting capabilities in SSIS.

7

Scripting in SSIS

Data Transformation Services has always had the ability to execute custom script tasks. This feature has been greatly enhanced in SQL Server Integration Services. Now you have the ability to develop scripts using Visual Basic.NET, a full-fledged programming language that has many improvements over interpreted scripting languages. In this chapter, we will show you the different scripting options, such as controlling execution flow and performing custom transformations, and demonstrate examples of each.

Scripting Overview

The scripting abilities of SSIS have come a long way from their predecessors in DTS for SQL Server 7.0 and 2000. Let's take a look at the possible scripting options in SSIS 2005.

❏ **ActiveX Script Task:** This task has been with DTS since SQL Server 7.0. It allows the execution of a script written in an ActiveX scripting language, such as VBScript. This task was included for backward compatibility with previous DTS packages and will be removed in the next version of SQL Server, so now is the time to upgrade to the newer components. This task will not be discussed further in this chapter.

❏ **Script Task:** This task is the replacement for the ActiveX script task and is used primarily for controlling package execution. It allows the execution of a script written in Visual Basic.NET. Unfortunately, Visual Basic.NET is the only language you can use to write a script using this task. From your script, however, you can use assemblies written in other .NET languages such as C# or COM components through COM-Interop.

❏ **Script Component:** This component allows for the creation of a totally custom transformation. This component is useful when the built-in transformations are not powerful or flexible enough for your needs.

❏ **Expression Language:** SQL Server Integration Services includes an expression language that allows you to set variable values and perform other operations.

There are three types of scripting that you can perform in SSIS: expressions, Control Flow scripting, and Data Flow scripting.

Expressions are written with the built-in expression language to define property values and provide the logic used to execute certain tasks and transformations. The Derived Column transformation, for example, uses the expression language to determine the value of a derived column.

Control flow scripting is achieved using the Script task. You can control the flow of package execution using a Script task. For example, perhaps you want a notification sent to one person when the package completes during normal business hours but to another person during off-hours. You could use a script task to evaluate the time and send the appropriate notification.

Data flow scripting is used for custom transformations. The Script Component accomplishes this task. An example of using this component would be evaluating the values from a source table and converting them to the expected values in a destination table. Suppose you are importing data from a mainframe, and the original system doesn't have much in the way of data validation, so you must make sure the data is valid before importing it. You may even want to correct the data in some situations. These are perfect tasks for the Script Component.

Expressions

An *expression* is a combination of elements that produces a single value. The elements that make up an expression can include variables, literal values, functions and procedures, and operators. An example expression would be 1 < 2, which produces the value `true`.

> *While the expression language syntax is derived from the C family of languages, it is not case-sensitive.*

Many items in SSIS support expressions. All tasks support expressions for properties, replacing the Dynamic Properties task from DTS. The For Loop and Foreach Loop containers use expressions to specify their looping conditions. See Chapter 4 for more information on these containers. Some tasks, such as the Derived Column task, use expressions to define their output.

Dynamic Properties

Integration Services provides a method of making your tasks dynamic by supporting expressions for task properties.

To view the property expressions for a task, right-click the task and select Edit. This will bring up the task editor window for that task. There will be a list on the left of the different property groupings you can edit. Each task will have an Expressions group that should be the last in the list, as seen in Figure 7-1.

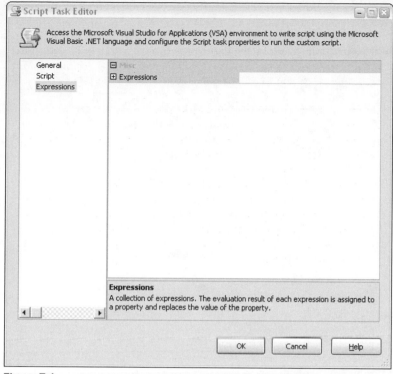

Figure 7-1

The Expressions property editor will have a plus sign next to it that you can use to expand it to see all the expressions set for any properties. To create a new expression or edit an existing one, click in the Expressions text box and then click the ellipsis button. This will bring up the Property Expressions Editor window, as shown in Figure 7-2.

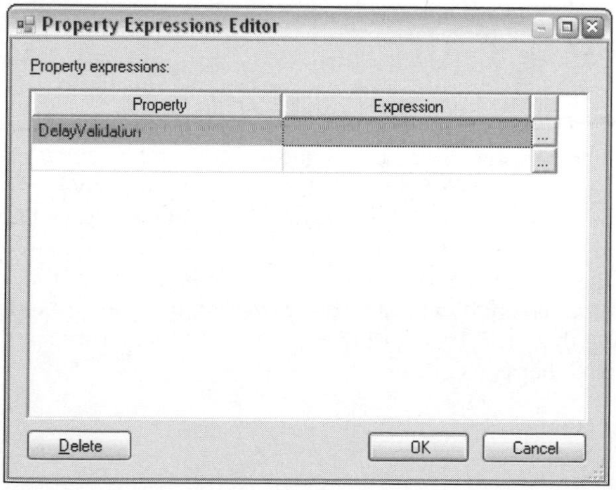

Figure 7-2

The Property Expressions Editor window has a Property column and an Expression column. The Property column provides a drop-down for selecting the task property you wish to create an expression for. Once you have selected the property, you can type the expression into the Expression column or you can click the ellipsis button to bring up the Expression Builder window as shown in Figure 7-3.

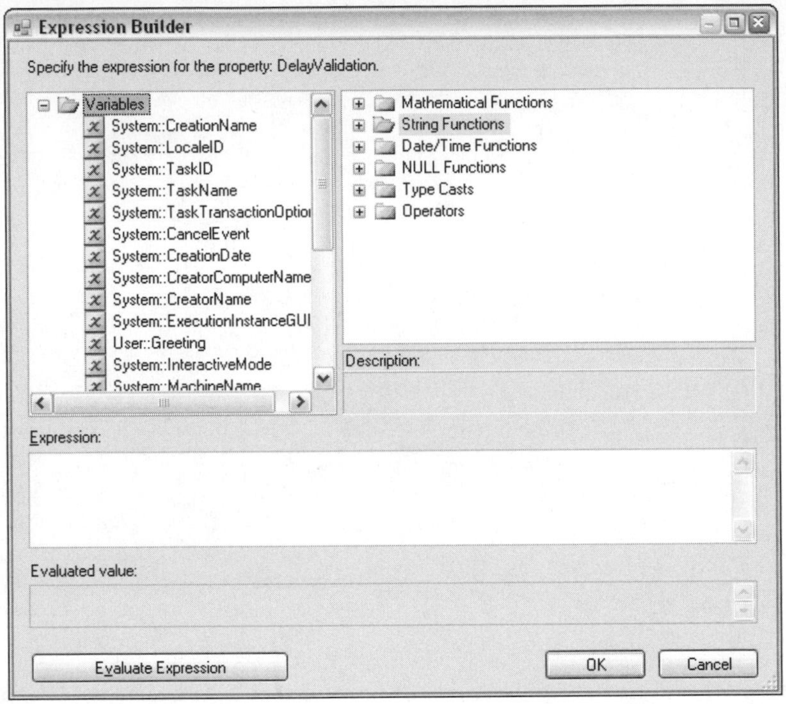

Figure 7-3

The Expression Builder window is simple but powerful. A label at the top lets you know the property whose expression you're editing. There is a tree view on the left of all the variables available to this task. On the right there is a tree view containing groups of all the available expression functions and operators. Selecting a function or operator provides a description of its purpose below the tree view. You can also drag a function to the Expression text box rather than typing it.

The Expression editing text box is located below the variable and function views. This is where you will enter your expression. Since you selected the DelayValidation property in Figure 7-2, you must enter an expression that evaluates to a Boolean value because DelayValidation is a Boolean property. For this example, try putting in 1 < 2. Once you are done, you can test the expression by clicking the Evaluate Expression button in the bottom left. The value will be displayed above this button. You should see the value True printed to the screen. If there is an error evaluating your expression, you will receive a message box explaining the error. Try entering an expression that returns a non-Boolean value such as GETDATE() and see what happens.

Expressions in Tasks

Expressions are also used in some containers and tasks to perform the work of the task. The Derived Column transformation works solely on expressions.

You will now see how expressions are used in the Derived Column transformation. Create a new SSIS package and add a Data Flow task. Open the Data Flow task and add an OLE DB Source. Use the AdventureWorks database and the [HumanResources].[vEmployee] view. Bring over only the FirstName, MiddleName, and LastName columns for this example.

Add a Derived Column task to the Data Flow and connect the OLE DB Source to it. Double-click the Derived Column task to bring up the Transformation Editor window. As you can see in Figure 7-4, this window is similar to the Expression Builder window. The big difference is that the Expression text box is gone. Now there is a grid that is used to define the derived columns.

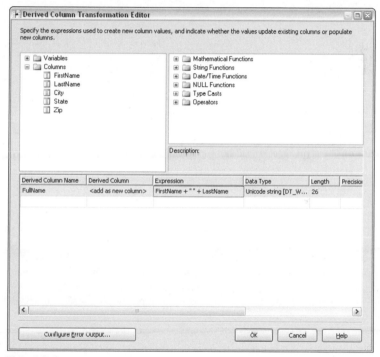

Figure 7-4

In the first row of the grid, type **FullName** in the Derived Column Name field. Next, select <add as new column> in the Derived Column field.

Finally, in the Expression field, enter the following expression:

```
FirstName + " " + MiddleName + " " + LastName
```

This expression is very simple. It concatenates each element of the person's name with a space between each element.

211

Click OK to close the Expression Builder window. Add a Flat File or Excel Destination to the Data Flow and connect the Derived Column task to it. Once you've got your destination set up, run the package.

Your package should run fine with no errors. Open up your destination file to see a list of all the employees with a FullName column at the end of each record. If you used the Excel Destination, you should have a file similar to the one displayed in Figure 7-5.

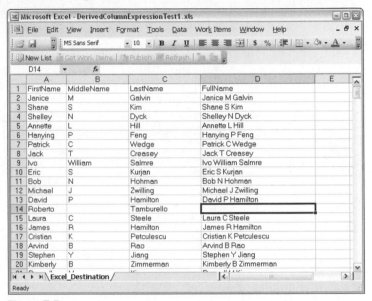

Figure 7-5

You should quickly notice that not every record will have a value in the FullName column. You might also notice that for these records, the person has no value for MiddleName. This is probably not what you expected. Since these records have a NULL value for MiddleName, they caused the expression to evaluate improperly. You must modify the expression to account for NULL values.

Open the Derived Column task again and change the FullName expression to the following:

```
FirstName + (ISNULL(MiddleName)? " " : " " + MiddleName + " ") + LastName
```

This expression uses the ISNULL() function along with the ternary operator to add the MiddleName only if its value is not NULL.

If you've developed only in Visual Basic or similar languages, you may not have heard of the ternary operator. The syntax of the expression language is derived from the C family of languages and inherits this operator from it. The ternary operator works much the same as the IIF() function in Visual Basic. The first argument is the Boolean condition to check — in this case, ISNULL(MiddleName). After the ? is the value returned if the condition is true, and after the colon is the value returned if the condition is false. In this example, a space is returned if MiddleName is NULL; otherwise, the value of MiddleName is returned with a spaced added to the front and back.

While some expression language functions have the same name as T-SQL functions, their syntax is not always the same.

Save the changes, and make sure that you close the Excel file before running the task again. With the new expression, every row should have a value for the FullName column. Your output should look like that in Figure 7-6.

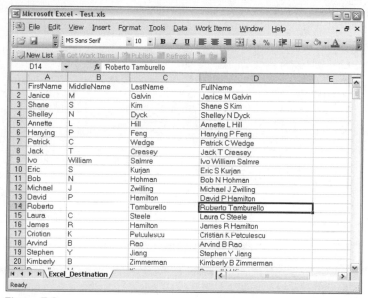

Figure 7-6

Notice that Robert Tamburello had an empty field in the first example, but his full name is now displayed properly.

The new expression language provided with SSIS is powerful and easy to use. For a full explanation of the expression language in SSIS, including documentation for all built-in functions, see SQL Server 2005 Books Online.

Script Tasks

The role of the Script task is primarily to control the flow of the SSIS package. When one of the existing Control Flow Items is not flexible enough to perform the action you desire, you should consider writing a script.

Here you'll create your very first SSIS script. You will create the most basic "Hello World!" example just to see how to add a script to a package, edit it, and execute it.

To create a SSIS project and add a Script task, do the following:

1. Create a new Integration Services Project.

2. Ensure that the Control Flow tab is selected and open the Toolbox.

3. Select the Script task from the Toolbox and drag it to the Control Flow container.

Your screen should look something like Figure 7-7.

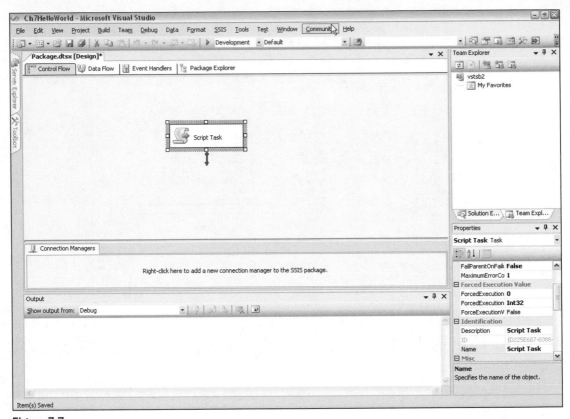

Figure 7-7

To open the Script task, you can double-click it or right-click it and select Edit. This will bring up the Script Task Editor window, as shown in Figure 7-8.

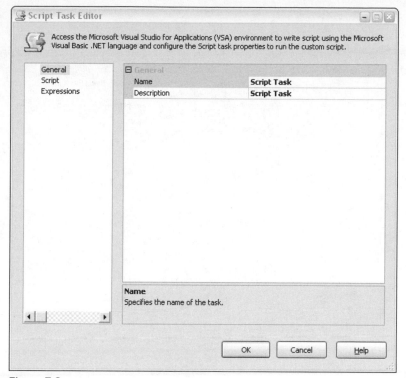

Figure 7-8

This window allows you to set a name for your script and give it a description. Never leave the name set to the default value; always give your script a meaningful name and description. Go ahead and change the Name property from Script Task to HelloWorldScriptTask. Change the description to "Prints 'Hello World!' to the screen."

Now select Script in the left pane. This opens the properties for the actual script as seen in Figure 7-9.

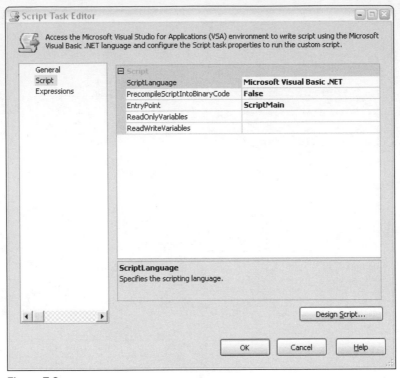

Figure 7-9

You will see five properties on this screen. The following is an explanation of each:

❑ **ScriptLanguage:** This is the language the script will be written in. While it seems that you can set this to something other than its default of Microsoft Visual Basic.NET, you can't. The drop-down provides only this option. Unfortunately, Visual Basic.NET is the only language supported by the Script task in SSIS 2005.

❑ **PrecompileScriptIntoBinaryCode:** When this property is set to true, your script will be compiled before the script executes. This will provide a speed bump on execution. When this flag is set to false, the script isn't compiled until the task is called. This property must be set to true in order to run on a 64-bit system or run as a SQL Server Agent job.

❑ **EntryPoint:** This is the name of the class that contains the Main method that will be called inside your script to begin execution. A class must declare a function named Main in order to be used as an entry point.

❑ **ReadOnlyVariables:** A comma-separated list of SSIS variables that can be read by your Script task.

❑ **ReadWriteVariables:** A comma-separated list of SSIS variables that can be read from and written to by your Script task.

You should also notice a button near the bottom of this window with the caption "Design Script..." This launches the Visual Studio for Applications editor for the script. We'll investigate this later.

The final page available on the left of this dialog is the Expression item. See the "Expressions" section earlier in this chapter for more information on this item.

Ensure that Script is selected in the left pane and then click Design Script. A new window should open that looks like Figure 7-10.

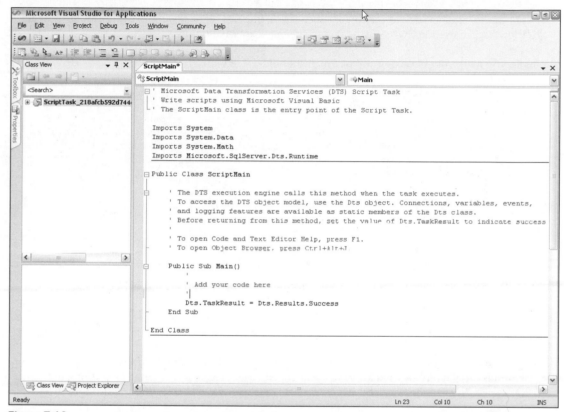

Figure 7-10

All your script editing is done inside the Visual Studio for Applications window. VSA gives you full access to the code editing and debugging features of Visual Studio, including syntax highlighting and IntelliSense.

This script is very basic, but there are a few important things to note. At the top there is a comment that should look like the following:

```
'Microsoft Data Transformation Services (DTS) Script Task
'Write scripts using Microsoft Visual Basic
'The ScriptMain class is the entry point of the Script Task.
```

It's a good idea to replace this comment with a description of the script you are writing. Replace this comment with "A script to display 'Hello World!' to the user."

Next you'll notices some `Import` statements.

```
Imports System
Imports System.Data
Imports System.Math
Imports Microsoft.SqlServer.Dts.Runtime
```

These imports are included at the top of every script. Imports serve two main purposes: to show the libraries that are used in this code file and to alleviate excessive typing.

Finally you have your class definition, which should look like this:

```
Public Class ScriptMain

    ' The DTS execution engine calls this method when the task executes.
    ' To access the DTS object model, use the Dts object. Connections, variables,
    ' events, and logging features are available as static members of the Dts class.
    ' Before returning from this method, set the value of Dts.TaskResult to indicate
    ' success or failure.

    ' To open Code and Text Editor Help, press F1.
    ' To open Object Browser, press Ctrl+Alt+J.

    Public Sub Main()
        '
        ' Add your code here
        '
        Dts.TaskResult = Dts.Results.Success
    End Sub

End Class
```

By now you've probably noticed all the references to DTS. This is because DTS was still the name for SSIS until pretty late in the development cycle. It just wasn't feasible to rename everything everywhere to SQL Server Integration Services, so you may still see references to DTS littered throughout SSIS.

This class definition is bare-bones. It contains a comment on how things work and a reminder to always set the value of `Dts.TaskResult`. You must always set this value to either a Success or Failure status, otherwise the SSIS runtime will not know if your script succeeded, regardless of any actions it may have performed.

Directly above the line setting Dts.TaskResult, add Msgbox("Hello World"). Now close the VSA editor, and your changes will be saved automatically. Click OK on the Script Task Editor window to close it. To run your script, press the F5 key. This simple task should execute and display "Hello World" in a message box. You must close the message box for the task to complete execution.

The Dts Object

The `Dts` object is an instance of `Microsoft.SqlServer.Dts.Tasks.ScriptTask.ScriptObjectModel`. The `Dts` object is your window into the package in which your script executes. The `Dts` object has seven properties and one method that allow you to interact with the package. Following is an explanation of these members.

❑   Connections — A collection of connections defined in the package. You can use these connections in your script to retrieve any extra data you may need.

❑   Events — A collection of events that are defined for the package. You can use this interface to fire off these predefined events and any custom events.

❑   ExecutionValue — A read-write property that allows you to specify additional information about your task's execution using a user-defined object. This can be any information you want.

❑   TaskResult — This property allows you to return the Success or Failure status of your script task to the package. This is your main way of controlling flow in your package. This property must be set before exiting your script.

❑   Transaction — Gets the transaction that is associated with the container in which your script is running.

❑   VariableDispenser — Gets the VariableDispenser object that you can use to retrieve variables.

❑   Variables — A collection of all the variables that are available to your script. Provides an easier-to-use alternative to the VariableDispenser object.

❑   Log — This method allows you to write to any log providers that have been enabled.

This may not seem like much, but the Dts object provides almost everything you need to interact with the executing package. The Dts object is available only in the Script task, not in the Script Component.

Accessing Variables

Variables are an important feature of the Script task. This type of variable is not the typical type that you would create in your script code. Rather, these variables are a communication device between your Script task and the rest of your package.

Variables in SSIS packages take on two forms: read-only and read-write. Read-only variables are variables that have been made available to your script for reading only. You cannot update the value of read-only variables using your script. Likewise, read-write variables can be updated through script code.

Variables can be accessed two ways in a Script task. The VariableDispenser object provides methods for locking variables for read-only or read-write access and then retrieving them. This was the standard way of accessing variables in scripts, but during early testing of SSIS, many users complained of the cumbersomeness of the API.

To retrieve a variable using the VariableDispenser object, you would have to write code like the following:

```
Dim vars As Variables
Dts.VariableDispenser.LockForRead("SomeVariable")
Dts.VariableDispenser.GetVariables(vars)
MsgBox(vars(0).Value)
```

Using four lines of code to read a variable value is not very efficient, so the Variables collection on the Dts object and the ReadOnlyVariables and ReadWriteVariables properties for the Script task were introduced.

The `ReadOnlyVariables` and `ReadWriteVariables` properties tell the Script task which variables to lock and how. The `Variables` collection in the `Dts` object then gets populated with these variables. The code to retrieve a variable then becomes much simpler, down to only one line:

```
Msgbox(Dts.Variables("SomeVariable").Value)
```

Attempting to read a variable from the `Variables` collection that hasn't been specified in one of the variable properties of the task will throw an exception. Likewise, attempting to write to a variable not included in the `ReadWriteVariables` property also throws an exception.

Although Visual Basic.NET is not case-sensitive, SSIS variables are.

To access `Variables` inside the Script Component, you must add them to the `ReadOnlyVariables` or `ReadWriteVariables` properties. Inside the component, you access them directly off the intrinsic `Variables` object. To access the value of a variable named `StringVariable` with a type of `String` from a Script Component, use code like this:

```
Variables.StringVariable
```

Unlike variables stored in the `Variables` collection, which must be accessed through a `Variable` object, these variables are of the type they are declared to be in the Variables editor. The above code returns a string since `StringVariable` is declared as a string.

While it is much easier to use variables in the Script Component, it is inconsistent and cumbersome to have so many different ways to access variables in SSIS scripts.

Events

The Script task can raise events, which can be logged with a log provider. If you have done any Windows GUI programming, you will be familiar with events. An *event* is a message sent from some object saying that something just happened or is about to happen.

Programs capture events with *event handlers*. You register an event handler for each event you wish to act upon. Your script can raise events, including custom ones you have defined.

To raise or *fire* an event, you use the `Events` property of the `Dts` object. The `Events` property is an instance of the `IDTSComponentEvents` interface. This interface specifies seven methods for firing events:

❑   `FireBreakpointHit` — Fires an event when a breakpoint is hit.

❑   `FireError` — Fires an event when an error occurs.

❑   `FireInformation` — Fires an event with information. You can fire this event when you want some set of information to be logged, possibly for auditing later.

❑   `FireProgress` — Fires an event when a certain progress level has been met.

❑   `FireQueryCancel` — Fires an event to determine if package execution should stop.

❑   `FireWarning` — Fires an event that is less serious than an error, but more than just information.

❑   `FireCustomEvent` — Fires a custom defined event.

In SSIS, any events you fire will be written to all enabled log handlers that are set to log that event. Logging allows you to see what happened with your script when you're not there to watch it run. This is useful for troubleshooting and auditing purposes.

To configure your SSIS package for logging, go to SSIS ⇨ Logging in the Business Intelligence Designer Studio. The Configure SSIS Log dialog will appear. Select SSIS log provider for XML files in the Provider Type drop-down and click Add. Select <new connection> for the configuration of the XML file provider to bring up the File Connection Manager Editor. For Usage type, select Create File and specify a path to a file name log.xml. Click OK to close the File Connection Manager. Make sure the box next to the provider name is checked so that the log will be used. Your screen should look something like Figure 7-11.

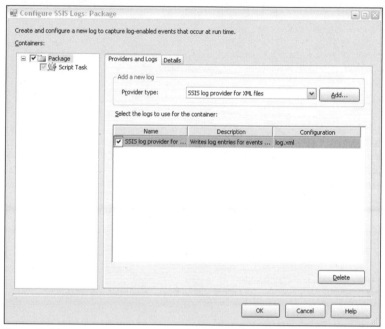

Figure 7-11

Now go to the Details tab and make sure the box next to OnInformation is checked. Only the events that are checked will be logged to the providers.

Edit the script of the HelloWorldScriptTask in your HelloWorld package. Replace the Msgbox("Hello World") line with the following code:

```
Dts.Events.FireInformation(1, "MyScriptTask", "Some Info here", "", 0, False)
```

The first argument to the FireInformation method is the information code. It can be anything you want; its purpose is to identify the message. The next argument specifies the source of the event. Again, it can really be anything you want. The third argument is the actual information message. The fourth argument is the path to the help file you wish to associate this information with. It's fine to pass an empty string; a help file is not required. The fifth argument is the help context that identities the help topic in the help file for this message. Since you're not using a help file, 0 is fine. The final argument is a

Boolean flag that indicates whether this event should be fired more than once. Firing events can be expensive, so if this flag is set to false, this event will not be fired again for the duration of the package execution, even if this script is called again.

If you run your package, the XML file you specified should be created and have content similar to the following:

```
<record>
  <event>OnInformation</event>
  <message>Some Info here</message>
  <computer>LAPTOP</computer>
  <operator>LAPTOP\Jason</operator>
  <source>Script Task</source>
  <sourceid>{84D266FB-16F7-44EB-B745-27645494AC9D}</sourceid>
  <executionid>{E2A4A645-F9CA-4027-A9B5-1C57E5337D98}</executionid>
  <starttime>8/7/2005 9:54:45 PM</starttime>
  <endtime>8/7/2005 9:54:45 PM</endtime>
  <datacode>1</datacode>
  <databytes>0x</databytes>
</record>
```

You'll have other events in the file such as Package Start and Package End, but this is the event that your code fired. This record contains the basic information on the event including the message, event execution time, and the computer and user that raised the event.

You can also specify event handlers to perform other operations when an event is fired. This is done on the Event Handlers view in the package designer. These event handlers, however, are not covered in this chapter. For more information on Event Handlers, see Chapter 13 of this book and also Books Online.

Logging

The Log method of the Dts object writes a message to all enabled log providers. The Log method has three arguments.

- ❑   messageText — The message to log
- ❑   dataCode — A field for logging a message code
- ❑   dataBytes — A field for logging binary data

The Log method is similar to the FireInformation method of the Events property, but it is easier to use and more efficient. The following code logs a simple message with some binary data to all available log providers. This is quite useful for troubleshooting and auditing purposes. You can write out information at important steps in your script and even print out variable values to help you track down a problem.

```
Dts.Log("my message", 0, myByteArray)
```

Script Task Debugging

Debugging is an important new feature of scripting in SSIS. Gone are the days of using the Msgbox() function to see the value of variables. Using the Visual Studio for Applications environment, you now have the ability to set breakpoints, examine variables, and even evaluate expressions interactively.

Breakpoints

Breakpoints allow you to flag a line of code where execution pauses while debugging. Breakpoints are invaluable in determining what's going on inside your code. They allow you to step into your code and see what happens as it executes.

You can set a breakpoint in several ways. One way is to click in the gray margin at the left of the text editor at the line where you wish to stop execution. Another way is to move the cursor to the line you wish to break on and hit F9. Yet another way is to select Debug ⇨ Toggle Breakpoint.

To continue execution from a breakpoint, press F10 to step to the next line or F5 to run all the way through to the next breakpoint.

When you have a breakpoint set on a line, the line gets a red highlight like the one shown in Figure 7-12.

Figure 7-12

When a Script task has a breakpoint set somewhere in the code, it will have a red dot on it similar to the one in Figure 7-13.

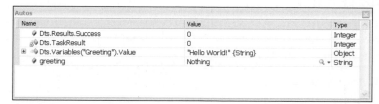

Figure 7-13

Autos, Locals, and Watches

The Visual Studio environment provides you with some powerful views into what is happening with the execution of your code. These views consist of three windows known as the Autos window, Locals window, and Watch window. These windows share a similar layout and display the value of expressions and variables, though each has a distinct method determining what data to display.

The Autos window displays the current statement, as well as three statements behind and in front of the current statement. For the running example, the Autos window would appear, as in Figure 7-14.

Autos			
Name	Value	Type	
Dts.Results.Success	0	Integer	
Dts.TaskResult	0	Integer	
Dts.Variables("Greeting").Value	"Hello World!" {String}	Object	
greeting	Nothing	String	

Figure 7-14

The Locals window displays variables that are local to the current context. It looks virtually identical to the Autos window.

Watches are another very important feature of debugging. Watches allow you to specify a variable to watch. You can set up a watch to break execution when a variable's value changes or some other condition is met. This will allow you to see exactly when something is happening, such as a variable that has an unexpected value.

To add a watch, select the variable you want to watch inside the script, right-click it, and select Add Watch. This will add an entry to the Watch window.

You can also use the Quick Watch window accessible from the Debug menu or through the Ctrl+Alt+Q key combination. The Quick Watch window is shown in Figure 7-15.

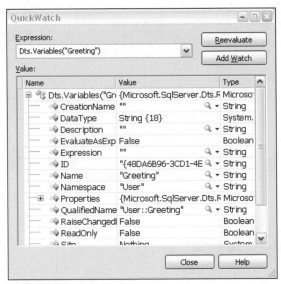

Figure 7-15

This window allows you to evaluate an expression at runtime and see the result in the window. You can then click the Add Watch button to move it to the Watch window.

The Immediate Window

The Immediate window allows you to evaluate expressions, execute procedures, and print out variable values. It is really a mode of the Command window, which allows you to issue commands to the IDE.

For more information on how to use the Command window and its available commands, see the MSDN documentation for Visual Studio.

The Immediate window is very useful while testing. You can see the outcome of several different scenarios. Suppose you have an object obj of type MyType. MyType declares a method called DoMyStuff() that takes a single integer as an argument. Using the Immediate window, you could pass different values into the DoMyStuff() method and see the results. To evaluate an expression in the Immediate window and see its results, you must start the command with a question mark (?).

```
?obj.DoMyStuff(2)
"Hello"
```

Commands are terminated by pressing the Enter key. The results of the execution are printed on the next line. In this case, calling DoMyStuff() with a value of 2 returns the string "Hello."

You can also use the Immediate window to change the value of variables. If you have a variable defined in your script and you want to change its value, perhaps for negative error testing, you can use this window, as shown in Figure 7-16.

Figure 7-16

In Figure 7-16, the value of the variable greeting is printed out. The value returned from an expression is always printed on the line directly below the expression. After the value is printed, it is changed to "Goodbye Cruel World." The value is then queried again and the new value is printed.

Using .NET Assemblies

The capability to reuse code written in other languages is the hallmark of COM and its successor, .NET. While you can only write SSIS scripts using Visual Basic.NET, you can reuse assemblies created using any .NET language including C#, J#, and even Delphi.

Using assemblies gives you the ability to reuse your existing code. You may have already written code that performs data validation; now you can reuse it in your SSIS package. No sense in rewriting code that is already tested and in use.

To use an assembly in your script, you must reference it. To reference it, in turn, you must put it in a location accessible to SSIS. SSIS can only use assemblies located in the .NET framework installation folder for version 2.0.

To add a reference, you must be in the Visual Studio for Applications environment for editing your script code. Go to the Project menu and select Add Reference. The Add Reference window will appear as shown in Figure 7-17.

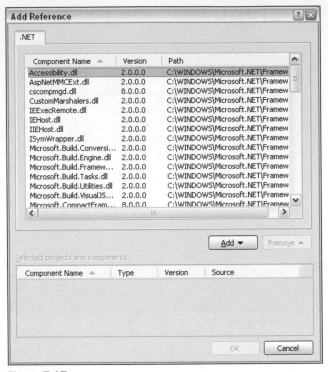

Figure 7-17

Select the assemblies from the list that you wish to reference and click the Add button. They will be added to the component list. Once you're done, click OK to add the references to your project. Now you can use any objects located in the referenced assemblies just like any other object.

Alternatively, you can add and remove references using the Project Explorer. Expand the References node to see all the references in your project. Right-click a reference and select Remove to remove it from the project. To add a reference, right-click the References node and select Add Reference to bring up the Add Reference window.

Open your HelloWorld package and edit the Script task. Add a reference to the System.Xml.dll by bringing up the Add Reference dialog, selecting the library from the list, and clicking Add. Click OK to close the dialog.

You can now use all the classes in the System.Xml namespace, and the VSA editor will provide full IntelliSense as with all the other objects.

Structured Exception Handling

Structured Exception Handling (SEH) allows you to catch specific errors as they occur and perform any appropriate action needed. In many cases, you just want to log the error and stop execution, but there are some instances where you may want to try a different plan of action, depending on the error.

Here is an example of exception handling in Visual Basic.NET.

```
Public Sub Main()
    Try
        Dim fileText As String
        FileIO.FileSystem.ReadAllText("C:\data.csv")
    Catch ex As System.IO.FileNotFoundException
        'Log Error Here
        Dts.TaskResult = Dts.Results.Failure
        Return
    End Try
    Dts.TaskResult = Dts.Results.Success
End Sub
```

This trivial example attempts to read the contents of the file at `C:\data.csv` into a string variable. That is why this code was placed in a `Try` block. It is trying to perform an action that has the potential for failure. If the file isn't there, a `System.IO.FileNotFoundException` is thrown. The `Catch` block is the error handler for this specific exception. You would probably want to add some code to log the error inside the `Catch` block. The result is set to `Failure` and the script is exited with the `Return` statement. If the file is found, no exception is thrown, and the next line of code is executed. In this case, it would go to the line that sets the `TaskResult` to Success, right after the `End Try` statement.

If an exception is not caught, perhaps because an appropriate `Catch` statement is not in place, the exception propagates up the call stack until an appropriate handler is found. If none is found, the exception stops execution.

The same code executed with the `Catch` statement removed will raise an error window like that in Figure 7-18.

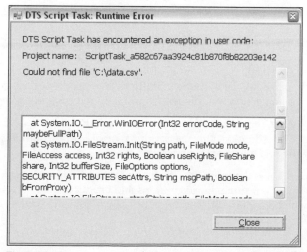

Figure 7-18

You can have as many `Catch` blocks associated with a `Try` block as you wish. When an exception is raised, the `Catch` blocks are walked from top to bottom until an appropriate one is found that fits the context of the exception. Only the first block that matches will be executed. Execution does not fall through to the next block, so it's important to place the most specific `Catch` block first and descend to the least specific. A `Catch` block specified with no filter will catch all exceptions.

Another feature of SEH is the `Finally` block. The `Finally` block exists inside a `Try` block and executes after any code in the `Try` block and any `Catch` blocks that were entered. Code in the `Finally` block is always executed, regardless of what happens in the `Try` block and in any `Catch` blocks. You would put code to dispose of any resources such as open files or database connections in the `Finally` block. Following is an example of using the `Finally` block to free up a connection resource.

```
Public Sub Main()
    Dim con As SqlConnection = New SqlConnection(myConStr)
    Try
        con.Open()
        'do stuff with con
    Catch ex As SqlException
        'Log Error Here
        Dts.TaskResult = Dts.Results.Failure
        Return
    Finally
        If Not con Is Nothing Then con.Dispose()
    End Try
    Dts.TaskResult = Dts.Results.Success
End Sub
```

For a full explanation of the Try/Catch/Finally structure in Visual Basic.NET, see the language reference in MSDN.

Script Component

The Script Component provides another type of scripting in SSIS. This component can be used only in the Data Flow portion of your SSIS package. The purpose of this component is to provide, consume, or transform data. Script components come in the following three types:

❑ **Source Type Component:** The role of this Script Component is to provide data to your Data Flow task. You can define outputs and their types and use script code to populate them. An example would be reading in a complex file format, possibly XML or something more archaic like a COBOL copybook file from the mainframe. I've worked with several files that were way too complex for any generic flat file reader and required custom coding to read.

❑ **Destination Type Component:** This type of Script Component consumes data much like an Excel or Flat File destination. One use for this type of Script Component is outputting data for batch processing to a mainframe system.

❑ **Transformation Type Component:** This type of Script Component can perform custom transformations on data. It consumes input columns and produces output columns. You would use the component when one of the built-in transformations just isn't flexible enough.

Using the Script Component

Here you'll see how to create and use a Script Component. In this example, you have to process a flat file and make sure the data is good. The good records will go on to their appropriate table while the questionable records will be sent to an error table for manual cleansing.

You're going to import contacts from a mainframe application that allowed the users to enter pretty much anything they wanted into a field. The database has a certain set of requirements for data. If the imported data doesn't meet these criteria, you'll put it in an error queue to be handled manually.

The contacts table is created with the following script:

```
CREATE TABLE dbo.Contacts
(
  ContactID int NOT NULL IDENTITY (1, 1),
  FirstName varchar(50) NOT NULL,
  LastName varchar(50) NOT NULL,
  City varchar(25) NOT NULL,
  State varchar(15) NOT NULL,
  Zip char(10) NULL
)  ON [PRIMARY]
```

The error queue table is virtually identical:

```
CREATE TABLE dbo.ContactsErrorQueue
(
  ContactErrorID int NOT NULL IDENTITY (1, 1),
  FirstName varchar(50) NULL,
  LastName varchar(50) NULL,
  City varchar(50) NULL,
  State varchar(50) NULL,
  Zip varchar(50) NULL
)  ON [PRIMARY]
```

The main difference is that all the data fields are nullable and all are varchar(50).

Finally, the data format is fixed-width and is defined as follows.

Field	Starting Position
First Name	1
Last Name	11
City	26
State	44
Zip	52

The data file will look something like the following:

```
Jason      Gerard       Jacksonville    FL       32276-1911
Joseph     McClung      JACKSONVILLE    FLORIDA  322763939
Andrei     Ranga        Jax             fl       32276
Chad       Crisostomo   Orlando         FL       32746
Andrew     Ranger       Jax             fl
```

Create a new package and add a Data Flow. Drag a Flat File Source to the Data Flow editor pane. Double-click the Flat File Source. In the Connection Manager, click New next to the Flat File Connection Manager drop-down. This will bring up the Flat File Connection Manager Editor. Name the Connection Manager "Contacts Mainframe Extract."

Click Browse and select the Contacts.dat file. Change the format to Fixed Width and click Columns on the left. Specify the Row Width as 62. Once you have the column boundaries marked, click Advanced on the left and give the columns meaningful names. Finally, click Preview on the left to see what your imported data will look like. Your preview should look like Figure 7-19.

Figure 7-19

Now, add a Script Component to the Data Flow. When you drop the Script Component, you will be prompted to pick the type of component to create, as shown in Figure 7-20. Select Transformation and click OK.

Drag a connection from the Flat File Source to the Script Component. Double-click the Script Component to bring up the Script Transformation Editor. You will notice that Input Name is a drop-down with a value of Input 0. You could have more sources pointed to this script component. You would select which columns from each input here.

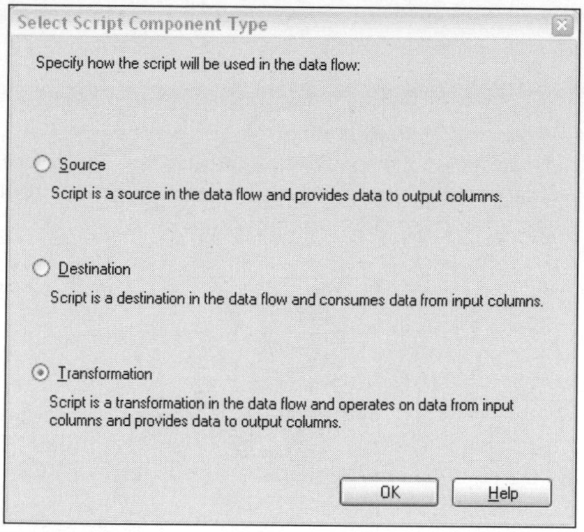

Figure 7-20

Select all of the input columns. Now click Input and Outputs on the left. Here you can see the properties for your input and output columns. You can also define multiple outputs.

Expand Output 0, select Output Columns, and then click Add Column at the bottom. Set the name of this column to GoodFlag and change the DataType property to Boolean [DT_BOOL].

Now click Script on the left and then click the Design Script button.

This will open up the now familiar Visual Studio for Applications environment. The script provided is different from the one provided with the Script task.

```
' Microsoft SQL Server Integration Services user script component
' This is your new script component in Microsoft Visual Basic .NET
' ScriptMain is the entrypoint class for script components

Imports System
Imports System.Data
Imports System.Math
Imports Microsoft.SqlServer.Dts.Pipeline.Wrapper
Imports Microsoft.SqlServer.Dts.Runtime.Wrapper

Public Class ScriptMain
  Inherits UserComponent

  Public Overrides Sub Input0_ProcessInputRow(ByVal Row As Input0Buffer)
    '
    ' Add your code here
    '
  End Sub

End Class
```

The imports are different. The three `System` namespace imports are the same, but the pipeline and runtime wrapper imports are new.

You will also notice that the `ScriptMain` class now inherits from `UserComponent`. Gone is the `Public Sub Main()`. Now you have a new method named `Input0_ProcessInputRow` that takes an `Input0Buffer` as its only parameter. If you had more inputs, you would see corresponding methods for each. The `Input0Buffer` class is auto-generated by the Script Component. It contains all the input and output columns as strongly typed properties (see Figure 7-21).

Figure 7-21

If you look in the Project Explorer, you will see three source files: `BufferWrapper`, `ComponentWrapper`, and `ScriptMain`.

`BufferWrapper` contains the custom-generated `ScriptBuffers` that your component will use. In this case, the only class in the file is `Input0Buffer`. Do not edit this code because it will be overwritten by the environment. The same goes for the code in `ComponentWrapper`, which contains `UserComponent`, the base class for your `ScriptMain` class. Finally, double-clicking `ScriptMain` will take you back to where you started with the `ScriptMain` class.

The rules for data validation are as follows:

❑   All fields are required except for the zip code.

❑   The zip code must be in the format DDDDD-DDDD or DDDDD where D is a digit from 0 through 9. If the zip code is valid for the first five characters but not afterward, strip the trailing records and use the first five.

❑   The state must be two uppercase characters.

The data will be validated using regular expressions. Regular expressions are a powerful utility that should be in every developer's tool belt. They allow you to perform powerful string matching and replacement routines. An excellent tutorial on regular expressions can be found at `http://www .regular-expressions.info`.

The regular expressions for matching the data are as follows:

`^\d{5}([\-]\d{4})?$`	Matches a five-digit or nine-digit zip code with dash
`\b([A-Z]{2})\b`	Ensures that the state is only two capital characters

Add the following code to the Script Component:

```vb
Imports System
Imports System.Data
Imports System.Math
Imports System.Text.RegularExpressions
Imports Microsoft.SqlServer.Dts.Pipeline.Wrapper
Imports Microsoft.SqlServer.Dts.Runtime.Wrapper

Public Class ScriptMain
    Inherits UserComponent

    Private zipRegex As Regex = New Regex("^\d{5}([\@@hy]\d{4})?$", RegexOptions.None)
    Private stateRegex As Regex = New Regex("\b([A@@hyZ]{2})\b", RegexOptions.None)
    Public Overrides Sub Input0_ProcessInputRow(ByVal Row As Iput0Buffer)
        'all fields except zip must have a value
        Dim isGood As Boolean = False
        If Row.FirstName_IsNull Or Row.LastName_IsNull Or Row.City_IsNull Or _
        Row.State_IsNull Then
            Row.GoodFlag = False
            Return
        End If

        If Not Row.Zip_IsNull Then
            Dim zip As String = Row.Zip.Trim()
            'zip must match regex if present
            If zipRegex.IsMatch(zip) Then
                Row.CleanedZip = zip
                isGood = True
            Else
                'try to clean up the zip

                If zip.Length > 5 Then
                    zip = zip.Substring(0, 5)
                    If zipRegex.IsMatch(zip) Then
                        Row.CleanedZip = zip
                        isGood = True
                    Else
                        isGood = False
                    End If
                End If
            End If
        End If

        If isGood Then

            Dim state As String
            state = Row.State.Trim().ToUpper()
            If stateRegex.IsMatch(state) Then
                Row.CleanedState = state
            Else
                isGood = False
            End If
        End If
        Row.GoodFlag = isGood

    End Sub
End Class
```

This code performs the data rules. First, the two regular expressions are defined that will be used to check the format of zip codes and states. In the `Input0_ProcessInputRow` method where execution starts, all fields are checked for NULL value except for the zip code. SSIS adds a property for each column in the row with the format `ColumnName_IsNull`. This property returns true if the particular column is NULL.

Next, if the Zip column is not NULL, its value is matched against the regular expression to see if it's in the correct format. If it is, the value is assigned to the CleanedZip column, since this is the column that will be stored in the destination table. If the value of the Zip column doesn't match the regular expression, the script checks to see if it is at least five characters long. If so, the first five characters are matched against the regular expression. If they match, these five characters are assigned to the CleanedZip column; otherwise, the GoodFlag is set to False.

Before checking the state, the GoodFlag is checked to make sure everything is good so far. If it's not, there is no point in checking the state.

The state is trimmed of any leading or trailing white space and then converted to uppercase. It is then matched against the regular expression. This expression simply checks to see if it's two uppercase letters between A and Z. If it is, the GoodFlag is set to true and the trimmed and uppercased value is assigned to the CleanedState field; otherwise, the GoodFlag is set to False.

To send the data to the appropriate table based on the `GoodFlag`, you must use the Conditional Split task. Add this task to the Data Flow designer. Connect the output of the Script Component task to the Conditional Split transformation. Edit the Conditional Split transformation and add an output with the condition `GoodFlag == TRUE`. The rows with this column set to true will be split from the rows where this column is false.

Now, add two OLE DB Destinations to the Data Flow designer. One should point to the Contacts table, the other to the ContactsErrorQueue table. Drag the output of the Conditional Split task to the OLE DB Destination for the Contacts table. Since this task has multiple outputs, select the output with the condition of `GoodFlag == TRUE`. Now drag the other output of the split to the ContactsErrorQueue destination.

Your final Data Flow should look something like Figure 7-22. A RowCount transformation and Data View have been added for debugging purposes. These will be discussed in the next section.

If you run this package with the Contacts.dat file provided in the downloadable source code package at www.wrox.com, 13 rows should go to the Contacts table and 2 should go to the error queue table.

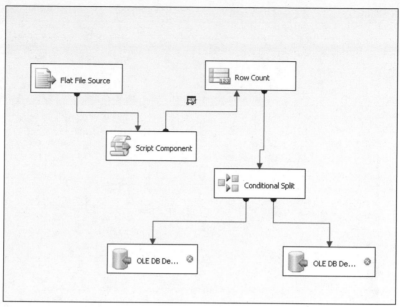

Figure 7-22

Debugging the Script Component

Previously, you looked at using the Visual Studio for Applications environment to debug a Script task using breakpoints and other tools. Unfortunately, you do not have the ability to debug the Script Component using this environment. Any breakpoints that you set will be ignored. Instead, you must resort to inspecting the data stream using the RowCount component or a Data Viewer.

The RowCount task is very straightforward; it simply states how many rows passed through it. The Data Viewer is a much better way to debug your component, however. To add a Data Viewer, select the connector arrow, leaving the component that you want to see data for. In the previous example, this would be the connector from the Script Component to the Conditional Split task. Right-click this connection and select Data Viewers. The Data Flow Path Editor will pop up. Click Add to add the data viewer. On the Configure Data Viewer screen, select Grid as the type. Click the Grid tab and make sure all the columns you wish to see are in the Displayed Columns list. Close out this window and the Data Path Flow Editor window by clicking OK. Figure 7-23 shows the Data Path Flow Editor with a Data Viewer configured on Output 0.

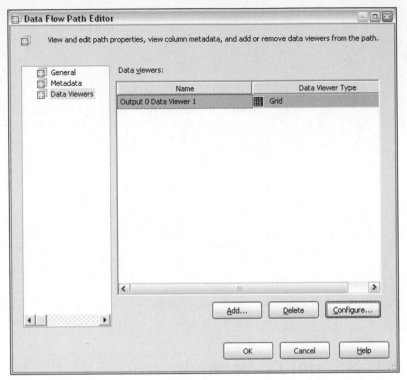

Figure 7-23

Now when you run this package again, you will get a Data Viewer window after the Script Component has executed. This view will show the data output by the Script Component. Figure 7-24 shows an example. Click the Play button to continue package execution, or simply close the window.

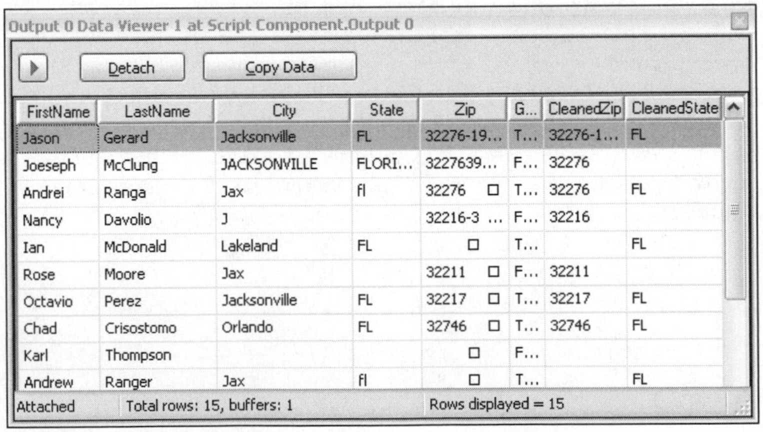

FirstName	LastName	City	State	Zip	G...	CleanedZip	CleanedState
Jason	Gerard	Jacksonville	FL	32276-19...	T...	32276-1...	FL
Joeseph	McClung	JACKSONVILLE	FLORI...	3227639...	F...	32276	
Andrei	Ranga	Jax	fl	32276 ☐	T...	32276	FL
Nancy	Davolio	J		32216-3 ...	F...	32216	
Ian	McDonald	Lakeland	FL	☐	T...		FL
Rose	Moore	Jax		32211 ☐	F...	32211	
Octavio	Perez	Jacksonville	FL	32217 ☐	T...	32217	FL
Chad	Crisostomo	Orlando	FL	32746 ☐	T...	32746	FL
Karl	Thompson			☐	F...		
Andrew	Ranger	Jax	fl	☐	T...		FL

Attached · Total rows: 15, buffers: 1 · Rows displayed = 15

Figure 7-24

While using the Data Viewer certainly helps with debugging, it is no replacement for being able to step into the code. Hopefully future versions of the Script Component will have this ability.

Summary

In this chapter, you learned about the available scripting options in SSIS. You learned how to use the expression language built into SSIS to set properties dynamically. You saw how the expression language is used in some tasks to perform their work. You learned how the Script task works and how it can be used in your package. Finally, you learned how to use the Script Component to transform your data.

Experiment with the scripting features of SSIS until you have a good handle on them, and you will find all kinds of uses for them. For more information on anything covered in this chapter, refer to SQL Server Books Online.

Accessing Heterogeneous Data

In Chapter 7 you discovered the many scripting enhancements available in SSIS. In this chapter, you'll learn about importing and working with data from heterogeneous, or non–SQL Server, sources. In today's Enterprise environment, data may exist in many diverse systems, such as mainframes, Oracle, Office documents, XML, or flat files, to name just a few. The data may be generated within the company, or it may be delivered through the Internet from a trading partner. Whether you need to import data from a spreadsheet to initially populate a table in a new database application, pull data from other sources for your data warehouse, or rely on a Web service to grab up-to-the-minute information, accessing heterogeneous data is probably a big part of your job.

You can load data into SQL Server using SSIS from any ODBC-compliant or OLE DB-compliant source. Many ODBC drivers and OLE DB providers are supplied by Microsoft for sources like Excel, Access, FoxPro, Paradox, Oracle, and dBase. Others are available from database vendors. A variety of data source components are found in SSIS. These include Excel, Flat File, XML, DataReader (which is used to connect to .NET sources), OLE DB (which allows connections to many different types of data), and Raw File (which is a special source used to read data that has been previously exported to a Raw File destination). If the supplied data sources do not meet your needs, it is also possible to create custom data sources.

This chapter will walk you through accessing data from several of the most common sources: Excel, MS Access, Oracle, XML, and Web Services. Each one is relatively easy to work with, but each is configured a bit differently. Excel is often used as a quick way to store data because spreadsheets are easy to set up and use. Access applications are frequently upsized to SQL Server as the size of the database and number of users increase. Even companies running their businesses on Oracle or another of SQL Server's competitors sometimes leverage SQL Server for its cost-effective reporting and business intelligence solutions. XML and Web Services (which is XML delivered through HTTP) are standards that allow very diverse systems to share data. The new XML data source allows you to work with XML as you would almost any other source of data. First, you'll take a look at Excel.

Excel

Excel is the favorite "database" software of many people without database expertise. We were amazed when an acquaintance of one of the authors confessed that she used Excel to do everything, even write letters. SQL Server Integration Services has Data Flow source and destination components made just for Excel. You can be sure that these components will be used in many SSIS packages, because data is often imported from Excel files into a SQL Server database or exported into Excel for many high-level tasks such as sales forecasting. Because Excel is so easy to work with, it is common to find inconsistencies in the data. For example, while possible to implement, it is less likely for an Excel workbook to have lookup lists or data type enforcement in place. It's often possible for the person entering data to type a note in a cell where a date should go. Of course, cleansing the data is part of the ETL process, but it may be even more of a challenge when importing from Excel.

In this section, you'll look at both exporting to and importing from Excel as the AdventureWorks staff performs their annual inventory.

Exporting to Excel

The easiest way to export data from SQL 2005 to an Excel file is to use the SQL Server Import and Export Wizard. Since using the wizard is covered in Chapter 2, you will use BIDS to create SSIS packages to import and export Excel data. The first example shows how to create a package that exports a worksheet the AdventureWorks inventory staff will use to record the physical inventory counts.

Create a new Integration Services Project in BIDS. Drag a Data Flow task from the Toolbox to the Control Flow design area and then switch to the Data Flow tab. Add an OLE DB Source and an Excel Destination. Drag the Data Flow path (green arrow) from the OLE DB Source to the Excel Destination.

It is always good practice to use meaningful names when designing your SSIS packages, so change the name of the OLE DB Source to Products. Name the Excel Destination Inventory Worksheet. You can name the components by using the Properties window or by directly clicking into the name of the actual component. The source and destination components in the Data Flow design area should resemble Figure 8-1.

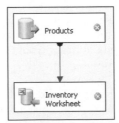

Figure 8-1

Create a Connection Manager pointing to the AdventureWorks database as described in Chapter 3. Create a second Connection Manager pointing to an Excel Workbook file. Right-click in the Connection Managers area and select New Connection. Choose Excel from the list of Types and click Add. The Excel Connection Manager window opens, where you can enter a file path to a new or existing Excel file. Select the appropriate version of Excel and make sure that First Row has Column Names is checked (see Figure 8-2). Click OK to dismiss the dialog box. You can rename the Excel Connection Manager in the Properties window. Name it Worksheet Destination.

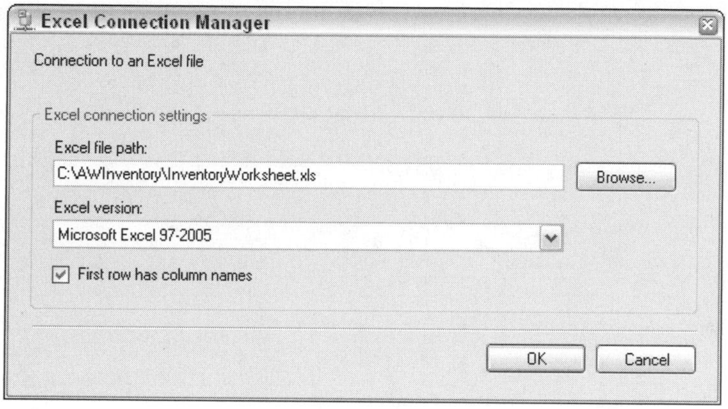

Figure 8-2

Double-click the Products component to bring up the OLE DB Source Editor. Make sure that Connection Manager is selected on the left. Choose the AdventureWorks Connection Manager for the OLE DB Connection Manager property. The Data access mode should be set to SQL Command. In this case, you will write a query to specify which data to export:

```
SELECT ProductID, LocationID, Shelf, Bin,
   Null as PhysicalCount
FROM Production.ProductInventory
ORDER by LocationID, Shelf, Bin
```

If you select Columns in the left pane, you have the opportunity to deselect some of the columns or change the name of the output columns (see Figure 8-3). Click OK to accept the configuration.

Double-click the Inventory Worksheet component to bring up the Excel Destination Editor. With Connection Manager tab selected, make sure that Worksheet Destination is set in the OLE DB Connection Manager property.

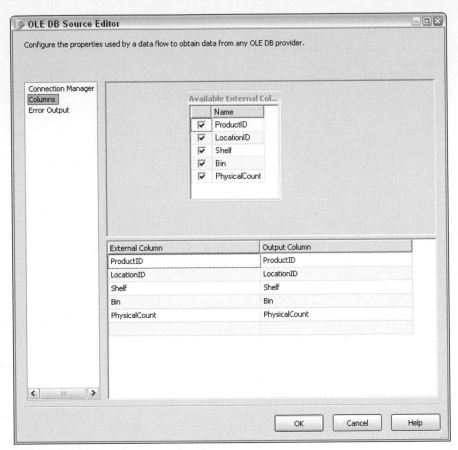

Figure 8-3

The Data Access Mode should be set to Table or View (more about this later). Next to Name of the Excel sheet, click New and a dialog box with a Create Table statement will pop up. You can modify the table name or the column properties if necessary in this dialog box (see Figure 8-4). Click OK to create a new worksheet with the appropriate column headings in the Excel file. Make sure that Name of the Excel Sheet is set to Inventory Worksheet.

You must click Mappings on the left to set the mappings between the source and destination. Each one of the Available Input Columns should match up exactly with an Available Output Column (see Figure 8-5). Click OK to accept the Inventory Worksheet settings.

Run the package to export the product list. The fields selected in the Production.Inventory table will be exported to the Excel file, and your inventory crew members can each use a copy of this file to record their counts.

Figure 8-4

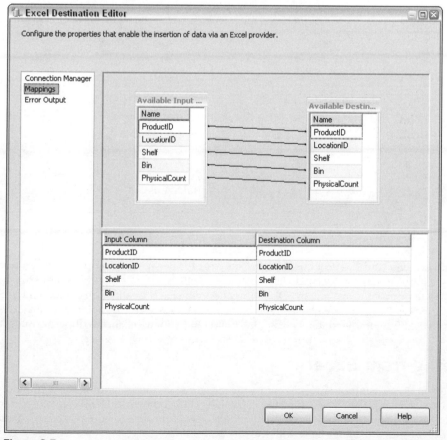

Figure 8-5

In this example, you started with a blank Excel workbook file. But what would happen if the file already had a worksheet set up with column headings that did not match up perfectly to the input columns? You can manually map input columns to output columns. Figure 8-6 shows the mappings when the Production.Product table is exported to an Excel spreadsheet with destination columns that are named differently than the source and an extra column that doesn't exist in the source.

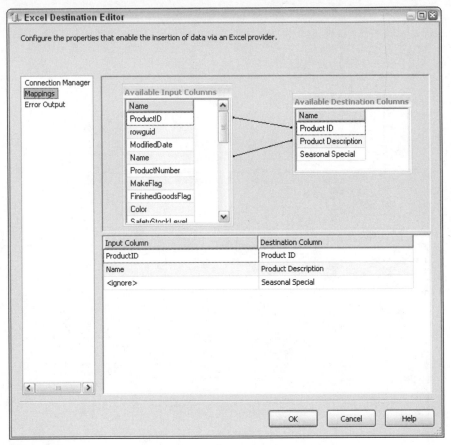

Figure 8-6

Alternatively, you could write a query in the source or the destination component to control how the fields match up. To write a query to select the correct columns from the spreadsheet, change the Data Access Mode from Table or View to SQL Command in the Excel Destination component. A SQL command text box will replace the Name of the Excel Sheet text box. At this point, you can either type a command into the SQL command text box or click Build Query for assistance writing the query.

Importing from Excel

Assume that the AdventureWorks inventory crew divided up the assignments according to the product location. As each assignment is completed, a partially filled-out worksheet file is returned to you. In this example, you'll create a package to import the data from each worksheet that is received and update the Production.ProductInventory table with the physical counts.

In order to follow along with the example, manually update the PhysicalCount column of a few of the rows in the spreadsheet that you created in the previous section. Look up and use the actual counts found in the AdventureWorks Production.ProductInventory table for some of the rows. In SQL Server Management Studio, click New Query and run the following query. It will give you the first 10 product ID numbers and quantities (see Figure 8-7).

```
USE AdventureWorks
GO
SELECT TOP 10 ProductID, Quantity
FROM Production.ProductInventory
ORDER BY LocationID, Shelf, Bin
```

	ProductID	Quantity
1	1	410
2	2	427
3	994	244
4	995	231
5	996	321
6	4	500
7	3	585
8	317	283
9	318	140
10	319	308

Figure 8-7

Make sure to update some of the rows in the spreadsheet with the exact count found in the AdventureWorks database and make up a count for the others (see Figure 8-8). Save and close the Excel file.

	A	B	C	D	E	F
1	ProductID	LocationID	Shelf	Bin	PhysicalCount	
2	1	1	A	1	415	
3	2	1	A	2	427	
4	994	1	A	3	244	
5	995	1	A	4	231	
6	996	1	A	5	322	
7	4	1	A	6	500	
8	3	1	A	7	585	
9	317	1	C	1	283	
10	318	1	C	2	144	
11	319	1	C	3	308	
12	320	1	C	4		
13	952	1	C	5		
14	321	1	C	6		
15	322	1	C	7		
16	359	1	C	8		

Figure 8-8

Open BIDS and create a new Integration Services Project. Drag a Data Flow task to the Control Flow design pane. Open the Data Flow tab and add an Excel Source and an OLE DB Destination component. Rename the Excel Source to Inventory Worksheet. Rename the OLE DB Destination to Inventory Import. Drag the Data Flow Path from the Inventory Worksheet component to the Inventory Import component.

The OLE DB Destination sometimes works better than the SQL Server Destination component for importing data from non–SQL Server sources! When using the SQL Server Destination component, you cannot import into integer columns or varchar columns from an Excel spreadsheet and must import into double precision and nvarchar columns. The SQL Server destination component does not support implicit data type conversions and works as expected when moving data from SQL Server to SQL Server.

Create a Connection Manager for the Excel file you have been working with by following the instructions in the previous section. Rename the Excel Connection Manager in the Properties window to Inventory Source. Create a Connection Manager pointing to the AdventureWorks database.

Double-click the Inventory Worksheet component to bring up the Excel Source Editor. For the OLE DB Connection Manager setting, select Inventory Source from the list. If you set the Data Access Mode to Table or view, you will see a list of spreadsheets and named areas under Name of the Excel spreadsheet (see Figure 8-9). The $ character designates a spreadsheet name.

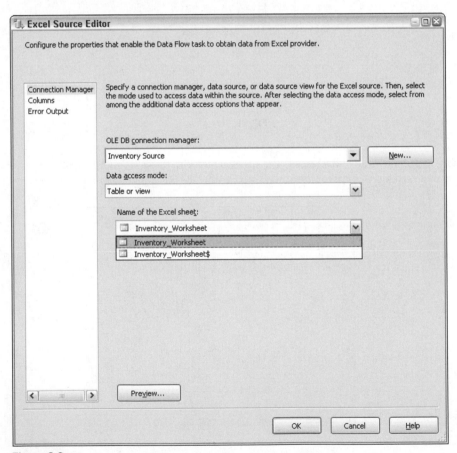

Figure 8-9

For this example the Data access mode should be set to SQL Command because we only want to import rows with the physical count filled in. Type the following query into the SQL command text box (see Figure 8-10):

```
SELECT ProductID, PhysicalCount, LocationID, Shelf, Bin
FROM Inventory_Worksheet
WHERE PhysicalCount IS NOT NULL
```

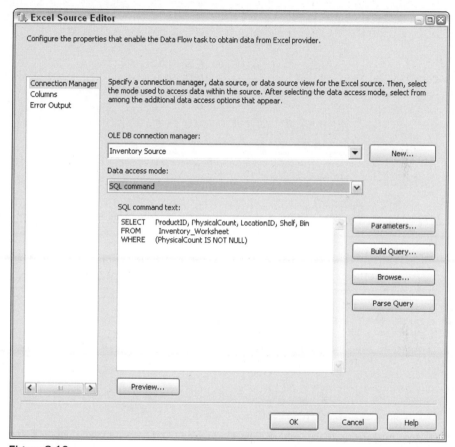

Figure 8-10

Double-click the Inventory Import component to bring up the OLE DB Destination Editor. Make sure the AdventureWorks connection is chosen. Under Data Access Mode, choose Table or View. Click the New button next to Name of the Table or the View to open the Create Table dialog box. Change the name of the table to InventoryImport and change the DOUBLE PRECISION columns to INTEGER in the script (see Figure 8-11).

Figure 8-11

Click OK to create the table. Select Mappings. Each field from the worksheet should match up to a field in the new table. Click OK to accept the configuration.

Move back to the Control Flow tab. Drag an Execute SQL Task from the Toolbox. Double-click it to view the properties. Change the name to Update Inventory. Make sure that the SQLSourceType is Direct Input. Click the ellipsis button next to the SQLStatement property for a dialog box where you can type in this query:

```
UPDATE PI
SET Quantity = PhysicalCount,
  ModifiedDate = getDate()
FROM Production.ProductInventory PI
INNER JOIN InventoryImport II
On II.ProductID = PI.ProductID
  and II.LocationID = PI.LocationID
  and II.Shelf = PI.Shelf
  and II.Bin = PI.Bin
```

Select the connection that points to the AdventureWorks database in the Connection property and click OK to accept the configuration. Drag the Precedence Constraint (green arrow) from the Data Flow task to the Update Inventory task.

Add a second Execute SQL task to the Control Flow pane. Change the name to Truncate Import Table. Double-click the component to open the Execute SQL Task Editor. Choose the connection pointing to AdventureWorks in the Connection property. Make sure that the SQLSourceType is set to Direct Input. Type the following in the SQLStatement property:

```
TRUNCATE TABLE InventoryImport
```

Click OK to accept the configuration. Drag the Precedence Constraint from the Truncate Import Table task to the Data Flow task. The Control Flow design area should now resemble Figure 8-12.

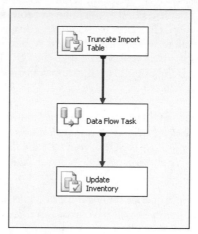

Figure 8-12

Now you're ready to run the package and see how it works. Once the package has completed, go back to SQL Server Management Studio and rerun the query to see the updated counts (see Figure 8-13):

```
Select top 10 ProductID, Quantity
From Production.ProductInventory
Order by LocationID, Shelf, Bin
```

	ProductID	Quantity
1	1	415
2	2	427
3	994	244
4	995	231
5	996	322
6	4	500
7	3	585
8	317	283
9	318	144
10	319	308

Figure 8-13

While this is a simple example, it illustrates just how easy it is to import from and export to a non–SQL Server data source. Now you'll move on to Access with its own interesting twists.

Access

MS Access is the database of choice for countless individual users and small workgroups. It has many great features and wizards that enable a small application or prototype to be quickly developed. Often, when an application has outgrown its humble Access origins, discussions of moving the data to SQL Server emerge. Many times, the client will be rewritten as a Web or desktop application using VB.NET or another language. Sometimes the plan will be to link to the SQL Server tables, utilizing the existing Access front-end. Unfortunately, if the original application was poorly designed, moving the data to SQL Server will not improve performance.

> *Designing an application with an SQL back-end and Access front-end that performs well is beyond the scope of this book. To learn more about creating Access applications where SQL Server hosts the data, read Microsoft Access Developer's Guide to SQL Server, by Andy Baron and Mary Chipman (SAMS, 2000) or Microsoft Access Projects with Microsoft SQL Server, by Ralf Albrecht and Natascha Nicol (Microsoft Press, 2002).*

Also, keep in mind that Access select queries will be imported into SQL Server as tables. Any queries that must be ported to the SQL Server database will have to be rewritten. Many select queries can be rewritten as views. Update, append, delete, create table and parameterized select queries can be rewritten as stored procedures if you need to move them to the SQL Server database. There may also be VBA (Visual Basic for Applications) functions used in queries. You may want to rewrite them as CLR User Defined Functions in SQL Server. What you do depends on the requirements for your application or solution, and that discussion could fill up a whole book in itself.

Importing Access tables is similar to importing Excel worksheets. It is very easy to accomplish using the Import and Export Wizard and, if you have several tables to import at once, that's probably the way to go. See Chapter 2 for detailed instructions on how to use the wizard. In this section you will learn how to import data from Access by building an SSIS package along with a few tips specific to Access.

Understanding Access Security

Connecting to an Access database is usually quite simple. If Access security has been enabled on the database, it gets a bit more complicated. Before you learn how to import from Access, take a quick look at how Access security works.

The simplest way to "secure" an Access database is to set a Database Password. This is done by opening the database in exclusive mode (see Figure 8-14) and then entering a password in the Set Database Password dialog box found at Tools ⇨ Security ⇨ Set Database Password. After that, the password must be supplied by anyone who opens the database, including your SSIS package.

The other method involves associating a database with a Workgroup Information file (system.mdw), setting up groups and users, and configuring permissions. Users attempting to open the database authenticate against the workgroup file. Access provides a wizard that can be used to set up groups and permissions, simplifying the process.

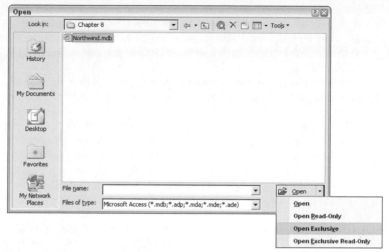

Figure 8-14

A default Workgroup file is specified in the registry for the user. If more than one individual shares the same database, usually a Workgroup Information file is stored on the network. Either that file can be the default workgroup file for the user or it can be used only for a specific database. If it is for the specific database, the path to the workgroup file must be specified as a startup command-line argument in a shortcut provided to the user. A user name and password can also be included in the command, like this:

```
"C:\Program Files\Microsoft Office\Office11\MSACCESS.EXE"
    c:\chapter8\Northwind.mdb /wrkgrp c:\chapter8\system.mdw
    /user kim /pwd kimspw
```

If the Access database does not have security enabled, all users actually open the database as the Admin user with a blank password. That enables the user to create, modify, and own all of the Access objects without even being aware that security, albeit not much security, is being used in the background. Creating a nonblank Admin password effectively enables security.

The Admin account is the same account no matter which Workgroup Information file is used, and it is a member of the Admins group by default. It seems counterintuitive, but moving the Admin account to a group with no object permissions and removing it from the Admins group is an Access security best practice. This keeps anyone with a copy of Access who opens the file using the Admin account from a different Workgroup file from viewing or modifying data. Before taking the rights away from Admin, another account must be added to the Admins group.

If you would like to learn more about how to set up Access security, refer to Microsoft Access Help for more information.

Configuring an Access Connection Manager

Once the Connection Manager is configured properly, importing from Access is simple. First, you'll look at the steps required to set up the Connection Manager.

Create a new SSIS project and create a new Connection Manager by right-clicking in the Connection Managers section of the design area of the screen. Select New OLE DB Connection to bring up the Configure OLE DB Connection Manager dialog box. Click New to open the Connection Manager. In the Provider drop-down list, choose the Microsoft Jet 4.0 OLE DB Provider and click OK.

The Connection Manager dialog box changes to an Access-specific dialog. Browse to the Access database file to set the Database File Name property. You are using the Northwind MS Access sample database for this example.

By default, the database user name will be Admin with a blank password. If security has been enabled for the Access database, a valid user name and password must be entered. Enter the password on the All pane in the Security section. The user Password property is also available in the properties window. Check the Save My Password option. Additionally, the path to the Workgroup Information File (system.mdw) must be set in the Jet ODBC:System Database property, also found by clicking the All tab.

If, on the other hand, a database password has been set, enter the database password in the Password property on the Connction pane. This also sets the Jet ODBC:Database Password property found on the All tab.

If both a database password and user security have been set up, enter both passwords on the All pane. In the Security section, enter the user password and enter the database password for the Jet OLEDB:New Database Password property (see Figure 8-15). Check the Save my password option. Be sure to test the connection and click OK to save the properties.

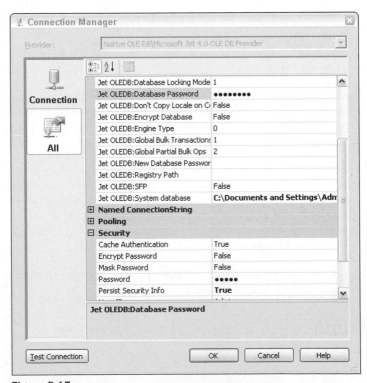

Figure 8-15

Importing from Access

Using the project you created in the last section with the Access Connection Manager already configured, add a Data Flow task to the Control Flow design area. Click the Data Flow tab to view the Data Flow design area. Add an OLE DB Source component and name it Customers.

Double-click the Customers icon to open the OLE DB Source Editor. Set the OLE DB Connection Manager property to the Connection Manager that you created in the last section. Select Table or View from the Data Access Mode drop-down list. Choose the Customers table from the list under Name of the Table or the View (see Figure 8-16). Click Columns on the left where you can choose which columns to import and change the output names if you need to. Click OK to accept the configuration.

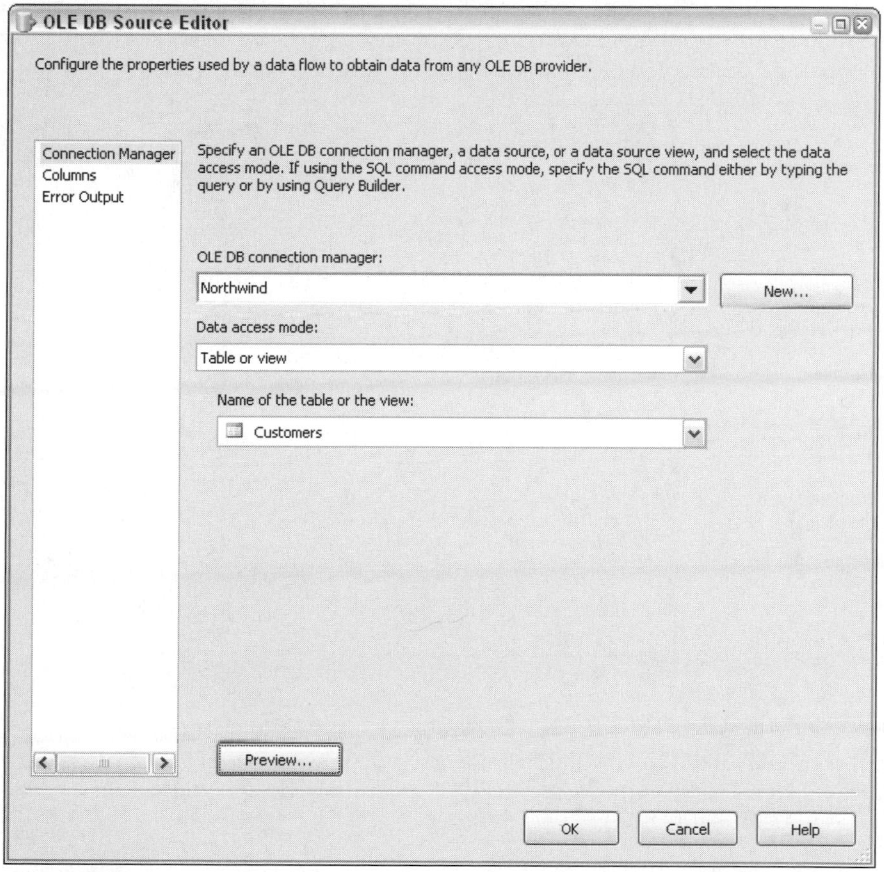

Figure 8-16

Create a Connection Manager pointing to AdventureWorks. Create an OLE DB Destination component and name it NW_Customers. Drag the connection (green arrow) from the Customers source component to the NW_Customers destination component. Double-click the destination component to bring up the OLE DB Destination Editor and configure it to use the AdventureWorks Connection Manager.

You can choose an existing table or you can click New to create a new table as the data destination. If you click New, you will notice that the Create Table designer does not script any keys, constraints, defaults, or indexes from Access. It makes its best guess as to the data types, which may not be the right ones for your solution. When building a package to be used in a production system, you will probably want to design and create the SQL Server tables in advance.

A tool that could save some time when porting Access tables to SQL is the Access Upsizing Wizard. This can be found in the Tools ⇨ Database Utilities menu of Access. This tool will enable you to upload the table and attributes along with or without the data. You still need to review the data types and the index names that the wizard creates, but it could save you quite a bit of time over the manual process.

For now, click New to bring up the table definition (see Figure 8-17). Notice that the table name is the same as the destination component, so change the name to NW_Customers if you did not name the OLE DB Destination as instructed previously. Click OK to create the new table. Click Mappings on the left to map the source and destination columns. Click OK to accept the configuration.

Figure 8-17

Run the package. All of the Northwind customers should now be listed in the SQL Server Table. Check this by clicking New Query in the Microsoft SQL Server Management Studio. Run the following query to see the results (see Figure 8-18):

```
USE AdventureWorks
GO
SELECT * FROM NW_Customers
```

Figure 8-18

Empty the table to prepare for the next example by running this query:

```
TRUNCATE TABLE NW_CUSTOMERS
```

Using a Parameter

Another interesting feature is the ability to pass a parameter from a package variable to a SQL Command.

In Access, you can create a query that prompts the user for parameters at runtime. You can import most Access select queries as tables, but data from an Access parameter query cannot be imported using SSIS.

Using the package you started in the last section, create a variable to hold the parameter value. Move back to the Control Flow tab and right-click the design area. Choose Variables. Add a variable by clicking the Add Variable icon. Name it CustomerID. Change the Data Type to String. Give it a value of ANTON (see Figure 8-19). Close the Variables window and navigate back to the Data Flow tab.

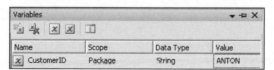

Figure 8-19

The design area or component that is selected determines the scope of the variable when it is created. The scope can be set to the package if it is created right after clicking the Control Flow design area. You can also set the scope to a Control Flow task, Data Flow component, or Event Handler task.

Double-click the Customers component to bring up the OLE DB Source Editor and change the Data
Access Mode to SQL Command. A SQL Command text box and some buttons appear. You can click the
Build Query button to bring up a designer to help build the command or click Browse to open a file with
the command you want to use. For this example, type in the following SQL statement (see Figure 8-20):

```
SELECT CustomerID, CompanyName, ContactName, ContactTitle,
    Address, City, Region, PostalCode, Country, Phone, Fax
FROM Customers
WHERE (CustomerID = ?)
```

Figure 8-20

The ? symbol is used as the placeholder for the parameter in the query. Map the parameters to variables
in the package by clicking the Parameters button. Set the name of the parameter to ?. Choose
User::CustomerID from the variable list and click OK (see Figure 8-21).

Figure 8-21

Variables in SSIS belong to a namespace. By default, there are two namespaces, User and System. Variables that you create belong to the User namespace. You can also create additional namespaces. See Chapters 6 and 7 to learn more about variables.

Note that you cannot preview the data after setting up the parameter because the package must be running to load the value into the parameter. Click OK to accept the new configuration and run the package. This time, only one record will be imported (see Figure 8-22).

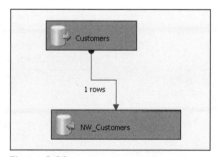

Figure 8-22

You can also go back to SQL Server Management Studio to view the results.

```
USE AdventureWorks
GO
SELECT * FROM NW_Customers
```

If you wish to use multiple parameters in your SQL Command, use Parameter0, Parameter1, etc., for your parameter names instead of the ?.

Set up a second Package-level variable for CompanyName and set the value to Island Trading. Change the query in the Customers component to the following:

```
SELECT CustomerID, CompanyName, ContactName,
    ContactTitle, Address, City, Region,
    PostalCode, Country, Phone, Fax
FROM Customers
WHERE (CustomerID = Parameter0) OR
    (CompanyName = Parameter1)
```

Now the Parameters dialog box will show the two parameters. Associate each parameter to the appropriate variable (see Figure 8-23).

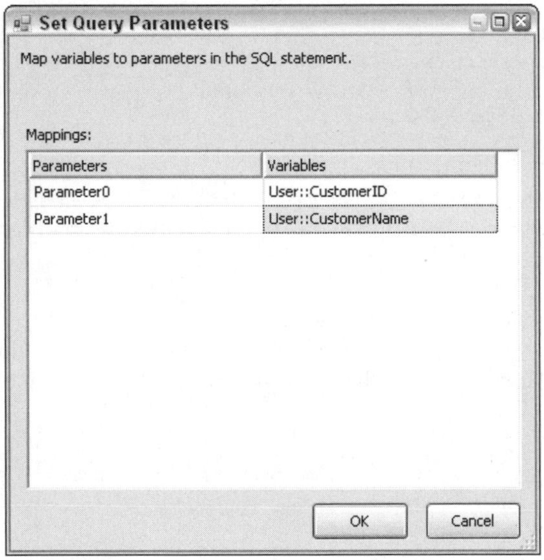

Figure 8-23

Delete the row from the table and run the package. Now two customers will be listed in the table.

Importing data from Access is a simple process as long as Access security has not been enabled. Often, porting an Access application to SQL Server is the desired result. Make sure you have a good book or resource to help ensure success.

Now you'll see just how easy it is to import from Oracle, as long as you do a bit of configuration first.

Oracle

Because of SQL Server's world-class reporting and business intelligence tools, more and more shops running Oracle rely on SQL Server for their reporting needs. Luckily, importing data from Oracle is much like importing from other sources, such as a text file or another SQL Server instance. In this section, you'll learn how to access data from a sample Oracle database.

Client Setup

An Oracle data provider is supplied with SQL Server 2005. The caveat is that the Oracle Client 8-1.7.0 or greater must be installed in order to use the data provider. The Oracle Client can be installed by running the Oracle Universal Installer. See your Oracle administrator for help. Alternately, the free Instant Client can be downloaded from the Oracle Web site at www.oracle.com/technology/tech/oci/instantclient/ instantclient.html. If you use the Instant Client, be sure to install the Basic and ODBC packages.

Installing the Instant Client is as simple as copying some files, setting some environment variables, and running a batch file. You are not going to look at the steps here, as Oracle could modify them in the future.

Once the Oracle Client is installed, a tnsnames.ora file must be placed in the Oracle Home directory. The tnsnames.ora file is used for the same purpose as ODBC Data Source connections. It contains all of the information required to locate the Oracle database. An alias for the database is defined. The alias is used later when setting up the connection in SSIS or any other client application.

Here is a sample section from a tnsnames.ora file:

```
ORCL =
  (DESCRIPTION =
    (ADDRESS = (PROTOCOL = TCP)(HOST = VPC-XP)(PORT = 1521))
    (CONNECT_DATA =
      (SERVER = DEDICATED)
      (SERVICE_NAME = orcl)
    )
  )
```

In this example, the alias, ORCL, is used to connect to an Oracle database named orcl. Your Oracle administrator can provide more information on how to set up your tnsnames.ora file to point to a test or production database in your environment.

Importing Oracle Data

Create a new Integration Services project using BIDS. Add a Data Flow task to the design area. On the Data Flow tab, add an OLE DB Source. Name the OLE DB Source Oracle.

In the Connection Managers area, right-click and choose New OLE DB Connection to open the Configure OLE DB Connection Manager dialog. Click New to open the Connection Manager dialog. Select Microsoft OLE DB Provider for Oracle from the list of providers and click OK. Type the alias from your tnsnames.ora file for Server Name. Type in the user name and password and check Save My Password (see Figure 8-24). This example illustrates connecting to the widely available scott sample database schema. The user name is scott with a password of tiger. Verify the credentials with your Oracle administrator. You will probably want to test the connection to make sure that everything is configured properly. Click OK to accept the configuration.

Figure 8-24

In the custom properties section of the Oracle component's property dialog, change the AlwaysUseDefaultCodePage property to True. Open the OLE DB Source Editor by double-clicking the Oracle source component. With the Connection Manager tab selected, choose the Connection Manager pointing to the Oracle database. Select Table or view from the Data Access Mode. Click the drop-down list under Name of the Table or the View to see a list of the available tables. Choose the "Scott"."Dept" table from the list (see Figure 8-25).

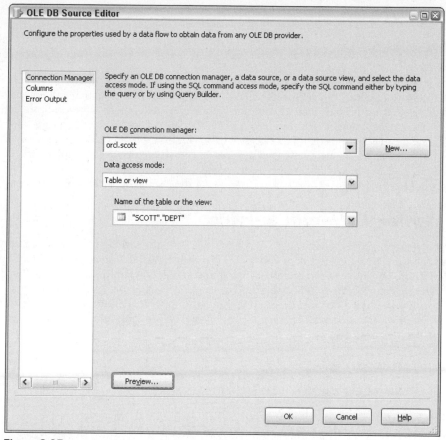

Figure 8-25

Select the Columns tab to see a list of the columns in the table. Click Preview to see sample data from the Oracle table. At this point, you can add a data destination component to import the data into SQL Server or another OLE DB destination. This is demonstrated several times elsewhere in the chapter, so you won't look at it again here.

Importing Oracle data is very straightforward, but there are a few things to watch out for. The current ODBC driver and OLE DB provider are designed for Oracle 7. At the time of this writing, Oracle 10g is the latest version available. Specific functionality and data types that were implemented after the 7 release will probably not work as expected. See Microsoft's Knowledge Base article 244661 for more information.

Now that you have seen how to import data from several sources using SSIS, you'll take a look at using the amazing new XML features.

Web Services

This has got to be the one of the coolest tools in the SSIS bag of tricks. You barely need to know what a Web service is to take advantage of this little gem.

In very simple terms, a Web service is to the Web as a function is to a code module. It accepts a message in XML, including arguments, and returns the answer in XML. The wonderful thing about XML technology is that it allows computer systems that are completely foreign to each other to communicate in this common language. When using Web services, this transfer of XML data occurs across the enterprise or across the Internet using the HTTP protocol. Many Web services — for example, stock-tickers and movie listings — are freely available for anyone's use. Some Web services, of course, are private or require a fee. Probably the most useful application is to allow orders or other data to be exchanged easily by trading partners. In this example, you'll learn how to use a Web service to get a listing of the hyperlinks on a Web page.

The Hyperlink Extractor Service

Start with a new project and create an HTTP Connection by right-clicking in the Connection Managers pane and choosing New Connection. Choose HTTP and click Add to bring up the HTTP Connection Manager Editor. Type **http://www.atomic-x.com/xmlservices/HyperlinkExtractor.asmx?wsdl** as the Server URL (see Figure 8-26). In this case, you'll use a publicly available Web service so you won't have to worry about any credentials or certificates. If you must supply proxy information to browse the Web, fill that in on the Proxy tab. Go ahead and test the connection before continuing, and then click OK to accept the Connection Manager.

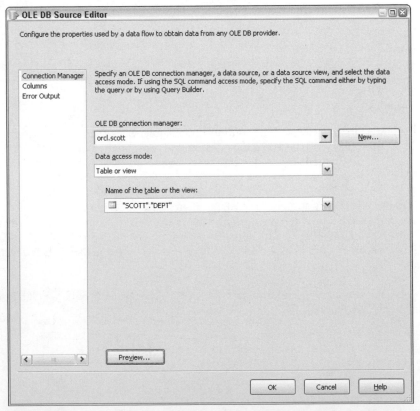

Figure 8-26

Add a Web Service task from the Toolbox. Double-click it to bring up the Web Service Task Editor. Select the General pane. Make sure that the HttpConnection property is set to the HTTP connection you created in the last step.

In order for a Web service to be accessed by a client, a Web Service Definition Language (WSDL) file must be available that describes how the Web service works—that is, the methods available and the parameters that the Web service expects. The Web Service task provides a way to automatically download this file. Enter the fully qualified path where the file will be created (see Figure 8-27). If the file already exists, set OverwriteWSDLFile to true. Click Download WSDL to create the file. If you are interested, you can open the file with Internet Explorer to learn more about its structure.

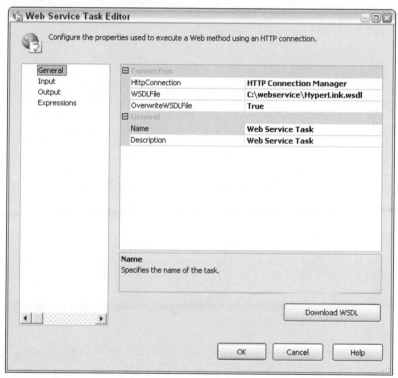

Figure 8-27

By downloading the WSDL file, the Web Service task now knows the Web service definition. Select the Input pane of the Web Service Task Editor. Select HyperLinkExtractor next to Service. Next to Method, select ExtractURL.

> *Web services are not limited to providing just one method. If multiple methods are provided, you'll see all of them listed.*

Once the Method is selected, a list of arguments appears. In this case, enter a URL for your favorite Web page, for example www.sqlservercentral.com (see Figure 8-28).

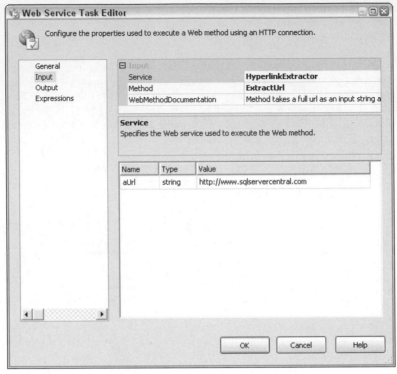

Figure 8-28

Now that everything is set up to invoke the Web service, you need to tell the Web Service task what to do with the result. Select Output in the left pane. You can store the results in a variable or in a file. For this example, choose File Connection. Next to the File property, click the drop arrow and choose <New Connection>. The File Connection Manager Editor opens. Next to Usage Type, select Create File. Type in a path for your new file, and click OK (see Figure 8-29). Click OK once more to accept the Web Service task configuration.

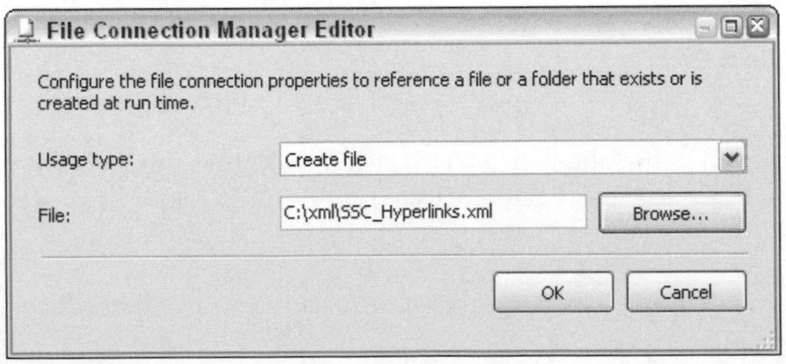

Figure 8-29

Now you're ready to run the project. If all went well, you can now open the XML file that was returned by the Web service and see a list of all the links on the page of the URL you entered previously.

The Currency Conversion Service

In this second example, you'll learn how to use a Web service to get back a value that can be used in the package to perform a calculation. You'll use the value with a very cool Data Flow Transformation component, the Derived Column, to convert a price list to another currency.

Begin by creating a new SSIS package. This example will require three variables. To set up the variables, make sure that the Control Flow tab is selected. If the variables window is not visible, right-click in the design area and select Variables. Set up the three variables as in the following table.

Name	Scope	Data Type
XMLAnswer	Package	String
Answer	Package	String
ConversionRate	Package	Double

Add a Connection Manager pointing to the AdventureWorks database. Add an HTTP Connection Manager and set the Server URL to http://www.webservicex.net/CurrencyConvertor .asmx?wsdl.

> Note that this Web service was valid at the time of this writing, but the authors cannot guarantee its future availability.

Drag a Web Service task to the design area. Double-click the task to open the Web Service Task Editor. Set the HTTPConnection property to the Connection Manager you just created. Download the WSDL file as you did in the last example.

Click Input to see the Web service properties. Select CurrencyConvertor in the Service property and ConversionRate as the Method. Two parameters will display, FromCurrency and ToCurrency. Set FromCurrency equal to USD and ToCurrency equal to EUR (see Figure 8-30).

Click Output and set the OutputType to Variable. The variable name to use is User::XMLAnswer. Click OK to accept the configuration.

> At this point, you may be interested in viewing the XML that it returned from the Web service. You can save the XML in a file instead of a variable. Then, after running the task, examine the file. Or, you can set a breakpoint on the task and view the variable at runtime. See Chapter 13 to learn more about breakpoints and debugging.

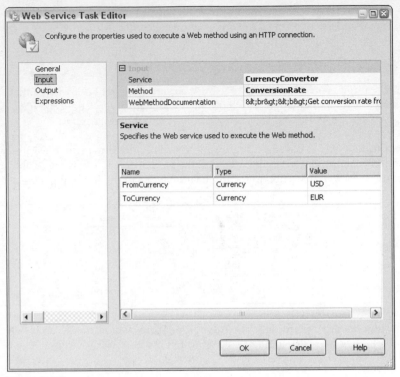

Figure 8-30

The value of the XML returned will look something like this:

```
<?xml version="1.0" encoding="utf-8">
<double>0.836</double>
```

You just need the number, not the XML, so add an XML task to the designer to evaluate the XML. Drag the Precedence Constraint from the Web Service task to the XML task. Open the XML Task Editor by double-clicking the XML task and change the OperationType to XPATH. The properties available will change to include those specific for the XPATH operation. Set the properties to match those in the following table.

Section	Property	Value
Input	OperationType	XPATH
	SourceType	Variable
	Source	User:XMLAnswer
Output	SaveOperationResult	True
Operation Result	OverwriteDestination	True
	Destination	User::Answer
	DestinationType	Variable
Second Operand	SecondOperandType	Direct Input
	SecondOperand	/
Xpath Options	PutResultInOneNode	False
	XpathOperation	Values

The XPATH query language is beyond the scope of this book and, luckily, this XML is very simple with only a root element that can be accessed by using the slash character (/). Values are returned from the query as a list with a one-character unprintable row delimiter. In this case, only one value is returned, but it still has the row delimiter that you can't use.

There are a couple of options here. You could save the value to a file, then import using a File Source component into a SQL Server table, and finally use the Execute SQL task to assign the value to a variable. But, in this example, you will get a chance to use the Script task to eliminate the extra character.

Add a Script task to the design area and drag the Precedence Constraint from the XML task to the Script task. Open the Script Task Editor and select the Script pane. In order for the Script task to access the package variables, they must be listed in the ReadOnlyVariables and ReadWriteVariables properties in a semicolon-delimited list. Enter User::Answer in the ReadOnlyVariable property and User::ConversionRate in the ReadWriteVariables property (see Figure 8-31).

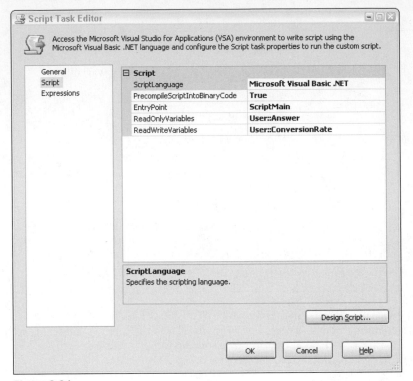

Figure 8-31

Click Design Script to open the code window. A Microsoft Visual Studio For Applications environment opens. With Intellisense and color-coding, the Script task bears little resemblance to the old ActiveX Script task from SQL 2000 DTS. The script will save the value returned from the Web service call to a variable. One character will be removed from the end of the value, leaving only the conversion factor. This will then be converted to a double and saved in the ConversionRate variable for use in a later step. Replace Sub Main with the following code:

```
Public Sub Main()
    Dim strConversion As String
    strConversion = Dts.Variables("User::Answer").Value.ToString
    strConversion.Remove(strConversion.Length -1,1)
    Dts.Variables("User::ConversionRate").Value = CType(strConversion,Double)
    Dts.TaskResult = Dts.Results.Success
End Sub
```

Close the scripting environment, and then click OK to accept the Script task configuration. Add a Data Flow task to the design area and connect the Script task to the Data Flow task. The Control Flow area should resemble what you see in Figure 8-32.

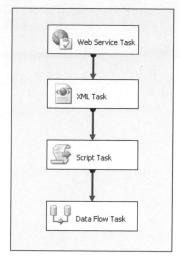

Figure 8-32

Move to the Data Flow tab. Add a Connection Manager pointing to the AdventureWorks database if you did not do so when getting started with this example. Drag an OLE DB Source component to the design area. Open the OLE DB Source Editor and set the OLE DB Connection Manager property to the AdventureWorks connection. Change the Data Access Mode property to SQL command. Type the following query in the command window:

```
SELECT ProductID, ListPrice
FROM Production.Product
WHERE ListPrice > 0
```

Click OK to accept the properties. Add a Derived Column transform to the design area. Drag the Data Flow Path from the OLE DB Source to the Derived Column component. Double-click to open the Derived Column Transformation Editor dialog box. Variables, columns, and functions are available for easily building an expression. Add a Derived column called EuroListPrice. In the Expression field type:

```
ListPrice * @[User::ConversionRate]
```

The Data Type should be decimal with a scale of 2. Click OK to accept the properties (see Figure 8-33).

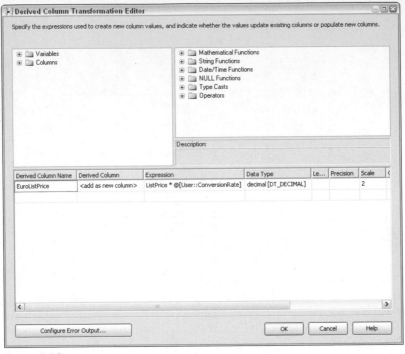

Figure 8-33

Add a Flat File Destination component to the Data Flow design area. Drag the Data Flow Path from the Derived Column component to the Flat File Destination component. Bring up the Flat File Destination Editor and click New to open the Flat File Format dialog. Choose Delimited and click OK (see Figure 8-34).

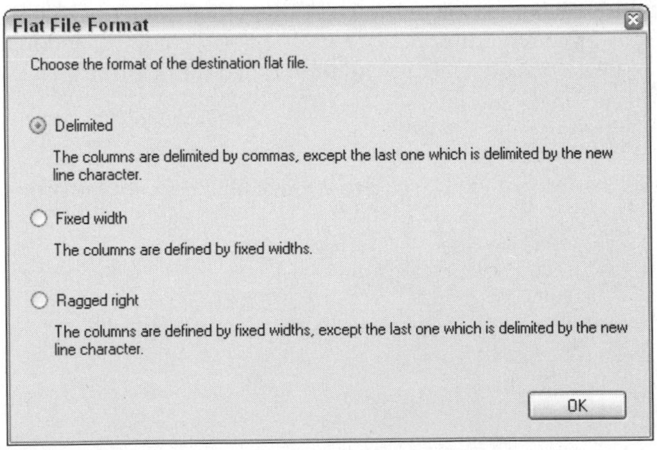

Figure 8-34

The Flat File Connection Manager Editor will open. Browse to or type in the path to a file. Here you can modify the file format and other properties if required (see Figure 8-35). Check Column Names in the First Data Row.

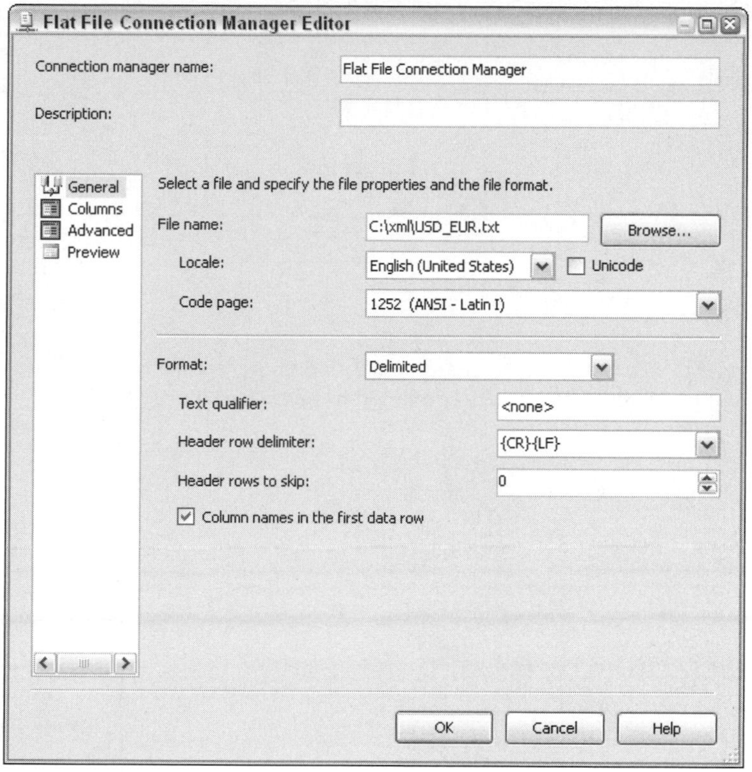

Figure 8-35

Click OK to dismiss the Flat File Connection Manager Editor dialog box. You should now be back at the Flat File Destination Editor. Click Mappings and then click OK. The Data Flow design area should resemble what you see in Figure 8-36.

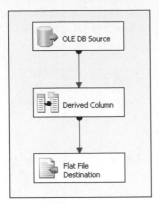

Figure 8-36

Run the package and then open the file that you defined in the last step. You should see a list of products along with the list price and the list price converted to Euros (see Figure 8-37).

USD_EUR.txt - Notepad
File Edit Format View Help
```
ProductID,ListPrice,EuroListPrice
514,133.34,109.99
515,147.14,121.37
516,196.92,162.43
517,133.34,109.99
518,147.14,121.37
519,196.92,162.43
520,133.34,109.99
521,147.14,121.37
522,196.92,162.43
680,1431.5,1180.84
706,1431.5,1180.84
707,34.99,28.86
708,34.99,28.86
```

Figure 8-37

Many free Web services are available for you to try. See www.xmethods.net for a list of services, some of which are free. In the next section, you will learn how to import an XML file into relational tables.

XML Data

SQL 2005 provides many ways to work with XML. The XML Data Source is yet another jewel in the SSIS treasure chest. It enables you to import an XML file directly into relational tables if that is what you need to do. In this example, you will import an RSS (Really Simple Syndication) file from the Web. You may not want to let your manager know how easy this is!

Create a new Integration Services project to get started. Add a Data Flow task to the Control Flow design area. Click the Data Flow tab to view the Data Flow design area. Add an XML Source and name it SQLNews. Double-click the SQLNews component to open the XML Source Editor. Make sure that Connections Manager is selected on the left. Select XML File Location for the Data Access Mode. For the XML location property, type in the following address:

```
http://www.sqlservercentral.com/sscrss.xml
```

If you click the Browse button, a regular file open dialog box opens. It is not obvious at first that you can use a URL address instead of a file on disk.

The XML file must be defined with an XML Schema Definition (XSD), which describes the elements in the XML file. Some XML files have an in-line XSD, which you can determine by opening the file and looking for xsd tags. There are many resources and tutorials available on the Web if you would like to learn more about XML schemas. If the file you are importing has an in-line schema, make sure that Use Inline Schema is checked. If an XSD file is available, you can enter the path in the XSD location property (see Figure 8-38). In this case, you will create the XSD file by clicking Generate XSD. Once the file is generated, you can open the file with Internet Explorer to view it if you are interested in learning more.

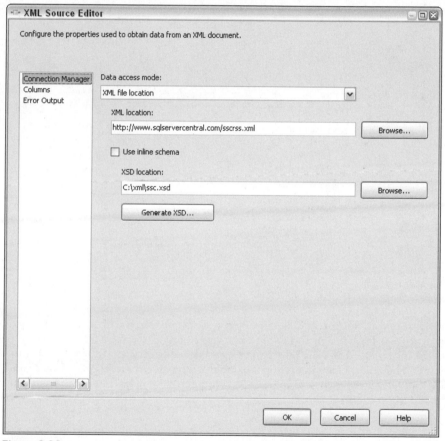

Figure 8-38

Now that the SQLNews component understands the XML file, click Columns. You will notice a drop-down box next to Output Name listing Channel and Item (see Figure 8-39).

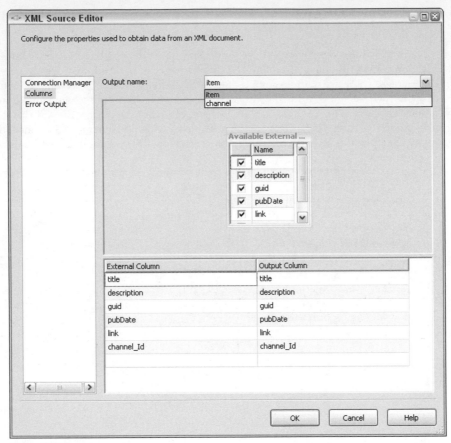

Figure 8-39

Even though the XML document is one file, it represents two tables with a one-to-many relationship. If you browse to www.sqlservercentral.com/sscrss.xml, you'll see a channel, which describes the source of the information, usually news, and several items, or articles, defined (see Figure 8-40). One note of caution here: If you are importing into tables with primary/foreign key constraints, there is no guarantee that the parent rows will be inserted before the child rows. Be sure to keep that in mind as you design your XML solution.

```
<?xml version="1.0" ?>
- <rss version="2.0">
  - <channel>
      <title>SQLServerCentral.com Articles</title>
      <link>http://www.sqlservercentral.com</link>
      <description>Articles posted on the SQLServercentral.com site.</description>
      <language>en-us</language>
      <ttl>360</ttl>
      <managingEditor>awarren@sqlservercentral.com (Andy Warren)</managingEditor>
    + <item>
    + <item>
    - <item>
        <title>The identity crisis in replication</title>
        <description>This article discusses three common problems DBAs are likely to encounter w
          identity property, which is defined as an attribute of int, smallint, bigint, decimal, numer
          auto-increment their value when data is inserted. These problems are humorously refer
          crisis.</description>
        <guid>www.sqlservercentral.com/articles/articlesexternal.asp?articleid=1996</guid>
        <pubDate>Thu, 28 Jul 2005 00:00:00 GMT</pubDate>
```

Figure 8-40

The properties of the channel and item tags match the columns displayed in the XML Source Editor. At this point, you can choose which fields you are interested in importing and change the output names if required.

Create a new Connection Manager pointing to the AdventureWorks database or to another test database. Add an OLE DB Destination component to the design area and name it Channel. Drag the Data Flow Path (green arrow) from the XML Source to Channel. Because the XML data represents two tables, an Input Output Select box opens (see Figure 8-41). Choose Channel in the Output drop-down and click OK.

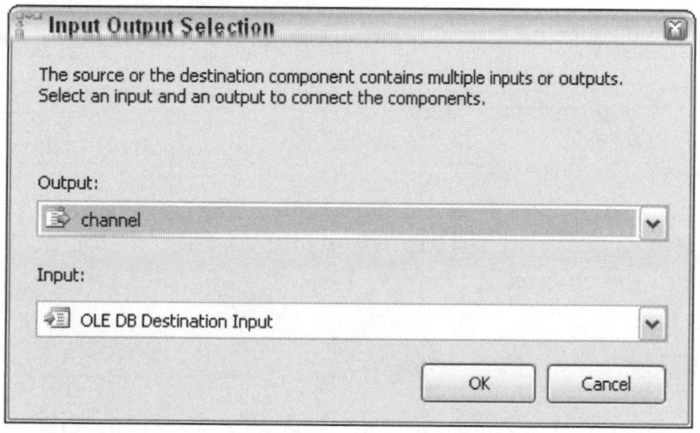

Input Output Selection

The source or the destination component contains multiple inputs or outputs. Select an input and an output to connect the components.

Output:

channel

Input:

OLE DB Destination Input

OK   Cancel

Figure 8-41

Double-click the Channel icon to bring up the OLE DB Destination Editor. Make sure that the OLE DB Connection Manager property is set to point to your sample database. Next to Use Table or View, click New. A window with a table definition will pop up. Click OK to create the table. Click Mappings and then click OK to accept the configuration.

Add a second OLE DB Destination component and name it NewsItem. Drag a Data Flow Path (green arrow) from the XML Source to the NewsItem component. This time, the designer will automatically set up the connection to use the Item table. Double-click the NewsItem destination component and verify that the Connection Manager property is set to the test database. Click the New button next to Name of the Table or the View to see a Create Table statement. Notice that the description field is only 255 characters. Modify the statement, increasing the number of characters to 2000, and click OK to create the table (see Figure 8-42). Click Mappings to view and set the mappings, and then click OK to accept the configuration.

Figure 8-42

Add one more OLE DB Destination component and name it Errors. Drag a red Data Flow Path from the XML Source to the Errors component. An Input Output Selection dialog box opens. Select Item Error Output (Error Output) in the Output option (see Figure 8-43). Click OK.

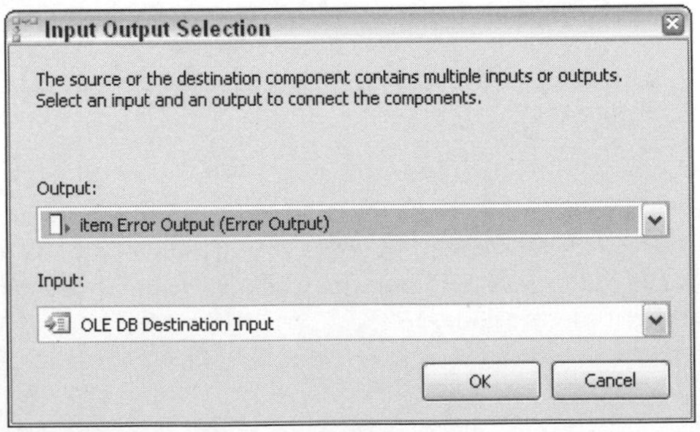

Figure 8-43

The Configure Error Output dialog box will then open. In the Truncation property of the Description row, change the value to Redirect row (see Figure 8-44) and click OK.

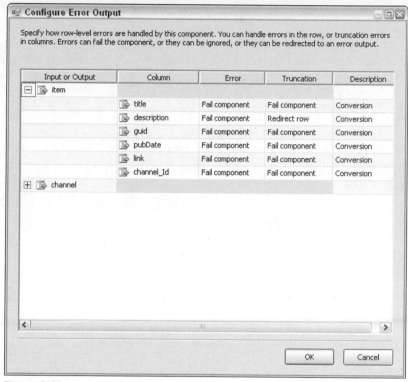

Configure Error Output

Specify how row-level errors are handled by this component. You can handle errors in the row, or truncation errors in columns. Errors can fail the component, or they can be ignored, or they can be redirected to an error output.

Input or Output	Column	Error	Truncation	Description
item				
	title	Fail component	Fail component	Conversion
	description	Fail component	Redirect row	Conversion
	guid	Fail component	Fail component	Conversion
	pubDate	Fail component	Fail component	Conversion
	link	Fail component	Fail component	Conversion
	channel_Id	Fail component	Fail component	Conversion
channel				

Figure 8-44

Double-click Errors and make sure it is pointing to the test database. Click New next to Name of the Table or the View and OK to create an Errors table. Click Mappings to accept the mappings and then click OK to save the configuration. The Data Flow design area should now resemble Figure 8-45.

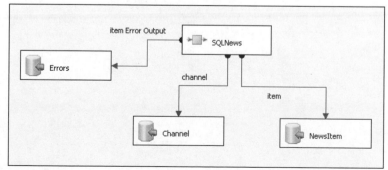

Figure 8-45

Run the package. If it completed successfully, some of the rows will be added to the NewsItem table. Any row with a description over 2000 characters long will end up in the Errors table.

Summary

Microsoft has made it easy to work with data from heterogeneous sources since DTS was first released. The addition of the XML data source and Web Service task in SSIS enhances this tremendously. In a perfect world, maybe all data would live in SQL Server. Until then, use SSIS to access data outside of SQL Server and even outside your Enterprise.

So far this book has covered the basic techniques of building SSIS packages. You now have enough knowledge to put all the pieces together and build a more complex package. The next chapter focuses on how to guarantee that your SSIS packages will scale and work reliably.

Reliability and Scalability

Reliability and scalability are goals for all your systems, yet they may seem like a strange combination for a chapter. Often, though, there are direct links, as you will see. Errors and the unexpected conditions that precipitate them are the most obvious threats to a reliable process. There are several features of SQL Server 2005 Integration Services that allow you to handle these situations with grace and integrity, keeping the data moving and systems running. Error outputs and checkpoints are the two features you will focus on in this chapter, and they highlight to you how these can be used in the context of reliability. The implementation of these methods can also have a direct effect on package performance, and therefore scalability, and you will learn how to take into account these considerations for your package and process design. The ability to provide checkpoints does not natively extend inside the Data Flow, but there are methods you can apply to achieve this. The methods can then be transferred almost directly into the context of scalability, allowing you to partition packages and improve both reliability and scalability at the same time. All of these methods can be combined, and while there is no perfect answer, you will look at the options and acquire the necessary information to make informed choices for your own SSIS implementations.

Restarting Packages

Everyone has been there — one of your overnight Data Transformation Services (DTS) packages failed overnight and you now have to completely rerun the package. This is particularly painful if some of the processes inside the package are expensive in terms of resources or time. In DTS, the ability to restart a package from where it left off did not exist, and picking apart a package to run just those tasks that failed was tedious and error-prone. There have been a variety of exotic solutions demonstrated, such as a post-execution process that goes into the package and re-creates the package from the failed step onward. Although this worked, it required someone with a detailed knowledge of the DTS object model, which most production DBAs did not have. If your process takes data from a production SQL Server that has a very small window of ETL opportunity, you can almost guarantee that the DBA is not going to be pleased when you tell him you need to run the extract again and that it may impact his users.

For this reason, the introduction of "Package Restartability" or checkpoints in SQL Server 2005 is manna from heaven. In this chapter, you are going to learn everything you need to know to make this happen in your SSIS packages.

Checkpoints are the foundation for restarting packages in SSIS, and they work by writing state information to a file after each task completes. This file can then be used to determine which tasks have run and which failed. More detail about these files is provided in the "Inside the Checkpoint File" section. To ensure that the checkpoint file is created correctly, there are three package properties and one task property that you must set, and they can be found on the property pages of the package and task. The package properties are as follows:

❑ **CheckpointFilename:** This is the file name of the checkpoint file, which must be provided. There are no specific conventions or requirements for the file name.

❑ **CheckpointUsage:** There are three values, which describe how a checkpoint file is used during package execution:

  ❑ **Never:** The package will not use a checkpoint file and therefore will never restart.

  ❑ **If Exists:** If a checkpoint file exists in the place you specified for the CheckpointFilename property, then it will be used, and the package will restart according to the checkpoints written.

  ❑ **Always:** The package will always use a checkpoint file to restart, and if one does not exist, the package will fail.

❑ **SaveCheckpoints:** This is a simple Boolean to indicate whether checkpoints are to be written. Obviously this must be set to true for this scenario.

The one property you have to set on the task is FailPackageOnFailure. This must be set for each task or container that you want to be the point for a checkpoint and restart. If you do not set this property to true and the task fails, no file will be written, and the next time you invoke the package, it will start from the beginning again. You'll see an example of this happening later.

> As you know, SSIS packages are broken down into Control Flow and Data Flow. Checkpoints only happen at the Control Flow; it is not possible to checkpoint transformations or restart inside a Data Flow. The Data Flow task can be a checkpoint, but it is treated as any other task. Implementing your own checkpoint and restart feature for data is described later in the chapter.

Remember also that if nothing fails in your package, no file will be generated. You shall have a look later at the generated file itself and try to make some sense out of it, but for now, you need to know that the file will contain all the information needed by the package when it is restarted to behave like nothing untoward had interrupted it. That's enough information to be able to make a start with using checkpoints in your packages, so now you can proceed with some examples.

Simple Control Flow

The basic idea of this first example package is that you have three ExecuteSQL tasks, as shown in Figure 9-1.

Figure 9-1

The second of those tasks, aptly named "2," is set to fail with a divide-by-zero error, as you can see in the Task Editor, shown in Figure 9-2.

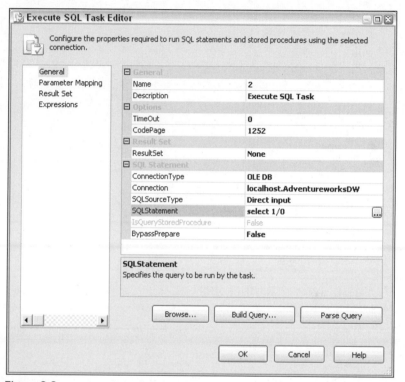

Figure 9-2

The task labeled "1" is expensive, so you want to make sure that you don't need to execute it twice, if it finishes and something else in the package fails. You now need to set up the package to use checkpoints and the task itself. First, set the properties of the package that you read about earlier, as shown in Figure 9-3.

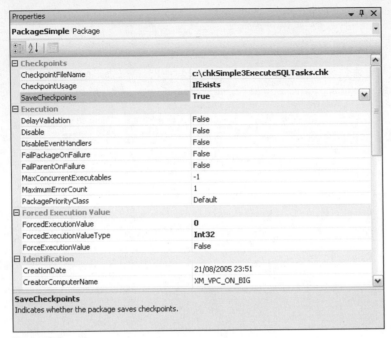

Figure 9-3

Now you need to set the properties of the task to use checkpoints, as you saw earlier (see Figure 9-4).

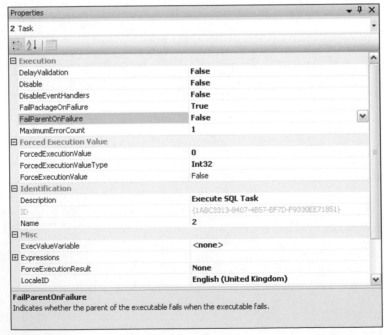

Figure 9-4

Now you can execute the package. The expected outcome is shown in Figure 9-5 — the first task completes successfully (green), but the second task fails (red).

Figure 9-5

If you had created this package in DTS, you would have had to write some logic to cope with the failure in order to not have to execute task 1 again. Because you are working in SSIS and have set the package up properly, you can rely on checkpoints. When the package failed, the error output window said something like this:

```
SSIS package "PackageSimple.dtsx" starting.
Information: 0x40016045 at PackageSimple: The package will be saving checkpoints to
file "C:\chkSimple3ExecuteSQLTasks.chk" during execution. The package is configured
to save checkpoints.
Information: 0x40016047 at 1: Checkpoint file "C:\chkSimple3ExecuteSQLTasks.chk"
was updated to record completion of this container.
Error: 0xC002F210 at 2, Execute SQL Task: Executing the query "select 1/0" failed
with the following error: "Divide by zero error encountered.". Possible failure
reasons: Problems with the query, "ResultSet" property not set correctly,
parameters not set correctly, or connection not established correctly.
Task failed: 2
Warning: 0x80014058 at PackageSimple: This task or container has failed, but
because FailPackageOnFailure property is FALSE, the package will continue. This
warning is posted when the SaveCheckpoints property of the package is set to TRUE
and the task or container fails.
SSIS package "PackageSimple.dtsx" finished: Failure.
```

As you can see, the output window says that a checkpoint file was written. If you look at the file system, you can see that this is true, as shown in Figure 9-6. You'll have a look inside the file later when you have a few more things of interest in there, but for the moment, just know that the package now knows what happened and where.

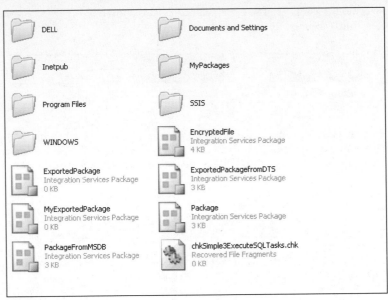

Figure 9-6

Now you need to fix the problem by removing the divide-by-zero issue with the second task and run the package again. Figure 9-7 shows what happens when you do that.

Figure 9-7

Task 2 was executed again and then task 3. Task 1 was oblivious to the package running again.

Earlier you saw that the task you want to be the site for a checkpoint must have the FailPackageOnFailure property set to true, otherwise no file will be written, and when the package executes again it will start from the beginning. Here is how that works. Set the task up to not use checkpoints by setting this property to false, as shown in Figure 9-8.

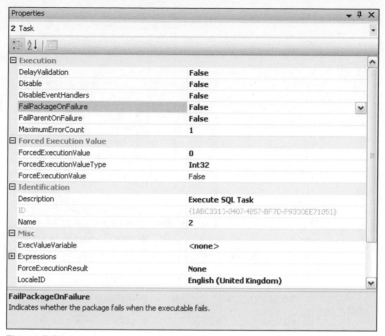

Figure 9 8

Execute the package once again, setting up task 2 to fail with a divide-by-zero error. No checkpoint file is written, as you expected. This means that after you've fixed the error in the task and rerun the package, the results look like Figure 9-9 (all tasks are green), which may or may not be what you want.

Figure 9-9

This example has been a very simple one and has simply involved three tasks joined by workflow. Hopefully this has given you an idea about restartability in packages; the examples that follow will be more complicated and involved than this one.

Containers within Containers and Checkpoints

Containers and transactions have an effect on checkpoints. You'll demonstrate that in this example and change some properties and settings while you're at it. First, create a package using sequence containers and checkpoints. In this package you have two sequence containers, which themselves contain ExecuteSQL tasks, as you can see in Figure 9-10.

285

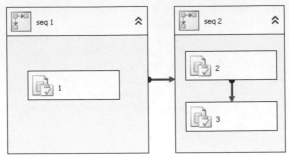

Figure 9-10

Make sure the package has all the settings necessary to use checkpoints, as in the previous example. On the initial run-through of this package, the only container that you want to be the site for a checkpoint is task 3, so set the FailPackageOnFailure property of task 3 to true. Figure 9-11 shows what happens when you deliberately set this task to fail perhaps with a divide-by-zero error; see the earlier example to see how to do that.

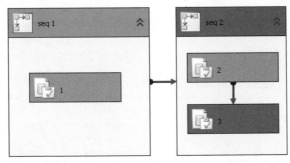

Figure 9-11

As expected, task 3 has failed, and the sequence container, seq2, has also failed because of this. If you now fix the problem with task 3 and re-execute the package, you will see results similar to those shown in Figure 9-12.

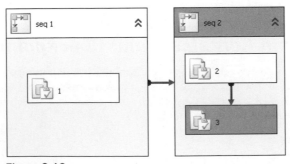

Figure 9-12

So there's no real difference here from the earlier example except that the sequence container "seq 2" is also colored green. Now you'll change the setup of the package to see the behavior change dramatically. What you're going to do is make the sequence container "seq 2" transacted. That means you're going to wrap "seq 2" and its child containers in a transaction. You will now see how to do that. Change the properties of the "seq 2" container to look like Figure 9-13.

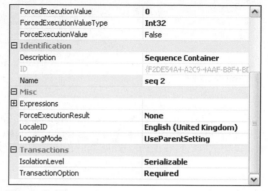

Figure 9-13

The "seq 2" container has its TransactionOption property set to Required, which means that it will start its own transaction. Now open the two child ExecuteSQL tasks and set their TransactionOption properties to Supported, as shown in Figure 9-14, so that they will join a transaction if one exists.

ForcedExecutionValueType	Int32
ForceExecutionValue	False
⊟ Identification	
Description	**Execute SQL Task**
ID	{E97A6058-04C4-4019-AB3C-15
Name	**3**
⊟ Misc	
ExecValueVariable	**<none>**
⊞ Expressions	
ForceExecutionResult	**None**
LocaleID	**English (United Kingdom)**
LoggingMode	**UseParentSetting**
⊟ Transactions	
IsolationLevel	**Serializable**
TransactionOption	**Supported**

Figure 9-14

Now execute the package again. On the first run-through, the package fails as before at task 3. The difference comes when you fix the problem with task 3 and re-execute the package. The result looks like Figure 9-15.

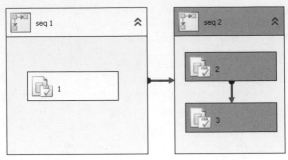

Figure 9-15

As you can see, because the container was transacted, the fact that task 3 failed is not recorded in the checkpoint file. The fact that the sequence container failed is recorded instead; hence the sequence container is re-executed in its entirety when the package is rerun.

Variations on a Theme

You may have noticed another property in the task property pages next to the FailPackageOnFailure property — the FailParentOnFailure property. In the previous example, the "seq 2" container is the parent to the two ExecuteSQL tasks 2 and 3. You'll run through a few variations of the parent/child relationship here so that you can see the differences. In each example, you will force a failure on the first run-through; you will correct whatever problem there is and then run the package through a second time.

Failing the Parent, Not the Package

So what happens then if instead of setting the FailPackageOnFailure property of task 3 to true, you set the FailParentOnFailure property to true? After fixing the issue, on the re-execution of the package the whole package will be run again. Why? Because no checkpoint file has been written.

> *Remember that if you want a checkpoint file to be written, the task that fails must have the FailPackageOnFailure property set to true; otherwise no file is written.*

Failing the Parent and the Package

In this variation, you still have a transacted sequence container and you still have task 3's FailParentOnFailure property set to true. What you also have is the "seq 2" sequence container's FailPackageOnFailure property set to true. Figure 9-16 shows what happens on the rerun of the package after a failure.

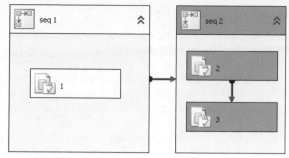

Figure 9-16

As you can see, the sequence container executes in its entirety and the output window from the package confirms that you used a checkpoint file and that you started a transaction.

```
SSIS package "PackageContainerFailures.dtsx" starting.
Information: 0x40016046 at PackageContainerFailures: The package restarted from
checkpoint file " C:\Restartability\CheckPoint Files\ContainerTest.chp ". The
package was configured to restart from checkpoint.
Information: 0x40016045 at PackageContainerFailures: The package will be saving
checkpoints to file "C:\Restartability\CheckPoint Files\ContainerTest.chp" during
execution. The package is configured to save checkpoints.
Information: 0x4001100A at seq 2: Starting distributed transaction for this
container.
Information: 0x4001100B at seq 2: Committing distributed transaction started by
this container.
SSIS package "PackageContainerFailures.dtsx" finished: Success.
```

Failing the Task with No Transaction

Remove the transactions from your package and simply run through this package again, getting it to fail the first time around at task 3; fix the problem and then re-execute the package. Remember that task 3 has its FailParentOnFailure property set to true, and the "seq 2" sequence container has its FailPackageOnFailure set to true. The outcome, shown in Figure 9-17, is not exactly what you expected. The sequence container has executed but nothing within has. The usage case for this scenario at the time of this writing escapes us.

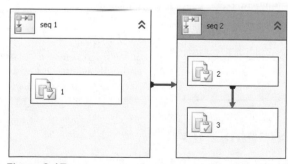

Figure 9-17

Failing the Package, Not the Sequence

You may think that if the tasks 2 and 3 have the sequence container as a parent, then the package itself must be the parent of the sequence container. If this is the case, would setting FailParentOnFailure on the sequence container not be the same as setting FailPackageOnFailure on the same container? The quick answer is no. If you try this option, you will see no checkpoint file being written, and by now you know what that means. The message here is that if you want a checkpoint file to be written, then make sure that the place you want to set as a restart point has FailPackageOnFailure set to true.

The following table summarizes all the cases you've looked at so far.

Test	Summary
Simple Control Flow	Three ExecuteSQL tasks in a row, joined by workflow. The middle of the three is set to fail. Set up the package and the tasks to use restarts. Run it through once; see the task fail and the checkpoint file generated. You then fix the issue with task 2 and rerun the package, which starts from task 2 now.
Containers within Containers and Checkpoints	Placing tasks within sequence containers on the package and having task 3 fail. The main point of this example is to watch the different effect that a transaction on the sequence containers has on the point of restart after a failure.
Failing the Parent, Not the Package	Instead of having task 3's FailParentOnFailure property set to true, you have its FailParentOnFailure property set to true. The effects of this can be seen on restarts.
Failing the Parent and the Package	Again in a transacted sequence container (seq 2), you have task 3 fail. The variation here is that the task has its FailParentOnFailure set to true and the sequence container itself has the FailPackageOnFailure property set to true.
Failing the Task with No Transaction	This is the exact same setup as the example above except the sequence container has not initiated a transaction.
Failing the Package, Not the Sequence	Show the difference between FailParentOnFailure and FailPackageOnFailure when your parent is the package itself. Isn't this logically the same thing?

Inside the Checkpoint File

Earlier it was mentioned that you would look inside the file and see what is actually inside once you had more things to put in there. In the package shown in Figure 9-18, although you have only three tasks, you also have a variable value being changed. The purpose of this package is to show you what kind of information is stored in a checkpoint file. To add a variable, simply click on the designer while in Workflow and choose Variables from the SSIS menu.

Figure 9-18

To alter the value of a variable using the Script task, you add the variable name to the ReadWriteVariables section on the Script task's editor. You then need to add some script to change the value. Below is that script.

```
Public Sub Main()
    '
    Dts.Variables.Item("v1").Value = 2
    '
    Dts.TaskResult = Dts.Results.Success
End Sub
```

Now, cause the package to fail as shown in Figure 9-19.

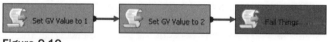

Figure 9-19

Instead of spending too much time figuring out an elaborate way to make your task or container fail, you can simply set the ForceExecutionResult on the task or container to Failure.

Inside the generated checkpoint file, you should find something like this:

```
<DTS:Checkpoint xmlns:DTS="www.microsoft.com/SqlServer/Dts"
DTS:PackageID="{5B59AB20-8B19-4C58-8021-6296A2F57158}"><DTS:Variables
DTS:ContID="{5B59AB20-8B19-4C58-8021-6296A2F57158}">
<DTS:Variable><DTS:Property DTS:Name="Expression"></DTS:Property><DTS:Property
DTS:Name="EvaluateAsExpression">0</DTS:Property><DTS:Property
DTS:Name="Namespace">User</DTS:Property><DTS:Property
DTS:Name="ReadOnly">0</DTS:Property><DTS:Property
DTS:Name="RaiseChangedEvent">0</DTS:Property><DTS:VariableValue
DTS:DataType="3">2</DTS:VariableValue><DTS:Property
DTS:Name="ObjectName">v1</DTS:Property><DTS:Property DTS:Name="DTSID">{A28969A0-
0633-4D43-9325-DF54B30EBF2D}</DTS:Property><DTS:Property
DTS:Name="Description">This is the variable being
changed</DTS:Property><DTS:Property
DTS:Name="CreationName"></DTS:Property></DTS:Variable></DTS:Variables><DTS:Containe
r DTS:ContID="{5BE98D21-AE77-4278-9784-BEE4D9115967}" DTS:Result="0"
DTS:PrecedenceMap=""/><DTS:Container DTS:ContID="{87431A77-CB01-4AFF-8A18-
0CB89209DD26}" DTS:Result="0" DTS:PrecedenceMap="Y"/></DTS:Checkpoint>
```

The file is better broken down into the constituent parts. The first part tells you about the package to which this file applies.

```
<DTS:Checkpoint xmlns:DTS="www.microsoft.com/SqlServer/Dts"
DTS:PackageID="{5B59AB20-8B19-4C58-8021-6296A2F57158}">
```

The next section of the file, the longest part, details the package variable that you were manipulating:

```
<DTS:Variables DTS:ContID="{5B59AB20-8B19-4C58-8021-6296A2F57158}">
<DTS:Variable><DTS:Property DTS:Name="Expression"></DTS:Property><DTS:Property
DTS:Name="EvaluateAsExpression">0</DTS:Property><DTS:Property
DTS:Name="Namespace">User</DTS:Property><DTS:Property
DTS:Name="ReadOnly">0</DTS:Property><DTS:Property
DTS:Name="RaiseChangedEvent">0</DTS:Property><DTS:VariableValue
DTS:DataType="3">2</DTS:VariableValue><DTS:Property
DTS:Name="ObjectName">v1</DTS:Property><DTS:Property DTS:Name="DTSID">{A28969A0-
0633-4D43-9325-DF54B30EBF2D}</DTS:Property><DTS:Property
DTS:Name="Description">This is the variable being
changed</DTS:Property><DTS:Property
DTS:Name="CreationName"></DTS:Property></DTS:Variable></DTS:Variables>
```

One of the most important things this part of the file tells you is that the last value assigned to the variable, v1, was 2. When the package re-executes, it is this value that will be used.

The final part of the file tells you about the tasks in the package and what their outcomes were. It only tells you about the two tasks that succeeded and not the one that failed.

```
<DTS:Container DTS:ContID="{5BE98D21-AE77-4278-9784-BEE4D9115967}" DTS:Result="0"
DTS:PrecedenceMap=""/><DTS:Container DTS:ContID="{87431A77-CB01-4AFF-8A18-
0CB89209DD26}" DTS:Result="0" DTS:PrecedenceMap="Y"/></DTS:Checkpoint >
```

The first container mentioned is the "Set GV Value to 2" task.

```
<DTS:Container DTS:ContID="{5BE98D21-AE77-4278-9784-BEE4D9115967}" DTS:Result="0"
DTS:PrecedenceMap=""/>
```

The next and final task to be mentioned is the "Set GV Value to 1" task.

```
DTS:Container DTS:ContID="{87431A77-CB01-4AFF-8A18-0CB89209DD26}" DTS:Result="0"
DTS:PrecedenceMap="Y"/></DTS:Checkpoint >
```

That concludes your whirlwind tour of package restartability in SSIS. Hopefully you will get something out of it, because using the features will save you hours of reloading time.

Package Transactions

In this part of the chapter, you will see how you can use transactions within your packages to handle data consistency. There are two types of transactions available in an SSIS package:

❑ **Distributed Transaction Coordinator (DTC) Transactions:** One or more transactions that require a DTC and can span connections, tasks, and packages

❑ **Native Transaction:** A transaction at a SQL Server engine level, using a single connection managed through using T-SQL transaction commands

Here is how Books Online defines MSDTC: "The Microsoft Distributed Transaction Coordinator (MS DTC) allows applications to extend transactions across two or more instances of SQL Server. It also allows applications to participate in transactions managed by transaction managers that comply with the X/Open DTP XA standard."

You will learn how to use them by going through four examples in detail. Each example builds on the previous example, except for the last one:

❑ Single Package: Single transaction using DTC

❑ Single Package: Multiple transactions using DTC

❑ Two Packages: One transaction using DTC

❑ Single Package: One transaction using a native transaction in SQL Server

For transactions to happen in a package and for tasks to join them, you need to set a few properties at both the package and the task level. As you go through the examples, you will see the finer print of what this means, but the following table will get you started with understanding the possible settings for the TransactionOption property.

Property Value	Description
Supported	If a transaction already exists at the parent, the container will join the transaction.
Not Supported	The container will not join a transaction, if one is present.
Required	The container will start a transaction if the parent has not; otherwise it will join the parent transaction.

So armed with these facts, you can get right into the thick of things and look at the first example.

Single Package, Single Transaction

To start the first example, create the simple package shown in Figure 9-20.

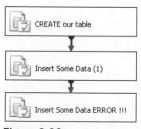

Figure 9-20

This package is quite basic in that all it does is create a table and insert some data into the table, and then the final task will deliberately fail. The first task contains the following as the code to be executed:

```
CREATE TABLE dbo.T1(col1 int)
```

The second task inserts some data into the table you just created:

```
INSERT dbo.T1(col1) VALUES(1)
```

To make the final task fail, you may like to try executing from this task a statement like the following:

```
INSERT dbo.T1(col1) VALUES('A')
```

Run the package with no transactions in place and see what happens. The results should look like Figure 9-21: The first two tasks succeed, and the third fails.

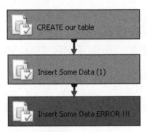

Figure 9-21

If you go to your database, you should see that the table was created and the data inserted, as shown in Figure 9-22.

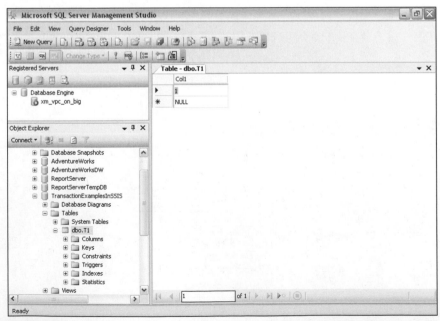

Figure 9-22

Now you want to make sure that the table should not be created if anything in the package fails. Drop the table and start again. The first thing you want to do is to tell the package to start a transaction that the tasks can join. You do that by setting the properties of the package as shown in Figure 9-23.

Figure 9-23

You now need to tell the tasks in the package to join this transaction, by setting their TransactionOption properties to "Supported," as shown in Figure 9-24.

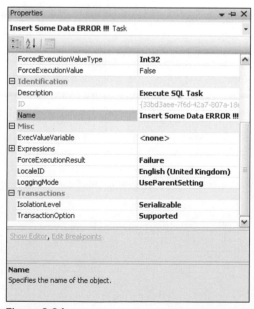

Figure 9-24

295

Now when you re-execute the package, a DTC transaction will be started by the package, all the tasks will join, and because of the failure in the last task, the work in the package will be undone. A good way to see that a DTC transaction was started is to look at the output window:

```
SSIS package "Transactions .dtsx" starting.
Information: 0x4001100A at Transactions: Starting distributed transaction for this
container.
Task failed: Insert Some Data ERROR !!!
Information: 0x4001100C at Insert Some Data ERROR !!!: Aborting the current
distributed transaction.
Information: 0x4001100B at Transactions: Committing distributed transaction started
by this container.
Warning: 0x8004D019 at Transactions: The transaction has already been aborted.
SSIS package "Transactions .dtsx" finished: Failure.
```

Single Package, Multiple Transactions

The aim of this second package is to be able to have two transactions running in the same package at the same time. Create the package as shown in Figure 9-25. If you're not feeling creative, you can use the same statements in the tasks as you used in the previous example.

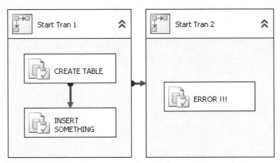

Figure 9-25

The package contains two sequence containers, each containing its own child tasks. The "Start Tran 1" container begins a transaction, and the child tasks will join the transaction. The "Start Tran 2" container also starts a transaction of its own, and its child task will join that transaction. As you can see, the task in "Start Tran 2" will deliberately fail. The "CREATE TABLE" task creates a table into which all the other child tasks of both sequence containers will insert. The idea here is that after this package has run, the table will be created and the data inserted by the "INSERT SOMETHING" task will be in the table even though the task in "Start Tran 2" fails. This could be useful when you have logical grouping of data manipulation routines to perform and they either all succeed or none of them do. The following table details the tasks and containers in the package along with the package itself and the setting of their TransactionOption properties.

Task/Container	TransactionOption Property Value
Package	Supported
"Start Tran 1"	Required
CREATE TABLE	Supported
INSERT SOMETHING	Supported
"Start Tran 2"	Required
ERROR !!!	Supported

After you execute the package, the results should look like Figure 9-26. The first container succeeded, but the second one failed because its child task failed.

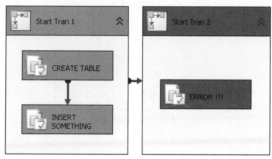

Figure 9-26

If you now look in the database, you will see that the table was created and a row inserted. To prove that two transactions were instantiated, take another look at the output window:

```
SSIS package "Multiple transactions same Package.dtsx" starting.
Information: 0x4001100A at Start Tran 1: Starting distributed transaction for this
container.
Information: 0x4001100B at Start Tran 1: Committing distributed transaction started
by this container.
Information: 0x4001100A at Start Tran 2: Starting distributed transaction for this
container.
Error: 0xC00291D7 at ERROR !!!, Execute SQL Task: No connection manager is
specified.
Error: 0xC0024107 at ERROR !!!: There were errors during task validation.
Information: 0x4001100C at ERROR !!!: Aborting the current distributed transaction.
Warning: 0x80019002 at Start Tran 2: The Execution method succeeded, but the number
of errors raised (3) reached the maximum allowed (1); resulting in failure. This
occurs when the number of errors reaches the number specified in MaximumErrorCount.
Change the MaximumErrorCount or fix the errors.
Information: 0x4001100C at Start Tran 2: Aborting the current distributed
transaction.
Warning: 0x80019002 at Multiple transactions same Package: The Execution method
succeeded, but the number of errors raised (3) reached the maximum allowed (1);
```

```
resulting in failure. This occurs when the number of errors reaches the number
specified in MaximumErrorCount. Change the MaximumErrorCount or fix the errors.
SSIS package "Multiple transactions same Package.dtsx" finished: Failure.
```

Two Packages, One Transaction

This example consists of two packages: "Caller" and "Called." What you want to do is to have a transaction span multiple packages. You'll have the Caller package create a table and then call a child package using an ExecutePackage task, Called, which itself will create a table and insert some data. You will then introduce an error in the Caller package that will cause it to fail. The result should be that the work done in both of the packages is undone. Figure 9-27 shows the "Caller" package.

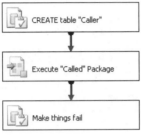

Figure 9-27

Figure 9-28 shows the "Called" package.

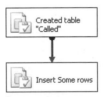

Figure 9-28

As before, you will need to set the TransactionOption properties on the tasks and containers, using the values in the following table.

Task/Container	TransactionOption Property Value
"Caller" Package	Required
CREATE TABLE "Caller"	Supported
EXECUTE "Called" Package	Supported
Make Things Fail	Supported
"Called" Package	Supported
Created Table "Called"	Supported
Insert Some Rows	Supported

The point to note here is that the child package "Called" becomes nothing more than another task. The parent of the "Called" package is the ExecutePackage task in the "Caller" package. Because the ExecutePackage task is in a transaction, and the Called package also has its TransactionOption set to Supported, it will join the transaction in the parent package.

If you change the TransactionOption property on the ExecutePackage task in the "Caller" package to Not Supported, when the final task in the "Caller" package fails, the work in the "Called" package will not be undone. To see how to change the option, please refer back to Figure 9-24.

Single Package Using a Native Transaction in SQL Server

This example differs from the others in that you are going to use the transaction-handling abilities of SQL Server and not those of MSDTC. Although the example is short, it does demonstrate the fact that transactions can be used in packages that are not MSDTC transactions. Native SQL transactions will allow you a finer level of granularity when deciding what data gets rolled back and committed, but they are possible only against SQL Server. The package for this example is shown in Figure 9-29.

Figure 9-29

The reason why we have a specific task to handle the COMMIT TRANSACTION and not the ROLL-BACK TRANSACTION is that, if the CREATE TABLE Transactions task fails, a ROLLBACK TRANSACTION is issued for us.

The following table lists the contents of the SQLStatement property for each of the ExecuteSQL tasks.

Task	SQLStatement Property Value
BEGIN TRANSACTION	BEGIN TRANSACTION
CREATE TABLE Transactions	CREATE TABLE dbo.Transactions(col1 int)
COMMIT	COMMIT TRANSACTION

The key to making the package use the native transaction capabilities in SQL Server is to have all the tasks use the same Connection Manager. In addition to this, you must make sure that the RetainSameConnection property on the Connection Manager is set to True, as shown in Figure 9-30.

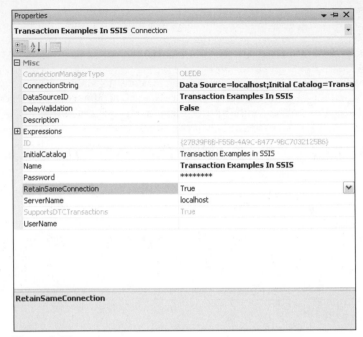

Figure 9-30

When the package is executed, SQL Server will fire up a transaction and either commit or rollback that transaction at the end of the package. You will now have a look at that happening on SQL Server by using Profiler, as shown in Figure 9-31. Profiler is really useful in situations like this. Here you simply want to prove that a transaction was started and that it either finished successfully or failed. You could also use it when firing SSIS packages to make sure that what you think you are executing is what you are actually executing.

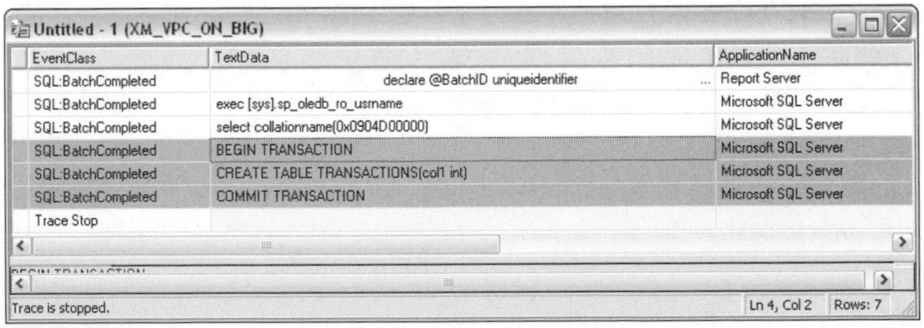

Figure 9-31

That ends your whistle-stop look at transactions within SSIS packages, and hopefully you can take something away from this section and use it in your packages.

Error Outputs

Error outputs can obviously be used to improve reliability, but they also have an important part to play for scalability as well. From a reliability perspective, they are a critical feature for coping with bad data. An appropriately configured component will direct failing rows down the error output as opposed to the main output. These rows are now removed from the main Data Flow path and may then receive additional treatment and cleansing to enable them to be recovered and merged back into the main flow. They can be explicitly merged, such as with a Union transform, or implicitly through a second adapter directed at the final destination. Alternatively they could be discarded. Rows are rarely discarded totally; more often they will be logged and dealt with at a later point in time.

The capability to recover rows is perhaps the most useful course of action. If a data item is missing in the source extract but required in the final destination, the error flow path can be used to fix this. If the data item is available from a secondary system, then a lookup could be used. If the data item is not available elsewhere, then perhaps a default value can be used instead.

In other situations, the data may be out of range for the process or destination. If the data causes an integrity violation, then the failed data could be used to populate the constraining reference with new values and then the data itself could be successfully processed. If a data type conflict occurs, then maybe a simple truncation would suffice, or an additional set of logic could be applied to try and detect the real value, such as with data time values held in strings. The data could then be converted into the required format.

When assumptions or fixes have been made to data in this way, it is best practice to always mark rows as having been manipulated so that if additional information becomes available later, they can be targeted directly. In addition, whenever an assumption is made, it should be clearly identified as such to the end user.

All of the scenarios described above revolve around trying to recover from poor data, within the pipeline and the current session, allowing processing to continue, and ideally fixing the problem such that data is recovered. This is a new concept when compared with DTS and several other products, but the ability to fix errors in real time is a very valuable option that you should always consider when building solutions.

The obvious question that then occurs is this: Why not include the additional transformations used to correct and cleanse the data in the main Data Flow path, so that any problems are dealt with before they cause an error? This would mean that all data flowed down a single path and the overall Data Flow design may appear simpler, with no branching and merging flows. This is where the scalability factor should come into your solution design. Ideally, you would always build the simplest Data Flow possible, using as few transformations as possible. The less work you perform, the greater the performance and therefore scalability.

Figure 9-32 illustrates a simple Data Flow used to load some data. In this contrived scenario, some of the rows will be missing values for SpecialtyCode and ConsultantCode. The source data contains text descriptions as well, so these are being used to perform a lookup to retrieve the missing values. The initial design logic goes that you evaluate the column for NULL values in a Conditional Split transform. Bad rows are directed to an alternate output that connects to the Lookup transform. Once the lookup has populated the missing value, the rows are then fed back into the main pipeline through the Union All transform. The same pattern is followed for the SpecialtyCode and ConsultantCode columns, ensuring that the final insert through the OLE DB Destination has all good data. This is the base design for solving your problem, and it follows the procedural logic quite closely.

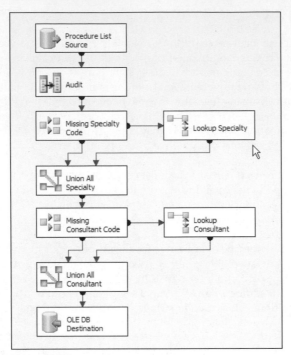

Figure 9-32

Figure 9-33 shows two alternative Data Flow designs, presented side by side for easy comparison. In the first design, you disregard any existing data in the SpecialtyCode and ConsultantCode columns and populate them entirely through the lookup. Although this may seem like wasted effort, the overall design is simpler and in testing it was 2% faster compared to the more complicated design in Figure 9-32. This was with a test data set that had a bad row ratio of 1 in 3, that is, one row in three had missing values. If the ratio dropped to 1 in 6 for the bad rows, then the two methods performed the same.

The second design assumes that all data is good until proven otherwise, so you insert directly into the destination. Rows that fail due to the missing values pass down the error output, "OLE DB Destination Error Output," and are then processed through the two lookups. The choice between the two designs is whether you fix all rows or only those that fail. Using the 1 in 3 bad rows test data, fixing only the failed rows was 20% faster than fixing all rows. When the bad row ratio dropped to 1 in 6, the performance gain also dropped, to only 10%.

As demonstrated by the previous examples, the decision on where to include the corrective transformations is based on the ratio of good rows to bad rows, when compared with how much work is required to validate the quality of the data. The cost of fixing the data should be excluded if possible, as that will be required regardless of the design, but often the two are inseparable.

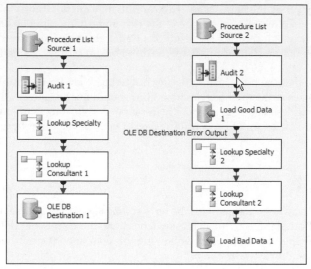

Figure 9-33

The performance characteristics of the corrective transforms should also be considered. In the examples above, you used lookups, which are inherently expensive transforms. The test data and lookup reference data included only six distinct values to minimize the impact on the overall testing. Lookups with more distinct values, and higher cardinality, will be more expensive, as the caching becomes less effective and itself will consume more resources.

In summary, the more expensive the verification, the more bad rows you require to justify adding the validation and fix to the main flow. For fewer bad rows, or a more expensive validation procedure, you have increased justification for keeping the main flow simple and for using the error flow to perform the fix-up work.

The overall number of rows should also influence your design, since any advantages or disadvantages will be amplified with a greater number of rows, regardless of the ratio. For a smaller number of rows, the fixed costs may outweigh the implied benefits, as any component has a cost to manage at runtime, so a more complicated Data Flow may not be worthwhile with fewer overall rows.

This concept of using error flows versus the main flow to correct data quality issues and related errors is not confined to those outputs that implement the error output explicitly. You can apply the same logic manually, primarily through the use of the conditional split transformation, as shown in the first example, Figure 9-32. You can perform a simple test to detect any potential issues and direct rows of differing quality down different outputs. Where expensive operations are required, your goal is to ensure that as few rows as possible follow this path and that the majority of the rows follow cheaper and usually simpler routes to their destination.

Finally, do not be put off by the name of an error output; they are not things to be avoided at all costs. Component developers often take advantage of the rich underlying pipeline architecture, using error outputs as a simple way of indicating the result of a transformation for a given row. They do not affect the overall success or failure state of a package, so don't be put off from using them.

You should be aware that the performance figures quoted here are for indicative purposes only. They illustrate the differences in the methods described but should not be taken as literal values that you can expect to reproduce, unless you're using exactly the same design, data, and environment. The key point is that testing such scenarios should be a routine part of your development practice.

Scaling Out

You will no doubt already be familiar with the term *scaling out*, and of course the concept can be applied to SSIS systems. Although there are no magic switches here, there are several interesting features of SSIS, and you will see how they can be applied. Following this combined theme, you will learn how these strategies benefit reliability as well.

Scale Out Memory Pressures

By design, the pipeline processing takes place almost exclusively in memory. This makes for faster data movement and transformations, and a design goal should always be to make a single pass over your data. In this way, you eliminate the time-consuming staging and the costs of reading and writing the same data several times. The potential disadvantage of this is that for large amounts of data and complicated sets of transformations, you need a large amount of memory, and it needs to be the right type of memory for optimum performance.

The virtual memory space for 32-bit Windows operating systems is limited to 2 GB by default. Although you can increase this amount through the use of the /3GB switch applied in the boot.ini file, this often falls short of the total memory available today. This limit is applied per process, which for your purposes means a single package during execution, so by partitioning a process across multiple packages, you can ensure that each of the smaller packages is its own process and therefore takes advantage of the full 2–3 GB virtual space independently. The most common method of chaining packages together to form a consolidated process is through the Execute Package task, in which case it is imperative that you set the child package to execute out of process. You must set the ExecuteOutOfProcess property to true to allow this to happen.

It is worth noting that unlike the SQL Server database engine, SSIS does not support Advanced Windowing Extensions (AWE), so scaling out to multiple packages across processes is the only way to take advantage of larger amounts of memory. If you have a very large memory requirement, then you should consider a 64-bit system for hosting these processes.

For more a more detailed explanation of how SSIS uses memory, and the in-memory buffer structure used to move data through the pipeline, see Chapters 10 and 11.

Scale Out by Staging Data

Staging of data is very much on the decline; after all, why incur the cost of writing to and reading from a staging area, when you can perform all the processing in memory with a single pass of data? With the inclusion of the Dimension and Partition Processing Destinations, you no longer need a physical data source to populate your SQL Server Analysis Services (SSAS) cubes — yet another reason for the decline of staging or even the traditional data warehouse. Although this is still a contentious subject for many, the issue here is this: Should you use staging during the SSIS processing flow? Although it may not be technically required to achieve the overall goal, there are still some very good reasons why you may want to, coming from both the scalability and reliability perspectives.

For this discussion, staging could also be described as partitioning. The process could be implemented within a single data flow, but for one or more of the reasons described below, it may be subdivided into multiple data flows. These smaller units could be within a single package, or they may be distributed through several as discussed below. The staged data will be used only by another Data Flow and does not need to be accessed directly through regular interfaces. For this reason, the ideal choices for the source and destinations are the raw file adapters. This could be described as vertical partitioning, but you could also overlay a level of horizontal partitioning, as by executing multiple instances of a package in parallel.

Raw file adapters allow you to persist the native buffer structures to disk. The in-memory buffer structure is simply dumped to and from the file, without any translation or processing as found in all other adapters, making these the fastest adapters for staging data. You can take advantage of this to artificially force a memory checkpoint to be written to disk, allowing you to span multiple Data Flows tasks and packages. Staging environments and raw files are also discussed later on in Chapter 11, but some specific examples will be illustrated here.

The key use for raw files is that by splitting a Data Flow into at least two individual tasks, the primary task can end with a raw file destination and the secondary task can begin with a raw file source. The buffer structure is exactly the same between the two tasks, so the split can be considered irrelevant from an overall flow perspective, but it provides perfect preservation between the two.

Data Flow Restart

As covered previously, the checkpoint feature provides the ability to restart a package from the point of failure, but it does not extended inside a Data Flow. However, if you divide a Data Flow into one or more individual tasks, each linked together by raw files, you immediately gain the ability to restart the combined flow. Through the correct use of native checkpoints at the (Data Flow) task level, this process becomes very simple to manage.

The choice of where to divide a flow is subjective, but two common choices would be immediately after extraction and immediately after transformation, prior to load.

The post-extraction point offers several key benefits. Many source systems are remote, so extraction may take place over suboptimal network links and can be the slowest part of the process. By staging immediately after the extraction, you do not have to repeat this slow step in the event of a failure and restart. There may also be an impact on the source system during the extraction, and very often this must take place during a fixed time window when utilization is low. In this case, it may be unacceptable to repeat the extract in the event of a failure, until the next time window, usually the following night.

Staging post-transformation simply ensures that the transformation is not wasted if the destination system is unavailable.

You may wish to include additional staging points mid-transformation. These would usually be located after particularly expensive operations and before those that you suspect are at risk to fail. Although you can plan for problems, and the use of error outputs described above should allow you to handle many situations, you can still expect the unexpected and plan a staging point with this in mind. The goal remains the ability to restart as close to the failure point as possible and to reduce the cost of any reprocessing required.

Figure 9-34 shows an example data load process that you may wish to partition into multiple tasks to take advantage of Data Flow restart.

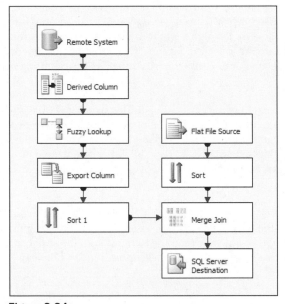

Figure 9-34

For this scenario, the OLE DB Source connects to a remote SQL Server over a slow network link. Due to the time taken for this data extraction and the impact on the source system, it is not acceptable to repeat the extract if the subsequent processing fails for any reason. For this reason, you choose to stage data through a raw file immediately after the source component. The resulting Data Flow layout is shown in Figure 9-35. This is a Data Flow task.

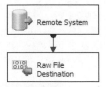

Figure 9-35

The flat file source data is accessed across the LAN, and it needs to be captured before it is overwritten. The sort operation is also particularly expensive due to the volume of data. For this reason, you choose to stage the data after the sort is complete. The resulting Data Flow is shown in Figure 9-36.

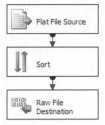

Figure 9-36

Finally, you use a third Data Flow task to consume the two staging raw files and complete the process. This is shown in Figure 9-37.

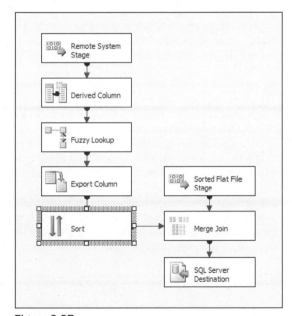

Figure 9-37

Following this example, a single Data Flow has been divided into three separate tasks. For the purposes of restarting a failed process, you would use a single package and implement checkpoints on each of the three Data Flow tasks.

Scale across Machines

In a similar manner to the Data Flow Restart just discussed, you can also use raw file adapters to partition the Data Flow. By separating tasks into different packages, you can run packages across machines. This may be advantageous if a specific machine has properties not shared with others. Perhaps the

machine capable of performing the extract is situated in a different network segment from the machine best suited for processing the data, and direct access is unavailable between the main processing machine and the source. The extract could be performed, and the main processing machine would then retrieve the raw data to continue the process. These situations will be organizational restrictions rather than decisions driven by the design architecture.

The more compelling story for scaling across machines is to use horizontal partitioning. A simple scenario would utilize two packages. The first package would extract data from the source system, and through the Conditional Split you produce two or more exclusive subsets of the data and write this to individual raw files. Each raw file would contain some of the rows from the extract, as determined by the expression used in the Conditional Split. The most common horizontal partition scheme is time-based, but any method could be used here. The goal is to subdivide the total extract into manageable chunks, so for example if a sequential row number is already available in the source, this would be ideal, or one could be applied. See the T-SQL ROW_NUMBER function. Similarly a Row Number transformation could be used to apply the numbering, which could then be used by the split, or the numbering and splitting could be delivered through a Script Component.

> *A Row Number transformation is freely available from www.sqlis.com and www.konesans.com.*

With a sorted data set, each raw file may be written in sequence, completing in order, before moving on to the next one. While this may seem uneven and inefficient, it is assumed that the time delay between completion of the first and final destinations is inconsequential compared to the savings achieved by the subsequent parallel processing.

Once the partitioned raw files are complete, they are consumed by the second package, which performs the transformation and load aspects of the processing. Each file is processed by an instance of the package running on a separate machine. This way, you can scale across machines and perform expensive transformations in parallel. For a smaller-scale implementation, where the previously described 32-bit virtual memory constraints apply, you could parallel process on a single machine, such that each package instance would be a separate thread, allowed its own allocation of virtual memory space.

For destinations that are partitioned themselves, such as a SQL Server data warehouse with table partitions or a partitioned view model, or Analysis Services partitions, it may also make sense to match the partition schema to that of the destination, such that each package addresses a single table or partition.

Figure 9-38 shows a sample package that for the purposes of this example you will partition horizontally.

In this scenario, the Fuzzy Lookup is processing names against a very large reference set, and this is taking too long. To introduce some parallel processing, you decide to partition on the first letter of a name field. It is deemed stable enough for matches to be within the same letter, although in a real-world scenario this may not always be true. You use a Conditional Split transformation to produce the two raw files partitioned from A to M and from N to Z. This primer package is illustrated in Figure 9-39.

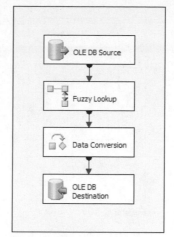

Figure 9-38

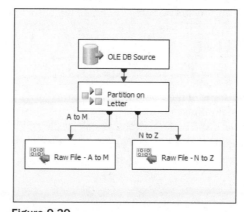

Figure 9-39

Ideally you would then have two instances of the second package, Figure 9-39, running in parallel on two separate machines. However, you need to ensure that the lookup data is filtered on name to match the raw file. Not all pipeline component properties are exposed as expressions, allowing you to dynamically control them, so you would need two versions of the package, identical except for a different Reference table name property in the Fuzzy Lookup, as shown in Figure 9-40. In preparation, you would create two views, one for names A to M and the other for names N to Z to match the two raw files. The two package versions would each use the view to match the raw file they will process.

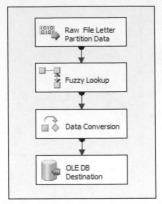

Figure 9-40

For any design that uses raw files, the additional I/O cost must be evaluated against the processing performance gains, but for large-scale implementations it offers a convenient way of ensuring consistency within the overall flow and incurs no translation penalty associated with other storage formats.

Summary

In this chapter, you looked at some of the obvious SSIS features provided to help you build reliable and scalable solutions, such as checkpoints and transactions. You also learned about some practices you can apply, such as Data Flow restarts and scaling across machines; although these may not be explicit features, they are nonetheless very powerful techniques that can be implemented in your package designs.

10

Understanding the Integration Services Engine

In this chapter, you will dive under the hood of Integration Services to consider the architecture of the engine and its components, including the following concepts:

- ❑ Control Flow and Data Flow comparison
- ❑ Data Flow transformation types
- ❑ Advanced workflow concepts in the Control Flow
- ❑ Data Flow buffer architecture and execution trees
- ❑ Monitoring Data Flow execution

Some of the discussions in this chapter are more abstract and theoretical, but you will start from a high level and work your way to the details of understanding SSIS. In the next chapter, you will take the knowledge you have developed here and bring it to application, considering a methodology to optimization and looking at a few real-world scenarios.

The Integration Services Engine: An Analogy

Before you learn about buffers, asynchronous components, and execution trees, you will start with an analogy — traffic management. Have you ever driven in a big city and wondered how the traffic system works? I find it remarkable to consider how the traffic lights are all coordinated in a city. In Manhattan, for example, a taxi drive can take you from midtown to downtown in minutes — in part because the lights are timed in a rolling fashion to maintain efficiency. The heavy fine assessed to anyone who "locks the box" (remains in the intersection after the light turns red) demonstrates how detrimental it is to interfere with the synchronization of such a complex traffic grid.

Contrast the efficiency of Manhattan with the gridlock and delay that result from a poorly designed traffic system. Everyone has been there before—sitting at a red light for minutes despite the absence of traffic on the intersecting streets, and then after the light changes, you find yourself at the next intersection in the same scenario! Even in a light-traffic environment, progress is impeded by poor coordination and inefficient design.

Bringing this back around to Integration Services, in some ways the engine is similar to the grid management of a big city because the Integration Services engine coordinates server resources and data flow for efficient information processing. Part of the process to make a package execution efficient requires your involvement. In turn, this requires knowing how the Integration Services engine works and some important particulars of components and properties that affect the data processing. That is the purpose of this chapter: to provide the groundwork of understanding Integration Services that will lead to better and more efficient design.

Understanding the SSIS Data Flow and Control Flow

From an architectural perspective, the difference between Integration Services Data Flow and Control Flow is important. One aspect that will help illustrate the distinction is to look at them from the perspective of how the components are handled. In the Control Flow, the *task* is the smallest unit of work, and tasks require completion (success, failure, or just completion) before the subsequent tasks are handled. In the Data Flow, the *transformation* is the basic component; however, a transformation functions very differently from a task. Instead of one transformation necessarily waiting for associated transformations before work can be done, the transformations work together to process and manage data.

Comparing and Contrasting the Data Flow and Control Flow

Although the Control Flow looks very similar to the Data Flow with processing objects (tasks and transformations) and green and red connectors that bridge them, there is a world of difference between them. The Control Flow, for example, does not manage or pass data between components; rather it functions as a task coordinator with isolated units of work. Here are some of the Control Flow concepts:

❑   Workflow orchestration

❑   Process-oriented

❑   Serial or parallel tasks execution

❑   Synchronous processing

As highlighted, the Control Flow tasks can be designed to execute both serially and in parallel—in fact, more often than not there will be aspects of both. A Control Flow task can branch off into multiple tasks that are performed in parallel as well as a single next step that is performed essentially in serial from the first. To show this, Figure 10-1 is a very simple Control Flow process where the tasks are connected in a linear fashion. The execution of this package shows that the components are serialized—only a single task is executing at a time.

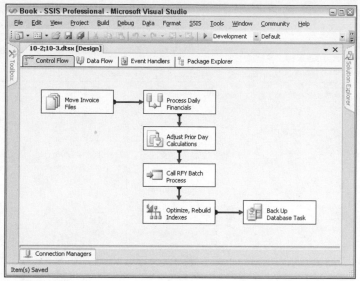

Figure 10-1

The Data Flow, on the other hand, can branch, split, and merge, providing parallel processing, but the concept is different from the Control Flow. Even though there may be a set of connected linear transformations, you cannot necessarily call the process serial, because the transformations in most cases will be running at the same time, handling subsets of the data in parallel. Here are some of the unique aspects of the Data Flow:

❑　Information-oriented

❑　Data correlation and transformation

❑　Coordinated processing

❑　Streaming in nature

❑　Sources and destinations

Similar to the Control Flow shown above, Figure 10-2 models a simple Data Flow where the components are connected one after the other. The difference between the Data Flow in Figure 10-2 and the Control Flow in Figure 10-1 is that only a single task is executing in the linear flow. In the Data Flow, however, all the transformations are doing work at the same time. In other words, the first batch of data flowing in from the source may be in the final destination step (Currency Rate Destination), while at the same time data is still flowing in from the source.

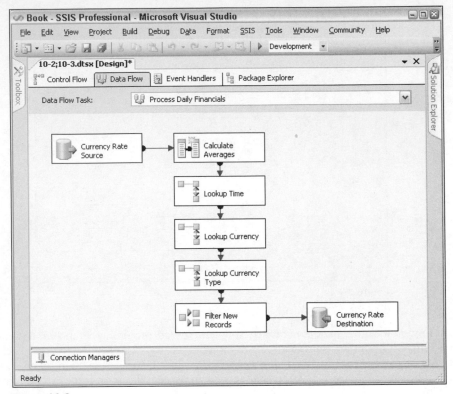

Figure 10-2

Multiple components are running at the same time because the Data Flow transformations are working together in a coordinated streaming fashion and the data is being transformed in groups as it is passed down from the source to the subsequent transformations.

SSIS Package Execution Times from Package Start to Package Finish

Since a Data Flow is merely a type of Control Flow task, and there can be more than one Data Flow embedded in a package, the total time it takes to execute a package is measured from the execution of the first Control Flow task or tasks through the completion of the last task being executed, regardless of whether the components executing are Data Flows transformations or Control Flow tasks. This may sound obvious, but it is worth mentioning, because when designing a package, maximizing the parallel processing where appropriate (with due regard to your server resources) will help optimize the flow and reduce the overall processing time.

The package in Figure 10-3 has several tasks executing a variety of processes and using precedence constraints in a way that demonstrates parallel execution of tasks.

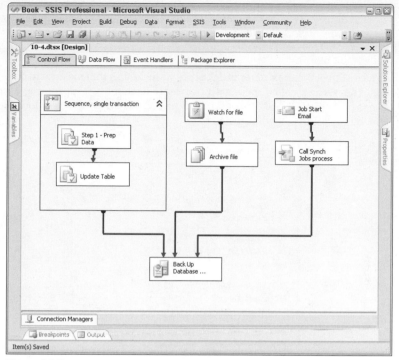

Figure 10-3

Because the Control Flow has been designed with parallelization, the overlap in tasks allows the execution of the package to complete faster than it would if the steps were executed in a serial manner as in Figure 10-1.

Enterprise Workflows with the Control Flow

Both of the components of the Control Flow have been discussed in Chapter 3 as well as the different types of precedence constraints. Since the Control Flow contains standard workflow concepts that are common to most scheduling and ETL tools, including DTS, the rest of this chapter will focus on the Data Flow; however, a brief look at the Control Flow parallelization and processing is warranted.

The Control Flow, as has already been mentioned, can be designed to execute tasks in parallel or serial, or a combination of the two. Tasks also are *synchronous* in nature, meaning that the task requires completion before handing off operation to another process. While it is possible to design a Control Flow that contains tasks that are not connected with constraints to other tasks, the tasks are still synchronously tied to the execution of the package. Said in another way, a package cannot kick off the execution of a task and then complete execution while the task is still executing. Rather, the SSIS execution thread for the task is synchronously tied to the task's execution and will not release until the task completes successfully or fails.

The synchronous nature of tasks should not be confused with the synchronous and asynchronous nature of transformations in the Data Flow. The concepts are slightly different. In the Data Flow, a transformation's synchronicity is a matter of communication (how data is passed between transformations) rather than the process orientation of the Control Flow.

Integration Services allows the maximum number of parallel tasks that execute to be set on a package-by-package basis. This setting, called the MaxConcurrentExecutables, is a property of the Control Flow. Click in a blank space on the Control Flow, and then pull up the Properties window. Figure 10-4 shows the property, which is settable to a whole number.

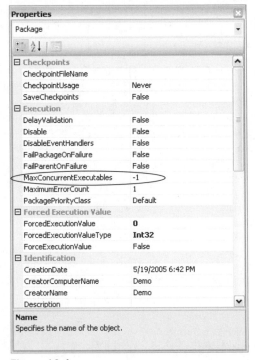

Figure 10-4

The default setting is -1, indicating to Integration Services to add 2 to the number of processors and use that value for the number of tasks to execute in parallel. For example, if the server has four processors and the default value is used, Integration Services will allow up to six tasks to be executed in parallel. Furthermore, if the number of possible parallel executing tasks (based on Control Flow design) is more than the number of allowable parallel tasks (allowable as specified by the MaxConcurrentExecutables setting), then some of the Control Flow tasks will have to wait to execute until parallel threads are available.

Some tasks require more server resources than others, so the package Concurrency should not be tied directly to the number of processors that your server contains. Rather, task workload should be evaluated across the tasks. For example, if your package contains a Data Flow, then most likely it will consume more server resources than the other tasks. In fact, each Data Flow can be set up to use multiple threads during execution, a property that is described in more detail in the Data Flow section that follows.

Enterprise Data Processing with the Data Flow

The Data Flow is the core data processing factory of Integration Services packages, where the primary data is handled, managed, transformed, integrated, and cleansed. Think of the Data Flow as a pipeline for data. A house, for example, has a primary water source, which is branched to all the different outlets in the house. If a faucet is turned on, water will flow out the faucet, while at the same time water is coming in from the source. If all the water outlets in a house are turned off, then the pressure backs up to the source to where it will no longer flow into the house until the pressure is relieved. On the contrary, if all the water outlets in the house are opened at once, then the source pressure may not be able to keep up with the flow of water and the pressure coming out of the faucets will be weaker. Of course, don't try this at home; it may produce other problems!

The Data Flow is appropriately named because the data equates to the water in the plumbing analogy. The data flows from the data sources through the transformations to the data destinations. In addition to the flowing concept, there are similarities to the data flow pressure within the pipeline. For example, while a data source may be able to stream 10,000 rows per second, if a downstream transformation consumes too much server resources, it could apply back pressure on the source and reduce the number of rows coming from the source. Essentially, this creates a bottleneck that may need to be addressed to optimize the flow. In order to understand and apply design principles in a Data Flow, an in-depth discussion of the Data Flow architecture is merited. Understanding several Data Flow concepts will give you a fuller perspective of what is going on under the hood of an executing package. Each of these will be addressed over the next few pages:

❑ Data buffer architecture

❑ Transformation types

❑ Transformation communication

❑ Execution trees

After your review of the architecture, your analysis will shift to monitoring packages in order to determine how the Data Flow engine is handling data processing.

Memory Buffer Architecture

The Data Flow manages data in groups of data called *buffers*. A buffer is merely memory that is allocated for the use of storing rows and columns of data where transformations are applied. This means that as data is being extracted from sources into the engine, it is put into these pre-allocated memory buffers. Buffers are dynamically sized based on row width (the cumulative number of bytes in a row) and other package and server criteria. A buffer, for example, may include 9000 rows of data with a few columns of data. Figure 10-5 shows a few groupings of buffers.

Buffer 1

row number	column 1	column 2	column 3	column 4	column 5	column 6	column 7
1	<data>	<data>	<data>	<data>	<data>	<data>	<data>
2	<data>	<data>	<data>	<data>	<data>	<data>	<data>
3	<data>	<data>	<data>	<data>	<data>	<data>	<data>
<data>	<data>	<data>	<data>	<data>	<data>	<data>	<data>
<data>	<data>	<data>	<data>	<data>	<data>	<data>	<data>
9000	<data>	<data>	<data>	<data>	<data>	<data>	<data>

Buffer 2

row number	column 1	column 2	column 3	column 4	column 5	column 6	column 7
9001	<data>	<data>	<data>	<data>	<data>	<data>	<data>
9002	<data>	<data>	<data>	<data>	<data>	<data>	<data>
9003	<data>	<data>	<data>	<data>	<data>	<data>	<data>
<data>	<data>	<data>	<data>	<data>	<data>	<data>	<data>
<data>	<data>	<data>	<data>	<data>	<data>	<data>	<data>
18000	<data>	<data>	<data>	<data>	<data>	<data>	<data>

Buffer N

row number	column 1	column 2	column 3	column 4	column 5	column 6	column 7
$9000*n+1$	<data>	<data>	<data>	<data>	<data>	<data>	<data>
$9000*n+2$	<data>	<data>	<data>	<data>	<data>	<data>	<data>
$9000*n+3$	<data>	<data>	<data>	<data>	<data>	<data>	<data>
<data>	<data>	<data>	<data>	<data>	<data>	<data>	<data>
<data>	<data>	<data>	<data>	<data>	<data>	<data>	<data>
$9000 * (n+1)$	<data>	<data>	<data>	<data>	<data>	<data>	<data>

Figure 10-5

Although it is easy to picture data being passed down from transformation to transformation in the Data Flow similar to the flow of water in the pipeline analogy, this is not a complete picture of what is going on behind the scenes. Instead of data being passed down through the transformations, groups of transformations pass over the buffers of data and make in-place changes as defined by the transformations. Think of how much more efficient this process is than if the data were copied from one buffer to the next every time a transformation specified a change in the data! To be sure, there are times when the buffers are copied and other times when the buffers are held up in cache by transformations. The understanding of how and when this happens will help determine the right design to optimize your solution.

The understanding of how memory buffers are managed requires knowing something about the different types of Data Flow components — transformations and adapters.

Types of Transformations

The adapters and the transformations in the Data Flow have certain characteristics that group each into different categories. The base-level differences between them are the way they communicate with each other and how and when data is handed off from one transformation to another. Evaluating transformations on two fronts will provide the background you need to understand how the buffers are managed.

❏ Blocking nature — streaming, blocking, and semi-blocking

❏ Communication mechanism — synchronous and asynchronous

In reality, these classifications are related, but from a practical standpoint, discussing them separately provides some context to data management in the Data Flow.

Non-Blocking, Semi-Blocking, and Blocking

The most obvious distinction between transformations is their blocking nature. All transformations fall into one of three categories: non-blocking, semi-blocking, or blocking. These terms describe whether data in a transformation is passed downstream in the pipeline immediately, in increments, or after all the data is fully received.

Non-Blocking Transformations, Streaming and Row-Based

Most of the Integration Services Transformations are non-blocking. This means that the transformation logic that is applied in the transformation does not impede the data from moving on to the next transformation after the transformation logic is applied to the row. Two categories of non-blocking transformations exist, streaming and row-based. The difference is whether the Integration Services engine can use internal information and processes to handle the transformations or whether the engine has to call an external process to retrieve information used for the transformation. Some transformations can be categorized as streaming or row-based depending on their configuration, and these have been indicated below.

Streaming transformations are able to apply transformation logic quickly, using pre-cached data and processing calculations within the engine. In these transformations, it is rarely the case that a transformation will slip behind the rate of the data being fed to it. Therefore, they are classified as streaming. The following transformations stream the data from transformation to transformation in the data flow:

❏ Audit

❏ Character Map

❏ Conditional Split

❏ Copy Column

❏ Data Conversion

❏ Derived Column

❏ Lookup (with a full cache setting)

❏ Multicast

❏ Percent Sampling

❏ Row Count

❏ Script Component (provided the script doesn't interact with a component outside the engine)

❏ Union All (can also be categorized as semi-blocking)

The second grouping of non-blocking transformation is identified as *row-based*. These transformations are still non-blocking in the sense that the data can flow immediately to the next transformation after the transformation logic is applied to the buffer. The row-based description indicates that the rows flowing through the transformation are acted on one-by-one with a requirement to interact with an outside process such as a database, file, or component. Given their row-based processes, in most cases these transformations may not be able to keep up with the rate at which the data is fed to them, and the buffers are held up until each row is processed. The following transformations are classified as row-based:

- ❑ Export Column
- ❑ Import Column
- ❑ Lookup (with a no cache or partial cache setting)
- ❑ OLE DB Command
- ❑ Script Component (where the script interacts with an external component)
- ❑ Slowly Changing Dimension (each row is looked up against the dimension in the database)

Figure 10-6 shows a Data Flow composed of only streaming transformations. If you look at the row counts in the design UI, you will notice that the transformations are processing the data nearly at the same time because the row counts are very close in range.

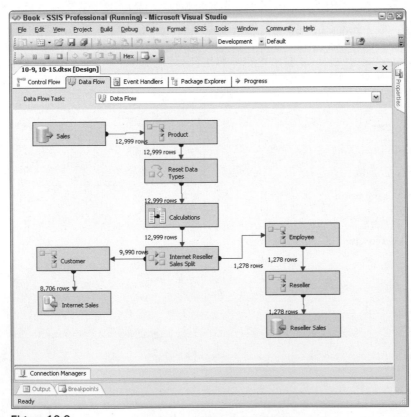

Figure 10-6

Also, notice in Figure 10-6 that data is still coming in from the source, but already records are being inserted into the destination. This very simple Data Flow is handling a high volume of data with minimal resources, such as memory usage, because of the streaming nature of the transformations components used.

Semi-Blocking Transformations

The next category of transformation components are the ones that hold up records in the Data Flow for a period of time before allowing the memory buffers to be passed downstream. These are typically called semi-blocking transformations, given their nature. Only a few out-of-the-box transformations are semi-blocking in nature:

❑ Data Mining Query

❑ Merge

❑ Merge Join

❑ Pivot

❑ Term Lookup

❑ Unpivot

❑ Union All (also included in the streaming transformations list, but given a limited number of threads, the Union All will be semi-blocking in nature)

The Merge and Merge Join transformations are described in detail in Chapter 4. But in relation to the semi-blocking nature of these components, note that they require the sources to be sorted on the matching keys of the merge. Both of these transformations function by waiting for key matches from both sides of the merge (or join), and when the matching sorted keys from both sides pass through the transformations, the records can then be sent downstream while the next set of keys is handled. Figure 10-7 shows how a merge join within a data flow will partially hold up the processing of the rows until the matches are made.

Typically the row count upstream of the Merge Join is much higher than the row count just below the Merge Join because the Merge Join waits for the sorted key matches as they flow in from both sides of the merge. Buffers are being released downstream, just not in a streaming fashion as in the non-blocking transformation components. You may also be wondering why there is not a Sort transformation on the right-side source of the Merge Join despite the fact that the transformations require the sources to be sorted. Stay tuned; the next chapter will cover one optimization technique, which is to sort the sources and tell the Data Flow that these sources are already sorted.

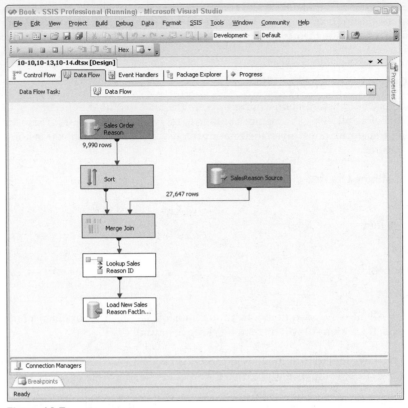

Figure 10-7

Semi-blocking transformations require a little more server resources since the buffers will need to stay in memory until the right data is received.

Blocking Transformations

The final category of the blocking nature is the actual blocking transformations. For one reason or another, these components require the full connected upstream data set before releasing any row downstream to the connected transformations and destinations. The list is also smaller than the list of non-blocking transformations because of the limited logic applications that require all the rows. Here is the list of the blocking transformations:

- ❑ Aggregate
- ❑ Fuzzy Grouping
- ❑ Fuzzy Lookup
- ❑ Row Sampling
- ❑ Sort
- ❑ Term Extraction

The two widely used examples of the blocking transformations are the Sort and Aggregate transforms; each of these requires the entire data set before handing off the data to the next transform. For example, in order to have an accurate average, all the records need to be held up by the Aggregate transform. Similarly, to sort data in a flow, all the data needs to be available to the Sort transformation before the component will know the order in which to release records downstream. Figure 10-8 shows a Data Flow that contains an Aggregate transformation. The screen capture of this process shows that the entire source has already been brought into the data flow, but no rows have been released downstream while the transformation is determining the order.

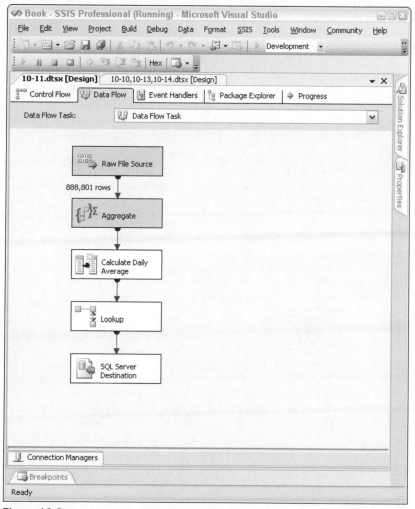

Figure 10-8

With a blocking component in the Data Flow, as you can see in Figure 10-8, the data is no longer streaming through the Data Flow, and there will not be a time when data can be inserted into the destination while data is being extracted from the source.

Blocking transformations are more resource-intensive for several reasons. First, since all the data is being held up, either the server must use a lot of memory to store the data or, in the case where the server does not have enough memory, a process of file staging happens, which requires the IO overhead of landing the data to disk temporarily. The second reason these transformations are intensive is that they usually put a heavy burden on the processor to perform the work of data aggregation, sorting, or fuzzy matching.

Synchronous and Asynchronous Transformation Outputs

Another important differentiation between transformations is how transformations that are connected to one another by a path communicate with one another. While closely related to the discussion on the blocking nature of transformations, *synchronous* and *asynchronous* refer more to the relationship between the input and output component connections.

Some transformations have an Advanced Editor window, which, among other things, drills into specific column-level properties of the transformations' input and output columns and is useful in explaining the difference between synchronous and asynchronous outputs. Figure 10-9 shows the Advanced Editor of the Sort transformation, highlighting the Input and Output Properties tab. This particular transformation has a Sort Input and Sort Output group with a set of columns associated with each.

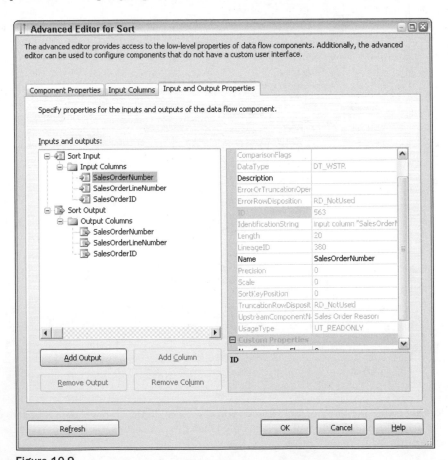

Figure 10-9

When a column is highlighted, the advanced properties of that column are displayed on the right, as Figure 10-9 shows. The advanced properties include such things as the data type of the column, the description, and so on. One important property to note is the LineageID. This is the integer pointer to the column within the buffers. Every column used in the Data Flow has at least one LineageID in the Data Flow. A column can have more than one Lineage ID as it passes through the Data Flow based on the types of transformation outputs (synchronous or asynchronous) that a column goes through in the Data Flow.

Asynchronous Transformation Outputs

You will begin with the *asynchronous* definition because it will be easier to explain first, and then you will come back to *synchronous* outputs for a comparison. A transformation output is asynchronous if the buffers used in the input are different from the buffers used in the output. In other words, many of the transformations cannot perform the given operation and at the same time preserve the buffers (the number of rows or the order of the rows), so a copy of the data must be made to accomplish the desired effect.

The Aggregate transformation, for example, may output only a fraction of the number of rows coming into it, or when the Merge Join transformation has to marry two data sets together, the resulting number of rows will not be equivalent to the number of input rows. In both cases, the buffers are received, the processing is handled, and new buffers are created.

The Advanced Editor of the Sort shown in Figure 10-9 highlights an input column. One of the properties of the input column is the LineageID. Notice that in this transformation, all the input columns are duplicated in the output columns list. In fact, as Figure 10-10 shows, the output column highlighted for the same input has a different LineageID.

The LineageIDs are different for the same column because the Sort transformation output is asynchronous and the data buffers in the input are not the same buffers in the output; therefore a new column identifier is needed for the output. In the preceding examples, the input LineageID is 380 while the output column LineageID is 566.

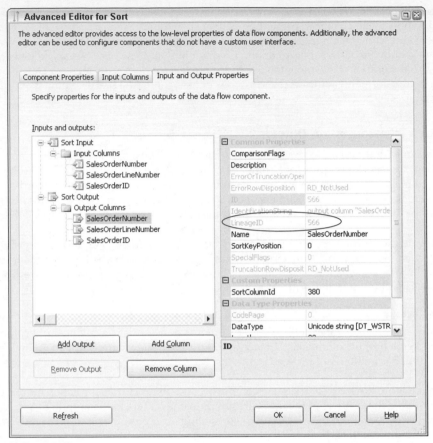

Figure 10-10

A list doesn't need to be included here, because all of the semi-blocking and blocking transformations already listed have asynchronous outputs by definition — none of them can pass input buffers on downstream because the data is held up for processing and reorganized.

One of the Integration Services engine components is called the buffer manager. For asynchronous component outputs, the buffer manager is busy at work, decommissioning buffers for use elsewhere (in sources or other asynchronous outputs) and reassigning new buffers to the data coming out of the transformation.

Synchronous Transformation Outputs

A synchronous transformation is one where the buffers are immediately handed off to the next downstream transformation at the completion of the transformation logic. This may sound like the definition given for streaming transformations, and it should, since there is almost complete overlap between streaming transformations and synchronous transformations. The word *buffers* was intentionally used in the definition, because the important point is that the same buffers received by the transformation input are passed out the output. Regarding the LineageIDs of the columns, they remain the same as the data is passed through the synchronous output, without a need to duplicate the buffers and assign a new LineageID as discussed previously in the asynchronous transformation output section.

Figure 10-11 shows the Advanced Editor of a synchronous component output, the Derived Column transformation. There is a big difference between the advanced Input and Output properties of the Derived Column compared with the Sort (shown in Figure 10-9 and Figure 10-10). As you saw, all of the columns in the Sort's input and output are duplicated, while Figure 10-11 shows that the Derived Column transformation contains only output columns.

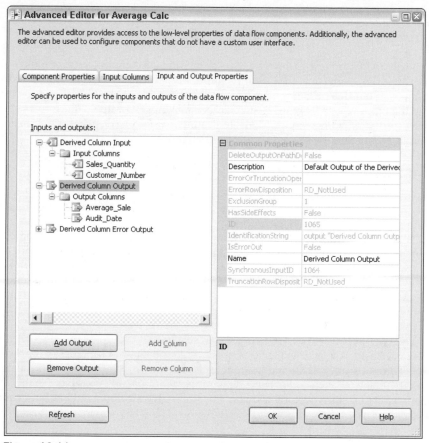

Figure 10-11

The rest of the columns are not included in the input or output list because they are not directly used by the transformation and because the Derived Column transformation output is synchronous. In other words, the columns coming from the upstream component flow through the Derived Column transformation (in this example) and are available to the next downstream component.

A transformation is not limited to a single synchronous output. Both the Multicast and the Conditional Split can have multiple outputs, but all the outputs are synchronous.

327

With the exception of the Union All, all of the non-blocking transformations listed in the previous section also have synchronous outputs. The Union All, while it functions like a streaming transformation, is really an asynchronous transformation. Given the complexity of unioning multiple sources together and keeping track of all the pointers to the right data from the different source inputs, the Union All instead copies the buffers as it receives them and passes them off to the downstream transformations.

> *Synchronous transformation outputs preserve the sort order of incoming data, while some of the asynchronous transformations do not. The Sort, Merge, and Merge Join asynchronous components of course have sorted outputs because of their nature, but the Union All, for example, does not.*

A definitive way to identify synchronous versus asynchronous components is to look at the SynchronousInputID property of the Column Output properties. If this value is 0, the component output is asynchronous, but if this property is set to a value greater than 0, the transformation output is synchronous to the input whose ID matches the SynchronousInputID value. Figure 10-11 shows the Derived Column transformation with a value of 1064, indicating that the Derived Column transformation output is synchronous and tied to the single Derived Column input.

Source and Destination Adapters

You should also briefly look at *adapters* in this section, since they are integral to the Data Flow. Because of their differences in functionality, sources and destinations are therefore classified differently.

In looking at the advanced properties of a source adapter, the source will have the same list of input columns and output columns. The external columns come directly from the source and are copied into the Data Flow buffers and subsequently assigned LineageIDs. While the external source columns do not have LineageIDs, the process is effectively the same as an asynchronous component output. Source adapters require buffers to be allocated where the incoming data can be grouped and managed for the downstream transformations to perform work against.

Destination adapters, on the other hand, function as synchronous components, since their buffers are de-allocated and data is loaded into the destinations. In the advanced properties of the destination adapter (as shown in Figure 10-12), an External Column list is also shown, which represents the destination columns used in the load. Notice that there is no primary Output container (besides the Error Output) for the destination adapter since the buffers do not flow through the component but rather are committed to a destination adapter as a final step in the Data Flow.

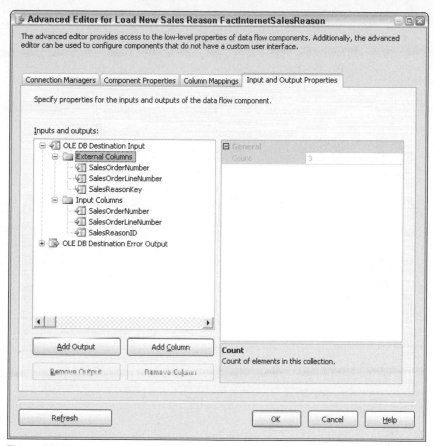

Figure 10-12

Advanced Data Flow Execution Concepts

You have already looked at several advanced Integration Services engine concepts that apply to transformations within the Data Flow. This section will take and apply the discussion of synchronous and asynchronous transformations and tie them together to provide the bigger picture of a package execution.

Relevant to this discussion is a more detailed understanding of buffer management within an executing package based on how the package is designed.

Execution Trees

In one sense, you have already looked at execution trees, although they weren't explicitly referred to by this name. An execution tree is the logical grouping of Data Flow components (transformations and adapters) based on their synchronous relationship to one another. Groupings are delineated by asynchronous component outputs that indicate the completion of one execution tree and the start of the next.

Figure 10-13 shows a moderately complex Data Flow that uses multiple components with asynchronous outputs.

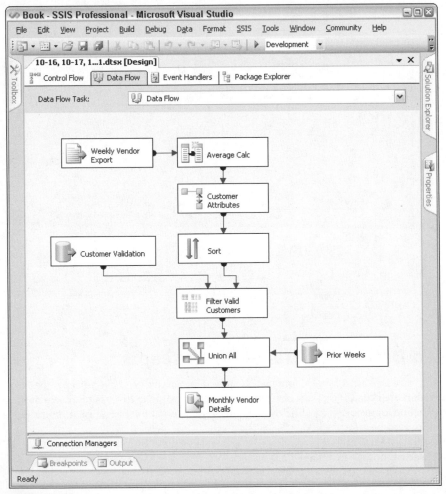

Figure 10-13

You will recall that components with asynchronous outputs use different input buffers. The input participates in the upstream execution tree, while the asynchronous output begins the next execution tree. In light of this, the execution trees for Figure 10-13 start at the source adapters and are then completed, and a new execution tree begins at every asynchronous transformation. The example in Figure 10-14 has six execution trees.

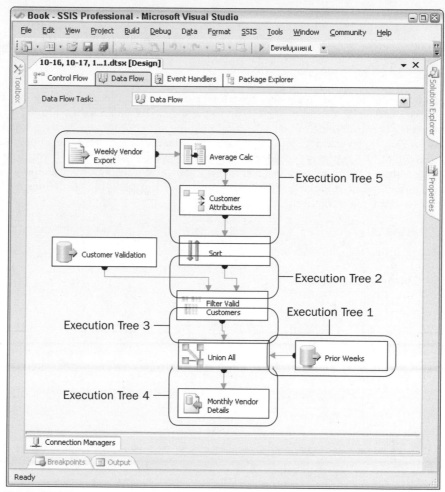

Figure 10-14

Execution trees are base 0, meaning you count them starting with a 0. In the next section, you will see how the pipeline logging identifies them. Although the execution trees seem out of order, you have used the explicit order given by the pipeline logging.

In the next section, you will address ways to log and track the execution trees within a Data Flow, but for now the discussion will emphasize the particulars of what happens in an execution tree.

> **Execution Trees Principle #1: Each component within an execution tree applies work (transformation logic) on the same set of buffers as the rest of the synchronous components in the same execution tree.**

As previously explained, the input and output buffers in a transformation with asynchronous outputs are different because the buffer data grouping cannot be preserved in both count and order. Rows within the input buffers may merge with other buffers, creating more (or fewer) rows in the output buffers than in either of the source buffers. Or input buffers may contain data that needs to be sorted or aggregated, which also fails to preserve the order or row count.

This means that when Integration Services executes a package, the buffer manager defines different buffer profiles based on the execution trees within a package. All the buffers used for a particular execution tree are identical in definition. When defining the buffer profile for each execution tree, the Integration Services buffer manager looks at all the transformations used in the execution tree and includes every column in the buffer that is needed at any point within the execution tree. If you focus on execution tree #1 in Figure 10-15, you'll see that it contains a source adapter, a Derived Column transformation, and a Lookup. Without looking at the source properties, the following list defines the four columns that the source adapter is using from the source:

❑   CurrencyCode

❑   CurrencyRate

❑   AverageRate

❑   EndofDayRate

A quick look at the Derived Column transformation in Figure 10-15 shows that two more columns are being added to the Data Flow: Average_Sale and Audit_Date.

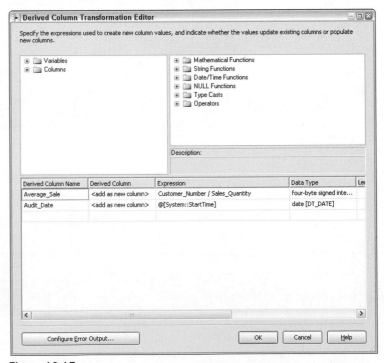

Figure 10-15

And finally, the Lookup transformation adds another three columns to the Data Flow, as Figure 10-16 highlights.

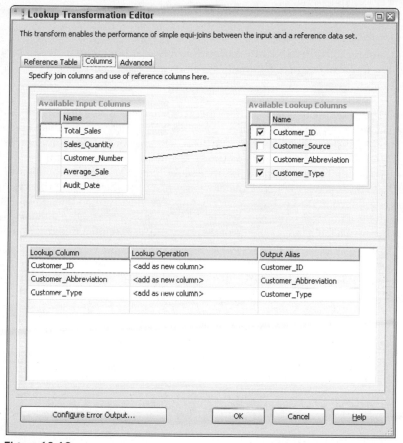

Figure 10-16

Added together, the columns used in these three components total nine. This means that the buffers used in this execution tree will have nine columns allocated, even though some of the columns are not used in the initial transformations or adapter. Optimization of a Data Flow can be compared with optimizing a relational table, where the smaller the width and number of columns, the more that can fit into a Data Flow buffer. This has some performance implications, and the next chapter will look in more detail at optimizing buffers.

> **Execution Trees Principle #2: Different execution trees use a different set of buffers, and therefore data in a new execution tree requires the transformed data to be copied into the new buffers allocated for the next in-line execution tree.**

When a buffer is used in an execution tree and reaches the transformation input of the asynchronous component (the last step in the execution tree), the data is subsequently not needed since it has been passed off to a new execution tree and new set of buffers. At this point, the buffer manager can use the allocated buffer for other purposes in the Data Flow.

> **Execution Trees Principle #3: Integration Services uses one process thread for each execution tree and one process thread for each source adapter.**

The final important point about execution trees involves situations where the Integration Services engine can multi-thread processes for parallelization. No matter how many synchronous transformations are used in an execution tree, the engine can use only one process thread per execution tree and one process thread per source adapter. Consequently, processing can be an Integration Services bottleneck if the execution threads have a large number of synchronous processes or if there are more execution trees than available system threads. In the first case, when a Data Flow uses many synchronous transformations that require intensive processes, such as the Lookup transformation, a single execution thread may have difficulty keeping up with the amount of work required. In the latter case, when there are many execution trees with a limited number of available threads, some of the downstream execution trees may have to wait for threads to be freed up in order to run their processes.

One advanced property of the Data Flow is the EngineThreads property. In the Control Flow, when a Data Flow task is highlighted, this property appears in the property window list, as Figure 10-17 shows.

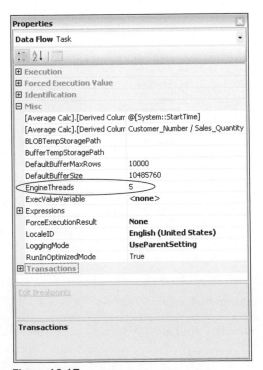

Figure 10-17

The EngineThreads property is the maximum number of threads available to the Data Flow in question. If there are multiple Data Flows in the package, each retains a separate EngineThreads setting and should be balanced between the Data Flows. In the last section of this chapter, you will look at the number of threads used in a Data Flow. The value for EngineThreads does not include the threads allocated for the number of sources in a Data Flow, which are allocated separate threads.

Monitoring Data Flow Execution

Built into the Integration Services logging is the ability to monitor specific pipeline events related to execution trees. This can be very useful in understanding your Data Flow and how the engine is managing buffers and execution.

Pipeline logging events are available in the Logging features of Integration Services. An overview of the general Integration Services logging is provided in Chapter 13, but for this discussion, you will focus on only the specific pipeline events that relate to the execution tree discussion. Two specific pipeline execution events are available to capture during the processing:

❑ PipelineExecutionPlan

❑ PipelineExecutionTrees

To capture the event, create a new log entry through the logging designer window under the SSIS menu Logging option. The pipeline events are available only when your Data Flow is selected in the tree menu navigator of the package executable navigator, as Figure 10-18 shows.

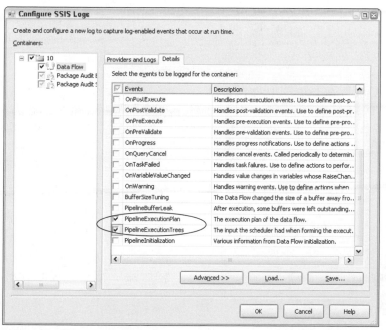

Figure 10-18

On the Details tab of the Configure SSIS Logs window, shown in Figure 10-18, the two execution information log events listed above are available to capture. When the package is run, these events can be tracked to the selected log provider as defined. However, during development, it is useful to see these events when testing and designing a package. Integration Services includes a way to see these events in the Business Intelligence Development Studio as a separate window. The Log Events window can be pulled up either from the SSIS menu by selecting "Log Events" or through the View menu, listed under the Other Windows submenu. As is standard, this window can float or be docked in the designer.

When the package is executed in design-time through the interface, the log events selected will be displayed in the Log Events window. For each Data Flow, there will be one event returned for the PipelineExecutionPlan event and one for the PipelineExecutionTrees event, as shown in Figure 10-19. These log details have been captured from the sample Data Flow used in Figure 10-13 and Figure 10-14.

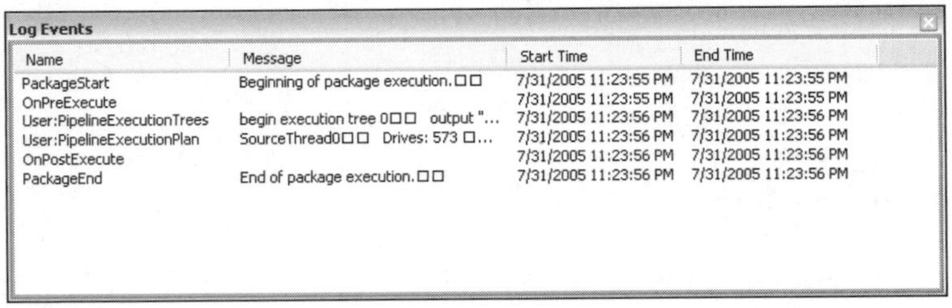

Figure 10-19

Note that all pipeline events selected in the Logging configuration are included in the Log window. To capture the details for a more readable view of the Message column, simply right-click on the log entry and copy, which will put the event message into the clipboard. A more detailed analysis of the message text is discussed in the following section.

Pipeline Execution Tree Log Details

The execution tree log event describes the grouping of transformation inputs and outputs that participate in each execution tree. Each execution tree is numbered for readability. The following text comes from the message column of the PipelineExecutionTrees log entry.

```
begin execution tree 0
   output "OLE DB Source Output" (582)
   input "Merge Join Right Input" (686)
end execution tree 0
begin execution tree 1
   output "OLE DB Source Output" (749)
   input "Union All Input 2" (976)
end execution tree 1
begin execution tree 5
   output "Flat File Source Output" (878)
   input "Derived Column Input" (1064)
   output "Derived Column Output" (1065)
   input "Lookup Input" (276)
   output "Lookup Output" (280)
   input "Sort Input" (553)
end execution tree 5
```

```
begin execution tree 2
   output "Sort Output" (554)
   input "Merge Join Left Input" (685)
end execution tree 2
begin execution tree 3
   output "Merge Join Output" (687)
   input "Union All Input 3" (1042)
end execution tree 3
begin execution tree 4
   output "Union All Output 1" (965)
   input "SQL Server Destination Input" (813)
end execution tree 4
```

In the log output, each execution tree evaluated by the engine is listed with a `begin` and an `end`, with the transformation input and outputs that participate in the execution tree. Some execution trees may have several synchronous component outputs participating in the grouping, while others may be composed of only an input and output between two asynchronous components. The listing of the execution trees is base 0, so the total number of execution trees for your Data Flow will be the numeral of the last execution tree plus one. In this example, there are six execution trees (note that execution tree 5 is listed higher in the output code).

A quick way to identify synchronous and asynchronous transformation outputs in your data flow is to review this log. Any transformation where both the inputs and outputs are contained within one execution tree is synchronous. Contrarily, any transformation where one or more inputs are separated from the outputs in different execution trees therefore has asynchronous outputs.

Pipeline Execution Plan Log Details

The second type of log detail that applies to the discussion of execution trees and execution threads is the PipelineExecutionPlan. This particular log detail dives one step deeper into the Integration Services engine process for a Data Flow by identifying the threads that will be allocated and used during the process. The following text comes from the message column of the PipelineExecutionPlan log output.

```
SourceThread0
   Drives: 573
   Influences: 684 800 963
   Output Work List
      CreatePrimeBuffer of type 1 for output ID 582.
      SetBufferListener: "WorkThread0" for input ID 686
      CallPrimeOutput on component "Customer Validation" (573)
   End Output Work List
End SourceThread0
SourceThread1
   Drives: 740
   Influences: 800 963
   Output Work List
      CreatePrimeBuffer of type 4 for output ID 749.
      SetBufferListener: "WorkThread1" for input ID 976
      CallPrimeOutput on component "Prior Weeks" (740)
   End Output Work List
End SourceThread1
SourceThread2
   Drives: 877
   Influences: 266 552 684 800 963 1063
```

```
        Output Work List
            CreatePrimeBuffer of type 11 for output ID 878.
            SetBufferListener: "WorkThread2" for input ID 1064
            CallPrimeOutput on component "Weekly Vendor Export" (877)
        End Output Work List
End SourceThread2
WorkThread0
    Drives: 684
    Influences: 684 800 963
    Input Work list, input ID 685 (1 EORs Expected)
        CallProcessInput on input ID 685 on component
          "Filter Valid Customers" (684) for view type 8
    End Input Work list for input 685
    Input Work list, input ID 686 (1 EORs Expected)
        CallProcessInput on input ID 686 on component
          "Filter Valid Customers" (684) for view type 2
    End Input Work list for input 686
    Output Work List
        CreatePrimeBuffer of type 7 for output ID 687.
        SetBufferListener: "WorkThread1" for input ID 1042
        CallPrimeOutput on component "Filter Valid Customers" (684)
    End Output Work List
End WorkThread0
WorkThread1
    Drives: 963
    Influences: 800 963
    Input Work list, input ID 976 (1 EORs Expected)
        CallProcessInput on input ID 976 on component
          "Union All" (963) for view type 5
    End Input Work list for input 976
    Input Work list, input ID 1042 (1 EORs Expected)
        CallProcessInput on input ID 1042 on component
          "Union All" (963) for view type 9
    End Input Work list for input 1042
    Output Work List
        CreatePrimeBuffer of type 7 for output ID 965.
        SetBufferListener: "WorkThread3" for input ID 813
        CallPrimeOutput on component "Union All" (963)
    End Output Work List
End WorkThread1
WorkThread2
    Drives: 1063
    Influences: 266 552 684 800 963 1063
    Input Work list, input ID 1064 (1 EORs Expected)
        CallProcessInput on input ID 1064 on component
          "Average Calc" (1063) for view type 14
        ActivateVirtualBuffer index 1
        CallProcessInput on input ID 276 on component
          "Customer Attributes" (266) for view type 12
        ActivateVirtualBuffer index 2
        CallProcessInput on input ID 553 on component
          "Sort" (552) for view type 13
    End Input Work list for input 1064
    Output Work List
```

```
        CreatePrimeBuffer of type 7 for output ID 554.
        SetBufferListener: "WorkThread0" for input ID 685
        CallPrimeOutput on component "Sort" (552)
    End Output Work List
End WorkThread2
WorkThread3
    Drives: 800
    Influences: 800
    Input Work list, input ID 813 (1 EORs Expected)
        CallProcessInput on input ID 813 on component
        "Monthly Vendor Details" (800) for view type 10
    End Input Work list for input 813
    Output Work List
    End Output Work List
End WorkThread3
    7/31/2005 11:23:56 PM     7/31/2005 11:23:56 PM
```

This text is a little more difficult to decipher. A few pointers will help determine some details of the pipeline execution plan. First of all, execution threads are identified by two types, SourceThread and WorkThread. As may be apparent, the SourceThreads are allocated for each of the source adapters. In the discussion of execution threads, recall that the number of possible threads used in a Data Flow is the number of sources plus the number of execution trees. Therefore, in this example, the number of SourceThreads is three and each is numbered (the SourceThread count is base 0, so the third thread is identified as SourceThread2).

The WorkThread is the second type of thread, which applies to the Data Flow execution trees. It is important to note that the WorkThreads are directly related to the EngineThread property. If the number of execution trees in a Data Flow exceeds the number of EngineThreads available, then a WorkThread may be assigned to more than one execution tree. Although there is not an explicit map between an execution tree and a WorkThread in the PipelineExecutionPlan output, the mapping can be inferred by looking at the CallProcessInput property, which shows the transformations assigned to the WorkThread.

By the using the two pipeline log entries just described, you can now better understand how the engine is processing your data. In any system, the road to applying design principles first requires a level of understanding.

Summary

Working from the high level of comparing the Control Flow and Data Flow, you have slowly drilled into the core details of the engine with the overall net effect of seeing how data is processed in Integration Services from the inside out. To be sure, this is not the end of the book, nor the end of the engine's story! Although there has been a sense of application throughout this chapter, the focus has mostly been on understanding the Integration Service's engine.

The next step is to take the understanding and turn it into application. In the next chapter, your focus will turn to bringing this knowledge to bear on your designs. You will look at overall design considerations and optimization to take advantage of the Integration Services engine's architecture.

11

Applying the Integration Services Engine

In the last chapter, you explored the core Integration Services Engine. You will now focus on bridging the gap between understanding its features and designing a solution based on those features.

DTS in SQL Server 2000 provided great capabilities to move data from one place to another or from one format to another. In fact, many data-processing architectures built on DTS adopted this model. In moving from DTS to Integration Services, however, should you continue to use this model? Using the DTS-based architecture as a comparative model, you will explore new ways of thinking about data integration.

In addition to data-processing best practices, you will also touch on package optimization techniques. Rounding out the chapter, you will examine the Perfmon counters targeted at the Data Flow, define them, and list what to look for when monitoring.

That Was Then: DTS

You may be familiar with SSIS's predecessor, SQL Server 2000 Data Transformation Services (DTS). If not, DTS is a widely used tool designed to move data from one source to another, and many organizations have developed compelling BI ETL solutions using DTS. The differences between SSIS and DTS are many, though. In fact, SSIS is not a new version of DTS; it is a new tool in the SQL Server 2005 platform that replaces and extends DTS's functionality.

Does Figure 11-1 look familiar? If you've developed any DTS-based solutions to handle data processing, then surely you recognize it.

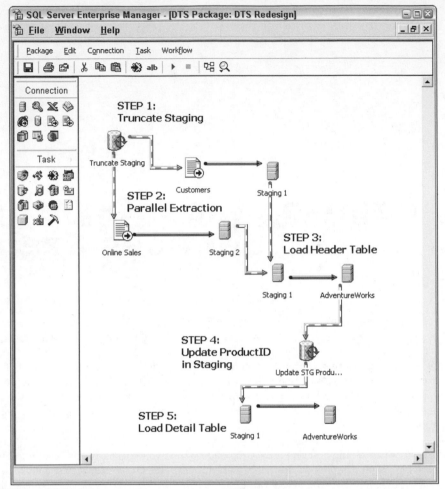

Figure 11-1

Since the topic in this chapter is Integration Services, the analysis of DTS will not be exhaustive; however, you will consider a few aspects of a typical DTS architecture in order to compare it with an Integration Services architecture. Ideally, the design of your ETL or data-processing solution will not be driven by your choice of ETL tool; however, a tool's capabilities inevitably influence the design. Source-to-destination data mappings are still the same and destination data structures do not change, but the process and logic to move and transform data from one to the other can be dependent on the capabilities of the tool. This was the case with DTS (in fact, this applies to any tool that is selected, but the difference is how much flexibility the tool will allow in data transformation design). The following sections consider the common design of a DTS package such as the one shown in Figure 11-1.

DTS Solution Architecture

DTS primarily uses a Data Pump task that moves data from a single source to a single destination with some interim transformation logic. The DTS interface focuses on the workflow features of the product, with the Data Pump being an object with configurable properties. A few built-in transformations can be defined, such as the built-in character mapping transforms. If transformation logic is included in the Data Pump, it is done in the form of a script. Some limitations are obvious, such as the one-to-one source-to-destination cardinality and the limitation of out-of-the-box transformations.

While scripting transforms can provide broad capabilities, scripting in itself introduces complexity, embedded code, and componentization scalability and support challenges. Because of these limitations, the approach that many DTS-based solutions use is to leverage the relational engine and use staging databases as interim layers of ETL. For example, if you needed the data source to split to multiple destinations, DTS would need to either make multiple passes from the source or stage the data and handle the partitioning of the data through another set of data pumps. Staging in DTS designs is also often used for cleansing, data correlation, and dimension lookups, again leveraging the relational engine. The pattern for data processing in DTS starts with a source. Then, raw data is staged. This data is transformed to an interim staging environment where lookups, data comparisons, and cleansing logic are applied. The final step in many cases loads the data to the destination, where perhaps a final cleanup may be applied.

Common DTS Processing Practices

The approach highlighted in Figure 11-1 and described previously contains two general features of this data transformation model. Figure 11-2 highlights the staging-intensive nature of the process.

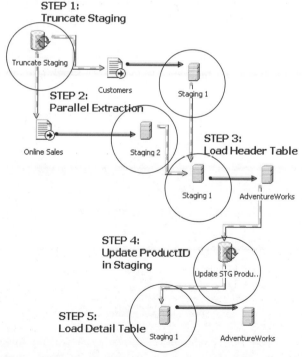

Figure 11-2

In this example, two staging tables have been used in between the source and destination in order to prepare the data for the load. Furthermore, when drilling into the data pumps that move the data from one table to another, oftentimes a SQL statement does some cleansing and correlating as the data is picked up from one staging table to another. The following code shows the source query used in Step 3 of the package that loads the header table.

```
SELECT STGOnlineDailyOrderBulk.OnlineCustomerID
     , STGOnlineDailyOrderBulk.OrderDate
     , SUM (UnitPrice) AS SubTotal
     , SUM (UnitPrice)* MAX(ISNULL(TaxRate,0.08)) AS TaxAmt
     , ISNULL(MAX(Address.AddressID), 1) AS BillToAddressID
     , ISNULL(MAX(Address.AddressID), 1) AS ShipToAddressID
     , SUM(freight) AS freight
     , DATEADD(D,7,OrderDate) AS DueDate
  FROM dbo.STGOnlineDailyOrderBulk
 INNER JOIN dbo.STGOnlineCustomers
    ON STGOnlineDailyOrderBulk.OnlineCustomerID
     = STGOnlineCustomers.OnlineCustomerID
  LEFT OUTER JOIN dbo.TaxRate
    ON STGOnlineCustomers.PostalCode = TaxRate.PostalCode
  LEFT OUTER JOIN AdventureWorks.Person.Address Address
    ON STGOnlineCustomers.AddressLine1 = Address.AddressLine1
   AND STGOnlineCustomers.PostalCode = Address.PostalCode
   AND STGOnlineCustomers.City = Address.City
 GROUP BY STGOnlineDailyOrderBulk.OnlineCustomerID
     , STGOnlineDailyOrderBulk.OrderDate
```

In this particular example, the transformation and data association is handled by an intense query on the relational staging database. Note the use of multiple joins between the staging and the destination tables and SQL logic to perform some in-process cleansing.

The second feature of this approach is the in-place set-based transformation using the RDBMS engine to update data within the staging or destination tables. Figure 11-3 highlights the DTS Execute SQL task that updates one of the staging tables in place to capture a primary key on the destination table.

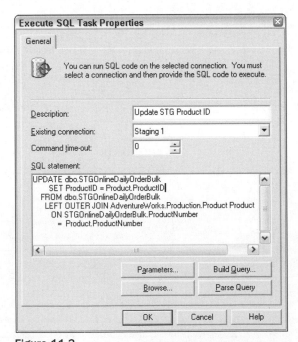

Figure 11-3

In Step 5, after the header table is loaded, the source SQL statement for the Data Pump joins the details staging table with the destination header table to return the IDENTITY column in the header.

```
SELECT SalesOrderHeader.SalesOrderID
     , STGOnlineDailyOrderBulk.*
  FROM dbo.STGOnlineDailyOrderBulk
  INNER JOIN AdventureWorks.Sales.SalesOrderHeader SalesOrderHeader
    ON SalesOrderHeader.CustomerID = STGOnlineDailyOrderBulk.OnlineCustomerID
   AND SalesOrderHeader.OrderDate = STGOnlineDailyOrderBulk.OrderDate
```

This example clearly does not represent all of the DTS-based solutions, nor does it leverage the lookup functionality embedded in the DTS Data Pump. The purpose of this example is to highlight the features of a typical DTS solution in order to compare it with an Integration Services solution.

DTS Limitations

As mentioned earlier, this architecture has a few limitations that affect scalability and may have an unnecessary impact on the destination systems. Generally, the DTS approach can be thought of as "ELT" instead of ETL. In other words, the common sequence for data processing is Extraction, Transformation, and Loading (ETL), but DTS solutions typically switch the order of the "T" and the "L." In this model, loading is commonly performed before transformation logic is applied. A few other limitations can be articulated from this generalized description.

One drawback to this approach is its synchronous nature. Some parallelization is used, but most data-processing steps require the full completion of the previous step in the workflow. Since this process is chained together, the total processing time will be a multiple of the duration of the extraction process, especially in a high-volume performance-driven environment. The Gantt chart in Figure 11-4 illustrates the total time taken to process the DTS package in Figure 11-1.

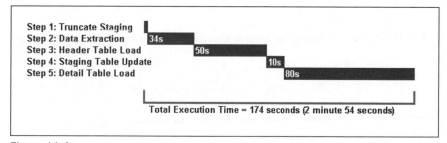

Figure 11-4

The second drawback to this approach is its disk-intensive nature. Every time data is inserted or updated in the database, it passes through several OSI layers, which adds resource overhead and stresses the system. Disk IO processes are expensive and generally slow down a system. To be sure, writing to the database is required in the loading phase, and often business requirements dictate that some interim database activities are necessary. The point, however, is that an architecture with data staging at its center has processing overhead that limits scalability. In fact, every step in the package from source to destination requires disk IO, including the set-based update statements, which at times may be more IO-intensive than pulling and writing data between data staging tables.

Related to the disk-intensive nature of this approach is the impact on the RDBMS when a process uses it for data correlation, lookups, and cleansing. This may or may not be relevant in every solution or even in the different layers of an ETL design, but consider a design where foreign keys are added to a staging table or queried in a custom source SQL statement through a series of database joins. Since the keys reside in a production destination database, even if the SQL statement is distributed across servers, there is a hit on the production system when that portion of the package runs. When the volume of the related destination tables starts to scale up, and if indexes are not optimized for loading, the load can really stress the RDBMS resources — processor, RAM, and IO. Whether the primary purpose of the destination database is to perform queries, report, or handle day-to-day transactions, this impact may affect the end users of your system. It may reduce productivity or, even worse, create a negative perception among end users of the value of the system.

These concerns notwithstanding, good design is possible using DTS, but the challenge comes with the required time, effort, and ongoing support. These DTS-based processes have also provided you with valuable lessons to apply when developing solutions with Integration Services. Finally, DTS may be perfectly appropriate for some systems; however, by examining the common pitfalls of DTS-based solutions, you will be better able to determine if DTS is a viable solution.

This Is Now: Integration Services

So here you are — a new tool and the opportunity to reconsider your data-processing architecture. In an ideal world, the tool would not be part of your conceptual design. This may never ultimately be achievable, but with Integration Services, solutions can be designed with much more flexibility and extensibility given the nature of the product. Designing a data-processing solution requires more than just sending the source data into a black-box transformation engine with outputs that push the data into the destination. And of course, system requirements will dictate the final design of the process, including but not limited to the following:

- ❏ Source and destination system impact
- ❏ Processing time windows and performance
- ❏ Destination system state consistency
- ❏ Hard and soft exception handling and restartability needs
- ❏ Environment architecture model, distributed hardware, or scaled-up servers
- ❏ Solution architecture requirements such as flexibility of change or OEM targeted solutions
- ❏ Modular and configurable solution needs
- ❏ Manageability and administration requirements

In reviewing this list, you can quickly map several of these to what you have learned about Integration Services already. In most cases, a good architecture will leverage the built-in functionality of the tool, which in the end reduces administration and support requirements. The tool selection process, if it is not completed before a solution is developed, should include a consideration of the system requirements and functionality of the available products.

The focus of this chapter is not to provide an exhaustive Integration Services architecture but rather to provide a framework for design that models true ETL (in that order). Integration Services brings with it a platform that is able to meet a broad variety of business data-processing needs and handle the required volume and integration complexity within the confines of the engine itself.

Integration Services Design Practices

In the previous analysis of DTS, you looked at a few challenges to the architecture. In doing so, however, you've uncovered a few good principles to follow when designing an Integration Services solution:

❑ Limit synchronicity

❑ Reduce staging and disk IO

❑ Reducing the reliance on an RDBMS

You've already looked at a few reasons why these are important principles to consider, and the result of following these will be more apparent as you compare your DTS solution to an Integration Services approach.

Keep in mind that solution requirements often drive design decisions, and there are situations where staging or the RDBMS are useful in data processing. Some of these are discussed in this section. Your goal, though, is to rethink your design paradigms with Integration Services.

Leveraging the Data Flow

For sure, the biggest value that Integration Services bring is the power of the Data Flow. Not to minimize the out-of-the-box functionality of restartability, configurations, logging, Event Handlers, or other Control Flow tasks, the primary goal of the engine is to "integrate," and the Data Flow is the key to realizing that goal. Accomplishing data-processing logic through Data Flow transformations brings performance and flexibility.

Most data architects come from DBA backgrounds, which means that the first thing that comes to their minds when trying to solve a data integration, processing, or cleansing scenario is to use an RDBMS, such as SQL Server. People gravitate to areas they are comfortable with, so this is a natural response. When your comfort in SQL is combined with an easy-to-use and low-cost product like DTS, which in many ways relies on relational databases, the result is a widely adopted tool.

Moving to Integration Services in some ways requires thinking in different terms — Data Flow terms. In previous chapters, you looked at the different Data Flow transformations, so the focus in this section will be on applying some of those components into design decisions and translating the SQL-based designs into Data Flow processes.

The three architecture best practices relate directly to the value that the Data Flow provides:

❑ **Limit synchronicity.** By bringing in more of the processing logic into the Data Flow, the natural result is fewer process-oriented steps that require completion before moving on. In the previous chapter, you looked at the general streaming nature of the Data Flow (streaming in terms of moving data, not audio or video streaming). This translates to reduced overall processing times.

❑ **Reduce staging and expensive IO operations.** The Data Flow performs most operations in memory (with occasional use of temp folders and some interaction with external systems). Whenever processing happens on data that resides in RAM, processing is more efficient. Disk IO operations rely on the performance of the drives, the throughput of the IO channels, and the overhead of the operating system to write and read information to the disk. With high volumes or bursting scenarios typical with data processing and ETL, disk IO is often a bottleneck.

❑ **Reduce reliance on RDBMS.** Relational engines are powerful tools to use, and the point here is not to detract from their appropriate uses to store and manage data. By using the Data Flow to cleanse and join data rather than the RDBMS, the result is reduced impact on the relational system, which frees it up for other functions that may be higher priority. Reading data from a database is generally less expensive than performing complex joins or complicated queries. In addition, related to the first bullet, all RDBMS operations are synchronous. Set-based operations, while they are very useful and optimized in a relational database system, still require that the operation be complete before the data is available for other purposes. The Data Flow, on the other hand, can process joins and lookups and other cleansing steps in parallel while the data is flowing through the pipeline.

Data Integration and Correlation

The Data Flow provides the means to combine data from different source objects completely independent of the connection source where the data originates. The most obvious benefit of this is the ability to perform in-memory correlation operations against heterogeneous data without having to stage the data. Said in another way, with Integration Services, you can extract data from a flat file and join it to data from a database table inside the Data Flow without first having to stage the flat file to a table and then perform a SQL join operation. This can be valuable even when the data is coming from the same source, such as a relational database engine; source data extractions are more efficient without complex or expensive joins, and data can usually begin to flow into the Data Flow immediately. In addition, single table SELECT statements provide less impact to the source systems than do pulls where join logic is applied. Certainly there are situations where joining data in the source system may be useful and efficient; in many cases, however, focusing on data integration within the Data Flow will yield better performance. When different source systems are involved, the requirement to stage the data is reduced.

Several of the built-in transformations can perform data correlation similar to how a database would handle joins and other more complex data relationship logic. The following transformations provide data association for more than one data source:

❑ Lookup

❑ Merge Join

❑ Merge

❑ Union All

❑ Fuzzy Lookup

❑ Term Lookup

❑ Term Extract

In the next section, you will also consider some of the features of the Data Flow that provide data cleansing and other in-line data operations.

Beyond the built-in capabilities of Integration Services, custom adapters and transformations allow more complex or unique scenarios to be handled. This will be discussed in Chapter 14.

The two most commonly used and powerful data correlation transformations are the Lookup and Merge Join. The functionality and properties of these transformations are described in Chapter 4, but for the purpose of applying Integration Services, a few descriptions and examples will be helpful to see how data integration can be applied.

Lookup Transformation

The Lookup transformation, particularly when it can be set up in fully cached mode, provides an efficient way to bring data objects together. Certainly there are many uses for the Lookup, but a few more common uses may be to look up a foreign key on a destination table or even check to see if a record exists in a related table to determine how to process downstream transformations. Figure 11-5 shows a Lookup transformation joined across a business key with the foreign key returned.

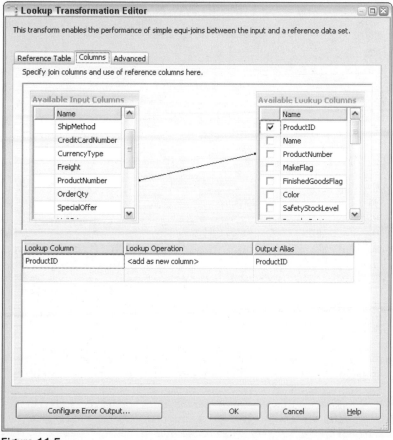

Figure 11-5

Using the Lookup to return foreign keys or other related columns in this way will relieve the need for joins across databases, or even distributed joins across servers, allowing scale-out models for processing — reducing resource needs and impact on the relational systems. Large set-based update statements can also be reduced by using a Lookup transformation to join data. When only a few columns are needed by the Lookup, such as a business key and one or two narrow return columns, a fully cached Lookup will scale very well.

The Lookup can also be used to check the existence of a related row in a table and provide information back to the Data Flow to inform downstream process on how to handle a row in the Data Flow, such as whether to do an insert or update. You can take a couple of different approaches to accomplish this, both of which require changing the error output. When you edit the Lookup transformation, the Configure Error Output property button is available on all the editor tabs. Figure 11-6 shows the Configure Error Output widow, highlighting the drop-down options that are settable for the error handling.

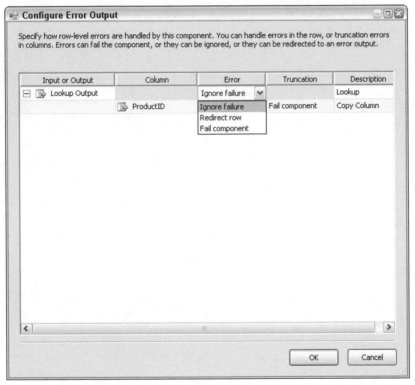

Figure 11-6

The three error-handling options are Fail Component (default), Redirect Row, and Ignore Failure. When set to Fail Component, the obvious result is a Data Flow failure when the Lookup table does not have a match with the input records. This option is not useful for the scenario you are considering. By setting the error handling to Redirect Row, the input row that does not match a record in the Lookup reference table is redirected out the error output (the red output path). This method can be useful when rows that do not match the Lookup reference table are needed immediately for operations. The red path may be confusing, however, since the purpose of Lookup would partially be to identify records that do not match the reference table, but the path name and annotations can help clarify the purpose.

The third error-handling option in the Lookup transformation, Ignore Failure, provides the most flexibility when you are trying to identify missing rows. When you set the error handling to Ignore Failure, the Lookup transformation will insert NULLs in all the return columns specified in the reference table when the reference table does not have a match. The flexibility comes when the Lookup output needs to be kept together (matches and non-matches) in the Data Flow either for the entirety of the downstream Data Flow path or when other transformations are required before checking the Lookup results. Figure 11-7 highlights a Data Flow containing a Lookup configured to ignore failures. Downstream of the Data Flow in this example are a few transformations before a Conditional Split, which evaluates the rows as they flow through this transformation based on the Lookup output.

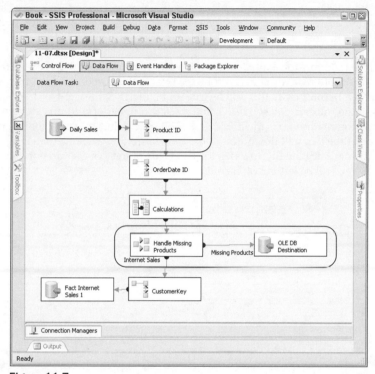

Figure 11-7

The Conditional Split evaluates whether the prior Lookup had a match in the reference by using an ISNULL function applied against a column specified to be returned from the Lookup reference table. The Conditional Split from Figure 11-7, named "Handle Missing Products," uses the ISNULL function, ISNULL([ProductID]), to identify previous Lookup records that did not have a match. Therefore, any row in the pipeline where the ProductID is NULL will be redirected out the named output, and the rest will be sent down the default output of the Conditional Split.

Of course, be aware that if the return column used in the Lookup reference table allows NULLs, then the filter logic in the Conditional Split would also evaluate this result as a match in the criteria. In the example, the return column does not allow NULLs; therefore the criterion is applied correctly. A common scenario, as this example highlights, is the use of Lookup to determine whether an input record should be inserted into a destination table or whether an update should be applied.

Take special note of how you used the Conditional Split and Multicast transformations. While these transformations do not bring data together, they are useful to split the data up once it is in the Data Flow. Some source data may be used in multiple ways during your data processing. Whether you need

to use the entire data set for multiple purposes (Multicast) or you need to break out each row for difference purposes (Conditional Split), these transformations will alleviate the need to pull from the same
source more than one time.

Merge Join Transformation

The second most useful data association transformation example is the Merge Join transformation,
which can take two different inputs and merge them together by comparing a set of key columns. The
Merge Join functionality is also described in detail in Chapter 4, so the discussion will focus on applying
the Merge Join in scenarios.

Because the Merge Join transformation allows three different types of joins (Left Outer Join, Inner Join,
and Full Join), the output row count may not be the total of the number of rows from either side of the
join added together. In most cases this will be true. In Figure 11-8, the right and left sides of the merge
are joined by a single column, SalesOrderID, and a select number of columns are returned by each side
of the join. Furthermore, the join is identified as a "Left outer join," meaning that all the output rows
from the left side of the join will flow through the transformation even if a matching record is not available on the right side. Additionally, rows on the right side of the join that do not match a record on the
left side of the merge will be left out of the output.

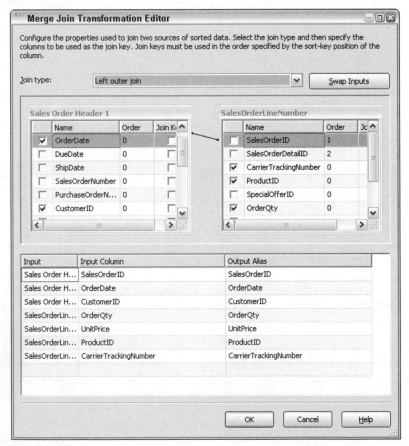

Figure 11-8

As an example of the output of this transformation, the following tables show some sample records within a range of OrderIDs.

Assume that the left input looks like the following table.

SalesOrderID	OrderDate	CustomerID
13452	8/1/2005	AW9987
18600	9/15/2005	AW540
21977	9/31/2005	AW2333

And the right input looks like this following table.

SalesOrderID	OrderQty	UnitPrice	ProductID	CarrierTracking
13452	1	$435.99	BK1055	A12227499
13452	1	$15.99	SH344	G977642
21977	3	$34.00	AC53	A12223445
23445	1	$799.95	BK1077	A12338890

When you apply the "Left outer join" logic as defined in Figure 11-9, you'll get the following results.

SalesOrderID	OrderDate	CustomerID	OrderQty	UnitPrice	ProductID	CarrierTracking
13452	8/1/2005	AW9987	1	$435.99	BK1055	A12227499
13452	8/1/2005	AW9987	1	$15.99	SH344	G977642
18600	9/15/2005	AW540	<NULL>	<NULL>	<NULL>	<NULL>
21977	9/31/2005	AW2333	3	$34.00	AC53	A12223445

You'll notice a few things about the output result set:

❏   Rows on the right side of the data set that do not have a match on the left are ignored, such as SalesOrderID 23445.

❏   Rows on the left that do not have matches on the right are in the output result set with NULLs in the columns returned from the right side, such as SalesOrderID 18600.

❏   When a row on either the left or right side of the Merge Join has multiple matches, multiple rows are returned in the output results. In other words, a row from either side may be used more than once in the output result set if the join results in more than one match. SalesOrderID 13452 has two matches on the right input and therefore produces two matches in the output.

As you can see, the Merge Join can be applied much like the Lookup transformation, because it integrates two different sources. There are, however, some very unique differences between the Merge Join and the Lookup transformation and some specific scenarios where the Merge Join transformation is very useful to accomplish data association based on the requirements. The Lookup, for example, will not duplicate rows when more than one match is made on the reference table; instead, a warning will be returned. Furthermore, the Lookup transformation Reference Table works only for database connections and not for flat file or other non-RDBMS sources.

The Merge Join transformation also requires that the sources be sorted by the join columns in the same order, whereas the Lookup does not require this. This may sound expensive from a resource perspective since a Sort transformation requires the entire data set to be cached; however, the source data may also be presorted coming in from the source adapter. In some situations, the join columns used in the Merge Join may have an index applied on the source database, or the source file may be ordered in the right order. You'll study this in more detail in the "Optimizing Package Processing" section later in this chapter. The purpose of mentioning it now is to illustrate that the Merge Join may not need the entire data set cached for performance. When you're determining whether to use the Merge Join or the Lookup transformation, if the sources can be efficiently presorted without adding overhead, and the volumes are moderate to high on both sides of the join (or the number of columns returned is high), then a Merge Join may be the right solution.

As you can see, the Merge Join transformation functions almost identically to a database join between tables (inner or outer join) where the join columns are equated (as opposed to nonequivalent comparisons: >, >=, <, <=, =!).

Data Cleansing and Transformation

The second major area of consideration where you can apply the Data Flow is data cleansing. Cleansing data involves managing missing values; correcting out-of-date, incomplete, or mis-keyed data; converting values to standard data types; changing data grain or filtering data subsets; and de-duplicating redundant data. Consistency is the goal of data cleansing whether the data source is a single system or multiple disparate sources.

Many of the Data Flow components provide data-cleansing capabilities or can participate in a data-cleansing process. Some of the more explicit transformations usable for this process include the following:

- ❑ Aggregate
- ❑ Character Map
- ❑ Conditional Split
- ❑ Data Conversion
- ❑ Derived Column
- ❑ Fuzzy Grouping
- ❑ Fuzzy Lookup
- ❑ Pivot
- ❑ Script Component
- ❑ Sort (with de-duplicating capabilities)
- ❑ Unpivot

Each of these transformations, or a combination of them, can handle many data-cleansing scenarios. A few of the transformations provide compelling data-cleansing features that even go beyond the capabilities of many relational engines. This makes use of the Data Flow. For example, the Fuzzy Lookup and Fuzzy Grouping (de-duplication) provide cleansing of dirty data by comparing data similarity within certain defined ranges. Pivot and Unpivot have the ability to transform data coming in by pivoting rows to columns or vice versa. Also, the Script transformation offers very powerful data-cleansing capabilities with the full features of VB.NET embedded; it is highlighted in detail in Chapter 7. Since the goal of this chapter is to highlight and discuss the application of Integration Services, the example will focus on a couple common examples of data cleansing using the Derived Column transformation and the Aggregate transformation. These two transformations have particular relevance in how data cleansing can be accomplished in the Data Flow in comparison with common query logic.

As Chapter 4 demonstrates, the Derived Column transformation's capabilities allow the ability to replace column values coming through the Data Flow. One of the more common data-cleansing scenarios that the Derived Column transformation can accomplish is to replace [blank] and NULL values extracted from various sources. Using the expression language, described in detail in Chapter 7, a check of values could be performed for both cases described. Figure 11-9 shows the Derived Column using the "Replace" column option on the AddressLine1 column coming through this transformation.

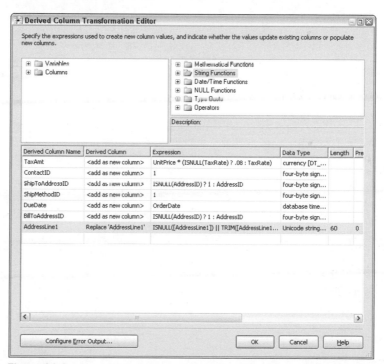

Figure 11-9

The following expression code is used to cleanse the [AddressLine1] input column in the example.

```
ISNULL([AddressLine1]) || TRIM([AddressLine1]) == "" ? @Unknown_Value :
TRIM([AddressLine1])
```

The expression checks for both conditions and also trims the value of the column to remove beginning and trailing spaces. If the input column value is NULL or blank, the expression uses a generic variable containing an "unknown" value as a replacement for the column output. Note that the expression uses a few of the different functions available in the language, particularly the conditional case expression (<Boolean> ? <True> : <false>). Rather than recursively embedding the conditional expression to evaluate both the NULL and blank ("") conditions, a Logical OR is used (||, double pipes) to check both conditions at once.

The second valuable transformation to highlight is the Aggregate. The Aggregate transformation brings GROUP BY logic to the Data Flow, but you can have multiple groups of aggregates with different outputs and different aggregations defined for each group. Many data transformation scenarios require changing the grain or the level of detail from the source to the destination, and in most situations the requirement is to roll up the data to higher levels of detail than what the source system makes available.

In Figure 11-10, the Aggregate transformation takes the input and groups by three source columns and applies aggregations across three other input columns.

Figure 11-10

Although not pictured, the Aggregate transformation can also provide multiple grouping with different outputs per grouping. This means if one grouping should be by CustomerID and another by CustomerID and OrderDate, they both can be accomplished in the same Aggregate component.

Putting It All Together, Seeing the Results

Now that you have considered a reengineered approach for data processing, compare it to the original DTS-based example. The DTS approach involved several steps that staged, cleansed, compared, updated, and loaded data into a destination table.

In reconstructing this approach, you were able to take the logic required and fit the entire process into a single Data Flow. Figure 11-11 shows the new design.

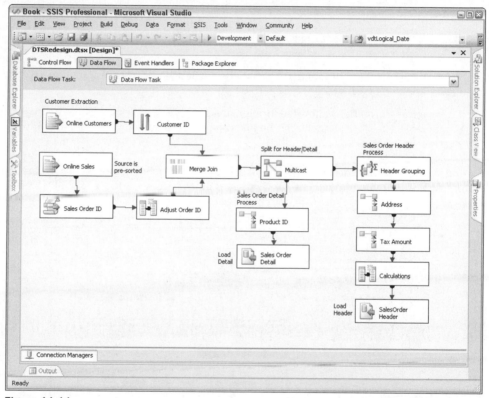

Figure 11-11

The Integration Services design takes advantage of the Data Flow by leveraging some of the built-in transformations just discussed, such as the Lookup, Derived Column, and Merge Join transformations. All of the logic that was accomplished in five DTS steps as described in Figure 11-1 has been retooled into a single Data Flow in Integration Services. Noticeably absent in the design is a staging environment. The following feature highlights of this redesign have been used to accomplish the identical data-processing task:

❏ A Merge Join transformation associates the Sales Detail flat file records with the Online Customer flat file records. Since the Sales Detail records were already presorted, a Sort transformation was not needed for the 480,000 records coming from this source adapter. A Sort transformation has been used for the 18,000 Online Customer records, which given its low record count performs very well in this scenario.

❏ Because the Sales Header table uses an IDENTITY column, SalesOrderID, which is required for the Sales Detail table, the Script transform creates a SalesOrderID value for each unique combination of sales grouping starting from the last SalesOrderID value in the Header table. The SQL Destination for the Sales Header table is set for Identity Insert to allow the created values to be inserted and the same keys to be available for the Sales Detail table without having to perform multiple passes on the data as the DTS solution did.

❏ A Multicast transformation allows the data to be separated for the Sales Detail and Sales Header tables.

❏ Using an Aggregate transformation, as shown in Figure 11-11, the input data is grouped by the Header criteria and the sales values are aggregated.

❏ A couple of Derived Column transformations are used to cleanse the data flowing through the Data Flow to replace NULL values with defaults.

❏ Lookup transformations allow the foreign keys for several tables to be acquired with limited single-table SELECT statements on the Lookup reference tables, which has little impact on the destination system.

Comparing the results, the redesigned DTS package in Integration Services was able to complete the same processing logic approximately two and one-half times faster than the original DTS package. Figure 11-12 shows the Gantt chart with both package execution times.

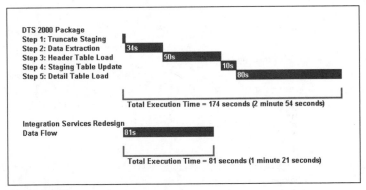

Figure 11-12

Although this is a simple example, it serves to point out the value of Integration Services. Not only does the performance speak for itself, but the simplicity in the design adds to the compelling nature of the tool and the architecture.

Staging Environments

A word must be mentioned about the appropriate use of staging environments. To this point, you have emphasized thinking in Data Flow terms by moving core data process logic into the Data Flow. And in most cases, this will yield high-performance results, especially when the timeliness of moving the data from point A to point B is the highest priority, such as near real-time or tight-processing-window scenarios. Doing this also mitigates some management overhead, limiting interim database usage.

A few situations merit staging environments and are worth mentioning for consideration.

❑ **Restartability.** The built-in checkpoint logic of Integration Services revolves around the Control Flow. What this means is that a failure in the Data Flow will not persist the data state. Rather, when the package is restarted, the Data Flow will restart from the beginning. The implications affect design if the source system is in flux and an error in the Data Flow causes a processing window to be missed. By landing the raw data first, the chance for data errors is minimized, and in the event of a failure during the load process, the package can be restarted from the staged data.

❑ **Processing Windows and Precedence.** Certain requirements may dictate that the various source extraction windows do not line up with each other or with the data load window for the destination. In these scenarios, it would be necessary to stage the data for a period of time until the full data set is available or the destination database load window has been reached.

❑ **Source Back Pressure.** At times, the Data Flow transformations may apply back pressure on the source extractions. This would happen when the flow of data coming in is faster than the performance of the transformations to handle the data processing in the pipeline. The back pressure created would slow down the extraction on the source system, and if the requirement is to extract the data in the fastest time with the least impact, then staging the raw data extract may help eliminate the back pressure.

❑ **Data Flow Optimization.** Staging certain elements, such as business keys, can actually provide valuable data to optimize the primary Data Flow. For example, if the Lookup source query can be filtered based on a set of keys that was pre-staged, this may allow overall gains in processing times by reducing the time it takes to load the Lookup plus the amount of memory needed for the operation. A second example is the use of staging to perform set-based table updates. Updates in a large system are often the source of system bottlenecks, and since Integration Services cannot perform set-based updates in the Data Flow, one consideration is to stage tables that can be used in a later Execute SQL task for a set-based update, which may provide a more efficient process.

Staged data can also prove useful in data validation and error handling. Given some of the uses of staging, is there a way to accomplish data staging but still retain the performance gain by leveraging the Data Flow? Yes. One emphasis that has been suggested is the reduction of synchronous processing in the Control Flow. In regard to data staging, the most natural thought when you have to introduce a staging environment is to first pick up the data from the source and land it to a staging environment and then pick the data back up from the staging environment and apply the transformation logic to it. What about landing the raw data to a staging environment at the same time that the transformations are applied? Figure 11-13 shows a Data Flow designed with a staging table that does not require the data to reside in the table before the transformation logic is applied.

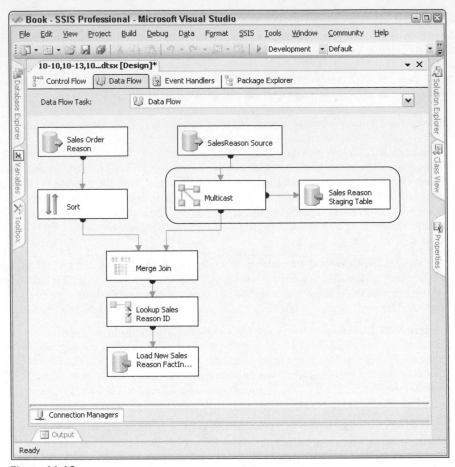

Figure 11-13

The Multicast transformation in this example is taking the raw source data and allowing it to stream down to the core Data Flow, while at the same time the raw source data is being staged to a table. The data within the table is now available to query for data validation and checking purposes; in addition, it provides a snapshot of the source system that can then be used for reprocessing when needed. Although the data is landed to staging, two differences distinguish this example from a model that first stages data and then uses the staged data as a source. First, as has been mentioned, the process is no longer synchronous; data can move from point A to point B in many cases in the time it takes simply to extract the data from A. Second, the staging process requires only a single pass on the staging table (for the writes) rather than the IO overhead of a second pass that reads the data from the staging. Overall, this approach may provide the best of both worlds — leveraging the Data Flow but providing the value of a stage environment.

Optimizing Package Processing

There are a few techniques you can apply when you're streamlining packages for performance. In the last chapter, you went under the covers of the Integration Services engine to understand buffer usage and the different types of Data Flow components. This section builds on that knowledge by applying certain optimization techniques to achieve better throughput.

Optimizing Buffers, Execution Trees, and Engine Threads

If you recall in the last chapter, for each Execution Tree in a Data Flow, a different buffer profile is used. This means that downstream execution trees may require different columns based on what is added or subtracted in the Data Flow. You also saw that the performance of a buffer within a Data Flow is directly related to the row width of the buffer. Narrow buffers can hold more rows, and therefore the throughput will be higher.

Some columns that are used in an Execution Tree may not be needed downstream. For example, if an input column to a Lookup transformation is used as the key match to the reference table, this column may not be needed after the Lookup and therefore should be removed before the next Execution Tree. Integration Services does a good job of providing warnings when columns exist in an Execution Tree but are not used in any downstream transformation or destination adapter. Figure 11-14 highlights the Progress tab within a package where column usage has not been optimized in the Data Flow. Each warning, highlighted with a yellow exclamation point, indicates the existence of a column not used later in downstream components and which therefore should be removed from the pipeline after initial use.

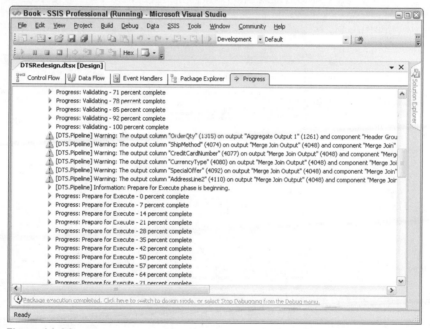

Figure 11-14

The warning text describes the optimization technique well:

```
[DTS.Pipeline] Warning: The output column "OrderQty" (1315) on output "Aggregate
Output 1" (1261) and component "Header Grouping" (1259) is not subsequently used in
the Data Flow task. Removing this unused output column can increase Data Flow task
performance.
```

Any asynchronous component whose input closes out an Execution Tree will have the option of removing columns in the output. You would normally do this through the edit dialog box of the transformation, but you can also do it in the Advanced Editor if the component provides an advanced properties window. For example, in the Union All transformation, you can highlight a row in the editor and delete it with the delete keyboard key. This will ensure that the column is not used in the next Execution Tree.

A second optimization technique in this area revolves around optimizing the processor utilization by adding the available use of more Execution Threads for the Data Flow. As was highlighted in the last chapter, increasing the EngineThreads Data Flow property to a value greater than the number of Execution Trees plus the number of Source components will ensure that Integration Services has enough threads to use. However, there may also be scenarios where an Execution Tree has so many synchronous components that the single Execution Thread allocated cannot handle the workload, and the result is a processing bottleneck, when in fact the server may still have unused processors that can perform the work. Even though breaking up the Execution Tree into multiple trees will require more buffer copies, the end result of allowing a second or third Execution Thread to process the transformations may improve overall performance. To accomplish this, one option is to use a Union All transformation with a single input and output at a natural balancing point of the Execution Tree. In Figure 11-15, notice how the entire Data Flow consists of synchronous transformations, which means that the entire process has only one Execution Tree.

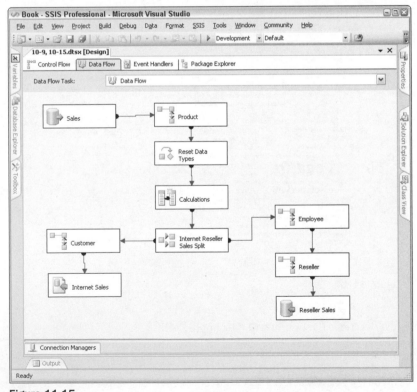

Figure 11-15

If you modify the Data Flow with the addition of a Union All transformation, the result would look like Figure 11-16.

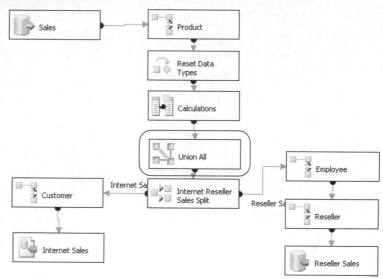

Figure 11-16

The Union All was placed before the Conditional Split, so that the first three transformations can be worked on in a different thread than the Conditional Split and the last three lookups in the Data Flow. The end result in both of these scenarios is more efficiency in handling the volumes and complexity within the Data Flow.

Careful Use of Row-Based Transformations

Row-based transforms, as described in Chapter 10, are non-blocking transformations, but they exhibit the functionality of interacting with an outside system (for example, a database or file system) on a row-by-row basis. Compared with other non-blocking transformations, these transformations are slower because of this nature. The other type of non-blocking transformation, streaming, can use internal cache or provide calculations using other columns or variables readily available to the Data Flow, making them perform very fast. Given the nature of row-based transformations, their usage should be cautious and calculated.

Of course, some row-based transformations have critical functionality, so this caution needs to be balanced with data-processing requirements. For example, the Export and Import Column transformation can read and write from files to columns, which is a very valuable tool, but has the obvious overhead of the IO activity with the file system.

Another useful row-based transformation is the OLE DB Command transformation, which can use input column values and execute parameterized queries against a database, row by row. The interaction with the database, although it can be optimized, still requires overhead to process. Figure 11-17 shows a SQL Server Trace run against a database that is receiving updates from an OLE DB Command transformation.

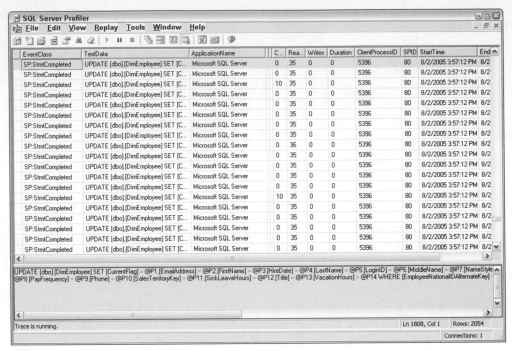

Figure 11-17

This is only a snapshot, but you can see that taking the duration, reads, and writes, the aggregated impact of thousands of rows will cause Data Flow latency at the transformation.

For this scenario, one alternative is to leverage set-based processes within databases. In order to do this, the data will need to be staged during the Data Flow, and you will need to add a secondary Execute SQL task to the Control Flow that runs the set-based update statement. The result may actually reduce the overall processing time when compared with the original OLE DB Command approach. This alternative approach is not meant to diminish the usefulness of the OLE DB Command but rather to provide an example of optimizing the Data Flow for higher-volume scenarios that may require optimization.

Understand Blocking Transformation Impacts

A blocking transformation requires the complete set of records cached from the input before it can release records downstream. In Chapter 10, a list of about a dozen transformations that meet this criterion was provided. The most common examples are the Sort and Aggregate transformations.

Blocking transformations are intensive because they require caching all the upstream input data, and they also may require more intensive processor usage based on their functionality. When not enough RAM is available in the system, the blocking transformations may also require temporary disk storage. You need to be aware of these limitations when you're working to optimize a Data Flow. The point of mentioning the nature of blocking transformations is not to minimize their usefulness but rather to advise that in some situations they are very useful and perform much better than alternative approaches. Rather, the intention here is to use these transformations in the right places and know the resource impact.

Since sorting data is a common requirement, one optimization technique is valuable to mention. Source data that can be sorted in the adapter through an ORDER BY statement or presorted in a flat file does not require the use of a Sort transformation. As long as the data is physically sorted in the right order when coming into the Data Flow, the source adapter can be configured to indicate that the data is sorted and which columns are sorted in what order. Figure 11-18 shows the Advanced Editor of a source adapter with the Source Output folder highlighted. The first step is to set the IsSorted property to True, as seen on the right-hand properties screen.

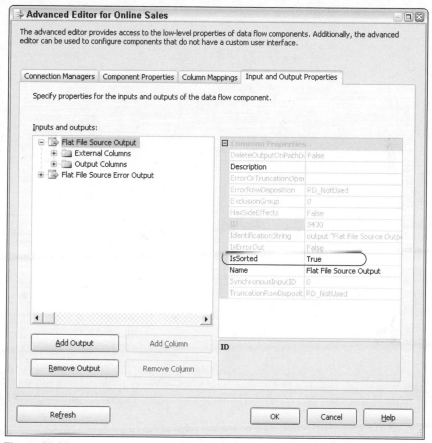

Figure 11-18

The second requirement is to indicate which columns are sorted. To do this, open the Source Output folder and then the Output Columns subfolder. This will open the list of columns that the adapter will send out into the pipeline. To set the sort column order and direction, highlight the first column that is sorted. The example in Figure 11-19 uses the presorted CustomerID column, which is highlighted in the figure.

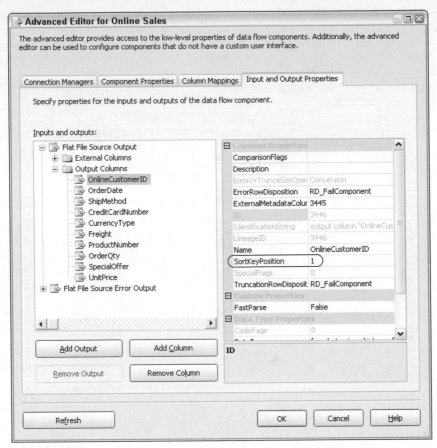

Figure 11-19

The SortKeyPosition should be set for the columns used in sorting. For the first column that is sorted, set the SortKeyPosition to a 1 or -1. A -1 indicates that the column is sorted in descending order. Continue to the next sorted column, if applicable, and set the value to a 2 or -2, and subsequently continue for all sorted columns.

Pipeline Performance Monitoring

In the last chapter, one of the things you looked at was the built-in Pipeline logging functionality and how it could help you understand what Integration Services was doing behind the scenes when running a package with one or more Data Flows. Another tool available to Integration Services is the Windows operating system tool called Performance Monitor (PerfMon for short), which is available to local administrators in the machine's Administrative Tools. When Integration Services is installed on a machine, a set of counters is added that allows the tracking of the Data Flow's performance.

As Figure 11-20 shows, the Pipeline counters can be used when selecting the SQLServer:SSIS Pipeline object.

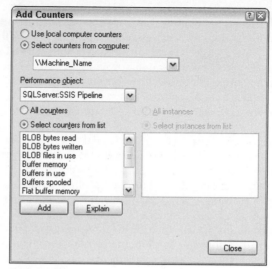

Figure 11-20

The following counters are available in the SQLServer:SSIS Pipeline object within PerfMon. Descriptions of these counters are provided below.

- ❏ BLOB bytes read
- ❏ BLOB bytes written
- ❏ BLOB files in use
- ❏ Buffer memory
- ❏ Buffers in use
- ❏ Buffers spooled
- ❏ Flat buffer memory
- ❏ Flat buffers in use
- ❏ Private buffers in use
- ❏ Rows read
- ❏ Rows written

The BLOB counters help identify the volume of the BLOB data types flowing through the Data Flow. Since handling large binary columns can be a huge drain on the available memory, understanding how your Data Flow is handling BLOB data types becomes important. Remember that BLOB data can be introduced to the Data Flow not only by Source adapters but also by the Import (and Export) Column transformations.

Since buffers are the mechanism that the Data Flow uses to process all data, the buffer-related counters provide the most valuable information to seeing how much and where memory is being used in the Data Flow. The Buffer Memory and Buffers in Use counters are the high-level counters that provide totals for the server, both memory use and total buffer count. Essentially, the Buffer Memory counter shows the total memory being used by Integration Services and can be compared with the amount of available system memory to know if Integration Services processing is bottlenecked by the available physical memory. Furthermore, the Buffers Spooled counter provides even more indication of resource limitations on your server. It shows the number of buffers temporarily written to disk if enough system memory is not available. Anything greater than zero shows that your Data Flow is having to utilize temporary disk storage to accomplish its work, which comes with an IO impact and overhead.

In regard to the buffer details, two types of buffers exist, flat and private. Flat buffers are the primary Data Flow buffers used when a Source adapter sends data into the Data Flow. Synchronous transformation outputs pass the flat buffers to the next component, and asynchronous outputs use reprovisioned or new flat buffers to be passed to the next transformation. On the other hand, some transformations require different buffers, called private buffers, which are received from upstream transformations or passed on to downstream transformations. Three primary examples of private buffer use are found in the Aggregate, Sort, and Lookup transformations, which use private buffers to cache data that is used for calculations and matching. These transformations still use flat buffers for data being received and passed, but they also use private buffers to manage and cache supplemental data used in the transformation. The flat and private buffer counters show the breakdown of these usages and help identify where buffers are being used and to what extent.

The last counters in the Pipeline counters list simply show the number of rows handled in the Data Flow, whether Rows Read or Rows Written. These numbers are aggregates of the rows processed since the counters were started.

When reviewing these counters, remember that they are an aggregate of all the Integration Services packages and embedded Data Flows running on your server. If you are attempting to isolate performance impacts of specific Data Flows or packages, run these by themselves and capture the Pipeline counters for review.

The Pipeline counters can be tracked in the UI of Performance Monitor in real time or captured at a recurring interval for later evaluation. Figure 11-21 shows the Pipeline counters tracked during the execution of Figure 11-11.

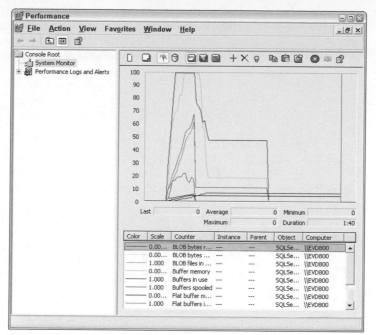

Figure 11-21

Notice that the buffer usage scales up and then drops and that the plateau lines occur during the database commit process when Integration Services has completed its processes and is waiting on the database to commit the insert transaction. When the package is complete, the buffers are released and the buffer counters drop to zero, while the row count buffers remain stable since they represent the aggregate rows processed since the PerfMon was started.

Summary

The flexibility of Integration Services brings more design options and in turn requires you to give more attention to establishing the architecture. As you've seen in this chapter, bringing over a DTS-based architecture to Integration Services also brings over the design and processing flaws with no real advantage gained from the new Integration Services features. Leveraging the Data Flow in Integration Services reduces processing time, eases management, and opens the door to scalability. Therefore, choose the right architecture up front and it will ease the design burden and give overall gains to your solution.

Once you have established a model for scalability, the reduced development time of Integration Services will allow attention to be given to optimization, where fine-tuning the pipeline and process will make every second count.

12

DTS 2000 Migration and Metadata Management

By now, you are probably pretty familiar with various basic aspects of SSIS. In earlier chapters, you've studied the new SSIS interface, the new object model, internal design, and how to write SSIS packages.

In this chapter, you will look at how to migrate DTS 2000 packages to SSIS and, if necessary, how to run DTS 2000 packages under SSIS. You will also learn about some advanced settings in SSIS, such as metadata management and managing DTS 2000 packages in SSMS.

Migrating DTS 2000 Packages to SSIS

Since SSIS is totally redesigned from the ground up and has a brand-new architecture, you may wonder, what do you do with your existing DTS 2000 packages?

The good news is that Microsoft provides the DTS Migration Wizard, which facilitates this process. The DTS Migration Wizard analyzes your current DTS 2000 package and tries to map all its tasks, components, and workflow constraints to their equivalent parts, where applicable, in SSIS. The bad news is that since SSIS is totally reengineered, it is not possible to migrate all packages that you can create in DTS 2000. The Migration Wizard provides a best-effort attempt. If your package cannot be migrated using the wizard, you will have to upgrade it manually. In fact, for those packages, you probably want to use manual upgrade anyway so that you can fully take advantage of the enhanced functions and capabilities.

In this section, you will see how to use the Migration Wizard to upgrade a sample DTS 2000 package. The sample package will use an ActiveX script (WMI) to query the system's services and their startup mode and to pipe the data captured into a CSV file. That data will then be imported into a table you'll create in the Northwind database.

Here are the steps to create a DTS 2000 package that will be used later in this chapter:

1. Create a table ServiceInfo within Northwind database using the following script:

```
Use Northwind
create table ServiceInfo (ServiceName varchar(100), StartupMode varchar(10))
```

2. Create a new package called GetServiceInfo. Create a connection to the Northwind database within the package.

3. Create an Execute SQL task to clean up the ServiceInfo table:

```
truncate table ServiceInfo
```

4. Create an ActiveX Script task that uses WMI to query the system's service info. Services present on the system and their startup mode will be retrieved and piped into a CSV file. Note that the folder in this example is C:\SSIS. If you use a different folder for your testing, you need to change that accordingly. Please see Chapter 16 if you want to learn more about WMI:

```vb
'***********************************************************************
'  Visual Basic ActiveX Script
'***********************************************************************
Option Explicit
Function Main()
Dim strLocalFolderName, strOutputFileName, strComputer
Dim objFSO, objWMIService, objMyFile, colServiceList, objService

strLocalFolderName = "c:\SSIS"
strOutputFileName = strLocalFolderName & "\ServiceAndStartMode.csv"
strComputer = "."

Set objWMIService = GetObject("winmgmts:" _
& "{impersonationLevel=impersonate}!\\" & strComputer & "\root\cimv2")
Set colServiceList = objWMIService.ExecQuery _
("Select * from Win32_Service")

Set objFSO = CreateObject("Scripting.FileSystemObject")

If (objFSO.FileExists(strOutputFileName)) Then
    objFSO.DeleteFile (strOutputFileName)
End If

Set objMyFile = objFSO.CreateTextFile(strOutputFileName, True)

objMyFile.WriteLine ("ServiceName,StartMode")


For Each objService In colServiceList
    objMyFile.WriteLine (objService.DisplayName & "," & objService.StartMode)
Next

objMyFile.Close

Set objFSO = Nothing
Set objWMIService = Nothing
```

```
Set objMyFile = Nothing
Set colServiceList = Nothing
Set objService = Nothing

Main = DTSTaskExecResult_Success
End Function
```

5. Create a Transform Data task to import data from the CSV file generated from the preceding step into the ServiceInfo table. Use the text file ServiceAndStartMode.csv as Source and the ServiceInfo table as Destination.

6. Create the appropriate workflow process.

Figure 12-1 shows what this DTS 2000 package should look like.

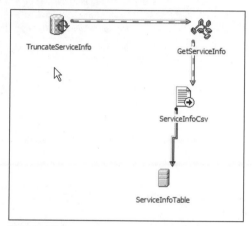

Figure 12-1

Your sample package is now set up and ready to go.

Using the Package Migration Wizard

You can invoke the Package Migration Wizard from multiple places. Depending on where you invoke the wizard from, the migrated package destination location will be different. For example, if you invoke the wizard from BIDS, it will assume that you want to migrate DTS 2000 packages into a SSIS package file (.dtsx). If the wizard is invoked from command line, it will assume that you want to migrate the package into the MSDB database on a server you define. Below are ways you can use to invoke the Package Migration Wizard:

❑ From SQL Server Management Studio, you can invoke the Package Migrate Wizard by using the right-click context menu of the Legacy node under the Management node in the Object Explorer, as shown in Figure 12-2.

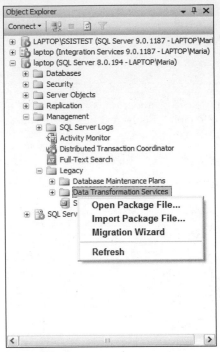

Figure 12-2

❑ From BIDS, right-click SSIS Packages in Solution Explorer and pick Migrate DTS 2000 Package, as shown in Figure 12-3.

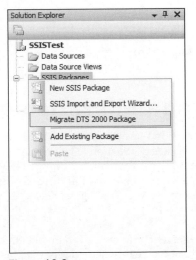

Figure 12-3

❑ From a DOS prompt, type **DTSMigrationWizard** to invoke the wizard. By default, the binary DTSMigrationWizard.exe resides at C:\Program Files\Microsoft SQL Server\90\DTS\Binn folder. This may be different in your environment if you customized your SQL Server 2005 installation.

Since BIDS is the home where you create, manage, and edit your SSIS packages, you'll use BIDS to see step-by-step how you can migrate the package you created in the previous section.

1. Invoke the Package Migration Wizard. You will see a welcome window from the wizard. Click Next to continue.

2. In the next page, shown in Figure 12-4, you choose the source type and location. In this case, you can assume that your package is stored in the local default SQL Server 2000 server. Click Next.

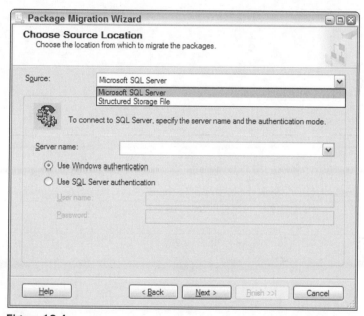

Figure 12-4

3. The next page of the wizard asks you to pick the destination location of the package you are migrating, as shown in Figure 12-5. As mentioned earlier, since the wizard is invoked within BIDS, it assumes that you want the package in a .dtsx file format. You can see from the figure that the Destination drop-down list box is grayed out and the default selection is DTSX File. If you want to migrate the package to a database server, invoke the package from command line instead. In this case, you can pick F:\SSIS as the destination folder. Click Next.

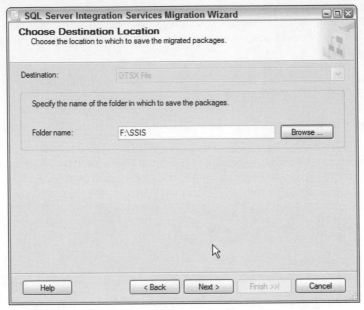

Figure 12-5

4. In the next step, the wizard lists the packages available on the source server that can be migrated, as shown in Figure 12-6. In this case, there's only one package, GetServiceInfo, which you created earlier. Check the box next to the package name. Note that it even gives you the choice of migrating previous versions of the package. Click Next.

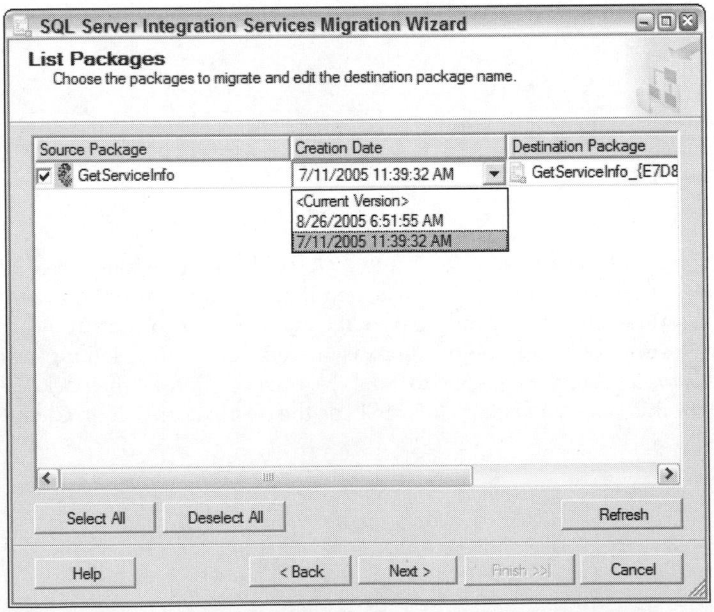

Figure 12-6

5. The wizard then asks you to provide a log file location, as shown in Figure 12-7. The log file will log the migration process. This information will be valuable if the migration is unsuccessful. You will use F:\SSIS\Migration.log file. Click Next.

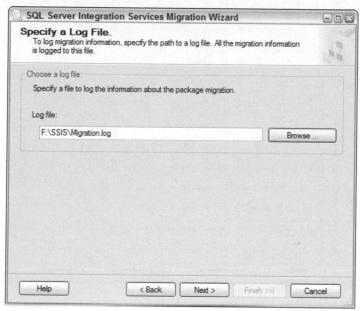

Figure 12-7

6. You now will see a summary screen of this migration-related information, as shown in Figure 12-8. You can scan over and go back and change settings, if desired. Otherwise, click Finish to migrate the package now.

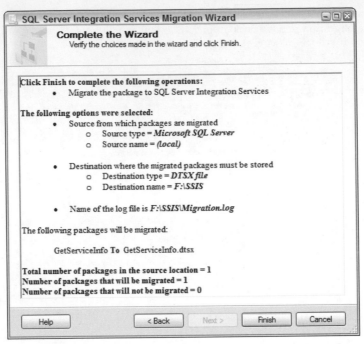

Figure 12-8

7. The migration process starts. You will see its progress in real time. After it is done, you can click the Report button to view the migration report. In this case, your GetServiceInfo package has migrated successfully, as shown in Figure 12-9. Click Close to finish the Package Migration Wizard. If for any reason the migration is not successful, the error will be in the final report. Based on the error message, you will be able to fix what is wrong to continue.

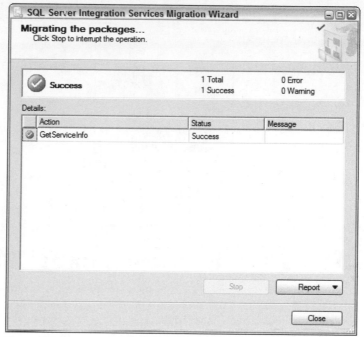

Figure 12-9

After the migration is complete, the GetServiceInfo.dtsx file will be opened within BIDS, as you can see in Figure 12-10.

Figure 12-10

Press F5 to start package execution and it will be successful, as shown in Figure 12-11.

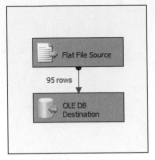

Figure 12-11

Running DTS 2000 Packages under SSIS

You could migrate the sample package created earlier successfully, because the tasks within are pretty simple. However, for a DTS 2000 package that uses lots of custom extensions, ActiveX scripts, and Dynamic Property tasks, the migration will not be that easy. These tasks have many interactions with the DTS 2000 object model, and the SSIS object model is not backward compatible. For those packages, you may have to do some new design and development work in order to migrate them to SSIS.

As a temporary solution, you can choose to run DTS 2000 packages under SSIS, if you have the Data Transformation Services 2000 runtime installed. You need to rerun the setup process to install the runtime if you did not do it the first time. You can choose to include this component by clicking the Advanced option during your installation process. However, if you already have SQL Server 2000 client tools installed, especially Enterprise Manager, then the runtime is already present on the server and you will not see this optional component during your installation process.

In this section, you will learn how to run a DTS 2000 package within SSIS. You will use your earlier sample package as an example.

1. Open BIDS, if it is not yet opened. Create an empty package.

2. Make sure the Control Flow tab is selected. Move to the Toolbox and select the task called Execute DTS 2000 Package task.

3. Drag the task to the Control Flow design surface. Right-click on this item and select Edit. Give this task a descriptive name, such as ExeDTS2kGetServiceInfo. Fill in the SQLServer name. Also, put in the authentication information. After this, click the ellipsis button next to the PackageName box.

4. The Select Package window opens, as shown in Figure 12-12. Here you will see all the packages present on that server. Select the GetServiceInfo package and then click OK.

Figure 12-12

5. Now that the DTS 2000 package is defined, you will see that you can edit this package within the DTS 2000 designer if necessary, as shown in Figure 12-13.

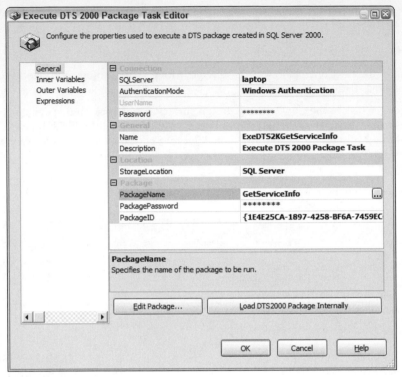

Figure 12-13

Click "Edit Package..." if you want to do that. You will see that the DTS 2000 package designer is launched, as shown in Figure 12-14. Since you have the DTS 2000 runtime component and the SQL Server 2000 client tools, you can edit this package.

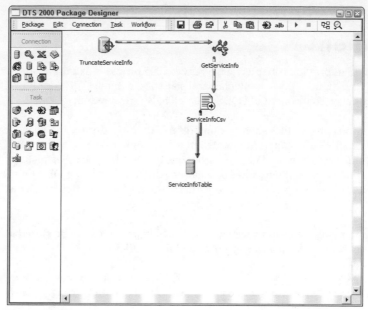

Figure 12-14

6. Don't make any changes to the package at this time. Close the DTS 2000 package designer and then click OK, and you will be at the design surface of the Control Flow tab, with the package showing, as shown in Figure 12-15.

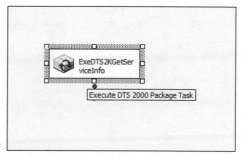

Figure 12-15

7. Test-run this package and it will be successful. If for any reason it is not, read the error message to find out what went wrong and make modifications accordingly.

Package Metadata and Storage Management

As you've learned in previous chapters, SQL Server 2005 provides extensive support for XML, such as the XML data type, XQuery, XML showplan and statistics, native HTTP endpoint XML Web service, and more. SSIS, as a major component of SQL Server 2005, is no exception.

For example, various project files such as .ssmssqlproj, .dwproj, .dtproj, and so on are saved as XML documents. In addition, SSIS Mapping files, located in the %ProgramFiles%\Microsoft SQL Server\90\DTS\MappingFiles folder, which map data types from one back-end to the other, also use XML extensively. If you're interested in learning the nuances of data type differences among DB2, Oracle, SQL Server, and Access, you can open them up and take a look there. The package configuration file, .dtsConfig, is also an XML file.

As was alluded to many times in previous chapters, SSIS packages can be stored as a dtsx file, which is an XML file. Data sources for the project are stored in *.ds files.

Traditionally, in SQL Server 2000 and SQL Server 7, the most popular storage type has been MSDB. In SQL Server 2000 and SQL Server 7, there are a few tables that store packages, as shown in Figure 12-16.

System Tables

LAPTOP\Databases\System Databases\msdb\Tables\System   55 Item(s)

Name	Schema	Created
sysdtscategories	dbo	8/6/2000
sysdtspackagelog	dbo	8/6/2000
sysdtspackages	dbo	8/6/2000
sysdtssteplog	dbo	8/6/2000
sysdtstasklog	dbo	8/6/2000
sysfilegroups	dbo	8/6/2000
sysfiles	dbo	8/6/2000
sysfiles1	dbo	8/6/2000
sysforeignkeys	dbo	8/6/2000
sysfulltextcatalogs	dbo	8/6/2000
sysfulltextnotify	dbo	8/6/2000
sysindexes	dbo	8/6/2000
sysindexkeys	dbo	8/6/2000
sysjobhistory	dbo	8/6/2000
sysjobs	dbo	8/6/2000
sysjobschedules	dbo	8/6/2000
sysjobservers	dbo	8/6/2000
sysjobsteps	dbo	8/6/2000
sysmembers	dbo	8/6/2000
sysnotifications	dbo	8/6/2000
sysobjects	dbo	8/6/2000
sysoperators	dbo	8/6/2000

Figure 12-16

In SQL Server 2005, you still have the option of saving packages into MSDB, although the table structure has changed somewhat, as you can see in Figure 12-17.

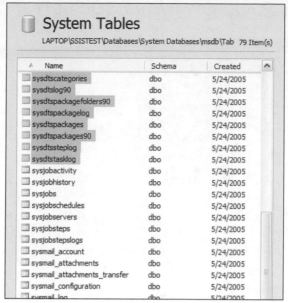

Figure 12-17

In general, XML files are easier to read and modify than packages saved in structured storage like MSDB, because XML files are text-based. In addition, there are more utilities and tools available for XML file processing. It is believed that XML file–based SSIS packages will be the future.

In addition, because of the separation of Control Flow and Data Flow in SSIS, it is much easier to change the properties of a package if it is XML-based. For example, you can easily modify the connection property, file directory, and other related properties of a package using a simple text editor, without having to using BIDS. That can be handy at times, especially when you deploy things to production servers.

On the other hand, MSDB-based storage has its merits, especially when it comes to backing up and restoring. Packages saved to MSDB can be backed up and restored using SQL Server's backup and restore features. Note that if packages are saved in MSDB, but their configuration files are not, then you need to make sure that the configuration files are backed up regularly as part of securing packages saved to MSDB. To include configurations in the backup of the MSDB database, you should consider using the SQL Server configuration type instead of file-based configurations.

The backup of packages that are saved to the file system should be included in the backup plan for securing those packages. The Integration Services service configuration file, which has the default name MsDtsSrvr.ini.xml, lists the folders on the server that the service monitors. You should make sure these folders are backed up. Additionally, packages may be stored in other folders on the server, and you should make sure to include these folders in the backup.

Managing SSIS Packages within SQL Server Management Studio

In SQL Server Management Studio, if you connect to an Integration Service instance in Object Explorer, you will see two folders: Running Packages and Stored Packages, as shown in Figure 12-18.

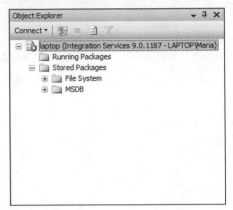

Figure 12-18

The Running Packages folder lists all packages that are currently running. Not surprisingly, the contents in this folder will change to reflect your current SSIS package activity. You must manually refresh this folder to display currently running packages.

The Stored Packages folder lists packages that have been saved and registered on this Integration Service instance. This folder has two default subfolders: File System and MSDB.

When you browse packages within SQL Server Management Studio, SQL Server Integration Services will go to the HKLM\SOFTWARE\Microsoft\MSDTS\ServiceConfigFile registry key to look for the SSIS service configuration file. Not surprisingly, the File System and MSDB Folder property is controlled by an XML configuration file. By default, this file is named MsDtsSrvr.ini.xml and is located at %ProgramFiles%\Microsoft SQL Server\90\DTS\Binn folder. The following is the default content of this XML file:

```xml
<?xml version="1.0" encoding="utf-8"?>
<DtsServiceConfiguration xmlns:xsd="http://www.w3.org/2001/XMLSchema"
xmlns:xsi="http://www.w3.org/2001/XMLSchema-instance">
  <StopExecutingPackagesOnShutdown>true</StopExecutingPackagesOnShutdown>
  <TopLevelFolders>
    <Folder xsi:type="SqlServerFolder">
      <Name>MSDB</Name>
      <ServerName>.</ServerName>
    </Folder>
    <Folder xsi:type="FileSystemFolder">
      <Name>File System</Name>
      <StorePath>..\Packages</StorePath>
    </Folder>
    <Folder xsi:type="FileSystemFolder">
      <Name>Dev Packages</Name>
      <StorePath>c:\SSIS</StorePath>
```

```
    </Folder>
  </TopLevelFolders>
</DtsServiceConfiguration>
```

You can customize this initialization file to suit your needs. For example, if you want to group your packages into Dev, QA, Cert, and Prod, you can add the following code to this file, along with the correct StorePath parameter. This way, all packages are grouped logically and therefore easier to manage.

For example, suppose you have a folder called C:\SSIS that you use for your packages. Underneath that, you can create subfolders called DevDTSX, QADTSX, CertDTSX, and ProdDTSX. You can then modify your configuration file using the following code:

```xml
<?xml version="1.0" encoding="utf-8"?>
<DtsServiceConfiguration xmlns:xsd="http://www.w3.org/2001/XMLSchema"
xmlns:xsi="http://www.w3.org/2001/XMLSchema-instance">
  <StopExecutingPackagesOnShutdown>true</StopExecutingPackagesOnShutdown>
  <TopLevelFolders>
    <Folder xsi:type="SqlServerFolder">
      <Name>MSDB</Name>
      <ServerName>.</ServerName>
    </Folder>
    <Folder xsi:type="FileSystemFolder">
      <Name>DevDTSX</Name>
      <StorePath>c:\SSIS\Dev</StorePath>
    </Folder>
    <Folder xsi:type="FileSystemFolder">
      <Name>QADTSX</Name>
      <StorePath>c:\SSIS\QA</StorePath>
    </Folder>
    <Folder xsi:type="FileSystemFolder">
      <Name>CertDTSX</Name>
      <StorePath>c:\SSIS\Cert</StorePath>
    </Folder>
    <Folder xsi:type="FileSystemFolder">
      <Name>ProdDTSX</Name>
      <StorePath>c:\SSIS\Prod</StorePath>
    </Folder>
  </TopLevelFolders>
</DtsServiceConfiguration>
```

After you make the modification to the configuration file, you need to restart SQL Server Integration Services for the new configuration to take effect. Figure 12-19 shows the new folder structure.

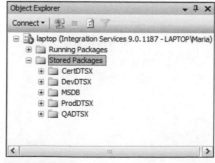

Figure 12-19

Notice that StorePath can be a UNC path. For example, if you store all your dtsx packages in one shared folder on a server, you can use that too. Just use \\PackageServerName\SharedPackageFolderName as StorePath. In fact, this is probably a good way to share packages among a group of developers.

In addition, if you decide to store some packages in MSDB, it probably is a good idea to store them on one server. That way, you can manage them centrally in one place.

In an environment where you have a lot of servers to manage, you can create a single MsDtsSrvr.ini.xml file and distribute it to all the servers that you use. That way, you will have all the packages you manage in one place and they will be uniform in all the servers you touch. That will truly make the management of packages portable.

Please note that although you can manage SSIS packages using SQL Server Management Studio, you cannot create packages with it. You will need BIDS to do that.

Managing DTS 2000 Packages within SQL Server Management Studio

If the SQL Server 2000 DTS runtime is installed, you can use SQL Server Management Studio to manage and even edit your DTS 2000 packages stored on a SQL Server 2000 MSDB database.

First, you need to connect to the SQL Server 2000 database instance in Object Explorer where those packages are stored. This is somewhat counterintuitive in that you do not connect to Integration Service to manage those packages.

Once you are connected, you need to expand the Management folder, then expand the Legacy folder, and then expand Data Transformation Services. As you can see in Figure 12-20, the DTS 2000 package you created earlier is listed.

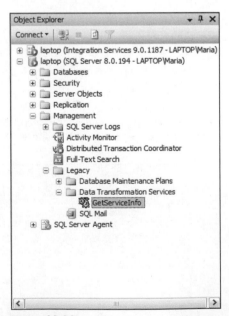

Figure 12-20

By right-clicking the package, you will see a context menu, where you can open, migrate, export, delete, rename, and refresh the highlighted package (see Figure 12-21).

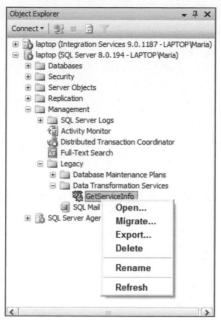

Figure 12-21

Summary

In this chapter, you learned about DTS 2000 package migration, about running DTS 2000 packages within SSIS, and about metadata management for packages.

Eventually, you will have to migrate all your DTS 2000 packages into SSIS packages. If you have many packages and they are fairly complex, you can choose to install DTS 2000 runtime and continue running them within SSIS. You can start migrating smaller and simpler packages with the Migration Wizard. As you gain more experience, you can start to tackle more complex packages. As mentioned earlier, you will probably have to rethink how the old package was designed and then redesign it using SSIS's enhanced functionality. This way, you will be able to fully take advantage of the richer functionality and better performance and scalability provided by SSIS.

As to metadata management and package storage, that depends on your environment and your particular needs. If you work in a team that has a few developers, you may want to use centralized storage for all your packages so that developers can share and manage those packages easily. If you choose to use dtsx XML files for storage, you can save them on the network or a shared folder. If you store them in MSDB, consider storing them in a centralized database. In any case, if you manage those packages within SSMS, you can create one single MsDtsSrvr.ini.xml file. You will then have a consistent view of all your packages, thus making package management easier.

13

Error and Event Handling

SQL Server Integration Services provides some valuable features to enable you to control the workflow of your SSIS packages at a very granular level. Functionality that you might expect to be available only by scripting can often be accomplished by setting a few properties of a component. In addition, powerful error-handling capabilities, the ability to log detailed information as the package runs, and impressive debugging functionality make SSIS a world-class ETL tool.

This chapter will walk you through controlling the package workflow, beginning at the highest level using precedence constraints and then drilling down to event handling. You'll see how trappable events play a role in breakpoints and logging. Finally, you will learn how these features can be used for troubleshooting, debugging, and enabling you to build robust SSIS packages.

Precedence Constraints

Precedence constraints, those green, red, and blue arrows, can be used to handle error conditions and the workflow of a package. Figure 13-1 shows a typical example. If the Initial Data Flow task completes successfully, the Success Data Flow task will execute. A green arrow (on the left) points to the Success Data Flow task. If the Initial Data Flow task fails, the Failure Send Mail task executes, sending notification of the failure. A red arrow (in the middle) points to the Failure Send Mail task. No matter what happens, the Completion Script task will always execute. A blue arrow (at the right) points to the Completion Script task.

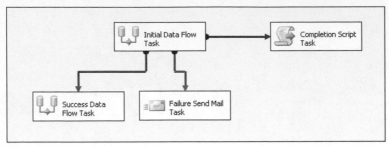

Figure 13-1

By default, the precedence constraint will be a green arrow designating success. To change how the precedence constraint is evaluated, you can right-click the arrow and choose a different outcome from the pop-up menu, as shown in Figure 13-2.

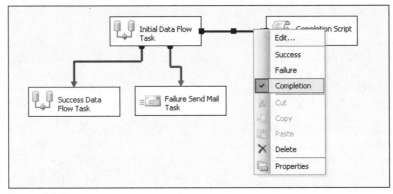

Figure 13-2

In addition to the success, failure, or completion of a task, you can combine the task outcome with a Boolean expression to determine the flow. Using Boolean expressions with precedence constraints will be discussed shortly. Tasks may also be combined into groups by using containers, and the workflow can be controlled by the success or failure of the container. For example, a package may have several Data Flow tasks that can run in parallel, each loading data from a different source. All of these must complete successfully before continuing on to the next step. These tasks can be added to a Sequence Container, and the precedence constraint can be drawn from the container to the next step. Figure 13-3 is an example showing how a Sequence Container might be used. After the Initialization Script runs, the Import Data container executes. Within it, three Data Flow processes run in parallel. A failure of any of the Data Flow tasks will cause the Import Data container to fail, and the failure message will be sent. If all three complete successfully, the Clean Up Script will run.

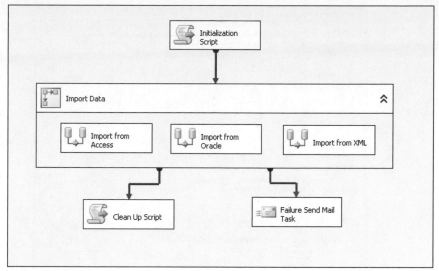

Figure 13-3

Precedence Constraints and Expressions

The workflow within a package can be controlled by using Boolean expressions in place of or in addition to the outcome of the initial task or container. Any expression that can be evaluated to True or False can be used. For example, the value of a variable that changes as the package executes can be compared to a constant. If the comparison resolves to True, the connected task will execute. The way a precedence constraint is evaluated can be based on both the outcome of the initial task and an expression. This allows the SSIS developer to finely tune the workflow of a package. The following table shows the four possibilities for configuring a precedence constraint.

Evaluation Operation	Definition
Constraint	Success, Failure, or Completion
Expression	Any expression that evaluates to True or False
Expression AND Constraint	Both conditions must be satisfied
Expression OR Constraint	One of the conditions must be satisfied

To configure a precedence constraint to use an expression, double-click the arrow to bring up the Precedence Constraint Editor (see Figure 13-4). There you can choose which type of Evaluation Operation to use and set the value of the constraint and/or supply the expression.

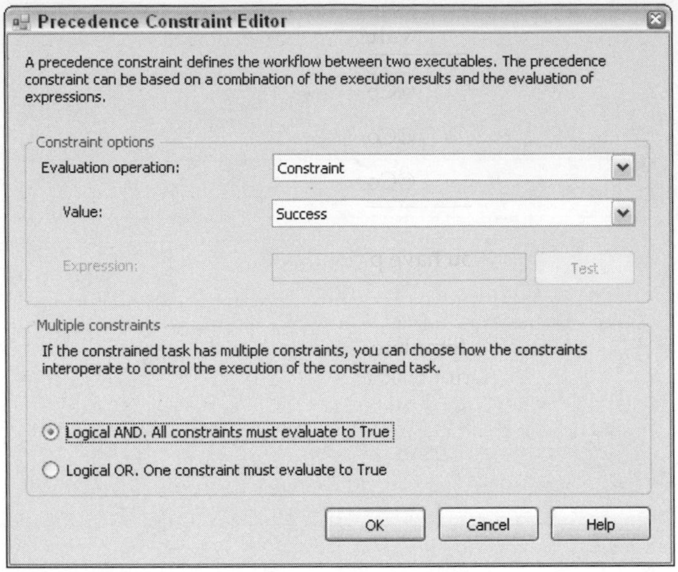

Figure 13-4

In this example, you will simulate flipping a coin to learn more about using expressions with precedence constraints. First, create a new table to hold the results. Connect to a test database in SQL Server Management Studio and run this script:

```
CREATE TABLE CoinToss (
    Heads INT NULL,
    Tails INT NULL )
GO
INSERT INTO CoinToss SELECT 0,0
```

Start a new SSIS project in BIDS. Create a Connection Manager pointing to the test database where the CoinToss table was created. The steps for creating a Connection Manager are covered in Chapter 3. Add an Execute SQL task to the Control Flow design area. Change the name of the task to Clear Results. Double-click the Clear Results task to open the Execute SQL Task Editor. Set the Connection property to point to the Connection Manager that you just created. Type the following code in the SQLStatement field:

```
UPDATE CoinToss
SET Tails = 0, Heads = 0
```

Click OK to accept the configuration and dismiss the dialog box. Right-click the Control Flow design area and select Variables from the pop-up menu to open the Variables window. Create a new package-level variable called Result. Set the Data Type to Int32.

Add a For Loop Container to the design area. You will use the container to simulate flipping the coin a given number of times, so name it Coin Toss Simulator. Drag the Precedence Constraint from the Clear Results task to the Coin Toss Simulator. Select the Coin Toss Simulator and open the Variables window. Add a variable called Count, with a Data Type of Int32. In this case, the variable will only be used by the For Loop and the scope will be Coin Toss Simulator. Double-click the Coin Toss Simulator container to open the For Loop Editor. Set the properties as in the following table and click OK.

Property	Value
InitExpression	@Count = 0
EvalExpression	@Count < 100
AssignExpression	@Count = @Count + 1

This should look familiar to you if you have programmed in almost any language: The For Loop will execute 100 times.

Drag a Script task into the Coin Toss Simulator. Since the Coin Toss Simulator is a container, you can drag other tasks into it. Name the Script task Toss. Double-click Toss to open the Script Task Editor. In the Script pane, ReadWriteVariables section, type in **User::Result**. The script will have access only to variables set up in this way.

Click Design Script to open the VSA design environment. Each time this script runs, it will randomly set the Result variable equal to a one or a two. Replace Sub Main with this code:

```
Public Sub Main()
    Randomize()
    Dts.Variables("User::Result").Value = Cint(Int((2 * Rnd()) + 1))
    Dts.TaskResult = Dts.Results.Success
End Sub
```

Close the VSA design area and click OK to accept the changes. Drag two Execute SQL tasks into the Coin Toss Simulator container. Name one Heads and the other Tails. Connect the Coin Toss Script task to each of the Execute SQL tasks. Double-click the Precedence Constraint pointing to Heads to bring up the Precedence Constraint Editor.

Change the Evaluation Operation from Constraint to Expression. The Expression text box will now become available. Type the following into the Expression property:

```
@Result == 1
```

Click OK. The precedence constraint will change from green to blue, meaning completion, and will have an *fx* symbol next to it specifying that the precedence uses an expression.

Open the properties of the precedence constraint pointing to Tails. Change the Evaluation Operation from Constraint to Expression. Type this in the Expression property:

```
@Result == 2
```

Click OK to accept the properties. At this point, the package should resemble Figure 13-5.

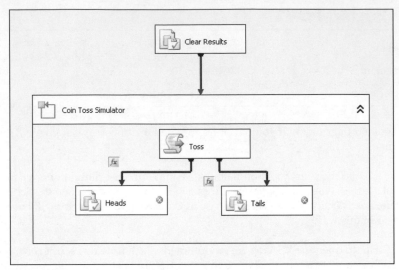

Figure 13-5

Just a couple more details and you'll be ready to run the package. Double-click Heads to open the Execute SQL Task Editor. In the Connection property, set the value to the test database Connection Manager. Type this in the SQLStatement property to increment the count in the CoinToss table:

```
UPDATE CoinToss SET Heads = Heads + 1
```

Click OK to accept the changes. Bring up the Execute SQL Task Editor for the Tails object. Set the Connection property to the test database Connection Manager. Type this code in the SQLStatement property:

```
UPDATE CoinToss SET Tails = Tails + 1
```

Click OK to accept the configuration and run the package. As the package runs, you can see that sometimes Heads will execute, and sometimes Tails will execute. Once the package execution completes, return to SQL Server Management Studio to view the results by running this query:

```
SELECT * FROM CoinToss
```

Out of 100 coin tosses, Heads should have come up approximately 50 times.

This simple example demonstrates how to use an expression to control the package workflow instead of or combined with the outcome of a task. In a business application, maybe the precedence constraint could be used to ensure that the number of rows affected by a previous step is less than a certain value. Or possibly, a task should execute only if it is a particular day of the week. Any variable within scope can be used and several functions and operators are available to build the expression. Any valid expression will work as long as it evaluates to True or False. See Chapter 7 to learn more about building and using expressions.

Multiple Constraints

In your package workflow, you can have multiple precedence constraints pointing to the same task. By default, the conditions of both must be True to enable execution of the constrained task. You also have the option of running a task if at least one of the conditions is True by setting the Multiple Constraint property to Logical Or. One Constraint Must Evaluate to True (see Figure 13-6).

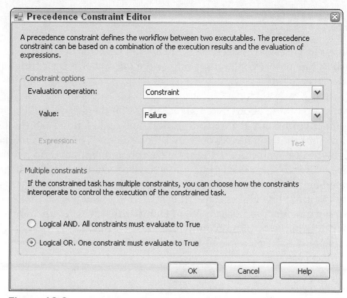

Figure 13-6

The solid arrows change to dotted arrows when the Logical Or option is chosen. Figure 13-7 shows how the Send Mail task will execute if either of the Data Flow tasks fails.

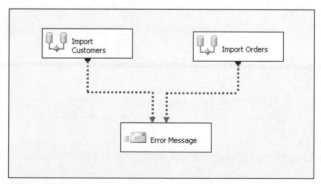

Figure 13-7

By using precedence constraints, you control the order of events within a package. After a task or container executes, and depending on how the precedence constraint between the two components was evaluated, the second task or container runs. With all of these options, you can control the workflow of your package at a very granular level. Drilling down a bit more, you will now learn another way to control package execution: event handling.

Event Handling

Each task and container raises events as it runs, such as an OnError event, among several others that will be discussed shortly. SSIS allows you to trap and handle these events by setting up workflows that will run when particular events fire.

The first really interesting thing about Event Handlers is that there is a whole tab devoted to them in the SSIS package design environment. Figure 13-8 shows the Event Handler tab right next to the Control Flow and Data Flow tabs that you have worked with up to now. The Event Handler design area is just like the Control Flow area — you can use the same component types and do anything that is possible at the Control Flow level. Once several event handlers have been added to a package, the workflow could get very complicated and difficult to understand if you had to view it all at once, so separating Event Handlers from the Control Flow makes sense. It is important, however, to make sure your packages are well designed and documented because an Event Handler that was set up and then forgotten could be the source of a hard-to-troubleshoot problem within the package.

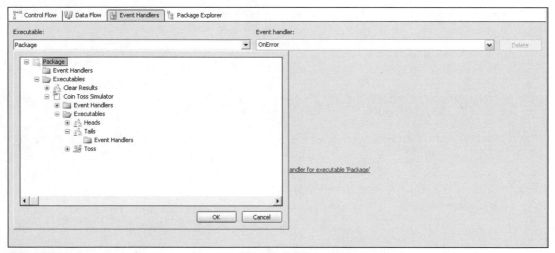

Figure 13-8

Events

As the package and each task or container executes, a dozen different events are raised. You can capture the events by adding Event Handlers that will run when the event fires. The OnError event may be the event most frequently handled, but some of the other events will be useful in complex ETL packages. Events can also be used to set breakpoints and control logging, which will all be covered later in the chapter.

The following table shows a list of all of the events.

Event	Description
OnError	The OnError event is raised whenever an error occurs. You can use this event to capture errors instead of using the failure precedence constraint to redirect the workflow.
OnExecStatusChanged	Each time the execution status changes on a task or container, this event fires.
OnInformation	During the validation and execution events of the tasks and containers, this event reports information. This is the information displayed in the Progress tab.
OnPostExecute	Just after task or container execution completes, this event fires. You could use this event to clean up work tables or delete no-longer-needed files.
OnPostValidate	This event fires after validation of the task is complete.
OnPreExecute	Just before a task or container runs, this event fires. This event could be used to check the value of a variable before the task executes.
OnPreValidate	Before validation of a task begins, this event fires.
OnProgress	As measurable progress is made, this event fires. The information about the progress of an event can be viewed in the Progress tab.
OnQueryCancel	The OnQueryCancel event is raised when an executable checks to see if it should stop or continue running.
OnTaskFailed	It's possible for a task or container to fail without actual errors. You can trap that condition with this event.
OnVariableValueChanged	Any time a variable value changes, this event fires. Setting the RaiseChangeEvent property to False prevents this event from firing. This event will be very useful when debugging a package.
OnWarning	Warnings are less critical than errors. This event fires when a warning occurs. Warnings are displayed in the Progress tab.

Inventory Example

This example will demonstrate how to use Event Handlers by setting up a simulation that checks the inventory status of some random products from AdventureWorks. Run this script in SQL Server Management Studio against the AdventureWorks database to create the tables and a stored procedure used in the example:

```
USE AdventurWorks
GO
CREATE TABLE InventoryCheck (
```

```
      ProductID INT )
GO
CREATE TABLE InventoryWarning (
    ProductID INT, ReorderQuantity INT )
GO
CREATE TABLE MissingProductID (
    ProductID INT )
GO
CREATE PROC usp_GetReorderQuantity @ProductID INT,
    @ReorderQuantity INT OUTPUT AS
    IF NOT EXISTS(SELECT ProductID FROM Production.ProductInventory
            WHERE ProductID = @ProductID) BEGIN
        RAISERROR('InvalidID',16,1)
        RETURN 1
    END

    SELECT @ReorderQuantity = SafetyStockLevel - SUM(Quantity)
    FROM Production.Product AS p
    INNER JOIN Production.ProductInventory AS i
    ON p.ProductID = i.ProductID
    WHERE p.ProductID = @ProductID
    GROUP BY p.ProductID, SafetyStockLevel
    RETURN 0
GO
```

Create a new SSIS package. Add a Connection Manager pointing to the AdventureWorks database using the ADO.NET provider. This example uses the Execute SQL task with parameters. The parameters work differently depending on which provider is being used. For example, parameters used with the OLE DB provider are numerically named starting with zero. Parameters used with ADO.NET providers use names beginning with the @ symbol.

Set up the variables in the following table. (Click the Control Flow area right before opening the variables window so that the scope of the variables will be at the Package level.)

Name	Scope	Data Type	Value
Count	Package	Int32	0
ProductID	Package	Int32	0
ReorderQuantity	Package	Int32	0

Drag a Sequence Container to the Control Flow design area and name it Inventory Check. You can use a Sequence Container to group tasks, treating the tasks as a unit in the workflow of the package. In this case, you will use it to experiment with the Event Handlers. Set the MaximumErrorCount property of Inventory Check to 9999 in the Property window. This example will raise errors by design, and setting the MaximumErrorCount property will allow the simulation to continue running after the errors fire.

Drag an Execute SQL task into the Inventory Check container, and name it Empty Tables. Double-click the task to open the Execute SQL Task Editor. First change the ConnectionType property to ADO.NET. Set the Connection property to the Connection Manager pointing to AdventureWorks. Click the ellipsis button next to the SQLStatement property and type the following into the Enter SQL Query window:

```
DELETE FROM MissingProductID
DELETE FROM InventoryWarning
DELETE FROM InventoryCheck
```

Click OK to accept the statements and OK once more to accept the Execute SQL Task Editor changes. Drag a For Loop container into the Inventory Check container, and name it Inventory Query Simulator. Double-click the Inventory Query Simulator and fill in the properties as shown in the following table.

Property	Value
InitExpression	@Count =1
EvalExpression	@Count <= 50
AssignExpression	@Count = @Count + 1

Click OK to accept the configuration. Set the MaximumErrorCount property of the Inventory Query Simulator to 9999 in the Properties window. Drag a precedence constraint from the Empty Tables task to the Inventory Query Simulator. Drag a Script task into the Inventory Query Simulator container, and name it Generate ProductID. Double-click to open the Script Task Editor. Select the Script pane. Set the ReadWriteVariables property to User::ProductID, as shown in Figure 13-9.

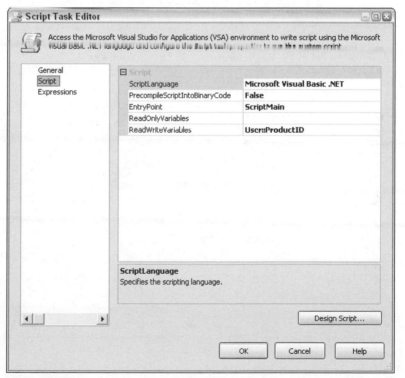

Figure 13-9

Click Design Script to open the VSA design environment. You will use this Script task to generate a random ProductID. Replace Sub Main with the following code:

```
Public Sub Main()
    Randomize()
    Dts.Variables("User::ProductID").Value = Cint(Int((900 * Rnd()) + 1))
    Dts.TaskResult = Dts.Results.Success
End Sub
```

Close the VSA environment and then click OK to accept the changes to the Script task.

Add an Execute SQL task to the Inventory Query Simulator and name it Check Inventory Level. Drag a Precedence Constraint from Generate ProductID to Check Inventory Level. Double-click the Check Inventory Level task to open the Execute SQL Task Editor. Set the ConnectionType property to ADO.NET. Find the Connection Manager for the AdventureWorks database in the list of Connections. Change the SQLStatement property to usp_GetReorderQuantity. Change the IsQueryStoredProcedure to True. This task will call the usp_GetReorderQuantity with the two parameters. The ResultSet property should be set to None since you are using an output parameter to get the ReorderQuantity value from the stored procedure. The General pane of the Execute SQL Task Editor should resemble Figure 13-10.

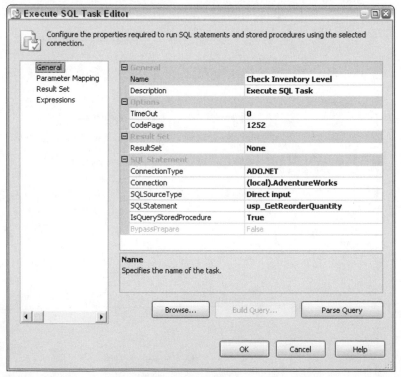

Figure 13-10

On the Parameter Mapping pane, set up the parameters as in the following table.

Variable Name	Direction	Data Type	Parameter Name
User::ProductID	Input	Int32	@ProductID
User::ReorderQuantity	Output	Int32	@ReorderQuantity

Click OK to accept the configuration. As described earlier, set the MaximumErrorCount property of the Check Inventory Level task to 9999 using the Properties window.

Add another Execute SQL task and name it Insert Warning. This task will be used to insert a row into the InventoryWarning table whenever the current inventory is less than the established reorder point for a particular product. Connect Check Inventory Level to Insert Warning. Double-click the Precedence Constraint and set the Evaluation operation property to Expression and Constraint. Set the Expression Property to @ReorderQuantity > 0 and leave the Value property at Success (see Figure 13-11). Click OK to accept the changes to the precedence constraint.

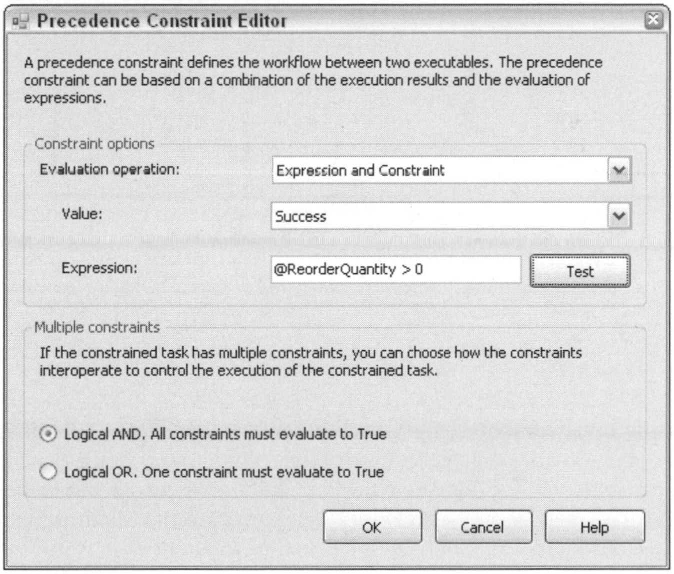

Figure 13-11

Double-click the Insert Warning object. Set the ConnectionType to ADO.NET. Choose the AdventureWorks Connection Manager from the Connection list. Click the ellipsis next to SQLStatement and type this into the Enter SQL Query dialog box:

```
INSERT INTO InventoryWarning (ProductID, ReorderQuantity)
SELECT @ProductID, @ReorderQuantity
```

Click OK to accept the command. On the Parameter Mapping pane, set up two parameters, as shown in the following table. In this case they will both be input parameters.

Variable Name	Direction	Data Type	Parameter Name
User::ProductID	Input	Int32	@ProductID
User::ReorderQuantity	Input	Int32	@ReorderQuantity

Click OK to accept the configuration. The package should now resemble Figure 13-12.

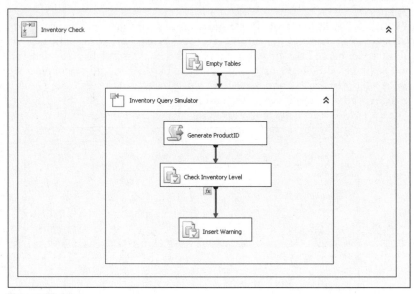

Figure 13-12

When you run the package, sometimes the Check Inventory Level task will fail. The Generate ProductID script will not always come up with a valid ProductID. When that happens, the stored procedure will raise an error and cause the Check Inventory Level task to fail. Because the FailParentOnFailure and FailPackageOnFailure properties are set to False by default, and the MaximumErrorCount property is set to 9999 on the task and parent containers, the package will continue to run through the simulation even after a failure of this task.

You will notice that once the Check Inventory Level task fails, it will turn red, but the simulation will continue running. It is a bit misleading, but once the task turns red, it stays red even though it will run each time the For Loop executes. A great way to view what is going on as the package runs is to click the Progress tab. This is also a fantastic troubleshooting tool, with detailed information about each step. Once the package completes and debugging is stopped, you can continue to view the information on the Execution Results tab.

After running the package, you can view the results by querying the InventoryWarning table to see the rows that were inserted when the User::ReorderQuantity variable was greater than 0. Run this query in SQL Server Management Studio:

```
SELECT * FROM InventoryWarning
```

The package is almost guaranteed to generate some errors at the Check Inventory Level task every time it runs. You could add a task connected to the Check Inventory Level with the Precedence Constraint set to Failure, but in this case you will create an Event Handler to add a row to the MissingProductID table each time the Check Inventory Level task fails.

Click the Event Handlers tab. Because you can have a large number of Event Handlers in a package, you must select the object and the event from the drop-down lists. Click the down arrow under Executable to see the package objects in a hierarchy. The Package has a child, Inventory Check, which has children Empty Tables and Inventory Query Simulator and so on (see Figure 13-13).

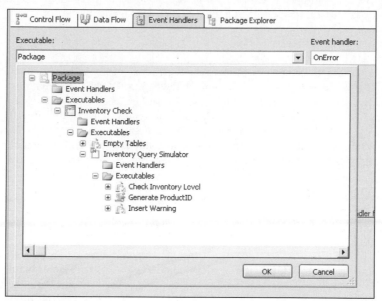

Figure 13-13

Select Check Inventory Level and click OK to close the list. Choose OnError in the Event Handler list if it isn't there by default. You must click the link "Click here to create an 'OnExecute' event handler for executable 'Check Inventory Level'" to create the new event handler. The screen will change to a design area very much like the Control Flow tab. You can now drag any Control Flow level task or container to the design area. In this case you will add an Execute SQL task that adds a row to the MissingProductID table whenever the Check Inventory Level task fails.

Event handlers can be as simple or as complex as you need them to be. All functionality available at the Control Flow level is available at the Event Handler level, including the ability to add an Event Handler to an Event Handler.

Drag an Execute SQL task to the Event Handler design area and name it Insert Missing ProductID. Double-click the task to bring up the Execute SQL Task Editor. Change the Connection Type to ADO.NET. Choose the AdventureWorks Connection Manager from the Connection list. Click the ellipsis next to the SQLStatement property to open the Enter SQL Query dialog box. Type the following statement:

```
INSERT INTO MissingProductID (ProductID) SELECT @ProductID
```

Click OK to accept the query. Switch to the Parameter Mapping pane. Add one parameter with the properties shown in the following table.

Variable Name	Direction	Data Type	Parameter Name
User::ProductID	Input	Int32	@ProductID

Click OK to accept the configuration. Now, when you run the package, the new Event Handler will fire whenever the Check Inventory Level task raises an error. You can query the MissingProductID table to see the results by running this query in SQL Server 2005 Management Studio:

```
SELECT * from MissingProductID
```

Suppose you would like to keep a record of all the ProductID numbers that were tested. To do that, add another Event Handler to the Check Inventory Level task. With Check Inventory Level selected in the Executable list, select OnPreExecute under Event Handler. Click the link to create the handler. Add an Execute SQL task to the Event Handler design area and name it Record ProductID. Double-click to open the Execute SQL Task Editor. Change the ConnectionType property to ADO.NET. Select the AdventureWorks Connection Manager from the Connection list. Add this statement to the SQLStatement property by typing in the Property text box or using the Enter SQL Query dialog box:

```
INSERT INTO InventoryCheck (ProductID) SELECT @ProductID
```

Add one parameter, @ProductID, on the Parameter Mapping pane with exactly the same properties as the one added to the OnError event task, as the following table shows.

Variable Name	Direction	Data Type	Parameter Name
User::ProductID	Input	Int32	@ProductID

Click OK to accept the configuration and run the package. Once execution of the package has completed, go back to SQL Server Management Studio to see the results by running the following queries:

```
SELECT * FROM InventoryCheck
SELECT * FROM MissingProductID
SELECT * FROM InventoryWarning
```

The InventoryCheck table should have one row for each ProductID that was generated. This row was entered at the Check Inventory Level OnPreExecute event, in other words, before the task actually executed. The MissingProductID table should have several rows, one for each ProductID that caused the usp_GetReorderQuantity to raise an error. These rows were added at the Check Inventory Level OnError event. Finally, the InventoryWarning table will have some rows if the inventory level of any of the products was low. These rows were added at the Control Flow level.

Event Bubbling

Events can "bubble" or travel up from child task to parent container. To demonstrate this, you'll move the OnError event handler from the task to a parent container. Using the package created in the previous section, navigate to the Check Inventory Level OnError event handler. Select the Insert Missing Product

ID task, right-click, and select Copy from the pop-up window. Create an OnError Event Handler for the Inventory Check container. Right-click the design area of the new event handler and select Paste. Go back to the Check Inventory Level OnError event and click the Delete button to completely remove the original Event Handler.

Run your package again. You will see that the errors are now trapped at the Inventory Check container level by viewing the error handler as the package runs. The OnError event bubbled up from the task to the For Loop container to the Inventory Check container.

What would happen if you had an OnError event handler on both the Check Inventory Level task and the Sequence container? Surprisingly, both will fire when an error is raised at the Check Inventory Level task. This could cause some unexpected results. For example, suppose you had an error handler at the parent container to perform a particular task, such as sending an e-mail message. An error in a child container that you expected to be handled at that level would also cause the parent's OnError Handler to execute. To prevent this from happening, you can set a system variable, Propagate, to False at the child task's Error Handler level.

To demonstrate this, add the OnError Event Handler back to the Check Inventory Level task. Once again, create an Event Handler for the Check Inventory Level OnError Event. You can copy and paste the Insert Missing Product ID task from the Inventory Check OnError event handler. While still working in the Check Inventory Level OnError Event design area, click the design area and open the Variables window. If the system variables are not visible, click the gray box X to display them (see Figure 13-14). Make sure that the Propagate property is set to True, the default.

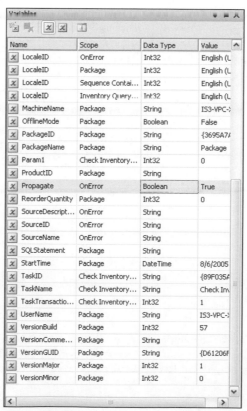

Figure 13-14

Run the package. While the package is running, navigate to each of the error handlers to watch as they execute. You will notice that both OnError events will fire and the MissingProductID table will end up with two rows for every invalid ProductID. After execution of the package is complete, change the Propagate property to False. Now only the Check Inventory Level OnError event handler will execute. The OnError event will no longer bubble to the parent containers. Run the package again. This time, you should find the expected behavior; the error will be handled only at the Check Inventory Level task.

When the Propagate property is set to False on an OnEvent handler, you no longer need to modify the MaximumErrorCount property of the parent containers from the default setting of 1 to keep the package running after the error.

Breakpoints

Many programmers use breakpoints to debug programs, viewing the value of variables and following the flow of the logic as they step through the source code. SSIS allows you to set breakpoints on the package or any Control Flow level task or container. You can also set breakpoints in Script task code just like most programming environments.

Using the Inventory Example package created in a previous section, right-click on the Inventory Query Simulator (For Loop) container, and choose Edit Breakpoints from the pop-up menu. The Set Breakpoints dialog box opens. A list of possible events where a breakpoint can be set is displayed, as shown in Figure 13-15.

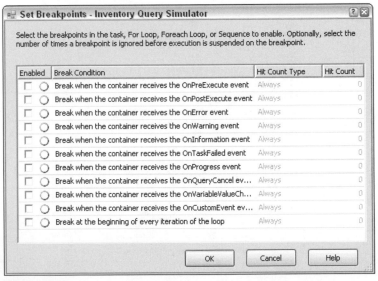

Figure 13-15

Enable the last item, Break at the Beginning of Every Iteration of the Loop, which is available only for looping containers. Under Hit Type Count, you can choose Always, Hit Count Equals, Hit Count Greater Than or Equal To, or Hit Count Multiple. The last item will suspend execution when the hit count is equal to a multiple of the value set for Hit Count. For example, setting the Hit Count Type to Hit Count Multiple and the Hit Count to 5 will cause the execution to be suspended every fifth time through the loop.

Go ahead and set the type to Hit Count Multiple and the Hit Count to 5 as in Figure 13-16.

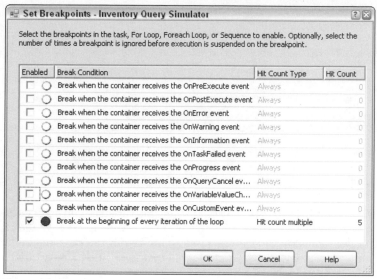

Figure 13-16

Click OK. The container will now have a red circle specifying that a breakpoint has been set (see Figure 13-17).

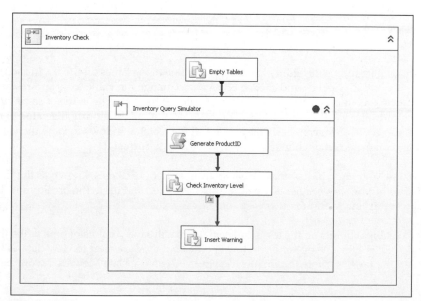

Figure 13-17

Run the package. When the Hit Count reaches 5, the execution will stop and the red dot will change to a red circle with an arrow. You can now view the values of the variables in the Locals window. If the Locals window is not visible, open it from Debug ➪ Windows ➪ Locals. Expand Variables and look for the User variables that were set up for the package (see Figure 13-18). User::Count should have a value of 5. If the value of a variable cannot be completely viewed in the window, such as a long string, you can mouse over to see the entire value in a tooltip.

Figure 13-18

Restart the package and it will run until the Hit Count reaches 10.

There are also Watch windows to make it easier to view the variables you are interested in viewing. Open the Watch window from Debug ➪ Windows ➪ Watch ➪ Watch 1. Type in the name of a variable, User::Count. The value automatically appears (see Figure 13-19). You can add additional variables to watch in this window or in new Watch windows. Alternately, right-click on a variable in the Locals window to add the variable to the Watch window.

Watch 1	
Name	Value
⊟ 🔖 User::Count	{10}
── ● Type	Int32
── ● Value	10

Figure 13-19

Another very cool feature is the ability to change the value of variables on the fly. In the Watch window, expand User::Count. Right-click and choose Edit Value. Change the value to 40 and restart the package. The next time the execution is suspended, the value should be at 45. The value of some system variables may also be interesting to view and change. For example, you might modify the value of a task property as the package executes. You can use breakpoints and the watch windows to view the value to make sure it is what you expected or change the value manually to correct it.

An additional debugging window may also help troubleshoot packages, known as the Call Stack Window. This window shows a list of the tasks that have executed up to the breakpoint. This could be very useful when trying to figure out a very complex workflow.

The ability to set breakpoints on the tasks and containers will save you lots of time while troubleshooting your packages. Data Viewers are similar to breakpoints, but they are used to view data as the package executes. See Chapter 4 for more information on how you can use Data Viewers in your packages.

Checkpoints

SSIS has a feature called Checkpoints that has absolutely nothing to do with the definition that probably came to mind when you read the section title. In SQL Server, a checkpoint occurs when the data is written to disk. In SSIS, you can enable a checkpoint on a package to allow a failed package to restart at the point of failure.

Say you have a package that does a lot of processing, but one task or container in the package is likely to fail occasionally. That task might require a connection to an Internet Web service, or another resource must be available. Maybe you really don't want to repeat all the heavy lifting that the package does before the failure. By configuring a checkpoint, the package can be restarted at the failed task. Information about the package as it runs is saved into a checkpoint file, which is then used when the package is restarted.

To learn more about using checkpoints, create a new SSIS project in BIDS. The package in this example will not do anything particularly useful, but it will illustrate the use of checkpoints. Add four Script tasks to the design area. Connect them as shown in Figure 13-20.

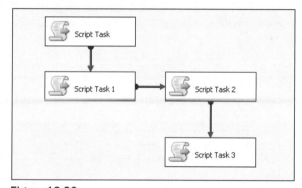

Figure 13-20

Click the Control Flow design area and open the Properties window of the package. In the Checkpoints section of the package Properties window, enter a path for the checkpoint file. Set SaveCheckpoints to True. These settings will cause the package to save information as it executes to the checkpoint file. Set the CheckpointUsage property to IfExists. If the package fails, it will use the information in the checkpoint file to restart execution at the point of failure. If the package completes, the file will be deleted afterward.

Select Script Task 2 and open the Properties window. Change the ForceExecutionResult property to Failure. This will cause the task to fail, regardless of any other conditions. In this example, the setting will be used to simulate a failure of the task.

If you run the package now, Script Task 2 will fail and Script Task 3 will not get a chance to execute. The package, however, will complete and the checkpoint file will be deleted. If you rerun the package, it will start at the first task. To get this to work as expected, the package must actually fail when Script Task 2 fails. Change the FailPackageOnFailure property of Script Task 2 to True in the Properties window of the task.

Go ahead and run the package. Once again, Script Task 2 should fail (see Figure 13-21). This time, however, the checkpoint file will still be available.

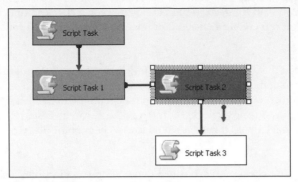

Figure 13-21

Go back to design mode and change the ForceExecutionResult property of Script Task 2 to None. Rerun the package. Package execution will start at Script Task 2 (see Figure 13-22), picking up where it left off from the previous run.

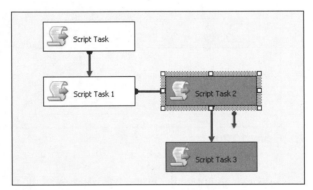

Figure 13-22

Any task or container can be configured to be a checkpoint by setting the FailPackageOnFailure property to True. With clever use of checkpoints, you have the chance to correct a problem and restart the process from the point of failure instead of from the beginning. But how will you know what caused the failure? Read on to learn about another feature, Logging, for the answer.

Logging

Just when you were truly amazed at all of the control flow, event-handling, and debugging features, you find out about Package Logging. Logging enables you to record information about events you are interested in as the package runs. The logging information can be stored in a text or XML file, to a SQL Server table, to the Windows Event Log, or to a file suitable for Profiler.

Logging can be enabled for all or some tasks and containers and for all or any events. Tasks and containers can inherit the settings from parent containers. Multiple logs can be set up, and a task or event can log to any or all logs configured. You also have the ability to control which pieces of information are recorded for any event.

Open one of the packages you created earlier in this chapter or any package with several Control Flow tasks. From the menu, navigate to SSIS ⇨ Logging to open the Configure SSIS Logs dialog box. To enable logging, you must first check the box next to Package in the left pane (see Figure 13-23).

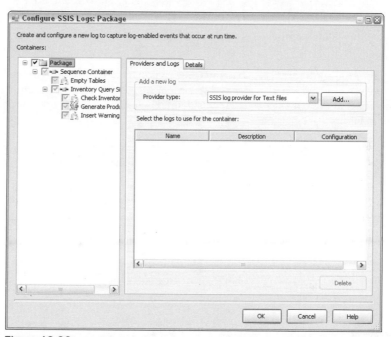

Figure 13-23

Notice that the checkboxes for the child objects in the package are grayed out. This means that they will inherit the logging properties of the package. You can click into any checkbox to uncheck an object. Clicking again to check the box will allow you to set up logging properties specific for that task or container.

To get started, the log providers must be defined at the package level. Select Package in the TreeView control on the left. Choose which type of provider you would like to configure; in this case, choose SSIS Log Provider for XML File. Click Add to add the provider to the list. Click the drop-down under Configuration and choose <New Connection>. The File Connection Manager Editor opens. Set the Usage Type property to Create File. Type the path for the XML file or click Browse to the XML file location as in Figure 13-24.

Figure 13-24

Click OK to accept the configuration and dismiss the dialog box. In the Configure SSIS Logs dialog box, you should now see the new log provider and its properties. Check the box next to the new logging provider to enable it at the package level. At this point, you can give the log provider a descriptive name if you wish as in Figure 13-25.

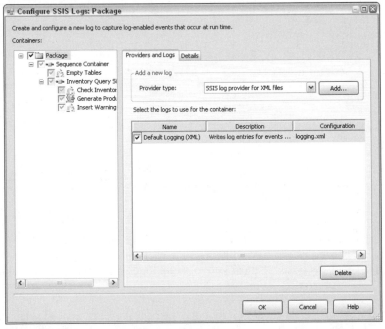

Figure 13-25

Click the Details tab to view a list of events that you can log. By clicking Advanced, you will also see a list of possible fields (see Figure 13-26). Choose one or two of the events. Notice that all of the fields are automatically chosen. You can uncheck some of the fields if you don't think the information will be useful.

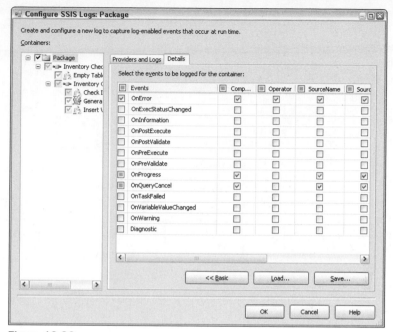

Figure 13-26

Move back to the Providers and Logs tab. When you checked the log provider as Package was selected on the left, you enabled that log for all components in the package that are set to inherit settings from their parent container. Even if that log provider is chosen for an object that does not inherit the log settings, you can use it to select different events and fields (see Figure 13-27).

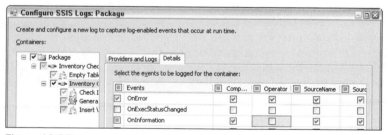

Figure 13-27

Once you modify the logging on a parent container, such as a For Loop container, the child objects will now inherit from the container, not the package.

When you are satisfied with the logging settings, click OK to close the dialog box. If you view the Properties window of a task or container, you will find the LoggingMode property. This property can be set to UseParentSetting, Enabled, or Disabled and will match the settings you just configured.

Run the package. Once the package execution has completed, open the log file to view the XML (see Figure 13-28).

```xml
<?xml version="1.0" ?>
- <dtslogs>
    <dtslog />
    <dtslog />
  - <dtslog>
    - <record>
        <event>PackageStart</event>
        <message>Beginning of package execution.</message>
        <computer>IS3-VPC-XP</computer>
        <operator>IS3-VPC-XP\Administrator</operator>
        <source>Package</source>
        <sourceid>{3695A7A0-0F4A-4B3E-9621-94DF21B65A4D}</sourceid>
        <executionid>{48BB428A-E907-42B6-95F2-5196E3C6B4BA}</executionid>
        <starttime>8/6/2005 6:54:51 PM</starttime>
        <endtime>8/6/2005 6:54:51 PM</endtime>
        <datacode>0</datacode>
        <databytes>0x</databytes>
      </record>
    - <record>
        <event>OnProgress</event>
        <message>Executing query "delete from MissingProductID ".</message>
```

Figure 13-28

Setting up logging for a package can be as complicated or as simple as you would like. It's possible that you may want to log similar information, such as the OnError event, for all packages. You can save the settings as a template by clicking Save when on the Detail tab of the Configure SSIS Logs dialog box. Alternately, you can load a previously saved template by clicking the Load button.

Summary

SSIS gives you a set of powerful tools to build, debug, and troubleshoot your packages. With enhanced precedence constraints, the event handlers, debugging features, checkpoints, logging, and Data Viewers (covered in Chapter 4), creating robust packages will be faster and easier than ever before. Now that you understand how to use these great tools, you'll move on to even more advanced topics.

14

Programming and Extending SSIS

Out of the box, Microsoft provides a huge list of components for you in SSIS. When you find that none of them fits your job, you need to be able to create your own. Initially this can be a steep learning curve, but hopefully with the help of this chapter you will be able to overcome this. In this chapter you will focus on the pipeline — not because it is better than any other area of programmability within SSIS but because it will probably be the area where you have the most benefit to gain, and it does require a slightly greater level of understanding. It also allows you to see some of the really interesting things that Microsoft has done in SSIS. All forms of extensibility are well covered in the SQL Server documentation and samples, so don't forget to leverage those resources as well.

The *pipeline*, for all intents and purposes, is the way your data moves from A to B and how it is manipulated, if at all. You can find it on the Data Flow tab of your packages after you have dropped a Data Flow task into the Control Flow. There's no need to go into any more detail about where to find the pipeline in your package, as this has been covered elsewhere in this book.

Most people think that even the most timid or "code scared" DBAs, when faced with not having what they want in the SSIS box, will be able to do a very reasonable job of designing and building the component they need themselves. Because SSIS is now hosted in the Visual Studio shell, traditional programmers may be most at home here, but that's no reason for everyone else to be left out in the cold. Hopefully by the end of this chapter you'll see that it doesn't have to be that way.

The Sample Components

Three sample components will be defined in this section to demonstrate the main component types. The transform component will then be expanded in Chapter 15 to include a user interface. All code samples will be available on the Web site for this book, which you can find at www.wrox.com.

Component 1: Source Adapter

The source adapter needs to be able to do quite a few things in order to be able to present the data to the downstream components in the pipeline in a format that the next component understands and is expecting. Here is a list of what the component needs to do:

- ❑ Accept a Connection Manager
- ❑ Validate the Connection Manager (did it get the right type of Connection Manager?)
- ❑ Add output columns to the component for the downstream processes
- ❑ Connect to the data source
- ❑ Get the data from the data source
- ❑ Assign the correct parts of the data to the correct output columns
- ❑ Handle any data errors

This component is going to need to do quite a bit of work in order to present its data to the outside world. Stick with it and you'll see how easy this can be. Your aim in the source adapter is to be able to take a file with a custom format, read it, and present it to the downstream components. The file will look like this:

```
<START>
Name:
Age:
Married:
Salary:
<END>
```

As you can see, this is a nonstandard format that none of the source adapters out of the box could deal with.

Component 2: Transformation

The transform is where you are going to take data from a source, manipulate it, and then present the newly arranged data to the downstream components. This component performs the following tasks:

- ❑ Create input columns to accept the data from upstream
- ❑ Validate the data to see that it is how the component expects it
- ❑ Check the column properties because this transform will be changing them in place
- ❑ Handle somebody trying to change the metadata of the transform by adding or removing inputs and/or outputs

The requirement here is to take data from the source and reverse the contents. The quirk, though, is that the column properties must be set correctly, and you can only perform this operation on certain data types.

Component 3: Destination Adapter

The destination adapter will take the data received from the upstream component and write it to the destination. This component will need to do the following:

- ❑ Create an input that accepts the data
- ❑ Validate that the data is correct
- ❑ Accept a Connection Manager
- ❑ Validate the Connection Manager (did you get the right type of Connection Manager?)
- ❑ Connect to the data source
- ❑ Write data from the data source

The destination adapter is basically a reverse of the source adapter. When it receives the input rows, it needs to create a new file with data resembling that of the source file except that some of the data will be the opposite way around compared to when it started out in the pipeline.

The components you'll build are really quite simple, but the point is not their complexity, but how you use the methods in Microsoft's object model.

The Pipeline Component Methods

Components are normally described as having two distinct phases: design-time and runtime. When you implement a component, you *inherit* from the base class, `Microsoft.SqlServer.Dts.Pipeline.PipelineComponent`, and provide your own functionality by *overriding* the base methods, some of which are primarily design-time, others runtime. If you are using native code, then the divide between the runtime and design-time is clearer because they are implemented on different interfaces. Commentary on the methods has been divided into these two sections, but there are some exceptions, notably the connection-related methods; a section on Connection Time–related methods is included later on.

> *In programming terms, a class can inherit functionality from another class, termed the base class. If the base class provides a method, and the inheriting class wishes to change the functionality within this method, it can override the method. In effect, you replace the base method with your own. From within the overriding method, you can still access the base method, and call it explicitly if required, but any consumer of the new class will see only the overriding method.*

Design-Time

The following methods are explicitly implemented for design-time, overriding the `PipelineComponent` methods, although they will usually be called from within your overriding method. Not all of the methods have been listed, because for some there is little more to say, and others have been grouped together according to their area of function. Refer to the SQL Server documentation for a complete list.

There are some methods that have been described as verification methods, and these are a particularly interesting group. They provide minor functions such as adding a column or setting a property value, and you could quite rightly think that there is little point in ever overriding them, as there isn't much to add to the base implementation. As mentioned, these are your verification methods, and code has been added for verification that the operation about to take place within the base class is allowed. The following sections expand on the types of checks you can do, and if you want to build a robust component, these are well worth looking into.

Another very good reason to implement these methods as described is actually to reduce code. These methods will be used by both a custom user interface (UI) and the built-in component editor, or Advanced Editor. If you raise an error saying that a change is not allowed, then both user interfaces can capture this and provide feedback to the user. Although a custom UI would not be expected to offer controls to perform blatantly inappropriate actions, the Advanced Editor is designed to offer all functionality, so you are protecting the integrity of your component regardless of the method used.

ProvideComponentProperties

This method is provided so you can set up your component. It is called when a component is first added to the Data Flow, and it initializes the component. It does not perform any column-level activity, as this is left to ReinitializeMetadata; when this method is invoked, there are generally no inputs to outputs to be manipulated anyway. The sorts of procedures you may want to set in here are listed below.

❑ Remove existing settings, such as inputs and outputs. This allows the component to be rebuilt and can be useful when things go wrong.

❑ Add inputs and outputs, ready for column work later on in the component lifetime. You may also define custom properties on them and specify related properties, such as linking them together for synchronous behavior.

❑ Define the connection requirements. By adding an item to the RuntimeConnectionCollection, you have a placeholder prepared for the Connection Manager at runtime, as well as informing the designer of this requirement.

❑ The component may have custom properties that are configurable by a user in addition to those you get for free from Microsoft. These will hold settings other than the column-related one that effect the overall component operation or behavior.

Validate

Validate is called numerous times during the lifetime of the component, both at design-time and at runtime, but the most interesting work is usually the result of a design-time call. As the name suggests, it validates that the content of the component is correct and will enable you to at least run the package. If the validation encounters a problem, then the return code used is important to determine any further actions, such as calling ReinitializeMetadata. The base class version of Validate performs its own checks in the component, and you will need to extend it further in order to cover your specific needs. Validate should not be used to change the component at all; it should only report the problems it finds.

ReinitializeMetaData

The ReinitializeMetaData method is where all the building work for your component is done. You add new columns, remove invalid columns, and generally build up the columns. It is called when the Validate method returns VS_NEEDSNEWMETADATA. It is also your opportunity in the component to do any repairs that need to be done, particularly around invalid columns as mentioned previously.

MapInputColumn and MapOutputColumn

These methods are used to create a relationship between an input/output column and an external metadata column. An external metadata column is an offline representation of an output or input column and can be used by downstream components to create an input. It allows you to validate and maintain columns even when the data source is not available. It is not required, but it makes the user experience better. If the component declares that it will be using External Metadata (IDTSComponentMetaData90 .ValidateExternalMetadata), then the user in the advanced UI will see upstream columns to the left and the external columns on the right; if you are validating your component against an output, you will see the checked listbox of columns.

Input and Output Verification Methods

There are several methods you can use to deal with inputs and outputs. The three functions you may need to perform are adding, deleting, and setting a custom property. The method names clearly indicate their functions:

- ❑ `InsertInput`
- ❑ `DeleteInput`
- ❑ `SetInputProperty`
- ❑ `InsertOutput`
- ❑ `DeleteOutput`
- ❑ `SetOutputProperty`

For most components, the inputs and outputs will have been configured during `ProvideComponent Properties`, so unless you expect a user to add additional inputs and outputs and fully support this, you should override these methods and fire an error to prevent this. Similarly, unless you support additions, you would also want to deny deletions by overriding the corresponding methods. Properties can be checked for validity during the `Set` methods as well.

Set Column Data Types

There are two methods used to set column data types: one for output columns and the other for external metadata columns. There is no input column equivalent, as the data types of input columns are determined by the upstream component.

- ❑ `SetOutputColumnDataTypeProperties`
- ❑ `SetExternalMetadataColumnDataTypeProperties`

These are verification methods that can be used to validate or prevent changes to a column. For example, in a source component, you would normally define the columns and their data types within `ReinitializeMetaData`. You could then override `SetOutputColumnDataTypeProperties`, and by comparing the method's supplied data types to the existing column, you could prevent data type changes but allow length changes.

There is quite a complex relationship between all of the parameters for these methods; please refer to SQL Server documentation for reference when using this method yourself.

PerformUpgrade

This method should allow you to take a new version of the component and update an existing version of the component on the destination machine.

RegisterEvents

This method allows you to register custom events in a pipeline component. You can therefore have an event fire on something happening at runtime in the package. This is then eligible to be logged in the package log.

RegisterLogEntries

This method decides which of the new custom events are going to be registered and selectable in the package log.

SetComponentProperty

In the `ProvideComponentProperties` method, you told the component about any custom properties that you would like to expose to the user of the component and perhaps allow them to set. This is a verification method, and here you can check what it is that the user has entered for which custom property on the component and ensure that the values are valid.

Set Column Properties

There are three column property methods, each allowing you to set a property for the relevant column type.

- ❑   `SetInputColumnProperty`
- ❑   `SetOutputColumnProperty`
- ❑   `SetExternalMetadataColumnProperty`

These are all verification methods and should be used accordingly. For example, you may set a column property during `ReinitializeMetaData`, and to prevent a user interfering with this, you could examine the property name and throw an exception if it is a restricted property, in effect making it read-only.

Similarly, if several properties are used in conjunction with each other at runtime to provide direction on the operation to be performed, you could enumerate all column properties to ensure that those related properties exist and have suitable values. You could assign a default value if a value is not present or raise an exception depending on the exact situation.

For an external metadata column, which will be mapped to an input or output column, any property set directly on this external metadata column can be cascaded down onto the corresponding Input or Output column through this overridden function.

SetUsageType

This method deals with the columns on inputs into the component. In a nutshell, you use it to select a column and to tell the component how you will treat each column. What you see coming into this method is the Virtual Input. What this means is that it is a representation of what is available for selection to be used by your component. These are the three possible usage types for a column:

❑ DTSUsageType.UT_IGNORED — The column will not be used by the component. What happens is that you will be removing from the InputColumnCollection this InputColumn. This differs from the other two usage types, which add a reference to the InputColumn to the InputColumnCollection if it does not exist already or you may be changing its Read/Write property.

❑ DTSUsageType.UT_READONLY — The column is read-only. The column is selected, and data can be read and used within the component but cannot be modified.

❑ DTSUsageType.UT_READWRITE — The column is selected, and you can both read and write or change the data within your component.

This is another of the verification methods, and you should use it to ensure that the columns selected are valid. For example, the Reverse String sample shown below can operate only on string columns, so you must check that the data type of the input column is DT_STR for string or DT_WSTR for Unicode strings. Similarly, the component performs an in-place change, so the usage type must be read/write. Setting it to read-only would cause an exception during execution when you tried to write the changed data back to the pipeline buffer. Therefore you want to validate the columns as they are selected to ensure that they meet the requirements for your component design.

On Path Attachment

There are three closely related path attachment methods, called when the named events occur, and the first two in particular can be used to improve the user experience:

❑ OnInputPathAttached

❑ OnOutputPathAttached

The reason these methods are here is to handle situations where the inputs or outputs are all identical and interchangeable, the multicast being the example, where you attach to the dangling output and another dangling output is created. You detach, and the output is deleted.

Runtime

Runtime, also known as execution-time, is when you actually work with the data, through the pipeline buffer, with columns and rows of data. The following methods are all about preparing the component, doing the job it was designed for, and then cleaning up afterward.

PrepareForExecute

This method is rather like the PreExecute method below and can be used for setting up anything in the component that you will need at runtime. The difference is that you do not have access to the Buffer Manager, so you cannot get your hands on the columns in either the output or the input at this stage. The distinction between the two is very fine apart from that, so usually you will end up using PreExecute exclusively, as you will need access to the Buffer Manager anyway.

PreExecute

PreExecute is called once and once only in the component, and it is the recommendation of Microsoft that you do as much preparation as possible for the execution of your component in this method. In this case, you'll use it to enumerate the columns, reading off values and properties, calling methods to get more information, and generally preparing by gathering all the information you require in advance. This is stored in a variable, making it faster to access multiple times rather than creating objects during the real execution for every row. This is the earliest point in the component that you will access the component's Buffer Manager, so you have the live context of columns, as opposed to the design-time representation. The live and design time representations of columns may not match. The design time may contain more information that you do not need at runtime. As mentioned, it is here that you do the Column Preparation for your component in this method, because it is called only once per component execution, unlike some of the other runtime methods, which are called multiple times.

PrimeOutput and ProcessInput

These two methods are dealt with together because they are so closely linked that to deal with them any other way would be disjointed. These two methods are essentially how the data flows through components. Sometimes you use only one of them, and sometimes you use both. There are some rules you can follow.

In a source adapter, the ProcessInput method is never called, and all of the work is done through PrimeOutput. In a destination adapter, it is the opposite way around. The PrimeOutput method is never called, and the whole of the work is done through the ProcessInput method.

Things are not quite that simple with a transform. There are two types of transforms, and the type of transform you are writing will dictate which method or indeed methods your component should call.

- ❏ **Synchronous:** PrimeOutput is not called and therefore all the work is done in the ProcessInput method. The buffer Lineage IDs remain the same. For a detailed explanation of buffers and Lineage IDs, please refer to Chapter 10.

- ❏ **Asynchronous:** Both methods are called here. The only difference really between a synchronous and an asynchronous component is that the asynchronous component does not reuse the input buffer. The PrimeOutput method hands the ProcessInput method a buffer to fill with its data.

PostExecute

This method would be where you clean up anything that you started in PreExecute. Although it can do this, it is not limited to just that. After reading the description of the Cleanup method in just a second, you're going to wonder about the difference between that and this method. The answer is, for this release, nothing. If you want to think about this logically, then PreExecute is married to PrepareForExecute.

Cleanup

As the method name suggests, this is called as the very last thing your component will do, and it is your chance to clean up whatever resources may be left. However, it is rarely used, like PostExecute.

DescribeRedirectedErrorCode

If you are using an error output and directing rows down there in case of errors, then you should expose this method to give more information about the error. When you direct a row to the error output, you specify an error code. This method will be called by the pipeline engine, passing in that error code, and it is expected to return a full error description string for the code specified. These two values are then included in the columns of the error output.

Connection Time

These two methods are called several times throughout the life cycle of a component, both at design-time and at runtime, and are used to manage connections within the component.

AcquireConnections

This method is called both in design and when the component executes. There is no explicit result, but the connection is normally validated and then cached in a member variable within the component for later use. At this stage, a connection should be open and ready to use.

ReleaseConnections

If you have any open connections, as set in the `AcquireConnections` method, then this is where they should be closed and released. If the connection was cached in a member variable, use that reference to issue any appropriate `Close` or `Dispose` methods. For some connections, such as a File Connection Manager, this may not be relevant as all that was returned was a file path string, but if you took this a stage further and opened a text stream or similar on the file, it should now be closed.

Building the Components

Now you can move on to actually building the components. These components are simple and demonstrate the most commonly used methods when building your own components. They also help give you an idea of what the composition of a component resembles, the order in which things happen, and which method is meant to do what. They will not implement all the available methods. The components have been built and they can be extended, so why not download them and give them a go? If you happen to break them, simply revert back to a previous good copy. No programmer gets things right the first time, so having the component break is part of the experience. Or at least that's what programmers tell themselves at two o'clock in the morning when they are still trying to figure out why the thing isn't doing what they asked. The component classes will be covered in the next sections. You will then be shown how to make sure your component appears in the correct folder, what to put in the AssemblyInfo file, how it gets registered in the GAC, and how to sign the assembly. This is common to all three components, so it will be dealt with as one also.

Preparation

In this section of the chapter, you'll go through the steps that are common to all the pipeline components. These are the basic sets of things you need to do before you fly into coding.

Start by opening Visual Studio 2005, and create a New Project, a Class Library project as shown in Figure 14-1.

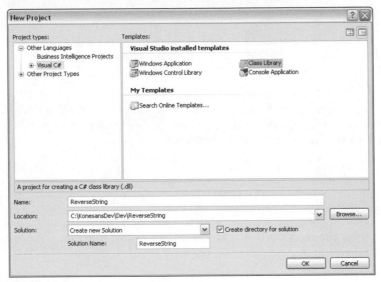

Figure 14-1

Now select the Add References option from the Project menu, and select the assemblies listed below, which are also illustrated in Figure 14-2.

- ❑   `Microsoft.SqlServer.DTSPipelineWrap`

- ❑   `Microsoft.Sqlserver.DTSRuntimeWrap`

- ❑   `Microsoft.Sqlserver.ManagedDTS`

- ❑   `Microsoft.SqlServer.PipelineHost`

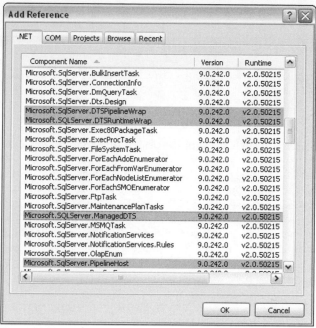

Figure 14-2

Once you have those set up, you can start to add the `using` directives. These are the directives:

```
#region Using directives

using System;
using System.Collections.Generic;
using System.Text;
using System.Globalization;
using System.Runtime.InteropServices;
using Microsoft.SqlServer.Dts.Pipeline;
using Microsoft.SqlServer.Dts.Pipeline.Wrapper;
using Microsoft.SqlServer.Dts.Runtime.Wrapper;
using Microsoft.SqlServer.Dts.Runtime;

#endregion
```

The first stage in building a component is to inherit from the `PipelineComponent` base class and to decorate the class with `DtsPipelineComponent`. From this point on, you are officially working on a pipeline component.

```
namespace Konesans.Dts.Pipeline.ReverseString
{
   [DtsPipelineComponent(
      DisplayName = "ReverseString",
      ComponentType = ComponentType.Transform,
      IconResource = "Konesans.Dts.Pipeline.ReverseString.ReverseString.ico")]
   public class ReverseString : PipelineComponent
   {
      ...
```

The `DtsPipelineComponent` attribute supplies design-time information about your component, and the first key property here is `ComponentType`. The three options — Source, Destination, or Transformation — reflect the three tabs within the SSIS designer Toolbox. This option determines which tab or grouping of components your component belongs to; it does not have any influence over the component behavior. The display name should be self-explanatory, and the `IconResource` is the reference to the icon in your project that will be shown to the user in both the Toolbox and when the component is dropped onto the package designer. This part of the code will be revisited later in the chapter when the attribute for the User Interface, which you'll be building later, is added.

Now type the following in the code window:

```
public override
```

Once you hit the spacebar after the word "override," you'll see a list of all the methods on the base class. You are now free to type away to your heart's content and code the component.

Once you've done that, though, the component will need to be built and it also needs a few other things to happen to it. If you are a seasoned developer, then this section will probably be old hat to you, but it's important for everybody to understand what needs to happen for the components to work. This is what needs to be covered:

❑ Provide a strong name key for signing the assembly.

❑ Set the build output location to the PipelineComponents folder.

❑ Use a post-build event to install the assembly into the global assembly cache (GAC).

❑ Set assembly-level attributes in the AssemblyInfo.cs file.

SSIS needs the GAC because it can execute in designer or agent, with different directories. Strong names are a consequence. The PipelineComponents folder allows the designer to discover the component and put it in the Toolbox. Assembly-level stuff is a consequence of the fact that the strong name, with version, is persisted in the package, making all your packages break if you rebuild the component unless you stop incrementing the version.

Probably the best way to go through the first three points is by way of screenshots. You can start by looking at how you sign the project. Right-click on your C# project and choose Properties from the context menu. You are not going to look at all of the tabs on the left-hand side of the screen, but you are going to look at the ones that are relevant to what you're doing here. Figure 14-3 shows the Application tab.

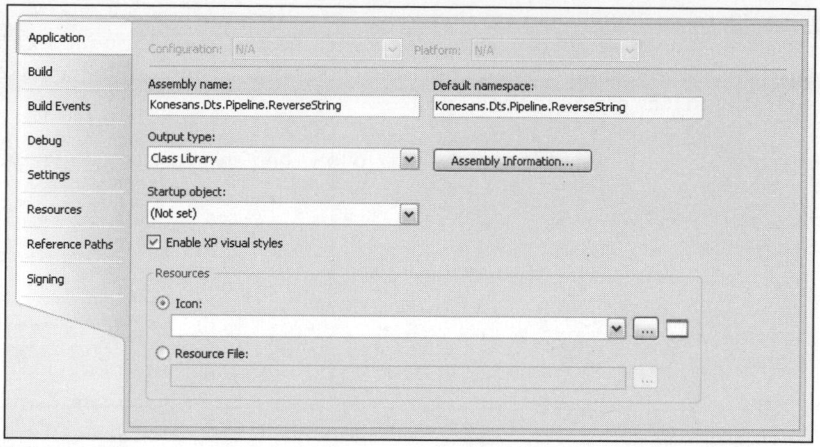

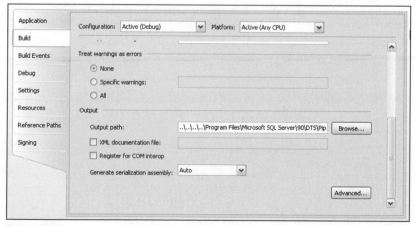

Figure 14-3

In this tab, the only thing you really need to do is change the assembly name to be the same as your default namespace.

On the Build tab, shown in Figure 14-4, you need to be concerned with the output path box toward the bottom of the dialog box. This tells the project that when it builds, the output should be placed in a certain folder. On your PC, this folder is:

```
C:\Program Files\Microsoft SQL Server\90\DTS\PipelineComponents
```

An alternative method of ensuring that the component assembly is automatically installed in the correct folder is to use a copy command to the post-build event command line, covered further below.

```
copy "$(TargetPath)" "%ProgramFiles%\Microsoft SQL
Server\90\DTS\PipelineComponents" /Y
```

Figure 14-4

For the designer to use a component, it must be placed in a defined folder, and for the runtime engine to work correctly, it must be placed in the global assembly cache. So setting the build location and installing into the GAC are both required steps, which you can do manually, but it makes for faster development if you do it as part of the build process.

Some example build event commands are shown as follows and are illustrated in Figure 14-5:

```
"$(DevEnvDir)\..\..\SDK\v2.0\Bin\gacutil" /if "$(TargetPath)"
```

or

```
"C:\Program Files\Microsoft Visual Studio 8\SDK\v2.0\Bin\Gacutil" /if
"$(TargetPath)"
```

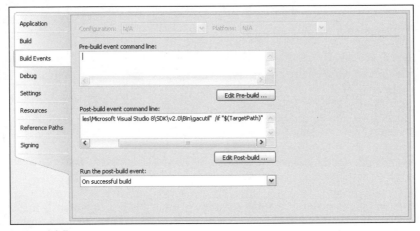

Figure 14-5

Because the assembly is to be installed in the GAC, you need to sign the assembly using a strong name key, which can be specified and created from the Signing page, as shown in Figure 14-6.

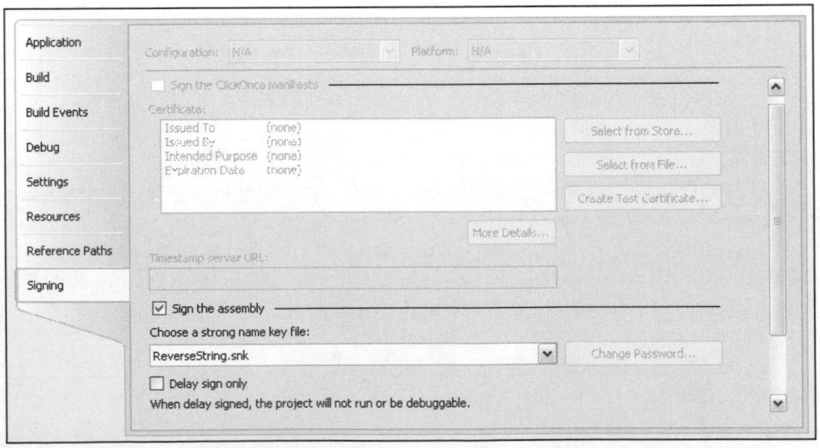

Figure 14-6

That is it as far as the project's properties are concerned, so now you can move on to looking at the AssemblyInfo file. While most assembly attributes can be set through the Assembly Information dialog box, available from the Application tab of Project Properties, shown previously in Figure 14-3, you require some additional settings. Shown below is the AssemblyInfo.cs file for the example project, which can be found under the Properties folder within the Solution Explorer of Visual Studio.

```
#region Using directives
using System;
using System.Security.Permissions;
using System.Reflection;
using System.Runtime.CompilerServices;
using System.Runtime.InteropServices;

#endregion

[assembly: AssemblyTitle("ReverseString")]
[assembly: AssemblyDescription("Reversing String Transformation for SQL Server
Integration Services")]
[assembly: AssemblyConfiguration("")]
[assembly: AssemblyCompany("Konesans Ltd")]
[assembly: AssemblyProduct("Reverse String Transformation")]
[assembly: AssemblyCopyright("Copyright (c) 2004-2005 Konesans Ltd")]
[assembly: AssemblyTrademark("")]
[assembly: AssemblyCulture("")]

[assembly: AssemblyVersion("1.1.0.0")]
[assembly: AssemblyFileVersion("1.1.0")]
[assembly: CLSCompliant(true)]
[assembly: PermissionSet(SecurityAction.RequestMinimum)]
[assembly: ComVisible(false)]
```

The first section of attributes listed represents primarily information, and you would change these to reflect your component and company, for example. The AssemblyCulture should be left blank unless you are experienced at working with localized assemblies and understand the implications of any change.

The AssemblyVersion attribute is also worth noting; as the version is fixed, it does not use the asterisk token to generate an automatically incrementing build number. The assembly version forms part of the fully qualified assembly name, which is how a package references a component under the covers. So if you changed the version for every build, you would have to rebuild your packages for every new version of the component. So that you can differentiate between versions, you should use AssemblyFileVersion, although you will need to manually update this.

The other attribute worth special note is CLSCompliant. Best practice dictates that the .Net classes and assemblies conform to the Command Language Specification (CLS), and compliance should be marked at the assembly level. Individual items of noncompliant code can then be decorated with the CLSCompliant attribute, marked as false. The completed samples all include this, and you can also refer to SQL Server documentation for guidance, as well as following the simple compiler warnings that are raised when this condition is not met.

Here is an example of how to deal with a method being noncompliant in your component.

```
[CLSCompliant(false)]
public override DTSValidationStatus Validate()
{
...
```

Building the Source Adapter

As mentioned earlier, the source adapter needs to be able to retrieve information from a file and present the data to the downstream component. The file is not your standard-looking file. The format is strange but consistent. When you design the destination adapter, you will write the contents of an upstream component to a file in a very similar format. After you have read this chapter, you may want to take the source adapter and alter it slightly so that it can read a file produced by the destination adapter.

The very first method to look at is `ProvideComponentProperties`. This gets called almost as soon as you drop the component onto the designer. Here is the method in full before you begin to break it down:

```
public override void ProvideComponentProperties()
{
    ComponentMetaData.RuntimeConnectionCollection.RemoveAll();
    RemoveAllInputsOutputsAndCustomProperties();

    ComponentMetaData.Name = "Professional SSIS Source Adapter";
    ComponentMetaData.Description = "Our first Source Adapter";
    ComponentMetaData.ContactInfo = "www.Konesans.com";

    IDTSRuntimeConnection90 rtc =
        ComponentMetaData.RuntimeConnectionCollection.New();
    rtc.Name = "File To Read";
    rtc.Description = "This is the file from which we want to read";

    IDTSOutput90 output = ComponentMetaData.OutputCollection.New();
    output.Name = "Component Output";
    output.Description = "This is what downstream Components will see";

    output.ExternalMetadataColumnCollection.IsUsed = true;

}
```

Now you can break down some of this code.

```
ComponentMetaData.RuntimeConnectionCollection.RemoveAll();
RemoveAllInputsOutputsAndCustomProperties();
```

The very first thing this code does is remove any runtime connections in the component, which you'll be adding back soon. You can also remove inputs, outputs, and custom properties. Basically your component is now a clean slate. This is not strictly required for this example; however, it's advantageous to follow this convention, as it prevents any unexpected situations that may arise in more complicated components.

```
ComponentMetaData.Name = "Professional SSIS Source Adapter";
ComponentMetaData.Description = "Our first Source Adapter";
ComponentMetaData.ContactInfo = "www.Konesans.com";
```

These three lines of code simply help to identify your component when you look in the property pages after adding it to the designer. The only property here that may not be obvious is `ContactInfo`, which simply identifies to the user the developer of the component. If a component throws a fatal error during loading or saving, for example — areas not influenced by the user-controlled settings — then the designer will show the contact information.

```
IDTSRuntimeConnection90 rtc = ComponentMetaData.RuntimeConnectionCollection.New();
rtc.Name = "File To Read";
rtc.Description = "This is the file from which we want to read";
```

Your component needs a runtime connection from which you can read and get the data. You removed any existing connections earlier in the method, so here is where you add it back. Simply give it a name and a description.

```
IDTSOutput90 output = ComponentMetaData.OutputCollection.New();
output.Name = "Component Output";
output.Description = "This is what downstream Components will see";
```

The way downstream components will see the data is to present it to them from an output in this component. Here you add a new output to the output collection and give it a name and a description. The final part of this component is to use `ExternalMetadataColumns`, which will allow you to view the structure of the data source with no connection.

```
output.ExternalMetadataColumnCollection.IsUsed = true;
```

Here, you tell the output you created earlier that it will use `ExternalMetaData` columns.

The next method to look at is the `AcquireConnections` method. In this method, you want to make sure that you have a runtime connection available and that it is the correct type. You then want to retrieve the file name from the file itself. Here is the method in full:

```
public override void AcquireConnections(object transaction)
{

    if (ComponentMetaData.RuntimeConnectionCollection["File To
Read"].ConnectionManager != null)
    {
        ConnectionManager cm =
Microsoft.SqlServer.Dts.Runtime.DtsConvert.ToConnectionManager(
ComponentMetaData.RuntimeConnectionCollection["File To Read"].ConnectionManager);

        if (cm.CreationName != "FILE")
        {
            throw new Exception("The Connection Manager is not a FILE Connection
Manager");
        }
        else
        {
            fil = (Microsoft.SqlServer.Dts.Runtime.DTSFileConnectionUsageType)
cm.Properties["FileUsageType"].GetValue(cm);

            if (_fil != DTSFileConnectionUsageType.FileExists)
            {
```

```
            throw new Exception("The type of FILE connection manager must be an
    Existing File");
            }
            else
            {
                _filename = ComponentMetaData.RuntimeConnectionCollection["File To
    Read"].ConnectionManager.AcquireConnection(transaction).ToString();
                if (_filename == null || _filename.Length == 0)
                {
                    throw new Exception("Nothing returned when grabbing the filename");
                }
            }
        }
    }
}
```

This method covers a lot of ground and is really quite interesting. The first thing you want to do is find out if you can get a Connection Manager from the runtime connection collection of the component. The runtime connection was defined during `ProvideComponentProperties` earlier. If it is null, then the user has not provided a runtime connection.

```
if (ComponentMetaData.RuntimeConnectionCollection["File To Read"].ConnectionManager
!= null)
```

The next line of code is quite cool. What it does is convert the native Connection Manager object to a managed Connection Manager. You need the managed Connection Manager to find out what type it is and the properties.

```
ConnectionManager cm =
Microsoft.SqlServer.Dts.Runtime.DtsConvert.ToConnectionManager(
ComponentMetaData.RuntimeConnectionCollection["File To Read"].ConnectionManager);
```

Once you have the managed Connection Manager, you can start to look at some of its properties and make sure that it is what you want. All Connection Managers have a `CreationName` property. For this component, you want to make sure that the `CreationName` property is `FILE`, as highlighted below.

```
if (cm.CreationName != "FILE")
```

If the Creation Name is not `FILE`, then you send an exception back to the component.

```
throw new Exception("The type of FILE connection manager must be an Existing
File");
```

You've established that a connection has been specified and that it is the right type. The problem with the `FILE` Connection Manager is that it can still be the wrong type of connection. To find out if it is the right type, you will have to look at another of its properties, the `FileUsageType` property. This can return to you one of four values, defined by the `DTSFileConnectionUsageType` enumeration:

❑ `DTSFileConnectionUsageType.CreateFile`—The file does not yet exist and will be created by the component. If the file does exist, then you can raise an error, although you may also accept this and overwrite the file. Use this type for components that create new files.

- ❑ `DTSFileConnectionUsageType.FileExists` — The file exists, and you would be expected to raise an error if this is not the case.

- ❑ `DTSFileConnectionUsageType.CreateFolder` — The folder does not yet exist and will be created by the component. If the folder does exist, then you can decide how to handle this situation as with `CreateFile` above.

- ❑ `DTSFileConnectionUsageType.FolderExists` — The folder exists, and you would be expected to raise an error if this is not the case.

The type you want to check for in your component is `DTSFileConnectionUsageType.FileExists` and you do that like this, throwing an exception if the type is not what you want:

```
fil = (Microsoft.SqlServer.Dts.Runtime.DTSFileConnectionUsageType)cm.Properties
["FileUsageType"].GetValue(cm);

if (_fil != Microsoft.SqlServer.Dts.Runtime.DTSFileConnectionUsageType.FileExists)
{...}
```

You're nearly done checking your Connection Manager now. At this point, you need the file name so you can retrieve the file later on when you need to read it for data. You do that like this:

```
_filename = ComponentMetaData.RuntimeConnectionCollection
["File To Read"].ConnectionManager.AcquireConnection(transaction).ToString();
```

That concludes the `AcquireConnections` method, so you can now move straight on to the `Validate` method.

```
[CLSCompliant(false)]
public override DTSValidationStatus Validate()
{
    bool pbCancel = false;

    IDTSOutput90 output = ComponentMetaData.OutputCollection["Component Output"];

    if (ComponentMetaData.InputCollection.Count != 0)
    {
        ComponentMetaData.FireError(0, ComponentMetaData.Name, "Unexpected input
found. Source components do not support inputs.", "", 0, out pbCancel);
        return DTSValidationStatus.VS_ISCORRUPT;
    }

    if (ComponentMetaData.RuntimeConnectionCollection["File To
Read"].ConnectionManager == null)
    {
        ComponentMetaData.FireError(0, "Validate", "No Connection Manager
Specified.", "", 0, out pbCancel);
        return DTSValidationStatus.VS_ISBROKEN;
    }

    // Check for Output Columns, if not then force ReinitializeMetaData
    if (ComponentMetaData.OutputCollection["Component
        Output"].OutputColumnCollection.Count == 0)
    {
```

```
        ComponentMetaData.FireError(0, "Validate", "No output columns specified.
Making call to ReinitializeMetaData.", "", 0, out pbCancel);
        return DTSValidationStatus.VS_NEEDSNEWMETADATA;
    }

    //What about if we have output columns but we have no ExternalMetaData
    // columns?  Maybe somebody removed them through code.

    if (DoesEachOutputColumnHaveAMetaDataColumnAndDoDatatypesMatch(output.ID) ==
false)
    {
        ComponentMetaData.FireError(0, "Validate", "Output columns and metadata
columns are out of sync.  Making call to ReinitializeMetaData.", "", 0, out
pbCancel);
        return DTSValidationStatus.VS_NEEDSNEWMETADATA;
    }
    return base.Validate();
}
```

The first thing this method does is check for an input. If it has an input, it raises an error back to the component using the `FireError` method and returns `DTSValidationStatus.VS_ISCORRUPT`. This is a source adapter and there is no place for an input.

```
if (ComponentMetaData.InputCollection.Count != 0)
```

The next thing you do is check that the user has specified a Connection Manager for your component. If not, then you return back to the user a message indicating that a Connection Manager is required. Again, you do this through the `FireError` method. If there is no Connection Manager specified, then you tell the component it is broken. Remember that you do the validation of any Connection Manager that is specified in `AcquireConnections()`.

```
if (ComponentMetaData.RuntimeConnectionCollection["File To Read"].ConnectionManager
== null)
{
    ComponentMetaData.FireError(0, "Validate", "No Connection Manager Specified.",
"", 0, out pbCancel);
    return DTSValidationStatus.VS_ISBROKEN;
}
```

The next thing to do is check to see if the output has any columns. On the initial drop onto the designer, the output will have no columns. If this is the case, the `Validate()` method will return `DTSValidationStatus.VS_NEEDSNEWMETADATA`, which in turn calls `ReinitializeMetaData`. You will see later what happens in that method.

```
if (ComponentMetaData.OutputCollection["Component
Output"].OutputColumnCollection.Count == 0)
{
    ComponentMetaData.FireError(0, "Validate", "No output columns specified.  Making
call to ReinitializeMetaData.", "", 0, out pbCancel);
    return DTSValidationStatus.VS_NEEDSNEWMETADATA;
}
```

So if the output has output columns, then one of the things you want to check for is whether the output columns have an ExternalMetaDataColumn associated with them. You'll recall that in ProvideComponentProperties it was stated that you would use an ExternalMetadata ColumnCollection. So for each output column, you need to make sure that there is an equivalent external metadata column and that the data type properties also match.

```
if (DoesEachOutputColumnHaveAMetaDataColumnAndDoDatatypesMatch(output.ID) == false)
{
    ComponentMetaData.FireError(0, "Validate", "Output columns and metadata columns
are out of sync.  Making call to ReinitializeMetaData.", "", 0, out pbCancel);
    return DTSValidationStatus.VS_NEEDSNEWMETADATA;
}
```

The rather long-named helper method here, DoesEachOutputColumnHaveAMetaDataColumnAndDo DatatypesMatch, accepts as a parameter the ID of an output, so you pass in the output's ID. There are two things that this method has to do. First, it has to check that each output column has an ExternalMetadataColumn associated with it, and second, it has to make sure that the two columns have the same column data type properties. Here is the method in full.

```
private bool DoesEachOutputColumnHaveAMetaDataColumnAndDoDatatypesMatch(int
outputID)
{

    IDTSOutput90 output =
ComponentMetaData.OutputCollection.GetObjectByID(outputID);
    IDTSExternalMetadataColumn90 mdc;
    bool rtnVal = true;

    foreach (IDTSOutputColumn90 col in output.OutputColumnCollection)
    {

        if (col.ExternalMetadataColumnID == 0)
        {
            rtnVal = false;
        }
        else
        {
            mdc =
            output.ExternalMetadataColumnCollection[col.ExternalMetadataColumnID];

            if (mdc.DataType != col.DataType || mdc.Length != col.Length ||
mdc.Precision != col.Precision || mdc.Scale != col.Scale || mdc.CodePage !=
col.CodePage)
            {
                rtnVal = false;
            }
        }
    }
    return rtnVal;
}
```

The first thing this method does is to translate the ID passed in as a parameter to the method into an output.

```
IDTSOutput90 output = ComponentMetaData.OutputCollection.GetObjectByID(outputID);
```

Once you have that, the code loops over the output columns in that output and asks if the ExternalMetadataColumnID associated with that output column has a value of 0 (that is, there is no value). If the code finds an instance of a value, then it sets the return value from the method to be false.

```
foreach (IDTSOutputColumn90 col in output.OutputColumnCollection)
{

    if (col.ExternalMetadataColumnID == 0)
    {
        rtnVal = false;
    }
...
```

If all output columns have a nonzero ExternalMetadataColumnID, then you move on to the second test:

```
mdc = output.ExternalMetadataColumnCollection[col.ExternalMetadataColumnID];

if (mdc.DataType != col.DataType || mdc.Length != col.Length || mdc.Precision !=
col.Precision || mdc.Scale != col.Scale || mdc.CodePage != col.CodePage)
{
    rtnVal = false;
}
```

In this part of the method, you are checking that all attributes of the output column's data type match those of the corresponding ExternalMetadataColumn. If they do not, then again you return false from the method, which causes the Validate() method to call ReinitializeMetadata. Notice how you are using the ID over a Name, since names can be changed by the end user.

ReinitializeMetaData is where a lot of the work happens in most components. In this component, it will fix up the output columns and the ExternalMetadataColumns. Here's the method:

```
public override void ReinitializeMetaData()
{
    IDTSOutput90 _profoutput = ComponentMetaData.OutputCollection["Component
Output"];

    if (_profoutput.ExternalMetadataColumnCollection.Count > 0)
    {
        _profoutput.ExternalMetadataColumnCollection.RemoveAll();
    }

    if (_profoutput.OutputColumnCollection.Count > 0)
    {
        _profoutput.OutputColumnCollection.RemoveAll();
    }

    CreateOutputAndMetaDataColumns(_profoutput);

}
```

This is a really simple way of doing things. Basically, you are going to remove all the ExternalMetaDataColumns and then remove the output columns. You will then add them back using the CreateOutputAndMetaDataColumns method.

As an exercise, you may want to see if you can work out which columns actually need fixing.

CreateOutputAndMetaDataColumns creates the output's output columns and the ExternalMetaData columns to go with them. This is very rigid, and it presumes that the file you get will be in one format only. There are actually two methods here, and the output you just created is passed in:

```
private void CreateOutputAndMetaDataColumns(IDTSOutput90 output)
{
    IDTSOutputColumn90 outName = output.OutputColumnCollection.New();
    outName.Name = "Name";
    outName.Description = "The Name value retrieved from File";
    outName.SetDataTypeProperties(DataType.DT_STR, 50, 0, 0, 1252);
    CreateExternalMetaDataColumn(output.ExternalMetadataColumnCollection, outName);

    IDTSOutputColumn90 outAge = output.OutputColumnCollection.New();
    outAge.Name = "Age";
    outAge.Description = "The Age value retrieved from File";
    outAge.SetDataTypeProperties(DataType.DT_I4, 0, 0, 0, 0);

    //Create an external metadata column to go alongside with it
    CreateExternalMetaDataColumn(output.ExternalMetadataColumnCollection, outAge);

    IDTSOutputColumn90 outMarried = output.OutputColumnCollection.New();
    outMarried.Name = "Married";
    outMarried.Description = "The Married value retrieved from File";
    outMarried.SetDataTypeProperties(DataType.DT_BOOL, 0, 0, 0, 0);

    //Create an external metadata column to go alongside with it
    CreateExternalMetaDataColumn(output.ExternalMetadataColumnCollection,
        outMarried);

    IDTSOutputColumn90 outSalary = output.OutputColumnCollection.New();
    outSalary.Name = "Salary";
    outSalary.Description = "The Salary value retrieved from File";
    outSalary.SetDataTypeProperties(DataType.DT_DECIMAL, 0, 0, 10, 0);

    //Create an external metadata column to go alongside with it
    CreateExternalMetaDataColumn(output.ExternalMetadataColumnCollection,
    outSalary);
}
```

This code follows the same path for every column you want to create, so you'll just look at one example here, as the rest are variations of the same code. In CreateOutputAndMetaDataColumns, you first need to create an output column and add it to the outputcolumncollection of the output, which is a parameter to the method. You give the column a name, a description, and a data type along with details about the data type.

SetDataTypeProperties takes the name, the length, the precision, the scale, and the code page of that data type. A list of what is required for these fields can be found in Books Online.

```
IDTSOutputColumn90 outName = output.OutputColumnCollection.New();
outName.Name = "Name";
outName.Description = "The Name value retrieved from File";
outName.SetDataTypeProperties(DataType.DT_STR, 50, 0, 0, 1252);
```

You now look to create an `ExternalMetaDataColumn` for the `OutputColumn`, and you do that by calling the method `CreateExternalMetaDataColumn`. This method takes as parameters the `ExternalMetaDataColumnCollection` of the output and the `Column` for which you want to create an `ExternalMetaDataColumn`.

```
CreateExternalMetaDataColumn(output.ExternalMetadataColumnCollection, outName);
```

The first thing you do in the method is create a new `ExternalMetaDataColumn` in the `ExternalMetaDataColumnCollection` that was passed as a parameter. You then map the properties of the output column that was passed as a parameter to the new `ExternalMetaDataColumn`. Finally, you create the relationship between the two by assigning the ID of the `ExternalMetaDataColumn` to the `ExternalMetadataColumnID` property of the output column.

```
IDTSExternalMetadataColumn90 eColumn = externalCollection.New();
eColumn.Name = column.Name;
eColumn.DataType = column.DataType;
eColumn.Precision = column.Precision;
eColumn.Length = column.Length;
eColumn.Scale = column.Scale;
eColumn.CodePage = column.CodePage;
column.ExternalMetadataColumnID = eColumn.ID;
```

At this point, the base class will call the MapOutputColumn method. You can choose to override this method to decide if you want to allow the mapping to occur, but in this case you should choose to leave the base class to simply carry on.

Now you will move on to looking at the runtime methods. `PreExecute` is the usual place to start for most components, but it is done slightly different here. Normally you would enumerate the output columns and enter them into a struct so you could easily retrieve them later. You're not going to do that here, but you do this in the destination adapter, so you could port what you do there into this adapter as well. The only method you are interested in with this adapter is `PrimeOutput`. Here is the method in full:

```
public override void PrimeOutput(int outputs, int[] outputIDs, PipelineBuffer[]
buffers)
{
    ParseTheFileAndAddToBuffer(_filename, buffers[0]);
    buffers[0].SetEndOfRowset();
}
```

On the face of this method, it looks really easy, but as you can see, all the work is being done by the `ParseTheFileAndAddToBuffer` method. To that, you need to pass the file name you retrieved in `AcquireConnections`, and the buffer is `buffers[0]`, because there is only one buffer and the collection is zero-based. You'll look at the `ParseTheFileAndAddToBuffer` method in a moment, but the last thing you do in this method is call `SetEndOfRowset` on the buffer. This basically tells the downstream component that there are no more rows to be had from the adapter. Now you will look at the `ParseTheFileAndAddToBuffer` method in a bit more detail.

```
private void ParseTheFileAndAddToBuffer(string filename, PipelineBuffer buffer)
{
    TextReader tr = File.OpenText(filename);
    IDTSOutput90 output = ComponentMetaData.OutputCollection["Component Output"];
    IDTSOutputColumnCollection90 cols = output.OutputColumnCollection;
    IDTSOutputColumn90 col;

    string s = tr.ReadLine();
    int i = 0;

    while (s != null)
    {
        if (s.StartsWith("<START>"))
            buffer.AddRow();

        if (s.StartsWith("Name:"))
        {
            col = cols["Name"];
            i = BufferManager.FindColumnByLineageID(output.Buffer, col.LineageID);
            string value = s.Substring(5);
            buffer.SetString(i, value);
        }

        if (s.StartsWith("Age:"))
        {
            col = cols["Age"];
            i = BufferManager.FindColumnByLineageID(output.Buffer, col.LineageID);
            Int32 value;
            if (s.Substring(4).Trim() == "")
                value = 0;
            else
                value = Convert.ToInt32(s.Substring(4).Trim());

            buffer.SetInt32(i, value);
        }

        if (s.StartsWith("Married:"))
        {
            col = cols["Married"];
            bool value;
            i = BufferManager.FindColumnByLineageID(output.Buffer, col.LineageID);
            if (s.Substring(8).Trim() == "")
                value = true;
            else
                value = s.Substring(8).Trim() != "1" ? false : true;

            buffer.SetBoolean(i, value);
        }

        if (s.StartsWith("Salary:"))
```

```
        {
            col = cols["Salary"];
            Decimal value;
            i = BufferManager.FindColumnByLineageID(output.Buffer, col.LineageID);

            if (s.Substring(7).Trim() == "")
                value = 0M;
            else
                value = Convert.ToDecimal(s.Substring(8).Trim());

            buffer.SetDecimal(i, value);
        }
        s = tr.ReadLine();
    }
    tr.Close();
}
```

Because this is not a lesson in C# programming, you will simply describe the points relevant to SSIS programming in this component. You start off by getting references to the output columns collection in the component.

```
IDTSOutput90 output = ComponentMetaData.OutputCollection["Component Output"];
IDTSOutputColumnCollection90 cols = output.OutputColumnCollection;
IDTSOutputColumn90 col;
```

The IDTSOutputColumn90 object will be used when you need a reference to particular columns. Now the problem with the file is that the columns in the file are in rows, and you need to pivot them into columns. The way to identify in the text file that you need to add a new row to the buffer is if when reading a line of text from the file it begins with the word <START>. You do that in this code here (remember that s is a line of text from the file):

```
if(s.StartsWith("<START>"))
    buffer.AddRow();
```

As you can see, you have added a row to the buffer. As you read lines in the file, you test the start of each line. This is important because you need to know this in order to be able to grab the right column from the output columns collection and assign it the value from the text file. The first column name you test for is the "Name" column.

```
if (s.StartsWith("Name:"))
{
    col = cols["Name"];
    i = BufferManager.FindColumnByLineageID(output.Buffer, col.LineageID);

    string value = s.Substring(5);
    buffer.SetString(i, value);
}
```

The first thing you do here is to check what the row begins with. In the example above, it is "Name:". Next, you set the IDTSColumn90 variable column to reference the Name column in the OutputColumnCollection. You need to be able to locate the column in the buffer, and to do this you need to look at the Buffer Manager. This has a method called FindColumnByLineageID, which returns the integer location of the column. You need this to assign a value to the column. To this method, you pass the output's buffer and the column's LineageID. Once you have that, you can use the SetString method on the buffer object to assign a value to the column by passing in the Buffer column index and the value you want to set the column to. You pretty much do the same with all the columns you want to set values for. The only variation is the method you call on the buffer object. The buffer object has a set<datatype> method for each of the possible data types. In this component, you need a SetInt32, a SetBoolean, and a SetDecimal method. They do not differ in structure from the SetString method at all.

Building the Transform

In this section, you will build the transform that is going to take data from the upstream source adapter. After reversing the strings, it will pass the data to the downstream component. In this example, the downstream component will be the destination adapter, which you'll be writing right after you're done with the transform. The component will need a few things during its lifetime, so you should have a look at those things now.

```
private ColumnInfo[] _inputColumnInfos;

const string ErrorInvalidUsageType = "Invalid UsageType for column '{0}'";
const string ErrorInvalidDataType = "Invalid DataType for column '{0}'";

CLSCompliant(false)]
public struct ColumnInfo
{
    public int bufferColumnIndex;
    public DTSRowDisposition columnDisposition;
    public int lineageID;
}
```

The structure or struct that you create here, called ColumnInfo, is something you use in various guises time and time again in your components. It is really useful for storing details about columns that you will need later in the component. In this component, you will store the BufferColumnIndex, which is basically where the column is in the buffer, so that you can retrieve the data. You'll store how the user wants the row to be treated in an error, and you'll also store the column's LineageID, which helps to retrieve the column from the InputColumnCollection.

Logically, it would make sense to code the component beginning with the design-time, followed by the runtime. The very first thing that happens when your component is dropped into the SSIS package designer surface is that it will make a call to ProvideComponentProperties. In this component, you want to set up an input and an output, and you also need to tell your component how it is going to handle data — as in whether it is a synchronous or an asynchronous transformation, as discussed earlier in the chapter. Just as you did with the source adapter, you'll look at the whole method first and then examine parts of the method in greater detail. Here is the method in full:

```
public override void ProvideComponentProperties()
{
    ComponentMetaData.UsesDispositions = true;

    ReverseStringInput = ComponentMetaData.InputCollection.New();
```

```
    ReverseStringInput.Name = "RSin";

    ReverseStringInput.ErrorRowDisposition = DTSRowDisposition.RD_FailComponent;

    ReverseStringOutput = ComponentMetaData.OutputCollection.New();
    ReverseStringOutput.Name = "RSout";

    ReverseStringOutput.SynchronousInputID = ReverseStringInput.ID;

    ReverseStringOutput.ExclusionGroup = 1;

    AddErrorOutput("RSErrors", ReverseStringInput.ID,
                   ReverseStringOutput.ExclusionGroup);


}
```

Now to break it down. The very first thing you do is to tell the component to use dispositions.

```
ComponentMetaData.UsesDispositions = true;
```

In this case, this tells your component that it can expect an error output. Now you move on to adding an input to the component.

```
// Add a new Input, and name it.
ReverseStringInput = ComponentMetaData.InputCollection.New();
ReverseStringInput.Name = "RSin";

// If an error occurs during data movement, then the component will fail.
ReverseStringInput.ErrorRowDisposition = DTSRowDisposition.RD_FailComponent;

// Add a new Output, and name it.
ReverseStringOutput = ComponentMetaData.OutputCollection.New();
ReverseStringOutput.Name = "RSout";

// Link the Input and Output together for a synchronous behavior
ReverseStringOutput.SynchronousInputID = ReverseStringInput.ID;
```

This isn't too different from adding the input, except that you tell the component that this is a synchronous component by setting the SynchronousInputID on the output to the ID of the input you created earlier. If you were creating an asynchronous component, you would set the SynchronousInputID of the output to be 0, like this:

```
ReverseStringOutput.SynchronousInputID = 0
```

This tells SSIS to create a buffer for the output that is separate from the input buffer. This is not an asynchronous component, though; you will revisit some of the subtle differences later.

```
AddErrorOutput("RSErrors",
ReverseStringInput.ID,ReverseStringOutput.ExclusionGroup);

ReverseStringOutput.ExclusionGroup = 1;
```

`AddErrorOutput` creates a new output on the component and tags it as being an error output by setting the `IsErrorOut` property to true. To the method, you pass the name of the error output you want, the input's `ID` property, and the output's `ExclusionGroup`. An `ExclusionGroup` is needed when two outputs use the same synchronous input. Setting the exclusion group allows you to direct rows to the correct output later in the component using `DirectRow`.

That's it for `ProvideComponentProperties`. Now you'll move on to the `Validate` method. As mentioned earlier, this method is called on numerous occasions, and it is your opportunity within the component to check whether what has been specified by the user is allowable by the component.

Here is your completed `Validate` method:

```
[CLSCompliant(false)]
public override DTSValidationStatus Validate()
{
    bool Cancel;

    if (ComponentMetaData.AreInputColumnsValid == false)
        return DTSValidationStatus.VS_NEEDSNEWMETADATA;

    foreach (IDTSInputColumn90 inputColumn in
ComponentMetaData.InputCollection[0].InputColumnCollection)
    {
        if (inputColumn.UsageType != DTSUsageType.UT_READWRITE)
        {
            ComponentMetaData.FireError(0, inputColumn.IdentificationString,
String.Format(ErrorInvalidUsageType, inputColumn.Name), "", 0, out Cancel);
            return DTSValidationStatus.VS_ISBROKEN;
        }

        if (inputColumn.DataType != DataType.DT_STR && inputColumn.DataType !=
DataType.DT_WSTR)
        {
            ComponentMetaData.FireError(0, inputColumn.IdentificationString,
String.Format(ErrorInvalidDataType, inputColumn.Name), "", 0, out Cancel);
            return DTSValidationStatus.VS_ISBROKEN;
        }
    }

    return base.Validate();
}
```

This method will return a validation status to indicate the overall result and may cause subsequent methods to be called. Refer to the SQL Server documentation for a complete list of values (see `DTSValidationStatus`).

Now to break down the `Validate` method. A user can easily add and take away an input from the component at any stage and add it back. It may be the same one, or it may be a different one, presenting the component with an issue. When an input is added, the component will store the lineage IDs of the Input columns. If that input is removed and another is added, those lineage IDs may have changed because something like the query used to generate those columns may have changed; therefore you are presented with different columns, so you need to check to see if that has happened and if it has invalidated the lineage IDs. If it has, the component will call `ReinitializeMetaData`.

```
if (ComponentMetaData.AreInputColumnsValid == false)
{ return DTSValidationStatus.VS_NEEDSNEWMETADATA; }
```

The next thing you should check for is that each of the columns in the `InputColumnCollection` chosen for the component has been set to READ WRITE. This is because you will be altering them in place. If they are not set to READ WRITE, you need to feed that back by returning VS_ISBROKEN. You can invoke the `FireError` method on the component, which will result in a red cross on the component along with tooltip text indicating the exact error.

```
if (RSincol.UsageType != DTSUsageType.UT_READWRITE)
{
    ComponentMetaData.FireError(0, inputColumn.IdentificationString,
String.Format(ErrorInvalidUsageType, inputColumn.Name), "", 0, out Cancel);
    return DTSValidationStatus.VS_ISBROKEN;
}
```

The last thing you do in `Validate` is to check that the columns selected for the component have the correct data types.

```
if (inputColumn.DataType != DataType.DT_STR && inputColumn.DataType !=
DataType.DT_WSTR)
...
```

If the data type of the column is not one of those in the list, you again fire an error and set the return value to VS_ISBROKEN.

Now you will look at the workhorse method of so many of your components: ReinitializeMetaData. Here is the method in full:

```
public override void ReinitializeMetaData()
{
    if (!ComponentMetaData.AreInputColumnsValid)
    {
        ComponentMetaData.RemoveInvalidInputColumns();
    }

    base.ReinitializeMetaData();
}
```

Remember back in the `Validate` method mentioned earlier that if `Validate` returns VS_NEEDSNEW METADATA, then the component internally would call `ReinitializeMetaData`. The only time you do that for this component is when you have detected that the lineage IDs of the input columns are not quite as expected, that is to say, they do not exist on any upstream column and you want to remove them.

```
if (!ComponentMetaData.AreInputColumnsValid)
{
    ComponentMetaData.RemoveInvalidInputColumns();
}
```

You finish off by calling the base class's `ReinitializeMetaData` method as well. This method really can become the workhorse of your component. You can perform all kinds of triage on your component here and try to rescue the component from the user.

The `SetUsageType` method is called when the user is manipulating how the column on the input will be used by the component. In this component, this method validates the data type of the column and whether the user has set the column to be the correct usage type. The method returns an `IDTSInputColumn`, and this is the column being manipulated.

```
[CLSCompliant(false)]
public override IDTSInputColumn90 SetUsageType(int inputID, IDTSVirtualInput90
virtualInput, int lineageID, DTSUsageType usageType)
{
    IDTSVirtualInputColumn90 virtualInputColumn =
virtualInput.VirtualInputColumnCollection.GetVirtualInputColumnByLineageID(
lineageID);

    if (usageType == DTSUsageType.UT_READONLY)
        throw new Exception(String.Format(ErrorInvalidUsageType,
            virtualInputColumn.Name));

    if (usageType == DTSUsageType.UT_READWRITE)
    {
        if (virtualInputColumn.DataType != DataType.DT_STR &&
            virtualInputColumn.DataType != DataType.DT_WSTR)
        {
            throw new Exception(String.Format(ErrorInvalidDataType,
                virtualInputColumn.Name));
        }
    }

    return base.SetUsageType(inputID, virtualInput, lineageID, usageType);
}
```

The first thing the method does is get a reference to the column being changed, from the virtual input, which is the list of all upstream columns available.

You then perform the tests to ensure the column is suitable, before proceeding with the request through the base class. Note that this method looks a lot like the `Validate` method. The only real difference is that the `Validate` method obviously returned a different object but also reported errors back to the component. `Validate` uses the `FireError` method, but `SetUsageType` throws an exception; in `SetUsageType` you are checking against the `VirtualInput`, and in `Validate()` you check against the `Input90`. (We used to use FireError in here also, but we found that it wasn't as predictable on what got bubbled back to the user, and we were advised that the correct way would be to throw a new exception.) These are important, as this is one of the key verification methods you can use, allowing you to validate in real time the change that is made to your component and prevent it if necessary.

The `InsertOutput` method is the next design-time method you'll be looking at, and it is called when a user attempts to add an output to the component. In your component, you want to prohibit that, so if the user tries to add an output, you should throw an exception telling them it is not allowed.

```
[CLSCompliant(false)]
public override IDTSOutput90 InsertOutput(DTSInsertPlacement insertPlacement, int
outputID)
{
    throw new Exception("You cannot insert an output (" +
        outputID.ToString() + ")");
}
```

You do the same when the user tries to add an input to your component in the `InsertInput` method:

```
[CLSCompliant(false)]
public override IDTSInput90 InsertInput(DTSInsertPlacement insertPlacement, int
inputID)
{
    throw new Exception("You cannot insert an output (" +
        outputID.ToString() + ")");
}
```

Notice again how in both methods you throw an exception in order to tell the user that what they requested is not allowed.

If the component were asynchronous, you would need to add columns to the output yourself. There exists a choice of methods in which to do this. If you want to add an output column for every input column selected, then the `SetUsageType` method is probably the best place to do that. This is something about which Books Online agrees. Another method for doing this might be the `OnInputPathAttached`.

The final two methods you'll look at for the design-time methods are the opposite of the previous two. Instead of users trying to add an output or an input to your component, they are trying to remove one of them. You do not want to allow this either, so you can use the `DeleteOutput` and the `DeleteInput` methods to tell them. Here are the methods as implemented in your component.

First the `DeleteInput` Method:

```
[CLSCompliant(false)]
public override void DeleteInput(int inputID)
{
    throw new Exception("You cannot delete an input");
}
```

Now the `DeleteOutput` method:

```
[CLSCompliant(false)]
public override void DeleteOutput(int outputID)
{
    throw new Exception("You cannot delete an ouput");
}
```

That concludes the code for the design-time part of your transformation component. Now you will move on to the runtime methods.

The first runtime method you'll be using is the `PreExecute` method. As mentioned earlier, this is called once in your component's life, and it is where you typically do most of your setup using the struct mentioned at the top of this section. It is the first opportunity you get to access the Buffer Manager, providing access to columns within the buffer, which you will need in `ProcessInput` as well. Keep in mind that you will not be getting a call to `PrimeOutput`, as this is a synchronous component and `PrimeOutput` is not called in a synchronous component. Here is the `PreExecute` method in full:

```
public override void PreExecute()
{
    // Prepare array of column information. Processing requires
```

```
    // lineageID so we can do this once in advance.

    IDTSInput90 input = ComponentMetaData.InputCollection[0];
    _inputColumnInfos = new ColumnInfo[input.InputColumnCollection.Count];

    for (int x = 0; x < input.InputColumnCollection.Count; x++)
    {
        IDTSInputColumn90 column = input.InputColumnCollection[x];
        _inputColumnInfos[x] = new ColumnInfo();
        _inputColumnInfos[x].bufferColumnIndex =
BufferManager.FindColumnByLineageID(input.Buffer, column.LineageID);
        _inputColumnInfos[x].columnDisposition = column.ErrorRowDisposition;
        _inputColumnInfos[x].lineageID = column.LineageID;
    }
}
```

The first thing this method does is get a reference to the input collection. The collection is zero-based, and because you have only one input, you have used the indexer and not the name, though you could have used the name as well.

```
IDTSInput90 input = ComponentMetaData.InputCollection[0];
```

At the start of this section was a list of the things your component would need later. This included a struct that you were told you would use in various guises, and it also included an array of these structs. You now need to size the array, which you do next by setting the size of the array to the count of columns in the InputColumnCollection for your component.

```
_inputColumnInfos = new ColumnInfo[input.InputColumnCollection.Count];
```

Now you loop through the columns in the InputColumnCollection. For each of the columns, you create a new instance of a column and a new instance of the struct.

```
IDTSInputColumn90 column = input.InputColumnCollection[x];
_inputColumnInfos[x] = new ColumnInfo();
```

You then read from the column the details you require and store them in the ColumnInfo object. The first thing you want to retrieve is the location of the column in the buffer. You cannot simply do this by the order that you added them to the buffer. Though this would probably work, it is likely to catch you out at some point. You can find the column in the buffer by the use of a method called FindColumnByLineageID on the BufferManager object. This method takes the buffer and the LineageID of the column that you wish to find as arguments.

```
_inputColumnInfos[x].bufferColumnIndex =
BufferManager.FindColumnByLineageID(input.Buffer, column.LineageID);
```

You now need only two more details about the input column: the LineageID and the ErrorRowDisposition. Remember, ErrorRowDisposition tells the component how to treat an error.

```
_inputColumnInfos[x].columnDisposition = column.ErrorRowDisposition;
_inputColumnInfos[x].lineageID = column.LineageID;
```

When you start to build your own components, you will see that this method really becomes useful. You can use it to initialize any counters you may need or to open connections to data sources as well as anything else you think of.

The final method you are going to be looking at for this component is `ProcessInput`. Remember, this is a synchronous transform as dictated in `ProvideComponentProperties`, and this is the method in which the data is moved and manipulated. This method contains a lot of information that will help you understand the buffer and what to do with the columns in it when you receive them. It is called once for every buffer passed.

Here is the method in full:

```
public override void ProcessInput(int inputID, PipelineBuffer buffer)
{

    int errorOutputID = -1;
    int errorOutputIndex = -1;
    int GoodOutputId = -1;

    IDTSInput90 inp = ComponentMetaData.InputCollection.GetObjectByID(inputID);


    #region Output IDs
    GetErrorOutputInfo(ref errorOutputID, ref errorOutputIndex);
    // There is an error output defined
    errorOutputID = ComponentMetaData.OutputCollection["RSErrors"].ID;
    GoodOutputId = ComponentMetaData.OutputCollection["ReverseStringOutput"].ID;
    #endregion

    if (!buffer.EndOfRowset)
    {
        while (buffer.NextRow())
        {
            // Check if we have columns to process
            if (_inputColumnInfos.Length == 0)
            {
                // We do not have to have columns. This is a Sync component so the
                // rows will flow through regardless. Could expand Validate to check
                // for columns in the InputColumnCollection
                buffer.DirectRow(GoodOutputId);
            }
            else
            {
                try
                {
                    for (int x = 0; x < _inputColumnInfos.Length; x++)
                    {
                        ColumnInfo columnInfo = _inputColumnInfos[x];

                        if (!buffer.IsNull(columnInfo.bufferColumnIndex))
                        {
                            // Get value as character array
                            char[] chars =
```

```
buffer.GetString(columnInfo.bufferColumnIndex).ToString().ToCharArray();

                    // Reverse order of characters in array
                    Array.Reverse(chars);

                    // Reassemble reversed value as string
                    StringBuilder outputValue = new StringBuilder(chars.Length);
                    for (int i = 0; i < chars.Length; i++)
                    {
                        outputValue.Append(chars[i]);
                    }

                    // Set output value in buffer
                    buffer.SetString(columnInfo.bufferColumnIndex,
outputValue.ToString());
                }
            }

            buffer.DirectRow(GoodOutputId);
        }
        catch(Exception ex)
        {
            switch (inp.ErrorRowDisposition)
            {

                case DTSRowDisposition.RD_RedirectRow:
                    buffer.DirectErrorRow(errorOutputID, 0, buffer.CurrentRow);
                    break;
                case DTSRowDisposition.RD_FailComponent:
                    throw new Exception("There was an error in your processing " +
ex.Message);
                            case DTSRowDisposition.RD_IgnoreFailure:
                    buffer.DirectRow(GoodOutputId);
                    break;
            }
        }
    }
}
```

There is a lot going on in this method, so you should break it down to make it more manageable. The first thing you want to do is find out from the component the location of the error output, as shown here:

```
int errorOutputID = -1;
int errorOutputIndex = -1;
int GoodOutputId = -1;

#region Output IDs
GetErrorOutputInfo(ref errorOutputID, ref errorOutputIndex);

errorOutputID = ComponentMetaData.OutputCollection["RSErrors"].ID;
GoodOutputId = ComponentMetaData.OutputCollection["ReverseStringOutput"].ID;
#endregion
```

The method GetErrorOutput returns the output ID and the Index of the error output. Remember that you defined the error output in ProvideComponentProperties.

Because you could have many inputs to a component, you want to isolate the input for this component. You can do that by finding the output that is passed in to the method.

```
IDTSInput90 inp = ComponentMetaData.InputCollection.GetObjectByID(inputID);
```

You need this because you want to know what to do with the row if you encounter an issue. You gave a default value for the ErrorRowDisposition property of the input in ProvideComponentProperties, but this can be overridden in the UI.

The next thing you want to do is check that the upstream buffer has not called SetEndOfRowset, which would mean that it has no more rows to send. You then loop through the rows in the buffer like this.

```
if (!buffer.EndOfRowset)
{
    while (buffer.NextRow())
...
```

You then check to see if the user asked for any columns to be manipulated. Remember, this is a synchronous component, so all columns and rows are going to flow through even if you do not specify any columns for this component. Therefore, you tell the component that if there are no input columns selected, the row should be passed to the normal output. You do this by looking at the size of the array that holds the collection of ColumnInfo struct objects.

```
if (_inputColumnInfos.Length == 0)
{
    buffer.DirectRow(GoodOutputId);
}
```

If the length of the array is not zero, the user has asked the component to perform an operation on the column. In turn, you need to grab each of the ColumnInfo objects from the array so you can look at the data. Here you begin your loop through the columns, and for each column you create a new instance of the ColumnInfo struct.

```
for (int x = 0; x < _inputColumnInfos.Length; x++)
{
    ColumnInfo columnInfo = _inputColumnInfos[x];
...
```

You now have a reference to that column and are ready to start manipulating it. You first convert the column's data into an array of chars.

```
char[] chars =
buffer.GetString(columnInfo.bufferColumnIndex).ToString().ToCharArray();
```

The interesting part of this line is the method GetString() on the buffer object. It returns the string data of the column and accepts as an argument the index of the column in the buffer. This is really easy, because you stored that reference earlier in the PreExecute method. Now that you have the char array, you can perform some operations on the data. This code won't be shown in detail here because it is not particular to SSIS, and you will move straight on to where you reassign the changed data back to the column using the SetString() method on the buffer.

```
buffer.SetString(columnInfo.bufferColumnIndex, outputValue.ToString());
```

Again this method takes as one of the arguments the index of the column in the buffer. It also takes the string you want to assign to that column. You can see now why it was important to make sure that this column was read/write. If there was no error, you point the row to the good output buffer.

```
buffer.DirectRow(GoodOutputId);
```

If you encounter an error, you want to redirect this row to the correct output or alternatively throw an error. You do that in the catch block like this:

```
catch(Exception ex)
{
    switch (inp.ErrorRowDisposition)
    {

        case DTSRowDisposition.RD_RedirectRow:
            buffer.DirectErrorRow(errorOutputID, 0, buffer.CurrentRow);
            break;
        case DTSRowDisposition.RD_FailComponent:
            throw new Exception("There was an error in your processing " +
ex.Message);
        case DTSRowDisposition.RD_IgnoreFailure:
            buffer.DirectRow(GoodOutputId);
            break;
    }
}
```

The code is pretty self-explanatory. If the input was told to redirect the row to the error output, then you do that. If it was told to either fail the component, or the user did not specify anything, then you throw an exception. Otherwise the user is asked just to ignore the errors and allow the error row to flow down the normal output.

Now how could this have looked had it been an asynchronous transform? You would get a buffer from both PrimeOutput and ProcessInput. ProcessInput would contain the data and structure that came into the component, and PrimeOutput would contain the structure that the component expects to pass on. The trick here is to get the data from one buffer into the other. Here is one way you can approach it.

At the class level, create a variable of type PipelineBuffer, something like this:

```
PipelineBuffer _pipelinebuffer;
```

Now in PrimeOutput, assign the output buffer to this buffer:

```
public override void PrimeOutput(int outputs, int[] outputIDs, PipelineBuffer[]
buffers)
{
    _pipelinebuffer = buffers[0];
}
```

You now have a cached version of the buffer from PrimeOutput, and you go straight over to ProcessInput. Books Online has a great example of doing this in an asynchronous component: navigate to "asynchronous outputs."

Do not be afraid to look through Books Online. Microsoft has done a fantastic job of including content that helps with good, solid examples.

Building the Destination Adapter

The requirement for the destination adapter is that it accepts an input from an upstream component of any description and converts it to a format similar to that seen in the source adapter. The component will accept a FILE Connection Manager, and as you have seen in earlier components, this involves a significant amount of validation. You also need to validate whether the component is structurally correct, and if it isn't, you need to correct things. The first thing you always need to do is declare some variables that will be used throughout the component. You also need to create the very valuable struct that is going to store the details of the columns, which will be needed in PreExecute and ProcessInput.

```
#region Variables
private ArrayList _columnInfos = new ArrayList();
private Microsoft.SqlServer.Dts.Runtime.DTSFileConnectionUsageType _fil;
private string _filename;
FileStream _fs;
StreamWriter _sw;
#endregion
```

You should quickly run through the meaning of these variables and when they will be needed. The _columnInfos variable will be used to store ColumnInfo objects, which describe the columns in the InputColumnCollection. The _fil variable will be used to validate the type of FILE Connection Manager the user has assigned to your component. _filename stores the name of the file that is retrieved from the FILE Connection Manager. The final two variables, _fs and _sw, are used when you write to the text file in ProcessInput. Now take a look at the ColumnInfo struct.

```
#region ColumnInfo
private struct ColumnInfo
{
    public int BufferColumnIndex;
    public string ColumnName;
}
#endregion
```

The struct will be used to store the index number of the column in the buffer and also to store the name of the column.

You will now move on to looking at the ProvideComponentProperties method, which is where you set up the component and prepare it for use by an SSIS package, as in the other two components. Here's the method in full.

```
public override void ProvideComponentProperties()
{

    ComponentMetaData.RuntimeConnectionCollection.RemoveAll();
```

```
        RemoveAllInputsOutputsAndCustomProperties();

        ComponentMetaData.Name = "Professional SSIS Destination Adapter";
        ComponentMetaData.Description = "Our first Destination Adapter";
        ComponentMetaData.ContactInfo = "www.Konesans.com";

        IDTSRuntimeConnection90 rtc =
    ComponentMetaData.RuntimeConnectionCollection.New();
        rtc.Name = "File To Write";
        rtc.Description = "This is the file to which we want to write";

        IDTSInput90 input = ComponentMetaData.InputCollection.New();
        input.Name = "Component Input";
        input.Description = "This is what we see from the upstream component";
        input.HasSideEffects = true;
    }
```

The first part of the method gets rid of any runtime Connection Managers that the component may have and removes any custom properties, inputs, and outputs that the component has. This makes the component a clean slate to which you can now add back anything it may need.

```
    ComponentMetaData.RuntimeConnectionCollection.RemoveAll();
    RemoveAllInputsOutputsAndCustomProperties();
```

The component requires one connection, as defined as follows:

```
    IDTSRuntimeConnection90 rtc = ComponentMetaData.RuntimeConnectionCollection.New();
    rtc.Name = "File To Write";
    rtc.Description = "This is the file to which we want to write";
```

This piece of code gives the user the opportunity to specify a Connection Manager for the component. This will be the file to which you write the data from upstream.

```
    IDTSInput90 input = ComponentMetaData.InputCollection.New();
    input.Name = "Component Input";
    input.Description = "This is what we see from the upstream component";
```

The next thing you do is add back the input. This is what the upstream component will connect to, and through which you will receive the data from the previous component. Now you need to make sure that the IDTSInput90 object of the component remains in the execution plan regardless of whether it is attached by making the HasSideEffects property true.

```
    input.HasSideEffects = true;
```

Having finished with the ProvideComponentProperties method, you now move on to the AcquireConnections method. This method is not really any different from the AcquireConnections method you saw in the source adapter; the method is shown in full but is not described in detail. If you need to get the line-by-line details of what's happening, you can look back to the source adapter. The tasks this method accomplishes are the following:

❑   Check that the user has supplied a Connection Manager to the component

❑   Check that the Connection Manager is a FILE Connection Manager

❑ Make sure that the FILE Connection Manager has a FileUsageType property value of DTSFileConnectionUsageType.FileExists

❑ Get the file name from the Connection Manager

```
public override void AcquireConnections(object transaction)
{
    bool pbCancel = false;

    if (ComponentMetaData.RuntimeConnectionCollection["File To
Write"].ConnectionManager != null)
    {
        ConnectionManager cm =
Microsoft.SqlServer.Dts.Runtime.DtsConvert.ToConnectionManager(
ComponentMetaData.RuntimeConnectionCollection["File To Write"].ConnectionManager);

        if (cm.CreationName != "FILE")
        {
            ComponentMetaData.FireError(0, "Acquire Connections", "The Connection
Manager is not a FILE Connection Manager", "", 0, out pbCancel);
            throw new Exception("The Connection Manager is not a FILE Connection
Manager");
        }
        else
        {
            _fil =
(DTSFileConnectionUsageType)cm.Properties["FileUsageType"].GetValue(cm);

            if (_fil != DTSFileConnectionUsageType.FileExists)
            {
                ComponentMetaData.FireError(0, "Acquire Connections", "The type of FILE
connection manager must be an Existing File", "", 0, out pbCancel);
                throw new Exception("The type of FILE connection manager must be an
Existing File");

            }
            else
            {
                _filename = ComponentMetaData.RuntimeConnectionCollection["File To
Read"].ConnectionManager.AcquireConnection(transaction).ToString();

                if (_filename == null || _filename.Length == 0)
                {
                    ComponentMetaData.FireError(0, "Acquire Connections", "Nothing
returned when grabbing the filename", "", 0, out pbCancel);
                    throw new Exception("Nothing returned when grabbing the filename");
                }
            }
        }
    }
}
```

There is a lot of ground covered in the AcquireConnections method. A lot of this code is covered again in the Validate method, which you will visit now. The Validate method is also concerned that the input to the component is correct, and if it isn't, you'll try to fix what is wrong by calling ReinitializeMetaData. Here is the Validate method:

```
[CLSCompliant(false)]
public override DTSValidationStatus Validate()
{
    bool pbCancel = false;

    if (ComponentMetaData.OutputCollection.Count != 0)
    {
        ComponentMetaData.FireError(0, ComponentMetaData.Name, "Unexpected Output
found. Destination components do not support outputs.", "", 0, out pbCancel);
        return DTSValidationStatus.VS_ISCORRUPT;
    }

    if (ComponentMetaData.RuntimeConnectionCollection["File To
Write"].ConnectionManager == null)
    {
        ComponentMetaData.FireError(0, "Validate", "No Connection Manager returned",
"", 0, out pbCancel);
        return DTSValidationStatus.VS_ISCORRUPT;
    }

    if (ComponentMetaData.AreInputColumnsValid == false)
    {
        ComponentMetaData.InputCollection["Component
Input"].InputColumnCollection.RemoveAll();
        return DTSValidationStatus.VS_NEEDSNEWMETADATA;
    }

    return base.Validate();
}
```

The first check you do in the method is to make sure that the component has no outputs:

```
bool pbCancel = false;

if (ComponentMetaData.OutputCollection.Count != 0)
{
    ComponentMetaData.FireError(0, ComponentMetaData.Name, "Unexpected Output found.
Destination components do not support outputs.", "", 0, out pbCancel);
    return DTSValidationStatus.VS_ISCORRUPT;
}
```

You now want to check to make sure the user specified a Connection Manager. Remember that you are only validating the fact that a Connection Manager is specified, not whether it is a valid type. The extensive checking of the Connection Manager is done in AcquireConnections().

```
if (ComponentMetaData.RuntimeConnectionCollection["File To
Write"].ConnectionManager == null)
{
    ComponentMetaData.FireError(0, "Validate", "No Connection Manager returned", "",
0, out pbCancel);
    return DTSValidationStatus.VS_ISCORRUPT;
}
```

The final thing you do in this method is to check that the input columns are valid. *Valid* in this instance means that the columns in the input collection reference existing columns in the upstream component. If this is not the case, you call the trusty `ReinitializeMetadata` method.

```
if (ComponentMetaData.AreInputColumnsValid == false)
{
    ComponentMetaData.InputCollection["Component
Input"].InputColumnCollection.RemoveAll();
    return DTSValidationStatus.VS_NEEDSNEWMETADATA;
}
```

The return value `DTSValidationStatus.VS_NEEDSNEWMETADATA` means that the component will now call `ReinitializeMetaData` to try to sort out the problems with the component. Here is that method in full.

```
public override void ReinitializeMetaData()
{
    IDTSInput90 _profinput = ComponentMetaData.InputCollection["Component Input"];
    _profinput.InputColumnCollection.RemoveAll();
    IDTSVirtualInput90 vInput = _profinput.GetVirtualInput();
    foreach (IDTSVirtualInputColumn90 vCol in vInput.VirtualInputColumnCollection)
    {
        this.SetUsageType(_profinput.ID, vInput, vCol.LineageID,
DTSUsageType.UT_READONLY);

    }
}
```

You will notice that the columns are blown away in ReinitializemetaData and built again from scratch. A better solution is to test what the invalid columns are and try to fix them. If you cannot fix them, you could remove them and then the user could reselect at leisure. Books Online has an example of doing this.

The `IDTSVirtualInput` and `IDTSVirtualInputColumnCollection` in this component need a little explanation. There is a subtle difference between these two objects and their input equivalents. The "virtual" objects are what your component could have as inputs—that is to say, they are upstream inputs and columns that present themselves as available to your component. The inputs themselves are what you have chosen for your component to have as inputs from the virtual object. In the `Reinitialize` method, you start by removing all existing input columns.

```
IDTSInput90 _profinput = ComponentMetaData.InputCollection["Component Input"];
_profinput.InputColumnCollection.RemoveAll();
```

You then get a reference to the input's virtual input.

```
IDTSVirtualInput90 vInput = _profinput.GetVirtualInput();
```

Now that you have the virtual input, you can add an input column to the component for every virtual input column you find.

```
foreach (IDTSVirtualInputColumn90 vCol in vInput.VirtualInputColumnCollection)
{
    this.SetUsageType(_profinput.ID, vInput, vCol.LineageID,
DTSUsageType.UT_READONLY);
}
```

The `SetUsageType` method simply adds an input column to the input column collection of the component or removes it depending on what your UsageType value is. When a user adds a connector from an upstream component that contains its output to this component and attaches it to this component's input, then the `OnInputAttached` is called. This method has been overridden in the component herein:

```
public override void OnInputPathAttached(int inputID)
{
    IDTSInput90 input = ComponentMetaData.InputCollection.GetObjectByID(inputID);
    IDTSVirtualInput90 vInput = input.GetVirtualInput();
    foreach (IDTSVirtualInputColumn90 vCol in vInput.VirtualInputColumnCollection)
    {
        this.SetUsageType(inputID, vInput, vCol.LineageID, DTSUsageType.UT_READONLY);
    }
}
```

This method is the same as the `ReinitializeMetaData` method except that you do not need to remove the input columns from the collection. This is because if the input is not mapped to the output of an upstream component, there can be no input columns.

You have now finished with the design-time methods for your component and can now move on to look at the runtime methods. You are going to be looking at only two methods: `PreExecute` and `ProcessInput`.

PreExecute is executed once and once only in this component, so you want to do as much preparation work as you can in this method. It is also the first opportunity in the component to access the Buffer Manager, which contains the columns. In this component, you use it for two things: getting the information about the component's input columns and storing essential details about them.

```
public override void PreExecute()
{
    IDTSInput90 input = ComponentMetaData.InputCollection["Component Input"];

    foreach (IDTSInputColumn90 inCol in input.InputColumnCollection)
    {
        ColumnInfo ci = new ColumnInfo();
        ci.BufferColumnIndex = BufferManager.FindColumnByLineageID(input.Buffer,
inCol.LineageID);
        ci.ColumnName = inCol.Name;
        _columnInfos.Add(ci);
    }

    // Open the file
    _fs = new FileStream(_filename, FileMode.Open, FileAccess.Write);
    _sw = new StreamWriter(_fs);
}
```

First, you get a reference to the component's input.

```
IDTSInput90 input = ComponentMetaData.InputCollection["Component Input"];
```

You now loop through the input's `InputColumnCollection`

```
foreach (IDTSInputColumn90 inCol in input.InputColumnCollection)
{
```

459

For each input column you find, you need to create a new instance of the `ColumnInfo` struct. You then assign to the struct values you can retrieve from the input column itself as well as the Buffer Manager. You assign these values to the struct and finally add them to the array that is holding all the `ColumnInfo` objects.

```
ColumnInfo ci = new ColumnInfo();
ci.BufferColumnIndex = BufferManager.FindColumnByLineageID(input.Buffer,
inCol.LineageID);
ci.ColumnName = inCol.Name;
_columnInfos.Add(ci);
```

Doing things this way will allow you to move more quickly through the `ProcessInput` method. The last thing you do in the `PreExecute` method is to get a reference to the file you want to write to.

```
_fs = new FileStream(_filename, FileMode.Open, FileAccess.Write);
_sw = new StreamWriter(_fs);
```

You will use this in the next method, `ProcessInput`. `ProcessInput` is where you are going to keep reading the rows that are coming from the upstream component. While there are rows, you will write those values to a file. This is a very simplistic view of what needs to be done, so you should have a look at how to make that happen.

```
public override void ProcessInput(int inputID, PipelineBuffer buffer)
{

    if (!buffer.EndOfRowset)
    {
        while (buffer.NextRow())
        {
            _sw.WriteLine("<START>");
            for (int i = 0; i < _columnInfos.Count; i++)
            {
                ColumnInfo ci = (ColumnInfo)_columnInfos[i];
                object o = buffer[ci.BufferColumnIndex];

                if (o == null)
                {
                    _sw.WriteLine(ci.ColumnName + ":");
                }
                else
                {
                _sw.WriteLine(ci.ColumnName + ":" +
                    buffer[ci.BufferColumnIndex].ToString());
                }
            }
            _sw.WriteLine("<END>");
        }
    }

    _sw.Close();
}
```

The first thing you do is check that the upstream component has not called `SetEndOfRowset`. You then check that there are still rows in the buffer.

```
if (!buffer.EndOfRowset)
{
   while (buffer.NextRow())
   {
...
```

You now need to loop through the array that is holding the collection of `ColumnInfo` objects that were populated in the `preExecute` method.

```
for (int i = 0; i < _columnInfos.Count; i++)
```

For each iteration, you create a new instance of the `ColumnInfo` object:

```
ColumnInfo ci = (ColumnInfo)_columnInfos[i];
```

You now need to retrieve from the buffer object the value of the column whose index you will pass in from the `ColumnInfo` object.

```
object o = buffer[ci.BufferColumnIndex];
```

If the value is not null, you write the value of the column and the column name to the text file. If the value is null, you write just the column name to the text file. Again, because you took the time to store these details in a `ColumnInfo` object earlier, the retrieval of these properties is easy.

```
if (o == null)
{
   _sw.WriteLine(ci.ColumnName + ":");
}
else
{
   _sw.WriteLine(ci.ColumnName + ":" + buffer[ci.BufferColumnIndex].ToString());
}
```

That concludes your look at the destination adapter. You are now going to look at how you get SSIS to recognize your components and what properties you need to assign to your components.

Debugging Components

Debugging components is a really great feature of SSIS. If you are a Visual Studio .NET developer, you should easily recognize the interface. If you're not familiar with Visual Studio, hopefully this section will allow you to become proficient in debugging your components.

There are two phases for debugging. The design-time can be debugged only while you're developing your package, so it makes sense that you will need to use BIDS to do this. The second experience, which is the runtime experience, is slightly different. You can still use BIDS, though, and when your package runs, the component will stop at breakpoints you designate. You need to set up a few things first, though. You can also use DTExec to fire the package straight from Visual Studio. The latter method saves you the cost of invoking another instance of Visual Studio.

The component you are going to debug is the Reverse String transform.

Design-Time

You will now jump straight in and start to debug the component at design-time. Open the component's design project and set a breakpoint at ProvideComponentProperties (breakpoints are discussed in Chapter 13). Now create a new SSIS project in BIDS. In the package, add a Data Flow task and double-click on it. If your component is not in the Toolbox already, add it now.

> To add a component to the Toolbox, right-click on the Toolbox and select Choose Items from the context menu. When the Choose Toolbox Items dialog box appears, click the SSIS Data Flow Items tab and scroll down until you see the component. Check your new component and click OK. When you go back to the Toolbox, you should see your new component.

You need to create a full pipeline in this package because you'll be using it later on when you debug the runtime, so get a Connection Manager and point it to the AdventureWorks database. Now add a source adapter to the design surface and configure it to use the Connection Manager you just created. It's now time to add your component to the designer. However, before you do that, you need to tell the component's design project to attach to the devenv.exe process you're working in so that it can receive the component's methods being fired. The way you do that is as follows. In the design project, select Tools ➪ Attach to Process. The Attach to Process dialog box opens (see Figure 14-7), which allows you to choose what you want to debug as well as which process.

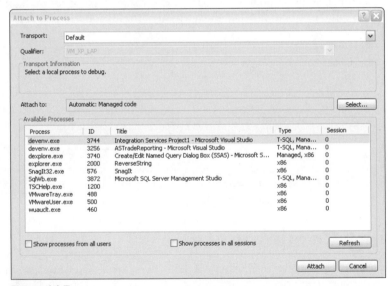

Figure 14-7

The process you're interested in is the package you're currently building. This shows up in the Available Processes list as Integration Services Project 1 – Microsoft Visual Studio (the name you see may differ). You can see just above this window a small box containing the words "Managed Code." This tells the debugger what you want to debug in the component. There are a number of options available, and if you click the Select button to the right of the label, you'll be able to see them. They are Managed, Native, and Script.

Highlight the process for your package and click Attach. If you look down now at the status bar in your component's design project, you should see a variety of debug symbols being loaded. Go back to the SSIS package and drop the ReverseString transform onto the design surface. Because one of the very first things a component does when it gets dropped into a package is call `ProvideComponentProperties`, you should immediately see your component break into the code in its design project, as shown in Figure 14-8.

```
ColumnInfo Structure

Ctor

#region Design Time

#region ProvideComponentProperties
public override void ProvideComponentProperties()
{
    // Perform component setup operations

    ComponentMetaData.UsesDispositions = true;

    // Add Input
    IDTSInput90 input = ComponentMetaData.InputCollection.New();
    input.Name = "ReverseStringInput";
    input.ErrorRowDisposition = DTSRowDisposition.RD_FailComponent;

    // Add Output
    IDTSOutput90 output = ComponentMetaData.OutputCollection.New();
    output.Name = "ReverseStringOutput";
```

Figure 14-8

As you can see, the breakpoint on ProvideComponentProperties in the component's design project has been hit. This is indicated by a yellow arrow inside the breakpoint red circle. You are now free to debug the component as you would with any other piece of managed code in Visual Studio.NET. If you're familiar with debugging, a number of windows appear at this point at the bottom of the IDE, things like "Locals," "Autos," and "Call Stack." These can help you get to the root of your problem, but you do not use them here. Don't be afraid of them.

Runtime

As promised, in this section you are going to look at two ways of debugging. As with design-time debugging, the first is through the BIDS designer. The other is by using DTExec and the package properties. Using BIDS is similar to the design-time method with a subtle variation.

You should now have a complete pipeline with the ReverseString transform in the middle. If you don't, quickly make up a pipeline like in Figure 14-9.

Figure 14-9

The Trash Destination you see terminating this pipeline is a simple destination adapter that requires no setup at all. Just drop it onto the design-sheet and go. It is used as a development aid, when you wish to test a partially completed workflow and you need a destination to quickly terminate the flow. The component is freely available for download from www.konesans.com or www.sqlis.com.

You then need to add a breakpoint to the Data Flow task that is hit when the Data Flow task hits the OnPreExecute event. You need to do this so that you can attach your debugger to the correct process at runtime. Right-click on the task itself and select Edit Breakpoints. The Set Breakpoints dialog box will appear, as shown in Figure 14-10.

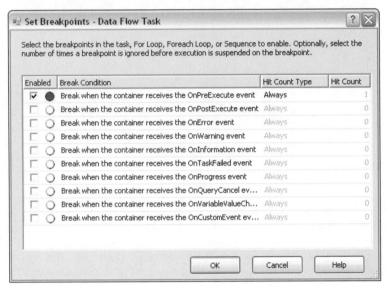

Figure 14-10

You are now ready to execute your package. Hit F5 and allow the breakpoint in the Data Flow task to be hit. When you hit the breakpoint, switch back to the component's design process and follow the steps detailed earlier when debugging the design-time in order to get to the screen where you chose what process to debug.

When you execute a package in the designer, it is not really the designer that is doing the work. It hands off the execution to a process called DtsDebugHost.exe. This is the package that you want to attach to, as shown in Figure 14-11.

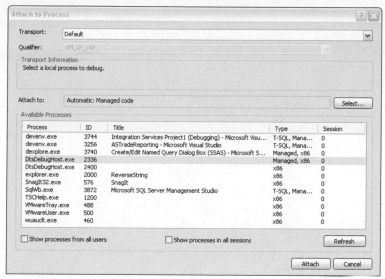

Figure 14-11

Click Attach and watch the debug symbols being loaded by the project. Before returning to the SSIS package, you need to set a breakpoint on one of the runtime methods used by your component, such as PreExecute. Now return to the SSIS project and press F5 again. This will release the package from its suspended state and allow the package to flow on. Now when the ReverseString component hits its `PreExecute` method, you should be able to debug what it is doing. In Figure 14-12, the user is checking to make sure that the LineageID of a column is being retrieved correctly and is ready to be used in the ProcessInput method that follows.

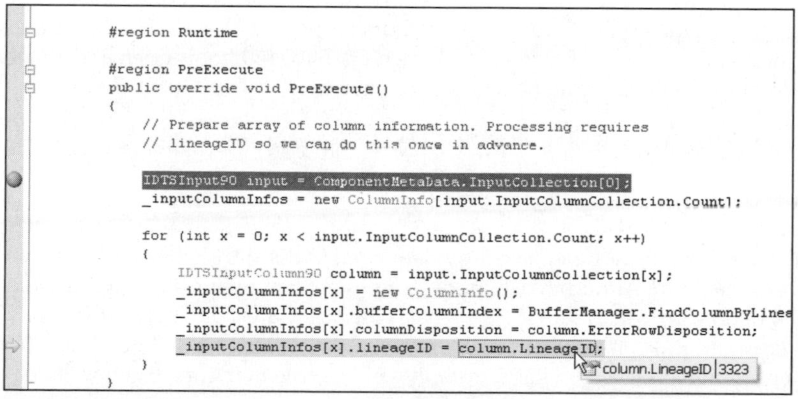

```
#region Runtime

#region PreExecute
public override void PreExecute()
{
    // Prepare array of column information. Processing requires
    // lineageID so we can do this once in advance.

    IDTSInput90 input = ComponentMetaData.InputCollection[0];
    _inputColumnInfos = new ColumnInfo[input.InputColumnCollection.Count];

    for (int x = 0; x < input.InputColumnCollection.Count; x++)
    {
        IDTSInputColumn90 column = input.InputColumnCollection[x];
        _inputColumnInfos[x] = new ColumnInfo();
        _inputColumnInfos[x].bufferColumnIndex = BufferManager.FindColumnByLine
        _inputColumnInfos[x].columnDisposition = column.ErrorRowDisposition;
        _inputColumnInfos[x].lineageID = column.LineageID;
    }
                                        column.LineageID  3323
}
```

Figure 14-12

465

That concludes your look at the first method for debugging the runtime. The second method involves BIDS indirectly because you need to create a package like this one that you can call later. After that, you do not need BIDS at all. You do, however, still need the component's design project open. Open your project's properties and look at the Debug tab on the left, which should look similar to Figure 14-13.

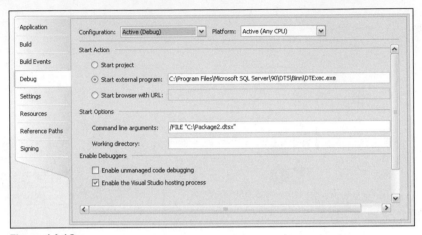

Figure 14-13

As you can see, you have said that you want to start an external program to debug. That program is DTExec, which is the new and more powerful version of DTSRun. On the command line, you will pass a parameter /FILE to DTExec. This tells DTExec the name and location of the package you just built. Make sure you still have a breakpoint set on PreExecute, and hit F5in your project. A DOS window will appear and you will see some messages fly past, which are the same messages you would see in the designer. Eventually you will get to your breakpoint, and it will break in exactly the same way as it did when you were using BIDS. So, why might you use one over the other? The most obvious answer is speed. It is much faster to get to where you want to debug your component using DTExec than it is doing the same in BIDS. The other advantage is that you do not need to have two tools open at the same time. You can focus on your component's design project and not have to worry about BIDS at all.

Summary

In this chapter, you have built pipeline components, but at the start, other types of components that you can build were alluded to. Although designing your own components isn't exactly like falling off a log, once you get a handle on what methods do what, when they are called, and what you can possibly use them for, you can certainly create them with only a moderate amount of knowledge in programming. The components you have designed are certainly very simple in nature, but hopefully this chapter will give you the confidence to experiment with some of your own unique requirements.

15

Adding a User Interface to Your Component

Now that you've learned how to extend the pipeline with your own custom components, the next step is to improve the user experience and efficiency, by adding a user interface. This will be demonstrated using the ReverseString example from the previous chapter.

Pipeline components do not require the developer to provide a user interface, and although this saves time and resources, the overall user experience can be poor. It can increase the package development time and requires the user to have an intimate knowledge of the component to be able to correctly set the required columns and properties. The more complex the configuration required, the more acute the lack of suitable prompts and real-time validation becomes, making configuration tedious and error-prone. For simple components, however, the built-in Advanced Editor, as used by several stock components, is perfectly acceptable. If you want to add that extra style and guidance for the end user, though, this is your chapter.

You will learn how to add a user interface to a component and look in detail at each of the stages. You will then be able to apply these techniques to your own components. It is worth noting that this chapter deals exclusively with managed components.

Three Key Steps

There are three steps in adding a user interface (UI) to any component, and each will be examined in detail below; first, here's a summary of each.

The first step is to add a class that implements the `IDtsComponentUI` interface. This defines the methods needed for the designer to interact with your user interface class. This class is not the visible UI itself; rather it provides a way for the designer to ask for what it needs when it needs it, as well as exposing several methods that allow you to hook into the life cycle of your UI. For example, you have a New method, which is called when a component is first added to a package, and an Edit method, called when you open an existing component inside your package. The interface will be expanded on in the following paragraphs.

The second step is to actually build the visible interface, normally a Windows Form. The form is invoked from the IDtsComponentUI.Edit method, and by customizing the constructor, you can pass through references to the base component and supporting services. The form then displays details such as component properties or data-handling options including inputs, outputs, and columns within each.

The final stage is to update the component itself to tell the designer that you have provided a user interface and where to find it, or specifically where to find the IDtsComponentUI implementation. You do this through the UITypeName property of the DtsPipelineComponent attribute, which decorates the component, your existing PipelineComponent inheriting class. The UITypeName is the fully qualified name of the class implementing your user interface, allowing the designer to find the assembly and class to invoke the user interface when required through the interface methods mentioned above.

In summary, you need a known interface with which the designer can interact and a form that you display to the user through the relevant interface method, and the component needs to advertise that it has a user interface and offer instructions of where to find the UI when required.

Building the User Interface

Now that the key stages have been explained, you can examine each of them in detail. This guidance makes very few assumptions, explaining all the actions required; so as long as you can open Visual Studio on your own, you should be able to follow these steps, and perhaps more importantly understand why.

Adding the Project

If you followed the example in the previous chapter, you currently have an existing solution in Visual Studio 2005 that contains the pipeline component project (ReverseString). Therefore, your first step is to add a new Class Library project to host the UI, as shown in Figure 15-1. Although the UI can be implemented within the pipeline component project, for performance reasons this is not the recommended approach. Because SSIS has distinct runtime versus design-time elements, the combination of the two functions leads to a larger assembly, which requires more memory and consequently lower runtime performance. The separate design practice also allows for easier code development and maintenance, reducing confusion and conflicts within the areas of code.

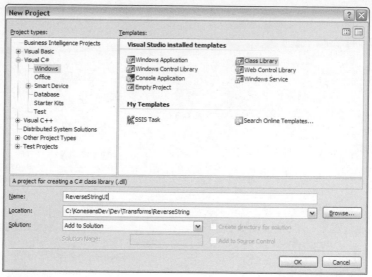

Figure 15-1

Starting with the empty project, the first task is to configure any project properties, so you need to set the Assembly name and Default namespace to be consistent with your development practices, as shown in Figure 15-2.

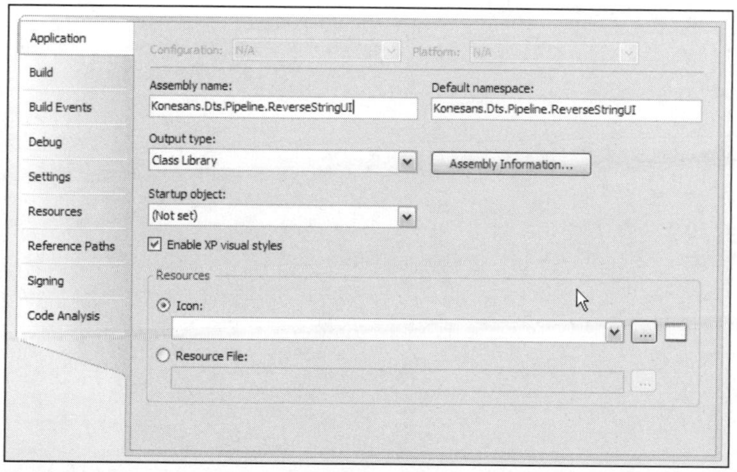

Figure 15-2

The user interface assembly does not need to be placed in a defined location like tasks and components (%Program Files%\Microsoft SQL Server\90\DTS\PipelineComponents or %Program Files%\ Microsoft SQL Server\90\DTS\Tasks), but it does need to be installed within the global assembly cache (GAC). So within the project properties, you can leave the build output path location as the default value, but for ease of development you can add a post-build event command on the Build Events page, as shown in Figure 15-3.

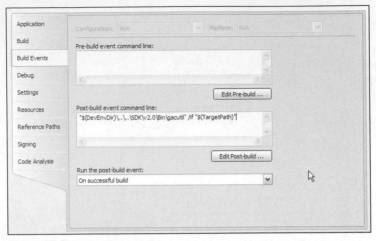

Figure 15-3

Because the assembly will be installed in the GAC, you will need to sign the assembly using a strong name key, which can be configured from the Signing page, as shown in Figure 15-4. For more information about strong names and their importance in .Net, see "Security Briefs: Strong Names and Security in the .NET Framework" (http://msdn.microsoft.com/library/default.asp?url=/library/en-us/dnnetsec/html/strongNames.asp).

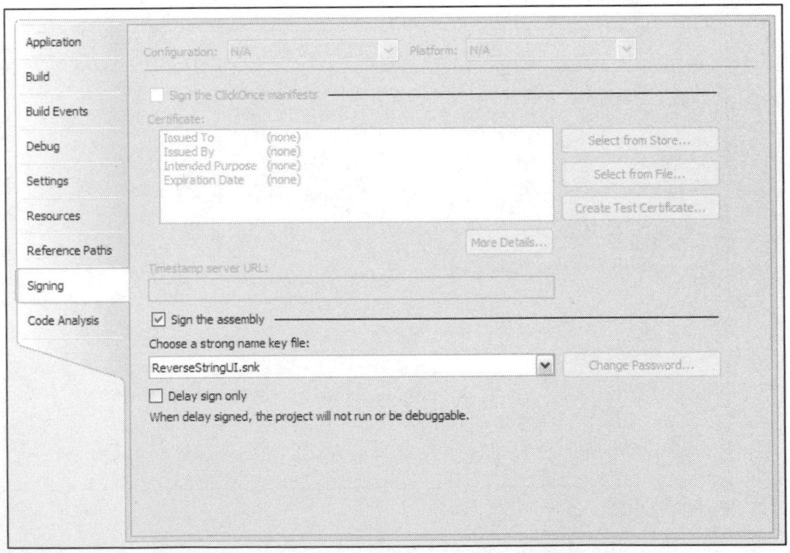

Figure 15-4

Although most assembly attributes can now be set through the Assembly Information dialog box accessed from the Application page of Project Properties, you still next need to manually edit AssemblyInfo.cs, adding the CLSCompliant attribute, as described in Chapter 14 and as shown here:

```
#region Using directives
using System;
using System.Security.Permissions;
using System.Reflection;
using System.Runtime.CompilerServices;
using System.Runtime.InteropServices;
#endregion

[assembly: AssemblyTitle("ReverseStringUI")]
[assembly: AssemblyDescription("Reversing String Transformation UI for SQL Server
Integration Services")]
[assembly: AssemblyConfiguration("")]
[assembly: AssemblyCompany("Konesans Ltd")]
[assembly: AssemblyProduct("Reverse String Transformation")]
[assembly: AssemblyCopyright("Copyright (c) 2005 Konesans Ltd")]
[assembly: AssemblyTrademark("")]
[assembly: AssemblyCulture("")]

[assembly: AssemblyVersion("1.1.0.0")]
[assembly: AssemblyFileVersion("1.1.0")]
[assembly: CLSCompliant(true)]
[assembly: PermissionSet(SecurityAction.RequestMinimum)]
[assembly: ComVisible(false)]
```

The AssemblyVersion *will form part of the* UITypeName *property described below; therefore it is important that this is not allowed to auto-increment using the * token, as this will break the linkage between the component and its user interface.*

You also require a Windows Form to actually display your component's interface to the user in addition to the default class you have in your project, so one can be added at this stage.

The final preparatory task is to add some additional references to your project. The recommended three are listed here:

❏ Microsoft.SqlServer.Dts.Design

❏ Microsoft.SqlServer.DTSPipelineWrap

❏ Microsoft.SQLServer.ManagedDTS

Implementing IDtsComponentUI

You now have the empty framework for the UI assembly, and you can start coding. The first step is to implement the Microsoft.SqlServer.Dts.Pipeline.Design IDtsComponentUI interface. Using the default class in the project, you can add the interface declaration and take advantage of the new context menu features, as well as use the Implement Interface command to quickly generate the five method stubs, saving you from manually typing them out.

The methods are documented in detail in the following list; however, it is useful to understand the scenarios in which each method is called, highlighting how the Initialize method is usually called before the real action method:

Chapter 15

- ❑ Adding a new component to the package:
    - ❑ `Initialize`
    - ❑ `New`

- ❑ Edit the component, through a double-click or by selecting Edit from the context menu:
    - ❑ `Initialize`
    - ❑ `Edit`

- ❑ Delete the component, through the Delete key or by selecting Delete from the context menu:
    - ❑ `Delete`

You will now look at the methods in more detail and examine how they are implemented in the example.

IDtsComponentUI.Delete

The `Delete` method is called when a component is deleted from the SSIS designer. It allows you to perform any cleaning operations that may be required or warn users of the consequences. This is not normally required, because the consequences should be fairly obvious, but the opportunity is available.

For this example, simply remove the placeholder exception, leaving an empty method.

IDtsComponentUI.Help

The `Help` method has not been implemented in SQL Server 2005. For this example, simply remove the placeholder exception. The method will not be called, but this should prevent any surprises in case of a service pack introducing the functionality, although this is unlikely.

IDtsComponentUI.New

The `New` method is called when a component is first added to your package through the SSIS designer. Use this to display a user interface specific to configuring the component for the first time, such as a wizard to help configure the component or an option dialog box that gathers some information that will influence the overall use of the component. The Script transformation uses this method to display a dialog box asking you to specify the type, source, destination, or transformation.

The `New` method is not widely used, because configuration of the component usually requires you to have wired up the data flow paths for the component. In addition, most people start by laying out the package and adding most or all of the components together, allowing them to visualize and validate their overall data flow design, before configuring each component in detail, but in specialized circumstances you have this option.

For this example, simply remove the placeholder exception, leaving an empty method.

IDtsComponentUI.Initialize

`Initialize` is the first method to be called when adding or editing a component, and although you do not actually perform any actions at this stage, the parameters provided are normally stored in private member variables for later use. At a minimum, you will store the `IDTSComponentMetaData90` reference, because a UI will always need to interact with the underlying component, and this is done through the IDTSComponentMetaData90 reference.

For components that use connections or variables, you would also store a reference to IServiceProvider. This allows you to access useful services like the connection service (IDtsConnectionService) and the variable service (IDtsVariableService). These designer services allow you to create new connections and variables, respectively. For connections, the service will invoke the Connection Manager user interface, provided by the connection author, and for variables you use the dialog box built into the SSIS designer. This is a good example of how Microsoft has made life easier for component developers, offering access to these services, saving you time and effort. There are two other services available, the IErrorCollectionService for retrieving error and warning event messages, and IDtsClipboardService, which allows component developers to determine if a component was created by a copy-and-paste operation.

In the Reverse String example, these services are not required, but you would follow the same pattern as you do with IDTSComponentMetaData90 here.

```
private IDTSComponentMetaData90 _dtsComponentMetaData;

[CLSCompliant(false)]
public void Initialize(IDTSComponentMetaData90 dtsComponentMetadata,
IServiceProvider serviceProvider)
{
// Store ComponentMetaData for later use
_dtsComponentMetaData = dtsComponentMetadata;
}
```

IDtsComponentUI.Edit

The Edit method is called by the designer when you edit the component, and this is the place where you actually display the visible window or form of the user interface component. The purpose of the Edit method is to display the form, passing through any references you need, stored in private variables during Initialize. The Edit method also has a Boolean return value that notifies the designer whether changes have been made.

This is perhaps one of the most useful features of the component UI pattern, as it allows you to make changes directly to the component, but they are persisted only if the return value is true. You get commit or rollback functionality for free, rather than having to write additional code to cache changes within the UI and only apply them when a user clicks the OK button. It also allows you to benefit from validation routines you have written into the component itself. For example, the ReverseString.SetUsageType method checks data types and the UsageType property for the column being selected, since this component supports only string types. Putting the validation into the component, rather than the UI, ensures that if a user bypasses your UI and uses the built-in Advanced Editor or the Visual Studio Properties instead, the same validation takes place.

Therefore, your UI should focus on the display side and leave as much validation as possible to the component. Inevitably, some validation will be implemented in the UI, but always bear in mind that you can use the existing component code in this way, saving time and simplifying maintenance through this reuse.

For ease of implementation, you can use the `DialogResult` functionality of the form to indicate the return value for the form. This is illustrated in the example implementation of `Edit`:

```
public bool Edit(IWin32Window parentWindow, Variables variables, Connections
connections)
{
    try
    {
        // Create UI form and display
        ReverseStringUIForm ui = new ReverseStringUIForm(_dtsComponentMetaData);
        DialogResult result = ui.ShowDialog(parentWindow);

        // Set return value to represent DialogResult. This tells the
    // managed wrapper to persist any changes made
        // on the component input and/or output, or properties.
        if (result == DialogResult.OK)
        {
            return true;
        }
    }
    catch (Exception ex)
    {
        MessageBox.Show(ex.ToString());
    }
    return false;
}
```

The `Edit` method also provides references to the `Variables` and `Connections` collections. You can use these collections to list the available variables and connections. The `Variables` collection is already limited to those in scope for the current Data Flow task.

If your component uses connections or variables, you would modify the form constructor to accept these, as well as the `System.IServiceProvider` reference you captured during `Initialize`. This allows you to offer the option of selecting an existing item or creating a new one as required. These are not required for the Reverse String component, but an example of an `Edit` method implementation using them is shown here:

```
public bool Edit(IWin32Window parentWindow, Variables variables, Connections
connections)
{
    try
{
        TraceSourceUIForm ui = new TraceSourceUIForm(_dtsComponentMetaData,
            variables, connections, _serviceProvider);
        DialogResult result = ui.ShowDialog(parentWindow);
        if (result == DialogResult.OK)
        {
            return true;
        }
    }
```

```
    catch (Exception ex)
    {
        Konesans.Dts.Design.ExceptionDialog.Show(ex);
    }
    return false;
}
```

Setting the UITypeName

This section deals with changes to the Reverse String component itself, rather than the user interface project. This is listed as the last of the three key steps for providing a user interface, but it is generally done fairly early on, because once it's complete, you can actually test your UI in the designer itself.

You need to tell the designer that your component has a user interface, in effect overriding the Advanced Editor dialog box provided by default. To do this, set the UITypeName property of the DtsPipelineComponentAttribute, which already decorates the component class in the transformation project. The required format of the property value is as follows:

```
<Full Class Name>,
<Assembly Name>,
Version=<Version>,
Culture=Neutral,
PublicKeyToken=<Public Key Token>
```

You may recognize the format as being very similar to an assembly strong name, because apart from the additional <Full Class Name> at the beginning, it is the assembly strong name. Using the strong name, the designer can find and load the assembly, and then using the class name, it knows exactly where to go for its entry point, the IDTSComponentUI implementation.

Setting this property often causes people problems, but if you know where to look, it is quite easy.

```
...
namespace Konesans.Dts.Pipeline.ReverseStringUI
{
    public class ReverseStringUI : IDtsComponentUI
    {
...
```

This code snippet from the main UI class file shows the namespace and the class name, so the first token on the UITypeName is Konesans.Dts.Pipeline.ReverseStringUI.ReverseStringUI.

The remainder is just the strong name of the assembly. The simplest way to obtain this is to compile the project, and if you set the post-build events as described above, your assembly will have been installed in the GAC. Open the assembly viewer (C:\WINDOWS\assembly) and locate your assembly. The tooltip for an assembly will show the string name, as shown in Figure 15-5.

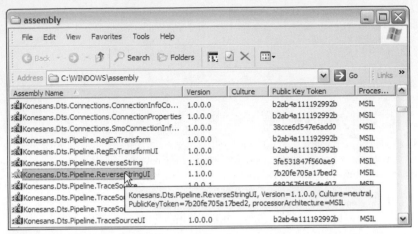

Figure 15-5

The individual tokens are shown again in the Properties dialog box, and there you can highlight the text for copy-and-paste operations to save typing mistakes, particularly with the public key token.

If you make a mistake in setting this property, you will get an error such as this one when you to use the component UI.

```
Could not load file or assembly 'Konesans.Dts.Pipeline.TrashDestination,
Version=1.0.1.0, Culture=neutral, PublicKeyToken=b8351fe7752642cc' or one of its
dependencies. The system cannot find the file specified. (mscorlib)
```

The completed attribute for the ReverseString component, referencing the ReverseStringUI assembly, is illustrated as follows:

```
[DtsPipelineComponent(
    DisplayName = "ReverseString",
    ComponentType = ComponentType.Transform,
    IconResource = "Konesans.Dts.Pipeline.ReverseString.ReverseString.ico",
    UITypeName = "Konesans.Dts.Pipeline.ReverseStringUI.ReverseStringUI,
    Konesans.Dts.Pipeline.ReverseStringUI, Version=1.1.0.0, Culture=neutral,
PublicKeyToken=7b20fe705a17bed2")]
public class ReverseString : PipelineComponent
...
```

Building the Form

The final stage of the development is to build the form itself, allowing it to capture the user input and apply the selections to the component. You are about to start building the form, but before you do, review the following summary of the progress so far.

You have implemented IDTSComponentUI, providing the methods required by the designer to support a custom user interface. The IDTSComponentUI.Edit method is used to display the form, passing through a reference to the base component (IDTSComponentMetaData90). This was gained initially through the IDTSComponentUI.Initialize method and stored in a private class-level variable.

Finally, you have updated the component itself to include the UITypeName property for the DtsPipelineComponentAttriute. This allows the designer to detect and then find your user interface class, thereby calling the IDTSComponentUI methods you have now implemented, leading to the display of the form.

The sample form for the user interface is shown in Figure 15-6.

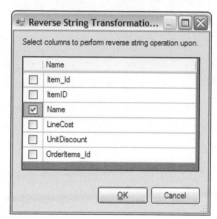

Figure 15-6

Form Constructor

As previously mentioned, the default form constructor is modified to accept the references you will need, such as the component and support objects, variables, and connections. For this example, you just have the component, IDTSComponentMetaData90. You should store these constructor parameters in private member variables for later use elsewhere in the form, as well as using them directly in the constructor itself.

The commit and rollback feature discussed above in the "IDtsComponentUI.Edit" section has one specific requirement. Any changes made must be done through a wrapper class, rather than applied directly to the IDTSComponentMetaData90 reference. This wrapper, the CManagedComponentWrapper design-time interface, is created within the constructor and stored in a private member variable for later use.

Changes can be made directly to IDTSComponentMetaData90, but they will be permanent, so even if you return false from IDtsComponentUI.Edit, the changes will persist. Users like recognizable and intuitive user interfaces, and the ability to recover from a mistake with the Cancel button is one of those design patterns that all users have been grateful for on numerous occasions. Writing code to implement this yourself would be a considerable amount of work, so make sure you issue changes only through the design-time interface.

The complete form constructor is shown as follows, including the call to the
`SetInputVirtualInputColumns` method, covered later in the chapter:

```
private IDTSComponentMetaData90 _dtsComponentMetaData;
private CManagedComponentWrapper _designTimeComponent;
private IDTSInput90 _input;

public ReverseStringUIForm(IDTSComponentMetaData90 dtsComponentMetaData)
{
    InitializeComponent();

    // Store constructor parameters for later
    _dtsComponentMetaData = dtsComponentMetaData;

    // Get design-time interface for changes and validation
    _designTimeComponent = _dtsComponentMetaData.Instantiate();

    // Get Input
    _input = _dtsComponentMetaData.InputCollection[0];

    // Set any form controls that host component properties or connections here
    // None required for ReverseString component

    // Populate DataGridView with columns
    SetInputVirtualInputColumns();

}
```

Column Display

Once all of the constructor parameters have been stored and the initial preparation is complete, you can
begin to interrogate the component and other objects that may have been supplied on the constructor to
populate the form controls.

The Reverse String transformation will operate on any column the user selects, so the user interface will
simply consist of a way to allow columns to be selected. For this example, you should use a
DataGridView control. Using the control designer, you'll preconfigure two columns, a checkbox column
for the selection state (`DataGridViewCheckBoxColumn`) and a text column for the column name
(`DataGridViewTextBoxColumn`). The individual form controls will not be covered in detail; rather the
focus will be on their use and interaction with the component, as the choice of control is entirely up to
you as the user interface developer. To see exactly how the controls have been configured, review the
completed project available at www.wrox.com.

Because you allow users to select columns, the initial requirement is to enumerate the columns and
determine their current selection state. To find out how to do this, you need to understand the architecture of a component in relation to data movement. For a simple synchronous transformation such as this
one, you have a single input. The input has a collection of input columns, which at runtime hold the data
provided in the pipeline buffer, so the transformation itself operates on these columns.

For more detail on pipeline architecture, see Chapter 10.

In the Reverse String component, the presence of an input column means that the user wants the operation to be performed on that column. By default, the input will contain no columns, because no columns have been selected for transformation. To select a column, you set the column usage type to something other than DTSUsageType.UT_IGNORED. For this component, because you do an in-place transformation on the column value, you require both read and write access as indicated by DTSUsageType.UT_READWRITE. This allows you to read the column value and reverse it before writing it back into the buffer.

It is important that you select only columns that are required for any transformation and minimize excess columns through all stages of the pipeline for performance reasons. The designer will display a warning like this when it detects unused columns:

```
[DTS.Pipeline] Warning: The output column "ProductPrice" (36) on output "OLE DB
Source Output" (10) and component "Products" (1) is not subsequently used in the
Data Flow task. Removing this unused output column can increase Data Flow task
performance.
```

Because the input column collection is empty by default, you actually work on the virtual input column collection instead. The virtual input represents all the upstream columns available to the transformation, allowing you to enumerate columns, as well as interrogating the virtual input column's UsageType property.

Calling GetVirtualInput to get the collection of virtual columns is a potentially expensive operation, depending on the number of upstream columns. You should therefore cache the result for later use in other methods. You should also be aware that since a virtual input is very much a snapshot of current state, it can become invalid. Simple changes to the current component do not affect the virtual columns, but deeper changes like ReinitializeMetaData can invalidate it. You should therefore plan the lifetime of the cached reference and periodically refresh it after major changes.

The use of the virtual input and the column usage type is the basis for the SetInputVirtualInputColumns helper method included in the form. This populates the DataGridView with a list of columns and their current selection state. This method is the final call in the form constructor and completes the initialization of the form.

```
private void SetInputVirtualInputColumns()
{

    _virtualInput = _input.GetVirtualInput();

    IDTSVirtualInputColumnCollection90 virtualInputColumnCollection =
        _virtualInput.VirtualInputColumnCollection;

    IDTSInputColumnCollection90 inputColumns = _input.InputColumnCollection;

    int columnCount = virtualInputColumnCollection.Count;
    for (int i = 0; i < columnCount; i++)
    {
        IDTSVirtualInputColumn90 virtualColumn = virtualInputColumnCollection[i];
        int row;

        if (virtualColumn.UsageType == DTSUsageType.UT_READONLY ||
            virtualColumn.UsageType == DTSUsageType.UT_READWRITE)
```

```
            {
               row = this.dgColumns.Rows.Add(    new object[]
                  { CheckState.Checked, " " + virtualColumn.Name });
            }
            else
            {
               row = this.dgColumns.Rows.Add(new object[]
                  { CheckState.Unchecked, " " + virtualColumn.Name });
            }

            this.dgColumns.Rows[rowIndex].Tag = i;

            DataGridViewCheckBoxCell cell =
                 (DataGridViewCheckBoxCell)dgColumns.Rows[row].Cells[0];
            cell.ThreeState = false;
         }
      }
```

The pipeline engine is implemented in native code for performance, so calls to pipeline objects normally use a wrapper class and incur the overhead of COM Interop. You should therefore minimize such calls through efficient coding practices. In the preceding example, the count from the virtual input column collection is retrieved only once, as opposed to being interrogated within the for loop test itself.

Column Selection

The next stage of the user interface is to react to user input and reflect any changes back to the component. In this example, the only choice offered is the selection of columns, made through the DataGridView, as captured through the CellContentClick event. You use this event rather than one of the others available such as CellValueChanged, as this is raised immediately and you can give timely feedback to the user.

Through the DataGridViewCellEventArgs, you can obtain the row and column indices for the cell. This is first used to validate that the row exists and that the column is the first column, because this column contains the checkboxes used for managing selection. You then use the virtual input again and set the usage type as indicated by the checkbox or cell value.

Since the example component includes validation within the overridden SetUsageType method, you need to ensure that you catch any exceptions thrown and can react and feedback to the component user as shown here:

```
private void dgColumns_CellContentClick(object sender, DataGridViewCellEventArgs e)
{
   if (e.ColumnIndex == 0 && e.RowIndex >= 0)
   {
      // Get current value and flip boolean to get new value
      bool newValue = !Convert.ToBoolean(dgColumns.CurrentCell.Value);

      // Get the virtual column to work with
      IDTSVirtualInputColumn90 virtualColumn =
         _virtualInput.VirtualInputColumnCollection[e.RowIndex];

      try
```

```
        {
            // Set the column UsageType to indicate the column is selected or not
            if (newValue)
                _designTimeComponent.SetUsageType(_input.ID, _virtualInput,
                    virtualColumn.LineageID, DTSUsageType.UT_READWRITE);
            else
                _designTimeComponent.SetUsageType(_input.ID, _virtualInput,
                    virtualColumn.LineageID, DTSUsageType.UT_IGNORED);
        }
        catch(Exception ex)
        {
            // Catch any error from base class SetUsageType here.
            // Display simple error message from exception
            MessageBox.Show(ex.Message, "Invalid Column", MessageBoxButtons.OK,
                MessageBoxIcon.Error);

            // Rollback UI selection
            dgColumns.CancelEdit();
        }
    }
}
```

To complete the description of the user interface example, there are two button controls on the form, named OK and Cancel, each with their respective `DialogResult` property values set. By using the dialog results in this way, you do not need any event handler bound to the click event and no additional code is required to close the form. The dialog result is then used within `IDTSComponentUI.Edit` to commit or roll back any changes made to the component wrapper, as shown previously.

This concludes the example, and if you have been building as you read, all that remains is to compile the project. If you configured the build events that were described at the beginning, the assemblies should be in the correct locations ready for use.

You will need to start a new instance of Visual Studio and open a SSIS project. Before you can use the component, it needs to be added to the Toolbox. To add a component to the Toolbox, right-click on the Toolbox and select Choose Items from the context menu. When the Choose Toolbox Items dialog appears, click the SSIS Data Flow Items tab and scroll down until you see the component. Check your new component and click OK. When you go back to the Toolbox, you should see your new component. Another method is to select Reset Toolbox from the context menu instead.

The completed example is available for download from www.wrox.com.

Further Development

The simple component that was used lacks some of the other features you may require. For example, components can use runtime connections or have properties. These would generally be represented through additional form controls, and their values would be interrogated and controls initialized in the form constructor. You will now look at these other methods in greater detail.

Runtime Connections

As previously discussed, components can use connections, and the `System.IServiceProvider` from `IDtsComponentUI.Initialize` and the `Connections` collection from `IDtsComponentUI.Edit` allow you to provide meaningful UI functions around them. Examples have been given of passing these as far as the form constructor, so now you will be shown what you then do with them. This example shows a modified constructor that accepts the additional connection-related parameters, performs some basic initialization, and stores them for later use. You would perform any column- or property-related work as shown in the previous examples, but for clarity none is included here. The final task is to initialize the connection-related control.

For this example, you will presume that the component accepts one connection, which would have been defined in the `ProvidedComponentProperties` method of the component. You will use a `ComboBox` control to offer the selection options, as well as the ability to create a new connection through the `IDtsConnectionService`. The component expects an ADO.Net SqlClient connection, so the list will be restricted to this, and the current connection, if any, will be preselected in the list. The preparatory work for this is all shown here:

```
private IDTSComponentMetaData90 _dtsComponentMetaData;
private CManagedComponentWrapper _designTimeComponent;
private IDtsConnectionService _dtsConnectionService;
private Microsoft.SqlServer.Dts.Runtime.Connections _connections;

// Constant to define the type of connection we support and wish to work with.
private const string Connection_Type =
"ADO.NET:System.Data.SqlClient.SqlConnection, System.Data, Version=2.0.0.0,
Culture=neutral, PublicKeyToken=b77a5c561934e089";

public ConnectionDemoUIForm(IDTSComponentMetaData90 dtsComponentMetaData,
IServiceProvider serviceProvider)
{
    InitializeComponent();

    // Store constructor parameters for later.
    _dtsComponentMetaData = dtsComponentMetaData;
    _connections = connections;

    // Get IDtsConnectionService and store.
    IDtsConnectionService dtsConnectionService =
serviceProvider.GetService(typeof(IDtsConnectionService)) as IDtsConnectionService;
    _dtsConnectionService = dtsConnectionService;

    // Get design-time interface for changes and validation.
    _designTimeComponent = _dtsComponentMetaData.Instantiate();

    // Perform any other actions, such as column population or
    // component property work.

    // Get Connections collection, and get name of currently selected connection.
    string connectionName = "";
    if (_dtsComponentMetaData.RuntimeConnectionCollection[0] != null)
    {
        IDTSRuntimeConnection90 runtimeConnection =
```

```
            _dtsComponentMetaData.RuntimeConnectionCollection[0];
        if (runtimeConnection != null
            && runtimeConnection.ConnectionManagerID.Length > 0
            && _connections.Contains(runtimeConnection.ConnectionManagerID))
        {
            connectionName = _connections[runtimeConnection.ConnectionManagerID].Name;
        }
    }

    // Populate connections combo.
    PopulateConnectionsCombo(this.cmbSqlConnections, Connection_Type,
        connectionName);
}
```

The final command in the constructor is to call your helper function, PopulateConnectionsCombo, to populate the combo box. The parameters for this are quite simple: the combo box to populate, the type of connection you wish to list, and the name of the currently selected connection. Using these three items, you can successfully populate the combo as shown here:

```
private void PopulateConnectionsCombo(ComboBox comboBox,
    string connectionType, string selectedItem)
{
    // Prepare combo box by clearing, and adding the new connection item.
    comboBox.Items.Clear();
    comboBox.Items.Add("<New connection...>");

    // Enumerate connections, but for type supported.
    foreach (ConnectionManager connectionManager in
        _dtsConnectionService.GetConnectionsOfType(connectionType))
    {
        comboBox.Items.Add(connectionManager.Name);
    }

    // Set currently selected connection
    comboBox.SelectedItem = selectedItem;
}
```

The ADO.Net connection is slightly different from most connections in that it has what can be thought of as subtypes. Because you need a specific subtype, the System.Data.SqlClient.SqlConnection, you need to use the full name of the connection, as opposed to the shorter creation name moniker, ADO.NET, which you may see elsewhere and which is the pattern used for other simpler types of Connection Managers.

Now that you have populated the combo box, you need to handle the selection of an existing connection or the creation of a new connection. When you author a Connection Manager yourself, you can provide a user interface by implementing the IDtsConnectionManagerUI, which is analogous to the way you have implemented IDtsComponentUI to provide a user interface for your component. The connection service will then display this user interface when you call the CreateConnection method.

The following example is the event handler for the connections combo box, which supports new connections and existing connections and ensures that the selection is passed down to the component:

```
private void cmbSqlConnections_SelectedValueChanged(object sender, EventArgs e)
{
    ComboBox comboxBox = (ComboBox)sender;

    // Check for index 0 and <New Item...>
    if (comboxBox.SelectedIndex == 0)
    {
        // Use connection service to create a new connection.
        ArrayList newConns = _dtsConnectionService.CreateConnection(Connection_Type);
        if (newConns.Count > 0)
        {
            // A new connection has been created, so populate and select
            ConnectionManager newConn = (ConnectionManager)newConns[0];
            PopulateConnectionsCombo(comboxBox, Connection_Type, newConn.Name);
        }
        else
        {
            // Create connection has been cancelled
            comboxBox.SelectedIndex = -1;
        }
    }

    // An connection has been selected. Verify it exists and update component.
    if (_connections.Contains(comboxBox.Text))
    {
        // Get the selected connection
        ConnectionManager connectionManager = _connections[comboxBox.Text];

        // Save selected connection
        _dtsComponentMetaData.RuntimeConnectionCollection[0].ConnectionManagerID =
            _connections[comboxBox.Text].ID;
        _dtsComponentMetaData.RuntimeConnectionCollection[0].ConnectionManager =
            DtsConvert.ToConnectionManager90(_connections[comboxBox.Text]);
    }
}
```

By following the examples shown here, you can manage connections from within your user interface, allowing the user to create a new connection or select an existing one, and ensure that the selection is persisted through to the component's RuntimeConnectionCollection, thereby setting the connection.

You can also use variables within your UI. Normally the selected variable is stored in a component property, so by combining the property access code from the Component Properties section and following the pattern for Runtime Connections, substituting the IDtsVariableService instead, you can see how this can be done.

Component Properties

As an example of displaying and setting component-level properties, you may have a string property that is displayed in a simple text box control and an enumeration value that is used to set the selected index for a combo box control. The following example assumes that the two component properties, StringProp and EnumProp, have been defined in the overridden ProvideComponentProperties method of your component class. You would then extend the form constructor to include some code to retrieve the property values and display them in the form controls. This assumes that you have added two new form controls, a `TextBox` control called `MyStringTextBox`, and a `ComboBox` called `MyEnumValComboBox`. An example of the additional form constructor code is shown here:

```
MyStringTextBox.Text =
_dtsComponentMetaData.CustomPropertyCollection["StringProp"].Value.ToString();

MyEnumValComboBox.SelectedIndex =
Convert.ToInt32(_dtsComponentMetaData.CustomPropertyCollection["EnumProp"].Value);
```

The appropriate events for each control would then be used to set the property value of the component, ensuring that this is done through the design-time interface. A variety of events could be used to capture the value change within the Windows Form control, and this may depend on the level of validation you wish to apply within the form, or if you wish to rely solely on validation routines within an overridden `SetComponentProperty` method in your component class. Capturing these within the control's validating event would then allow you to cancel the change in the form, as well as displaying information to the user. A simple example is shown here for the two properties:

```
private void MyStringTextBox_Validating(object sender, CancelEventArgs e)
{
    // Set the property, and capture any validation errors
    // thrown in SetComponentProperty
    try
    {
      _designTimeComponent.SetComponentProperty("StringProp",
MyStringTextBox.Text);
    }
    catch(Exception ex)
    {
      // Display exception message
      MessageBox.Show(ex.Message);

      // Cancel event due to error
      e.Cancel = true;
    }
}

private void MyEnumValComboBox_SelectedIndexChanged(object sender, EventArgs e)
{
    try
    {
      _designTimeComponent.SetComponentProperty("EnumProp ",
        ((ComboBox)sender).SelectedIndex);
    }
    catch(Exception ex)
    {
      // Display exception message
      MessageBox.Show(ex.Message);

      // Cancel event due to error
      e.Cancel = true;
    }
}
```

Providing an overridden `SetComponentProperty` is a common requirement. The most obvious reason is that component properties are stored through the object type, but you may require a specific type, such as integer, so the type validation code would be included in `SetComponentProperty`. A simple example of this is shown here, where the property named `IntProp` is validated to ensure that it is an integer:

```
public override IDTSCustomProperty90 SetComponentProperty(string propertyName,
object propertyValue)
{
    int result;
    if (propertyName == "IntProp" &&
        int.TryParse(propertyValue.ToString(), out result) == false)
    {
        bool cancel;
        ComponentMetaData.FireError(0, ComponentMetaData.Name, "The IntProp property
            is required to be a valid integer.", "", 0, out cancel);
        throw new ArgumentException("The value you have specified for IntProp is not
            a numeric value");
    }

    return base.SetComponentProperty(propertyName, propertyValue);
}
```

You will build on this example and learn how to handle the exceptions and events in the following section, "Handling Errors and Warnings."

Handling Errors and Warnings

The previous example and the column selection method in the main example both demonstrated how you can catch exceptions thrown from the base component when you apply settings. Although it is recommended that you use managed exceptions for this type of validation and feedback, you may also wish to use the component events such as `FireError` or `FireWarning`. Usually, these would be called immediately prior to the exception and used to provide additional information in support of the exception. Alternatively you could use them to provide the detail and only throw the exception as a means of indicating that an event has been raised. To capture the event information, you can use the `IErrorCollectionService`. This service can be obtained through `System.IServiceProvider`, and the preparatory handling is identical to that of `IDtsConnectionService` as illustrated in the previous example. For the following examples, you will assume that a class-level variable containing the `IErrorCollectionService` has been declared, `_errorCollectionService`, and populated through in the form constructor.

The following example demonstrates how we can use the `GetErrorMessage` method of the `IErrorCollectionsrevice` to retrieve details of an event. This will also include details of any exception thrown as well. The validating method of a text box control is illustrated, and `SetComponentProperty` is based on the overridden example shown previously, to validate the property value is an integer:

```
private void txtIntPropMessage_Validating(object sender, CancelEventArgs e)
{
    // Clear any existing errors in preparation for setting property
```

```
    _errorCollectionService.ClearErrors();

    try
    {
        // Set property through CManagedComponentWrapper
        _designTimeComponent.SetComponentProperty("IntProp",
            this.txtIntPropMessage.Text);
    }
    catch
    {
        // Display message
        MessageBox.Show(_errorCollectionService.GetErrorMessage());

        // Cancel event due to error
        e.Cancel = true;
    }
}
```

If a non-integer value is entered, the following message is displayed:

```
Error at Data Flow Task [ReverseString]: The IntProp property is required to be a
valid integer.
Error at Data Flow Task [ReverseString [84]]: System.ArgumentException: The value
you have specified for IntProp is not a numeric value
    at Konesans.Dts.Pipeline.ReverseString.ReverseString.SetComponentProperty(String
propertyName, Object propertyValue)
    at
Microsoft.SqlServer.Dts.Pipeline.ManagedComponentHost.HostSetComponentProperty(IDTS
ManagedComponentWrapper90 wrapper, String propertyName, Object propertyValue)
```

This second example demonstrates the GetErrors method and how to enumerate through the errors
captured by the service individually:

```
private void txtIntPropErrors_Validating(object sender, CancelEventArgs e)
{
    // Clear any existing errors in preparation for setting property
    _errorCollectionService.ClearErrors();

    try
    {
        // Set property through CManagedComponentWrapper
        _designTimeComponent.SetComponentProperty("IntProp",
            this.txtIntPropErrors.Text);
    }
    catch
    {
        // Get ICollection of IComponentErrorInfo and cast into
        // IList for accessibility
        IList<IComponentErrorInfo> errors =
            _errorCollectionService.GetErrors() as IList<IComponentErrorInfo>;

        // Loop through errors and process into message
        string message = "";
        for (int i = 0; i < errors.Count; i++)
```

```
    {
        IComponentErrorInfo errorInfo = errors[i] as IComponentErrorInfo;
        message += "Level: " + errorInfo.Level.ToString() + Environment.NewLine +
            "Description : " + Environment.NewLine + errorInfo.Description
            + Environment.NewLine + Environment.NewLine;
    }

    // Display message
    MessageBox.Show(message);

    // Cancel event due to error
    e.Cancel = true;
    }
}
```

If a non-integer value is entered, the following message is displayed:

```
Level: Error
Description :
The IntProp property is required to be a valid integer.

Level: Error
Description :
System.ArgumentException: The value you have specified for IntProp is not a numeric
value
    at Konesans.Dts.Pipeline.ReverseString.ReverseString.SetComponentProperty(String
propertyName, Object propertyValue)
    at
Microsoft.SqlServer.Dts.Pipeline.ManagedComponentHost.HostSetComponentProperty(IDTS
ManagedComponentWrapper90 wrapper, String propertyName, Object propertyValue)
```

As you can see, both the event and exception information are available through the
IErrorCollectionService. You can also see the use of the Level property in this example, which may
be useful for differentiating between errors and warnings. For a complete list of IComponentErrorInfo
properties, please refer to the SQL Server documentation.

Column Properties

When you require column-level information, beyond the selection state of a column, it is best practice to
store this as a custom property on the column. This applies to all column types. An example of this can
be seen with the stock Character Map transform. If you select a column and perform an in-place operation, such as the Lowercase operation, this is stored as a custom property on that input column. To confirm this, select a column as described and view the component through the Advanced Editor. If you
then navigate to the Input and expand to select the column, you will see a custom property called
MapFlags. This stores the operation enumeration, as shown in Figure 15-7.

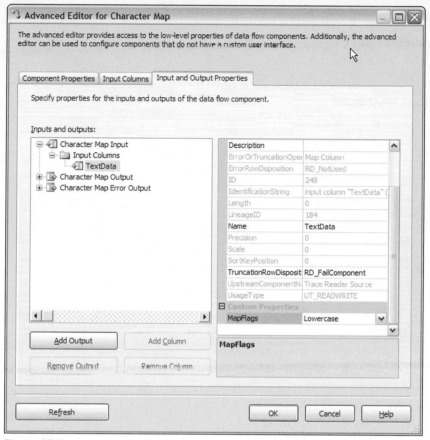

Figure 15-7

If your component uses custom column properties in this way, these are perhaps the best candidates for a custom user interface. Using the Advanced Editor to navigate columns and set properties correctly carries a much higher risk of error and is more time-consuming for the user than a well-designed user interface. Unfortunately this does raise the complexity of the user interface somewhat, particularly from the Windows Forms programming perspective, as the effective use of form controls is what will determine the success of such a UI. However, if you are still reading this chapter, you will probably be comfortable with such challenges.

To persist these column level properties, simply call the appropriate SetColumnTypeProperty method on the design-time interface, CManagedComponentWrapper. For example, in the following code, a property is being set on an input column:

```
_designTimeComponent.SetInputColumnProperty(_input.ID, inputColumn.ID,
    "PropertyName", propertyValue);
```

Summary

You will now hopefully have a good understanding of what is required to implement your own custom user interface for a pipeline component. We hope that you have understood how to apply this guidance for yourself and, perhaps more importantly, why certain practices are to be followed, allowing you to go on and confidently develop your own components further and really exploit the power and extensibility of SQL Server Integration Services.

16

External Management and WMI Task Implementation

Chapter 3 gave an explanation of the management operations that can be performed through the SQL Server Management Studio. This chapter will expand on those operations by providing an overview of the ways in which you can externally manage your packages through managed code. Almost all package management operations that you can perform through the SQL Server Management IDE can be accomplished through managed code classes exposed by the `Microsoft.SqlServer.Dts.Runtime` namespace. This chapter will investigate the uses of managed classes encapsulated by this namespace such as the `Application` and `Package` classes.

The second half of this chapter will detail the capabilities of the WMI Data Reader task and the WMI Event Watcher task. These tasks provide access to system information via the Windows Management Interface model, better known as WMI. Through a query-based language called WQL, similar to SQL in structure and syntax, you can obtain information about a wide variety of system resources. In addition, WMI can be used to monitor a Windows-based system for events that occur in the system and then trigger actions to be performed when the monitored event occurs.

But first you will investigate what package management operations you can implement through managed code.

External Management with Managed Code

The SSIS development team has done a terrific job in providing a robust architecture to manage SSIS through managed code. Managed code in this case refers to the use of the .Net Framework Common Language Runtime that hosts code written in C# or VB.NET.

Through a rich object model, you can customize your applications to control almost every aspect of a SSIS server instance. This section will attempt to provide a brief overview of the SSIS programming model as it applies to externally managing a SSIS server instance and the SSIS packages it contains.

To start using these objects exposed by the `Microsoft.SqlServer.Dts.Runtime` namespace, you must first have created a project in Visual Studio 2005. If you are unfamiliar with how to do this, the example presented later in this chapter will walk you through the creation of a simple Web page that utilizes these operations. But for now, I will generally describe the functionality available through code snippets. If you are unfamiliar with C#, I would suggest you investigate the language to fully understand these code snippets and how the example works.

The classes in this namespace are encapsulated by the `Microsoft.SQLServer.ManagedDTS` class library. Add this reference to a new console application and investigate the classes exposed for your use. Pay particular attention to the members exposed by the `Application` and `Package` objects. These are the core objects you will be working with.

The `Application` object is the core class that exposes methods used to connect to and interface with a SSIS service instance. The following typical management operations can be performed through this class:

❑   Load, save, execute, and delete SSIS packages on the Windows files system, SQL Server, or Integration Services repository

❑   Add, remove, and rename folders in SQL Server or Integration Services repository folders

❑   Control package permissions stored within a SQL Server

❑   Obtain state information and status regarding the execution of packages in SQL Server or the SSIS package repository

The `Package` object represents an instance of a single SSIS package. Although this object exposes many methods that allow you to control every aspect of a package, this chapter will only deal with functionality as it could apply to maintenance-type operations. So, keeping that in mind, the `Package` object exposes the following functionality that you can use in maintenance-type scenarios like these:

❑   Configure Log Providers

❑   Manage Package Configurations

❑   Manage Connection Managers in SQL Server and Integration Services

Application Object Maintenance Operations

The following methods of the `Application` object allow you to manage a SSIS package in the Windows file system, in the SSIS package store, or within the SQL Server DBMS. In addition, packages can be managed across server instances. Note that methods that contain `DtsServer` in their names will apply the operation to the SSIS package store, and methods that contain `SqlServer` in their names will address operations against the SQL Server package store.

Package Maintenance Operations

The Application object exposes the following methods to manage packages in the Windows file system, the SSIS package store, and SQL Server database instance.

- ❑ LoadPackage — Loads a package from the file system
- ❑ LoadFromDtsServer — Loads a package from the specified SSIS package store
- ❑ LoadFromSqlServer — Loads a package to the specified SQL Server instance
- ❑ LoadFromSqlServer2 — Loads a package to the specified SQL Server instance by supplying a valid connection object
- ❑ SaveToXML — Saves a package object to the file system with a dtsx file extension
- ❑ SaveToDtsServer — Saves a package to the SSIS package store
- ❑ SaveToSqlServer — Saves a package to the specified SQL Server instance
- ❑ SaveToSqlServerAs — Saves a package as a different name to the specified SQL Server instance
- ❑ RemoveFromDtsServer — Removes a package from the SSIS package store
- ❑ RemoveFromSqlServer — Removes a package from the specified SQL Server instance
- ❑ ExistsOnDtsServer — Indicates whether a specified package already exists in the SSIS package store at the specified path
- ❑ ExistsOnSqlServer — Indicates whether a specified package already exists on a specified SQL Server

The following C# code snippets exhibit the use of a few of the package maintenance functions outlined above. The following C# code snippet loads a package into an object variable from the file system. Once this object has been instantiated, you can obtain information about the package and control its execution.

```
public void LoadPackage()
{
    Application dtsapp = new Application();
    Package pac =  dtsapp.LoadPackage(@"C:\Documents and Settings\SSISPackages\
                                    Package1.dtsx", void);
}
```

The next C# code snippet obtains a reference to a package object that exists on SQL Server "Server1" instance. Note that the path to the object is not a file system path but rather the path to the root of the SQL Server package store. The package is then transferred to the SQL Server "Server2" instance by calling the SaveToSqlServer method.

```
public void TransferPackage()
{
    Application dtsapp = new Application ();
    Package package1 = dtsapp.LoadFromSqlServer(@"\\Package1", "Server1",
                                        "user1", "password", void);
    dtsapp.SaveToSqlServer(package1, void, "Server2", "user1", "password");
}
```

493

Server Folder Maintenance

The following methods of the `Application` object allow for the common maintenance operations on the folder structures:

❏ `CreateFolderOnDtsServer` — Creates a new folder in the "Stored Packages" node of the application objects server

❏ `CreateFolderOnSqlServer` — Create a new folder in the specified server's "Stored packages" node using the specified user name and password

❏ `RemoveFolderFromDtsServer` — Removes the specified folder from the application objects server

❏ `RemoveFolderFromSqlServer` — Removes the specified folder from the specified server using the supplied user name and password

❏ `RenameFolderOnDtsServer` — Renames the specified folder on the application objects server

❏ `RenameFolderOnSqlServer` — Renames the specified folder on the specified server using the supplied user name and password

❏ `FolderExistsOnDtsServer` — Determines if the specified folder currently exists on the application objects server

❏ `FolderExistsOnSqlServer` — Determines if the specified folder currently exists on the specified server using the supplied user name and password

To exhibit the use of folder maintenance operations, the following examples show how to employ a few of these methods. The first example will create a new folder named "Primary Packages" in the parent folder "SSIS packages" on the VSTSB2 server instance:

```
public static void CreateFolder()
{
    Application dtsapp = new Application();
    dtsapp.CreateFolderOnDtsServer("SSIS Packages", "Primary Packages", "VSTSB2");
}
```

In this next C# code snippet, the `FolderExistsOnSqlServer` method returns a Boolean value indicating whether the folder called "Primary Folder" exists on the "VSTSB2" SQL Server instance:

```
public static void CreateFolder()
{
    Application dtsapp = new Application();

    bool exists = dtsapp.FolderExistsOnSqlServer("Primary Folder", "VSTSB2", null,
                                                 null);
}
```

Package Role Maintenance

The `Application` object exposes methods that allow for SQL Server roles to be referenced and then assigned to SSIS packages. These methods are valid only for packages stored in the SQL Server package store.

❑ `GetPackageRoles` — This method takes two string parameters that return the assigned reader role and writer role for the package.

❑ `SetPackageRoles` — This method sets the reader role and writer role for a package.

Packages installed on a SSIS Instance or SQL Server Instance can be assigned SQL Server roles, giving the users assigned to those roles read and/or write access to the package. Read access gives the user the ability to view and run the package. To be able to modify the package, a user must have been assigned write access. To detail this capability, the following C# code snippet assigns the "dbcreater" role to a package and then checks to ensure that the assignment is in effect:

```
public static void GetPackageRoles()
{
    Application dtsapp = new Application();
    string readerRole;
    string writerRole;
    dtsapp.SetPackageRoles("VSTSB2", @"MSDB\package", "dbcreator", "dbcreator");

    dtsapp.GetPackageRoles(@"VSTSB2", @"MSDB\package", out readerRole, out
                       writerRole);

    System.Diagnostics.Debug.WriteLine(readerRole);
    System.Diagnostics.Debug.WriteLine(writerRole);

}
```

Package Monitoring

The `Application` class exposes a method to enumerate all the packages that are currently being executed on a SSIS server. By accessing a running package, you can gain access to handle package events and control a package's execution status. The methods that can be used here are as follows:

❑ `GetRunningPackages` — Returns a `RunningPackages` object that enumerates all the packages currently running on a server

❑ `RunningPackages` — A collection of `RunningPackage` objects

❑ `RunningPackage` — An informational object that includes such information as package start time and current running duration

The following C# code snippet uses the `GetRunningPackage` object to enumerate information about each running package such as the package's start time and running duration:

```
public static void GetRunningPackageInformation()
{
    Application dtsapp = new Application();
    RunningPackages RunPks = dtsapp.GetRunningPackages("VSTSB2");

    RunningPackagesEnumerator RunPksEnum = RunPks.GetEnumerator();

    while (RunPksEnum.MoveNext())
    {
        RunningPackage RunPk = RunPksEnum.Current;
        Console.WriteLine("InstanceID: {0}", RunPk.InstanceID);
        Console.WriteLine("PackageID: {0}", RunPk.PackageID);
        Console.WriteLine("Packagename: {0}", RunPk.PackageName);
        Console.WriteLine("UserName: {0}", RunPk.UserName);
        Console.WriteLine("Execution Start Time: {0}", RunPk.ExecutionStartTime);
        Console.WriteLine("Execution Duration {0}", RunPk.ExecutionDuration);
    }
}
```

A Package Management Example

The following example will demonstrate how to incorporate package management operations in a Web-based application. This example will demonstrate how to enumerate the folder structure of a SQL Server SSIS package store, enumerate the packages that are contained in a selected folder, and allow you to execute a package from the Web page itself.

To start, first create a new Web project in Visual Studio 2005. Launch VS2005 and select File ➪ New ➪ Web Site. In the New Web Site dialog (see Figure 16-1), choose Visual C# as the language. Leave the rest of the fields as they are.

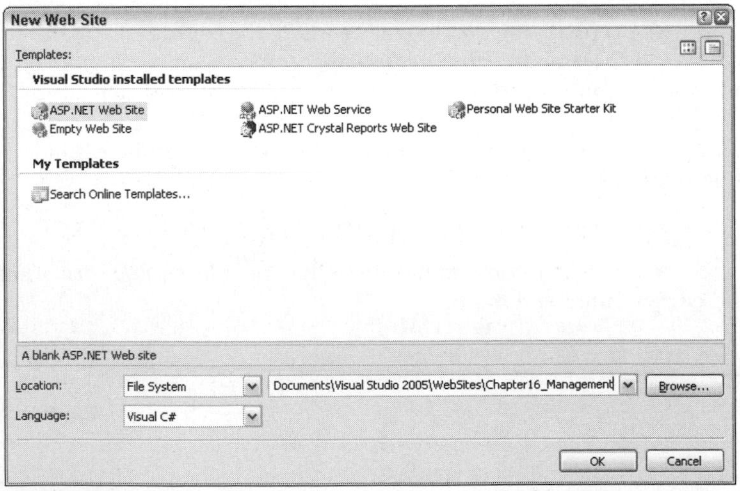

Figure 16-1

Click the OK button and the Web site project will be initialized. By default, the Default.aspx page is created and displayed automatically. Now you'll start building the page that will display the information you want. First, you must add the Web controls to the page.

To do this, select the Design view from the bottom-left corner of the Default.aspx tab. This puts the interface into graphics designer mode. From the Toolbox on the left-hand side of the window, drag a TreeView control onto the page. The TreeView control is in the Navigation group of the Toolbox. Now drag a GridView control onto the page. The DataGrid is located in the Data group of the Toolbox. And finally drag over a Button control from the Toolbox. The Button control can be found in the Standard group. The page should look like Figure 16-2.

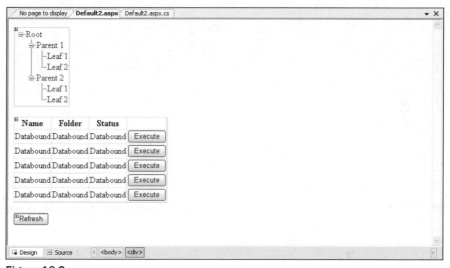

Figure 16-2

Before you leave this screen, you need to create a few event handlers on these controls. To do this, select the TreeView control. Go to the Properties tab in the bottom right of the Visual Studio IDE. On the toolbar of the Properties window, select the lightning bolt symbol that signifies the Events view. The Events view allows you to configure what event handlers you will need to handle for this page. With the TreeView selected and the Events view shown in the Properties window, double-click in the SelectedNodeChanged event in the Behavior group. Notice that the Default.aspx.cs code-behind page is automatically loaded and the event handler code for the SelectedNodeChanged event is automatically created. Switch back to the Default.apsx tab and do the same thing for the TreeView Load event. Now repeat the same process for the GridView RowCommand event and the Button Click events. To view a description of what these events do, you can search for the event name in the Help screen.

Now you need to add some supporting HTML in the source view of the page to configure the columns of the GridView control. To do so, select the Source button on the bottom left of the Default.aspx page tab. This switches the view to show you the HTML code that defines this page. Add the following HTM code between the `<asp:GridView1>` elements. The `<asp:BoundField>` elements you're adding configure the GridView to display three data columns and a button column. This could be done through the design interface, but this is a bit quicker for your purposes:

```
<Columns>
    <asp:BoundField DataField="PackageName" HeaderText="Name" />
    <asp:BoundField DataField="PackageFolder" HeaderText="Folder" />
    <asp:BoundField DataField="Status" HeaderText="Status" />
    <asp:ButtonField Text="Execute"  ButtonType=Button/>
</Columns>
```

The full HTML code of the page should now look something like this:

```
<%@ Page Language="C#" AutoEventWireup="true"  CodeFile="Default.aspx.cs"
Inherits="_Default2" %>

<!DOCTYPE html PUBLIC "-//W3C//DTD XHTML 1.1//EN"
"http://www.w3.org/TR/xhtml11/DTD/xhtml11.dtd">

<html xmlns="http://www.w3.org/1999/xhtml" >
<head runat="server">
    <title>Untitled Page</title>
</head>
<body>
    <form id="form1" runat="server">
    <div>
        <asp:TreeView ID="TreeView1" runat="server" ShowLines="True"
            OnLoad="TreeView1_Load" OnSelectedNodeChanged=
            "TreeView1_SelectedNodeChanged">

        </asp:TreeView>
        <br />
        <asp:GridView ID="GridView1" runat="server" AutoGenerateColumns=False
            OnRowCommand="GridView1_RowCommand" >
            <Columns>
                <asp:BoundField DataField="PackageName" HeaderText="Name" />
                <asp:BoundField DataField="PackageFolder" HeaderText="Folder" />
                <asp:BoundField DataField="Status" HeaderText="Status" />
                <asp:ButtonField Text="Execute"  ButtonType=Button/>
            </Columns>
        </asp:GridView>
         <br />
        <asp:Button ID="Button1" runat="server" OnClick="Button1_Click"
                    Text="Refresh" /></div>
    </form>
</body>
</html>
```

Now you need to start adding the code behind the page that makes this page work. For this example, you will be creating a few custom classes to support code you will be writing in the code-behind page of the Web form. First, you need to add two new class files. To do this, select File ➪ New ➪ File from the main menu. In the Add New File dialog box that appears, select a new Class object and name it PackageGroup.cs. The PackageGroup object will be used to wrap a PackageInfo object and enhance its functionality. Next, add another Class object and call this one PackageGroupCollection.cs. Notice that these two files have been added to the App_Code directory of the solution. In Visual Studio 2005, your code external modules are stored in the App_Code directory. Next, open the PackageGroup.cs file and add the following code to the file. You can overwrite the code that was automatically generated with this code.

```csharp
using System;
using System.Data;
using System.Configuration;
using System.Web;
using System.Web.Security;
using System.Web.UI;
using System.Web.UI.WebControls;
using System.Web.UI.WebControls.WebParts;
using System.Web.UI.HtmlControls;
using Microsoft.SqlServer.Dts.Runtime;

/// <summary>
/// Summary description for PackageGroup
/// </summary>
///

public class PackageGroup
{
  Application dtsapp;

  public PackageGroup(PackageInfo packageInfo, string server)
  {
    dtsapp= new Application();
    _packageinfo = packageInfo;
    server = server;
  }

  private PackageInfo _packageinfo;
  private string _server;

  public string PackageName
  {
    get { return _packageinfo.Name;}
  }

  public string PackageFolder
  {
    get{return _packageinfo.Folder;}
  }

  public string Status
  {
    get { return GetPackageStatus(); }
  }

  public void ExecPackage()
  {
    Package p = dtsapp.LoadFromSqlServer(string.Concat(_packageinfo.Folder + "\\" +
              _packageinfo.Name) , _server, null, null, null);
    p.Execute();
```

```
  }

  private string GetPackageStatus()
  {
    RunningPackages rps= dtsapp.GetRunningPackages(_server);
    foreach( RunningPackage rp in rps)
    {
      if (rp.PackageID == new Guid(_packageinfo.PackageGuid))
      {
        return "Executing";
      }
    }
    return "Sleeping";
  }
}
```

As you can see, this object wraps a PackageInfo object. You could just link the PackageInfo objects to the GridView, but I wanted to create a wrapper with additional functionality to determine a package's execution status and execute a package. The ExecutePackage method can be called to execute the package, and the GetPackageStatus method searches the currently running packages on the server and returns an execution status to the calling object.

But to store information on multiple packages, you need to roll all the PackageGroup objects you create into a collection object. To do this, you created a strongly typed PackageGroup collection class called PackageGroupCollection to house PackageGroup objects. Open the PackageGroupCollection.cs file and add the following code to the file. Once again, you can overwrite the code that was automatically created when the file was created with this example code.

```
using System;
using System.Data;
using System.Configuration;
using System.Web;
using System.Web.Security;
using System.Web.UI;
using System.Web.UI.WebControls;
using System.Web.UI.WebControls.WebParts;
using System.Web.UI.HtmlControls;

/// <summary>
/// Summary description for PackageGroupCollection
/// </summary>
///

public class PackageGroupCollection : System.Collections.CollectionBase
{
  public PackageGroupCollection()
  {
  }

  public void Add(PackageGroup aPackageGroup)
  {
    List.Add(aPackageGroup);
```

```
  }

  public void Remove(int index)
  {
    if (index > Count - 1 || index < 0)
    {
      throw new Exception("Index not valid!");
    }
    else
    {
      List.RemoveAt(index);
    }
  }

  public PackageGroup Item(int Index)
  {
    return (PackageGroup)List[Index];
  }
}
```

This class simply inherits from the System.CollectionBase class to implement a basic IList interface. To learn more about strongly typed collections and the CollectionBase class, search the Help files.

Next you will add the code-behind page of the Default.aspx page. Select the Default.aspx.cs tab and add the following code to this page.

```
using System;
using System.Data;
using System.Data.SqlClient;
using System.Configuration;
using System.Web;
using System.Web.Security;
using System.Web.UI;
using System.Web.UI.WebControls;
using System.Web.UI.WebControls.WebParts;
using System.Web.UI.HtmlControls;
using System.Threading;
using Microsoft.SqlServer.Dts.Runtime;

public partial class _Default : System.Web.UI.Page
{
  Application dtsapp;
  PackageGroupCollection pgc;

  protected void Page_Load(object sender, EventArgs e)
  {
    //Initialize Application object
    dtsapp = new Application();
  }

  protected void TreeView1_Load(object sender, EventArgs e)
  {
    //Clear TreeView and Load root node
    //Load the SqlServer SSIS folder structure into tree view and show all nodes
```

```
    TreeView1.Nodes.Clear();
    TreeView1.Nodes.Add(new TreeNode("MSDB", @"\"));
    LoadTreeView(dtsapp.GetPackageInfos(@"\", "localhost", null, null));
    TreeView1.ExpandAll();
}

protected void TreeView1_SelectedNodeChanged(object sender, EventArgs e)
{
    //Build Collection of PackageGroups
    pgc = BuildPackageGroupCollection(dtsapp.GetPackageInfos(
            TreeView1.SelectedNode.ValuePath.Replace('/', '\\'),
            "localhost", null, null));
    //Rebind the GridView to load Package Group Collection
    LoadGridView(pgc);
    //Store the Package Group Collection is Session State
    Session.Add("pgc", pgc);
}

protected void GridView1_RowCommand(object sender, GridViewCommandEventArgs e)
{
    if (((Button)e.CommandSource).Text == "Execute")
    {
        pgc = (PackageGroupCollection)Session["pgc"];
        PackageGroup pg = pgc.Item(Convert.ToInt32(e.CommandArgument));
        Thread oThread = new System.Threading.Thread(new
                        System.Threading.ThreadStart(pg.ExecPackage));
        oThread.Start();
        LoadGridView(pgc);
    }
}

protected void LoadTreeView(PackageInfos pis)
{
    foreach (PackageInfo p in pis)
    {
        if (p.Flags == DTSPackageInfoFlags.Folder)
        {
            TreeNode n = TreeView1.FindNode(p.Folder);
            n.ChildNodes.Add(new TreeNode(p.Name));
            LoadTreeView(dtsapp.GetPackageInfos(p.Folder + '/' + p.Name, "localhost",
                    null, null));
        }
    }
}

protected void LoadGridView(PackageGroupCollection pgc)
{
    GridView1.DataSource = pgc;
    GridView1.DataBind();
}

protected PackageGroupCollection BuildPackageGroupCollection(PackageInfos
        packageInfos)
{
    PackageGroupCollection pgc = new PackageGroupCollection();
```

```
      foreach (PackageInfo p in packageInfos)
      {
        if (p.Flags == DTSPackageInfoFlags.Package)
        {
          PackageGroup pg = new PackageGroup(p, "localhost");
          pgc.Add(pg);
        }
      }
      return pgc;
   }

   protected void Button1_Click(object sender, EventArgs e)
   {
      LoadGridView((PackageGroupCollection)Session["pgc"]);
   }
}
```

The preceding code handles the execution of the page request. First is the Page_Load method that is run every time the asp worker process loads the page to be processed. In this method, an Application object is loaded for use during the processing of the page.

When the page is processed, there are several additional methods that are called. The TreeView_Load method is called. This method in turn calls the LoadTreeView method that accepts a PackageInfos collection. This collection of PackageInfo objects is processed one by one, and the information is loaded into the TreeView according to the hierarchy of the SQL Server SSIS package folders. When the page is first loaded, just the TreeView is displayed. By selecting a folder in the TreeView, the page is posted back to the server, and the TreeView1_SelectedNodeChanged method is called. This method calls another method in this page called BuildPackageGroupCollection, which accepts a PackageInfos collection. The PackageInfos collection is processed to look for valid package objects only. To determine this, the PackageInfo class exposes a Flag property that identifies the PackageInfo object as a Folder or a Package object. Once the collection is built, the LoadGridView method is called to link the PackageGroupCollection to the GridView. In the LoadGridView method, the collection is bound to the GridView object. This action automatically loads all the objects in the PackageGroupCollection into the GridView.

So how does the GridView know which columns to display? Remember back in the beginning of this example when you added the <asp:BoundColumn> elements to the GridView object. Notice that the DataField attributes are set to the properties of the PackageGroup objects in the PackageGroupCollection object. So in your walk-through of the code, the page is basically finished processing and the results would be displayed to the user in the Web page. So try it and inspect what you have so far. Go ahead and build and then run the project. Figure 16-3 shows a sample of what you may see when you run the Web page. Your results may vary depending on the folders and packages you have configured in your server.

So now take a look at how the status field and Execute button work. When the GridView is loaded with PackageGroup objects, the status property of the PackageGroup class is called. Look in the PackageGroup.cs file and you will see that when the status property is called, a collection of RunningPackages is created. By iterating through all the RunningPackage objects, if the GUID of the package in question matches the GUID of a running package, a result of Executing is returned to the GridView. Otherwise, the Sleeping status result is returned. The Execute button works in a similar fashion.

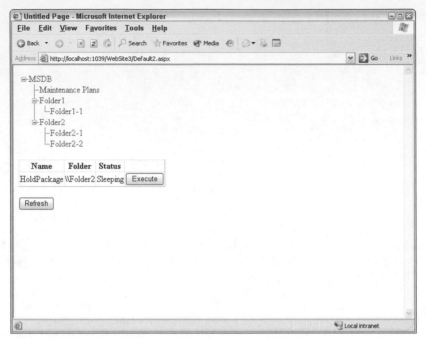

Figure 16-3

When the Execute button is clicked, the GridView1_RowCommand method is called in the page's code-behind file. This method re-instantiates the PackageGroup object from the page's viewstate cache. When found, the package is executed by calling the Execute method of the PackageGroup object. Notice that this call is being done in a newly created thread. By design, a Web page is processed synchronously. This means that if the package was executed in the same thread, the Execute method would not return until the package was finished executing. So by starting the package in a new thread, the page can return, and the status of the package can be displayed in the GridView. So give it a try. Make sure your package runs long enough for you to refresh the Web page and see the status value change.

That's just a basic implementation of some of the functionality exposed by the Microsoft.SqlServer.Dts.Runtime namespace to manage your SSIS packages through managed code. You saw how to obtain a collection of PackageInfo objects and how to leverage the functionality of the objects in an application. In addition, you learned how to run a package and determine which packages are currently running. Obviously, this is a simple application and could stand to be greatly improved with error handling and additional functionality. For example, you could add functionality to cancel a package's execution, load or delete package files to SQL Server through the Web site, or modify the code to support the viewing of packages in the SSIS file storage hierarchy.

Package Log Providers

Log providers are used to define the destination for the log information that is generated when a package executes. For instance, if you require a record of the execution of your package, a log provider could persist the events and actions that had transpired in a log file, recording not only the execution but also, if required, the values and results of the execution. Defining what should be logged during a package's execution is a two-step process. First, you must define which log providers to use. You can define multiple providers in a single package. The second step is to define what information should be sent to the defined log providers.

To configure logging for a package, open a valid package file and select Tools, and then select SSIS ⇨ Logging from the main menu. The Configure SSIS Logs dialog box that is displayed shows all the containers that currently exist in the package. The first step is completed by configuring SSIS Log Providers on the Providers and Logs tab, shown in Figure 16-4.

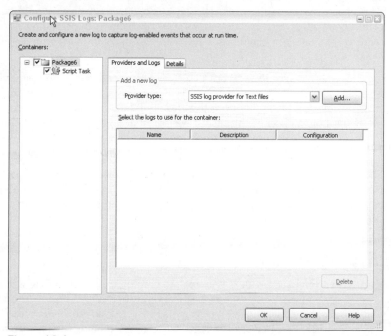

Figure 16-4

SQL Server Integration Services includes several default log providers. These providers are selected in the Provider type combo box and are defined as follows.

❑ **SSIS Log Provider for Text Files:** This provider is used to store log information to a CSV file on the file system. This provider requires you to configure a File Connection object that defines the location of the file. Storing log information in a text file is the easiest way to persist a package's execution. Text files are portable and the CSV format is a simple-to-use industry-wide standard.

❑ **SSIS Log Provider for SQL Profiler:** This provider produces a SQL Provider trace file. The file must be specified with a `trc` file extension so that you can open it using the SQL Profiler diagnostic tool. Using SQL profiler trace files is an easy way for DBAs to view log information. Using Profiler, you could view the execution of the package step-by-step, even replaying the steps in a test environment.

❑ **SSIS Log Provider for SQL Server:** This provider sends package log events to a table in the specified SQL Server database. The database is defined using an OLEDB Connection. The first time this package is executed, a table called sysdtslog90 will be created automatically. Storing log information in a SQL Server database inherits the benefits of persisting information in a relational database system. You could easily retrieve log information for analysis across multiple package executions.

❑ **SSIS Log Provider for Windows Event Log:** This provider sends log information to the Application event store. The entries created will be under the Source name SQLISPackage. No additional configuration is required for this provider. Logging package execution to the Windows Event Log is possibly the easiest way to store log events. The Windows Event Log is easy to view and can be viewed remotely if required.

❑ **SSIS Log Provider for XML Files:** This provider stores log information in a specified XML file on the file system. The file is specified through a File Connection object. Make sure you save the file with an `xml` file extension. Logging events to XML inherits the advantages of the XML specification. XML files are very portable across systems and can be validated against a Schema definition.

Specifying Events to Log

Once you have configured the log providers you wish to employ, you must define what events in the package to log. This is done in the Details tab of Log Configuration dialog box, as shown in Figure 16-5. To enable an event to be logged, check the box next to its name. For instance, in Figure 16-5, the OnError event for the package has been selected to be logged. By selecting other containers on the left-hand side of the dialog box, additional events can be selected down to an individual task or Data Flow event level. To select all events at once, check the box in the header row of the table. By selecting individual containers in the tree view on the left, you can configure the logging of events on an individual task level. By configuring logging at the task level, the special events exposed by a task can additionally be included in the log.

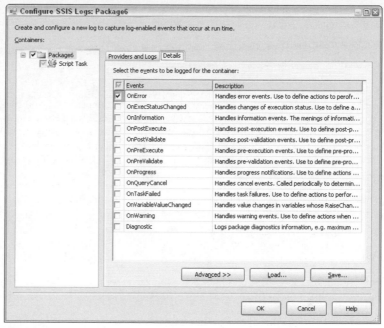

Figure 16-5

Programming Log Providers

The package object exposes the LogProviders collection object, which contains the configured log providers in a package. The LogProvider object encapsulates a provider's configuration information.

The LogProvider object exposes the following key properties.

- ❑ Name — A descriptive name for the log provider.

- ❑ ConfigString — The name of a valid Connection object within the package that contains information on how to connect to the destination store.

- ❑ CreationName — The ProgID of the log provider. This value is used in the creation of log providers dynamically.

- ❑ Description — Describes the type of provider and optionally the destination to which it points.

The following example enumerates all the log providers that have been configured in a package and writes the results to the console window:

```
public static void GetPackageLogs()
{
    Application dtsapp = new Application();
    Package p = dtsapp.LoadFromDtsServer(@"MSDB\Package6x (1)", "VSTSB2", null);
    p.Execute();

    Console.WriteLine("LogProviders");
```

```
        LogProviders logProviders = p.LogProviders;
        Console.WriteLine("LogProviders Count: {0}", logProviders.Count);
        LogProviderEnumerator logProvidersEnum = logProviders.GetEnumerator();

        while (logProvidersEnum.MoveNext())
        {
            LogProvider logProv = logProvidersEnum.Current;
            Console.WriteLine("ConfigString:    {0}", logProv.ConfigString);
            Console.WriteLine("CreationName     {0}", logProv.CreationName);
            Console.WriteLine("DelayValidation {0}", logProv.DelayValidation);
            Console.WriteLine("Description      {0}", logProv.Description);
            Console.WriteLine("HostType        {0}", logProv.HostType);
            Console.WriteLine("ID              {0}", logProv.ID);
            Console.WriteLine("InnerObject      {0}", logProv.InnerObject);
            Console.WriteLine("Name            {0}", logProv.Name);
            Console.WriteLine("-----------------");

        }
}
```

You can of course dynamically configure a package's log providers. The following C# code snippet details the creation of a SQL Server log provider in a package:

```
public static void CreatePackageLogProvider()
{
    Application dtsapp = new Application();
    Package p = dtsapp.LoadFromDtsServer(@"File System\Package6", "VSTSB2", null);

    ConnectionManager dbConMgr = p.Connections.Add("OLEDB");
    dbConMgr.Name = "VSTSB2.AdventureWorks";
    dbConMgr.ConnectionString = "Data Source=VSTSB2;Initial Catalog=AdventureWorks;
        Provider=SQLOLEDB.1;Integrated Security=SSPI;Auto Translate=False;";

    LogProvider logProvider = p.LogProviders.Add("DTS.LogProviderSQLServer.1");
    logProvider.ConfigString = "VSTSB2.AdventureWorks";
    logProvider.OpenLog();

    p.Execute();
}
```

In this example, a valid connection must initially be created to support the communications to the database. Next, the log provider is instantiated by passing the ProgID of the provider you wish to create. The following is a list of the ProgIDs for each type of log provider available:

❑ **Text File Log Provider:** DTS.LogProvider.TextFile.1

❑ **SQL Profiler Log Provider:** DTS.LogProvider.SQLProfiler.1

❑ **SQL Server Log Provider:** DTS.LogProvider.SQLServer.1

❑ **Windows Event Log Provider:** DTS.LogProvider.EventLog.1

❑ **XML File Log Provider:** DTS.LogProvider.XMLFile.1

Package Configurations

Package configurations are a flexible method of dynamically configuring a package at runtime. This allows you a high degree of flexibility in the execution of SSIS packages. This allows you to design the package to run in different environments without having to modify the package file itself. When a package is written, not all operational parameters may be known, such as the location of a file or the value of a variable. By supplying this information at runtime, the user does not have to hard-code these values into a package. When a package is run, the values stored in the specified configuration store are loaded for use during the package's execution. The configuration capabilities of SSIS support the storage of data in five different data stores. The following list describes each type of data store and its capabilities:

❑ **XML File Configuration:** The XML File Configuration option stores package information in an XML file on the file system. This configuration provider lets you store multiple configuration settings in a single file. As an alternative to hard-coding the path to the XML file, the path can be stored in a user-defined environment variable. This option allows you to modify the XML file easily and distribute the configuration easily with the package.

❑ **Environment Variable:** The Environment Variable option allows you to store a configuration value in an Environment variable. This option will only allow you to save a single configuration parameter. By specifying an environment variable that is available on each machine the package will run on, you can be sure that the package configuration will be valid for each environment. Also, the setup of the environment variable can be done once during initial setup of package's environment.

❑ **Registry Entry:** The Registry Entry option allows you to store a configuration value in a registry value. Only a single value can be specified. Optionally, you can specify an environment variable that contains a registry key where the value is stored. Configuration entries in the registry are a secure and reliable way to store configuration values.

❑ **Parent Package Variable:** The Parent Package Variable option allows you to specify a fully qualified variable in a different package as the source for the configuration value. Only a single value can be stored in a specified configuration store. This is a good way to link packages and pass values between packages at runtime. If one package depends on the results from another package, this option is perfect.

❑ **SQL Server:** The SQL Server option creates a SSIS Configuration table in a database that you specify. Since this table could hold the configurations for multiple packages, a configuration filter value should be specified to allow the system to return the correct configuration values. This option allows you to specify multiple configuration values that will be stored under the filter name specified. Optionally, you can specify the database, table, and filter in an environment variable in the following format:

```
<database connection>;<configuration table>;<filter>;
```

For example:

```
VSTSB2.WroxTestDB;[dbo].[SSIS Configurations];Package1;
```

Creating a Configuration

To create a configuration for a package, select SSIS ⇨ Package Configurations. In the dialog that is displayed, select the "Enable Package Configurations" checkbox. From here, you must define which package configuration provider to use. This can be accomplished through the Package Configuration Wizard that is started when you click the Add button.

On the first page of the wizard, shown in Figure 16-6, you must decide which configuration provider you wish to use to store the configuration information. For this example, choose the XML File Configuration option. Now specify the path where the configuration file will reside. Having a standard location to store your configuration files will help ensure that as a package is moved from environment to environment, the links to the configuration will not be broken. If the path to the configuration is not standard, you can store the path to the configuration file in an environment variable and reference the environment variable in the package wizard. Remember, if you have recently added the environment variable to your system, you may need to reboot for it to be available for use in your package.

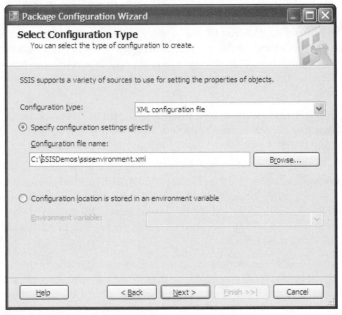

Figure 16-6

Once you've chosen a configuration storage provider, the next step is to specify the properties to save in the configuration store, as shown in Figure 16-7. You can either select a single value from the property tree view or select multiple values at one time. Because you selected the XML File Configuration provider, you can select multiple values to store.

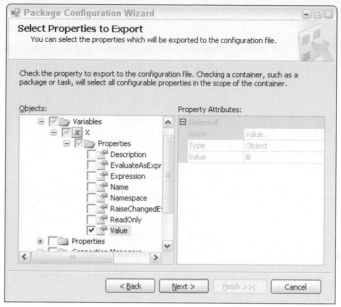

Figure 16-7

Notice that not only can you store default values to load at the time the package is executed, but you can also load entire object definitions at runtime. This is useful if you just want to load a variable's value or actually specify an entire variable configuration at runtime. This would be useful if you wanted to configure the actual properties of a variable. Almost every aspect of a package can be persisted to a configuration store. These include package properties, configured values in defined tasks, configuration information for log providers, and Connection Manager information. About the only thing you can't store in a package configuration store is information about the package configurations.

Once finished, the package configuration information is stored in the package. When the package is executed, the configuration providers will load the values from the specified data stores and substitute the values found for the default values saved in the package.

Programming the Configuration Object

You can also programmatically configure a package's configuration through the `Configuration` object. This is useful if you would like to configure a package through managed code as shown at the beginning of this chapter. You could also configure a configuration file through managed code. All package configurations can be accessed through the `Configurations` collection of the package object.

The `Configuration` object exposes functionality to dynamically configure a package's configuration settings. This allows you to programmatically configure a package based on the environment in which it will run. Since a package can contain multiple configuration sources, you can discover all the configurations in a package by enumerating the configuration objects in the `Configurations` object.

Configuration Object

The Configuration object exposes the following members:

❑   ConfigurationString — The path describing where the physical configuration store is located.

❑   ConfigurationType — Sets the configuration provider to be used to interface to the configuration data store. The configuration type is referenced in from the DTSConfigurationType enumeration. Note that a DTSConfigurationType that starts with an "I" denotes that the configurationstring is stored in an Environment variable.

❑   Name — The unique name for the package.

❑   PackagePath — Defines the path of the actual data that is being accessed.

The following example details how to add an existing configuration store to a package. First, the EnableConfiguration property is set to true. Then, an empty configuration object is added to the package. The configuration object is then set to the Config File type, which directs the configuration to expect a valid dtsconfig file to be specified in the configurationstring property. Finally, the path to the configuration information is supplied and the package's path is stored. The package is then saved, thus persisting the configuration setup to the package file.

```
public static void CreatePackageConfiguration()
{
    Application dtsapp = new Application();
    string packagePath = @"C:\Package6.dtsx";
    Package package = dtsapp.LoadPackage(packagePath, null);

    package.EnableConfigurations = true;

    Configuration config = package.Configurations.Add();
    config.Name = @"ConfigurationMain";
    config.ConfigurationType = DTSConfigurationType.ConfigFile;
    config.ConfigurationString = @"C:\ConfigMain.dtsconfig";
    config.PackagePath = package.GetPackagePath();

    dtsapp.SaveToXml(packagePath, package, null);

}
```

Windows Management Instrumentation Tasks

SSIS includes two special tasks that allow you to query system information and monitor system events. These tasks are the WMI Data Reader task and the WMI Event Watcher task. WMI uses a specialized query language known as WQL, which is similar to SQL, to obtain information about a Windows system. I am not going to get into all the features and capabilities of WMI in this section, but here are a few possible uses:

❑ You can get information on files and directories, such as file size, or enumerate the files in a folder. You can also monitor the file system for events, such as whether a file has been modified recently. This could be required in a package if your package is importing data from a CSV or XML file. A change in the file could trigger tasks to fire in your package.

❑ You can find out if an application is currently running. In addition, you can find out how much memory that application is using or how much processor time it has used. This would be useful if your package needed to know if a companion process was running before creating some sort of output result.

❑ You can obtain information about users in Active Directory, such as whether a user is active or if they have certain permissions on a resource. This would be useful in a package if information about a user or machine on the network is required for your package's execution.

❑ You can control services that are running on a computer system and actually start and stop them as required. This would be useful if your package needed to stop a service during a data transfer.

This is just a small sample of the information you can glean from a computer system. You can obtain information not only on the current system but also on remote systems. As you can see, this gives you access to a great deal of information that could be used in the execution of a SSIS package. For example, you could determine if enough disk space existed on a drive before copying a backup file from a remote system to the current system. You could also monitor a file for updates and automatically import the changes into a database table. Later in this chapter you will see how to actually implement these two examples.

WMI Reader Task Explained

The WMI Data Reader task has the following parameters that must be configured properly for the task object to work:

❑ WmiConnection — A configured WMI Connection Object.

❑ WqlQuerySourceType — This setting specifies where the WQL query is referenced. The query can be manually typed in or can be stored in a file or a variable.

❑ WqlQuerySource — This field sets the actual source of the WQL query source selected in the WqlQuerySourceType.

❑ OutputType — This parameter sets the structure that the results of the WQL query are stored in when executed.

❑ Overwrite Destination — This parameter determines if the previous results are retained or overwritten when the task is executed.

❑ Destination Type — This allows you to specify how the results will be stored.

❑ Destination — This parameter allows you to specify the location of the destination type.

To start configuration of the WMI Data Reader task, you must first create a WMI Connection Manager object. The WMI Connection Manager specifies the WMI namespace that the query will run against. The WMI class used in the query must be contained within that namespace. The standard namespace is the \root\cimv2 namespace. This namespace contains the majority of WMI classes that can be called to get system information. Also, the connection object specifies the target computer system that the query will be run against. By default, the WMI Connection Object points to the localhost machine, but remote systems can be specified as well. As security is always an issue, the WMI Connection Object specifies the user that the query will be run against. Whether it is Windows Authentication or a specified user, the user must have permissions to query the WMI repository on the system for it to work.

Next, the WQL query must be designed. Since WMI is so expansive a subject, I couldn't possibly start to explain the intricacies of the model. I would suggest that you locate a good book on WMI scripting to learn the details of how WMI works. Another resource I suggest you check out are the free tools available through MSDN downloads. There are two applications I would suggest. The first is the Scriptomatic V2 application, which allows you to browse the classes in WMI namespace and generate WMI queries in several different scripting formats. The second is the WMI Administrative tools package. This package includes several apps to enumerate the classes in various namespaces and monitor WMI filter events, among other useful features. These two tools can help you derive WMI queries quickly and easily.

Once you have figured out the structure of your query, you must decide into which object type to store your query results. The WMI Data Reader Task Object gives you basically two choices, a String or a Data Table. Either object can be stored in a user-defined variable or in a file on the file system. When storing the result in a user-defined variable, the variable must be defined as a String data type or Object data type. This means that when obtaining numeric information from the system, you must convert the resultant string to the appropriate data type for use in a mathematical expression. My file transfer example will suggest one way to accomplish this transformation. When storing a Data Table to file, the result is a basic comma-separated file with the properties listed in the first row and the actual values returned in the second row.

WMI Event Watcher Task

As outlined above, not only can WMI obtain information about a computer system, but it can also monitor that system for certain events to occur. This capability could allow you to monitor the file system for a change in a file or monitor the Windows system for the start of an application. The WMI Event Watch task has the following options to configure:

❏ WmiConnection—This is a configured WMI Connection Manager.

❏ WqlQuerySourceType—This setting specifies where the WQL query is referenced. The query can be manually typed in or can be stored in a file or a variable.

❏ WqlQuerySource—This field sets the actual source of the WQL query source selected in the WqlQuerySourceType.

❏ ActionAtEvent—This option sets the actions that are to occur when the WMI event being monitored occurs. This option has two settings, Log the Event and Fire the SSIS Event or just Log the Event.

❏ `AfterEvent` — This field is used to determine what should happen after the WMI event occurs. This setting could be Return with Success, Return with Failure, or Watch for the Event Again.

❏ `ActionAtTimeout` — Should the task time-out waiting for the WMI Event to occur, this option details what action should be taken. This could be Log the Time-Out and Fire the SSIS event, or just Log the Time-Out.

❏ `AfterTimeout` — Should the task time out, this option sets what should happen after the `ActionAtTimeout` occurs. This could be Return with Failure, Return with Success, or Watch for the Event Again.

❏ `NumberOfEvents` — This option specifies how many events must occur before the specified action is taken.

❏ `Timeout` — This sets how long the task should wait, in seconds, before the specified time-out action is taken. A setting of zero (0) denotes that the task will never time-out.

The WMI Event Watcher task is similar to the WMI Data Reader task in that the basic query setup is the same in both cases. You must define a WMI Connection Object and create a WMI query to monitor for an event. The specific options available in this task define how the task will react when the event occurs.

There are two basic types of actions: what should happen when the event actually occurs, and what should happen if the event does not occur within a specified time. Both these actions can either log the event to the package log or, in addition to logging the event, fire an event that can be used to perform additional specified tasks. Also, both actions can dictate what happens after the event occurs or the task times out. These after-events can be to pass to subsequent tasks a success or failure of the WMI Event Watcher task or simply to continue to monitor for the event to occur again.

WMI Data Reader Example

The best way to explain the WMI Data Reader task is to see an example of it in action. The idea of this example is to query the file system for the size of a database file and for the amount of free space on a drive. With this information, you can then determine if the drive has enough space to handle the new file. For simplicity, this example will copy from directories on the same drive. At the end of the example, I will show you how to modify the WMI queries to query the same information from remote systems.

To set up this example, you must first create a file you would like to copy. This example uses a backup of the AdventureWorks database. If you don't know how to create a backup of the AdventureWorks database, you can create your own file or use a file from one of many examples in this book. I would, however, suggest that you do use the AdventureWorks backup, as it will tie into the WMI Event Watcher task example later in this chapter.

First, open a new Integration Services Project and call it WMI Data Copy. Drag a new WMI Data Reader task object from the Toolbox to the Control Flow page of the package. First, give this task a unique name; call it WMI Data Reader Task - Read Free Space on C. Now, right-click on the task and select Edit from the pop-up menu. The WMI Data Reader Task Editor will open, as shown in Figure 16-8.

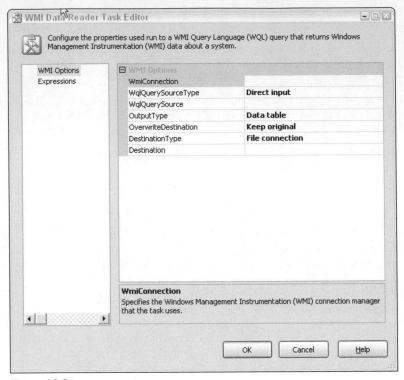

Figure 16-8

Click in the WmiConnection parameter field and select the button to the right. Select <New WMI Connection...> from the drop-down list. The dialog box shown in Figure 16-9 will be displayed.

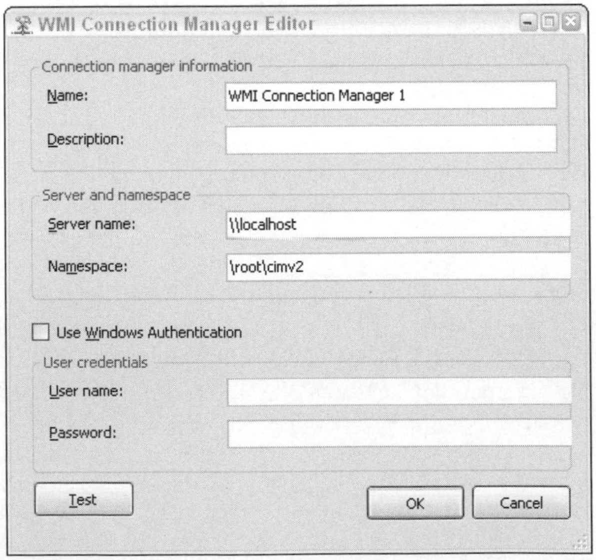

Figure 16-9

Give the new WMI connection a name and enter a description. Enter the computer system you wish to query. Leave the server name set to the default of \\LocalHost to query the local computer, and leave the default namespace as \root\cimv2. CimV2 is the main WMI repository that contains the core WMI classes to access information on the system. Finally check the box to use Windows Authentication or enter a user name and password that has rights to query the CIM repository on this computer. Click the test button to verify the settings, and then click OK to close the dialog box.

Back in the WMI Data Reader Task Editor dialog box, leave the WqlQuerySourceType as DirectInput. This means you will manually enter the WQL query into the WqlQuerySource field. Next, select the WqlQuerySource field and click on the ellipsis button on the right-hand side. In the dialog box that appears, enter the following WQL query in the WqlQuerySource window:

```
SELECT FreeSpace FROM Win32_LogicalDisk Where DeviceID ='C:'
```

This query will return the amount of free space that exists on drive C.

Next, change the OutputType to Property Value and leave the OverwriteDestination field set to Overwrite Destination. Now change the OutputDestination to Variable, and then click in the Destination field and choose the ellipsis button to the right and select <New variable...>. In the Create variable dialog box that appears (shown in Figure 16-10), enter FreeSpaceOnC in the Name field and give the variable a default of zero. Leave the rest of the fields at their default values and click OK to close the dialog box.

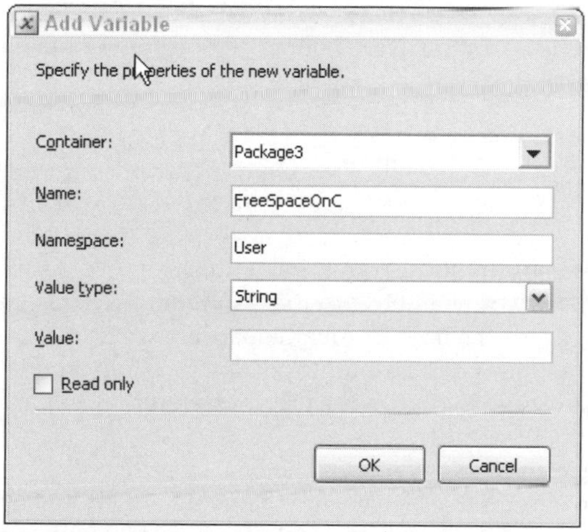

Figure 16-10

Now, you'll add another WMI Data Reader task and configure it to return the size of the AdventureWorks backup file. Call this task WMI Data Reader Task - Read DB File Size. Open the WMI Data Reader Task dialog box for this new task. Click in the WMI Connector field and choose the WMI Connection Manger 1 connection. Since the CIM class you will be using to obtain the file size of the backup file is in the same CIM namespace, you can reuse the same WMI Connection Object.

Leave the WqlQuerySourceType as DirectInput. Now, click the SqlQuerySource field and click on the ellipsis to the right to open the query editor dialog box. Enter the following query:

```
Select FileSize FROM CIM_Datafile WHERE Name = 'C:\\Program Files\\Microsoft SQL
Server\\MSSQL.1\\MSSQL\\Backup\\AdventureWorks.bak'
```

Now, in the OutputType field, choose Property Value. Then, in the DestinationType, choose Variable and then click in Destination field and choose <New Variable...>. Call the new variable DBBackupFileSize with a data type of string and an initial value set to zero (0).

That's all there is to configuring the tasks themselves, so now you'll add some logic to handle the data the WQL query will return. It was stated previously that the WMI Data Reader can only write to strings and Datatable objects. Well, when a string is returned, it has several extraneous characters at the end that will cause a data conversion from String to Integer to fail. You can see these characters by setting a breakpoint on the PostExecute event of one of the WMI Data Reader tasks and running the package. When the tasks turns green, go to the Variables tab and look at the data in the two user-defined variables.

To massage this data into a usable form suitable for conversion to an Integer data type, you will create a VB.Net Script task to strip the extra characters from the string, leaving just numeric digits in the string. To start, click on the Event Handler tab of the package. In the Executables drop-down box, choose the WMI Data Reader task called WMI Data Reader Task - Read Free Space on C. Now select the OnPostExecute event handler and click the hyperlink in the middle of the page to create the event. Drag a Script Task object from the Toolbox and drag it onto the page. Change the name of the object to FileSizeOnC Data Massage. Right-click on the task and select Edit from the pop-up menu. On the left-hand side of the Script Editor dialog box, choose the Script page. In the ReadWriteVariables property, type in "User::FreeSpaceOnC." This will give you read/write access to the variable from within the VB.Net script. Now, click on the Design Script... button in the bottom-right corner of the window. In the Script Host editor that appears, add the following code immediately after the start of the Main subroutine:

```
Dim s As String
s = CType(Dts.Variables("User::FreeSpaceOnC").Value, String)
Dts.Variables("User::FreeSpaceOnC").Value = Int64.Parse(s).ToString()
```

As you can see, this code parses the string to return an Int64 value as a string. In short, it will strip all the extraneous characters from the string and return the result into the same variable. The result is that the contents of the string are ready to be used in a mathematical expression. To finish, close the Script Host windows and hit OK to close the Script Task Editor dialog box. Repeat this same setup for the ReadDBFileSize task, making sure to change the variable references to the appropriate variable names.

You're now in the home stretch of this example. The final steps to complete are to set up the file transfer and add the precedence constraint that will ensure that you have enough space on the drive before you initiate the transfer. First drag a File System task onto the Control Flow page. Name this task Copy Db File. Right-click on the task and click on Edit in the pop-up menu. In the File System Task Editor, set the following properties as shown in Figure 16-11.

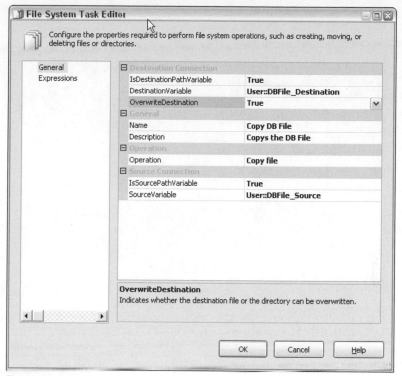

Figure 16-11

In the Source and Destination variable fields, create two variables called DBFile_Source and DBFile_Destination as string variables. In the default field of the DBFile_Source variable, enter the full path to the AdventureWorks backup file. In the DBFile_Destination, enter **C:\Test**. Click OK to close the dialog box. At this time, you will need to go ahead and create a directory under the root of C called Test. The File System task will not create the directory automatically.

The final step is to link these tasks with precedence constraints. Link the tasks as shown in Figure 16-12.

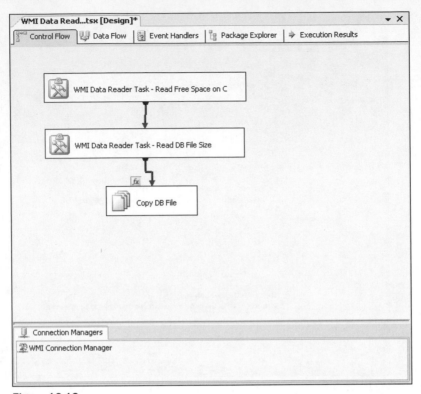

Figure 16-12

After adding the links, right-click on the constraint between the Read DB File Size task and the Copy Db File task. Click on the Edit option in the pop-up menu to open the Precedence Constraint Editor. Set the Evaluation option to Expression and Constraint and then enter the following line of code in the Expression field:

```
(DT_I8)@FreeSpaceOnC > (DT_I8)@DBFileSize
```

As you can see, this is where the massaging of the data in the Script task pays off. If you had not stripped the extraneous characters from the string, then the cast from string data type to the Integer data type would fail. Click OK to close the Precedence Constraint Editor dialog box.

Now you are ready for the moment of truth: running the package. If all went well, all the tasks should green up and the file should have been copied to the C:\Test directory. That is assuming you had enough space available on the drive.

I mentioned earlier about ways you could improve this example. It seem a waste that you have to hard-code the WQL query with the path to the file being checked for size, especially since the path to the file is already stored in the DBFile_Source variable. One option is to build the WQL query on the fly with a Script task. This would allow you to construct the path in the WQL in the proper format, namely changing the single backslash in the path to double backslashes. Also, in a more advanced scenario, the file could be located on another computer system. This could easily be handled by creating a separate WMI

Connection Object pointing to the second system and assigning it to the WmiConnection property in the WMI Data Reader Task - Read DB File Size task. You can check out these enhancements in the samples included with this book.

WMI Event Watcher Task Example

In the previous example, you used WMI to check the size of a file before you copied it to the drive. But what if you want this action to occur whenever the file is updated? To do that, you would use the WMI Event Watcher task to monitor the file and kick off the WMI Data Reader package created earlier.

To start, create a new SSIS package called WMI Event Watcher Package. Now add a WMI Event Watcher task to the Control Flow page of the package. Name this task WMI Event Watcher Task - Monitor DB File. Right-click on the task and select Edit from the pop-up menu. You are now presented with the WMI Event Watcher Task Editor. Select WMI Option from the listbox and configure the properties as outlined in the following code.

First, create a `WmiConnection` pointing to the machine where the backup file exists. You can use the same connection properties as outlined in the previous example. Next, enter the WqlQuerySource that will monitor the file system for changes to the AdventureWorks.bak file.

```
Select * from __InstanceModificationEvent within 30 where targetinstance isa
'CIM_DataFile' and targetinstance.name = 'C:\\Program Files\\Microsoft SQL
Server\\MSSQL.1\\MSSQL\\Backup\\AdventureWorks.bak'
```

As you can see, this query monitors the AdventureWorks.bak file for changes every 30 seconds.

The rest of the properties are specific to the WMI Event Watcher task. Set the ActionAtEvent property to Log the Event and Fire the SSIS Event. As you'll see in a moment, this event will be used to launch the Db Data File Copy package created in the previous example. Next, set the AfterEvent property to Watch for this Event Again. This setting will essentially set up a monitoring loop that will perpetually monitor the file for changes as long as the package is running. Since you do not care if the task times out, leave the time-out settings at their default values. Click the OK button to close the dialog box.

Now that the task is configured, you need to configure the event handler that will be fired when a file change is detected. Click on the Event Handler tab and select the WMI Event Watcher Task - Monitor DB File in the executable combo box and then the WMIEventWatcherEventOccurred in the Event Handlers combo box. Click on the hyperlink in the middle of the page to create this event. Now drag an Execute Package Task from the Toolbox to the event page. Rename this task as Execute WMI Data Reader Package. Right-click the task and select Edit from the pop-up menu. In the execute Package Task Editor dialog box, click on the Package item in the listbox. For this example, you will be referencing the package via the file system, but in real life you would probably be calling a package that had been deployed to a SQL Server instance. For demonstration purposes, the WMI Data Reader Package file will be referenced so that you can see the package execute in the Visual Studio IDE. So in the Location property, choose File System. In the Connection property, create a new file connection pointing to the WMI Data Reader Package.dtsx file. Leave the rest of the properties at their default values. Click OK to finish configuration of this example.

Now test out your new package. Run the WMI Event Watcher Package. The WMI Event Watcher task should turn yellow. The WMI Event Watcher is now monitoring the AdventureWorks.bak file for changes. Now open the SQL Server Management Studio IDE and initiate the start of a backup of the AdventureWorks database. Make sure you back up the DB to the directory you're monitoring. At some point during the backup process, you should see the WMI Data Reader Package kick off and copy the backup file to the C:\Test directory.

When the copy is complete, the package will continue to monitor the backup file for change. So by initiating another backup, the package will detect the change and copy the file again.

Summary

Congratulations, you now have the basic information to manage your SSIS packages from managed code. You've seen how easy it is to transfer packages between your environments. You've also seen how to create and maintain package configurations to customize packages at runtime. In addition, you've seen how to configure log providers, which allow you to store the history of a package's execution.

In the second half of the chapter, you saw how to use the WMI Reader task and WMI Event Watcher task in your packages. Using these two tasks, you discovered how you can gain access to a huge amount of system information to use in your packages. Plus, you learned how to monitor the system for events to occur and perform actions in your SSIS package when those events occur.

17

Using SSIS with External Applications

SQL Server 2005 Integration Services accepts data from nearly any source and presents output, including ADO.NET datasets and SSIS datareaders, that are consumable by external applications. These features allow SSIS to sink and source external applications with ease. In this chapter, you will take a look at three examples of external applications that utilize SSIS. This chapter is not intended to exhaust all possible combinations of external interface with SSIS but rather to provide a sampling of some available functionality.

SSIS is flexible and configurable, so there are many ways to approach interaction with external applications. This book is rife with examples, including the following:

❑ Sources and Destinations — Implicit objects inside SSIS that provide connectivity to data sources and destinations. See Chapter 4 for more information.

❑ Scripting — Arguably provides the most flexibility when interacting with external applications. See Chapter 16 for an example and more information.

Because interface scenarios can vary, it is difficult to define best practices. That said, generally accepted software development practices apply, including the following:

❑ Employ a methodology — Chapter 18 provides an introduction to Software Development Life Cycles (SDLCs). A development methodology is not a prescribed recipe; it is a framework that assists you in creating the proper recipe for your software development project.

❑ Debug — Execute your SSIS package in Debug Mode in either the Business Intelligence Developer Studio or the Visual Studio Integrated Development Environment (IDE).

❑ Test — Wherever possible, obtain a sample of actual ("live") data and execute your package against this data. In the absence of access to a copy of live data, populate tables with dummy data and execute your package against them.

In the first example, SSIS will read data from an RSS feed and output results to a Reporting Services report. This demonstration was inspired by Kamal Hathi, who presented an MSDN TV demonstration of this SSIS capability. Mr. Hathi's presentation shows that this is feasible—the example in this chapter demonstrates configuration, functional considerations, and pitfalls.

RSS In, Reporting Services Report Out

RSS (Really Simple Syndication) is a popular standard for summarizing content-driven Web sites, such as news outlets and Weblogs. Typically referred to as an *RSS feed*, the RSS file contains XML-formatted headlines and descriptions of content items on the site. The standardized format and availability of RSS feeds has driven their popularity. In addition, most RSS is automatically updated when the site content changes. This makes it easy to build applications and Web sites that provide real-time links to RSS-published content. An *aggregator* is a Web site or application that collects and displays RSS feeds.

SQL Server Reporting Services (SSRS) is an integrated tool that allows you to create Web-based reports. This example assumes that you have SQL Server Reporting Services installed and configured on an available server.

SSRS is not configured to consume SSIS data by default. For instructions on how to configure Reporting Services to consume Integration Services data, search the MSDN Library for "Configuring Reporting Services to Use Integration Services Package Data."

In Business Intelligence Development Studio or Visual Studio, start a new Business Intelligence/Integration Services project. Drag a new Data Flow task onto the Control Flow tab. On the Data Flow tab, drag an XML Source, Term Extraction, and DataReader Destination.

Configure the XML Source by double-clicking it. On the XML Source Editor screen, supply the URL to an RSS feed document in the Connection Manger page, such as `www.sqlservercentral.com/sscrss.xml`. The following is an example of some of the XML in an RSS feed:

```xml
<?xml version="1.0" ?>
<rss version="2.0">
<item>
  <title>Executing the result set</title>
  <description>SQL Server Database administrators often generate SQL Statements and
execute the generated SQL statement in order to simplify certain tasks. It has
always been a twin operation. This article illustrates how to use un-documented
stored procedures to execute the generated SQL Statements directly.</description>
<guid>www.sqlservercentral.com/articles/articlesexternal.asp?articleid=2036</guid>
  <pubDate>Mon, 29 Aug 2005 00:00:00 GMT</pubDate>
<link>http://www.sqlservercentral.com/articles/articlesexternal.asp?articleid=2036
</link>
</item>
<item>
  <title>Generating Test Data with Integration Services</title>
  <description>DTS was one of the most amazing new features of SQL Server 7 and in
SQL Server 2005 it has been renamed to Integration Services. This component has
some incredible new capabilities, many of which come at a steep learning curve. New
author Kristian Wedberg brings us a basic article and some code on how you can SSIS
to generate test data.</description>
```

```
<guid>http://www.sqlservercentral.com/columnists/kwedberg
/generatingtestdatawithintegrationservices.asp</guid>
  <pubDate>Mon, 29 Aug 2005 00:00:00 GMT</pubDate>
<link>http://www.sqlservercentral.com/columnists/kwedberg/
generatingtestdatawithintegrationservices.asp</link>
</item>
```

Click the Generate XSD button to automatically generate the XML schema definition document, as shown in Figure 17-1. You can store the XSD file anywhere, but it is a good practice to store related project files together.

An XML Schema provides a definition of the expected data format in an XML document.

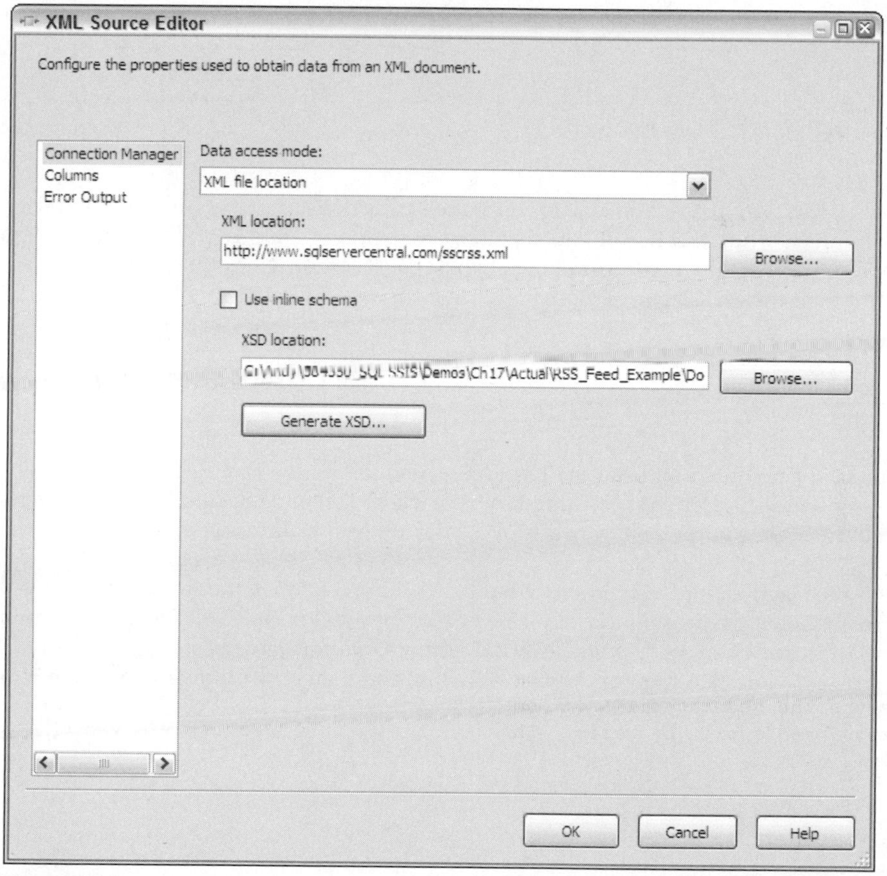

Figure 17-1

On the Columns page, select "item" from the Output drop-down list and check the description field in the Available External Columns table. This defines mapping between the contents on the description field and an output column named Description. On the Error Output page, select Ignore failure for all Error and Truncation conditions. Click OK to close the XML Source configuration editor.

Drag a precedence constraint (represented by a green connection arrow) from the XML Source task to the Term Extraction task. Select the item output as shown in Figure 17-2 and click OK to define the transformation.

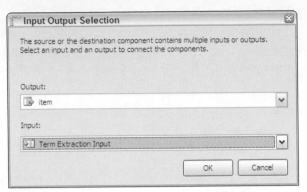

Figure 17-2

Double-click the Term Extraction task to configure it. Check the description column in the Available Input Columns table on the Term Extraction tab, as shown in Figure 17-3. Click the Configure Error Output button and set the Error drop-down list to Ignore failure. Click OK to close the Error Output screen, and then click OK again to close the Term Extraction Editor.

The Term Extraction task is described in Chapter 4. You will recall that it outputs two columns: term and score. Term contains a list of repeated terms in the input. Score contains the number of times each term appears in the input.

Drag a precedence constraint from the Term Extraction task to the DataReader Destination task. Define a Data Viewer on this precedence constraint by right-clicking it and clicking Data Viewers from the context menu. Click Add and then OK to accept the default grid Data Viewer configuration.

Configure the DataReader Destination by double-clicking it to open the Advanced Editor for the Data Reader Destination. Change the Name property to RSSFeedOutput. Click the Input Columns tab and check the Term and Score items in the Available Input Columns table as shown in Figure 17-4. Click OK to exit the DataReader Destination Advanced Editor, and then click OK again to exit the Data View Path Editor dialog box.

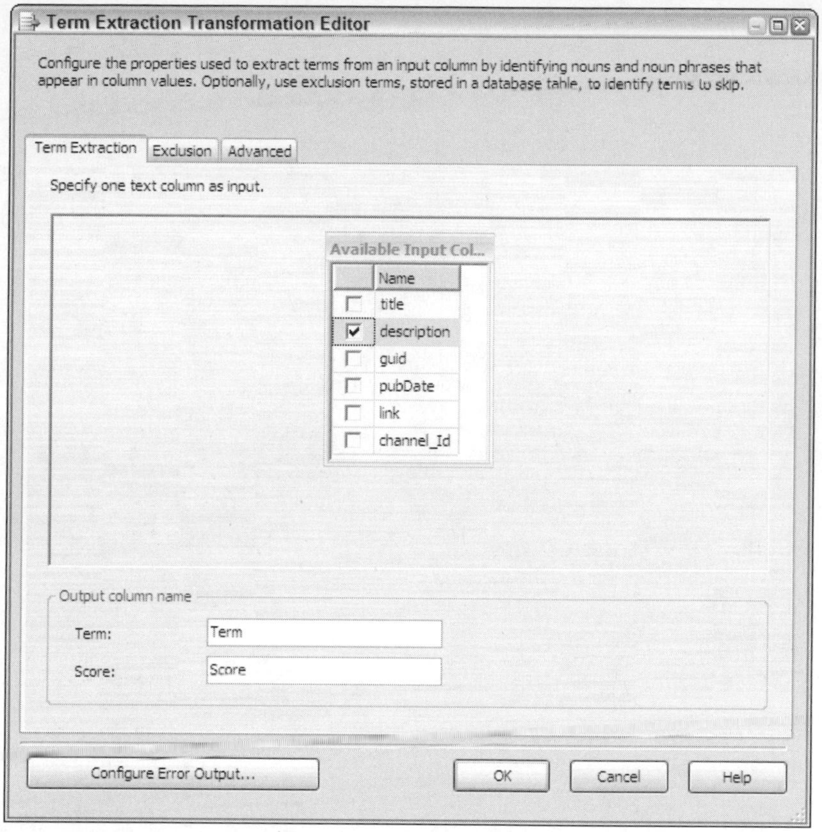

Figure 17-3

Save your work and test it by clicking the Play button. The Data Flow executes and displays results in the Data Viewer as shown in Figure 17-5. Click the Play button on the Data Viewer. The package will continue executing in debug mode until execution completes (this may take some time). After the objects on the screen turn green, indicating that the tasks have completed, halt execution by clicking the Stop button.

Figure 17-4

Add a new Reporting Service project by clicking File ⇨ Add ⇨ New Project. Click Business Intelligence Projects and select Report Server Project from the New Project dialog box. Name the project RSS_Feed_Report.

Right-click the Reports folder, and then click Add New Report to create a new report. Define a new data source for the report, selecting SSIS as the data source type. Name the data source RSS_Feed_SSIS. Enter the connection string manually. Enter **-f** for a file path, followed by the full path in double quotes to the package file. Check the Make This a Shared Data Source checkbox as shown in Figure 17-6.

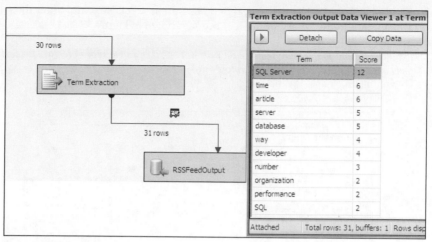

Figure 17-5

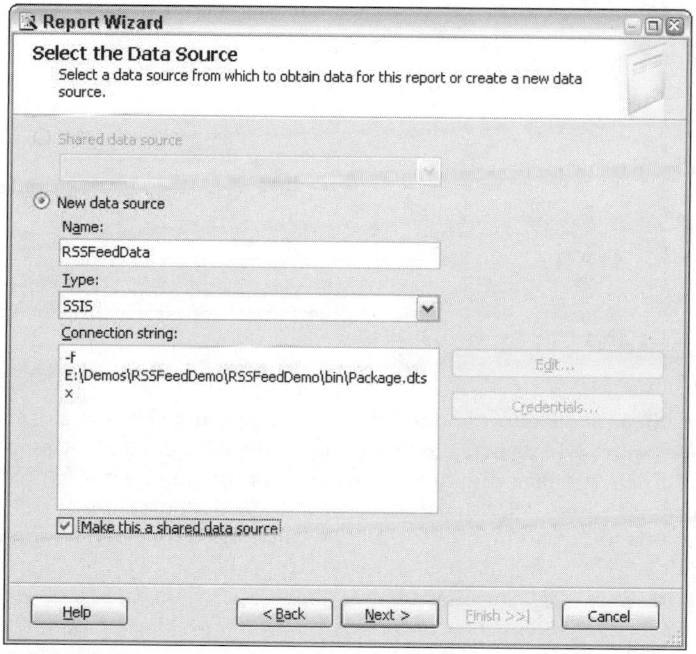

Report Wizard

Select the Data Source

Select a data source from which to obtain data for this report or create a new data
source.

Shared data source

⦿ New data source

Name:

RSSFeedData

Type:

SSIS

Connection string:

-f
E:\Demos\RSSFeedDemo\RSSFeedDemo\bin\Package.dts
x

Edit...

Credentials...

☑ Make this a shared data source

Help   < Back   Next >   Finish >>| Cancel

Figure 17-6

Click the Credentials tab and select the No Credentials option. Click Next and enter the name of the DataReader Destination in the Query String text box, as shown in Figure 17-7.

The DataReader Destination is more than just a new feature; it is a new type of feature for SSIS developers. This is apparent at this step in the example as you reference the name of an object in a Query string.

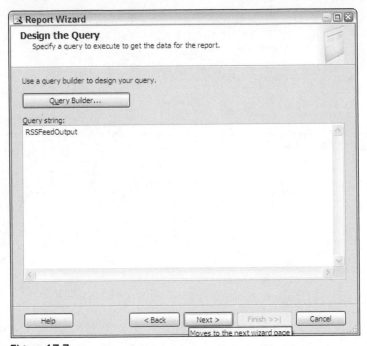

Figure 17-7

The wizard screens that follow allow you to select report type and choose fields, field hierarchy, and table style, but no changes will be made to them. Click through them to the Completing the Wizard screen to continue. The last screen displays the selected configuration options and allows you to name the report as shown in Figure 17-8. Name the report RSS_Feed_Report and click Finish to complete the wizard.

For more information on SQL Server Reporting Services, see Professional SQL Server Reporting Services by Paul Turley, Todd Bryant, James Counihan, George McKee, and Dave DuVarney (Wiley, 2004).

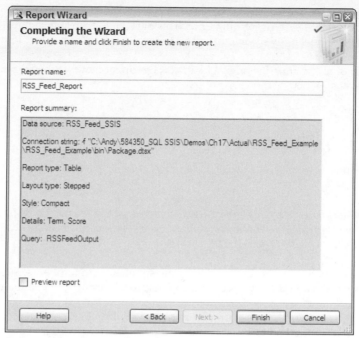

Figure 17-8

Click the Preview tab to view the report as shown in Figure 17-9. Your results will vary, based on the terms extracted when you execute the report.

RSS Feed Report	
Term	Score
SQL Server	12
time	6
article	6
server	5
database	5
way	4
developer	4
number	3
organization	2
performance	2

Figure 17-9

Another use for term extraction reports like the one you just developed is text mining. One application of text mining is gathering statistics on technical support messages and calls.

If the example above were adapted so that the XML input contained a summary of technical support issues, the report would reflect trouble-call trends. This data could then be used by a support center to schedule support personnel or by the manufacturer to identify areas for product improvement.

Other applications of text mining include Weblog, newsgroup, or news site aggregation to detect trends in topics or reader comments.

InfoPath Document

This example demonstrates the ability of SSIS to interact with an external Microsoft Office application, namely InfoPath 2003.

> *Microsoft InfoPath 2003 is a desktop forms client that provides a rich interface to XML-based documents. For more information about Microsoft InfoPath 2003, see Professional InfoPath 2003 by Ian Williams and Pierre Greborio (Wiley, 2004).*

Using a document created from the Timecard template supplied with InfoPath 2003, you will import portions of data stored in an InfoPath document and output the results to a comma-delimited flat file.

Portions of imported data in this demonstration appear disconnected in the Data Flow task. This example demonstrates an SSIS method to join disconnected data. This example also covers some troubleshooting.

> *Many thanks to Wenyang Hu for permission to reuse some elegant XSL!*

Create a new Integration Services project in SSIS. Drag an XML task onto the Control Flow. Double-click the XML task to open the editor. Configure the XML task as follows:

- ❑ Operation Type: XSLT.
- ❑ Source Type: File Connection.
- ❑ Source: New File Connection. Configure the New File Connection as follows:
    - ❑ Usage Type: Existing File.
    - ❑ File: Click Browse to locate and select an InfoPath timecard directory and file. The timecard file may be generated using the InfoPath 2003 Timecard template, or you can get the Timecard_ARay.xml file from the Resources.
- ❑ Save Operation Result: True.
- ❑ Overwrite Destination: True.
- ❑ Destination Type: File Connection.
- ❑ Destination: New File Connection. Configure the New File Connection as follows:
    - ❑ Usage Type: Create File.
    - ❑ File: Use the same InfoPath directory containing the Timecard files. File name: TimecardResult.xml.

❑ Second Operand Type: File Connection.

❑ Second Operand: New File Connection. Configure the New File Connection as follows:

  ❑ Usage Type: Existing File.

  ❑ File: SSISInfoPath.xsl (Wenyang Hu's XSL file — see Resources).

Why transform the Timecard XML file? Because the SSIS XML task does not support multiple namespaces.

Click OK to proceed as shown in Figure 17-10.

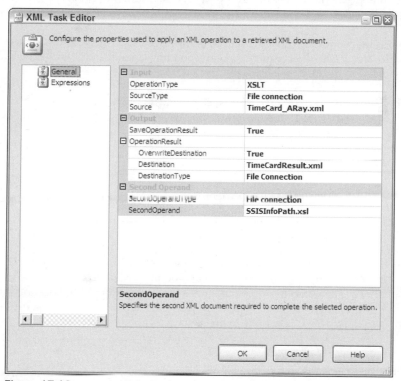

Figure 17-10

Now take a brief look at some XML task properties before moving on.

The top property of the task, OperationType, defines the remaining properties. The XML Task Editor changes to present different properties for different OperationTypes. There are six OperationTypes:

❑ **Diff:** Creates a *Diffgram* (an XML document consisting of the differences between two XML documents) XML document from the differences between the XML defined in the Source property and the XML defined in the SecondOperand property.

❑ **Merge:** Adds XML defined in the SecondOperand property to the XML defined in the Source property.

❑ **Patch:** Adds a Diffgram defined in the SecondOperand property to the XML defined in the Source property.

❑ **Validate:** Validates the XML defined in the Source property by the XML Schema Definition (XSD) or Document Type Definition (DTD) defined in the SecondOperand property.

❑ **XPath:** Specifies an XPath query in the SecondOperand property executed against the XML defined in the Source property to evaluate or aggregate or to return a node or value list. For more information about using XPath, see *XPath 2.0 Programmer's Reference* by Michael Kay (Wiley, 2004).

❑ **XSLT**: Applies XML Stylesheet Language (XSL) documents defined in the SecondOperand property to the XML defined in the Source property. For more information about XSLT, see *XSLT 2.0 Programmer's Reference, 3rd Edition,* by Michael Kay (Wiley, 2004).

The OperationResult property defines the output of the XML task. The DestinationType property can be set to File Connection or Variable, requiring a corresponding Connection Manager or Variable, respectively, to be assigned to the *Destination* property.

To generate the TimecardResult.xml file, you must execute this task.

> *This is also a good development practice: Create a task and then test it before moving on. You may find that you cannot accomplish what you wish with this type of task, and this discovery may impact downstream development decisions.*

Right-click the XML task and click Execute Task. You may receive a validation error in the Errors window — especially on the first execution of the task. If everything is configured properly, however, the task will succeed and the TimecardResult.xml file will be created in the Timecards directory.

Drag a Data Flow task onto the Control Flow. Connect the XML task to the Data Flow task using the available Precedence Constraint (the green arrow on the XML task). Double-click the Data Flow task to proceed. Drag an XML Source onto the Data Flow and double-click it to edit. Browse to the location of TimecardResult.xml — generated in a previous step — to configure the XML Location parameter. Click the Generate XSD button to automatically generate a schema definition for the file (this is such a timesaver!) as shown in Figure 17-11. Click OK to proceed.

> *If you receive the error "Unable to infer the XSD from the XML file. The XML contains multiple namespaces" while stepping through this example, make sure you are using the SSISInfoPath.xsl file supplied in Resources. If you are adapting this example, make sure your transformation eliminates multiple namespaces from your source XML.*

Drag a merge join onto the Data Flow. Merge joins, discussed in Chapter 4, are designed to join rows of data from disparate sources. This example uses them to join disconnected data from the same source: the same XML file. The desired result is one row from the file containing the employee name and information about the work week.

> *This merge could be accomplished many other ways; this is an example of the flexibility of SSIS.*

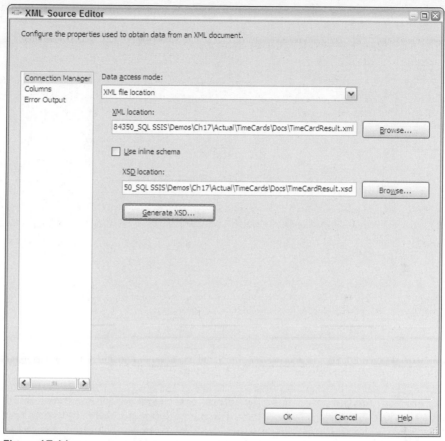

Figure 17-11

In order to join the disconnected data, the merge join needs a field upon which to join. To create this field, drag two Derived Column transformations onto the Data Flow. Connect the XML Source to one of the Derived Column transformations. Select timecard_employee_name from the Output drop-down list on the Input Output Selection dialog box. Connect the XML Source to the other Derived Column transformation, and select Week as the Derived Column input. Double-click each Derived Column in turn to open their respective editors. Configure the same Derived Column for each as follows (as shown in Figure 17-12):

❑ Derived Column: <add as new column>

❑ Derived Column Name: JoinID

❑ Expression: 1

❑ Data Type: 4-byte signed integer [DT_I4]

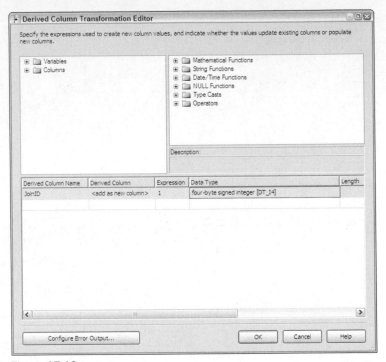

Figure 17-12

Click OK to proceed. You can now connect the outputs of the Derived Column transformations to the Merge Join transformation, except for one thing: The merge join requires the input data to be sorted. So drag and drop two Sort transformations onto the Data Flow. Connect the output of each Derived Column transformation to a respective Sort transformation. Double-click each Sort transformation to configure it. Select the JoinID for each Sort, allowing all other columns to pass through the transformation, as shown in Figure 17-13.

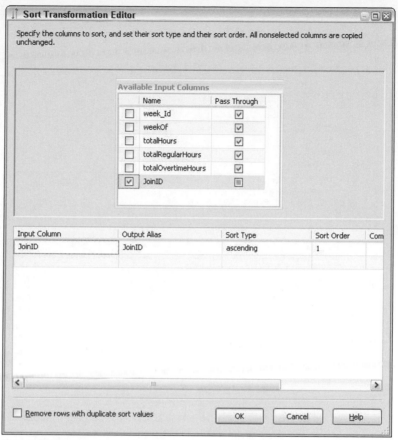

Figure 17-13

Connect the outputs of each Sort to the Merge Join transformation. Assign the output of the first Sort transformation to the merge join. When prompted, select Merge Join Left Input as the input for the first Sort output — the second will connect by default to the remaining available input. Double-click the Merge Join transformation to edit it. Make sure that Inner Join is selected in the Join Type drop-down list and that the Join Key checkbox for each JoinID field is checked in the Available Columns tables. Check the Select checkbox for the JoinID columns in the join, as shown in Figure 17-14. Click OK to close the editor.

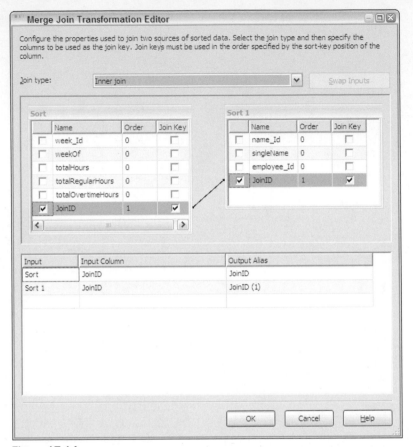

Figure 17-14

Add a Flat File Destination to the Data Flow and connect the merge join to it. Double-click the Flat File Destination to configure it. Click the new Flat File Connector to configure a new file destination named TimeCardOutput. Select Delimited as the Flat File Type. The Flat File Connection will be created, and the Flat File Connection Manager Editor will display. Click Browse to choose a File Name and enter TimecardOutput.csv. Click OK to return to the Flat File Destination Editor. Click the Mappings item to generate the column mappings as shown in Figure 17-15, and then click OK to close the editor.

Right-click each Sort output, respectively, and click Data Viewers. Make sure Data Viewers is selected in the left pane of the Data Flow Path Editor, and then click the Add button. Accept the default name of the Data Viewer and make sure Grid is selected on the General tab of the Configure Data Viewer wizard. Click OK to add a Data Viewer to the Sort output. Add another Grid Data Viewer to the output of the merge join. Test the Data Flow by clicking the Play button and observing the results. In this instance, the error shown in Figure 17-16 is detected during package validation.

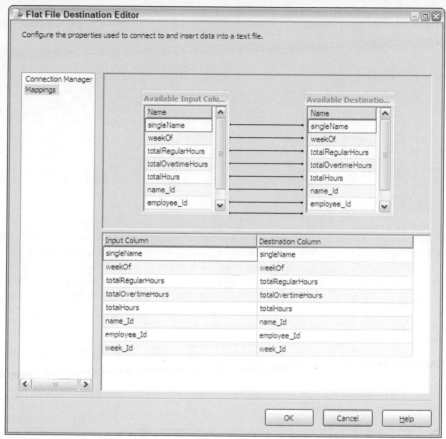

Figure 17-15

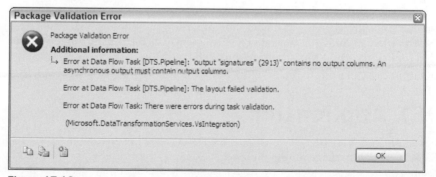

Figure 17-16

To troubleshoot this problem, open the Data Flow and double-click the XML Source transformation. An Editing Component dialog box (shown in Figure 17-17) displays a message that the component is not in a valid state.

Figure 17-17

This dialog box references the same field identified in the validation error and then asks, "Do you want the component to fix these errors automatically?" Clicking the Yes button resolves this issue but creates two more. Red X's display downstream in each Sort transformation, but these are easily resolved by editing and resetting them to the desired state. The error next propagates to the Merge Join transformation, but again it is addressed by resetting to the desired state previously defined. After these items are addressed, the package validates and runs when the Play button is clicked, displaying the data in Data Viewers (an example is shown in Figure 17-18) as it does so.

Figure 17-18

This example demonstrated some techniques for importing and filtering a subset of data from an XML document. You used an InfoPath-generated XML document as the source, but the approach to the solution is valid for loading any XML document into SSIS.

ASP.NET Application

The first example in this chapter demonstrated the DataReader Destination in SSIS, which adds flexibility to SSIS by exposing package output. In the first example, the output was consumed by a Reporting Services Report. This example demonstrates the capability of SSIS to interact with custom external applications by interfacing with a simple ASP.NET application.

This example application is written in VB.NET 2005 and displays the output from an SSIS package in an ASP.NET GridView control. Thanks to Ashvini Sharma and Ranjeeta Nanda for technical support!

In Visual Studio 2005, create a new Integration Services project. Drag a Data Flow task onto the Control Flow and double-click it to open the Data Flow tab. Drag an OLE DB Source onto the Data Flow and double-click to edit. Configure the OLE DB Source as follows (shown in Figures 17-19 and 17-20):

❑ OLE DB Connection Manager: Click New to open the Configure OLE DB Connection Manager dialog box, and then click New to open the Connection Manager dialog box. Configure the connection as follows:

  ❑ Server Name: [Your server name]

  ❑ Log on to the server: Use Windows Authentication

  ❑ Select or enter a database name: AdventureWorks

Click the Test Connection button to confirm connectivity, as shown in Figure 17-19, and then click OK to proceed.

❑ Data Access Mode: SQL Command

❑ SQL Command Text:

```
SELECT Title, FileName FROM Production.[Document]
```

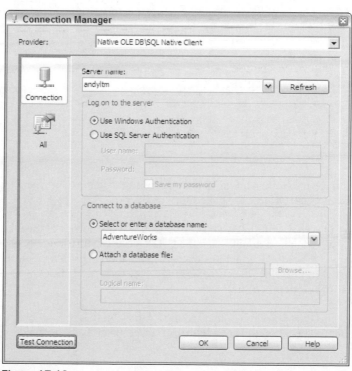

Figure 17-19

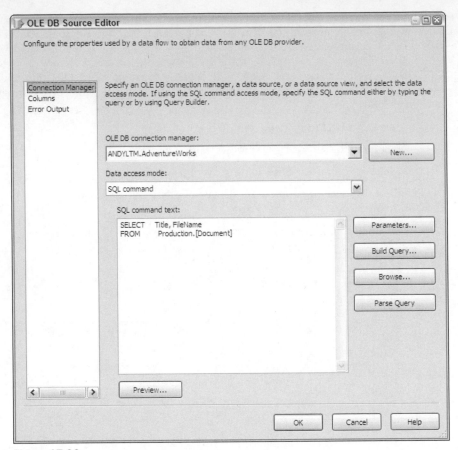

Figure 17-20

Select the fields you wish to return by clicking Columns in the listbox and checking the Title and Filename checkboxes. Click OK to close the editor.

Drag a DataReader Destination onto the Data Flow. Connect the output of the OLE DB Source to the DataReader Destination and double-click the DataReader Destination to begin editing. Click the Input Columns tab on the Advanced Editor for the DataReaderDest dialog. Select the Title and Filename fields (selected earlier in the OLE DB Source) for the DataReader and click OK to close the editor. Test the SSIS functionality before proceeding.

Add a new Web site to the solution by clicking File ⇨ Add ⇨ New Web Site. Name the Web project ASP_Feed_Web. Set the Location to File System and select Visual Basic as the Language as shown in Figure 17-21.

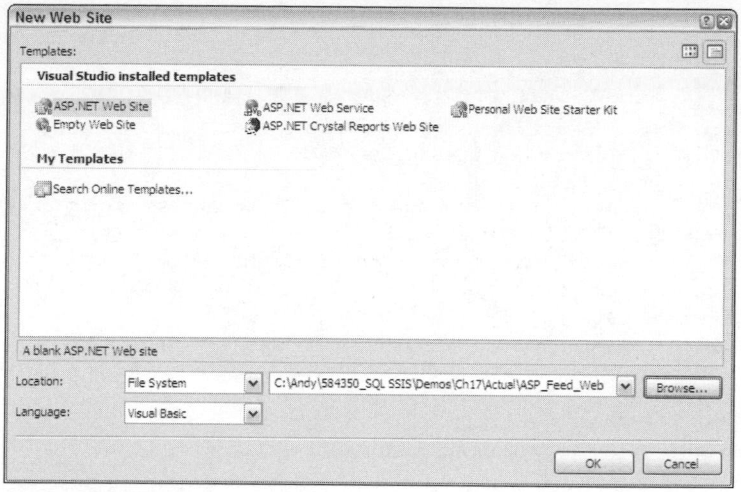

Figure 17-21

In Solution Explorer, right-click the Web site project and click Add Reference. If Microsoft.SqlServer .Dts.DtsClient appears in the list of References on the .Net tab, double-click it to add a reference to the project. If not, click the Browse tab and navigate to `%Program Files%\Microsoft SQL Server\90\ DTS\Binn\Microsoft.SqlServer.Dts.DtsClient.dll` and click OK.

> *The DTSClient DLL contains interfaces to SSIS connection and command objects. See Books Online and MSDN for more information about this library.*

Right-click the Default.aspx object and click View Designer. Drag a GridView control onto the Web page. Double-click the page to open the code viewer. Add the following code at the top of the page:

```
Imports Microsoft.SqlServer.Dts.DtsClient
Imports System.Data.SqlClient
```

In the `Page_Load` subroutine, add the following line of code, replacing [your package directory] with the actual name of the directory containing your SSIS package:

```
connectToSSISPackage("[your package directory]\Package.dtsx")
```

Add the following function to the `_Default` partial class:

```
Private Function connectToSSISPackage(ByVal path As String) As Integer

    ' create new SSIS connection...
    Dim ssisCN As DtsConnection = New DtsConnection
    ' set new SSIS connection's connectionstring property to path
    '    passed into function as an argument...
    ssisCN.ConnectionString = String.Format("-f ""{0}""", path)

    ' open the new SSIS connection...
```

```
    ssisCN.Open()

    '  create new SSIS command and assign it's connection...
    Dim ssisCmd As DtsCommand = New DtsCommand(ssisCN)
    '  assign new SSIS command's cpmmandtext property...
    ssisCmd.CommandText = "DataReaderDest"

    '  create a datareader to receive the SSIS command's output...
    Dim ssisReader As Data.IDataReader = _
        ssisCmd.ExecuteReader(Data.CommandBehavior.Default)
    '  create and populate a new dataset from the datareader...
    Dim ssisDs As Data.DataSet = New Data.DataSet _
    ssisDs.Load(ssisReader, Data.LoadOption.OverwriteChanges, _
        ssisReader.GetSchemaTable().TableName)
    '  populate the gridview from the dataset...
    GridView1.DataSource = ssisDs
    '  bind the gridview (refresh data bindings)...
    GridView1.DataBind()

    '  close the SSIS connection...
    ssisCN.Close()

End Function
```

The connectToSSISPackage function receives a path to an SSIS package through the "path" argument. A new SSIS connection (of DTSConnection type) called ssisCN is created.

> *If your environment does not recognize the DTSConnection data type, make sure you have a reference properly defined and have included the Imports Microsoft.SqlServer.Dts.DtsClient statement at the beginning of your code.*

The path argument is the connection string for the SIS connection. After the SSIS connection is opened, a new SSIS command (of DTSCommand type) is created and assigned to the SSIS connection. The CommandText property of the SSIS command object is set to the *name* of the DataReader Destination in the SSIS package.

Next, a DataReader object is defined and populated with the results of the SSIS command's execution. A data set is created and filled with the datareader's data. The gridview's datasource property is assigned to the data set and the gridview is refreshed with a call to DataBind. Finally, the SSIS connection is closed.

Click the Play button to test. A list of document names and file paths should populate the grid as shown in Figure 17-22.

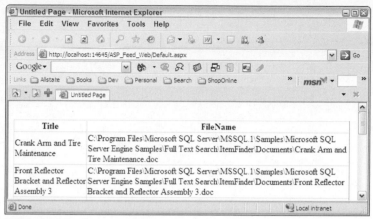

Figure 17-22

This example demonstrates a simple yet powerful feature of SSIS—the ability to expose output directly to ASP.NET applications. The DataReader Destination provides a flexible interface for SSIS package output.

Summary

This chapter presented three examples that demonstrate how SSIS relates to external applications—as both a source to external applications and a method for reading external sources.

The examples covered four interfaces with external applications:

❑   A Web-based XML data source (RSS)

❑   An output to a Reporting Services report

❑   An InfoPath 2003 data source

❑   An output to ASP.NET

In these four examples, only one used the database—and that was a source of sample data. SSIS is designed to interface with the world beyond SQL Server—what's more, this enterprise development tool ships with this functionality "off the shelf."

The good folks at Microsoft have delivered a powerful enterprise development solution that reaches well beyond the SQL Server database.

Learn more by participating in the Developer Community. A good place to start is the Microsoft TechNet Web site for SQL Server 2005 at www.microsoft.com/technet/prodtechnol/sql/2005.

18

SSIS Software Development Life Cycle

Software Development Life Cycles play an important role in any type of application development. Many SQL Server database administrators and DTS developers have little experience with Microsoft Source Control tools because the tools themselves have been less than "database project-friendly." Microsoft has responded with a more reliable version of Visual SourceSafe and a new source control architecture called Team System.

In addition, many SQL Server DBAs have not been involved with Software Development Life Cycles beyond executing scripts attached to change control documentation. Recent legislation in the United States has changed the role of the SQL Server DBA in the enterprise. Regarding Software Development Life Cycles, DBAs now must participate in ever-earlier phases of the project development.

In addition, SQL Server DBAs — especially SSIS developers — will realize greater productivity and development cycle fault tolerance as they employ source-controlled development practices. These practices produce code that is auditable, an added benefit in the current corporate climate.

This chapter provides an overview of some of the available features in Microsoft's new offerings. It includes a brief description of how to store a project in Visual SourceSafe and a detailed walk-through that describes creating a Team Project — using Visual Studio Team System — for SSIS. In practice, Team Projects will most likely be created by someone else in the software development enterprise.

A more detailed examination of Team System is beyond the scope of this book but may be found in Professional Visual Studio 2005 Team System by Jean-Luc David et al. (Wrox, 2006).

Because the line between database administrator and software developer has blurred and blended over the years, the Team Project walk-through is built in Visual Studio 2005. In the Team Project walk-through, you are going to put together a project that uses the source control and collaboration functionality provided by Visual Studio Team System to demonstrate working with the tool and complying with your SDLC process.

This chapter also contains information about debugging and breakpoints — highlighting features new to database administrators and DTS developers in SSIS.

Included is a discussion regarding development and testing with an admitted bias toward the agile development methodology. In the author's humble opinion, there are two types of developers: those who use agile methodologies and those who will.

The chapter concludes with a discussion about managing package deployment.

Introduction to Software Development Life Cycles

Software Development Life Cycles (or *SDLCs*) are a systematic approach to each component of application development — from the initial idea to a functioning production application. A *step* (or *phase*) is a unit of related work in an SDLC. A *methodology* is a collection of SDLC steps in action, applied to a project. *Artifacts* are the recorded output from steps.

For example, the first step of an SDLC is Analysis. The methodology requires a requirements document as an Analysis artifact.

Software Development Life Cycles: A Brief History

Software Development Life Cycles have existed in some form or other since the first software applications were developed. The true beginning of what is now termed "software" is debatable. For your purposes, the topic is confined to binary operations based on Boolean algebra.

In 1854, mathematician George Boole published *An Investigation of the Laws of Thought, on which are founded the Mathematical Theories of Logic and Probabilities*. This work became the foundation of what is now called Boolean algebra. Some 80 years later, Claude Shannon applied Boole's theories to computing machines of Shannon's era. Shannon later went to work for Bell Labs.

Another Bell Labs employee, Dr. Walter Shewhart, was tasked with quality control. Perhaps the pinnacle of Dr. Shewhart's work is statistical process control (SPC). Most quality control and continuous improvement philosophies in practice today utilize SPC. Dr. Shewhart's work produced a precursor to Software Development Life Cycles, a methodology defined by four principles: Plan, Do, Study, and Act (PDSA).

Dr. Shewhart's ideas influenced many at Bell Labs, making an accurate and formal trace of the history difficult. Suffice it to say that Dr. Shewhart's ideas regarding quality spread throughout many industries; one industry influenced was the software industry.

Types of Software Development Life Cycles

SQL Server Integration Services provides integrated support for many SDLC methodologies. This chapter will touch on a few of them. In general, SDLCs can be placed into one of two categories: waterfall and iterative.

Waterfall SDLCs

The first formal Software Development Life Cycles are sequential or linear. That is, they begin with one step and proceed through subsequent steps until reaching a final step. A typical example of linear methodology steps is the following:

- ❏ **Analysis:** Review the business needs and develop requirements.

- ❏ **Design:** Develop a plan to meet the business requirements with a software solution.

- ❏ **Development:** Build the software solution.

- ❏ **Implementation:** Install and configure the software solution.

- ❏ **Maintenance:** Address software issues identified after implementation.

These methodologies are referred to as *waterfall* methodologies because information and software "fall" one-way from plateau to plateau (step to step).

Waterfall methodology has lots of appeal for project managers. It is easier to determine the status and completeness of a linear project: It's either in analysis, in development, in implementation, or in maintenance.

A potential downside to the waterfall methodology is that the analysis and design steps are traditionally completed in a single pass at the beginning of the project. This does not allow much flexibility should business needs change after the project starts. In addition, the development and implementation steps are expected to be defined prior to any coding.

Iterative SDLCs

Iterative methodology begins with the premise that it's impossible to know all requirements for a successful application before development starts. Conversely, iterative development holds that software is best developed within the context of knowledge gained during earlier development of the project. Development therefore consists of several small, limited-scope, feature-based iterations that deliver a product ever closer to the customer's vision.

The following are examples of iterative SDLCs:

- ❏ **Spiral:** Typified by ever-expanding scope in hopes of identifying large design flaws as soon as possible.

- ❏ **Agile:** A collection of methodologies fall into this category, including Scrum, Feature-Driven Development, Extreme Programming, Test-Driven Design, and others.

- ❏ **Microsoft Solutions Framework:** Microsoft's own practice gleaned from a sampling of best practices from different methodologies.

What happens if, hypothetically, an iteration fails to produce the desired functionality? The developer or DBA must remove the changes of the last iteration from the code and begin again. This is much easier to accomplish if the developer or DBA has stored a copy of the previous version someplace safe, hence the need for *source control*.

Source control is defined as preserving the software source code in a format that allows recovery to a previous state of development or version, and it is a basic tenet of all iterative Software Development Life Cycles.

Versioning and Source Code Control

SQL Server 2005 and SQL Server Integration Services (SSIS) integrate with source control products such as Microsoft Visual SourceSafe (VSS) and the new Team System. Visual SourceSafe is Microsoft's current source control product. Team Foundation Server is Microsoft's new suite of SDLC management tools — which includes a source control engine.

Microsoft Visual SourceSafe

Visual SourceSafe 2005, which ships with the 2005 developer product suites, is an upgrade to previous versions of the product. It boasts improved stability, performance, access, and capacity. In this section, you'll create a project in SQL Server Business Intelligence Development Studio (BIDS) and use it to demonstrate integrated source control with Microsoft Visual SourceSafe.

To configure SSIS source control integration with Microsoft Visual SourceSafe 2005, open the SQL Server Business Intelligence Development Studio. You don't need to connect to an instance of SQL Server to configure integrated source control.

To configure Visual SourceSafe as your SSIS source control, click Tools ➪ Options. Click Source Control and select Microsoft Visual SourceSafe. Expand the Source Control node and click Environment for detailed configuration, as shown in Figure 18-1.

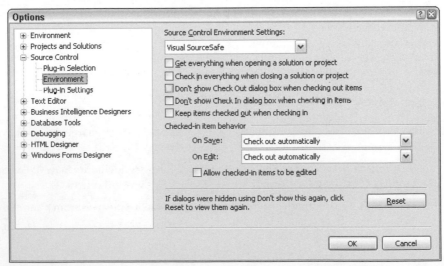

Figure 18-1

The Source Control Environment Settings drop-down list contains three options that represent source control environment roles: Visual SourceSafe, Independent Developer, and Custom.

The Custom role is automatically selected if you begin customizing the source control behaviors in the environment. The following options are available for customization:

- Get everything when opening a solution or project:
    - **Checked:** Retrieves all solution or project files from source control when a solution or project is opened.
    - **Not checked:** You must manually retrieve files from source control.

- Check in everything when closing a solution or project:
    - **Checked:** Automatically checks in all files related to a solution or project on close.
    - **Not checked:** Does not automatically check in all files related to a solution or project on close.

- Don't show Check Out dialog box when checking out items:
    - **Checked:** Hides Check Out dialog box when checking out items.
    - **Not checked:** Displays Check Out dialog box when checking out items.

- Don't show Check In dialog box when checking in items:
    - **Checked:** Hides Check In dialog box when checking in items.
    - **Not checked:** Displays Check In dialog box when checking in items.

- Keep items checked out when checking in:
    - **Checked:** Allows you to continue editing items that have been checked into source control.
    - **Not checked:** You must manually check out the file before editing it.

- Checked-in item behavior on Save:
    - **Prompt for checkout:** You are prompted to check out the files after each Save.
    - **Check out automatically:** Files are checked out automatically when you Save.
    - **Save as:** When Save is clicked, a Save As dialog box appears.

- Checked-in item behavior on Edit:
    - **Prompt for checkout:** You are prompted to check out the files when you begin editing.
    - **Prompt for exclusive checkouts:** You are prompted to exclusively check out the files when you begin editing.
    - **Check out automatically:** Files are checked out automatically when you begin editing.
    - **Do nothing:** When you begin editing, SQL Server Management Studio does nothing.

❑   Allow checked-in items to be edited:

❑   **Checked:** When you begin editing a checked-in file, the Checkout on Edit dialog box appears. This option allows you to check out the file or continue editing without checking out the file.

This is not a best practice. The only situation where this has any useful application is if you intend to save the contents as a new file. If this is the case, it is recommended that you open the existing source-controlled version, save it as the other file, and then make your edits.

❑   **Not checked:** Edits to checked-in items are not allowed.

The following predefined roles, and their settings, are available:

❑   **Visual SourceSafe** — A generic role with the following settings:

❑   Keep items checked out when checking in: Not checked.

❑   Checked-in item behavior on Save: Check out automatically.

❑   Checked-in item behavior on Edit: Check out automatically.

❑   Allow checked-in items to be edited: Not checked.

❑   **Independent Developer** — A role defined for stand-alone development with the following settings:

❑   Keep items checked out when checking in: Checked.

❑   Checked-in item behavior on Save: Check out automatically.

❑   Checked-in item behavior on Edit: Check out automatically.

❑   Allow checked-in items to be edited: Not checked.

Check out automatically is the default behavior for checked-in items when saving or editing a project. By not requiring developers to manually check out code, this feature alone saves hours of development time.

One of the options for Source Control (or the Plug-in Selection) is Microsoft Visual SourceSafe (Internet). You can configure Visual SourceSafe for remote access through and intranet or the Internet. This allows you to store source files off-site. A detailed description is beyond the scope of this book, but you can learn more by browsing the "How to: Enable the Internet Service for Remote Access" topic in the Microsoft Visual SourceSafe Documentation.

For the purposes of this demo, select Visual SourceSafe from the Source Control Environment Settings drop-down list and configure source control options as shown in Figure 18-1.

Open the SQL Server Business Intelligence Development Studio by clicking Start ➪ All Programs ➪ Microsoft SQL Server 2005 ➪ SQL Server Business Intelligence Development Studio (BIDS). Because BIDS uses the Visual Studio Integrated Development Environment (IDE), opening SQL Server Business Intelligence Development Studio will open Visual Studio 2005 if you have Visual Studio 2005 installed. When the BIDS IDE opens, click File ➪ New ➪ Project to start a new project. Enter a project name in the New Project dialog box. For now, do not check the Add to Source Control checkbox as shown in Figure 18-2.

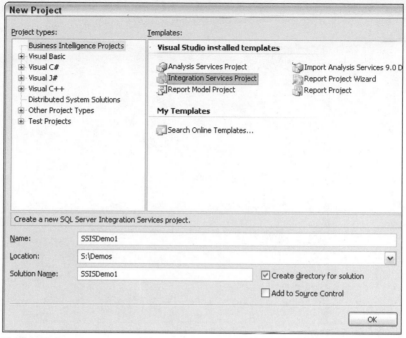

Figure 18-2

Click OK to proceed, and a new project is created in the BIDS IDE.

Add the project to Microsoft Visual SourceSafe by right-clicking the project name in the Solution Explorer and selecting Add to Source Control. You will be prompted to log in to Microsoft Visual SourceSafe. Enter your credentials and click OK as shown in Figure 18-3.

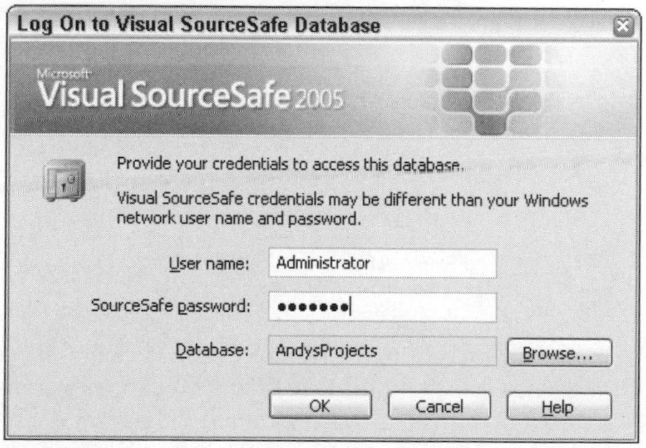

Figure 18-3

The Add to SourceSafe dialog box appears, as shown in Figure 18-4. SSISDemo1.root is the default VSS project name assigned to your project. Accept the default by clicking OK.

Figure 18-4

Since an SSISDemo1 project does not currently exist in your instance of Visual SourceSafe, you will be prompted to create a project. Click Yes on the dialog box.

After successfully creating a VSS project to maintain your source code, you are returned to the BIDS development environment. Notice the source control "lock" beside your project and Package file as shown in Figure 18-5. The lock icons indicate that the objects are checked in.

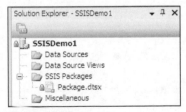

Figure 18-5

Manually check out Package.dtsx for editing by right-clicking Package.dtsx in the Solution Explorer and clicking Check Out for Edit. The Check Out for Edit dialog box appears as shown in Figure 18-6. You may enter a comment to identify why you are checking out the package. This is a good location for change control documentation references, or at a minimum, good notes.

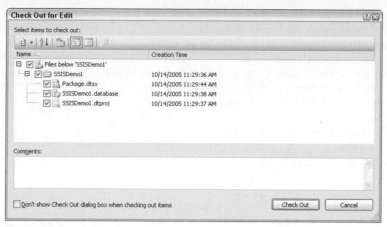

Figure 18-6

Click Check Out to start the checkout process. A Microsoft Visual SourceSafe dialog box will appear, prompting you overwrite your local file or keep your changes. Select the Replace Your Local File with this Version from SourceSafe? option and check the Apply to All Items checkbox. Click OK to begin editing. The Solution Explorer icon beside the Package.dtsx item will change to a red check mark to indicate that the item is checked out exclusively to you, as shown in Figure 18-7.

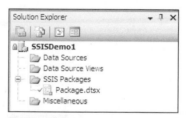

Figure 18-7

Click View ⇨ Pending Checkins to open the Pending Checkins window. The Pending Checkins window displays checked-out files awaiting check-in, as shown in Figure 18-8.

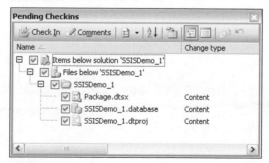

Figure 18-8

Click the Comments button to add any notes to your check-in operation. Again, this is an excellent place to add change control documentation references and bug fixes. Click the Check In button to check your code back into source control. The Source Control confirmation dialog box appears.

If you check the Don't Show this Dialog Box Again (Always Check In) checkbox, you will not see this dialog box on check-in operations. Click the Check In button to continue. Note that the Pending Checkins window is now empty, as no items are checked out for the project.

Observe the Package.dtsx item in the Solution Explorer as you drag a Data Source task onto the Control Flow workspace. A red check mark appears beside the Package.dtsx item. This is the "automatic check-out on edit" feature in action. The Pending Checkins window will now contain the Package.dtsx item, as well as its parent items.

Continue the package construction by right-clicking the Connection Managers workspace just below the Control Flow workspace. Click New ADO.Net Connection to launch the Configure ADO.NET Connection Manager. Click the New button to open the Connection Manager editor. Type or select a server name in the Server Name drop-down list. Select Use Windows Authentication to log on to the server, and select AdventureWorks in the Database Name drop-down list, as shown in Figure 18-9.

Figure 18-9

Click OK to continue, and OK again to close the ADO.Net Connection Manager.

Double-click the Data Flow task on the Control Flow workspace to edit it. Drag a DataReader Source onto the Data Flow workspace and double-click it to edit. On the Connection Managers tab, in the Connection Manager drop-down list, select the ADO.Net Connection Manager you just defined.

> The ADO.Net Connection Manager I defined shows up as AndyLTM.AdventureWorks because my machine is named AndyLTM and the database is named AdventureWorks. Your ADO.Net Connection Manager will be named something different.

Click the Component Properties tab and enter the following SQL query in the SQLCommand property:

```
SELECT * FROM Purchasing.vVendor
```

Your Component Properties tab will look like Figure 18-10.

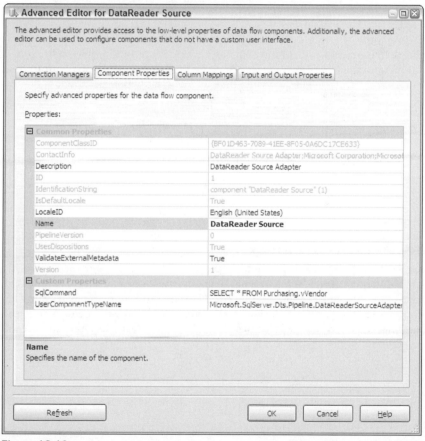

Figure 18-10

Click the Column Mappings tab, and then click OK to close the Advanced Editor for DataReader Source. Save your code, and then open the Pending Checkins window by clicking View ➪ Pending Checkins. Click the Comments button and enter **Added Connection and DataReader** in the Comment text box as shown in Figure 18-11.

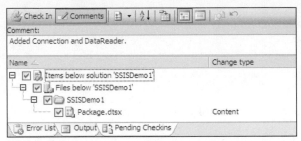

Figure 18-11

Click the Check In button to add current changes to source control. Continue editing by dragging a Flat File Destination onto the Data Flow workspace. Drag the DataReader Source output (represented by a green arrow) from the DataReader Source to the Flat File Destination as shown in Figure 18-12.

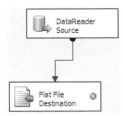

Figure 18-12

Double-click the Flat File Destination to edit. Click the New button beside the Flat File Connection Manager drop-down list. The Flat File Format dialog box will appear; select Delimited and click OK. The Flat File Connection Manager appears. Enter **File 1** in the Connection Manager Name text box. Click the Browse button beside the File Name text box and enter **C:\File1.txt** in the File Name text box. Click Open to continue. Check the Column Names in the First Data Row check box and accept the remaining defaults as shown in Figure 18-13.

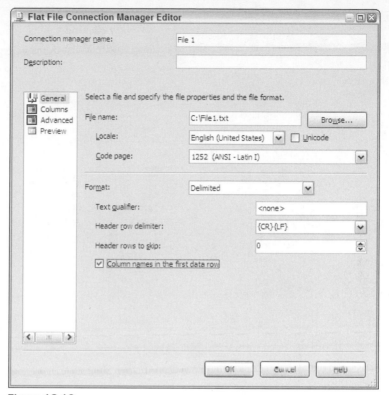

Figure 18-13

Click OK to close the Flat File Connection Manager Editor. This returns you to the Flat File Destination Editor. Click the Mappings item from the list on the left to configure column mappings for the connection, as shown in Figure 18-14.

Click OK to close the Flat File Destination Editor. Click View ⇨ Pending Checkins to view the Pending Checkins window. Enter **Added File1.txt destination** in the Comments text box and click the Check In button.

You now have a functional version of a package in source control. Don't take my word for it — click the Play button (or press F5) to execute the package. After some validation completes, you should see the Data Flow items turn green, as shown in Figure 18-15.

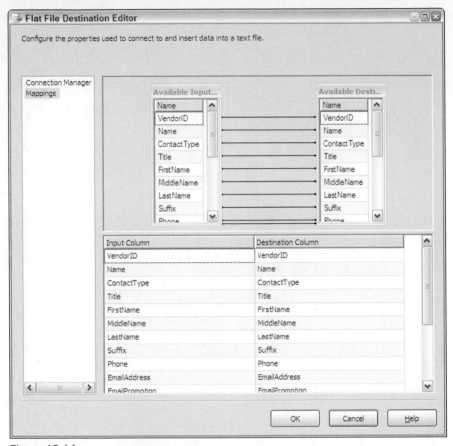

Figure 18-14

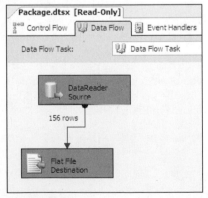

Figure 18-15

Note that the Package.dtsx item is read-only as it is now saved in VSS.

Click the Stop button (or press Shift+F5) to stop the debugger. You can view the resulting output by opening Windows Explorer and double-clicking the C:\File1.txt file, as shown in Figure 18-16.

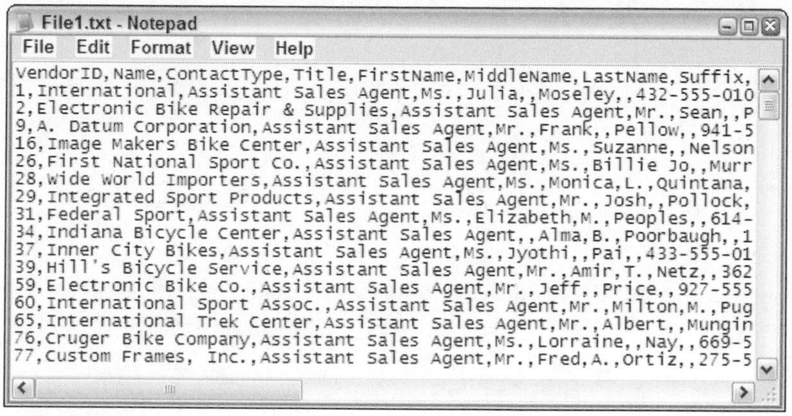

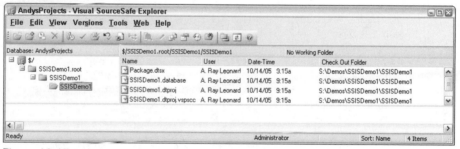

Figure 18-16

You will now roll back to an earlier version of the package. To begin, click File ➪ Source Control ➪ Launch Microsoft Visual SourceSafe. Navigate to the SSISDemo1 folder containing Package.dtsx as shown in Figure 18-17.

Figure 18-17

View the history of the project by clicking Tools ➪ Show History (or Ctrl+H). The Project History dialog box displays as shown in Figure 18-18.

Figure 18-18

For the purposes of this demo, click the OK button to accept the defaults. The History of Project dialog box appears, showing all source control activity and items, as shown in Figure 18-19.

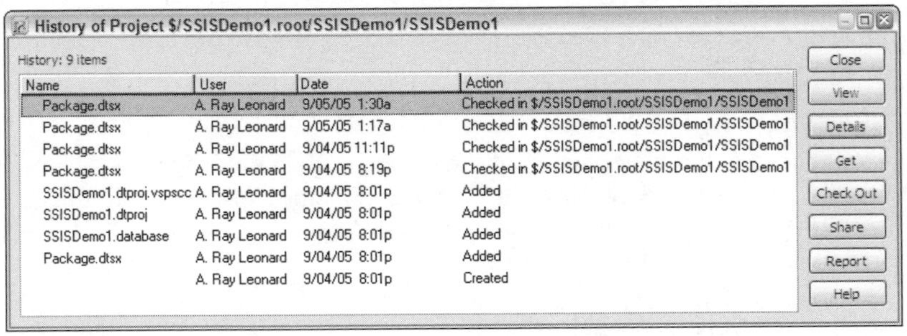

Name	User	Date	Action
Package.dtsx	A. Ray Leonard	9/05/05 1:30a	Checked in $/SSISDemo1.root/SSISDemo1/SSISDemo1
Package.dtsx	A. Ray Leonard	9/05/05 1:17a	Checked in $/SSISDemo1.root/SSISDemo1/SSISDemo1
Package.dtsx	A. Ray Leonard	9/04/05 11:11p	Checked in $/SSISDemo1.root/SSISDemo1/SSISDemo1
Package.dtsx	A. Ray Leonard	9/04/05 8:19p	Checked in $/SSISDemo1.root/SSISDemo1/SSISDemo1
SSISDemo1.dtproj.vspscc	A. Ray Leonard	9/04/05 8:01p	Added
SSISDemo1.dtproj	A. Ray Leonard	9/04/05 8:01p	Added
SSISDemo1.database	A. Ray Leonard	9/04/05 8:01p	Added
Package.dtsx	A. Ray Leonard	9/04/05 8:01p	Added
	A. Ray Leonard	9/04/05 8:01p	Created

Figure 18-19

Click on the version of Package.dtsx that is the second newest and click the Get button. A dialog box asking if you wish to get the entire project with this version displays. Click the Yes button, and another dialog box prompts you for the location of the project files, as shown in Figure 18-20.

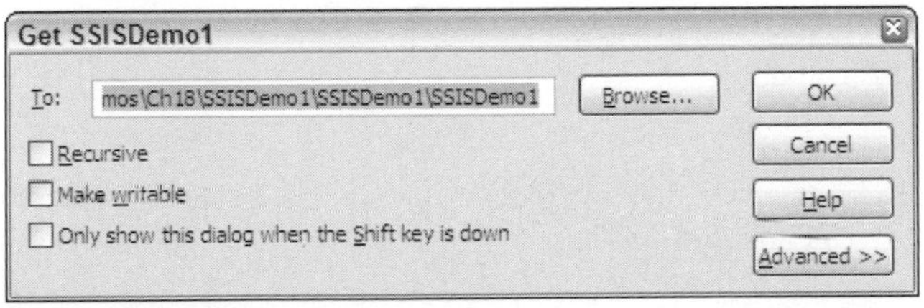

Figure 18-20

Clicking the OK button restores the previous version of code over your existing version. After clicking the OK button, return to the SQL Server Business Intelligence Development Studio environment. A prompt to reload displays as shown in Figure 18-21.

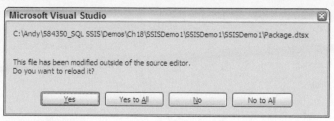

Figure 18-21

Click the Yes To All button to reload all files in the project. Click the Data Flow tab to observe that the Flat File Destination and File1 Connection Manager are no longer part of this project, as shown in Figure 18-22. They have been removed from the project due to your version rollback from source control.

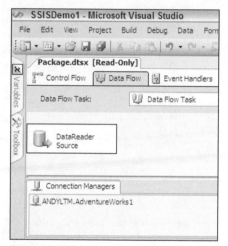

Figure 18-22

Add another Flat File Destination to the Data Flow workspace. Configure this Flat File Destination exactly like the first, except change the file and Connection Manager names from File1 to File2 as shown in Figure 18-23.

Figure 18-23

Open the Pending Checkins window and add the following comment: "Rolled back and added File2.txt destination." Click the Check In button to store this version in source control.

Execute the package by clicking the Play button. Verify C:\File2.txt is created and populated with Vendor data from the AdventureWorks database.

Return to Visual SourceSafe and click Tools ⇨ Show History to view the project history. As before, select the second Package.dtsx in the history list and click the Get button as shown in Figure 18-24.

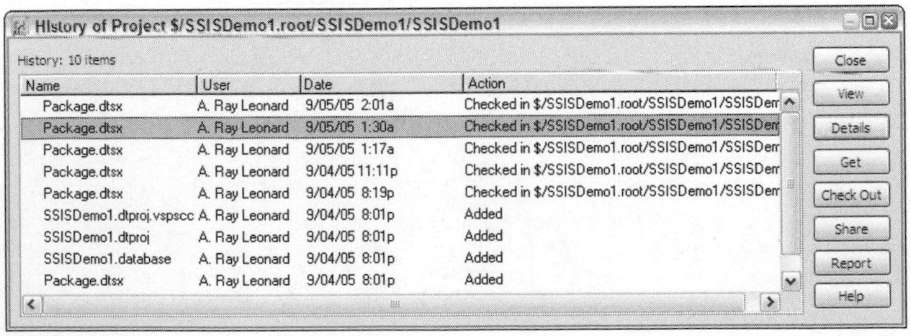

Figure 18-24

Click OK when the location confirmation dialog box displays and return to the BIDS environment. Click the Data Flow Task tab and confirm that you now see the original working version of the package. The File1 Connection Manager and Flat File Destination should now reflect this status, as shown in Figure 18-25.

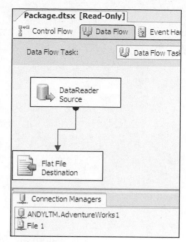

Figure 18-25

This example has provided a rudimentary procedure for manually accomplishing *branching* — a topic that will be covered in a section to come.

Visual SourceSafe is a familiar source control tool to many with application development experience. For this reason, it has been updated and integrated into the 2005 integrated development environments. The new version addresses many complaints and shortcomings of previous versions of the product that were not touched on in this section. One example of this is the native Internet connectivity functionality.

The next section provides a brief introduction to Microsoft's new source control (and so much more) server and client tools known collectively as Team System.

Team Foundation Server, Team System, and SSIS

With the coordinated release of SQL Server 2005 and Visual Studio 2005, Microsoft introduced Team System and Team Foundation Server—a powerful enterprise software development life cycle suite and project management repository consisting of collaborative services, integrated functionality, and an extensible application programming interface (API). Team System seamlessly integrates software development, project management, testing, and source control into the Visual Studio 2005 IDE.

To configure Team Foundation Server as your SSIS source control, click Tools ⇨ Options. Click Source Control and select Visual Studio Team Foundation. Expand the Source Control node for detailed configuration, as shown in Figure 18-26.

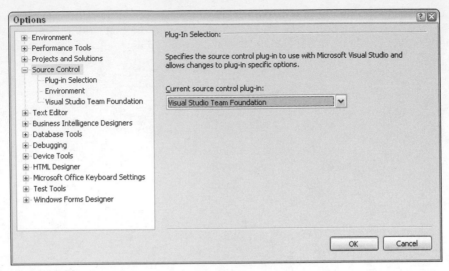

Figure 18-26

This section discusses the relationship between Team System and SQL Server Integration Services. The walk-through is shown using Visual Studio 2005, but it can be completed in SQL Server Business Intelligence Developer Studio (BIDS).

If Visual Studio 2005 is installed, opening BIDS will open Visual Studio 2005. If Team System is specified as the source controller for either environment, the environment, upon opening, will attempt to connect to a Team Foundation Server. Open Visual Studio 2005 to proceed.

Once Visual Studio 2005 is open, press Shift+Alt+T or click the Team Explorer tab to view the Team System properties. Click the Connect to the Team Foundation Server icon (as shown in Figure 18-27) to connect to the Team System server.

Figure 18-27

Click the Servers button to browse for a Team Foundation Server or select a TF Server from the drop-down list as shown in Figure 18-28.

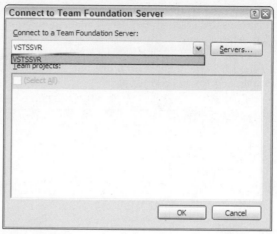

Figure 18-28

Once you've connected to the Team Foundation Server, open the Team Explorer and click the New Team Project icon, or right-click the Team Foundation Server and click New Team Project. The New Team Project wizard starts. Enter a name and optional description for the new team project, and click Next to continue. Select a Process Template on the next step of the New Team Project wizard, as shown in Figure 18-29.

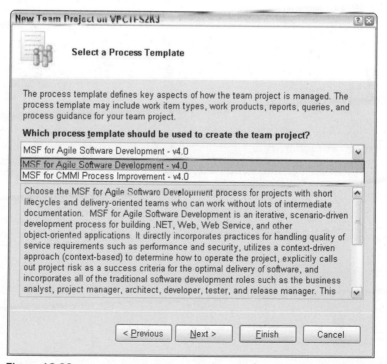

Figure 18-29

Click Next to continue. Here's where Team System gets fun: The good people on the Team System team at Microsoft automated the process of creating a project management Web site using Windows SharePoint Services and Reporting Services.

Click Next to proceed and enter a Team Project Portal title and description in the next step of the wizard as shown in Figure 18-30, and click Next to continue.

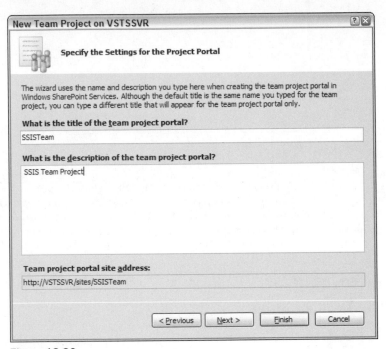

Figure 18-30

In the next step of the wizard, you'll initialize source control and click Next to continue. The confirmation dialog box displays a summary of selections made. Click Finish to set up the new Team Project. A new Team Project is defined according to the configuration you specified. Creation status is indicated by a progress bar as setup scripts execute. If all goes as expected, the wizard will display a Project Created Successfully dialog box as shown in Figure 18-31.

At this point, you have created a Team System container for your SSIS projects. A Team Project is similar to a Visual Studio solution, in that you can add several SSIS projects (or any other type of project) to it.

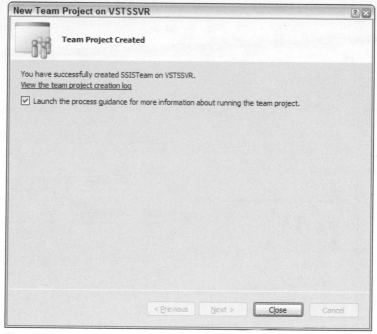

Figure 18-31

If this is your first Team Project, leave View Project Creation Log File checked, and click the Close button to complete the New Team Project wizard and view the log file. The project creation log file provides a lot of information that is helpful in troubleshooting should the project creation fail. If the project is created successfully, there is no need to view the project creation log.

View Process Guidance Page is checked by default. Team System provides a great overview of the process in the Process Guidance page as shown in Figure 18-32. These pages provide a wealth of information, useful to beginners and the experienced alike.

> *"Why create a Team Project?" you ask? The short answer is, "The practice of database development is changing." Team development is becoming practical, even required for DBAs, in software shops of all sizes. It is no longer confined to the enterprise with dozens or hundreds of developers.*

Team System provides a mechanism for DBAs to utilize team-based methodologies, perhaps for the first time. The Team Project is the heart of Team System's framework for the database developer.

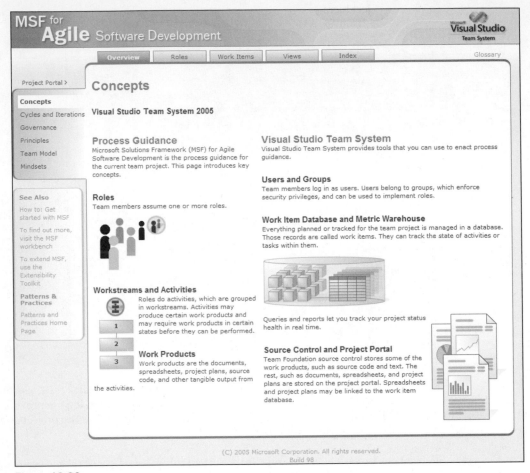

Figure 18-32

MSF Agile and SSIS

MSF Agile is an iterative methodology template included with Team System. In a typical agile software project, a time- and scope-limited project—called an *iteration*—is defined by collaboration with the customer. Deliverables are established, but they may be de-scoped in the interests of delivering a completed feature-set at the end of the iteration. An important aspect of agile iterations is that features slip, but timelines do not slip. In other words, if the team realizes that all features cannot be developed to completion during the time allotted, the time is not extended, and features that *cannot* be developed to completion are removed from the feature-set.

The author advocates agile methodologies.

No one uses a single methodology alone. There are facets of waterfall thinking in any iterative project. In practice, your methodology is a function of the constraints of the development environment imposed by regulatory concerns, personal style, and results.

Once an MSF Agile Team Project hierarchy has been successfully created, the following subitems are available under the project in Team Explorer (see Figure 18-33):

❑ Work Items

❑ Documents

❑ Reports

❑ Team Builds

❑ Source Control

Figure 18-33

Take a moment now to examine some subitems.

Work Items

In MSF Agile projects, work items consist of Tasks, Bugs, Scenarios, and Quality of Service Requirements. Bugs are self-explanatory — they are deficiencies or defects in the code or performance of the application. Scenarios map to requirements and are akin to Use Cases in practice. Quality of Service (QoS) Requirements include acceptable performance under attack or stress. QoS includes scalability and security. Tasks are a catchall category for work items that includes features yet to be developed.

Documents

The MSF Agile template includes several document templates to get you started with project documentation. Included are the following:

❑ Process Guidance — An HTML document that describes the MSF Agile process

❑ Development and Testing Project Plans — Microsoft Project templates for development and testing efforts

❑ Project Checklist — A template containing a project "to do" list

❑   Scenarios Spreadsheet—Listing requirements for validation scenarios

❑   Persona document—A template for listing all parties connected to the project

❑   QoS Requirements document—Defining the Quality of Service Requirements and conditions

Reports

The MSF Agile template contains several built-in Reporting Services project status reports. These reports are accessible directly from Reporting Services or from the Project Portal (SharePoint Portal Services) Web site.

The Reporting Services home page contains links to several reports as shown in Figure 18-34.

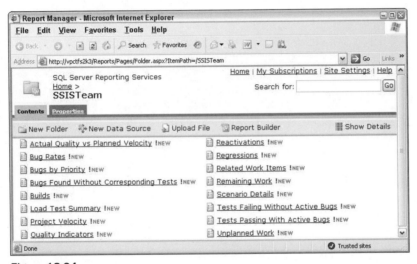

Figure 18-34

The reports are formatted in a style sheet that complements the SharePoint Portal Web site. The Remaining Work report is shown in Figure 18-35.

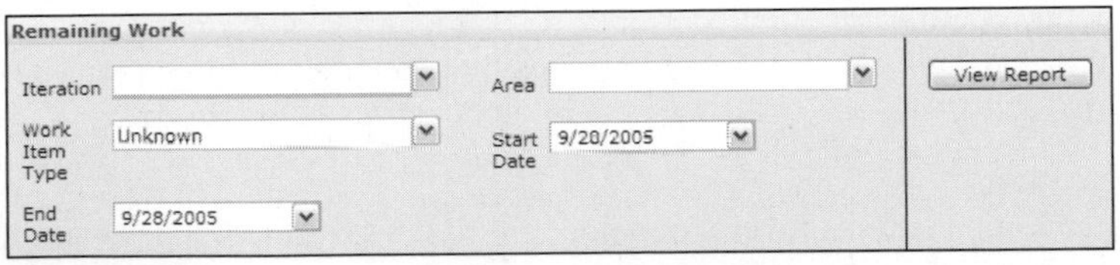

Figure 18-35

The Remaining Work report is part of the larger reporting solution provided by the Project Portal. The Project Portal provides a nice interface for the development team, but project managers are the target audience. The Project Portal can also serve to inform business stakeholders of project status.

To navigate to the Project Portal home page, right-click the Team Project in the Team Explorer and click Show Project Portal.

The Project Portal

The Project Portal (see Figure 18-36) is implemented in SharePoint Portal Services and contains several helpful portals, including the following:

- ❑ Main Menu
- ❑ Announcements
- ❑ Links
- ❑ Reports (Bug Rates, Builds, and Quality Indicators)

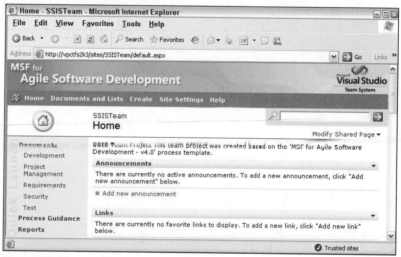

Figure 18-36

Putting It to Work

In this section, you'll create a small SSIS package to demonstrate some fundamental Team System features. To begin, create a new SSIS package in Visual Studio 2005 by clicking File ➪ New ➪ Project. From the Project Types treeview, select Business Intelligence Projects. From the Templates listview, select Integration Services Project. Do not check the Add to Source Control check box. Enter **SSISDemo** as the project name in the Name text box as shown in Figure 18-37.

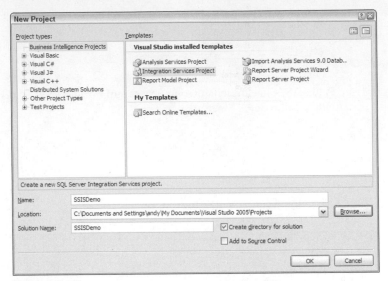

Figure 18-37

Click OK to create the new project. Drag a Data Flow task onto the Control Flow workspace as shown in Figure 18-38.

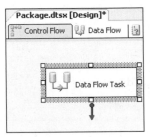

Figure 18-38

Right-click in the Connection Managers tab and select New OLE DB Connection to add a database connection. Click the New button to create a new OLE DB Connection and complete the configuration dialog box, as shown in Figure 18-39.

Figure 18-39

Select your local server from the Server Name drop-down list. Configure the connection for Windows or SQL Server authentication. Select AdventureWorks as the database name. You can click the Test Connection button to test connectivity configuration. Click OK to close the Connection Manager dialog, and OK again to continue.

Double-click the Data Flow task to edit. Drag an OLE DB Source onto the Data Flow workspace. Double-click the OLE DB Source to edit. Select the AdventureWorks connection in the OLE DB connection manager drop-down list. Select Table or View in the Data Access Mode drop-down list. Select [Sales].[vStoreWithDemographics] in the Name of Table or View drop-down list, as shown in Figure 18-40.

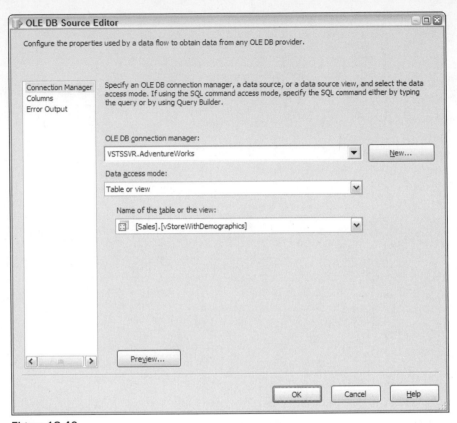

Figure 18-40

Click OK to continue. Drag an Aggregate transformation onto the Data Flow workspace. Connect the output of the OLE DB Source to the Aggregate transformation by dragging the green arrow from the source to the transformation. From the Available Input Columns table, select StateProvinceName, SquareFeet, and AnnualSales. In the grid below, ensure that the operation for StateProvinceName is Group by, the operation for SquareFeet is Average, and the operation for AnnualSales is Sum as shown in Figure 18-41.

Click OK to close the Aggregate editor, and drag an OLE DB Source Output (denoted by the green arrow) from the OLE DB Source to the Aggregate as shown in Figure 18-42.

Drag an Excel Destination onto the Data Flow workspace and connect the Aggregate output to it. Double-click the Excel Destination to open the Excel Destination Editor. Click the New button beside the OLE DB Connection Manager drop-down list to create a new Excel connection object. Enter or browse to the path of an Excel file as shown in Figure 18-43.

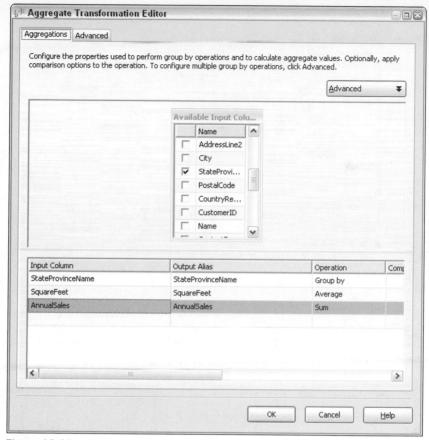

Figure 18-41

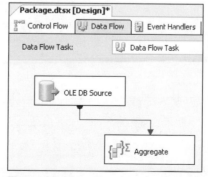

Figure 18-42

Figure 18-43

Click OK to continue.

You can create an Excel spreadsheet in this step. If you enter the desired name of a spreadsheet that does not yet exist, the Excel Destination Editor will not be able to locate a worksheet name. The "No tables or views could be loaded" message to this effect will appear in the Name of Excel Worksheet drop-down list as shown in Figure 18-44.

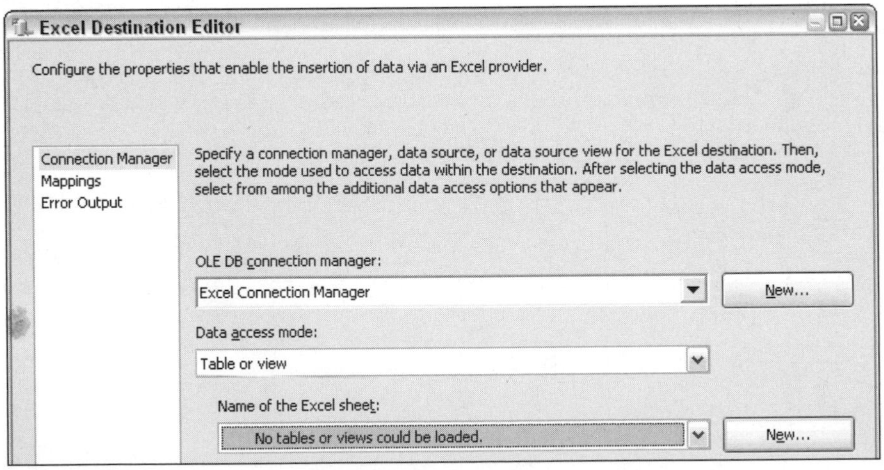

Figure 18-44

To create a worksheet, click the New button beside the Name of the Excel Sheet drop-down list. A Create Table dialog box will appear as shown in Figure 18-45. Click OK to accept the defaults and create the worksheet and Excel workbook.

Figure 18-45

Click Mappings in the Excel Destination Editor to configure column-to-data mappings. Accept the defaults by clicking OK.

Click File ⇨ Save All to save your work.

Version and Source Control with Team System

To add your SSIS project to the Team Project, open the Solution Explorer, right-click the project, and click Add to Source Control.

The Add Solution SSISDemo to Source Control dialog box appears containing a list of Team Projects. Select the SSISTeam Team Project you created earlier, as shown in Figure 18-46.

Figure 18-46

Click OK to continue.

You have successfully created a Team Project and a SSIS project. The Team Project contains version control information—even now.

> *Source control is loosely modeled after a library. Items are checked out for modification and checked in when modifications are complete.*

Click View ➪ Other Windows ➪ Pending Changes to view the current source control status for the SSIS project, as shown in Figure 18-47.

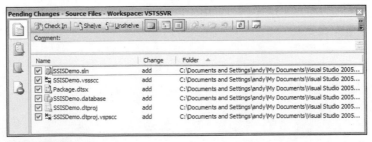

Figure 18-47

The Change column indicates that the files are currently in an Add status. This means the files are not yet source-controlled but are ready to be added to source control.

Click the Check In button to add the current SSISDemo project to the SSISTeam Team Project's source control. This clears the Pending Checkin list. Editing the SSISDemo SSIS project will cause the affected files to reappear in the Pending Checkin list.

> *Any change to the SSISDemo project is now tracked against the source-controlled version maintained by the SSISTeam Team Project. Seemingly insignificant changes count: For instance, moving any of the items in the Data Flow workspace is considered an edit to the package item and is tracked.*

The default behavior for source control in Visual Studio 2005 is that checked-in items are automatically checked out when edited. You can view the current status of all Team Projects on your Team Foundation Server in the Source Control Explorer. To access the Source Control Explorer, double-click Source Control in the Team Explorer or click View ➪ Other Windows ➪ Source Control Explorer as shown in Figure 18-48.

Figure 18-48

The example will now implement a larger change to demonstrate practical source control management before moving into some advanced source control functionality. In your SSIS project, add an Execute SQL task to the Control Flow workspace. Configure the task by setting the Connection Type to OLE DB, the Connection to your AdventureWorks connection, and the SQLSourceType to Direct input, as shown in Figure 18-49.

Set the SQLStatement to the following:

```
if not exists(select * from sysobjects where id = object_id('Log')
 and ObjectProperty(id, 'IsUserTable') = 1)
begin
   CREATE TABLE Log (
     LogDateTime datetime NOT NULL,
     LogLocation VarChar(50) NOT NULL,
     LogEvent VarChar(50) NOT NULL,
     LogDetails VarChar(1000) NULL,
     LogCount Int NULL
   ) ON [Primary]
   ALTER TABLE Log ADD CONSTRAINT DF_Log_LogDateTime DEFAULT (getdate()) FOR
        LogDateTime
 end

INSERT INTO Log
(LogLocation, LogEvent, LogDetails, LogCount)
VALUES('SSISDemo', 'DataFlow', 'Completed', '1st Run')
```

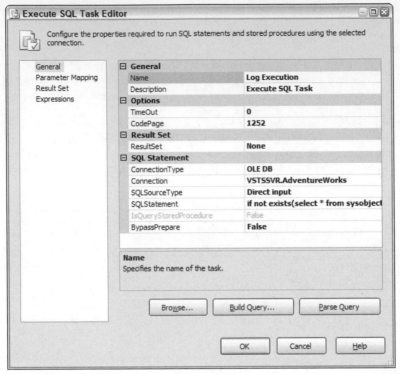

Figure 18-49

It is always a good practice to check your SQL before execution. Do so by clicking the Parse Query button and correct if necessary. Then click OK to continue.

Connect the Data Flow task to the Execute SQL task by dragging the output (green arrow) of the Data Flow task over the Execute SQL task as shown in Figure 18-50.

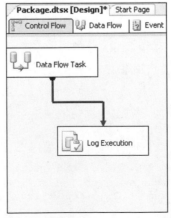

Figure 18-50

Save your changes by clicking the Save button on the toolbar. You now have updated your SSIS project and saved the changes to disk, but you have not committed the changes to source control. You can verify this in the Pending Changes window by clicking View ➪ Other Windows ➪ Pending Changes as shown in Figure 18-51.

Figure 18-51

The Change column indicates that the Package.dtsx is in an Edit status. This means that changes to the existing source-controlled Package.dtsx file have been detected. Click the Check In button. The next section introduces shelving and unshelving changes, using the code in its current state.

Shelving and Unshelving

Shelving is a new concept in Microsoft source control technology. It allows you to preserve a snapshot of the current source state on the server for later retrieval and resumed development. You can also shelve code and pass it to another developer as part of a workload reassignment. In automated nightly build environments, shelving provides a means to preserve semi-complete code in a source control system without fully checking it into the build.

To shelve code, click the Shelve button on the Pending Checkin toolbar. The Shelve dialog box appears, as shown in Figure 18-52.

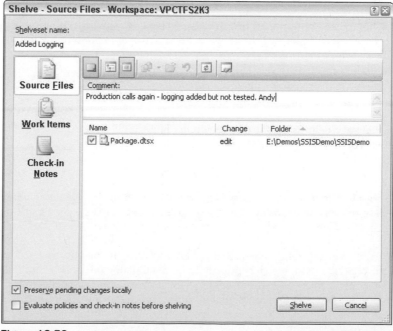

Figure 18-52

The "Preserve pending changes locally" checkbox allows you to choose between rolling back or keeping the edits since the last source code check-in. Checking the checkbox will keep the changes. Unchecking the checkbox will roll changes back to the last source-controlled version.

The rollback will effectively "undo" all changes—even changes saved to disk.

Leave the Preserve Pending Changes Locally checkbox checked and click Shelve to proceed.

To unshelve code, click the Unshelve button on the Pending Checkin toolbar. You'll see the dialog box shown in Figure 18-53.

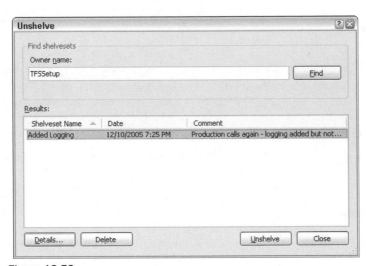

Figure 18-53

Click Unshelve to proceed with unshelving. The Unshelve Details wizard opens, providing options for unshelving metadata and preserving the shelve set on the server as shown in Figure 18-54.

Unshelving code with conflicts will roll the project back to its state at the time of shelving. For this reason, you may wish to consider shelving your current version of the code prior to unshelving a previous version.

If you see the dialog box similar to the one shown in Figure 18-55 and respond by clicking Yes or Yes to All, your current version will be rolled back to the shelve set version.

Branching

The ability to *branch* code provides a mechanism to preserve the current state of a SSIS project *and* modify it in some fashion. Think of it as driving a stake in the sod of project space marking the status of the current change set as "good."

To branch, open Source Control Explorer. Right-click the project name you wish to branch and click Branch from the context menu, which brings up the Branch dialog box shown in Figure 18-56. Select a name for the branched project and enter it into the To text box. Note the option to lock the new branch—thus preserving it indefinitely from accidental modification. You can further secure the branched code by including the option to not create local working copies for the new branch.

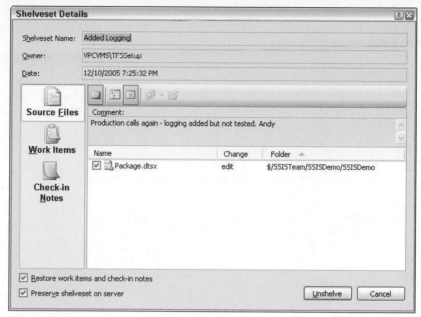

Figure 18-54

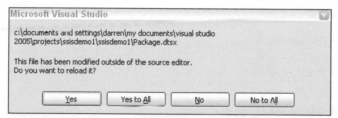

Figure 18-55

Figure 18-56

Merging

Merging is the inverse operation for branching. It involves recombining code that has been modified with a branch that has not been modified.

To merge projects, open Source Control Explorer. Right-click the name of the branched project containing the changes and click Merge. The project you right-clicked in the previous step should appear in the Source Branch text box of the Version Control Merge Wizard. Select the Target branch (the branch containing no changes) from the Target Branch drop-down, as shown in Figure 18-57. Note the options to merge all or selected changes from the Source branch into the Target branch. Click Next to proceed.

The Source Control Merge Wizard allows users to select the version criteria during merge. The options include Latest Version (default), workspace, label, date, and change set. Click Finish to proceed.

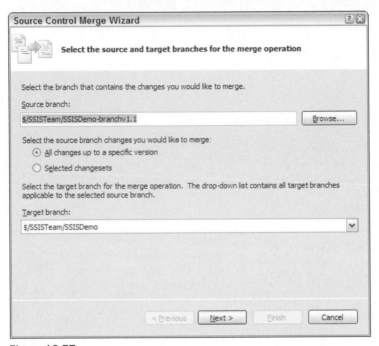

Figure 18-57

If the Version Control Merge Wizard encounters errors while attempting the merge, the Resolve Conflicts dialog box is displayed. Click Auto-Merge All to attempt an automatic merge. Click Resolve to manually merge branches.

When all conflicts have been resolved, the Resolve Conflicts dialog will reflect this condition.

Labeling (Striping) Source Versions

Labeling provides a means to mark (or "stripe") a version of the code. Generally, labeling is the last step performed in a source-controlled version of code — marking the version as complete. Additional changes require a branch.

To label a version, open Source Control Explorer. Right-click the project and click Apply Label. Enter a name for the Label and optional comment. Click the Add button to select files or project(s) to be labeled as shown in Figure 18-58.

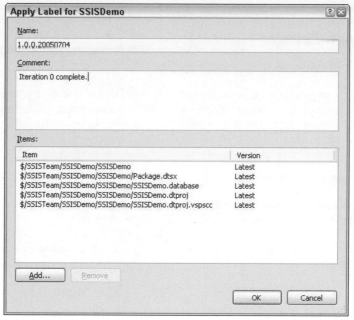

Figure 18-58

Click OK to complete labeling.

Much has been debated about when to Shelve, Branch, or Label. The following advice is based on years of utilizing many software source control products:

❑ **Shelve** — When your code is not code complete. In other words, if your code isn't ready for the nightly or weekly build, shelve it for now.

❑ **Branch** — When you need to add functionality and features to an application that can be considered complete in some form. Some shops will have you branch if the code can be successfully built; others will insist on no branching unless the code can be labeled.

❑ **Label** — When you wish to mark a version of the application as "complete." In practice, labels *are* the version; for instance "1.2.0.2406."

Code Deployment and Promotion from Development to Test to Production

In DTS, you had the option to store packages in SQL Server or persist them to disk as either a Visual Basic or Structured Storage file. But most DTS development occurred within the context of a SQL Server.

SQL Server Integration Services is decoupled from the SQL Server engine. Packages are developed in either Business Intelligence Development Studio or Visual Studio 2005. Because of this, code promotion is addressed in different ways.

For instance, in DTS you would likely develop a package on a local or development server. You would unit test the package to ensure proper functionality and desired results, and then you would click Package ⇨ Save As to promote the package to a test server. This was by no means the only method available, but it was a popular method for accomplishing package migration through the SDLC hierarchy in many SQL Server 2000 shops.

Now that SSIS is decoupled from the SQL Server environment, developing packages is equivalent to external software development. Some DBAs have experience as developers. To them, this will pose no challenge or threat. To others, this may be outside their comfort zone. To the uncomfortable, I say, "Relax. You can do this!"

The Deployment Wizard

You will now look at one method for migrating a package created in Visual Studio 2005 into an instance of SQL Server 2005 Integration Services: using the Deployment wizard.

For the example, you'll use a project you built in Chapter 17. You can substitute the previous project or a project of your own.

In Solution Explorer, right-click the project and click Properties to display the project Property Pages. Click Deployment Utility beneath Configuration Properties and set CreateDeploymentUtility to True as shown in Figure 18-59.

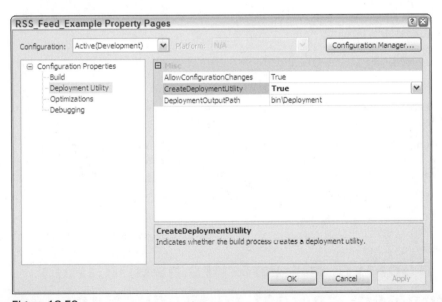

Figure 18-59

Click OK to close the Property Pages.

Build the solution in Visual Studio 2005 (or Business Intelligence Development Studio) by clicking Build ⇨ the Build Solution (or Build [Solution Name]). A \Deployment folder is created in the project \bin directory if you accepted the Configuration Property defaults in a previous step. The Deployment folder contains the package dtsx files (one per package in the project) and a file of type SSISDeploymentManifest (one per project). To deploy the package, right-click the SSISDeploymentManifest file and click Deploy to start the Package Installation Wizard.

The Package Installation Wizard allows you to install a SSIS package to an instance of Integration Services or to a File System location. For SQL Server or File System installations, a folder is created (the default directory is in %Program Files%) to hold support files only or support and package dtsx files, respectively — as shown in Figure 18-60.

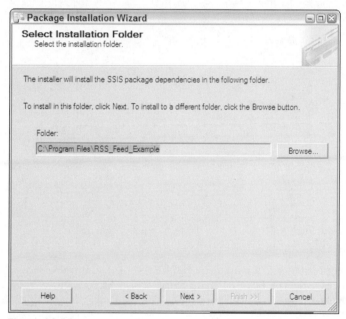

Figure 18-60

After you select the installation location, click Next to continue. A confirmation wizard screen displays; click Next to continue. A summary displays showing the location of the files installed; click Finish to complete the installation.

Import a Package

Another method for migrating a code-complete package is to import it directly into an instance of Integration Services on a target server, as follows:

First, build the solution. The Output window will display a message indicating the status of the build. If the Output window is not visible, click View ⇨ Other Windows ⇨ Output to view it.

Once the solution has been successfully built, open Microsoft SQL Server Management Studio and connect to an instance of Integration Services on the destination SQL Server. In the Integration Services treeview, expand the Stored Packages item. There are two subitems listed beneath Stored Packages: File System and MSDB. The package may be imported into either (or both — with the same name, if desired). Right-click File System or MSDB and click Import Package to begin the import.

Select a Package location (SQL Server, File System, or SSIS Package Store). Choosing File System disables the Server text box and Authentication controls. Select File System. Click the ellipsis beside the Package Path text box and navigate to the dtsx file of the package you desire to import as shown in Figure 18-61. Enter a Package name in the appropriate text box and click OK to import the package.

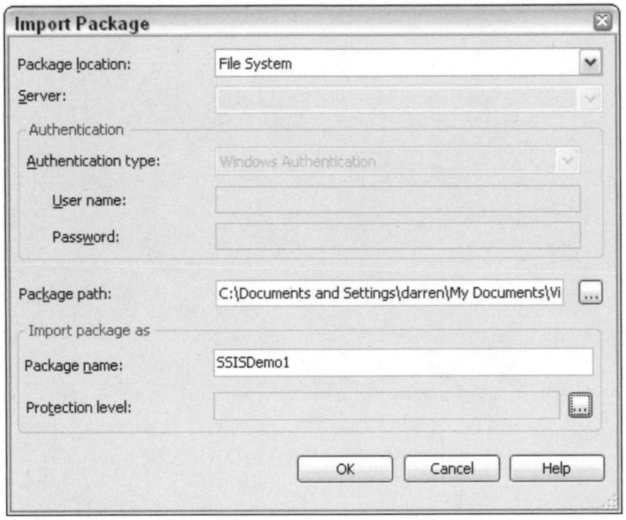

Figure 18-61

Once a package is imported into an instance of SQL Server Integration Services, it may be exported to another instance of SQL Server, File System, or SSIS Package Store via the Export Package functionality as shown in Figure 18-62. To start the export, right-click the Package name and click Export Package.

Export functionality can be used to promote SSIS packages from development to test to production environments.

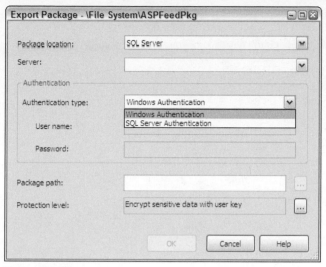

Figure 18-62

Summary

You now have a clearer picture of the Software Development Life Cycle of SSIS projects. In this chapter, you learned how to use the new Integrated Development Environment (IDE) to add SSIS projects to Microsoft Visual SourceSafe. You also learned how to do the following:

❏ Create a Team Project in Team System

❏ Add a SSIS project to the Team Project

❏ Manage and report project status

❏ Control the SSIS source code

Finally, you have more experience with code promotion — deploying an SSIS package from Development to an Integration Services server, as well as exporting a package to another Integration Services server.

You know more about software development methodologies and about how Team Foundation Server allows you to customize Team System to clearly reflect your methodology of choice. Team System is a fascinating framework! I encourage you to learn more about Team System and Team Foundation Server from the *Professional Visual Studio 2005 Team System,* by Jean-Luc David, et al. (Wiley, 2006), and the MSDN Team System Developer center (http://lab.msdn.microsoft.com/teamsystem).

Case Study: A Programmatic Example

Typically a book like this has to cover so much material that there is not enough space to really dig into some of the typical issues that you run into when you put the book down and start putting together your first solution. You end up coming back to the book to flip through all of the one-off examples, but they just don't seem to provide any insight or applicability to your current project or deadline. The case study is your best chance to get specific, to get into the ring, to take a business issue and run with it. Hopefully you'll be the beneficiary of this.

You will use the SSIS environment to solve a payment processing problem with varying levels of quality payment data that has to be validated against corporate billing records. This example is a little different from the typical data-warehouse-type ETL case study; it's a little more programmatic. You'll combine the need to import heterogeneous data formats and to validate and apply programming logic into a solid learning opportunity that showcases the new capabilities of SSIS.

Background

Company ABC is a small benefits company that sells several niche products to other small business owners. They offer these products directly to the employees of the small businesses, but the employers are billed, not the employees. Company ABC considers the employers to be their customer and creates monthly invoices for the employee-selected services. Each invoice contains an invoice number for reference purposes. Company ABC's customers deduct the cost of the products from the employee paychecks. These payments are then submitted back to Company ABC in a lump sum, but because of timing issues and ever-changing worker populations, the payment doesn't always match the billed amount. Customers have the option of paying invoices using one of the following payment methods:

❑ Pay by using PayPal or an e-mail payment service. These services directly credit a corporate bank account and typically provide a small description of the service being paid, the amount, and an e-mail address or other type of surrogate user identity. These entries are downloaded daily from an online bank account and are available within an OLE DB–compliant data source.

❑ Pay by check. The customer sends a copy of the invoice and a check in the mail to a special address that is serviced by a bank. The invoice could fully, partially, or not even accompany the payment. The bank credits the account for each check received and provides an output file containing as much data as practicable from the supporting material to help the company identify and apply the payment. A payment that is serviced like this is commonly known as a *lockbox*.

❑ Pay by wire. Payments can be made by direct debit of customer bank accounts or direct credit to the corporate account. These payments are known as wires. This type of entry is usually provided through large banks or automated clearinghouses (ACH).

Business Problem

Just working with the low-quality payment data involves a significant amount of manual lookup to match payments to customers and invoices. Since Company ABC is growing, the volume of payments is exceeding their capacity to continue to process payments manually. If the invoice number was always received with the payment, an automated process could easily identify the customer from the invoice and make some decisions about the payment by comparing the paid and billed amounts. So far, attempts at automating even the paper invoice through the mail have failed because customers don't always send in copies of invoices, or they send in old, outdated invoices. Using the bank lockbox has helped ease the burden of getting the deposits processed, but the bank makes mistakes too, truncating and transposing customer name or invoice data. Opening up the company to wires and PayPal accounts has really complicated matters, since very little corroborating data is provided in these transactions.

Approximately 60% of the incoming payments can't be automatically identified using a strict compare of invoice number and payment amount. The good news is that they can almost all be manually identified by a small group of subject matter experts (SMEs) who really understand the process and know how to use the corporate data. The bad news is that once a customer and invoice are identified by the SMEs, the method of making the match is not recorded. The next month the process of identification starts all over again. Company ABC needs a way to wade through the payments automatically, to take the place of the SMEs. This process should match items by invoice number, name, and e-mail address with some measurable certainty and leave only the most troublesome payments for research activity. They need a solution that runs continuously to meet the demands of a 24-hour turnaround standard for their industry.

Solution Summary

Company ABC has made the need to resolve this payment processing hurdle their top priority. They already have a custom software application that gives users the ability to break the bulk payments down to an employee level, but the application requires that the customer and invoice be identified. The solution is to use SSIS to develop a package that can process data from these heterogeneous data sources. This solution should require no human intervention on items that can be identified as paid-as-billed items. The solution should be as "smart" as possible and be able to identify bank items that have been manually identified before. Items that can't be identified will still need to be processed manually, but it is expected that this number should drop 20 to 40 percent.

In preparation for the design of the SSIS package, specification documents for the two input files, ACH and Lockbox, have been gathered. The files contain multiple payment transactions and can be sent by both the bank and ACH clearinghouse to specific folders. Your process should be able to access these folders and continuously look for new files to process. When a file is located in the input folder, it needs to be validated for proper format, for previous processing, so a file is not processed more than once, and for each payment to summarize and balance to the total deposit. Files not meeting these criteria will be rejected. Once a file is verified, each payment in the file should be examined for matches to existing invoices. If no match is found, the data should be examined against previously matched data. Matched data will flow into a completed queue to be broken into employee-level charges by another piece of software. Unmatched data will flow into a working queue that will require user intervention. User matches will be stored for future matching. Finally, statistics will be created for the input for reporting purposes. Figure 19-1 is a diagram of the business solution.

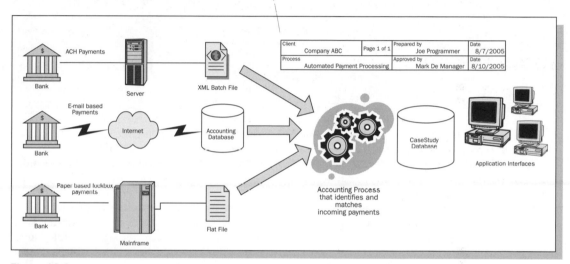

Figure 19-1

Solution Architecture

Before you jump into building this integration service, you should lay out what you want to accomplish. You have two sets of tasks: first, to import files of different formats, to validate, and to load them into your data structures; and second, to process the payments to find customer and invoice matches. Figure 19-2 shows a design where the logic is divided into two packages. Since the main job of the first task is to load, you'll name the first package CaseStudy_Load. This package will perform the loading process for each of the three import types. (There is also a good argument for having three separate packages: CaseStudy_ACH_Load, CaseStudy_LB_Load, and CaseStudy_Epay_Load.) The identification logic to apply to each transaction in the payment data is universal, so it makes sense to put this logic into a separate package. You can name this package CaseStudy_Process.

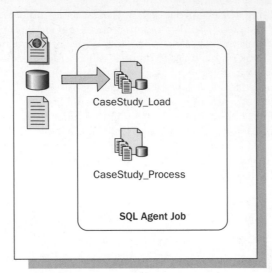

Figure 19-2

When you are building packages that have external dependencies such as file hierarchies, it is a good idea to programmatically validate the locations for existence before processing. You'll check for default paths and create them if they don't exist. If files for the Lockbox or ACH processes exist, you should read the files, parse the transaction information, validate totals against a control record in the file, and then persist the information from the file into permanent storage. You should also confirm the acceptance of the transaction with the bank. The toughest part of this processing logic is that the validation routines have to validate file formats, proper data types, and file balances and check for file duplication. When processing any flat file from an external source, be aware of how that import file was generated and what you might find in it. Don't be surprised to find that some systems allow a date of 02/30/2005 or amount fields with data like .0023E2.

The downloaded bank transactions for the PayPal or E-Pay transactions will be easier to process — at least from an import standpoint. You only need to read information from a table in another OLE DB–compliant data source. You'll be creating a batch from the transactions, so balancing also shouldn't be an issue. The hardest part will be identifying these payments, since usually only an amount and an e-mail address are embedded in the transaction. All this information can be summarized in a flowchart like the one in Figure 19-3.

In the CaseStudy_Process package, you are required to complete a matching process of the payment information to find customers and invoices. You'll first attempt a high-confidence match using an exact match to the invoice number. If a match is not made, you'll move to a fuzzy lookup on the invoice number. If a match is still not made, you'll keep moving down to lower-confidence-level matches until you can retrieve an invoice or at least customer identification. Transactions identifiable only by customer will be checked against available invoices for a match within a billed-to-paid tolerance of 5 percent. Transactions that simply don't have enough certainty to be identified will be left at this point to subject-matter experts who will individually review and research the transactions to identify the customer or refund the payment. Research can be saved via software outside this SSIS project into the CustomerLookup table. A summary flowchart for the CaseStudy_Process package is shown in Figure 19-4.

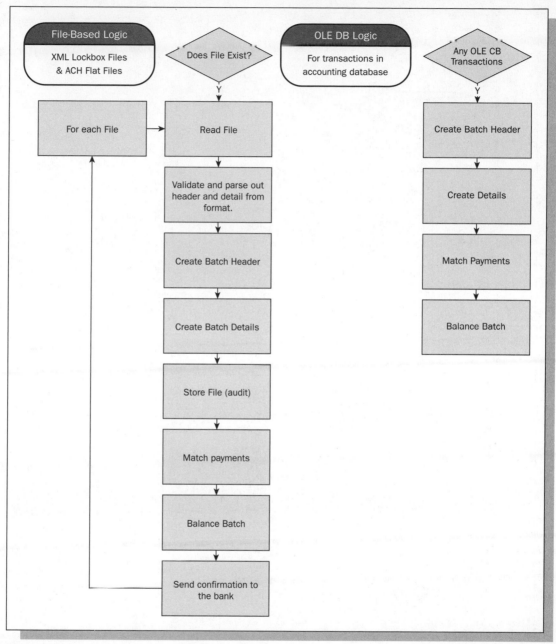

Figure 19-3

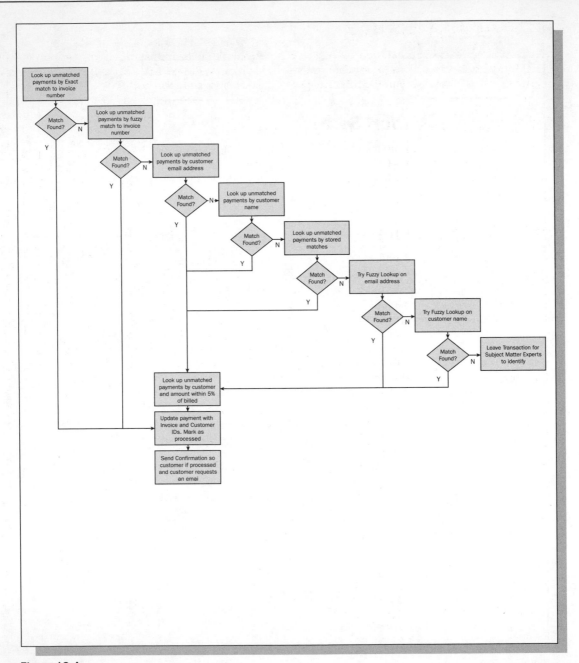

Figure 19-4

Data Architecture

This section will detail the data sources both in SQL Server and in the format of each of the input files. First, create default locations to simulate your receiving area for the external files, and then you'll take a closer look at each of the input files that are part of the business requirements.

File Storage Location Setup

Create a base directory to store the file-based imports to this project. Throughout the case study, the base location will be referred to as C:\casestudy\ for file-based imports. In the base directory, create two sub-directories: ACH\ and LOCKBOX\. You will use these locations to store the files you'll create in the next few sections.

Bank ACH Payments

Customers make payments within their own banks or electronic payment systems to ABC Company through an automated clearinghouse. The automated clearinghouse bundles up all the payments for the day and sends one XML file through an encrypted VPN connection to an encrypted folder. The bank wires contain only a little bit of information at the transactional level. Each XML file does contain a header row with a unique ID that identifies the file transmission. The header also contains a total deposit amount and a transaction count that can be used to further verify the file transmission. Each transactional detail row represents a deposit and contains two date fields: the date the deposit item was received and the date the deposit item was posted to ABC Company's deposit account. Each payment contains the amount of the deposit and a free-form field that could contain the customer's name on a bank account, an e-mail address, or anything the customer adds to the wire. More commonly the description contains the name on the customer's bank account—which is often very different from the name in Company ABC's customer data. To make the sample ACH file, and for each file in this example, you'll need to re-create these files manually or download the files from this book's page at www.wrox.com. Download or create a file named c:\casestudy\ach\sampleach.xml that looks like the following:

```
<BATCH>
<HEADER><ID>AAS22119289</ID>
<TOTALDEPOSIT>180553.00</TOTALDEPOSIT>
<DEPOSITDATE>07/15/2005</DEPOSITDATE>
<TOTALTRANS>6</TOTALTRANS>
</HEADER>
<DETAIL><AMOUNT>23318.00</AMOUNT>
<DESC>Complete Enterprises</DESC>
<RECEIVEDDATE>07/15/2005</RECEIVEDDATE>
<POSTEDDATE>07/15/2005</POSTEDDATE></DETAIL>
<DETAIL><AMOUNT>37054.00</AMOUNT>
<DESC>Premier Sport</DESC>
<RECEIVEDDATE>07/15/2005</RECEIVEDDATE>
<POSTEDDATE>07/15/2005</POSTEDDATE></DETAIL>
<DETAIL><AMOUNT>34953.00</AMOUNT>
<DESC>Intl Sports Association</DESC>
<RECEIVEDDATE>07/15/2005</RECEIVEDDATE>
<POSTEDDATE>07/15/2005</POSTEDDATE></DETAIL>
<DETAIL><AMOUNT>22660.00</AMOUNT>
<DESC>Arthur Datum</DESC>
```

```
<RECEIVEDDATE>07/15/2005</RECEIVEDDATE>
<POSTEDDATE>07/15/2005</POSTEDDATE></DETAIL>
<DETAIL><AMOUNT>24759.00</AMOUNT>
<DESC>Northwind Traders</DESC>
<RECEIVEDDATE>07/15/2005</RECEIVEDDATE>
<POSTEDDATE>07/15/2005</POSTEDDATE></DETAIL>
<DETAIL><AMOUNT>37809.00</AMOUNT>
<DESC>Wood Fitness</DESC>
<RECEIVEDDATE>07/15/2005</RECEIVEDDATE>
<POSTEDDATE>07/15/2005</POSTEDDATE></DETAIL>
</BATCH>
```

Lockbox Files

Company ABC has starting using a lockbox service that their bank provides for a nominal fee. This service images all check and invoice stubs sent to a specific address that the bank monitors. The bank provides a data file containing the following data attributes for each deposit item: the amount, a reference number for the invoice, and an image key that can be used to review the images of the item online. The terms of the service dictate that if the bank can't determine the invoice number because of legibility issues, or if the invoice is not sent in with the deposit item, either a customer account number or a customer name may be used in place of the invoice number. Periodically during the day, the bank will batch a series of payments into one file containing a header that includes a batch number, the posted deposit date for all deposit items, and an expected total for the batch.

The structure of the file from the bank is as follows:

```
HEADER:
TYPE            1A          TYPE OF LINE H-HEADER
POSTDATE        6A          DATE DEPOSIT POSTED
FILLER          1A          SPACE(1)
BATCHID         12A         UNIQUE BATCH NBR

DETAIL (TYPE I):
TYPE            1A          TYPE OF LINE I-INVOICE
IMGID           10A         IMAGE LOOK UP ID (2-6 IS ID)
DESC            25A         INVOICE OR DESC INFO

DETAIL (TYPE C)
TYPE            1A          TYPE OF LINE C-CHECK
IMGID           10A         IMAGE LOOK UP ID (2-6 IS ID)
DESC            8S 2        CHECK AMOUNT
```

Download or create using the following code a file named c:\casestudy\lockbox\samplelockbox.txt to simulate the Lockbox transmission in this example:

```
H080105 B1239-99Z-99 0058730760
I4001010003 181INTERNAT
C4001010004   01844400
I4002020005 151METROSPOOO1
C4002020006   02331800
I4003030009 MAGIC CYCLES
C4003030010   02697000
```

```
I4004040013 LINDELL
C4004040014   02131800
I4005040017 151GMASKI0001
C4005040019   01938800
```

PayPal or Direct Credits to Corporate Account

Company ABC has started a pilot program to allow customers to make payments using PayPal and other similar online electronic payment services. Customers like this option because it is easy to use. However, these payments are difficult to process for the Accounting group, because not all e-mail addresses have been collected for the customers and that is the most common description on the transactions. Accounting personnel have to do some research to determine who the customer is and to release the deposit to the payment systems. They would like to be able to input the e-mail address into the customer records and have that data used in future processing. Currently the accounting department uses a data synch process in their accounting software to download these transactions directly from a special bank account periodically during the day. This information is available through a read-only view in the database called [vCorpDirectAcctTrans]. Figure 19-5 shows the structure of this view.

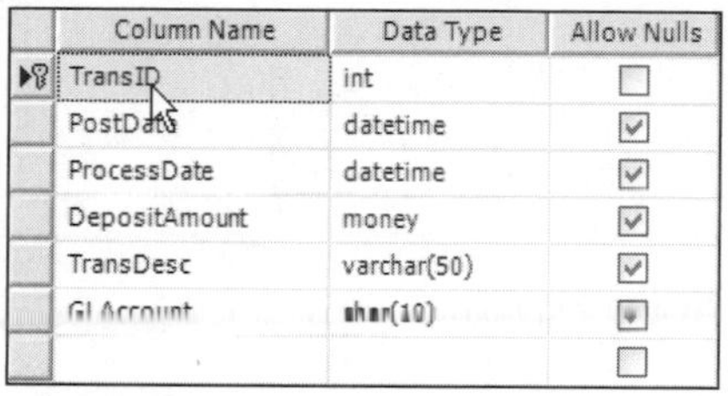

Column Name	Data Type	Allow Nulls
TransID	int	☐
PostDate	datetime	☑
ProcessDate	datetime	☑
DepositAmount	money	☑
TransDesc	varchar(50)	☑
Gl Account	char(10)	☑
		☐

Figure 19-5

Case Study Database Model

The case study database model (see Figure 19-6) is limited to only the information relevant to the case study. The core entities are the following:

❑ **Customer:** An entity that utilizes products and services from Company ABC. To keep it simple, only the customer name, account number, and e-mail address attributes are represented in the table.

❑ **Invoice:** A monthly listing of total billed products and services for each customer. Each invoice is represented by a unique invoice number. Invoice details are not shown in the case study data model for simplicity.

❑ **BankBatch:** Any set of transactions from a bank or deposit institution that is combined. Auditable information expected for the exchange of monetary data is a major part of this entity. Files, or batches, of transactions must be validated in terms of the number of transaction lines and most importantly by amount. Care must be taken not to load a batch more than once. Recording the bank batch number or BankBatchNbr field and comparing incoming batches should allow you to keep this from happening.

❏ **BankBatchDetail:** Each bank batch will be composed of many transactions that break down into essentially a check and an invoice. You could receive as much as both pieces of information or as little as none of this information. For auditing purposes, you should record exactly what you received from the input source. You'll also store in this table logically determined foreign keys for the customer and invoice dimension.

❏ **CustomerLookUp:** This lookup table will be populated by your SSIS package and an external application. This will allow users to store matching information to identify customers for future processing. This will allow the data import processes to "learn" good matches from bad data.

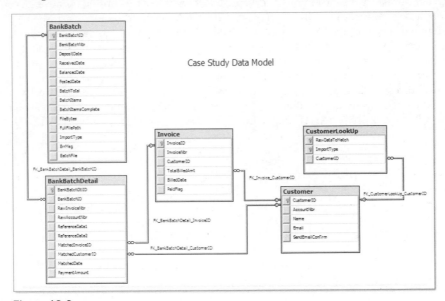

Figure 19-6

Database Setup

To get started, you need to set up the database named CaseStudy. The database and all objects in it will become the basis for your solution to this business issue. Of course, as mentioned earlier, all input files and scripts are available from the www.wrox.com Web site. There are two ways to create a new database. Use the Microsoft SQL Management Studio to connect to a server or database engine of your choice. On the Databases node, right-click and select the pop-up menu option New Database. In the New Database editor, provide the Database name as CaseStudy. Press the OK button to accept the other defaults. The second easy option is to run the following SQL script in a new query editor:

```
USE [master]
GO
CREATE DATABASE [CaseStudy] ON  PRIMARY
( NAME = N'CaseStudy', FILENAME = N'C:\Program Files\Microsoft SQL
Server\MSSQL.1\MSSQL\DATA\CaseStudy.mdf' , SIZE = 3072KB , MAXSIZE = UNLIMITED,
FILEGROWTH = 1024KB )
 LOG ON
( NAME = N'CaseStudy_log', FILENAME = N'C:\Program Files\Microsoft SQL
```

```
Server\MSSQL.1\MSSQL\DATA\ CaseStudy_log.ldf' , SIZE = 1024KB , MAXSIZE = 2048GB ,
FILEGROWTH = 10%)
 COLLATE Latin1_General_CI_AI
GO
EXEC dbo.sp_dbcmptlevel @dbname=N'CaseStudy', @new_cmptlevel=90
GO
EXEC [CaseStudy].[dbo].[sp_fulltext_database] @action = 'disable'
GO
```

Customer

The customer table can be created in the Microsoft SQL Server Management Studio. Click on the New Query button in the toolbar to open a New Query window. Run the following SQL statement in the window.

```
use casestudy
GO
CREATE TABLE [dbo].[Customer](
   [CustomerID] [int] IDENTITY(1,1) NOT NULL,
   [AccountNbr] [char](15) NOT NULL,
   [Name] [varchar](50)    NOT NULL,
   [Email] [varchar](50)    NULL,
   [SendEmailConfirm] [bit] NOT NULL CONSTRAINT [DF_Customer_SendEmailConfirm]
DEFAULT ((0)),
 CONSTRAINT [PK_Customer] PRIMARY KEY CLUSTERED
(
   [CustomerID] ASC
) ON [PRIMARY]
) ON [PRIMARY]
```

To fill the table with potential customers, you'll need access to an AdventureWorks database. You'll use the vendor table to create your customers.

```
use casestudy
GO
INSERT INTO CaseStudy..Customer(AccountNbr, [Name])
SELECT AccountNumber, [Name] as CustName
FROM adventureworks.purchasing.vendor
GO
```

You'll also use the AdventureWorks data to create some e-mail addresses. Run the following SQL script to populate the e-mail field in the customer table.

```
use casestudy
GO
UPDATE Customer
SET Email = subqry.email,
    SendEmailConfirm = case when len(subqry.email) > 0 then 1 else 0 end
FROM Customer cust
INNER JOIN (
    SELECT v.vendorid as CustomerID, email =
        case when len(replace(replace(replace(replace([name], '&', ''), ' ', ''),
        '.', ''), ',', '')) > 15
```

```
        and ascii(left(c.firstname, 1)) < 70 then
            left(c.firstname, 1) + rtrim(c.lastname) + '@msn.com'

        when len(replace(replace(replace(replace([name], '&', ''), ' ', ''), '.',
    ''), ',', '')) < 15
        and (len(rtrim(c.lastname)) + 1) < 16 then
            left(c.firstname, 1) + rtrim(c.lastname) + '@' +
            replace(replace(replace(replace([name], '&', ''), ' ', ''), '.', ''),
                ',', '') + '.com'

        else NULL end
    FROM adventureworks.purchasing.vendor v
    INNER JOIN adventureworks.person.contact c
    ON vendorid = contactid
) subQry
ON cust.CustomerID = subQry.CustomerID
```

Invoice

To create the invoice table, run the following SQL statement:

```
USE [CaseStudy]
GO
CREATE TABLE [dbo].[Invoice](
  [InvoiceID] [int] IDENTITY(1,1) NOT NULL,
  [InvoiceNbr] [varchar](50) NOT NULL,
  [CustomerID] [int] NOT NULL,
  [TotalBilledAmt] [money] NOT NULL,
  [BilledDate] [datetime] NOT NULL,
  [PaidFlag] [smallint] NOT NULL CONSTRAINT [DF_Invoice_PaidFlag]  DEFAULT ((0)),
 CONSTRAINT [PK_Invoice] PRIMARY KEY CLUSTERED
(
  [InvoiceID] ASC
) ON [PRIMARY]
) ON [PRIMARY]
GO
ALTER TABLE [dbo].[Invoice]  WITH NOCHECK ADD  CONSTRAINT [FK_Invoice_CustomerID]
FOREIGN KEY([CustomerID])
REFERENCES [dbo].[Customer] ([CustomerID])
GO
ALTER TABLE [dbo].[Invoice] CHECK CONSTRAINT [FK_Invoice_CustomerID]
```

You will use the customer table to generate three months' worth of invoice data. In doing so, you are creating invoice numbers with the customer account number embedded in the invoice number. Companies commonly do this because it provides an extra piece of identification as a cross-check in an environment where there is very limited data. Use the following SQL script to create the invoice entries:

```
INSERT INTO Invoice(InvoiceNbr, CustomerID, TotalBilledAmt, BilledDate, PaidFlag)
SELECT  InvoiceNbr = '151' + Accountnbr,
        CustomerID,
        TotalBilledAmt = cast(131 * (ascii(left(name, 1)) + ascii(substring(name,
                         2, 1))) as money),
        BilledDate = '06/01/2005 00:00:00',
        PaidFlag = 0
```

```
FROM customer
UNION
SELECT   InvoiceNbr = '181' + Accountnbr,
         CustomerID,
         TotalBilledAmt = case
            when left(Accountnbr, 1) in ('A', 'B', 'C', 'D', 'E', 'F', 'G')
            then cast(131 * (ascii(left(name, 1)) + ascii(substring(name, 2, 1)))
                 as money)
            else
                cast(191 * (ascii(left(name, 1)) + ascii(substring(name, 2, 1)))
                as money)
            end,
         BilledDate = '07/01/2005 00:00:00',
         PaidFlag = 0
FROM customer
UNION
SELECT   InvoiceNbr = '212' + Accountnbr,
         CustomerID,
         TotalBilledAmt = case
            when left(Accountnbr, 1) in ('A', 'F', 'G')
            then cast(132 * (ascii(left(name, 1)) + ascii(substring(name, 2, 1)))
                 as money)
            else
                cast(155 * (ascii(left(name, 1)) + ascii(substring(name, 2, 1)))
                as money)
            end,
         BilledDate = '08/01/2005 00:00:00',
         PaidFlag = 0
FROM customer
GO
UPDATE invoice set totalbilledamt = 18444.00
WHERE invoicenbr = '151INTERNAT0002' and totalbilledamt = 23973
```

CustomerLookUp

The customer lookup table will be used to verify some repeated bad data that continues to be sent through the accounting feeds. A bad data string can be stored for each import type as long as the data has been resolved into an existing customer. The structure can be created using the following SQL script:

```
USE [CaseStudy]
GO
CREATE TABLE [dbo].[CustomerLookUp](
  [RawDataToMatch] [varchar](50) NOT NULL,
  [ImportType] [char](10) NOT NULL,
  [CustomerID] [int] NOT NULL,
 CONSTRAINT [PK_CustomerLookUp] PRIMARY KEY CLUSTERED
(
  [RawDataToMatch] ASC,
  [ImportType] ASC
) ON [PRIMARY]
) ON [PRIMARY]
GO
ALTER TABLE [dbo].[CustomerLookUp]  WITH NOCHECK ADD  CONSTRAINT
[FK_CustomerLookUp_CustomerID] FOREIGN KEY([CustomerID])
```

```
REFERENCES [dbo].[Customer] ([CustomerID])
GO
ALTER TABLE [dbo].[CustomerLookUp] CHECK CONSTRAINT [FK_CustomerLookUp_CustomerID]
BankBatch
```

The BankBatch table will not only store the summary data from the batch file but also store the file itself in the BatchFile field. This table can be created using the following SQL statement.

```
USE [CaseStudy]
GO
CREATE TABLE [dbo].[BankBatch](
   [BankBatchID] [int] NOT NULL,
   [BankBatchNbr] [nvarchar](50) NULL,
   [DepositDate] [datetime] NULL,
   [ReceivedDate] [datetime] NULL,
   [BalancedDate] [datetime] NULL,
   [PostedDate] [datetime] NULL,
   [BatchTotal] [money] NULL,
   [BatchItems] [int] NULL,
   [BatchItemsComplete] [int] NULL,
   [FileBytes] [int] NULL,
   [FullFilePath] [nchar](100) NULL,
   [ImportType] [char](1) NULL,
   [ErrMsg] [varchar](100) NULL,
   [BatchFile] [ntext] NULL,
 CONSTRAINT [PK_BankBatch] PRIMARY KEY CLUSTERED
(
   [BankBatchID] ASC
) ON [PRIMARY]
) ON [PRIMARY] TEXTIMAGE_ON [PRIMARY]
```

BankBatchDetail

The detail to the BankBatch table can be created using the following SQL script:

```
USE [CaseStudy]
GO
CREATE TABLE [dbo].[BankBatchDetail](
   [BankBatchDtlID] [int] NOT NULL,
   [BankBatchID] [int] NOT NULL,
   [RawInvoiceNbr] [nvarchar](15) NULL,
   [RawAccountNbr] [nvarchar](15) NULL,
   [ReferenceData1] [nvarchar](15) NULL,
   [ReferenceData2] [nvarchar](15) NULL,
   [MatchedInvoiceID] [int] NULL,
   [MatchedCustomerID] [int] NULL,
   [MatchedDate] [datetime] NULL,
 CONSTRAINT [PK_BankBatchDtlID] PRIMARY KEY CLUSTERED
(
   [BankBatchDtlID] ASC
) ON [PRIMARY]
) ON [PRIMARY]

ALTER TABLE [dbo].[BankBatchDetail]  WITH NOCHECK ADD  CONSTRAINT
```

```
[FK_BankBatchDetail_BankBatchID] FOREIGN KEY([BankBatchID])
REFERENCES [dbo].[BankBatch] ([BankBatchID])
GO
ALTER TABLE [dbo].[BankBatchDetail] CHECK CONSTRAINT
[FK_BankBatchDetail_BankBatchID]
GO
ALTER TABLE [dbo].[BankBatchDetail]  WITH CHECK ADD  CONSTRAINT
[FK_BankBatchDetail_CustomerID] FOREIGN KEY([MatchedCustomerID])
REFERENCES [dbo].[Customer] ([CustomerID])
GO
ALTER TABLE [dbo].[BankBatchDetail]  WITH CHECK ADD  CONSTRAINT
[FK_BankBatchDetail_InvoiceID] FOREIGN KEY([MatchedInvoiceID])
REFERENCES [dbo].[Invoice] ([InvoiceID])
```

Corporate Ledger Data

To simulate a view into your Direct Credits to the Corporate Account, you need to create the
GLAccountData structure and your view [vCorpDirectAcctTrans]. Run the following SQL to create the
physical table:

```
USE [CaseStudy]
GO
CREATE TABLE [dbo].[GLAccountData](
  [TransID] [int] IDENTITY(1,1) NOT NULL,
  [PostDate] [datetime] NULL,
  [ProcessDate] [datetime] NULL,
  [DepositAmount] [money] NULL,
  [TransDesc] [varchar](50) NULL,
  [GLAccount] [char](10) NULL,
 CONSTRAINT [PK_GLAccountData] PRIMARY KEY CLUSTERED
(
  [TransID] ASC
) ON [PRIMARY]
) ON [PRIMARY]
```

Run the following SQL to create the logical view to this data.

```
USE [CaseStudy]
GO
CREATE VIEW dbo.vCorpDirectAcctTrans
AS
SELECT      TransID, PostDate, ProcessDate, DepositAmount, TransDesc
FROM        dbo.GLAccountData
```

Run this SQL batch to load the GLAccountData with some sample deposit transactions from the direct-
pay customers:

```
INSERT INTO GLACCOUNTDATA(postdate, processdate, depositamount, transdesc,
glaccount)
SELECT '08/09/05', '08/10/05', 22794.00, 'PAYPAL*MBlack@Marsh.com', 'BANK'
UNION
SELECT '08/09/05', '08/10/05', 21484.00, 'PAYPAL*JBrown@CapitalCycles.com', 'BANK'
UNION
```

```
SELECT '08/09/05', '08/10/05', 22008.00, 'PAYPAL*DBlanco@msn.com', 'BANK'
UNION
SELECT '08/09/05', '08/10/05', 22794.00, 'PAYPAL*CBooth@MagicCycle', 'BANK'
UNION
SELECT '08/09/05', '08/10/05', 22401.00, 'PAYPAL*ABaltazar@msn.com', 'BANK'
```

ErrorDetail

Although there are some great new logging options in SSIS, there is still a need to log detailed errors that can occur at the column level when processing. This table will allow you to store that information, and by storing the Execution ID, you can later join the custom-logged error detail with the step-level error information logged during package execution.

```
USE [CaseStudy]
GO
CREATE TABLE [dbo].[ErrorDetail](
  [ExecutionID] [nchar](38) NOT NULL,
  [ErrorEvent] [nchar](20) NULL,
  [ErrorCode] [int] NULL,
  [ErrorColumn] [int] NULL,
  [ErrorDesc] [nvarchar](1048) NULL,
  [ErrorDate] [datetime] NULL,
  [RawData] [varchar](2048) NULL
) ON [PRIMARY]
```

Usp_BankBatch_Add

This stored procedure will be used to add a new bank batch to the payment processing system. Run the script to add this procedure to CaseStudy:

```
Use CaseStudy
GO
CREATE PROC usp_BankBatch_Add(
  @BankBatchID int OUTPUT,
  @BankBatchNbr nvarchar(50)=NULL,
  @DepositDate datetime=NULL,
  @ReceivedDate datetime=NULL,
  @BatchTotal money=NULL,
  @BatchItems int=NULL,
  @FileBytes int=NULL,
  @FullFilePath nvarchar(100)=NULL,
  @ImportType char(10)
)
AS
  /*=====================================================
   PROC: usp_BankBatch_Add
   PURPOSE: To Add BankBatch Header Basic info
            and to validate that the batch is new.
   OUTPUT: Will return BankBatchID if new or 0 if exists
   HISTORY: 08/01/05 Created
   =====================================================*/
  SET NOCOUNT ON
  If @ReceivedDate is null
```

```
                SET @ReceivedDate = getdate()

            IF LEN(@BankBatchNbr) <= 1 OR Exists(Select top 1 *
                FROM BankBatch
                WHERE BankBatchNbr = @BankBatchNbr
                AND ImportType = @ImportType)
            BEGIN
                SET @BANKBATCHID = 0
                RETURN -1
            END
        ELSE
            BEGIN
                INSERT INTO BankBatch(BankBatchNbr, DepositDate, ReceivedDate,
                                    BatchTotal, BatchItems, FileBytes, FullFilePath,
                                    ImportType)
                SELECT UPPER(@BankBatchNbr), @DepositDate, @ReceivedDate,
                            @BatchTotal, @BatchItems, @FileBytes, UPPER(@FullFilePath),
                            UPPER(@ImportType)

                SET @BANKBATCHID = Scope_Identity()
            END

    SET NOCOUNT OFF

GO
```

usp_BankBatchDetail_Match

This stored procedure will be used to update a payment with a matching invoice or customer identification number relating back to the dimension tables. Run the script to add this procedure to CaseStudy:

```
CREATE PROC dbo.usp_BankBatchDetail_Match(
            @BankBatchDtlID int,
            @InvoiceID int=NULL,
            @CustomerID int=NULL)
AS
    /*===============================================
     PROC: usp_BankBatchDetail_Match
     PURPOSE: To update as paid an incoming payment
              with matched invoice and customerid
     HISTORY: 00/01/05 Created
    ===============================================
    */

    SET NOCOUNT ON

    --UPDATE BANKBATCH DETAIL WITH INVOICE AND CUSTOMERID
    --NOTE: IF EITHER IS NULL THEN DON'T UPDATE
    --MATCHED DATE. THIS WILL PUSH THE ITEM INTO A SUBJECT-
    --MATTER-EXPERT'S QUEUE TO IDENTIFY.
    UPDATE BankBatchDetail
    SET MatchedInvoiceID = @InvoiceID,
        MatchedCustomerID = @CustomerID,
        MatchedDate = case when @InvoiceID is NULL or @CustomerID is NULL then NULL
```

```
                              else getdate() end
          WHERE BankBatchDtlID = @BankBatchDtlID

          SET NOCOUNT OFF
```

usp_BankBatch_Balance

This stored procedure is used to examine all payments in a batch and to mark the batch as complete when all payments have been identified with an invoice and a customer:

```
GO
CREATE PROC usp_BankBatch_Balance
AS
  /*=======================================================
   PROC: usp_BankBatch_Balance
   PURPOSE: To update batchdetails when they are matched
            Then keep BankBatches balanced by matching all
            line items
   =======================================================
  */
UPDATE bankbatchdetail
SET MatchedDate = GetDate()
where (matchedinvoiceid is not null
and matchedcustomerid is not null)
and  (matchedinvoiceid <> 0
and matchedcustomerid <> 0)

UPDATE BANKBATCH
SET BatchItemsComplete = BatchItems - b.NotComplete
FROM BANKBATCH A
INNER JOIN (
select bankbatchid, count(*) as NotComplete
from bankbatchdetail
where
(matchedinvoiceid is null
OR matchedcustomerid is null
OR matcheddate is null)
group by bankbatchid
) B
on A.BankBatchID = B.BankBatchID

UPDATE BankBatch
SET BalancedDate = getdate()
WHERE BalancedDate IS NULL
and BatchItems = BatchItemsComplete
```

Case Study Load Package

The import integration service will be the first of the two packages you will build for this project. To keep this from becoming a 100-step process, you'll break it up into several sections: Naming Conventions and Tips, Package Setup and File System Tasks, Lockbox Control Flow Processing, Lockbox

File Validation, Lockbox Processing, ACH Control Flow Processing, ACH Validation, ACH Processing, Email Control Flow Processing, and Email Data Flow Processing. Each step will be explained in detail the first time, and as things become repetitive, you'll pick up some speed.

Naming Conventions and Tips

There's nothing like opening up a package that fails in production and seeing tasks named Execute SQL Task, Execute SQL Task1, and Execute SQL Task2. What do they do? There is also something to be said when there is so much annotation that it is a nightmare to maintain. The balance depends on your philosophy and your team, but for now, the following rules seem to make sense in your SSIS development processes.

❑ Name the package. Name it something other than package.dtsx.

❑ Name packages with ETL verb extensions: <PACKAGE NAME>_Extract, <Package Name>_Transform, or <Package Name>_Load. The extension _Process seems to be explicit enough for those packages that don't fall into the other three categories.

❑ Provide some brief annotation about what the package does, where it gets inputs and outputs, and what to do if it fails. Can it be rerun again? Is it part of a larger set of packages? Should it be restarted on checkpoints?

❑ Add short descriptive words to SSIS tasks and transforms, but don't alter the name altogether. For example, change an Execute SQL task to Execute SQL Task to Retrieve Invoice ID. Use the description field on the object to provide the detailed information. (You'll see this info in a tooltip when the mouse hovers over the object.) It is important to document, but completely changing the name of an Execute SQL task to Retrieve Invoice ID obscures information about the "how" that is embedded with the knowledge that the task is an Execute SQL task. You could of course learn the pictures, but then you'd . . . just get the picture.

Both of these packages will be fairly large, so a few additional tips may be in order before you start:

❑ Packages save themselves when you run them, so just be aware.

❑ Packages don't save themselves as you are working, so save periodically as you work on these large development packages. There is a nice recovery feature that sometimes will save you — don't depend on it.

❑ Data Viewers are your friends. They are like grid message boxes. Add them in temporarily to see what is in your transformation stream.

❑ Default data types aren't your friend. If your tables don't use Unicode text fields, watch your settings when you are adding columns or source data.

❑ If you are at a point where you want to experiment, stop and save the SSIS project directory for the package you are working on. Experiment with the copy until you figure out what is wrong. Go back to the original project folder, make your corrections, and continue.

❑ Disable tasks or groups of tasks as you work through large packages to focus only on specific functional areas until they work. (To disable a task, right-click it and select Disable from the pop-up menu.)

Package Setup and File System Tasks

This load package will be set up to look in specific file directories for Lockbox and ACH files. External dependencies like file folders can be a headache during package deployment when you have to remember to have them set up in each environment. Instead of having to set up the locations outside the package, you are going to build in the ability of your package to get these paths from variables and build them as needed. You can then use configuration files to set up the package in each environment without any further intervention. However, you could still have some issues if the directories that you provide are not created, so you need to take this into consideration as you set up the precedence and control of flow in your package. It means adding a few extra steps, but it will allow your package to adjust during initial deployment and any future change to these file locations.

1. Create a new SSIS project. Name the project CaseStudy_Load. When the project is built, go to the Solution Explorer and click on the Package.dtsx file. In the Property window, find the Name property and change the name from package.dtsx to casestudy_load.dtsx. Answer Yes to change the name of the package object as well.

2. Because the File System tasks only allow the source and destination properties to be set to variables — not expressions derived from variable values — you are going to have to create a few variables. Use the menu SSIS ⇨ Variables to access the Variables editor and add the elements shown in the following table. (*Note:* Some variables are intentionally left blank.)

Variable Name	Scope	Data Type	Value
ACHBASEFILEPATH	CaseStudy_Load	String	c:\casestudy\ach
ACHCURRENTFILE	CaseStudy_Load	String	c:\casestudy\lockbox\sample ach.xml
ACHERRORFILE	CaseStudy_Load	String	
ACHERRORFILEPATH	CaseStudy_Load	String	
ACHIMPORTTYPE	CaseStudy_Load	String	ACH
ACHPROCESSEDFILE	CaseStudy_Load	String	
ACHPROCESSEDFILEPATH	CaseStudy_Load	String	
BANKBATCHID	CaseStudy_Load	Int32	-999
BANKBATCHNBR	CaseStudy_Load	String	
BATCHITEMS	CaseStudy_Load	UInt64	0
BATCHTOTAL	CaseStudy_Load	Double	0
DEPOSITDATE	CaseStudy_Load	DateTime	12/30/1899

Variable Name	Scope	Data Type	Value
FILEBYTES	CaseStudy_Load	Int64	0
LBBASEFILEPATH	CaseStudy_Load	String	c:\casestudy\lockbox
LBCURRENTFILE	CaseStudy_Load	String	c:\casestudy\lockbox\sample lockbox.txt
LBERRORFILE	CaseStudy_Load	String	
LBERRORFILEPATH	CaseStudy_Load	String	
LBIMPORTTYPE	CaseStudy_Load	String	LOCKBOX
LBPROCESSEDFILE	CaseStudy_Load	String	
LBPROCESSEDFILEPATH	CaseStudy_Load	String	
EMAILIMPORTTYPE	CaseStudy_Load	String	EMAIL
EMAILCNT	CaseStudy_Load	Int32	0

3. Add an OLE DB Connection to the Connection Managers to connect to the CaseStudy database. Name the connection CaseStudy.OLEDB.

4. Add an ADO.NET Connection to the Connection Managers to connect to the CaseStudy database. Name the connection CaseStudy.ADO.NET.

5. Add an SMTP Connection to the Connection Managers that connects to a viable SMTP mail server. Name the connection Mail Server.

6. The variables with the string FILEPATH in the names, like @LBPROCESSEDFILEPATH, need to retrieve their values relative to the base file paths. The variable @LBPROCESSEDFILEPATH should be set up relative to the base Lockbox file path in a subdirectory called processed\. To do this, you'll use an expression for the value of the variable. Click on the variable in the Variables Editor. In the Property window, set the property EvaluateAsExpression to True. In the Expression property, add the expression to match Figure 19-7. The \\ is required as an escape sequence for the backslash in the expressions editor. Set the other three variables up to be evaluated as expressions the same way. Notice in the Variables Editor, and as shown in Figure 19-8, that the values change immediately.

For Variable Name	Set Expression To
LBERRORFILEPATH	@LBBASEFILEPATH + "\\error"
ACHERRORFILEPATH	@ACHBASEFILEPATH + "\\error"
ACHPROCESSEDFILEPATH	@ACHBASEFILEPATH + "\\processed"

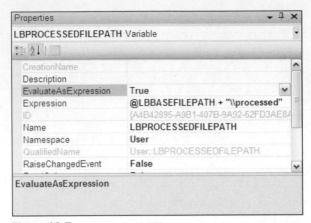

Figure 19-7

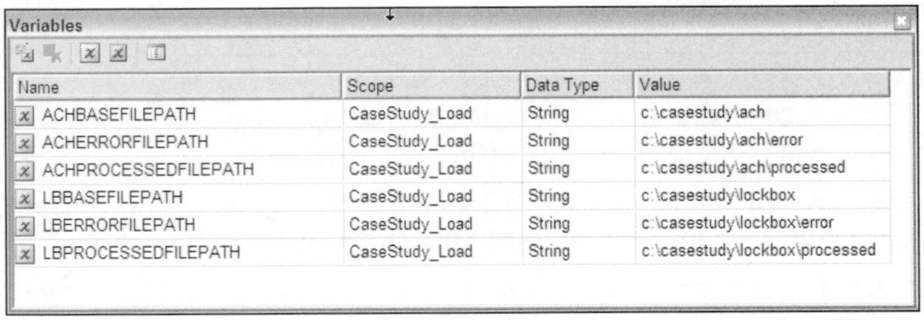

Figure 19-8

7. The variables ending in the string FILE, like @LBERRORFILE, @LBPROCESSEDFILE, @ACHERRORFILE, and @ACHPROCESSEDFILE, need to retrieve a unique value that can be used to rename the file into its respective destination file path. Set these variables up to be evaluated using expressions similar to the following formula, but change the variable represented in the example with @LBERRORFILEPATH for each of the four variables. This formula will generate a name similar to 20050816055208016000000.txt. For the ACH files, use the same formula but end the string with an ".xml" extension.

```
@LBERRORFILEPATH + "\\" + REPLACE(REPLACE(REPLACE(REPLACE((DT_WSTR,
50)GETUTCDATE(),"-",""),"  ", ""),".", ""),":", "") + (DT_WSTR, 50)@FILEBYTES +
".txt"
```

If you are manually typing the expression, there are no hard returns.

8. Add four File System tasks to the Control Flow design surface. Change the name and description properties to use the settings in the following table.

Name	Description
File System Task Folder LB Processed Folder	Ensures that the LB Processed Folder exists
File System Task Folder LB Error Folder	Ensures that the LB Error Folder exists
File System Task Folder ACH Processed Folder	Ensures that the ACH Processed Folder exists
File System Task Folder ACH Error Folder	Ensures that the ACH Error Folder exists

9. You want each of these four tasks to ensure that the directories needed for your load package exist. A File System task can perform the operation of creating a directory. One nifty thing that it will do when it creates a directory is create all the subdirectories in the hierarchy down to the last subdirectory. That is why you don't need two additional File System tasks to create the paths for the variables @LBBASEFILEPATH and @ACHBASEFILEPATH. You get these for free when you check for their subdirectories. For each of the four File System tasks, set the properties shown in the following table.

Property	Setting
Operation	Create Directory
UseDirectoryIfExists	True
IsSourcePathVariable	True
SourceVariable	Choose the corresponding variable for each task. (Notice how easy this is when the task is named properly?)

10. Connect the two lockbox File System tasks together by setting a precedence constraint between the File System Task Folder LB Processed Folder task and the File System Task Folder LB Error Folder task. Connect the two ACH File System tasks together the same way. Both precedence constraints should automatically be set to Success.

11. Run the package to validate that this section has been set up correctly. You should see a file hierarchy created on your machine resembling Figure 19-9.

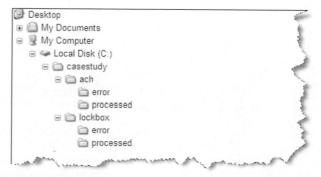

Figure 19-9

Executing these four File System tasks at the beginning of your load package helps ensure that the paths will exist for the tasks and transforms downstream. Almost all tasks and transforms that depend on paths or files will generate package failures if they are executed and the paths are invalid. Right now would be a good time to close and save this package and make a copy in another directory for insurance purposes. The CaseStudy_Load package at this point should look like Figure 19-10.

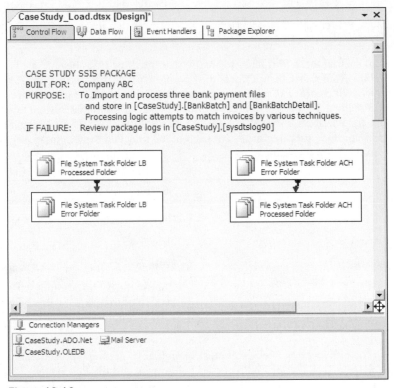

Figure 19-10

Lockbox Control Flow Processing

If all you had to do were load the Lockbox file, your task would be simple. You could build a Data Flow task to just split the file into header and detail rows and insert them. However, you need to validate that the file has not been previously loaded before you insert the payment information. If the batch has already been loaded, you need to divert the file to an error folder. The problem is that you don't know whether the file has already been processed until you open it up and process it. The other problem is that once you are inside a transformation, you lose the ability to alter the flow of control. In other words, you can't shift gears once you are inside the transformation and use precedence-type logic.

The strategy in this section is to retrieve a file name from the lockbox folder, to parse the header information from the file, and then to store the information in variables. If the batch number hasn't been processed, a [BankBatch] row will be inserted. Finally, you will reparse the Lockbox file for the detail records and insert them using the [BankBatchID] retrieved from the inserted [BankBatch] row. If everything works, you'll e-mail the bank and confirm the receipt of the file. If anything goes wrong, the file will get moved into the error folder.

Make sure you have created and copied the samplelockbox.txt file to the base lockbox directory before starting this section.

1. Drop a Sequence Container on the Control Flow design surface. Change the Name property to Sequence of Lockbox Processing. Connect the precedence from the last Lockbox File Systems task to the Sequence Container so that the Sequence Container is not executed unless the File Systems task completes successfully.

2. Add a Foreach Loop container inside the Sequence Container. Change the Name property to For Each Lockbox File. The Foreach Loop is expecting a literal path to poll. You want the loop to rely on a variable, so you'll have to use an expression. This task object is a little confusing because there are actually two sets of expression collections: One set in the left tab is for the container; the second set appears only when the Collections tab is selected. The second set of expressions is the collection of properties for the Foreach Enumerator. It is this second set of expressions that you want to alter. Click on the ellipsis to the right of this Expressions collection.

3. In the Expressions Editor, the property folder doesn't exist. It does, but it is named Directory. Select the Directory property and set its value to the variable @LBBASEFILEPATH. Evaluate the expression to ensure that it matches the base lockbox path.

@LBBASEFILEPATH and @[User::LBBASEFILEPATH] are the same thing since they are both in the same namespace.

4. Set the property files to "*.txt". Leave the Retrieve File value as Name Fully Qualified.

5. To store the name of the file you are processing into a variable, click the Variable Mappings tab on the left side of the Foreach Loop container. Select the variable named LBCURRENTFILE to retrieve the value of the Foreach loop for each file found. Leave the index on the variable mapping set to zero (0). This represents the first position in a files collection or the file name returned by the loop. Press OK to complete this task.

6. One of the things you have to save into the BankBatch data table is the file name and the number of bytes in the file. Now that you have the file name stored in the variable @LBCURRENTFILE, you can retrieve the file size using a Script task and some VB.NET code. Add a Script task to the Foreach Loop. Change the name to Script LB File Size into Variable.

7. For the Script task to be able to read and write to variables, you have to pass them into the container. Provide the variable LBCURRENTFILE for the ReadOnlyVariables property. Provide the variable FILEBYTES as the ReadWriteVariables property. Note that when passing variables into the Script task, the @ sign should not be used.

8. Click the Design Script button. This opens up a .NET development environment. Add an imports reference to the System.IO namespace and update the script to pull the file bytes from the file name provided in the DTS Variables collection:

```
Imports System
Imports System.Data
Imports System.Math
Imports Microsoft.SqlServer.Dts.Runtime
Imports System.IO  '<--Added Input/Output library

Public Class ScriptMain
    Public Sub Main()
        '**
```

```
'SCRIPT
'PURPOSE: To take file bytes and save to global variable
'================================================================
Dim oFile As FileInfo
Dim lDefault As Int64
lDefault = 0
Try
    oFile = New FileInfo(Dts.Variables("LBCURRENTFILE").Value.ToString)
    Dts.Variables("FILEBYTES").Value = oFile.Length
Catch ex As Exception
    Dts.Variables("FILEBYTES").Value = lDefault
End Try
Dts.TaskResult = Dts.Results.Success


    End Sub
End Class
```

At this point, you would know the file name and file size. The Foreach Loop stored the file name into a variable. The Script task retrieved the file size and stored the data into the FILEBYTES variable. You still need to figure out whether you have seen this file before. A unique batch number by import type is embedded in the header of the file. There are a few ways to retrieve that information. One way is to use a Data Flow task to examine the file. You could also use a Script task to open up and examine the file header row, but the Data Flow task will provide the added advantage of failure upon encountering a bad format. You can then alter your Control Flow to push this file to the error folder.

1. Add a Data Flow task. Connect the successful completion of the Script task to this task. Change the Name property to Data Flow Lockbox Validate File and Header Info. This task will parse out the batch header information into variables and then perform a lookup for a similar batch. An existing BankBatchID will be returned in the BankBatchID variable. You'll come back and configure the Data Flow in the next section, Lockbox File Validation. Disable the task for now.

2. Add an Execute SQL task. This task will use a stored procedure, usp_BankBatch_Add, to add the parsed information in the Lockbox file as a row in the BankBatch table to represent a new batch file. You don't want this task or any other tasks connected to it to be executed unless the Data Flow task returned a no-match condition or a BankBatchID of zero (0). To create a conditional precedence with an expression, connect the successful completion of the Data Flow task to this task. Then right-click on the precedence connector and select Edit. Set up the Precedence Constraint editor to look like Figure 19-11.

3. If the Data Flow task finds an existing BankBatchID, you also need to move the file into an error folder. Add a File System task and connect with similar precedence and constraint conditions — except change the expression to apply when the BankBatchID does not equal zero (0) OR if the Data Flow task fails. Set the Evaluation Operation to Expression OR Constraint. Set the Value to Failure and the Expression to @BANKBATCHID != 0. Select the Multiple constraint option of Logical OR.

4. It seems that the operation you want to perform with the File System task is Move File, but since you created a variable earlier, @LBERRORFILE, that is created with a full file path and a unique file name, the better option is to Rename the file. Update the variable @LBCurrentFile to c:\casestudy\lockbox\samplelockbox.txt and then set the File System properties to the values shown in the following table.

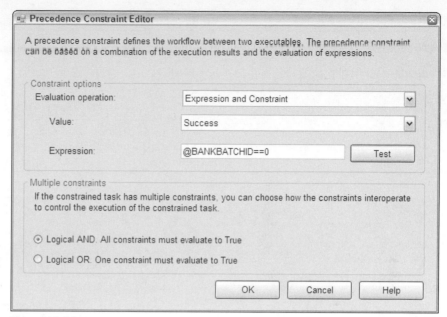

Figure 19-11

Property	Value
IsDestinationPathVariable	True
Destination Variable	User::LBERRORFILE
OverwriteDestination	True
Name	File System Task Error Folder
Description	Moves bad files to an error folder
Operation	Rename File.
IsSourcePathVariable	True
SourceVariable	User::LBCURRENTFILE

The File System task here will complain that the value for User::LBCurrentFile is empty if it doesn't have a default value.

5. Finish up the Execute SQL task by setting the properties to match the table below. Then set up the Parameter Mapping page to look like Figure 19-12.

Property	Value
Name	Execute SQL task to add Bank Batch Hdr
ConnectionType	ADO.Net
Connection	CaseStudy.ADO.Net
SQLStatement	EXEC usp_BankBatch_Add @BankBatchID OUTPUT, @BankBatchNbr, @DepositDate, @ReceivedDate, @BatchTotal, @BatchItems, @FileBytes, @FullFilePath, @ImportType

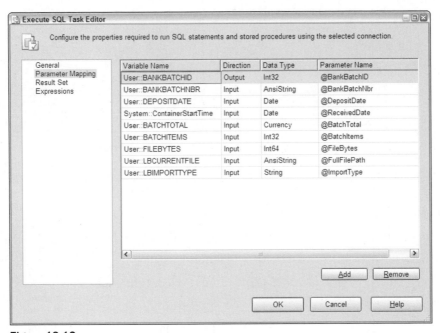

Figure 19-12

6. Add a second Data Flow task to the Foreach Loop. Connect the successful completion of the Execute SQL task to this task. Add an expression to check for a nonzero BankBatchID, and add a successful completion constraint between the Execute SQL task and this new Data Flow task. The stored procedure will return via an output parameter either a zero (0), which indicates that the batch already exists, or a new BankBatchID. If the Execute SQL task were to fail, or if the BankBatchID is returned as a zero, the Lockbox file should be moved to the error folder and you should move on to the next file. Add a Failure constraint and an expression that looks for a zero BankBatchID value. Set the condition to an OR so that if either occurs, the file moves to the error folder.

7. Change the name property to Data Flow Lockbox Detail Data Load. You'll come back and configure the Data Flow in the section "Lockbox Processing." Disable the task for now.

8. Add a Send Mail task to the Foreach Loop. Connect the successful completion of the Data Flow Lockbox Detail Data Load to this task. Set the SMTPConnection property of the task to the SMTP Mail Server connection. Fill in the To, From, and Subject properties. Create an expression for the MessageSource property similar to the following code:

```
" COMPANY ABC, 123 Main St, Somewhere, FL 99999  received and successfully
processed lockbox file -" +  @[User::BANKBATCHNBR] + "- for the amount of $" +
(DT_WSTR, 15) @[User::BATCHTOTAL] + " on " + (DT_WSTR, 50) GETUTCDATE()  +".  If
this is not correct please contact Minnie in accounts payable at 555-1111 ext 211
or minnie@companyabc.com " + "This is an automated response."
```

9. If the file is processed successfully, you need to move it to the "processed" folder. Add another File System task and connect it to the successful completion of the second Data Flow task. Set up this task just like the Error Folder File System task but point everything to the processed folder.

Property	Value
IsDestinationPathVariable	True
Destination Variable	User::LBPROCESSEDFILE
OverwriteDestination	True
Name	File System Task Processed Folder
Description	Moves completed files to an error folder
Operation	Rename File.
IsSourcePathVariable	True
SourceVariable	User::LBCURRENTFILE

You now have the basic structure set up for the Lockbox control flow. You still need to go back and build your transforms. You'll get to that in the next steps. Right now would be a good time to close and save this package and make a copy in another directory for insurance purposes. The CaseStudy_Load package at this point should look like Figure 19-13.

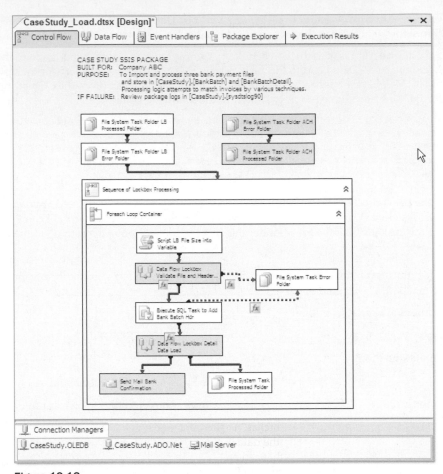

Figure 19-13

Lockbox Validation

In this section of the package, you are going to fill in the details of the Data Flow container. The strategy will be to open up the Lockbox file and retrieve information from the header to pass back to the control flow via variables. You'll use a Flat File connection to read the file, a conditional split transform to separate out the header and the check lines, derived columns to parse out the header line, and an aggregate count transform to count the check transactions. You'll use Script Component transforms to pull this information from the transformation stream and store it in your variables.

1. Start by setting up a New Flat File Connection in the Connection Managers tab. Configure the properties in the following table on the connection.

Property	Setting
Name	Lockbox Flat File
Description	Flat File for Lockbox processing
File Name	c:\casestudy\lockbox\samplelockbox.txt
Format	Ragged right
Advanced:OutputColumnWidth	80
Advanced:DataType	string[DT_STR]
Advanced:Name	line (case is important)

2. The only problem with the previous step is that you had to set a file name to a literal to set up the connection. At runtime you want to retrieve the file name from your variable @LBCURRENTFILE. Save the Flat File Connection, and then access the expressions collection in the Properties tab. Use the expression editor to set the ConnectionString property to @LBCURRENTFILE.

3. To use the Flat File connection in your Data Flow, add a Flat File Source to the Data Flow design surface. Select the Flat File connection created in the previous step named Lockbox Flat File. Name this transform source Flat File Lockbox.

4. One of the main purposes of this Data Flow is to perform an extraction of the header information and then perform a lookup on the batch number. You will use the Lookup transformation for this task, and one of the "gotchas" to using this task is that it is case-sensitive. Since at this point your source contains all the data in a single column, it makes sense to go ahead and run the data through a transform that can convert the data to uppercase in one step. Add a Character Map transform to the Data Flow. It should be connected to the output of the Flat File Source and be configured to perform an in-line change to uppercase with both input column and output alias as "line."

5. The Lockbox file contains three types of data formats: header, invoice, and check. At this stage, you are trying to determine whether this batch has been previously processed, so you only need the information from the header and a count of the check transactions. To split the one-column flat file input, add a Conditional Split transform to the Data Flow. Set up the transform to use the leftmost character of the input stream to split the line into two outputs: Header and Check. The transform should look like Figure 19-14.

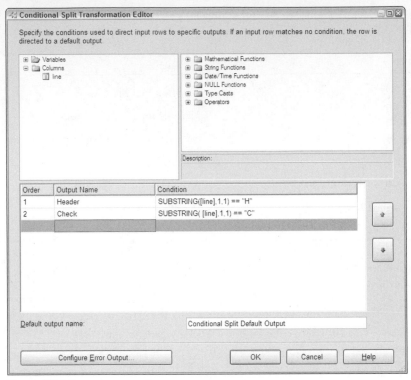

Figure 19-14

6. Add a Derived Column task to the Data Flow. Name it Derived Columns from Header.Connect to the Header output of the Conditional Split. This task will allow you to easily split up the line into the pieces of data that it represents. With the Derived Column task, you also get the conversion utilities as an added benefit. With the import stream being a string type, this is where you have to think ahead on your conversions. To add a row to the BankBatch table, you are going to need to extract a Batch Number from this input stream. Notice that the BatchNbr field in the BankBatch table is a Unicode variable text field. If you parse the text string into the data type of [DT_WSTR], you will match the destination field. Paying attention to data types early will save you many headaches further into the package. Set up the derived columns to match Figure 19-15.

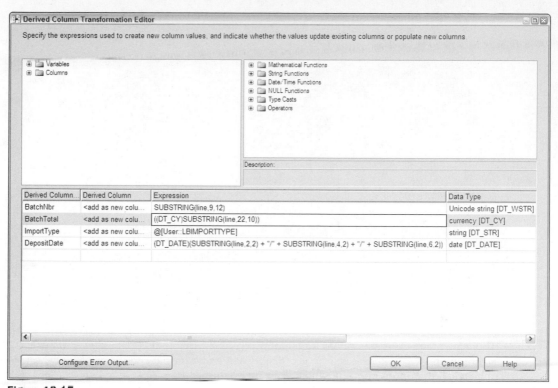

Figure 19-15

7. Wait a minute! These explicit castings of string data could be disastrous. What if the bank provides some bad data in the Batch Total field? Good question. If you just left the default error handling in place, the package would fail. You don't want that to happen; you just want to reject the file. To do that, you need the Control Flow to recognize that something is wrong and divert the file to the error folder. Notice that we said Control Flow — not Data Flow. The precedence and constraint you set up between this Data Flow task and the Execute SQL task to add a Bank Batch header is set up to reject the file if it returns any nonzero bank batch ID. For your transform to set the variable, you'll need to divert the whole row. In fact, it would be a good idea to divert the output stream of the header row if you have any problems converting this data into proper types. Click on the Configure Error Output button and set all actions for error or truncations to divert and redirect the output to another output stream. See Figure 19-16 for the completed error output.

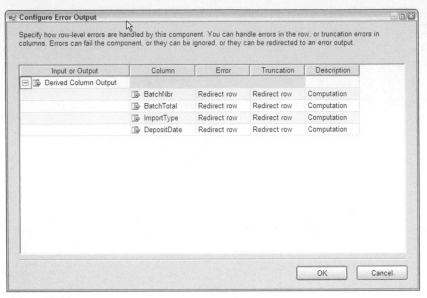

Figure 19-16

8. There are many different options for handling errors in SSIS. In this Data Flow, if there is an error parsing the lockbox header, it is probably an invalid format-type error, so you want to be able to capture information about that error. To do this, add a Script Component task to make use of the error stream you created from the Derived Column task. Set it up as a transformation. The error stream currently contains your raw data, an error code, and a column number for each error generated. You can use the Script Component to add the error description to your stream, and then in another transform task you can log the information into your [ErrorDetail] table. Connect the error output of the Derived Column task to the Script Component task to capture the original input stream. Name this task Script Component Get Error Desc. Open the Script Transformation Editor and select all the input columns. Then, in the Inputs and Outputs tab, expand the Output0 collection and add an output column (not an output) named ErrorDesc. Set the type to [DT_WSTR] with a length of 1048. Open up the design environment for the Script Component. Change your processinputrow event code to the following:

```
Public Overrides Sub Input0_ProcessInputRow(ByVal Row As Input0Buffer)
    'SCRIPT
    'PURPOSE: To retrieve the error description to write to error log
    '============================================================
    Row.ErrorDesc= ComponentMetaData.GetErrorDescription(Row.ErrorCode)
End Sub
```

9. Add a Derived Column transform and name it Derived Column System Variables. Along with the detailed error message, it will be helpful to add other information like the ExecutionInstanceGUID to log in to your custom ErrorDetail table. The ExecutionInstanceGUID is a unique ID given to each run of an SSIS package that will allow you to combine your custom error logging with other package error logging to give you a complete picture of what occurred when a package failed. Create the Derived Columns shown in Figure 19-17.

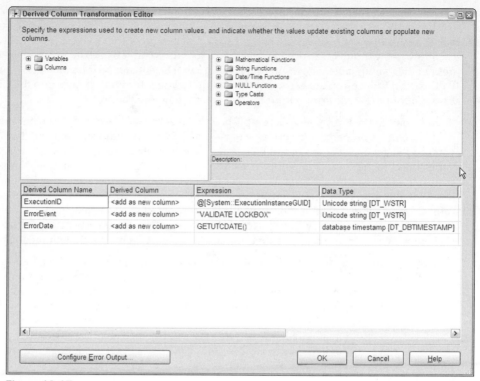

Figure 19-17

10. Add an OLE DB Destination to save this data into the ErrorDetail table. Name the transform OLE DB Destination Error Log. Set up the OLE DB connection and the name of the table to ErrorDetail. Map the columns. Most input columns should match the destination columns in the table. Map the column [Line] to the [RawData] column. Now you've handled the worst-case scenario of bad batch header data. Not only do you store the error of a bad conversion or batch header, but the flow of data will now stop at this transform. This leaves the value of the BankBatchID to the default of –999, which will cause the Control Flow to divert the file to the error folder — just what you want.

11. The other Data Flow back at the Derived Columns from Header transform should contain data that was successfully converted to proper data types. You now have to determine if the BatchNbr has been sent and received earlier by checking to see if it matches any existing BatchNbr in the BankBatch table by import type. Add a Lookup transformation task to the flow of the Derived column. Change the name to Lookup BankBatchID. Connect the CaseStudy.OLEDB connection. In the reference tab, instead of using the BankBatch table, specifically select the BankBatchID, BankBatchNbr, and ImportType columns using a SQL Query. One of the many reasons to use a query in the Lookup transformations is that the task is case-sensitive. You made sure that the batch number parsed from the input file is in uppercase. To ensure that you get matches to the stored data, use an UPPER statement in the SQL statement.

```
SELECT BANKBATCHID, UPPER(BANKBATCHNBR) AS BANKBATCHNBR, UPPER(IMPORTTYPE) AS
IMPORTTYPE FROM BankBatch
ORDER BY BANKBATCHNBR
```

In the Columns tab, connect the BatchNbr input column to the BankBatchNbr column. Connect the ImportType input column to the ImportType column. This is the equivalent of running a query against the BankBatch table looking for a matching row ImportType and BatchNbr for each row in the input stream. In the grid, add a lookup column BankBatchID by selecting the field in the lookup table. The result of the lookup will be either a NULL value or a retrieved BankBatchID. Since you are expecting the lookup task to return no matches, use the Configure Error Output to set the error output for the lookup to Ignore Failure.

12. At this point in the flow, you've accomplished the mission of determining whether the Lockbox file is formatted properly, and you have retrieved header-level information from the file that you need to get back to the Control Flow. Add a new Script Component task to the Data Flow and connect to the successful output stream of the Lookup task as a destination. Name this task Script Component to Store Variables. In this task, select the columns BankBatchID, BatchNbr, BatchTotal, ImportType, and DepositDate from the input stream. They will be added automatically as input columns and will be available in a row object. Add the matching variables to the ReadWriteVariable property: BANKBATCHID, BANKBATCHNBR, DEPOSITDATE, BATCHTOTAL. Remember, variables are case-sensitive and must be passed as a comma-delimited list.

13. In the script component, this time you want to access the row object to retrieve the values that are in the input row stream. Since you are processing the header row, you'll have only one row to process. Accessing the row values is not a problem. However, saving the value to a package variable is not allowed when processing at a row level. You can only access package variables in the PostExecute event stub. To retrieve the values, use variables to capture the values in the row-level event, and then update the package variables in the PostExecute event. If you have a need to retrieve information from your Data Flow into variables as in this example, this technique will be really useful to you. To continue with this example, replace the Script Component script with the following code:

```
'CASE STUDY 2005
Imports System
Imports System.Data
Imports System.Math
Imports Microsoft.SqlServer.Dts.Pipeline.Wrapper
Imports Microsoft.SqlServer.Dts.Runtime.Wrapper

Public Class ScriptMain
    Inherits UserComponent
    Public LocalBankBatchID As Int32 = -999
    Public LocalBatchTotal As Double = 0
    Public LocalBankBatchNbr As String = ""
    Public LocalDepositDate As Date = #12/31/1899#
    Public Overrides Sub Input0_ProcessInputRow(ByVal Row As Input0Buffer)
        'SCRIPT
        'PURPOSE: This sub will fire for each row processed
        '         since we only have one header row we only
        '         this sub will fire only one time.
        '         Store values in variables
        '=============================================================
        Try
            If Row.DepositDate_IsNull = True Or _
                Row.BatchTotal_IsNull = True Or _
                  Row.BatchTotal = 0 Then
                'KEEP DEFAULTS
```

```
                Else
                    LocalBankBatchNbr = Row.BatchNbr + ""
                    LocalBatchTotal = Row.BatchTotal
                    LocalBankBatchID = Row.BANKBATCHID
                    LocalDepositDate = Row.DepositDate
                End If
            Catch ex As Exception
                'KEEP DEFAULTS
            End Try

        End Sub
        Public Overrides Sub PostExecute()
            'SCRIPT
            'PURPOSE: To set SSIS variables with values retrieved earlier
            '=============================================================
            Try
                'Attempt to accept the values
                Variables.BANKBATCHNBR = LocalBankBatchNbr
                Variables.BANKBATCHID = LocalBankBatchID
                Variables.DEPOSITDATE = LocalDepositDate
                Variables.BATCHTOTAL = LocalBatchTotal / CDbl(100)
            Catch ex As Exception
                'If any failure occurs fail the file
                Variables.BANKBATCHID = -999
                Variables.BATCHTOTAL = 0
            End Try

            MyBase.PostExecute()
        End Sub
    End Class
```

14. The last variable that you need to retrieve is the number of transactions in the lockbox batch. The Lockbox file has detail lines separated into invoice and check types. You are really only interested in the check lines. Add an Aggregation transformation to the Conditional Split transform to capture the Check output stream. Name the transform Aggregate Check Count. Select the line column from the input columns. Set the Output Alias to BatchItems. Set the operation to Count. This will count the number of checks and put that count into your Data Flow. Now you just need to save the count of the checks into a variable.

15. Add a Script Component task to the Data Flow and attach the Aggregate output as a Destination. Change the name to Script Component to Capture BatchItems. Select the BatchItems column from the input stream. Add the variables BATCHITEMS and BANKBATCHID to the ReadWriteVariables property. A common issue at this point is that the type returned by the Aggregate output is a Unicode Long data type. That's why your BatchItems variable was preset to UINT64. Add the following script to the task in the ProcessInputRow stub:

```
' CASE STUDY 2005
Imports System
Imports System.Data
Imports System.Math
Imports Microsoft.SqlServer.Dts.Pipeline.Wrapper
Imports Microsoft.SqlServer.Dts.Runtime.Wrapper

Public Class ScriptMain
```

```
Inherits UserComponent
Public LocalBatchItems As UInt64
Public Overrides Sub Input0_ProcessInputRow(ByVal Row As Input0Buffer)
    '**
    'SCRIPT
    'PURPOSE: Attempt to save the value of batch items
    '         from aggregation to local variables b/c we
    '         can't set DTS Variables in this sub
    Try
        If Row.BatchItems_IsNull = True Then
            LocalBatchItems = 0
        Else
            LocalBatchItems = Row.BatchItems
        End If
    Catch ex As Exception
        LocalBatchItems = 0
    End Try
End Sub
Public Overrides Sub PostExecute()
    '**
    'SCRIPT
    'PURPOSE: Sets the value of DTS variables to
    '         local values
    Variables.BATCHITEMS = LocalBatchItems
    MyBase.PostExecute()
End Sub
End Class
```

This will complete the Lockbox Validation Data Flow — which should at this point look like Figure 19-18. Enable the Data Flow Lockbox Validate File and Header Info in the Control Flow and disable the Execute SQL task to run a test of the package. Remember that the only purpose of this Data Flow is to determine whether the file is properly formatted and whether it is indeed a new file to process. All it will do is open the file and parse the information from the file. Play around with the header of the file and put in invalid data such as '02/31/05'. You should see the transformation move through the error section of the Data Flow and store a row in the ErrorDetail table. The text file will then be moved into the error folder in the c:\casestudy\lockbox\ directory.

This Data Flow is by no means complete and ready for production. The batch lines making up the detail should also be validated for proper data types using the same techniques in this step. Essentially the default BANKBATCHID is set prior to this set of transformations to fail. If the transformation flows completely to the script component and stores the batch header information, it will be considered a success. If not, this step will be considered suspect, and the file will be rejected. This should give you a good idea of what you can do without having to stage the data before processing it.

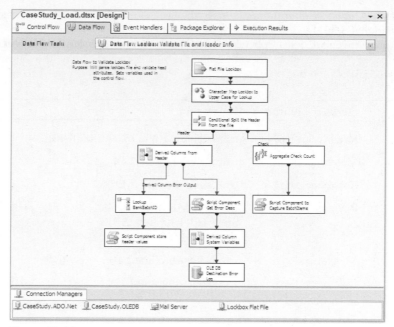

Figure 19-18

Lockbox Processing

Once you've validated your file, loading the detail data into the BankBatchDetail table will be rather simple. You have all the header-related information. The Execute SQL task will create a row in the BankBatch table to store the batch, and you'll store the primary key in the BANKBATCHID variable. You now just need to re-examine the text file and process the detail transactions. Your strategy will be to separate the invoice lines into two parts: a part containing individual payment invoice information, and a part containing check lines from the batch file. After validating the contents, you will recombine the two rows into one. That will give you the ability to do a straight insert using one row into the BankBatchDetail table.

Enable the Data Flow Lockbox Detail Data Load task in the Control Flow. Double-click it to expose the Data Flow design surface.

1. You already have a file connection in the Connection Managers for the Lockbox Flat File. Add a Flat File Source onto the design surface and set it up to use the Lockbox Flat File connection. Name it Flat File Lockbox Source.

2. Because the lookup transactions are case-sensitive, it is better to add a Character Map transform to convert the stream to uppercase while all the data is in one column. Name the Character Map, and set the operation to Uppercase and the destination to In-place.

3. Add a Conditional Split transform similar to what you did earlier when validating the batch file. This time you'll split the file into each of its parts: the header, check, and invoice lines. Set up the transform to use the leftmost character of the input stream to split the line into three outputs: Header, Check, and Invoice, based on the characters "H," "C," and "I," respectively.

4. Add two Derived Column transforms to the Data Flow. Attach one to the Checks output of the Conditional Split transform. Name it Derived Column Check. Attach the other to the Invoice output of the Conditional Split transform. Name it Derived Column Invoice. Don't worry about the header portion for the moment. Using the business specs, create the following new columns to parse out of each line type.

Transform	Derived Column	Expression	Data Type
Invoice	RawInvoiceNbr	trim(substring(line,13,len([line])-13))	[DT_STR] 50
Invoice	MatchingKey	trim(substring(line,2,4))	[DT_STR] 50
Invoice	ReferenceData1	trim(substring(line,2,10))	[DT_STR] 50
Check	PaymentAmount	((DT_NUMERIC,11,2)_ SUBSTRING([line],15,8) / (DT_NUMERIC,11,2)100.00)	[DT_CY]
Check	MatchingKey	trim(s.ubstring(line,2,4))	[DT_STR] 50
Check	ReferenceData2	trim(substring(line,2,10))	[DT_STR] 50

Notice the use of the [DT_STR] data type, which is a NULL-Terminated Non-Unicode data type—not the [DT_WSTR] Unicode data type. You are doing this because ultimately you are going to insert this data into the table BankBatchDetail where the data types are VARCHAR. I'm mentioning this here because the default data types and lengths are inferred from the field that you are using to design the package. It can be annoying that your settings will be overwritten if you change anything in the expression. However, if you don't get the data type right here, you'll need to add a Data Conversion transform to convert the data into a compatible format or the SSIS validation engines will complain—and may not compile. The other thing to notice here is the use of TRIM statements. In flat file data, the columns are tightly defined, but that doesn't mean the data within them lines up exactly to these columns. Use the TRIM statements to remove leading and trailing spaces that will affect your lookup processes downstream.

5. Now at this point you've got two output streams: one from the invoice lines and one from the check lines. You want to put them back together into one row. Any transformation you use is going to require that you sort these outputs and then find something in common to join them together. To put them together, you have to have some data that matches between the outputs. Luckily the bank provides the matching information and you parsed it out in the Derived Column task. The column name shared by both outputs that contains the same data is ReferenceData1. Look at a two-line sample from the Lockbox file. Columns two through six (2–6) contain the string 4001, which is defined in your business specs as the lookup key that ties the transaction together. (The entire sequence 4001010003 refers to an image system lookup ID.)

```
I4001010003 181INTERNAT
C4001010004   01844400
```

Add two new Sort transformations to the Data Flow and connect one to each Derived Column output. Select the field MatchingKey in both sorts and sort ascending. Select all columns for pass-through, except for the Line column. You will no longer use the line data, so there is no need to continue to drag this data through your transformation process. Now you are ready to merge the outputs.

6. Add a Merge Join transformation to connect the two outputs to the component. In the editor, select the RawInvoiceNbr and ReferenceNbr1 columns from the Invoice sort stream. Select the PaymentAmount and ReferenceData2 columns from the Check sort stream. There is no need to bring the Matching key data forward since that information is embedded in the ReferenceData fields. Make sure the JOIN type is set to INNER Join.

7. This stream is now one row per check and invoice combination. You are almost ready to insert the data into the BankBatchDetail table. All you need now is the Foreign Key for the BankBatch table. Earlier you stored this information in a global variable. To merge this into your stream, add a Derived Column task and add the variable BANKBATCHID to the stream. (You could have done this earlier in either the check or invoice processing steps as well.) You automatically get all the other fields in the Data Flow as pass-through.

8. Add an OLE DB destination and connect to the CaseStudy.OLEDB connection. Connect the transform and select the table BankBatchDetail. Map the columns from the output to the BankBatchDetail table where the column names match.

9. You still have one task left to do before closing out this Data Flow, and that is saving a snapshot of the file contents into the BankBatch row. Everything else you are doing in this Data Flow is saving data at the payment or detail level. Saving the entire file contents for audit purposes is a batch-level task. To do this, you'll need to create a separate stream that will use the Header portion of the Conditional stream you split off early in the Data Flow. Start by adding a Derived Column task connecting to the header-based output. Add the following columns to the stream.

Derived Column	Expression	Data Type
LBCurrentFile	@[User::LBCURRENTFILE]	[DT_WSTR] 100
BankBatchID	@[User::BANKBATCHID]	[DT_I4]

10. Add an Import Column transformation and connect it to this Header Derived Column transform. On the Input Columns tab, select the field that contains the file path in the stream: LBCurrentFile. Then go to the Advanced Input Output property tab and expand the Import Column Input and Import Column Output nodes. Add an output column to the output column node called FileStreamToStore. Set the DataType property to [DT_NTEXT]. The editor should look similar to Figure 19-19, but the Lineage IDs will be different. Note the LineageID and set the property in the LBCurrentFile Input Column named FileDataColumnID to that LineageID. Using Figure 19-19, the ID would be 1080.

11. Add an OLE DB Command transform to the output of the Header Derived Column transform. Set the OLEDB connection to CaseStudy.OLEDB. Then set the SQL Command to Update BankBatch Set BatchFile = ? where BankBatchID = ? and press Refresh. In the Mappings tab, connect the FileStreamToStore to the Destination Column Param_0, which is the [BatchFile] field in the BankBatch table. Connect the BankBatchID to the Destination column Param_1. Click Refresh and save.

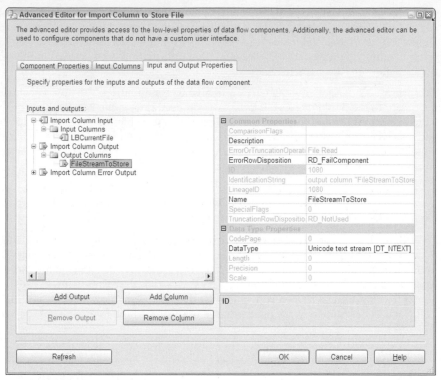

Figure 19-19

This completes the Data Flow task. The task will parse and save the lockbox detail file into your BankBatchDetail data table. The entire Data Flow should look similar to Figure 19-20. Now would be a good time to save the package. If you've run the package up to this point, check to see that a lockbox sample file exists in the c:\casestudy\lockbox\ folder. Enable the Execute SQL task and run the package to watch it execute.

> To run the test file through multiple times, you'll need to reset the database by truncating the BankBatch and BatchBatchDetail tables between runs. Otherwise in subsequent runs the package will fail upon finding that the file has been previously processed.

The remaining two processing options for ACH (which involve processing an XML file and e-mail payments) are not required to be completed, if you want to go on to building the Case Study Process package.

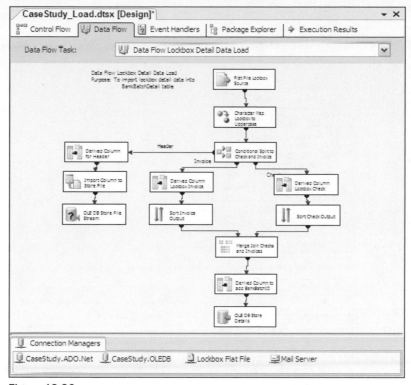

Figure 19-20

ACH Control Flow Processing

In the business specs, you have to process ACH files that represent the payment wire detail. The approach to this problem will resemble closely what you did for the Lockbox.

1. Move the two File System tasks that you built to validate the ACH paths in the Package Setup & File System Tasks section of the Case Study down under the Lockbox Sequence Container. Connect these tasks with a precedence type of Completion. You are using this condition because you don't want the ACH processing logic to be skipped just because the Lockbox has an error, but you also don't want the ACH process to take place until the Lockbox process completes. Minimize the Sequence Loop to give yourself more room to work. The Control Flow surface should look similar to Figure 19-21.

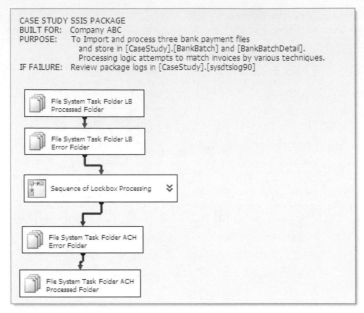

```
CASE STUDY SSIS PACKAGE
BUILT FOR:   Company ABC
PURPOSE:     To Import and process three bank payment files
             and store in [CaseStudy].[BankBatch] and [BankBatchDetail].
             Processing logic attempts to match invoices by various techniques.
IF FAILURE:  Review package logs in [CaseStudy].[sysdtslog90]
```

File System Task Folder LB Processed Folder

File System Task Folder LB Error Folder

Sequence of Lockbox Processing

File System Task Folder ACH Error Folder

File System Task Folder ACH Processed Folder

Figure 19-21

2. Add a Sequence Container named Sequence of ACH Processing. Connect to the last File Systems task for the ACH Processed folder.

3. Add a Script task to the Sequence container to reset the variables. Add the following variables in the ReadWriteProperty of the Script task: BANKBATCHID, BANKBATCHNBR, BATCHITEMS, BATCH-TOTAL, DEPOSITDATE, FILEBYTES. Open the script design mode and replace the Sub Main with this code:

```
'SCRIPT
'PURPOSE: To reset variables used by each payment file process
'=================================================================
Public Sub Main()
    Dts.Variables("BANKBATCHID").Value = System.Convert.ToInt32(-999)
    Dts.Variables("BANKBATCHNBR").Value = ""
    Dts.Variables("BATCHITEMS").Value = System.Convert.ToUInt64(0)
    Dts.Variables("BATCHTOTAL").Value = (0.0)
    Dts.Variables("DEPOSITDATE").Value = #12/31/1899#
    Dts.Variables("FILEBYTES").Value = System.Convert.ToInt64(0)
    Dts.TaskResult = Dts.Results.Success
End Sub
```

4. Add a Foreach Loop to loop through the XML files. Connect it to the Script task with a success precedence. Set this task up just like the Lockbox Foreach Loop, using expressions for the Directory property, but use the variable ACHBASEFILEPATH. In the Collections tab, set the folder up to start with the path c:\casestudy\ach\. Set the Files property to *.xml. Capture the file in the Foreach Loop in the variable ACHCURRENTFILE.

5. Add a Script task to take the file name stored in the variable ACHCURRENTFILE and retrieve the file size into the variable FILEBYTES. This task is set up the same as the one for scripting the lockbox.

6. Add a Data Flow task. Connect the successful completion of the Script task to this task. Change the Name property to Data Flow ACH Validate File and Header Info. This task will parse out the batch header information into variables and then perform a lookup for a similar batch. An existing BankBatchID will be returned in the BankBatchID variable. You'll come back and configure the Data Flow in the section "ACH Validate Data Flow." Disable the task for now.

7. Add an Execute SQL task. Copy this task directly from the Lockbox Foreach Loop. This task will use a stored procedure, usp_BankBatch_Add, to add the parsed information in the Lockbox file as a row in the BankBatch table to represent a new batch file. You don't want this task, or any other tasks connected to it, to be executed unless the Data Flow task returns a no-match condition or a BankBatchID of zero (0). Create a successful conditional precedence with an expression between the Data Flow task and this task. The expression should confirm that the value of @BANKBATCHID==0 is true. Change the mappings to parameters @FullFilePath and @ImportType to [User::ACHCURRENTFILE] and [User::ACHIMPORTTYPE].

8. If the Data Flow task finds an existing BankBatchID, you also need to move the file into an error folder. Add a File System task and connect with similar precedence and constraint conditions — except change the expression to apply when the BankBatchID does not equal zero (0) OR if the Data Flow task fails. Set the Evaluation Operation to Expression OR Constraint. Set the Value to Failure and the Expression to @BANKBATCHID != 0. Select the Multiple Constraint property to the option of Logical OR.

9. Set up the File System task to match the same step for the lockbox — except for the properties in the following table.

Property	Value
Destination Variable	User::ACHERRORFILE
SourceVariable	User::ACHCURRENTFILE

10. Add a second Data Flow task to the Foreach Loop. Connect the successful completion of the Execute SQL task to this task. Add an expression to check for a nonzero BankBatchID and a successful completion constraint between the Execute SQL task. The stored procedure will return via an output parameter either a zero (0), which indicates that the batch already exists, or a new BankBatchID. If the Execute SQL task were to fail, or if the BankBatchID is returned as a zero, the Lockbox file should be moved to the error folder and you should move on to the next file. Add a Failure constraint and an expression that looks for a zero BankBatchID value. Set the condition to an OR so that if either condition is true, the file moves to the error folder.

11. Change the name property on the Data flow task to Data Flow ACH Detail Data Load. You'll come back and configure the Data Flow in the section "Data ACH Detail Data Load" later in the chapter. Disable the task for now.

12. Add a Send Mail task to the Foreach Loop. Connect the successful completion of the Data Flow ACH Detail Data Load to this task. Set the SMTPConnection property of the task to the SMTP

Mail Server connection. Fill in the To, From, and Subject properties. Create an expression for the MessageSource property similar to the following code:

```
" COMPANY ABC, 123 Main St, Somewhere, FL 99999  received and successfully
processed ACH file -" +  @[User::BANKBATCHNBR] + "- for the amount of $" +
(DT_WSTR, 15) @[User::BATCHTOTAL] + " on " + (DT_WSTR, 50) GETUTCDATE() +".  If
this is not correct please contact Minnie in accounts payable at 555-1111 ext 211
or minnie@companyabc.com " + "This is an automated response."
```

13. If the file is processed successfully, you need to move it to the "processed" folder. Add another File System task and connect it to the successful completion of the second Data Flow task. Set up this task just like the Error Folder File System task, but point everything to the processed folder. The properties in the following table are different.

Property	Value
Destination Variable	User::ACHPROCESSEDFILE
SourceVariable	User::ACHCURRENTFILE

You now have the basic structure set up for the ACH Control Flow. You still need to go back and build your transforms. But you'll get to that in the next steps. Right now would be a good time to close and save this package and make a copy in another directory for insurance purposes. The CaseStudy_Load ACH Sequence container at this point should look like Figure 19-22.

To test the progress so far, disable the Execute SQL task so that a batch row won't be created. Disable the Lockbox Sequence Container, so it won't be run. Save, and then execute the package to ensure that everything so far is set up properly.

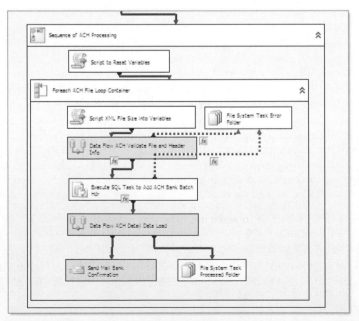

Figure 19-22

ACH Validation

In this section of the package, you are going to fill in the details for the ACH Data Flow container. The strategy will be to open up the ACH file, retrieve information from the header, and pass the information back to the Control Flow via variables. You'll use an XML data source combined with an XSD file that you'll create and edit to read the file. Since the data is structured and hierarchical, you don't have the parsing tasks that are associated with flat files. However, you can still have bad data in the structure, so you'll have to validate the file. You'll use a lookup on the header to look for matches by batch number, and a Script Component will pull this information from the transformation stream and send it back into your Control Flow.

1. Start by enabling the ACH Validate File and Header Info Data Flow. Click on the task to enter the Data Flow.

2. Add an XML Source to the Data Flow. In the XML Source editor, set the XML Location to the SampleAch.xml file that should be in the c:\casestudy\ach\ folder. You should immediately see the message shown in Figure 19-23. This message is acknowledging that an XML formatted file has been selected, but the task needs schema information from the XSD file to set up data types and sizes. Since you don't have an XSD file, you'll use a utility provided with this component to generate one.

> ⚠ XML Schema (XSD) is not specified. Select an existing XSD or click Generate XSD to create an XSD from the XML file.

Figure 19-23

3. Provide the XML source with a path to build the XSD as `c:\casestudy\ach\ach.xsd`. Then press the Generate XSD button to create the file. Unfortunately, the XSD generator is not perfect, so if you use this tool, manually validate the XSD file. Here's where error-handling strategy and design come into play. You can set up the XSD with all text fields, and the file will always parse successfully. However, you will have to type check all the fields yourself. If you strongly type your XSD, the task could fail and you won't get a chance to make any programmatic decisions. Another thing to note is that the automatically generated XSD is based on the available data in the XML file, so in the case of your header, which has only one row, it doesn't have much data to review to pick data types. That's why the XSD type designation for the BATCHITEMS variable is incorrect. Open the XSD up in Notepad and change the XSD type designation from xs:unsignedByte to xs:UnsignedInt. Now you match the data type of your global BATCHITEMS variable.

4. In the XML source component, go to the Error Output tab. For both header and detail output and for every column and every error type, set the action to Redirect Row. Since you are dealing with an ACH file, the effect of truncating numbers and dates is a big deal. You want the file to fail, and redirecting the output will allow you to record what went wrong and then end the current Data Flow task that exists solely to validate the incoming file.

5. In the same way as the lockbox, if you do get row errors, you would like to gather as much information about the error to assist in the troubleshooting process. The XML Source has two error outputs, Header and Detail, so you'll have twice as much work to do. Create two Script Component tasks as transformations like you did to capture errors in the Lockbox Data Flow for each of the error outputs from the XML Source. Select the ErrorCode and ErrorColumn columns from the input. Create a new Output Column named ErrorDesc of type Unicode string [DT_WSTR] and size 1048. Open up the design environment for the Script Component. Change your ProcessInputRow event code to the following:

```
Public Overrides Sub Input0_ProcessInputRow(ByVal Row As Input0Buffer)
    'SCRIPT
    'PURPOSE: To retrieve the error description to write to error log
    '=================================================================
    Row.ErrorDesc= ComponentMetaData.GetErrorDescription(Row.ErrorCode)
End Sub
```

6. Add two Derived Column transforms with the following derived columns. Connect them to the output of the two Script component transformations.

Derived Column	Expression	DataType
ExecutionID	@[System::ExecutionInstanceGUID]	DT_WSTR 38
ErrorEvent	"ACH"	DT_WSTR 20
ErrorDate	@[System::ContainerStartTime]	DT_DATE

For the Detail output only, add the following derived column.

RawData	(DT_STR, 1028, 1252) ErrorDesc	DT_STR 1048

7. Add two OLE DB destination components and connect them to the output of the Derived Columns mapping the fields to the table ErrorDetail exactly as you did for the Lockbox Data Flow. Map the converted [rawdata] field to the [rawdata] field for the detail output. Map the ID field of the header output to the output [rawdata] field. The error handling of the bad XML file should look like Figure 19-24.

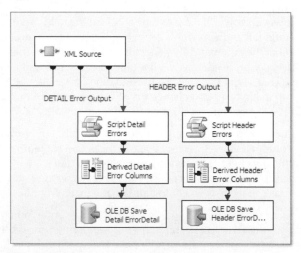

Figure 19-24

8. If the XML data is good, you want to perform a lookup on the batch number. Don't forget about the lookup being case-sensitive. Add a Character Map transform task and convert the Header output ID field (a batch number) to uppercase as an in-place change.

9. You also need a value in your stream to allow a lookup on import type. Batch numbers are only guaranteed to be unique by this type, and it is stored in the global variables. Add a Derived Column transform to add a column ImportType to your output stream. Since the [ImportType] field in the BankBatch table is of type CHAR(10), add the derived column as a type string [DT_STR] of size 10.

10. Add the Lookup transform to the Data Flow. Set the OLE DB connection to CaseStudy.OLEDB. Set the Lookup to the results of the following query:

```
SELECT BANKBATCHID, UPPER(BANKBATCHNBR) AS BANKBATCHNBR, UPPER(IMPORTTYPE) AS
IMPORTTYPE
FROM BANKBATCH
ORDER BY BANKBATCHNBR
```

In the Columns tab, link the Input Column ID to the Lookup column of BankBatchNbr. Link the ImportType columns. Add BankBatchID as the Lookup column with an output alias of BANKBATCHID. Since you are expecting that you will not get a match on the lookup and that this is indeed a new file, use the Configure Error output button and set the Lookup step to Ignore Failure on the Lookup Output.

11. Add a script component task as a destination to capture the successful end of your transformation Data Flow. Connect it to the Lookup output. Open the editor and select all the available input columns. Add the following global variables as ReadWriteVariables: BANKBATCHNBR, BANKBATCHID, BATCHTOTAL, BATCHITEMS, DEPOSITDATE. Insert the following code to store the variables. This code uses a technique of creating global variables, setting the global variables for the one row representing the header, and then setting the values of your passed-in variables to the variables stored temporarily in the script global variables:

```
'CASE STUDY 2005
Imports System
Imports System.Data
Imports System.Math
Imports Microsoft.SqlServer.Dts.Pipeline.Wrapper
Imports Microsoft.SqlServer.Dts.Runtime.Wrapper

Public Class ScriptMain
    Inherits UserComponent
    Public LocalBankBatchID As Int32 = -999
    Public LocalBatchTotal As Double = 0
    Public LocalBankBatchNbr As String = ""
    Public LocalDepositDate As Date = #12/31/1899#
    Public LocalBatchItems As UInt64 = 0

    Public Overrides Sub Input0_ProcessInputRow(ByVal Row As Input0Buffer)
        'SCRIPT
        'PURPOSE: This sub will fire for each row processed
        '         since we only have one header row we only
        '         this sub will fire only one time.
        '         Store values in variables
        '=========================================================
        Try
            If Row.TOTALDEPOSIT_IsNull = True Or _
                Row.TOTALDEPOSIT = 0.0 Or _
                 Row.TOTALTRANS_IsNull = True Or _
                    IsDate(Row.DEPOSITDATE) = False Then
                'KEEP DEFAULTS
```

```
                    Else
                        LocalBatchItems = Row.TOTALTRANS
                        LocalBankBatchNbr = Row.ID + ""
                        LocalBatchTotal = System.Convert.ToDouble(Row.TOTALDEPOSIT)
                        If Row.BANKBATCHID_IsNull Then
                            LocalBankBatchID = CInt(0)
                        Else
                            LocalBankBatchID = System.Convert.ToInt32(Row.BANKBATCHID)
                        End If
                        LocalDepositDate = System.Convert.ToDateTime(Row.DEPOSITDATE)
                    End If
                Catch ex As Exception
                    'KEEP DEFAULTS
                    Variables.BANKBATCHID = -999
                    Variables.BATCHTOTAL = 0
                End Try

        End Sub
        Public Overrides Sub PostExecute()
            'SCRIPT
            'PURPOSE: To set dts variables with values retrieved earlier
            '=============================================================
            Try
                'Attempt to accept the values
                Variables.BANKBATCHNBR = LocalBankBatchNbr
                Variables.BANKBATCHID = LocalBankBatchID
                Variables.BATCHTOTAL = LocalBatchTotal
                Variables.BATCHITEMS = LocalBatchItems
                Variables.DEPOSITDATE = LocalDepositDate
            Catch ex As Exception
                'If any failure occurs fail the file
                Variables.BANKBATCHID = -999
                Variables.BATCHTOTAL = 0
            End Try
            MyBase.PostExecute()
        End Sub
    End Class
```

The ACH Validation Data Flow is now complete. The final Data Flow should look like Figure 19-25. Make sure you've still got the Lockbox Sequence container disabled, and then go ahead and run the package. Once you get it working properly, archive a copy, because you've got another Data Flow to build to import this ACH XML file. Play around with the XML file by adding bad data and malforming the structure of the file to see how the Data Flow handles it.

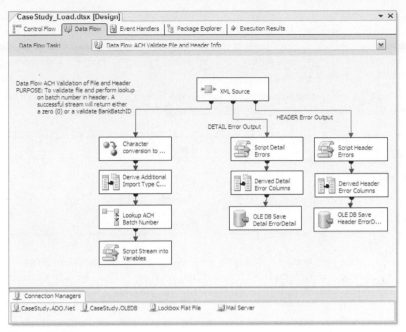

Figure 19-25

ACH Processing

This section in a lot of ways mirrors the Data Flow for Lockbox Processing. Once you've validated the ACH XML file, the Control Flow will create a [BankBatch] row and start the process of importing the detail. You have all the header-related information just as you did for the Lockbox process, and since the file has been validated, you can simply transform the data into the [BankBatchDetail] table.

1. Enable the Data Flow task named Data Flow ACH Validate File and Header Info and drill down into its design surface. Add an XML Source and set it up exactly the same as you did for the Validation Data Flow. However, this time you already have an XSD file, so just point the component to it. Leave the ErrorOutput settings to Fail component if an error is encountered while processing the file. You'll also leave the error-handling components out in this Data Flow, although in production you should add them back in.

    If you ran the package to test the ACH Validation section, you'll need to put a new ACH XML File back into c:\casestudy\ach\.

2. This time, you are concerned mainly with the detail portion of the XML data. You have the foreign key information stored in a variable so you don't need to perform any lookups on data, but you will want to use the Lookup later on the DESC field that you are going to import to the RawInvoiceNbr field in the CaseStudy_Processing package. Add a Character Map transform to convert the DESC field to uppercase and replace its current value in the stream.

643

3. The only other thing you need is that foreign key stored in the variable @BANKBATCHID. Add a Derived Column transform to add that variable to the current stream. Add another column named RAWINVOICENBR and select the [DESC] field from the Columns input collection as a string [DT_STR] type of length 50. This selection of string type has the result of conversion in one step.

4. Add an OLE DB destination and connect to the CaseStudy.OLEDB connection. Select the [BankBatchDetail] table and map the columns in the following table.

Input Column	Destination Column
BankBatchID	BankBatchID
Amount	PaymentAmount
RawInvoiceNbr	RawInvoiceNbr

5. The final thing you need to do is save the entire XML file in the [BankBatch] table. You'll use exactly the same technique from the Lockbox process. Add a Derived Column transform and connect to the Header output of the XML file. Add columns for the variables BANKBATCHID and ACHCURRENTFILE. Make sure the ACHCURRENTFILE column is set to [DT_WSTR] 100. Refer back to the "Lockbox Processing" section to see an example of this transform.

6. Add an Import Column transform and connect to this Header Derived Column transform. On the Input Columns tab, select the field that contains the file path in the stream: ACHCURRENT-FILE. Then go to the Advanced Input Output property tab and expand the Input Column Input and Import Column Output nodes. Add an output column to the output columns node named FileStreamToStore. Set the DataType property to [DT_NTEXT]. The editor should look similar to Figure 19-19, but the Lineage IDs may be different. Note the LineageID and set the property in the ACHCurrentFile Input Column named FileDataColumnID to that LineageID.

7. Add an OLE DB Destination to the output of the Header Derived column transform. Set the OLEDB connection to CaseStudy.OLEDB. Then set the SQL Command to Update BankBatch Set BatchFile = ? WHERE BANKBATCHID = ? and press Refresh. In the Mappings tab, connect the FileStreamToStore to the Destination Column Param_0, which is the [BatchFile] field in the BankBatch table. Connect the field BankBatchID to the Destination Column Param_1. Click Refresh and save.

The final Data Flow for ACH processing should look similar to Figure 19-26. Because the logic of this package is designed to process files only once, you may need to truncate the BankBatch and BankBatchDetail table in order to test repeatedly. As an alternative, alter the batch number in the input files to a new batch number. After you've gotten a successful run of this Data Flow, archive the package.

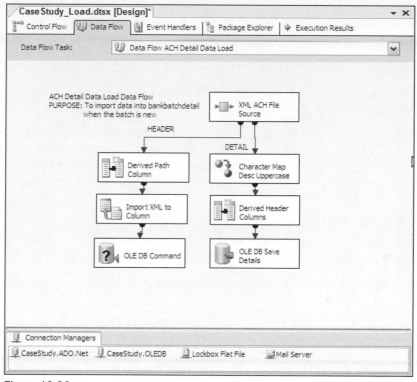

Figure 19-26

E-mail Payment Processing

The e-mail payment processing is interesting. The payment transactions are stored in a relational database, so you don't have data issues. You just need to check to see if there are any to process. You also have to make sure that you haven't picked the transaction up before. To be safe, you'll store the transactional primary key from the accounting system as your [ReferenceData1] field. You can then use this field in your extraction to keep from pulling a transaction more than once.

1. Add another Sequence container to the Control Flow surface. Name the container Sequence of Email Payment Processing and connect with a completion constraint to the ACH Processing sequence container.

2. Copy and paste the Script task named Script to Reset Variables Task from the ACH Payment Processing sequence container. (This task, as you recall, will reset the variables that you are sharing across processes.)

3. Add an Execute SQL task named Execute SQL to check for Trans. This task will count the number of transactions in the accounting system not yet processed. The task will set the variables EMAILCNT and BATCHTOTAL equal to the number and total amounts of available transactions to work. Set up the properties using the following table.

Property	Setting
ResultSet	SingleRow
ConnectionType	OLE DB
Connection	CaseStudy.OLEDB
SQLSourceType	Direct Input
SQLStatement	SELECT count(*) as TranCnt, sum(depositamount) as TotAmt FROM vCorpDirectAcctTrans Corp LEFT OUTER JOIN BANKBATCHDETAIL DTL ON cast(CORP.TRANSID as varchar(50)) = DTL.REFERENCEDATA1 WHERE DTL.REFERENCEDATA1 is null
ResultSet:ResultName	0
ResultSet:Variable	User::EMAILCNT
ResultSet:ResultName	1
ResultSet:Variable	User::BATCHTOTAL

4. Copy a new Execute SQL task into the sequence container from the ACH processing container named Execute SQL Task to Add ACH Bank Batch Hdr. This task will create the batch header for your e-mail-based transactions. Add a conditional constraint in combination with an expression between the two SQL tasks that won't allow the second SQL task to be executed if there are no items to be worked as e-mail payments. The expression should be set to:

```
EMAILCNT>0
```

5. In the Add Batch Execute SQL task, you don't have all the variable values like you did for the text and XML files. Navigate to the Parameter Mapping tab and change some of these variables to match Figure 19-27.

6. The last step is to add the Data Flow task and connect it to the Execute SQL Batch task. At the moment, the Email Control Flow tasks should resemble Figure 19-28. Continue on to the next section before testing this Control Flow.

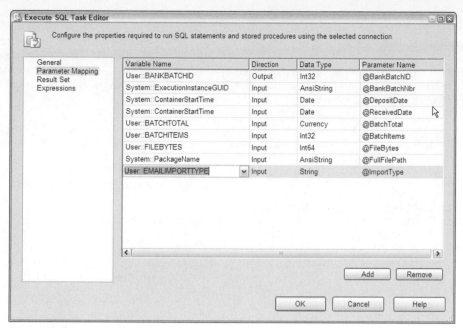

Figure 19-27

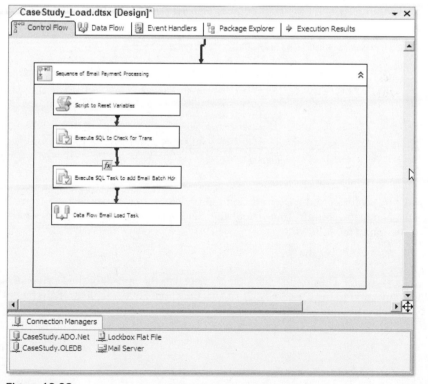

Figure 19-28

E-mail Data Flow Processing

If the package initiates the Email Data Flow, there must be some e-mail-based accounting transactions in the accounting database and the Execute SQL task will have already created a new row with a BankBatchID from the BankBatch table for you that is stored in the BANKBATCHID variable. All you have to do is extract the data from the accounting view, add the foreign key to the data, and insert the rows into the [BankBatchDetail] table.

1. Start by entering the Data Flow Email Load Task design surface. Add an OLE DB Source to the Data Flow. Connect to the CaseStudy.OLE.DB connection and supply the following SQL command text for the extract:

```
SELECT TransID, DepositAmount, TransDesc
FROM vCorpDirectAcctTrans Corp
LEFT OUTER JOIN BANKBATCHDETAIL DTL
ON CAST(CORP.TRANSID as VARCHAR(50)) = DTL.REFERENCEDATA1
WHERE DTL.REFERENCEDATA1 is null
```

2. You also need to add that BankBatchID foreign key to your stream, so add a Derived Column Transform to add the BANKBATCHID variable to the stream. Connect the OLE DB Source and the Derived Column transforms.

3. Look at a sample of the TransDesc data that is being brought over in Figure 19-29. To get this to match the e-mail addresses in the customer table, it would be better to strip the PAYPAL* identifier. Since the BankBatchDetail file expects a varchar field of 50 characters and you are also watching out for case-sensitivity, convert the type and case at the same time by adding an additional column named RawInvoiceNbr as a string [DT_STR] of 50 characters, and set the expression to the following:

```
TRIM(UPPER(REPLACE(REPLACE(TransDesc,"PAYPAL",""),"*",""))) 
```

	transdesc
1	PAYPAL*JBrown@CapitalCycles.com
2	PAYPAL*DBlanco@msn.com
3	PAYPAL*ABaltazar@msn.com
4	PAYPAL*CBooth@MagicCycle
5	PAYPAL*MBlack@Marsh.com

Figure 19-29

4. Add a last column to the Derived Column transform to also convert the TransID to a string value. Name the column TransIDtoString. Set the Data Type to [DT_STR] length 50, and set the Expression to the following:

```
(DT_STR, 50, 1252)[TransID]
```

5. Add an OLE DB Destination task and connect it to the output of the Derived Column task. Set the connection to the CaseStudy.OLEDB connection. Set the table to [BankBatchDetail]. Map the fields in the Mapping tab to those shown in the following table.

Input Field	Destination in [BankBatchDetail]
DepositAmount	PaymentAmount
TransDesc	ReferenceData2
BankBatchID	BankBatchID
RawInvoiceNbr	RawInvoiceNbr
TransIDasString	ReferenceData1

This completes the construction of the Data Flow for the e-mail load task — and for the CaseStudy_Load package as well. The Email Load Data Flow should look like Figure 19-30.

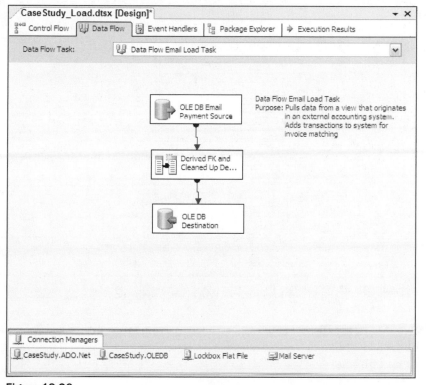

Figure 19-30

The final package, with everything enabled, should look like Figure 19-31.

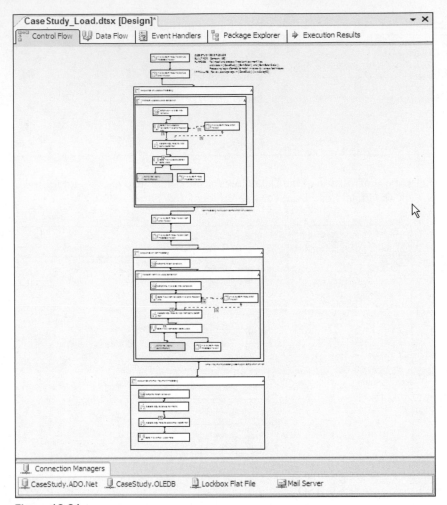

Figure 19-31

A more reasonable view of the CaseStudy_Load package, with the sequence and Foreach containers collapsed, is shown in Figure 19-32.

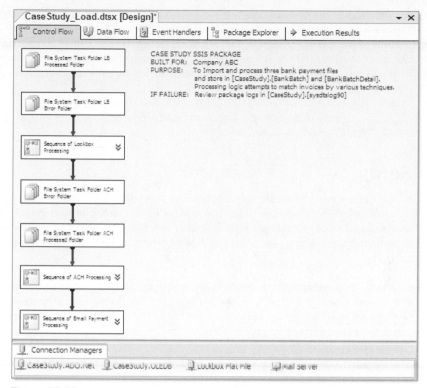

CaseStudy_Load.dtsx [Design]*   ▼ ×

Control Flow | Data Flow | Event Handlers | Package Explorer | Execution Results

File System Task Folder LB
Processed Folder

File System Task Folder LB
Error Folder

Sequence of Lockbox
Processing

File System Task Folder ACH
Error Folder

File System Task Folder ACH
Processed Folder

Sequence of ACH Processing

Sequence of Email Payment
Processing

CASE STUDY SSIS PACKAGE
BUILT FOR: Company ABC
PURPOSE: To Import and process three bank payment files
             and store in [CaseStudy].[BankBatch] and [BankBatchDetail].
             Processing logic attempts to match invoices by various techniques.
IF FAILURE: Review package logs in [CaseStudy].[sysdtslog90]

Connection Managers

CaseStudy.ADO.Net   CaseStudy.OLEDB   Lockbox Flat File   Mail server

Figure 19-32

Testing

Test the package by disabling all the sequence containers. Work your way through each of the tasks, enabling them as you go. Use this SQL script to delete rows that you may be adding to the database during repeated testing that may change the flow of logic in the Control Flow sections:

```
DELETE FROM BANKBATCHDETAIL
GO
DELETE FROM BANKBATCH
```

Case Study Process Package

The Load package put the data into the database. The Process package is going to perform the magic. All this payment data from different sources with varying degrees of quality needs to be matched by invoice or customer attributes against your dimension tables of Invoice and Customer. Having it combined in one place allows this package to apply the logic of payment matching to all payments at once. Hopefully, every time the package runs, it is money in the bank for Company ABC.

The strategy for this package is to mimic the logic provided from the business specifications in Figure 19-4. You will queue all the payment transactions that are unmatched for a moment in time. Then you will run that stream of payments through a gauntlet of matching options until you break through your confidence level for matching. This design will make it easy to add further matching scenarios in the future but will allow you to use the advanced fuzzy matching logic available today in the Integration Services.

You'll be breaking the construction of the package into these sections: Package Setup, High-Confidence Data Flow, and Medium-Confidence Data Flow.

Package Setup

This portion of the Case Study will create the Control Flow steps that you need to systematically review pending and unmatched payment transactions. You will set up the variables that you need to store unmatched payment counts at each stage of the matching process. You will create placeholder Data Flow tasks that will perform the matching, and then you'll send out an e-mail to report on the statistics for the matching operations.

1. Create a new SSIS project. Name the project CaseStudy_Process. When the project is created, go to the Solution Explorer and click on the Package.dtsx file. In the Property window, find the Name property and change the name from package.dtsx to casestudy_process.dtsx. Answer Yes to change the name of the package object as well.

2. Add an OLE DB Connection to the Connection Managers that connects to the CaseStudy database. Name the connection CaseStudy.OLEDB.

3. Add an SMTP Connection to the Connection Managers that connects to a viable SMTP mail server. Name the connection Mail Server.

4. Use the menu SSIS ⇨ Variables to access the Variables editor and add what's shown in the following table.

Variable Name	Scope	Data Type	Value
HIGHCONFMATCHCNTSTART	CaseStudy_Process	Int32	0
HIGHCONFMATCHCNTEND	CaseStudy_Process	Int32	0
MEDCONFMATCHCNTEND	CaseStudy_Process	Int32	0

5.   Add an Execute SQL task to the Control Flow. This task needs to query the database for the pending payments and record the total number and dollar amount prior to starting the High Confidence Data Flow task. Name the task Execute SQL Get High Conf Stats. Connect to the OLEDB connection. Set up two result columns to retrieve first an amount value into the variable that represents a count of the pending transactions at this point. Use the following SQL in the SQLStatement Property:

```
SELECT
        count(*) as ToCnt
FROM bankbatchdetail d
INNER JOIN BANKBATCH h
ON h.bankbatchid = d.bankbatchid
WHERE matcheddate is null
AND RawInvoiceNbr is not null
AND RawInvoiceNbr <> ''
```

6.   Add a Data Flow task to the Control Flow. Name the task High Confidence Data Flow Process Task Start. Connect the tasks. You'll cover this task in the "High-Confidence Data Flow" section.

7.   Add another Execute SQL task by copying the first SQL task. Name the task High Confidence Data Flow Process Task End. Connect the tasks. Change the variable mappings in the result column to HIGHCONFMATCHCNTEND.

8.   Add another Data Flow task to the Control Flow. Name the task Medium Confidence Data Flow Process Task. Connect the task to the Execute SQL task. You'll cover this task in the "Medium-Confidence Data Flow" section.

9.   Add another Execute SQL task by copying the first SQL task. Name the task Medium Confidence Data Flow Process Task End. Connect the tasks. Change the variable mappings in the result column to MEDCONFMATCHCNTEND.

10.   Add an Execute SQL task from the Toolbox. Name the task Execute SQL to Balance by Batch. Set the OLE DB connection. Set the SQLStatement property to EXEC usp_BankBatch_Balance. This procedure will update and balance batch level totals based on the payments that are processed.

11.   Add a Send Mail task. Set it up to connect to the Mail Server SMTP connection. Fill in the To, From, and Subject properties. (If you don't have access to an SMTP connection, disable this task for testing.) Create an expression for the MessageSource property similar to the following code:

```
" COMPANY ABC, Automated Payment Matching Results: Starting with " + (DT_WSTR, 25)
@[User::HIGHCONFMATCHCNTSTART] + " payments, We received and successfully
processed " + (DT_WSTR, 25) (@[User::HIGHCONFMATCHCNTSTART]-
@[User::HIGHCONFMATCHCNTEND]) + " payments automatically with a High-Level of
confidence. We processed " + (DT_WSTR, 25) (@[User::HIGHCONFMATCHCNTEND]-
@[User::MEDCONFMATCHCNTEND]) + " payments with a Medium-Level of confidence. This
is an automated message."
```

The completed Control Flow should look similar to Figure 19-33.

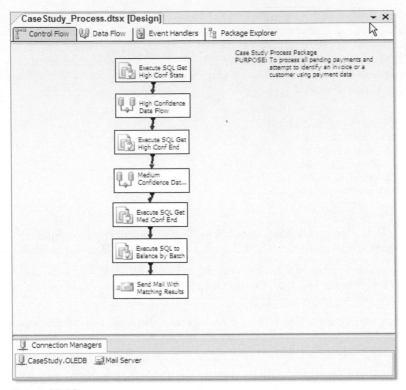

Figure 19-33

High-Confidence Data Flow

Your first level of matching should be on the data attributes that are most likely to produce the highest-quality lookup against the target invoice table. The attribute that would provide the highest-quality lookup and confidence level when matching would be the Invoice Number. An invoice number is a manufactured identification string generated by Company ABC for each created bill. If you get a match by invoice number, you can be highly confident that payment should be applied against this invoice number.

1. First you need to create a stream of items to process in your Data Flow. You'll do this by querying all pending payments that at least have some sort of data in the RawInvoiceNbr Field. If there is no data in this field, the items can't be matched through an automated process until a subject-matter expert can look up the item or identify it in another way. Add an OLE DB Source to the Data Flow. Set up these properties. Notice that the [RawInvoiceNbr] field has been converted to uppercase before it is delivered into your data stream to better enable the lookup matches.

Property	Value
Connection	CaseStudy.OLEDB Connection
DataAccessMode	SQLCommand
SQLCommandText	SELECT h.ImportType, BankBatchDtlID, UPPER (RawInvoiceNbr) as RawInvoiceNbr, PaymentAmount FROM bankbatchdetail d INNER JOIN BANKBATCH h ON h.bankbatchid = d.bankbatchid WHERE matcheddate is null AND RawInvoiceNbr is not null AND RawInvoiceNbr <> ''

2. Add a Sort transform to the output of the OLE DB Source and sort the data by the [BankBatchDtlID] field in ascending order. Even though you could order the incoming data by BankBatchDtlID by adding an ORDER BY clause to the SQLCommandText property in the OLE DB Source, you still need this Sort transform to sort the stream for a later Merge Join operation.

3. Add the first Lookup transform, which is going to be a lookup by Invoice. You are going to add many of these, so you'll go over this first one in detail. For each item in the stream, you want to set up an attempt to match the information in the [RawInvoiceNbr] field from the different payment data sources to your real invoice number in the invoice dimension table. In other lookups, you may attempt name or e-mail lookups. The invoice number is considered your highest-confidence match because it is a unique number generated by the billing system. If you find a match to the invoice number, you have identified the payment. Set up the following properties on the component.

Property	Value
Connection	CaseStudy.OLEDB Connection
SQL Query	SELECT InvoiceID, UPPER(ltrim(rtrim(InvoiceNbr))) As InvoiceNbr, CustomerID FROM INVOICE ORDER BY InvoiceNbr

4. In the Columns tab, connect the Input Column [RawInvoiceNbr] to the Lookup Column [InvoiceNbr]. If there is a match on the lookup, pull back the InvoiceID and CustomerID. This information will be in the Lookup data. Do this by adding these columns as Lookup columns to the Lookup Column Grid.

    The default behavior of the Lookup transform is to fail if there is a no-match condition. You don't want this to happen, because you expect that you aren't going to get 100 percent matches on each transform. What you'd like to be able to do is separate the matches from the non-matches so that you only continue to look up items in the stream that are unmatched. To do that, you will use this built-in capability to "know" if a match has been made, and instead of failing the component or package, you will divert the stream to another lookup. In the Lookup transform, use the Configure Error Output button to set up the action of a failed lookup to be Redirect Row as in Figure 19-34.

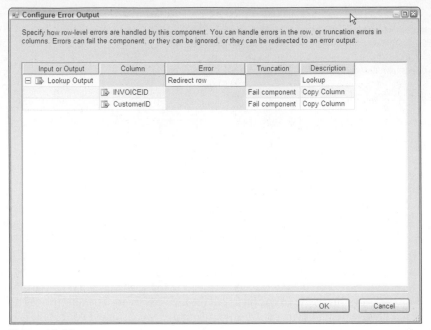

Figure 19-34

5. Because the Invoice number can be keyed incorrectly at the bank or truncated, it may be off by only a few digits, or by an "O" instead of a "0." Using only inner-join matching, you may miss the match, but there may still be a good chance of a match if you can use the Fuzzy Lookup. This package is also going to use a lot of Fuzzy Lookup tasks. They all need to be set up the same way, so you'll do this one in detail and then just refer to it later.

    a.   Add a Fuzzy Lookup task to the Data Flow to the right of the Lookup task. Connect the Error Output of the previous Invoice Lookup transform to the Fuzzy Lookup. Set up the OLE DB connection to CaseStudy.OLEDB.

    b.   Select the option to Generate a New Index with the reference table set to [Invoice]. (Later it will be more efficient to change these settings to store and then use a cached reference table.)

    c.   In the Columns tab, match the [RawInvoiceNbr] Fields to the [InvoiceNbr] field.

    d.   Deselect the extra Error columns from being passed through from the input columns. These columns were added to the stream because it was diverted using the error handler. You aren't interested in these columns because a no-match is not considered an error for this transform.

    e.   Right-click the line between the two columns. Click Edit Relationship on the pop-up menu. Check all the comparison flags starting with Ignore.

    f.   Select the InvoiceID and CustomerID fields to return as the lookup values if a match can be made with the fuzzy logic.

    g.   In the Advanced tab, set the Similarity Threshold up to .78 for the Invoice fuzzy match.

6. Since the output of the Fuzzy Lookup contains a number indicating the similarity threshold, you can use this number to separate the stream into high- and low-similarity matches. Low-similarity matches will continue through further matching attempts. High similarity matches will be remerged with other high-similarity matches. Add a Conditional Split task to separate the output into two streams based on the field [_Similarity] which represents a mathematical measurement of "sameness" between the [RawInvoiceNbr] provided by ABC Company's customers and the InvoiceNbr that you have on file. The splits should always be set up like Figure 19-35.

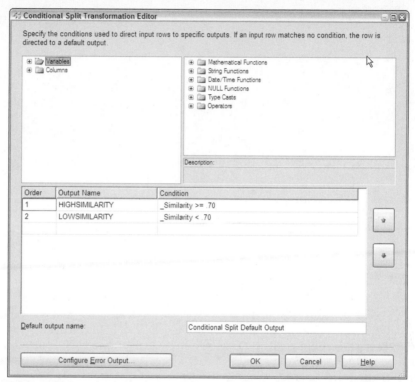

Figure 19-35

7. You want to merge any high-similarity matching from the Fuzzy Lookup and the previous Inner-Join Lookup transform, but to do that, the Fuzzy Lookup output must be sorted. This step will also be repeated many times. Add a Sort transform and select to sort the column [BankBatchDtlID] field in ascending order. The Sort transforms do two things: They sort data, and they also allow you to remove the redundant fuzzy-data-added columns by deselecting them for pass-through. Remove references to these fields (_Similarity, Confidence, ErrorCode, and ErrorColumn) when passing data through sorts.

8. Add a Merge Component to the Data Flow. Connect the output of the Invoice Lookup to the High Similarity output of the Fuzzy Lookup (via the Sort transform). In the Merge Editor you can see all the fields from both sides of the merge. Sometimes a field will come over with the value to <IGNORE> the field. Make sure you match these fields or some of the data is going to be dropped from your stream. A merge transaction will look like Figure 19-36.

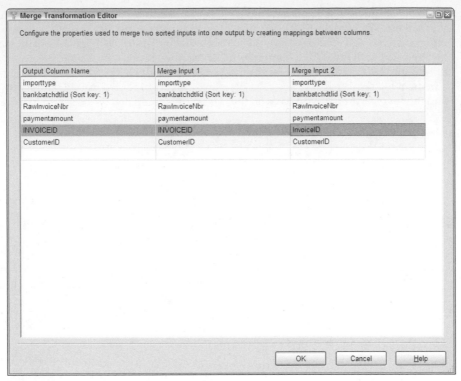

Figure 19-36

9. At this point, the only items in the Merge are matched by Invoice, and you should have foreign keys for both the customer and the invoice. These keys can now be updated by executing the stored procedure usp_BankBatchDetail_Match for each of the matching items in your merged stream. Add an OLE DB command to the Data Flow and set up the OLEDB connection. Set the SQLCommand Property up as `usp_BankBatchDetail_Match ?, ?, ?`. Press Refresh to retrieve the parameters to match. Match the InvoiceID, CustomerID, and BankBatchDtlID fields from the input and output. The stored procedure will run for each row in your stream and automatically update the foreign keys. If a row is found with both invoice and customer keys, the stored procedure will also mark that transaction as complete.

This completes the High-Confidence Data Flow. At this point, your Data Flow should look like Figure 19-37. When this Data Flow returns to the Control Flow, the Execute SQL task will recalculate the number of remaining pending transactions by count and by amount. The next step is the Medium-Confidence Data Flow.

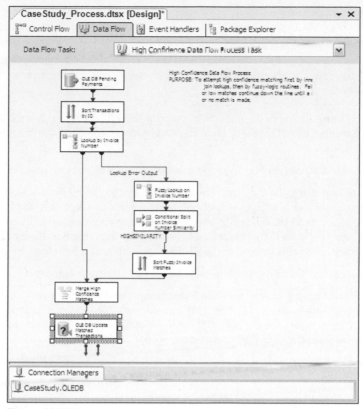

Figure 19-37

Medium-Confidence Data Flow

The Medium-Confidence Data Flow is made up of matches using customer information. Since names and e-mail addresses are more likely to be similar, this level of matching is not as high on the confidence-level continuum as an invoice number. And even after you have the customer identified, you will still need to identify the invoice. To find the invoice, you'll attempt to match on the closest non-paid invoice by amount for the customer. All of these tasks, until you get to the end, are similar to the High-Confidence Data Flow. The only difference is that the lookups use the customer table instead of the invoice table. For this reason, you'll just list the basic steps. Refer to Figure 19-40 to see a picture of the final result.

1. Add an OLE DB Source set up exactly the same way as for the High-Confidence Data Flow.

2. Add a Lookup to the Data Flow connecting to the OLEDB source. Name it Email Lookup. Look for exact matches between RawInvoiceNbr and the field [Email] in the customer table. Set the error handling to Redirect when encountering a Lookup error. Use this SQL Query:

```
Select CustomerID, UPPER(rtrim(Email)) as Email FROM Customer WHERE Email is not
null AND Email <> ''
```

3. Add another Lookup by Customer Name beside the Email Lookup. Feed it the error output of the Email Lookup. Look for exact matches between RawInvoiceNbr and the field [Name] in the customer table. Set the error handling to Redirect when encountering a Lookup error. Use this SQL Query:

```
SELECT CustomerID, UPPER(rtrim([Name])) as [Name] FROM CUSTOMER WHERE [Name] is not null and [Name] <> ''
```

4. Add Sort Components to the outputs of both lookups. Place them directly under each lookup. Sort by BankBatchDtlID ascending. In the sort by name matches, don't forget to deselect the error columns.

5. Add a Merge Component to merge the two outputs of the Sorts for matches by Email and Name.

6. Add a Lookup using the CustomerLookup table next to the Name Lookup. Feed it the error output of the Customer Name Lookup. Look for exact matches between the fields [RawInvoiceNbr] and the lookup field [RawDataToMatch]. This lookup requires an additional match on the fields [ImportType] for both the input and output data. Set the error handling to Redirect. Use the table name [CustomerLookup] as the source. Look up and return the CustomerID.

7. Add a Sort to the CustomerLookup task. Deselect the extra columns.

8. Add a Fuzzy Lookup task to the Data Flow. Connect it to the error output of the CustomerLookup Lookup. Connect to the customer table, and match by RawInvoiceNbr to Email Address. Select the CustomerID for the lookup. Set the Similarity to .70. Remove the columns for pass-through that start with lookup.

9. Add the Conditional Split component to the output of the Fuzzy Lookup to separate the matches by similarity values above and below .70.

10. Moving to the left, add a new Merge task to merge the results of the e-mail and name merge with the customer lookup matched sort results. Combine the matched results of the two sorted outputs.

11. Add a Sort to the High Similarity Results of the Fuzzy Lookup by Email. Deselect the columns that were added by the Fuzzy Lookup starting with "_". Sort by BatchDetailID.

12. Add a new Merge task to combine the Email Fuzzy Lookup Sort to the Email, Name, and CustomerLookup merged results.

13. Add a Fuzzy Lookup task to the Data Flow beside the conditional split from the last Email Fuzzy Lookup. Name it Fuzzy Name Lookup. Move it to the same level to the right of the conditional lookup. Connect the Low Similarity Output from the Email Fuzzy Lookup to the new Fuzzy Name Lookup. Use the [Customer] table to look for matches matching [RawInvoiceNbr] to [Name]. Uncheck the pass-through checkbox for the input column [CustomerID] that is being fed by the Low Similarity stream. Retrieve a new lookup of CustomerID. In the Advanced tab, move the Similarity setting to .65.

14. Add another conditional split below the Fuzzy Name Lookup and split the output into High and Low Similarity, again using the .70 number.

15. Add a sort to sort the HIGHSIMILARITY output from the Conditional Split you just created. Remove the extra columns.

16. Add the last Merge task to merge the Sort from the high-similarity fuzzy name match with all the other matches that have been merged so far. At this point, you have captured in the output of this Merge task all the transactions that you were not able to identify by invoice number but

that you have been able to identify by customer attributes of e-mail or name. These are all of your medium-confidence matches. Knowing the customer might be good, but finding the payment invoice would be even better.

17. Add another Lookup task to the Data Flow below the last Merge task. Name it Lookup Invoice By Customer. Connect the output of the Merge task to it. Open the editor. Put the following basic SQL query in as the reference table:

```
"SELECT INVOICEID, CUSTOMERID, TotalBilledAmt FROM INVOICE"
```

In the Columns tab, link the CustomerID that you have discovered to the CustomerID in the invoice lookup table. Connect the paymentamount field to the TotalBilledAmount field. Go to the Advanced tab and check the box Enable Memory Restriction. Then check the box to Modify the SQL Statement. Update the contents of the Caching SQL statement to the following:

```
select * from (SELECT INVOICEID, CUSTOMERID, TotalBilledAmt FROM INVOICE) as
refTable  where [refTable].[CUSTOMERID] = ? and (ABS([refTable].[TotalBilledAmt] -
?)<([RefTable].[TotalBilledAmt]*.05))
```

18. Click on the Parameters button. A box for parameters will appear as in Figure 19-38. Select the field PaymentAmount to substitute for Parameter1. This query looks for matches using the CustomerID field and an amount that is within 5 percent of the billed premium.

To have the result return an Invoice Number, click back on the Columns tab and select the InvoiceID field in the grid. At this stage, you don't care if you don't get a match in terms of error handling. Set the error-handling behavior to Ignore Error, and just send the data through regardless of whether it matches or not. If you have the customer ID and that's it, fine. If you have both, that's even better, but you'll send your results through regardless.

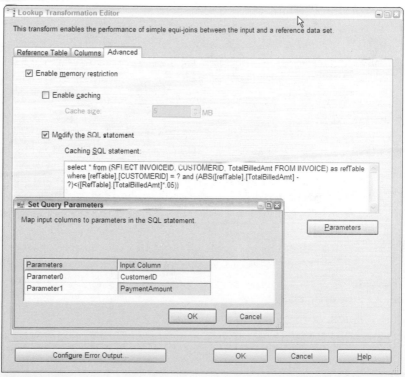

Figure 19-38

19.   Add an OLE DB Command transform to the Data Flow at the bottom. Attach a connection to the results of the last invoice lookup by amount. Set the connection to CaseStudy.OLEDB. Set the SQLCommand Property to usp_BankBatchDetail_Match ?, ?, ?. Press Refresh to retrieve the parameters to match. Match the InvoiceID, CustomerID, and BankBatchDtlID fields from the input and output. The stored procedure will run for each row in your stream and automatically update the foreign keys. If a row is found with both invoice and customer keys, the stored procedure will also mark that transaction as complete.

This completes the task of building the Medium-Confidence Data Flow and the CaseStudy_Process package. The Data Flow should look similar to Figure 19-39.

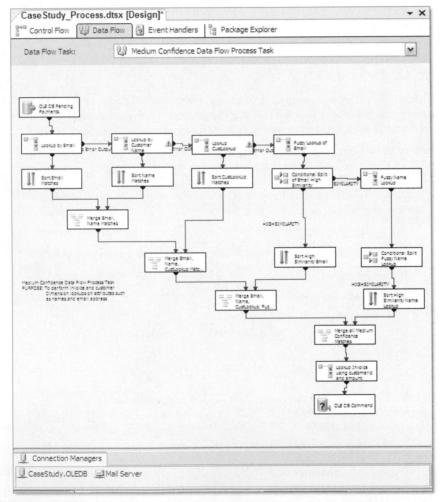

Figure 19-39

Interpreting the Results

Before you started this exercise of creating the CaseStudy_Process SSIS package, you had loaded a set of 16 payment transactions for matching into the BankBatchDetail table. By running a series of SQL statements comparing the RawInvoiceNbr with invoices and customers, you could only retrieve a maximum of 7 matches. This translates into a 44 percent match of payments to send to the payment processors without any further human interaction. The development of this package with heavy usage of Fuzzy Lookup transforms increases your identification hit-rate to 13 out of 16 matches, or an 81 percent matching percentage. The results can be broken out as shown in the following table.

Stage in Process	# of New Matches	Match Percent
High-Confidence Invoice Match	2	12%
Med-Confidence Invoice Match	9	56%
Med-Confidence Customer Match	2	12%

As you may recall, the business expectations were to make an improvement to match all but 20 to 40 percent of every payment that comes into Company ABC. You are right at, or just under, the best percentage with your test data — and this is just a beginning. Remember that the unidentified items will be worked by SMEs who will store the results of their matching customer information in the CustomerLookup table. Incidentally, you used this data even though the table is empty within the Lookup CustLookup transform in the Medium-Confidence Data Flow. As SME-provided information is stored, the Data Flow will become "smarter" in matching incoming payments by referring to this matching source as well.

Now look at the three items that weren't matched by your first run.

Item Matching Information	Payment Amount
Intl Sports Association	$ 34,953.00
JBROWN@CAPITALCYCLES.COM	$ 21,484.00
181INTERNA	$ 18,444.00

The first item looks like a customer name, and if you search in the customer table, you'd find a similar customer named International Sport Assoc. Since it is highly likely that future payments will be remitted in the same manner, you'll store the match between the customer's actual name and the string Intl Sports Association in the CustLookup table.

The second item looks like a customer e-mail address. If you can find the customer to whom this e-mail address belongs, you can update that information directly into the customer table to facilitate a future match. There is one customer named Capital Road Cycles that has several invoices at or around $20,000. You'll update the customer data with this e-mail address.

If you query the invoice table using an invoice number like 181INTERNA, you find several, but they are all for an amount of $34,953.00. This payment is for $18,444.00. Because the payment is significantly different from your billed amount, someone is going to have to look at this payment. This transaction will be manually processed based on your current business rules regardless of anything you could have done. Because the matching is against an invoice number, you also don't have anything of use for your customer lookup table.

If you were to now delete all the rows from the BankBatch and BankBatchDetail tables and rerun both the CaseStudy_Load and CaseStudy_Process packages, the payment matching process now improves to 15 out of 16 matches — a whopping 94 percent match. Company ABC will be highly pleased with the capabilities that you have introduced them to with this SSIS solution.

Running in SQL Agent

These packages were designed to run together in a sequence. The CaseStudy_Load would be scheduled to run first. It may or may not have anything to process based on the time of day or the workload of the external payment processing vendors. The CaseStudy_Process will continue to perform the matching activity all throughout the day. When users have to manually identify an item, their identification can be stored either by updating the data in the dimension tables or in your lookup tables. The sample packages here would then use that information in the medium-confidence-level Data Flow on the next run of the job.

Figure 19-40 shows an example of the two jobs residing in the SQL Agent running in sequence.

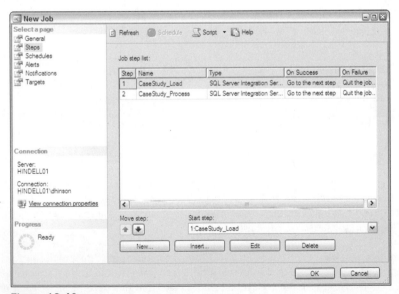

Figure 19-40

Summary

During this project, you gained some experience with most of the transforms and more than a few of the common tasks in the Toolbox. You learned firsthand that the new Data Flow is powerful, because you worked through typical staging logic in memory without having to commit the data and witnessed the results of the new Fuzzy Lookup transformations. You saw how visual the environment is and how easy it is to understand what is going on with the stream as it is being transformed. Transforming is what you do in the Data Flow, not in the Control Flow — even though it looks like a Control Flow page.

This case study provided an in-depth look at the new capabilities of the SSIS development environment. It is a real development environment now. That is why you first started with some business requirements and worked through the exercise like a development project. You focused on the nuts and bolts of error handling, naming conventions, and some practical tips for testing. Hopefully you saw a few things that you can use to solve that problem on your desk with SSIS 2005.

Index

SYMBOLS AND NUMERICS

&& (ampersands), logical AND operator, 147

... (ellipses button), 72, 146

== (equal signs), equality operator, 146–147

? (question mark), placeholder for query parameter, 256

|| (vertical bars), OR login, 131

010305c.dat file, 125, 134

A

Access database

configuring Connection Manager for, 251–252

importing from, 253–255

parameter, passing to SQL Command, 255–258

porting to SQL Server, 250

security for, 250–251

Access Upsizing Wizard, 254

ACH file, payment processing case study

Control Flow for, 635–638

description of, 595, 599–600

processing for, 643–645

processing requirements, 596

validation for, 639–643

AcquireConnections **method, 425, 433–435, 455–456**

ActionAtEvent option, WMI Event Watcher task, 514

ActionAtTimeout option, WMI Event Watcher task, 67, 515

ActiveX Script task, 5, 60, 61

adapters

Data Flow and, 328

destination adapters

building from pipeline components, 419, 454–461

definition of, 328

source adapters

building from pipeline components, 418, 432–443

definition of, 328

execution trees and, 330, 332

Admin account, Access, 251, 252

ADO enumerator, Foreach Loop container, 78

ADO.NET schema enumerator, Foreach Loop container, 78

Advanced Editor window

Import Column transformation using, 150–152

OLE DB Command transformation using, 105, 163

overriding with custom user interface, 475

Pivot transformation using, 182

Row Count transformation using, 161

synchronous and asynchronous transformations in, 324–328

Union All transformation using, 362

Unpivot transformation using, 188

when used by transformations, 91

Advanced Windowing Extensions (AWE), 304

AdventureWorksExtract.dtsx file, 110

AfterEvent option, WMI Event Watcher task, 67, 515

AfterTimeout option, WMI Event Watcher task, 67, 515

Aggregate transformation

as blocking transformation, 322–323

configuring, 91–92

data cleansing and, 354, 356–357

definition of, 13, 91

example using, 112

agile SDLCs
definition of, 549
MSF Agile template, 570–572
Allow Append option, Export Column transformation, 100
ampersands (&&), logical AND operator, 147
*An Investigation of the Laws of Thought, on which are
founded the Mathematical Theories of Logic and
Probabilities* (Boole), 548
**Analysis Services Dimension Processing Destination
transformation, 17**
Analysis Services Execute DDL task, 5, 70
**Analysis Services Partition Processing Destination
transformation, 17**
Analysis Services Processing task, 5, 70
annotations, 35–36
`Application` **object**
definition of, 492
methods of
example using, 496–504
package maintenance, 493
package monitoring, 495–496
package role maintenance, 495
server folder maintenance, 494
architecture of DTS, 342–343
architecture of SSIS
components of, 3–5
containers, 10
destinations, 12
DSVs (data source views), 8–9
packages, 5
precedence constraints, 9–10
sources, 7, 11–12
tasks in, 5–6
transformations, 13–14
variables, 10–11
arrows for precedence constraints, 391–392
ASP.NET applications, interfacing with, 540–545
assemblies, using in scripts, 225–226
AssemblyInfo.cs file, 428, 470–471
asynchronous transformation outputs
definition of, 325–326
execution trees and, 330
Audit transformation
configuring, 93
definition of, 13, 93
example using, 135–138
as streaming, non-blocking transformation, 319
auditing, system variables used for, 37–38
Auto Extend Factor option, Aggregate transformation, 92
Autos window, 32, 223–224

Average operation, Aggregate transformation, 91
AWE (Advanced Windowing Extensions), 304

B

back pressure on source extractions, 359
**BankBatchDetail table, payment processing database,
606–607**
BatchSize option, Bulk Insert task, 46
`bcp.exe` **tool, 46**
BIDS (Business Intelligence Development Studio)
definition of, 3, 25
navigation pane, 31
project, creating, 26, 27–28
runtime mode, 32
starting, 25
windows in, 32
BLOB counters, Performance Monitor, 367
BLOB data types
exporting, 100–101, 159–160
importing, 101, 150–157
blocking nature of transformations
blocking transformations
as asynchronous, 326
definition of, 322–324
when to use, 364–366
definition of, 319
non-blocking transformations
definition of, 319–321
as synchronous, 328
semi-blocking transformations
as asynchronous, 326
definition of, 321–322
blue arrows for precedence constraints, 391
Boole, George (*An Investigation of the Laws of Thought,
on which are founded the Mathematical Theories
of Logic and Probabilities***), 548**
branching code, 565, 584
breakpoints
definition of, 223, 408
setting, 223, 408–410
Breakpoints window, 32
bubbling of events, 406–408
buffer counters, Performance Monitor, 367, 368–369
buffers used by Data Flow
definition of, 317–318
execution trees and, 332–334
optimizing, 361–363

Bulk Insert task
configuring, 46–48
definition of, 5, 46
example using, 48–51
BulkLoadZip.dtsx file, 48
Business Intelligence Development Studio (BIDS)
definition of, 3, 25
navigation pane, 31
project, creating, 26, 27–28
runtime mode, 32
starting, 25
windows in, 32
BypassPrepare option, Execute SQL task, 45
Byte Reversal operation, Character Map transformation, 94

C

Call Stack window, 32, 410
case study. See payment processing case study
CaseStudy_Load package
ACH Control Flow, 635–638
ACH processing, 643–645
ACH validation, 639–643
description of, 595, 610–611
c-mail Data Flow processing, 648–651
e-mail payment processing, 645–647
File System tasks for, 612–616
Lockbox Control Flow, 616–622
Lockbox processing, 631–635
Lockbox validation, 622–631
naming conventions for, 611
setting up, 612–616
testing, 651
CaseStudy_Process package
description of, 595–596, 651–652
high-confidence matching, Data Flow for, 654–659
medium-confidence matching, Data Flow for, 659–662
results of, interpreting, 663–664
setting up, 652–654
Catch block, 227–228
Character Map transformation
configuring, 94
data cleansing and, 354
definition of, 13, 94
as streaming, non-blocking transformation, 319

Check Constraints option, Bulk Insert task, 47
CheckpointFilename property, 280
checkpoints
checkpoint file generated by, 290–292
configuring, 411–412
in Data Flow, 280, 305
definition of, 280, 411
enabling, 280
examples of
in containers with transactions, 285–288
failing package, not sequence, 290
failing parent and package, 288–289
failing parent, not package, 288
list of, 290
in simple Control Flow, 280–285
without transactions, 289
CheckpointUsage property, 280, 411
Chinese characters, converting to simplified or traditional, 94
circles for breakpoints, 409–410
cleansing (scrubbing) data
definition of, 354
example of
Conditional Split transformation, 130–131
connection for, 127–129
Data Flow for, 129
Derived Column transformation, 129–130
description of, 125–127
error handling, 134–138
Lookup transformation, 132
sending data to destination, 133–134
Union All transformation, 132–133
transformations used for, 354–357
Cleanup method, 424
clients, 3
CLSCompliant attribute, 470–471
column chart Data Viewer, 116
ColumnDelimiter option, Bulk Insert task, 46
comma-delimited files as data source. See Flat File source
Command window, 32
comments in scripts, 217
communication mechanism of transformations, 319, 324–328
Completion constraint value, 9

components, pipeline
building, 426–432
connection-time components, 425
debugging
definition of, 461
design-time, 462–463
runtime, 463–466
definition of, 417
design-time components
definition of, 419–420
DeleteInput method, 421
DeleteOutput method, 421
InsertInput method, 421
InsertOutput method, 421
MapInputColumn method, 421
MapOutputColumn method, 421
OnInputPathAttached method, 423
OnOutputPathAttached method, 423
PerformUpgrade method, 422
ProvideComponentProperties method, 420
RegisterEvents method, 422
RegisterLogEntries method, 422
ReinitializeMetaData method, 420
SetComponentProperty method, 422
SetExternalMetadataColumnDataType
    Properties method, 421
SetExternalMetadataColumnProperty
    method, 422
SetInputColumnProperty method, 422
SetInputProperty method, 421
SetOutputColumnDataTypeProperties
    method, 421
SetOutputColumnProperty method, 422
SetOutputProperty method, 421
SetUsageType method, 422–423
Validate method, 420
examples of
destination adapter, 419, 454–461
source adapter, 418, 432–443
transformation, 418, 443–454
runtime components
Cleanup method, 424
definition of, 423
DescribeRedirectedErrorCode method, 425
PostExecute method, 424
PreExecute method, 424
PrepareForExecute method, 423
PrimeOutput method, 424
ProcessInput method, 424

user interface (UI) for
assembly for, 468–471
column properties for, 488–489
component properties for, 484–486
configuring component for, 468, 475–476
error handling, 486–488
form for, 468, 476–481
IDtsComponentUI interface, implementing,
    467–468, 471–475
procedure for, 467–468
runtime connections for, 482–484
**conditional expressions, precedence constraints, 9, 34,
    393–396**
Conditional Split transformation
configuring, 94–97
data cleansing and, 354
definition of, 13, 94
example using, 130–131, 351–352
as streaming, non-blocking transformation, 319
Configuration **object, 511–512**
Configurations **object, 511**
configurations, package
changing at runtime, 148–150
creating, 510–511
nonstatic configuration, 146
programming, 511–512
types of, 509
Configure Error Output property, 350
Configure SSIS Logs dialog box, 413
Connection Manager
for Access database, 251–252
configuring offline, 7
creating, 120–122
destinations specified in, 84
sources specified in, 80
Connection Managers tab, SSIS Package Designer, 36
Connection option
Analysis Services Execute DDL task, 70
Bulk Insert task, 46
Execute SQL task, 45, 145
connections
data source
for Access database, 251–252
acquiring programmatically, 425, 433–435, 455–456
for Analysis Services Execute DDL task, 70
for Bulk Insert task, 46
configuring offline, 7
creating, 36, 120–122
for Execute SQL task, 45, 145
for File System task, 53

releasing programmatically, 425
for runtime components, 482–484
shared connections, adding to Connection Manager, 36
shared connections, creating, 120–122
shared connections, residing in project, 28
FTP, 54
HTTP, 63
Connections property, Dts object, 219
connection-time components, pipeline, 425
ConnectionType option, Execute SQL task, 45, 145
Constraint option, EvalOp property, 9, 34
constraints, precedence. See also paths
arrow indicators for, 391–392
conditional expressions for, 9–10, 34, 393–396
constraint values, 9, 34
creating, 33–34
definition of, 5, 9–10
error handling using, 391–398
multiple, 397–398
containers
checkpoints in, 285–288
creating, 35
definition of, 5, 10, 73
failing when task fails, 44
For Loop container
configuring, 75
definition of, 10, 74
example using, 75–78
Foreach Loop container
definition of, 10, 78
example using, 78–80, 139–140
types of, 78
logging, 413
sequence container, 10, 73–74
task host container, 10, 73
in transactions, 285–288
types of, 10
Control Flow. See also tasks
adding tasks to, 43
bound to Data Flow by Data Flow task, 32
checkpoints in, 280
compared to Data Flow, 312–314
definition of, 312
parallel processing in, 315–316
synchronous task execution in, 315–316
Control Flow scripting, 208
Control Flow tab, SSIS Package Designer, 33–36
Copy Column transformation
configuring, 97
definition of, 13, 97
as streaming, non-blocking transformation, 319

CorporationLoad.dtsx file, 127
correlation, data, 348–354
Count Distinct operation, Aggregate transformation, 91
Count Distinct Scale option, Aggregate transformation, 92
Count operation, Aggregate transformation, 91
Create Temp Table task, 157–159
CreateFolderOnDtsServer method, Application object, 494
CreateFolderOnSqlServer method, Application object, 494
CreateOutputAndMetaDataColumns method, 439–440
CreationDate system variable, 38
CreationName property, 434
Currency Conversion service, 265–272
Customer table, payment processing database, 603–604
CustomerLookUp table, payment processing database, 605–606

D

data. See also files; text
bad data
error outputs for, 301–304
finding with Fuzzy Grouping transformation, 13, 101, 178–182
finding with Fuzzy Lookup transformation, 13, 101, 173–178
cleansing (scrubbing)
definition of, 354
example of, Conditional Split transformation, 130–131
example of, connection for, 127–129
example of, Data Flow for, 129
example of, Derived Column transformation, 129–130
example of, description, 125–127
example of, error handling, 134–138
example of, Lookup transformation, 132
example of, sending data to destination, 133–134
example of, Union All transformation, 132–133
transformations used for, 354–357
correlation of, 348–354
loading into a table with Bulk Insert task, 5, 46–51
loading into an OLE DB destination with Data Flow task, 5, 51
staging data, 305–310

Data Access Mode option
  OLE DB destination, 88
  OLE DB source, 80
data buffers, 317–318
Data Conversion transformation
  configuring, 97–98
  data cleansing and, 354
  definition of, 13, 97
  as streaming, non-blocking transformation, 319
Data Flow. See also transformations
  adapters and, 328
  bound to controller flow by Data Flow task, 32
  checkpoints not possible in, 280
  compared to Control Flow, 312–314
  creating, 123–124
  definition of, 312, 317
  dividing
    to allow checkpoints, 305
    to scale across machines, 307–310
  elements of
    destinations, 12
    sources, 11–12
    transformations, 13–14
  execution trees for, 330–335
  memory buffers used by, 317–318
  monitoring execution of, 335–339
  optimizing, 359
  restarting, 305–307, 359
Data Flow engine
  definition of, 3, 311–312
  optimizing, 361–363
Data Flow scripting, 208
Data Flow tab, SSIS Package Designer, 38–39, 123
Data Flow task
  definition of, 5, 51
  example using, 122
Data Mining Model Training destination, 12, 86
Data Mining Query Component transformation, 17
Data Mining Query task
  available only in Enterprise Edition, 17
  definition of, 5, 71
Data Mining Query transformation
  definition of, 13, 98–99
  as semi-blocking transformation, 321
Data Mining Training Destination transformation, 17
Data Pump task, 342–343
Data Reader source, 12, 84
data source connections
  for Access database, 251–252
  acquiring programmatically, 425, 433–435, 455–456
  for Analysis Services Execute DDL task, 70

  for Bulk Insert task, 46
  configuring offline, 7
  creating, 36, 120–122
  for Execute SQL task, 45, 145
  for File System task, 53
  releasing programmatically, 425
  for runtime components, 482–484
  shared connections
    adding to Connection Manager, 36
    creating, 120–122
    residing in project, 28
data source views (DSVs), 8–9. See also Data Viewers
Data Source Wizard, 120
data sources
  back pressure on, 359
  Data Reader source, 12, 84
  definition of, 11, 80
  Excel source
    configuring, 83
    definition of, 12, 83
    importing from, 244–249
    uses of, 240
  Flat File source
    configuring, 84
    creating, 121–122
    definition of, 12, 84
  heterogeneous, 239
  list of, 12, 239
  .NET provider as (Data Reader source), 12, 84
  OLE DB source
    configuring, 80–83
    definition of, 12, 80
  Raw File source, 12, 84
  XML source
    configuring, 84
    definition of, 12, 84, 272
    importing from, 272–278
data stores for package configuration, 509
Data Transformation Services (DTS)
  architecture of, 342–343
  definition of, 341–342
  history of, 1
  limitations of, 345–346
  managing packages with SQL Server Management
    Studio, 388–389
  migrating packages to SSIS, 371, 373–380
  packages from SQL Server 2000, executing, 5
  processing practices of, 343–345
  relationship to controller flow, 33
  running packages in SSIS, 380–383

data types
BLOB data types
exporting, 100–101, 159–160
importing, 101, 150–157
changing in DDL, 123
converting for columns, 13, 97–98
default, not using, 611
mapping from one back-end to another, 384
setting for pipeline components, 421
specifying for connections, 122
SQL Server and, 246
Data Viewers. *See also* **DSVs (data source views)**
for debugging, 235–237
definition of, 116
types of, 116
using, 116–117
when to use, 611
Database Password, Access, 250, 252
database, payment processing case study
BankBatchDetail table, 606–607
creating, 602–603
Customer table, 603–604
CustomerLookUp table, 605–606
ErrorDetail table, 608
GLAccountData table, 607–608
Invoice table, 604–605
model of, 601–602
usp_BankBatch_Add table, 608–609
usp_BankBatch_Balance table, 610
usp_BankBatchDetail_Match table, 609–610
databases
logins for, transferring, 201–203, 204–205
moving or copying, 201–202
objects in, transferring, 204–205
DataFileType option, Bulk Insert task, 46
DataReader destination
configuring, 86–87
definition of, 12, 86
David, Jean-Luc (*Professional Visual Studio 2005 Team System*), 547
DDL statements. *See also* **SQL statements**
changing data types in, 123
executing in Analysis Services, 5, 70
debugging
pipeline components, 461–466
for Script Component, 235–237
for Script task, 222–225
DelayValidation property, 43
Delete **method,** IDtsComponentUI **interface, 472**

DeleteInput **method, 421, 448**
DeleteOutput **method, 421, 448**
denormalizing data. *See* **Pivot transformation**
deploying packages, 587–591
Deployment Wizard, 588–589
Derived Column transformation
configuring, 99
data cleansing and, 354, 355–356
definition of, 13, 99
example using, 111
expressions in, 211–213
as streaming, non-blocking transformation, 319
DescribeRedirectedErrorCode **method, 425**
Description property, 43–44
Design **assembly, 471**
design surface, 14
design-time components, pipeline
debugging, 462–463
definition of, 419–420
DeleteInput method, 421
DeleteOutput method, 421
InsertInput method, 421
InsertOutput method, 421
MapInputColumn method, 421
MapOutputColumn method, 421
OnInputPathAttached method, 423
OnOutputPathAttached method, 423
PerformUpgrade method, 422
ProvideComponentProperties method, 420
RegisterEvents method, 422
RegisterLogEntries method, 422
ReinitializeMetaData method, 420
SetComponentProperty method, 422
SetExternalMetadataColumnDataType
Properties method, 421
SetExternalMetadataColumnProperty
method, 422
SetInputColumnProperty method, 422
SetInputProperty method, 421
SetOutputColumnDataType Properties
method, 421
SetOutputColumnProperty method, 422
SetOutputProperty method, 421
SetUsageType method, 422–423
Validate method, 420
destination adapters
building from pipeline components, 419, 454–461
definition of, 328
Destination option, WMI Data Reader task, 66, 513

Destination Type Component, 228

**DestinationConnection option, File System
    task, 53**

destinations

configuring, 84–85

Data Mining Model Training destination, 12, 86

DataReader destination

configuring, 86–87

definition of, 12, 86

definition of, 12, 84

Dimension Processing destination

configuring, 87

definition of, 12, 87

staging and, 305

Excel destination

configuring, 87

definition of, 12, 87

exporting to, 240–244

Flat File destination

configuring, 88

definition of, 12, 88

example using, 114

list of, 12

OLE DB destination

configuring, 88–89

definition of, 12, 88

when to use, 246

Partition Processing destination

definition of, 12, 87

staging and, 305

Raw File destination, 12, 89

Recordset destination, 12, 89

SQL Server destination

configuring, 90

creating, 123–124

definition of, 12, 90

when to use, 246

SQL Server Mobile destination, 12, 90

DestinationTable option, Bulk Insert task, 46

**DestinationType option, WMI Data Reader
    task, 513**

Dimension Processing destination

configuring, 87

definition of, 12, 87

staging and, 305

dimension tables. *See* **Slowly Changing Dimension
    (SCD) transformation**

directories, manipulating, 6, 52–58

dirty data, cleansing (scrubbing)

definition of, 354

example of

Conditional Split transformation, 130–131

connection for, 127–129

Data Flow for, 129

Derived Column transformation, 129–130

description of, 125–127

error handling, 134–138

Lookup transformation, 132

sending data to destination, 133–134

Union All transformation, 132–133

transformations used for, 354–357

Disable property, 43

Distributed Transaction Coordinator transactions.
    See **DTC transactions**

document templates, MSF Agile, 571

Drop Temp Table task, 157–159

.ds files, 29, 384

.dsv files, 29

DSVs (data source views), 8–9. *See also* **Data Viewers**

DTC (Distributed Transaction Coordinator) transactions

definition of, 293

single package

multiple transactions using, 296–298

single transaction using, 293–296

two packages, one transaction using, 298–299

DTExec program, 466

.dtproj files, 29, 384

DTS (Data Transformation Services)

architecture of, 342–343

definition of, 341–342

history of, 1

limitations of, 345–346

managing packages with SQL Server Management
    Studio, 388–389

migrating packages to SSIS, 371, 373–380

packages from SQL Server 2000, executing, 5

processing practices of, 343–345

relationship to controller flow, 33

running packages in SSIS, 380–383

DTS Designer, relationship to BIDS, 3

DTS Migration Wizard, 371, 373–380

Dts object, 218–219

DTSClient DLL, 543

.dtsConfig file, 384

**DTSFileConnectionUsageType enumeration,
    434–435**

DtsPipelineComponent attribute

definition of, 427–428

UITypeName property, 468, 475

DTSPipelineWrap **assembly, 426, 471**
DTSRuntimeWrap **assembly, 426**
dtswizard.exe **tool, 19**
.dtsx **files**
 definition of, 29
 saving packages as, 5, 384
.dwproj **file, 384**
dynamic packages, 140–142
dynamic properties. *See* **property expressions**
Dynamic Properties task, 1

E

Edit **method,** IDtsComponentUI **interface, 473–475,**
 482
ellipses button (...), 72, 146
e-mail, sending with Send Mail task, 6, 62
e-mail transactions, payment processing case study
 Data Flow processing for, 648–651
 description of, 594, 596, 601
 payment processing for, 645–647
Enable Identity Insert option, Bulk Insert task, 47
engines
 Data Flow engine
  definition of, 3, 311–312
  optimizing, 361–363
 runtime engine, 3, 5
Enterprise Edition, SQL Server 2005, 16–17
EntryPoint option, Script task, 60, 216
Environment Variable option, package configuration,
 509
equal signs (==), equality operator, 146–147
Error List window, 32
ErrorDetail table, payment processing database, 608
errors. *See also* **events; logging**
 in Aggregate transformation, 92
 in Bulk Insert task, 48, 51
 constraints acting on, 33–34
 in data scrubbing, 134–138
 detected at design time, 32
 in Dimension Processing destination, 87
 division by zero, in Aggregate transformation, 92
 error outputs from bad data, 301–304, 425
 in Execute Process task, 51
 in Export Column transformation, 101
 firing an event when errors occur, 220
 handling, features for, 14–16
 IErrorCollectionService service, 473, 486
 in Import and Export Wizard, 23

 in Lookup transformation, 350–351
 in OLE DB source, 82
 OnError event, 40, 399
 precedence constraints handling, 391–398
 Structured Exception Handling (SEH) for, 227–228
 in task, failing package or parent, 44
 in user interface for components, 486–488
ETL (extraction, transformation, and loading)
 example of
  copying data from source to destination, 119–124
  creating derived columns during, 110–116
  scrubbing data, 125–138
 SSIS features for, 3
EvalOp property, 9
event handlers
 definition of, 5, 14–15, 398
 example of, 399–406
 for Script task, 220–222
 WMI Event Watcher task
  configuring, 67–68, 514–515
  definition of, 6, 67
  example using, 521–522
Event Handlers tab, SSIS Package Designer, 39–40
events
 bubbling, 406–408
 definition of, 398
 list of, 40, 399
 logging, 414–416, 506–507
Events **property,** Dts **object, 219, 220**
examples. *See also* **payment processing case study**
 Access
  importing from, 253–255
  using parameters with, 255–258
 Aggregate transformation, 112
 Application object, 496–504
 Audit transformation, 135–138
 Bulk Insert task, 48–51
 checkpoints
  in containers with transactions, 285–288
  failing package, not sequence, 290
  failing parent and package, 288–289
  failing parent, not package, 288
  list of, 290
  in simple Control Flow, 280–285
  without transactions, 289
 Conditional Split transformation, 130–131, 351–352
 copying data from source to destination, 119–125
 Currency Conversion service, 265–272
 Data Flow task, 122
 data scrubbing (cleansing)

examples (continued)

Conditional Split transformation, 130–131

connection for, 127–129

Data Flow for, 129

Derived Column transformation, 129–130

description of, 125–127

error handling, 134–138

Lookup transformation, 132

sending data to destination, 133–134

Union All transformation, 132–133

Derived Column transformation, 111

design practices, 357–358

DTC transactions

single package, multiple transactions using, 296–298

single package, single transaction using, 293–296

two packages, one transaction using, 298–299

ETL (extraction, transformation, and loading)

copying data from source to destination, 119–124

creating derived columns during, 110–116

scrubbing data, 125–138

event handlers, 399–406

Excel

exporting to, 240–244

importing from, 244–249

Execute SQL task, 48–51, 124, 148–150

File System task, 55–58

Flat File destination, 114

For Loop container, 75–78

Foreach Loop container, 78–80, 139–140

FTP task, 55–58

Fuzzy Grouping transformation, 180–182

Fuzzy Lookup transformation, 176–178

Hyperlink Extractor service, 262–265

images, importing, 151–154

Import Column transformation

file iteration, 155–157

importing images, 151–154

InfoPath documents, importing, 532–540

Lookup transformation, 132

massaging data, 110–115

Multicast transformation, 351–352

native transactions, 299–300

OLE DB Command transformation, 163–165

Oracle, importing from, 259–261

package management, 496–504

pipeline components

destination adapter, 419, 454–461

source adapter, 418, 432–443

transformation, 418, 443–454

producing Reporting Services report from RSS, 524–532

Row Count transformation, 161–162

Slowly Changing Dimension transformation, 192–200

Sort transformation, 113

Team System

branching code, 584

creating package, 573–579

labeling (striping) versions of code, 586–587

merging code, 585–586

shelving and unshelving, 583–584

version and source control, 579–583

Term Extraction transformation, 166–170

Term Lookup transformation, 172–173

Union All transformation, 132–133

Unpivot transformation, 186–189

Visual SourceSafe

branching, 565

checking in project, 555–556, 558, 559

checking out project, 554–555

creating project, 552–554

creating project in, 556–558

debugging project, 559–561

rolling back to earlier version, 561–564

Web site for, 417

WMI Data Reader task, 515–521

WMI Event Watcher task, 521–522

WQL queries, 66–67

XML, importing from, 272–278

Excel destination

configuring, 87

definition of, 12, 87

exporting to, 240–244

Excel source

configuring, 83

definition of, 12, 83

importing from, 244–249

uses of, 240

exceptions. See errors

Executable option, Execute Process task, 51

Execute DTS 2000 Package task, 5

Execute Package task, 6, 59

Execute Process task

configuring, 51–52

definition of, 6, 51

Execute SQL task

checkpoint in, example of, 280–285

configuring, 44–45, 144–145

definition of, 6, 44

example using, 48–51, 124, 148–150

uses of, 144

ExecuteOutofProcess option, Execute Package task, 59
Execution Instance GUID option, Audit
    transformation, 93
execution trees
    definition of, 330–335
    monitoring, 335–339
    optimizing, 361–363
ExecutionStartTime option, Audit transformation, 93
ExecutionValue property, Dts object, 219
ExecValueVariable property, 44
ExistsOnDtsServer method, Application
    object, 493
ExistsOnSqlServer method, Application
    object, 493
Export Column transformation
    configuring, 100–101
    definition of, 13, 100, 159
    example using, 159–160
    as row-based, non-blocking transformation, 320
exporting data, to Excel, 240–244. See also Import and
    Export Wizard
Express Edition, SQL Server 2005, 16
Expression Builder, 72, 146–148, 210
Expression option, EvalOp property, 9, 34
Expression page, 72
ExpressionAndConstraint option, EvalOp property, 9, 34
ExpressionOrConstraint option, EvalOp property, 9, 34
expressions
    conditional, for precedence constraints, 9, 34, 393–396
    definition of, 208
    property expressions
        creating, 72, 146–148, 208–210
        definition of, 72, 146, 208
    regular expressions, 232
    for task or transformation logic, 208, 211–213
external applications, using SSIS with, 523
Extract Column option, Export Column transformation,
    100
extraction, transformation, and loading (ETL)
    example of
        copying data from source to destination, 119–124
        creating derived columns during, 110–116
        scrubbing data, 125–138
    SSIS features for, 3

F

FailPackageonFailure property, 44, 280, 288–289, 412
FailParentonFailure property, 44, 288–289

FailtaskIfReturncodeIsNotSuccessValue option,
    Execute Process task, 52
Failure constraint value, 9
Fast Load option, OLE DB destination, 88
File Connection Manager, Web Service task, 64
file enumerator, Foreach Loop container, 78
File Extractor transformation. See Export Column
    transformation
File Inserter transformation. See Import Column
    transformation
File option, Bulk Insert task, 46
File Path Column option, Export Column transformation,
    100
File System option, Execute Package task, 59
File System task
    configuring, 53
    definition of, 6, 52–53
    example using, 55–58
FileConnection option, Execute SQL task, 45
FileCopy.dtsk file, 55
files
    creating from blob-type fields in database with Export
        Column transformation, 100–101, 159–160
    as data source
        Flat File source, 12, 84, 121–122
        Raw File source, 12, 84
    iteration through, example of, 155–157
    manipulating, 6, 52–58
    storing as blob-type fields in database with Import
        Column transformation, 101, 150–157
FileUsageType property, 434
Finally block, 228
Fire Triggers option, Bulk Insert task, 47
FireBreakpointHit method, IDTSComponent
    Events interface, 220
FireCustomEvent method, IDTSComponentEvents
    interface, 220
FireError method, IDTSComponentEvents
    interface, 220, 486
FireInformation method, IDTSComponentEvents
    interface, 220, 221
FireProgress method, IDTSComponentEvents
    interface, 220
FireQueryCancel method, IDTSComponentEvents
    interface, 220
FireWarning method, IDTSComponentEvents
    interface, 220, 486
fixed-width files as data source. See Flat File source
flat buffers, 367, 368

Flat File destination
configuring, 88
definition of, 12, 88
example using, 114
Flat File source
configuring, 84
creating, 121–122
definition of, 12, 84
`FolderExistsOnDtsServer` **method,** `Application`
object, 494
`FolderExistsOnSqlServer` **method,** `Application`
object, 494
folders, manipulating, 6, 52–58
For Loop container
configuring, 75
definition of, 10, 74
example using, 75–78
Force Truncate option, Export Column transformation,
100
ForceExecutionResult property, 411
Foreach Loop container
definition of, 10, 78
example using, 78–80, 139–140
types of, 78
ForeachLoop.dtsx file, 78
ForLoop.dtsx file, 75
Format option, Bulk Insert task, 46
FTP task
configuring, 54–55
definition of, 6, 54
example using, 55–58
FTPConnection option, FTP task, 54
Full Width operation, Character Map transformation, 94
Fuzzy Grouping transformation
available only in Enterprise Edition, 17
as blocking transformation, 322
configuring, 179–180
data cleansing and, 354, 355
definition of, 13, 101, 178
example using, 180–182
Fuzzy Lookup transformation
available only in Enterprise Edition, 17
as blocking transformation, 322
configuring, 174–175
data cleansing and, 354, 355
data correlation by, 348
definition of, 13, 101, 173–174
example using, 176–178

G
GAC (global assembly cache), 428, 430
`GetPackageRoles` **method,** `Application` **object,**
495
`GetRunningPackages` **method,** `Application` **object,**
495
GLAccountData table, payment processing database,
607–608
global assembly cache (GAC), 428, 430
global variables, 10, 37
Greborio, Pierre (*Professional InfoPath 2003***), 532**
green arrows for precedence constraints, 391–392
grid Data Viewer, 116
Group By operation, Aggregate transformation, 91
groups of tasks. *See* containers
GUID for execution instance, 93

H
Half Width operation, Character Map transformation, 94
Hathi, Kamal (demonstration of RSS to Reporting
Services), 524–532
`Help` **method,** `IDtsComponentUI` **interface, 472**
heterogeneous data sources, 239
Hiragana operation, Character Map transformation, 94
histogram Data Viewer, 116
HTTP Connection Manager, Web Service task, 63
Hu, Wenyang (InfoPath example), 532
Hyperlink Extractor service, 262–265

I
ID property, 44
`IDtsClipboardService` **service, 473**
`IDTSComponentEvents` **interface, 220**
`IDtsConnectionService` **service, 473, 482**
`IDtsVariableService` **service, 473**
`IErrorCollectionService` **service, 473, 486**
images, importing, 151–154
Immediate window, 32, 224–225
Import and Export Wizard
accessing, 19
columns, mapping, 22
definition of, 2, 19
destination
creating table in, 22
specifying, 20

identity column, enabling, 22
package
  executing, 22, 23
  location of, 24
  opening, 24
  saving, 22, 23
protecting sensitive data, 23
source, specifying, 20
tables, specifying, 20
transaction, specifying, 21
Import Column transformation
configuring, 150–151
definition of, 13, 101, 150
examples of
  file iteration, 155–157
  importing images, 151–154
as row-based, non-blocking transformation, 320
Import **statement, 218**
importing data. *See also* **Import and Export Wizard**
from Access, 253–255
from Excel, 244–249
images, 151–154
from InfoPath documents, 532–540
from Oracle, 259–261
from RSS (Really Simple Syndication) file, 272–278
from XML file, 272–278
importing packages, 589–591
InfoPath documents, importing, 532–540
Initialize **method,** IDtsComponentUI **interface,**
  472–473, 482
InsertInput **method, 421, 448**
InsertOutput **method, 421, 447–448**
Instant Client, Oracle, 259
Integration Services. *See* **SSIS (SQL Server Integration Services)**
InteractiveMode **system variable, 38**
Invoice table, payment processing database, 604–605
IsDestinationPathVariable option, File System task, 53
IServiceProvider **assembly, 473, 482**
IsLocalPathVariable option, FTP task, 54
IsolationLevel property, 44
IsQueryStoredProcedure option, Execute SQL task, 45
IsRemotePathVariable option, FTP task, 54
IsTransferAscii option, FTP task, 54
item enumerator, Foreach Loop container, 78
iteration, MSF Agile, 570
iterative SDLCs, 549–550

K
Katakana operation, Character Map transformation, 94
Keep Identity option, OLE DB destination, 89
Keep Nulls option, Bulk Insert task, 47
Key Scale option, Aggregate transformation, 92

L
labeling (striping) versions of code, 586–587
lazy-add, 173
Legacy folder, 388
Linguistic Casing operation, Character Map transformation, 94
LoadFromDtsServer **method,** Application **object, 493**
LoadFromSqlServer **method,** Application **object, 493**
LoadFromSqlServer2 **method,** Application **object, 493**
LoadPackage **method,** Application **object, 493**
LocalPath option, FTP task, 54
Locals window, 32, 223–224
Lockbox file, payment processing case study
Control Flow for, 616–622
description of, 595, 600–601
processing for, 631–635
processing requirements, 596
validation for, 622–631
Log **method,** Dts **object, 219, 222**
log providers
defining events to log, 506–507
definition of, 505
programming, 507–508
types of, 506
logging
for Bulk Insert task, 48
definition of, 16, 412–413
for packages, 412–416
pipeline logging events, 335–339
for Script task, 221
for tasks, 44, 413
LoggingMode property, 44, 415
logins for databases, transferring, 201–203, 204–205
LogProvider **object, 507**
LogProviders **object, 507**

Lookup transformation
configuring, 101–102
data correlation by, 348, 349–352
definition of, 13, 101
example using, 132
as row-based, non-blocking transformation, 320
as streaming, non-blocking transformation, 319
looping
For Loop container
configuring, 75
definition of, 10, 74
example using, 75–78
Foreach Loop container
definition of, 10, 78
example using, 78–80, 139–140
types of, 78
Lowercase operation, Character Map transformation, 94
LTRIM **function, 131**

M

MachineName option, Audit transformation, 93
MachineName **system variable, 38**
mail, sending with Send Mail task, 6, 62
managed code, 491
ManagedDTS **assembly, 426, 471, 492**
Management folder, 388
Management Studio
managing DTS packages with, 388–389
managing SSIS packages with, 386–388
MapInputColumn **method, 421**
MapOutputColumn **method, 421**
MappingFiles folder, 384
MaxConcurrentExecutables property, 316
MaxErrors option, Bulk Insert task, 48
Maximum Insert Commit Size option, OLE DB
destination, 88
Maximum operation, Aggregate transformation, 91
memory buffers, 317–318
Merge Join transformation
configuring, 104
data correlation by, 348, 352–354
definition of, 13, 103–104
as semi-blocking transformation, 321
Merge transformation
configuring, 103
definition of, 13, 102
restrictions on, 102
as semi-blocking transformation, 321

merging code, 585–586
Message option, Message Queue task, 63
Message Queue task, 6, 63
MessageSource option, Send Mail task, 62
MessageSourceType option, Send Mail task, 62
MessageType option, Message Queue task, 63
Method option, Web Service task, 64
methods, executing from Web service, 6, 63–65
Microsoft Distributed Transaction Coordinator
(MSDTC), 293
Microsoft InfoPath documents, importing, 532–540
Microsoft Message Queue (MSMQ), sending or receiv-
ing messages from, 6, 63
Microsoft Solutions Framework SDLCs, 549
Microsoft Visual SourceSafe. See Visual SourceSafe
Microsoft.SqlServer.Dts.Runtime **namespace,**
492
Microsoft.SQLServer.ManagedDTS **assembly, 492**
migrating DTS packages to SSIS, 371, 373–380
Migration Wizard, 371, 373–380
Minimum operation, Aggregate transformation, 91
msdb database, saving packages in, 5, 384–385
MSDTC (Microsoft Distributed Transaction
Coordinator), 293
MsDtsSrvr.ini.xml file, 386
MSF Agile template, 570–572
MSMQ (Microsoft Message Queue), sending or
receiving messages from, 6, 63
MSMQConnection option, Message Queue task, 63
Multicast transformation
configuring, 104–105
definition of, 13, 104
example using, 351–352
staging data and, 360
as streaming, non-blocking transformation, 319
multiphase data pump, history of, 1

N

Name property, 44
Nanda, Ranjeeta (ASP.NET example), 540
native transactions
definition of, 293
example using, 299–300
navigation pane, BIDS, 31
.NET assemblies, using in scripts, 225–226
.NET provider as data source (Data Reader source),
12, 84
New **method,** IDtsComponentUI **interface, 472**

nodelist enumerator, Foreach Loop container, 78
non-blocking transformations
    definition of, 319–321
    as synchronous, 328
nonstatic configuration, 146
normalized data, denormalizing. *See* Pivot transformation
Number of Keys option, Aggregate transformation, 92
NumberOfEvents option, WMI Event Watcher task,
    67, 515

O

OLE DB Command transformation
    configuring, 163
    definition of, 13, 105, 162–163
    example using, 163–165
    optimizing, 363–364
    as row-based, non-blocking transformation, 320
OLE DB destination
    configuring, 88–89
    definition of, 12, 88
    when to use, 246
OLE DB source
    configuring, 80–83
    definition of, 12, 80
OLTP (On-Line Transaction Processing) system, 190
OnError event, 40, 399
OnExecStatusChanged event, 40, 399
OnInformation event, 40, 399
OnInputPathAttached method, 423
On-Line Transaction Processing (OLTP) system, 190
OnOutputPathAttached method, 423
OnPostExecute event, 40, 399
OnPostValidate event, 40, 399
OnPreExecute event, 40, 399
OnPreValidate event, 40, 399
OnProgress event, 40, 399
OnQueryCancel event, 40, 399
OnTaskFailed event, 40, 399
OnVariableValueChanged event, 40, 399
OnWarning event, 40, 399
Operation option
    Aggregate transformation, 91
    File System task, 53
    FTP task, 54
OperationType option, XML task, 68–69
Oracle database
    client setup for, 259
    importing from, 259–261
    version of driver for, 261

Output window, 32
OutputType option, WMI Data Reader task, 66, 513
OverwriteDestination option
    File System task, 53
    WMI Data Reader task, 66, 513
OverwriteFileAtDestination option, FTP task, 54

P

package configurations
    changing at runtime, 148–150
    creating, 510–511
    nonstatic configuration, 146
    programming, 511–512
    types of, 509
Package Designer
    Connection Managers tab, 36
    Control Flow tab, 33–36
    Data Flow tab, 38–39
    definition of, 32
    Event Handlers tab, 39–40
    executing package, 41
    Package Explorer tab, 40
    Variables Window, 37–38
Package Explorer tab, SSIS Package Designer, 40
Package Installation Wizard
    definition of, 25
    installing to SSIS instance or File System, 589
Package Migration Wizard, 371, 373–380
Package object, 492
PackageID option, Audit transformation, 93
PackageID system variable, 38
PackageName option, Audit transformation, 93
PackageName system variable, 38
packages. *See also* projects
    annotations for, 35–36
    backups for, 385
    checking whether it exists, 493
    configuring at runtime, 509–512
    creating, 27–28, 119–124
    definition of, 5
    deploying, 587–591
    dynamic, 140–142
    executing, 27, 41, 125
    executing external program from, with Execute Process
        task, 6, 51–52
    executing from within another package, with Execute
        Package task, 6, 59
    execution time of, 314–315
    failing when task fails, 44

packages (continued)

files in, 29

importing to Integration Services instance, 589–591

loading, 493

log providers for, 505–508

logging, 412–416

managing

with `Application` object, 493

with SQL Server Management Studio, 386–388

migrating DTS packages to SSIS, 371, 373–380

monitoring, 495–496

optimizing processing of, 360–366

parallel processing in, 314–315

removing, 493

restarting

checkpoints for, 280–290, 411–412

reasons for, 279–280

roles, assigning to, 495

running across machines, 307–310

running DTS packages in SSIS, 380–383

saving, 27, 125, 493, 611

saving as `.dtsx` file, 5, 384

saving in msdb database, 5, 384–385

storage of, 384–385

viewing in Solution Explorer, 28

parallel processing

in Control Flow, 312, 315–316

in Data Flow, 313

in package, 314–315

parameter, passing to SQL Command, 255–258

Parent Package Variable option, package configuration, 509

`ParseTheFileAndAddToBuffer` **method, 441–443**

Partition Processing destination

definition of, 12, 87

staging and, 305

paths. See also precedence constraints

definition of, 38

specifying based on conditions, 13, 94–97, 130–131

patterns in data, finding. See Fuzzy Grouping transformation

payment method options, payment processing case study

check payments (lockbox), 594

e-mail payments (E-Pay), 594, 596

list of, 594

PayPal payments, 594, 596

wire payments (ACH), 594

payment processing case study

ACH file, 595, 596, 599–600

CaseStudy_Load package

ACH Control Flow, 635–638

ACH processing, 643–645

ACH validation, 639–643

description of, 595, 610–611

e-mail Data Flow processing, 648–651

e-mail payment processing, 645–647

File System tasks for, 612–616

Lockbox Control Flow, 616–622

Lockbox processing, 631–635

Lockbox validation, 622–631

naming conventions for, 611

setting up, 612–616

testing, 651

CaseStudy_Process package

description of, 595–596, 651–652

high-confidence matching, Data Flow for, 654–659

medium-confidence matching, Data Flow for, 659–662

results of, interpreting, 663–664

setting up, 652–654

database for

BankBatchDetail table, 606–607

creating, 602–603

Customer table, 603–604

CustomerLookUp table, 605–606

ErrorDetail table, 608

GLAccountData table, 607–608

Invoice table, 604–605

model of, 601–602

usp_BankBatch_Add table, 608–609

usp_BankBatch_Balance table, 610

usp_BankBatchDetail_Match table, 609–610

description of, 593–594

e-mail transactions, 601

file locations, 599

Lockbox file, 595, 596, 600–601

payment method options

check payments (lockbox), 594

e-mail payments (E-Pay), 594, 596

list of, 594

PayPal payments, 594, 596

wire payments (ACH), 594

PayPal transactions, 601

running in SQL Agent, 664

solution for, 594–598

PayPal transactions, payment processing case study, 601

PDSA (plan, do, study, act), 548

Percentage Sampling transformation
configuring, 105–106
definition of, 13, 105
as streaming, non-blocking transformation, 319
Performance Monitor (PerfMon), 366–369
PerformUpgrade **method, 422**
phrases
frequency of, determining with Term Extraction transformation, 14, 108–109, 165–170
matching with text, using Term Lookup transformation, 14, 109, 171–173
similar
finding with Fuzzy Grouping transformation, 13, 101, 178–182
finding with Fuzzy Lookup transformation, 13, 101, 173–178
pipeline
building components, 426–432
connection-time components, 425
debugging components
definition of, 461
design-time, 462–463
runtime, 463–466
definition of, 417
design-time components
definition of, 419–420
DeleteInput method, 421
DeleteOutput method, 421
InsertInput method, 421
InsertOutput method, 421
MapInputColumn method, 421
MapOutputColumn method, 421
OnInputPathAttached method, 423
OnOutputPathAttached method, 423
PerformUpgrade method, 422
ProvideComponentProperties method, 420
RegisterEvents method, 422
RegisterLogEntries method, 422
ReinitializeMetaData method, 420
SetComponentProperty method, 422
SetExternalMetadataColumnDataType Properties method, 421
SetExternalMetadataColumnProperty method, 422
SetInputColumnProperty method, 422
SetInputProperty method, 421
SetOutputColumnDataTypeProperties method, 421
SetOutputColumnProperty method, 422
SetOutputProperty method, 421

SetUsageType method, 422–423
Validate method, 420
example components
destination adapter, 419, 454–461
source adapter, 418, 432–443
transformation, 418, 443–454
runtime components
Cleanup method, 424
definition of, 423
DescribeRedirectedErrorCode method, 425
PostExecute method, 424
PreExecute method, 424
PrepareForExecute method, 423
PrimeOutput method, 424
ProcessInput method, 424
user interface (UI) for components
assembly for, 468–471
column properties for, 488–489
component properties for, 484–486
configuring component for, 468, 475–476
error handling, 486–488
form for, 468, 476–481
IDtsComponentUI interface, implementing, 467–468, 471–475
procedure for, 467–468
runtime connections for, 482–484
pipeline logging events, 335–339
pipeline performance monitoring, 366–369
PipelineComponent **class, 419, 427**
PipelineComponents folder, 428, 429
PipelineExecutionPlan event, 335–336, 337–339
PipelineExecutionTrees event, 335–337
PipelineHost **assembly, 426**
Pivot transformation
configuring, 182
data cleansing and, 354, 355
definition of, 13, 106–107, 182
example using, 183–186
as semi-blocking transformation, 321
plan, do, study, act (PDSA), 548
PostExecute **method, 424**
precedence constraints. See also paths
arrow indicators for, 391–392
conditional expressions for, 9–10, 34, 393–396
constraint values, 9, 34
creating, 33–34
definition of, 5, 9–10
error handling using, 391–398
multiple, 397–398

PrecompileScriptIntoBinaryCode option, Script task, 60, 216

`PreExecute` **method, 424, 440, 448–450, 459–460**

`PrepareForExecute` **method, 423**

`PrimeOutput` **method, 424, 440, 453–454**

private buffers, 367, 368

`ProcessInput` **method, 424, 450–454, 460–461**

Professional InfoPath 2003 (Williams and Greborio), 532

Professional Visual Studio 2005 Team System (David), 547

Project Portal, 573

projects. *See also* **packages**

creating, 29

definition of, 28

files in, 29

Team System container for, creating, 567–568

viewing in Solution Explorer, 28

properties for tasks

setting to expressions, 72, 146–148, 208–210

shared, list of, 43–44

validating at runtime, 43

Properties Window, 30–31

property expressions

creating, 72, 146–148, 208–210

definition of, 72, 146, 208

Property Expressions Editor, 72, 146–147, 209

`ProvideComponentProperties` **method**

building destination adapter using, 454–455

building source adapter using, 432–433

building transformation using, 443–445

definition of, 420

publications

An Investigation of the Laws of Thought, on which are founded the Mathematical Theories of Logic and Probabilities (Boole), 548

Professional InfoPath 2003 (Williams; Greborio), 532

Professional Visual Studio 2005 Team System (David), 547

Q

question mark (?), placeholder for query parameter, 256

R

Raw File destination, 12, 89

Raw File source, 12, 84

raw files, for staging data, 305

RDBMS, reducing reliance on, 348

read-only variables, 219

ReadOnlyVariables option, Script task, 60, 216, 219–220

read-write variables, 219

ReadWriteVariables option, Script task, 60, 216, 219–220

Really Simple Syndication (RSS) file

importing, 272–278

producing Reporting Services report from, 524–532

Recordset destination, 12, 89

red arrows for precedence constraints, 391

red circle for breakpoints, 409–410

`RegisterEvents` **method, 422**

`RegisterLogEntries` **method, 422**

Registry Entry option, package configuration, 509

regular expressions, 232

`ReinitializeMetaData` **method, 420, 438–439, 446, 458**

`ReleaseConnections` **method, 425**

reliability

definition of, 279

error outputs and, 301–304

restarting packages for

checkpoints for, 280–290, 411–412

reasons for, 279–280

transactions for

checkpoints and, 285–288, 289

DTC (Distributed Transaction Coordinator) transactions, 293–299

in Import and Export Wizard, 21

native transactions, 293, 299–300

for script container, getting, 219

for tasks, 44

types of, 293

RemotePath option, FTP task, 54

`RemoveFolderFromDtsServer` **method,** `Application` **object, 494**

`RemoveFolderFromSqlServer` **method,** `Application` **object, 494**

`RemoveFromDtsServer` **method,** `Application` **object, 493**

`RemoveFromSqlServer` **method,** `Application` **object, 493**

`RenameFolderOnDtsServer` **method,** `Application` **object, 494**

`RenameFolderOnSqlServer` **method,** `Application` **object, 494**

Reporting Services, producing report from RSS, 524–532

reports, MSF Agile, 572

RequireFullFileName option, Execute Process task, 51

restarting Data Flow, 305–307, 359

restarting packages
  checkpoints for, 280–290, 411–412
  reasons for, 279–280

ResultSet option, Execute SQL task, 44–45, 145

roles, assigning to packages, 495

Row Count transformation
  for debugging, 235
  definition of, 14, 107, 160–161
  example using, 161–162
  as streaming, non-blocking transformation, 319

Row Number transformation, 308

Row Sampling transformation
  as blocking transformation, 322
  configuring, 105–106
  definition of, 14, 105

row-based transformations
  definition of, 320–321
  when to use, 363–364

RowDelimiter option, Bulk Insert task, 46

Rows Per Batch option, OLE DB destination, 88

Rows Read counter, Performance Monitor, 367, 368

Rows Written counter, Performance Monitor, 367, 368

RSS (Really Simple Syndication) file
  importing, 272–278
  producing Reporting Services report from, 524–532

Running Packages folder, 386

RunningPackage method, Application object, 495

RunningPackages method, Application object, 495

runtime components, pipeline
  Cleanup method, 424
  debugging, 463–466
  definition of, 423
  DescribeRedirectedErrorCode method, 425
  PostExecute method, 424
  PreExecute method, 424
  PrepareForExecute method, 423
  PrimeOutput method, 424
  ProcessInput method, 424

runtime engine, 3, 5

runtime mode, BIDS, 32

Runtime namespace, 492

S

SaveCheckpoints property, 280, 411

SaveToDtsServer method, Application object, 493

SaveToSqlServer method, Application object, 493

SaveToSqlServerAs method, Application object, 493

SaveToXML method, Application object, 493

scalability
  across machines, 307–310
  definition of, 279
  DTS and, 345–346
  error outputs and, 301–304
  memory requirements for, 304
  staging data for, 305–310

scaling out
  definition of, 304
  memory requirements, 304
  staging data, 305–310

scatter plot Data Viewer, 116

SCD (Slowly Changing Dimension) transformation
  configuring, 190–192
  definition of, 14, 107, 189–190
  example using, 192–200
  as row-based, non-blocking transformation, 320
  Type I, II, III changes for, 190, 191

Script Component transformation
  creating, 229–235
  data cleansing and, 354
  debugging, 235–237
  definition of, 14, 107, 228
  as row-based, non-blocking transformation, 320
  as streaming, non-blocking transformation, 319
  types of, 228

Script task
  comments in, 217
  configuring, 60–61, 216
  creating, 213–218
  debugging, 222–225
  definition of, 6, 60, 213
  events raised by, handling, 220–222
  interacting with package, using Dts object, 218–219
  logging for, 221, 222
  .NET assemblies in, 225–226
  variables, accessing from, 219–220

ScriptLanguage option, Script task, 60, 216

scripts. See also expressions
  ActiveX, executing, 5, 60, 61
  for Control Flow, 208
  for custom transformations, using Script Component
    transformation, 14, 107, 228–235
  for Data Flow, 208
  executing with Script task, 60–61, 213–218

scripts (continued)

language for, 225

.NET assemblies in, 225–226

Structured Exception Handling (SEH) for, 227–228

types of, 208

scrubbing (cleansing) data

definition of, 354

example of

Conditional Split transformation, 130–131

connection for, 127–129

Data Flow for, 129

Derived Column transformation, 129–130

description of, 125–127

error handling, 134–138

Lookup transformation, 132

sending data to destination, 133–134

Union All transformation, 132–133

transformations used for, 354–357

SDLCs (Software Development Life Cycles)

definition of, 547, 548

history of, 548

types of, 549–550

security

for Access database, 250–251, 252

transferring logins to another database, 201–203, 204–205

for WMI connection, 514

SEH (Structured Exception Handling), 227–228

semi-blocking transformations

as asynchronous, 326

definition of, 321–322

Send Mail task, 6, 62

sequence container, 10, 73–74

serial processing, in Control Flow, 312

server folders, maintaining, 494

server instances, managing externally, 491–492

Server Name option, FTP task, 54

Server Port option, FTP task, 54

Server URL option, Web Service task, 63

Service option, Web Service task, 64

Service, SSIS, 3–4

Set Breakpoints dialog box, 408–409

SetComponentProperty **method, 422, 486**

SetExternalMetadataColumnDataType Properties **method, 421**

SetExternalMetadataColumnProperty **method, 422**

SetInputColumnProperty **method, 422, 489**

SetInputProperty **method, 421**

SetOutputColumnDataTypeProperties **method, 421**

SetOutputColumnProperty **method, 422**

SetOutputProperty **method, 421**

SetPackageRoles **method,** Application **object, 495**

settings. See configurations, package

SetUsageType **method, 422–423, 447, 459**

Shannon, Claude (application of Boole's theories), 548

shared connections

adding to Connection Manager, 36

creating, 120–122

residing in project, 28

shared properties for tasks, 43–44

Sharma, Ashvini (ASP.NET example), 540

shelving and unshelving code, 583–584

Shewhart, Walter (statistical process control), 548

Simplified Chinese operation, Character Map transformation, 94

.sln **files, 29**

Slowly Changing Dimension (SCD) transformation

configuring, 190–192

definition of, 14, 107, 189–190

example using, 192–200

as row-based, non-blocking transformation, 320

Type I, II, III changes for, 190, 191

SMO (SQL Management Object) enumerator, Foreach Loop container, 78

Software Development Life Cycles (SDLCs)

definition of, 547, 548

history of, 548

types of, 549–550

Solution Explorer Window

definition of, 28

projects, creating, 29

windows in, 29–32

solutions. See also projects

definition of, 28

files in, 29

Sort transformation

as blocking transformation, 322–323

configuring, 107–108

data cleansing and, 354

definition of, 14, 107

example using, 113

optimizing, 365–366

SortedData option, Bulk Insert task, 48

source adapters

building from pipeline components

`AcquireConnections` method, 433–435

`CreateOutputAndMetaDataColumns` method, 439–440

`ParseTheFileAndAddToBuffer` method, 441–443

`PrimeOutput` method, 440

`ProvideComponentProperties` method, 432–433

`ReinitializeMetaData` method, 438–439

requirements for, 418

`Validate` method, 435–438

definition of, 328

execution trees and, 330, 332

source code control. *See* **Team System; Visual SourceSafe**

Source Type Component, 228

sources, data

back pressure on, 359

Data Reader source, 12, 84

definition of, 11, 80

Excel source

configuring, 83

definition of, 12, 83

importing from, 244–249

uses of, 240

files as

Flat File source, 12, 84, 121–122

Raw File source, 12, 84

Flat File source

configuring, 84

creating, 121–122

definition of, 12, 84

heterogeneous, 239

list of, 12, 239

.NET provider as (Data Reader source), 12, 84

OLE DB source

configuring, 80–83

definition of, 12, 80

Raw File source, 12, 84

XML source

configuring, 84

definition of, 12, 84, 272

importing from, 272–278

SourceSafe

configuring, 550–552

definition of, 550

example using

branching, 565

checking in project, 555–556, 558, 559

checking out project, 554–555

creating project, 552–554

creating project in, 556–558

debugging project, 559–561

rolling back to earlier version, 561–564

Internet version of, 552

SourceType option, Analysis Services Execute DDL task, 70

SourceVariable option, Execute SQL task, 45

SPC (statistical process control), 548

spiral SDLCs, 549

spreadsheet, Excel, as data source

configuring, 83

definition of, 12, 83

importing from, 244–249

uses of, 240

SQL Agent, 664

SQL Command, passing parameter to, 255–258

SQL Management Object (SMO) enumerator, Foreach Loop container, 78

SQL objects, transferring, 204–205

SQL Profiler Log Provider, 506, 508

SQL Server 2000

DTS Designer, 3

executing DTS packages from, 5

global variables, 10, 37

history of, 1

native transactions in, 293, 299–300

Workgroup Edition, 16

SQL Server 2005, editions of, 16–17

SQL Server destination

configuring, 90

creating, 123–124

definition of, 12, 90

when to use, 246

SQL Server Integration Services (SSIS)

architecture of

components of, 3–5

containers, 10

destinations, 12

DSVs (data source views), 8–9

packages, 5

precedence constraints, 9–10

sources, 7, 11–12

tasks in, 5–6

SQL Server Integration Services (SSIS) (continued)
transformations, 13–14
variables, 10–11
definition of, 1
design practices
data cleansing, 354–357
data correlation, 348–354
example of, 357–358
factors in, 346–347
RDBMS, reducing reliance on, 348
staging data, reducing, 348
staging environments, 359–360
synchronicity, limiting, 347
features in, based on SQL Server edition, 16–17
history of, 1–2
migrating DTS packages to, 371, 373–380
running DTS packages in, 380–383
using with external applications, 523
SQL Server Log Provider, 506, 508
SQL Server Management Studio
managing DTS packages with, 388–389
managing SSIS packages with, 386–388
SQL Server Mobile destination, 12, 90
SQL Server option, Execute Package task, 59
SQL Server option, package configuration, 509
SQL Server package store, object maintenance operations on, 492–496
SQL Server Reporting Services (SSRS), producing report from RSS, 524–532
SQL statements. *See also* **DDL statements**
executing for each input row with OLE DB Command transformation
configuring, 163
definition of, 13, 105, 162–163
example using, 163–165
optimizing, 363–364
as row-based, non-blocking transformation, 320
executing with Execute SQL task
checkpoint in, example of, 280–285
configuring, 44–45, 144–145
definition of, 6, 44
example using, 48–51, 124, 148–150
uses of, 144
SQLSourceType option, Execute SQL task, 45, 145
SQLStatement option, Execute SQL task, 45, 145, 299
SSIS clients, 3
SSIS Data Flow engine
definition of, 3, 311–312
optimizing, 361–363

SSIS Package Designer
Connection Managers tab, 36
Control Flow tab, 33–36
Data Flow tab, 38–39
definition of, 32
Event Handlers tab, 39–40
executing package, 41
Package Explorer tab, 40
Variables Window, 37–38
SSIS package store, object maintenance operations on, 492–496
SSIS runtime engine, 3, 5
SSIS Service, 3–4
SSIS (SQL Server Integration Services)
architecture of
components of, 3–5
containers, 10
destinations, 12
DSVs (data source views), 8–9
packages, 5
precedence constraints, 9–10
sources, 7, 11–12
tasks in, 5–6
transformations, 13–14
variables, 10–11
definition of, 1
design practices
data cleansing, 354–357
data correlation, 348–354
example of, 357–358
factors in, 346–347
RDBMS, reducing reliance on, 348
staging data, reducing, 348
staging environments, 359–360
synchronicity, limiting, 347
features in, based on SQL Server edition, 16–17
history of, 1–2
migrating DTS packages to, 371, 373–380
running DTS packages in, 380–383
using with external applications, 523
.SSISDeploymentManifest files, 25
`.ssmssqlproj` **file, 384**
SSRS (SQL Server Reporting Services), producing report from RSS, 524–532
staging data
Data Flow restart using, 305–307
definition of, 305
reducing, 348
scaling across machines using, 307–310
when to use, 359

staging environments, 359–360
Standard Edition, SQL Server 2005, 16
StandardErrorVariable option, Execute Process task, 51
StandardInputVariable option, Execute Process task, 51
StandardOutputVariable option, Execute Process task, 51
StartTime system variable, 38
statistical process control (SPC), 548
Stored Packages folder, 386
stored procedures
    executing
        for each input row, with OLE DB Command
            transformation, 13, 104, 162–165
        with Execute SQL task, 44–45, 144–145, 148–150
    transferring, 203–204
streaming transformations
    definition of, 319
    as synchronous, 326
striping (labeling) versions of code, 586–587
Structured Exception Handling (SEH), 227–228
SUBSTRING function, 129–130
Success constraint value, 9
SuccessValue option, Execute Process task, 52
Sum operation, Aggregate transformation, 91
synchronous processing
    definition of, 315–316
    in DTS, 345
    limiting, 347
synchronous transformation outputs, 326–328
SynchronousInputID property, 328
system variables
    definition of, 37
    list of, 38
system.mdw file, 250

T

tab-delimited files as data source. See Flat File source
Table Lock option
    Bulk Insert task, 47
    OLE DB destination, 88
tables
    dimension tables, 14, 107, 189–192
    pivot tables, 106–107, 182–189
    temporary, 157–159
task host container, 10, 73
task List window, 32
taskID option, Audit transformation, 93
taskName option, Audit transformation, 93
taskResult property, Dts object, 219

tasks. See also containers; packages; specific tasks
    adding to controller flow, 43
    available only in Enterprise Edition, 17
    configuring, 33
    creating, 27, 33
    definition of, 5, 43–44
    disabling, 43, 611
    expressions for logic of, 208, 211–213
    failure of, specifying effects of, 44
    ID for, 44
    list of, 5–6
    logging for, 44, 413
    name of, 44
    outcome of, precedence constraints indicating, 391–393
    output of, 44
    precedence constraints for
        arrow indicators for, 391–392
        conditional expressions for, 9–10, 34, 393–396
        constraint values, 9
        creating, 33–34
        definition of, 5, 9–10
        error handling using, 391–398
        multiple, 397–398
    properties of
        setting to expressions, 72, 146–148, 208–210
        shared, list of, 43–44
        validating at runtime, 43
    synchronous execution of, 315–316
    transaction for
        isolation level of, 44
        support for, 44
Team Foundation Server, 565–566
Team System
    creating project in, 567–570
    definition of, 547, 565
    example using
        branching code, 584
        creating package, 573–579
        labeling (striping) versions of code, 586–587
        merging code, 585–586
        shelving and unshelving, 583–584
        version and source control, 579–583
    MSF Agile template for, 570–572
    Project Portal, 573
temporary tables, 157–159
Term Extraction transformation
    available only in Enterprise Edition, 17
    as blocking transformation, 322
    data correlation by, 348
    definition of, 14, 108–109, 165–166
    example using, 166–170

Term Lookup transformation
available only in Enterprise Edition, 17
configuring, 171–172
data correlation by, 348
definition of, 14, 109, 171
example using, 172–173
as semi-blocking transformation, 321
TerminateProcessAfterTimeOut option, Execute Process task, 52
text. *See also* **data; files**
frequency of words in, determining with Term Extraction transformation, 14, 108–109, 165–170
matching, using Term Lookup transformation, 14, 109, 171–173
similar words in
finding with Fuzzy Grouping transformation, 13, 101, 178–182
finding with Fuzzy Lookup transformation, 13, 101, 173–178
Text File Log Provider, 506, 508
threads, optimizing, 361–363
Timeout option
Execute Process task, 52
Execute SQL task, 44
WMI Event Watcher task, 67, 515
tnsnames.ora file, 259
Toolbox, 29–30
Traditional Chinese operation, Character Map transformation, 94
Transaction **property,** Dts **object, 219**
TransactionOption property, 44
transactions
checkpoints and, 285–288, 289
DTC (Distributed Transaction Coordinator) transactions
definition of, 293
single package, multiple transactions using, 296–298
single package, single transaction using, 293–296
two packages, one transaction using, 298–299
in Import and Export Wizard, 21
native transactions
definition of, 293
example using, 299–300
for script container, getting, 219
for tasks, 44
types of, 293
Transfer Database task, 201–202
Transfer Logins task, 202–203
Transfer SQL Objects task, 204–205
Transfer Stored Procedures task, 203–204
Transformation Type Component, 228

transformations. *See also specific transformations*
available only in Enterprise Edition, 16–17
blocking nature of, 319–324
building from pipeline components
DeleteInput method, 448
DeleteOutput method, 448
InsertOutput method, 447–448
PreExecute method, 448–450
ProcessInput method, 450–454
ProvideComponentProperties method, 443–445
ReinitializeMetaData method, 446
requirements for, 418
SetUsageType method, 447
Validate method, 445–446
communication mechanism of, 324–328
configuring, 90, 91
definition of, 13, 90
in DTS, 343–345
example of
copying data from source to destination, 119–124
scrubbing data, 125–138
expressions for logic of, 208, 211–213
list of, 13–14
types of, 318–319
Try **block, 227–228**

U
UI for components. *See* **user interface (UI) for components**
UITypeName **property, 468, 471, 475–476**
Union All transformation
configuring, 109
data correlation by, 348
definition of, 14, 109
example using, 132–133
optimizing Data Flow and, 363
as semi-blocking transformation, 321
as streaming, non-blocking transformation, 319
Unpivot transformation
data cleansing and, 354, 355
definition of, 14, 107, 186
example using, 186–189
as semi-blocking transformation, 321
unshelving and shelving code, 583–584
Uppercase operation, Character Map transformation, 94
Use Passive Mode option, FTP task, 54

user interface (UI) for components
assembly for, 468–471
column properties for, 488–489
component properties for, 484–486
configuring component for, 468, 475–476
error handling, 486–488
form for
description of, 468, 476–477
form constructor, 477–478
populating controls, 478–480
responding to user input, 480–481
`IDtsComponentUI` interface, implementing,
467–468, 471–475
procedure for, 467–468
runtime connections for, 482–484
user variables, 37
UserName option, Audit transformation, 93
`UserName` **system variable, 38**
**usp_BankBatch_Add table, payment processing
database, 608–609**
**usp_BankBatch_Balance table, payment processing
database, 610**
**usp_BankBatchDetail_Match table, payment
processing database, 609–610**

V

`Validate` **method, 420, 435–438, 445–446, 456–458**
variable enumerator, Foreach Loop container, 78
`VariableDispenser` **object, 219**
`VariableDispenser` **property,** `Dts` **object, 219**
variables
accessing from Script task, 219–220
adding, 37
changing in Watch windows, 410
definition of, 10–11, 37
nonstatic configurations using, 146
for output of task execution, 44
read-only variables, 219
read-write variables, 219
scope of, 11, 37, 145–146
system variables
definition of, 37
list of, 38
types of, 37
user variables, 37
`Variables` **collection, 219–220**
`Variables` **property,** `Dts` **object, 219**
Variables Window, 37–38

`VersionBuild` **system variable, 38**
VersionID option, Audit transformation, 93
versioning. See Team System; Visual SourceSafe
vertical bars (||), OR **login, 131**
views. See Data Viewers; DSVs (data source views)
Visual SourceSafe (VSS)
configuring, 550–552
definition of, 550
example using
branching, 565
checking in project, 555–556, 558, 559
checking out project, 554–555
creating project, 552–554
creating project in, 556–558
debugging project, 559–561
rolling back to earlier version, 561–564
Internet version of, 552
Visual Studio 2005, relationship to BIDS, 3, 25

W

**Warn On Division by Zero option, Aggregate
transformation, 92**
Watch windows, 32, 223–224, 410
waterfall SDLCs, 549
Web Service Description Language (WSDL), 64, 263
Web Service task
configuring, 63–65
definition of, 6, 63
Web services
Currency Conversion service, using, 265–272
definition of, 262
Hyperlink Extractor service, using, 262–265
list of, 272
**WebMethodDocumentation option, Web Service
task, 64**
Williams, Ian (*Professional InfoPath 2003*), 532
Windows Event Log Provider, 506, 508
Windows Management Instrumentation (WMI)
events, handling with WMI Event Watcher task, 6,
67–68, 514–515, 521–522
running WQL queries with WMI Data Reader task, 6,
65–67, 513–521
WindowStyle option, Execute Process task, 52
WMI Data Reader task
configuring, 66–67, 513–514
definition of, 6, 65
example using, 515–521

WMI Event Watcher task

configuring, 67–68, 514–515

definition of, 6, 67

example using, 521–522

WMI (Windows Management Instrumentation)

events, handling with WMI Event Watcher task, 6, 67–68, 514–515, 521–522

running WQL queries with WMI Data Reader task, 6, 65–67, 513–521

WMIConnection option

WMI Data Reader task, 66, 513

WMI Event Watcher task, 514

words

frequency of, determining with Term Extraction transformation, 14, 108–109, 165–170

matching with text, using Term Lookup transformation, 14, 109, 171–173

similar

finding with Fuzzy Grouping transformation, 13, 101, 178–182

finding with Fuzzy Lookup transformation, 13, 101, 173–178

work items, MSF Agile, 571

Workgroup Edition, SQL Server 2000 and 2005, 16

Workgroup Information file, Access, 250–251

WorkingDirectory option, Execute Process task, 51

WQL queries

example of, 66–67

running with WMI Data Reader task, 6, 65–67, 513–521

WQLQuerySource option

WMI Data Reader task, 66, 513

WMI Event Watcher task, 514

WQLQuerySourceType option

WMI Data Reader task, 66, 513

WMI Event Watch task, 514

Write BOM option, Export Column transformation, 100

WSDL (Web Service Description Language), 64, 263

X

XML File Configuration option, package configuration, 509

XML File Log Provider, 506, 508

XML files

comparing, 69

merging, 69

parsing or processing with XML task, 6, 68–69

project files stored as, 384–385

validating, 69

XPATH query, performing on, 69

XSL transformation, performing on, 69

XML Schema Definition (XSD)

definition of, 273

generating from XML source, 84

XML source

configuring, 84

definition of, 12, 84, 272

importing from, 272–278

XML task

configuring, 68–69

definition of, 6, 68

XPATH query, performing, 69

XPathStringSource option, XML task, 69

XSD (XML Schema Definition)

definition of, 273

generating from XML source, 84

XSL transformation, performing, 69

Z

010305c.dat file, 125, 134

ZipCode.txt file, 48, 119

ZipLoad.dtsx file, 120